150 Best Jobs for a Better World™

for a

Better World

Part of JIST's Best Jobs™ Series

The Editors @ JIST and Laurence Shatkin, Ph.D.

Also in JIST's *Best Jobs* Series

- *Best Jobs for the 21st Century*
- *200 Best Jobs for College Graduates*
- *300 Best Jobs Without a Four-Year Degree*
- *250 Best Jobs Through Apprenticeships*
- *50 Best Jobs for Your Personality*

- *40 Best Fields for Your Career*
- *225 Best Jobs for Baby Boomers*
- *250 Best-Paying Jobs*
- *150 Best Jobs for Your Skills*
- *175 Best Jobs Not Behind a Desk*
- *150 Best Jobs Through Military Training*
- *200 Best Jobs for Introverts*

JIST Works
America's Career Publisher®

150 Best Jobs for a Better World

© 2008 by JIST Publishing

Published by JIST Works, an imprint of JIST Publishing
7321 Shadeland Station, Suite 200
Indianapolis, IN 46256-3923

Phone: 800-648-JIST   Fax: 877-454-7839   E-mail: info@jist.com   Web site: www.jist.com

Some Other Books by the Authors

The Editors at JIST
EZ Occupational Outlook Handbook
Salary Facts Handbook
Enhanced Occupational Outlook Handbook
Guide to America's Federal Jobs
Health-Care CareerVision Book and DVD

Laurence Shatkin
90-Minute College Major Matcher

Quantity discounts are available for JIST products. Have future editions of JIST books automatically delivered to you on publication through our convenient standing order program. Please call 800-648-JIST or visit www.jist.com for a free catalog and more information.

Visit www.jist.com for information on JIST, free job search information, book excerpts, and ordering information on our many products.

Printed on 30% post-consumer recycled paper.

Acquisitions Editor: Susan Pines
Development Editor: Stephanie Koutek
Cover and Interior Designer: Aleata Howard
Interior Layout: Aleata Howard
Proofreaders: Paula Lowell, Jeanne Clark
Indexer: Cheryl Lenser

Printed in the United States of America

12 11 10 09 08 07   9 8 7 6 5 4 3 2 1

Library of Congress Cataloging-in-Publication Data
150 best jobs for a better world / the editors at JIST and Laurence Shatkin.
    p. cm. -- (JIST's best jobs series)
    Includes bibliographical references and index.
    ISBN 978-1-59357-476-5 (alk. paper)
1. Vocational guidance--United States. 2. Occupations--United States. 3.
    Social action--United States. I. Shatkin, Laurence. II. JIST Works, Inc.
    III. Title: One hundred fifty best jobs for a better world.
    HF5382.5.U5A59 2008
    331.7020973--dc22

                                        2007035650

All rights reserved. No part of this book may be reproduced in any form or by any means, or stored in a database or retrieval system, without prior permission of the publisher except in the case of brief quotations embodied in articles or reviews. Making copies of any part of this book for any purpose other than your own personal use is a violation of United States copyright laws. For permission requests, please contact the Copyright Clearance Center at www.copyright.com or (978) 750-8400.

We have been careful to provide accurate information throughout this book, but it is possible that errors and omissions have been introduced. Please consider this in making any career plans or other important decisions. Trust your own judgment above all else and in all things.

Trademarks: All brand names and product names used in this book are trade names, service marks, trademarks, or registered trademarks of their respective owners.

ISBN 978-1-59357-476-5

This Is a Big Book, But It Is Very Easy to Use

Wouldn't it be nice to work in a career where your work helps improve the world? Imagine having a job in which your work addresses problems of disease, ignorance, hunger, crime, pollution, or natural disasters. Instead of just earning a paycheck, you would be improving people's lives or the natural environment.

This book can help you identify and explore jobs that make a difference. We provide lists of jobs that contribute to physical health, mental health, education, social well-being, the arts, and public safety.

And the 150 jobs we chose for this book allow you to *do well* while you're doing good. They don't commit you to a life of poverty, and they have lots of job openings so you won't be forced to go into some less-rewarding line of work. In fact, we order many of the lists in this book to emphasize those with the highest earnings and the highest demand for workers. Other lists arrange these jobs by interest fields and personality types. You can also see lists of jobs that have high percentages of part-time, self-employed, female, or male workers.

Every job is described in detail later in the book, so you can explore the jobs that interest you the most. You'll learn the major work tasks, all the important skills, the work conditions, and many other informative facts.

Using this book, you'll be surprised how quickly you'll get new ideas for career goals that can inspire you to improve the world and can suit you in many other ways.

Some Things You Can Do with This Book

- ◎ Develop long-term career plans for world-improving jobs.
- ◎ Identify jobs that can better people's lives in specific ways.
- ◎ Develop plans for getting the education or training you need for a job in one of these helpful careers.
- ◎ Prepare for interviews by learning how to connect your skills and interests to your career goals.

These are a few of the many ways you can use this book. We hope you find it as interesting to browse as we did to put together. We have tried to make it easy to use and as interesting as occupational information can be.

When you are done with this book, pass it along or tell someone else about it. We wish you well in your career and in your life.

(continued)

(continued)

Credits and Acknowledgments: While the authors created this book, it is based on the work of many others. The occupational information is based on data obtained from the U.S. Department of Labor and the U.S. Census Bureau. These sources provide the most authoritative occupational information available. The job titles and their related descriptions are from the O*NET database, which was developed by researchers and developers under the direction of the U.S. Department of Labor. They, in turn, were assisted by thousands of employers who provided details on the nature of work in the many thousands of job samplings used in the database's development. We used the most recent version of the O*NET database, release 11.0. We appreciate and thank the staff of the U.S. Department of Labor for their efforts and expertise in providing such a rich source of data.

Table of Contents

Summary of Major Sections

Introduction. A short overview to help you better understand and use the book. *Starts on page 1.*

Part I. The Best Jobs Lists: Jobs for a Better World. Very useful for exploring career options! Lists are organized into groups. The first group of lists presents the 150 best world-saving jobs. What makes them best overall is their outstanding combinations of earnings, job growth, and job openings. Another series of lists gives the 50 best-paying jobs, the 50 fastest-growing jobs, and the 50 jobs with the most openings. More-specialized lists follow, presenting the best jobs that are rated high for various world-improving characteristics (for example, using knowledge of Medicine and Dentistry); have a high concentration of certain kinds of workers (for example, part-time workers or female workers); and are associated with specific levels of education and training, personality types, and interest areas. The column starting at right presents all the list titles. *Starts on page 15.*

Part II. Descriptions of the Best Jobs for a Better World. Provides complete descriptions of the jobs that appear on the lists in Part I. Each description contains information on work tasks, skills, earnings, projected growth, job duties, work environment, and many other details. *Starts on page 123.*

Appendix A. Resources for Further Exploration. Lists several helpful resources for researching the facts about jobs and for learning how to conduct a successful job hunt. *Starts on page 405.*

Appendix B. The GOE Interest Areas and Work Groups. This list of the 16 GOE Interest Areas and their related Work Groups can help you narrow down your career interests. *Starts on page 407.*

Detailed Table of Contents

Introduction

Improving the World Through Your Work

Many people want their work to do more than just earn a paycheck or keep a business running. They want to be engaged in work that makes the world a better place—by easing suffering, increasing knowledge, promoting safety and security, improving the natural environment, or creating things of beauty.

If you're one of those people, perhaps you've been influenced by the many philosophers and religious figures through the ages who have argued that *the best thing we can do for ourselves is to help other people.* Perhaps you're taking the long view of your life, thinking about how you'll look back on your career later in life and will ask yourself, "What did I accomplish that had real significance? How did I touch people's lives?" Perhaps you're troubled by the amount of hunger, disease, or crime in the world; the degradation of the natural environment; or the lackluster performance of the nation's schools.

Some people just throw up their hands and say, "What can one person do to improve the world?" But others make plans to do what they can, however small, to contribute to improving the lives of others or the environment. And what better way than through work? After all, you're going to be devoting a major chunk of your life to your career. Why not use that time and energy in a way that makes the world a better place?

In truth, *every* job makes the world better in *some* way. Every job helps keep a business or organization running. That business or organization keeps people employed so they can pay their bills and raise their families. The business also pays taxes that keep the government running—unless it is a nonprofit organization, in which case it is serving some social good.

If your job pays well enough that you don't have to work two jobs, you have leisure time that you can devote to volunteer work. For example, you could spend a few Saturdays swinging a hammer for Habitat for Humanity, you could spend some evenings making fund-raising phone calls for the American Cancer Society, or you could host an evening meeting to organize a neighborhood watch program. And if your job pays well enough to cover the basic costs of living, you can contribute some of your income to charities. So no matter what your job is, it probably allows you to improve people's lives through off-the-job activities.

Another way to help other people through your job is to be one of the workers (about seven percent nationwide) who work for a nonprofit organization with a world-improving mission. It might be a charity, an educational institution, a government agency that improves people's lives or the environment, or a hospital. And you wouldn't have to play a conspicuous role of feeding the hungry, teaching people, catching criminals, tagging birds, or binding wounds. You could be balancing the account books, maintaining the computer network, ordering supplies, or doing something else that has no *direct* impact on people's lives, yet you would be helping your employer accomplish its mission. And that would add a satisfaction to your work that you would not get if you worked somewhere else.

The Focus of This Book

Even though all jobs do something to make the world better, this book focuses on jobs where the *main job functions* are activities that improve people's lives. The jobs in this book have this world-improving nature regardless of the employer. So you won't find job titles here such as "Peace Corps Volunteer," "Nonprofit Manager," or "Church Organist," because these job titles reflect the nature of the *employer* rather than the kind of work done. The actual occupation of the Peace Corps volunteer might be Elementary School Teacher or Health Educator; the nonprofit manager might be a General and Operations Manager or a Social and Community Service Manager; the church organist is a Musician, Instrumental. The jobs in this book are defined by their functions, not by their employers.

This book also focuses on jobs with good economic rewards. We don't believe that the best way for you to improve the world is to live a life of poverty. You can have a greater impact on people's lives if you bring a high level of skill to your work, and highly skilled workers are usually paid better. You also cannot help people through your work if you are unemployed, so we emphasize careers that are growing and have a lot of job openings.

Besides their economic rewards, these jobs can bring great personal satisfaction. In a survey about job satisfaction conducted by the National Opinion Research Center at the University of Chicago, 57 percent of the workers holding the jobs in this book said they were "very satisfied" with their jobs, compared to 49 percent of the workers holding all jobs. Of the top 15 most satisfying jobs identified by the survey, 10 are included in this book.

The sage Hillel once remarked, "If I am not for myself, who will be for me? If I am not for others, what am I? And if not now, when?" This book suggests career choices that allow you to do good for both yourself and others. And the time to get started on your world-improving career is *now.*

Where the Information Came From

The information we used in creating this book came mostly from databases created by the U.S. Department of Labor and the U.S. Census Bureau:

⊚ We started with the jobs included in the Department of Labor's O*NET (Occupational Information Network) database, which is now the primary source of detailed information on occupations. The Labor Department updates the O*NET on a regular basis, and we used the most recent one available—O*NET release 11.

⊚ Because we wanted to include earnings, growth, number of openings, and other data not in the O*NET, we cross-referenced information on earnings developed by the U.S. Bureau of Labor Statistics (BLS) and the U.S. Census Bureau. This information on earnings is the most reliable data we could obtain. For data on earnings, projected growth, and number of openings, the BLS uses a slightly different set of job titles than the O*NET uses, so we had to match similar titles. Data about part-time workers, age brackets of workers, and the male-female breakdown of workers was derived from the Census Bureau, which also uses a slightly different set of job titles. By linking the BLS and Census data to the O*NET job titles in this book, we tied information about growth, earnings, and characteristics of workers to all the job titles in this book.

Of course, information in a database format can be boring and even confusing, so we did many things to help make the data useful and present it to you in a form that is easy to understand.

How the Best Jobs for a Better World Were Selected

Different people have different opinions about which jobs make the world a better place. We decided that the jobs should involve a lot of helping people, teaching people, improving people's health and well-being, protecting people from harm, or enriching people's lives by advancing knowledge or creating works of art. In terms of the descriptors used in the O*NET database, that meant we were looking for occupations that are rated high on one or more of the following characteristics:

⊚ The value Social Service

⊚ The knowledge Education and Training

⊚ The knowledge Fine Arts

⊚ The knowledge Medicine and Dentistry

⊚ The knowledge Public Safety and Security

⊚ The knowledge Therapy and Counseling

We sorted the O*NET database using these characteristics and created a preliminary list of jobs. However, we decided that this list would need further pruning to focus on jobs in which the work contributes to people's lives *directly*. Therefore, we eliminated a few jobs in which workers are acting primarily as managers—for example, Medical and Health Services Managers and Administrative Law Judges, Adjudicators, and Hearing Officers. We removed some scientific jobs that are in fields impacting people's lives only very indirectly, such as Archeologists and Astronomers. We also eliminated some jobs that have an artistic component but are mainly about advancing commercial goals, such as Fashion Designers, Producers, and Graphic Designers. These judgments admittedly are somewhat subjective, but we believe most people will agree that they help refine the book's definition of jobs that make the world a better place.

We also had to eliminate a few jobs, such as Actors, because annual average earnings figures are not available.

We decided to collapse some jobs that were very closely related. From 36 very similar college teaching jobs we created one job called Teachers, Postsecondary. And from seven jobs for which people get a medical degree, we created one job called Physicians and Surgeons. (All 43 of these collapsed jobs are described separately in Part II, however, so this book actually covers 201 jobs rather than 150.)

Our reduced list now contained 160 world-improving jobs. We then matched these to information from the U.S. Department of Labor so we could evaluate the economic rewards of the jobs and select the best jobs to include in this book. We followed these procedures for creating our list of best jobs:

1. We created three lists that ranked the 160 jobs based on three major criteria: median annual earnings, projected growth through 2014, and number of job openings projected per year.

2. We then added the numerical ranks for each job from all three lists to calculate its overall score.

3. To emphasize jobs that tend to pay more, are likely to grow more rapidly, and have more job openings, we selected the 150 job titles with the best numerical scores for our final list. These jobs are the focus of this book.

For example, Computer Security Specialists and Teachers, Postsecondary, were tied for having the best combined score for earnings, growth, and number of job openings, so Computer Security Specialists (because it comes first in alphabetical order) is listed first in our "150 Best Jobs Overall" list even though it is not the best-paying job (which is a tie between Orthodontists, Prosthodontists, and Physicians and Surgeons), the fastest-growing job (which is Home Health Aides), or the job with the most openings (which is a position shared by Child Care Workers and Nannies).

Understand the Limits of the Data in This Book

In this book we use the most reliable and up-to-date information available on earnings, projected growth, number of openings, and other topics. The earnings data came from the U.S. Department of Labor's Bureau of Labor Statistics. As you look at the figures, keep in mind that they are estimates. They give you a general idea about the number of workers employed, annual earnings, rate of job growth, and annual job openings.

Understand that a problem with such data is that it describes an average. Just as there is no precisely average person, there is no such thing as a statistically average example of a particular job. We say this because data, while helpful, can also be misleading.

Take, for example, the yearly earnings information in this book. This is highly reliable data obtained from a very large U.S. working population sample by the Bureau of Labor Statistics. It tells us the average annual pay received in May 2005 by people in various job titles (actually, it is the median annual pay, which means that half earned more and half less).

This sounds great, except that half of all people in that occupation earned less than that amount. For example, people who are new to the occupation or with only a few years of work experience often earn much less than the median amount. People who live in rural areas or who work for smaller employers typically earn less than those who do similar work in cities (where the cost of living is higher) or for bigger employers. People in certain areas of the country earn less than those in others. Other factors also influence how much you are likely to earn in a given job in your area. For example, dentists in the New York metropolitan area earn an average of $124,540 per year, whereas dentists in six metropolitan areas in North Carolina earn an average of more than $145,600 per year. Although the cost of living tends to be higher in the New York area, North Carolina has only one dentistry school, and therefore dentists there experience less competition for patients and can command higher fees. So you can see that many factors can cause earnings to vary widely.

Also keep in mind that the figures for job growth and number of openings are projections by labor economists—their best guesses about what we can expect between now and 2014. They are not guarantees. A major economic downturn, war, or technological breakthrough could change the actual outcome.

Finally, don't forget that the job market consists of both job openings and job-*seekers*. The figures on job growth and openings don't tell you how many people will be competing with you to be hired. The Department of Labor does not publish figures on the supply of job candidates, so we are unable to tell you about the level of competition you can expect. Competition is an important issue that you should research for any tentative career goal. In some cases the *Occupational Outlook Handbook* provides informative statements. You should speak to people who educate or train tomorrow's workers; they probably have a good idea of how many of their graduates find rewarding employment and how quickly. People in the workforce also can provide insights into this issue. Use your critical thinking skills to evaluate what people tell you. For example, recruiters for training programs are highly motivated to get you to sign up, whereas people in the workforce may be trying to discourage you from competing. Get a variety of opinions to balance out possible biases.

So, in reviewing the information in this book, please understand the limitations of the data. You need to use common sense in career decision making as in most other things in life. We hope that, using that approach, you find the information helpful and interesting.

The Data Complexities

For those of you who like details, we present some of the complexities inherent in our sources of information and what we did to make sense of them here. You don't need to know this to use the book, so jump to the next section of the introduction if you are bored with details.

We include information on earnings, projected growth, and number of job openings for each job throughout this book.

Earnings

The employment security agency of each state gathers information on earnings for various jobs and forwards it to the U.S. Bureau of Labor Statistics. This information is organized in standardized ways by a BLS program called Occupational Employment Statistics, or OES. To keep the earnings for the various jobs and regions comparable, the OES screens out certain types of earnings and includes others, so the OES earnings we use in this book represent straight-time gross pay exclusive of premium pay. More specifically, the OES earnings include the job's base rate; cost-of-living allowances; guaranteed pay; hazardous-duty pay; incentive pay, including commissions and production bonuses; on-call pay; and tips but do not include back pay, jury duty pay, overtime pay, severance pay, shift differentials, non-production bonuses, or tuition reimbursements. Also, self-employed workers are not included in the estimates, and they can be a significant segment in certain occupations. When data on earnings for an occupation is highly unreliable, OES does not report a figure, which meant that we reluctantly had to exclude from this book a few occupations such as Actors. The median earnings for all workers in all occupations were $29,430 in May 2005. The jobs in this book were chosen partly on the basis of their earnings, so they average $38,327.

The OES earnings data uses a system of job titles called the Standard Occupational Classification system, or SOC. We cross-referenced these titles to the O*NET job titles we use in this book so we can rank the jobs by their earnings and include earnings information in the job descriptions. In some cases, an SOC title cross-references to more than one O*NET job title. For example, the O*NET has separate information for Radiologic Technicians and Radiologic Technologists, but the SOC reports earnings for a single occupation called Radiologic Technologists and Technicians. Therefore you may notice that we report the identical salaries for Radiologic Technicians and Radiologic Technologists: $45,950. In reality there probably is a difference, but this is the best information that is available.

Projected Growth and Number of Job Openings

This information comes from the Office of Occupational Statistics and Employment Projections, a program within the Bureau of Labor Statistics that develops information about projected trends in the nation's labor market for the next ten years. The most recent projections available cover the years from 2004 to 2014. The projections are based on information about people moving into and out of occupations. The BLS uses data from various sources in projecting the growth and number of openings for each job title—some data comes from the Census Bureau's Current Population Survey and some comes from an OES survey. The projections assume that there will be no major war, depression, or other economic upheaval.

Like the earnings figures, the figures on projected growth and job openings are reported according to the SOC classification, so again you will find that some of the SOC jobs crosswalk to more than one O*NET job. To continue the example we used earlier, SOC reports growth (23.2%) and openings (17,000) for one occupation called Radiologic Technologists and Technicians, but in this book we report these figures separately for the occupation Radiologic Technicians and for the occupation Radiologic Technologists. When you see Radiologic Technicians with 23.2% projected growth and 17,000 projected job openings and Radiologic Technologists with the same two numbers, you should realize that the 23.2% rate of projected growth represents the *average* of these two occupations—one may actually experience higher growth than the other—and that these two occupations will *share* the 17,000 projected openings.

While salary figures are fairly straightforward, you may not know what to make of job-growth figures. For example, is projected growth of 15% good or bad? You should keep in mind that the average (mean) growth projected for all occupations by the Bureau of Labor Statistics is 13.0%. One-quarter of the occupations have a growth projection of 3.2% or lower. Growth of 12.2% is the median, meaning that half of the occupations have more, half less. Only one-quarter of the occupations have growth projected at 17.4% or higher.

Remember, however, that the jobs in this book were selected as "best" partly on the basis of high growth. Furthermore, many of the jobs are in the fast-growing field of health care. In fact, the median growth for the best 150 jobs is *almost twice* that of the median for all jobs: 22.2%. Among these 150 outstanding jobs, the job ranked 38th by projected growth has a figure of 25.5%, and the job ranked 113th has a projected growth of 14.3%.

The news about job openings for world-improving jobs is actually the reverse of the news about job growth: It's not as good as the national average for all occupations. The Bureau of Labor statistics projects an average of about 35,000 job openings per year for each of the 750 occupations that it studies, but for each of the 150 occupations included in this book, the average is about 31,000 openings. The job ranked 37th for job openings has a figure of 21,000 annual openings, the job ranked 75th (the median) has 10,000 openings projected, and the job ranked 132nd has 1,000 openings projected.

This contrast between the news about job growth and number of job openings highlights the reasons why we include *both* figures in this book. It demonstrates that these are not two ways of saying the same thing. As a single example, consider the occupation Occupational Therapist Assistants, which is projected to grow at the astounding rate of 34.1%. There should be lots of opportunities in such a fast-growing job, right? Not exactly. This is a very small occupation, with only about 21,000 people currently employed, so even though it is growing rapidly, it is expected to create only 2,000 job openings per year. A lot of the occupations in this book resemble Occupational Therapist Assistants: growing fast, but small in size and therefore with relatively few job openings. Fortunately this book also features a number of occupations with lots of job openings, like Security Guards. This occupation is growing at the rate of 12.6%—about the same as the average for all occupations. Nevertheless, this is a very large occupation that employs almost one million workers, so even though its growth rate is unimpressive, it is expected to take on 230,000 new workers each year. We base our selection of the best jobs on both of these economic indicators—growth and openings—and you should pay attention to both when you scan our lists of best jobs.

How This Book Is Organized

The information in this book about job options for a better world moves from the general to the highly specific.

Part I. The Best Jobs Lists: Jobs for a Better World

For many people, the 101 lists in Part I are the most interesting section of the book. Here you can see titles of jobs that make a better world and that have the best combination of high salaries, fast growth, and plentiful job openings. You can see which jobs are best in terms of each of these factors combined or considered separately. The list of high performers is broken out further according to the interest fields and several other features of the jobs. Look in the table of contents for a complete list of lists. Although there are a lot of lists, they are not difficult to understand because they have clear titles and are organized into groupings of related lists.

People who prefer to think about careers in terms of personality types will want to browse the lists that show the best world-improving jobs with Realistic, Investigative, Artistic, Social, Enterprising, and Conventional personality types. On the other hand, some people think first in terms of interest fields, and these people will prefer the lists that show the best world-improving jobs using the interest categories of the *New Guide for Occupational Exploration*.

We suggest that you use the lists that make the most sense for you. Following are the names of each group of lists along with short comments on each group. You will find additional information in a brief introduction provided at the beginning of each group of lists in Part I.

Best Jobs Overall for a Better World: Lists of Jobs with the Highest Pay, Fastest Growth, and Most Openings

This group has four lists, and they are the ones that most people want to see first. The first list presents all 150 jobs that are included in this book in order of their combined scores for earnings, growth, and number of job openings. These jobs are used in the more-specialized lists that follow and in the descriptions in Part II. Three more lists in this group present specialized lists of jobs that make the world a better place: the 50 best-paying jobs, the 50 fastest-growing jobs, and the 50 jobs with the most openings.

Best Jobs Rated High on Various World-Improving Criteria

To select world-improving jobs for this book, we looked for jobs that the O*NET database rates high on one or more of certain beneficial factors: the value Social Service, the knowledge Education and Training, the knowledge Fine Arts, the knowledge Medicine and Dentistry, the knowledge Public Safety and Security, and the knowledge Therapy and Counseling.

These sets of lists show the best jobs that are rated high on *each* of these factors, plus a set of lists based on all of the factors *combined*.

Best Jobs Lists by Demographic

This group of lists recognizes the diversity of world-improving jobs by presenting interesting information for a variety of types of workers based on data from the U.S. Census Bureau. The lists are arranged into groups for workers 16–24, workers 55 and over, part-time workers, self-employed workers, women, and men.

Best Jobs Lists Based on Levels of Education and Experience

We created separate lists for each level of education and training as defined by the U.S. Department of Labor. We put each of the 150 jobs into one of the lists based on the education and training required for entry. Jobs within these lists are presented in order of their total combined scores for earnings, growth, and number of openings. The lists include jobs in these groupings:

- Short-term on-the-job training
- Moderate-term on-the-job training
- Long-term on-the-job training
- Work experience in a related job
- Postsecondary vocational training
- Associate degree

- Bachelor's degree
- Work experience plus degree
- Master's degree
- Doctoral degree
- First professional degree

Best Jobs Lists Based on Interests

These lists organize the 150 jobs into groups based on interests. Within each list, jobs are presented in order of their combined scores for earnings, growth, and number of openings. Here are the 15 interest areas used in these lists: Agriculture and Natural Resources; Architecture and Construction; Arts and Communication; Education and Training; Finance and Insurance; Government and Public Administration; Health Science; Hospitality, Tourism, and Recreation; Human Service; Information Technology; Law and Public Safety; Manufacturing; Retail and Wholesale Sales and Service; Scientific Research, Engineering, and Mathematics; and Transportation, Distribution, and Logistics. (This classification of interest areas includes one additional area, Business and Administration, but none of the 150 jobs falls into that category.)

Best Jobs Lists Based on Personality Types

These lists organize the 150 jobs into six personality types, which are described in the introduction to the lists: Realistic, Investigative, Artistic, Social, Enterprising, and Conventional. The jobs within each list are presented in order of their combined scores for earnings, growth, and number of openings.

Part II: Descriptions of the Best Jobs for a Better World

This part describes each of the best world-improving jobs, using a format that is informative yet compact and easy to read. The descriptions contain statistics such as earnings and projected percent of growth; lists such as major work tasks, skills, and work environment; and key descriptors such as personality type and interest field. Because the jobs in this section are arranged in alphabetical order, you can easily find a job that you've identified from Part I and that you want to learn more about.

We used the most current information from a variety of government sources to create the descriptions. Although we've tried to make the descriptions easy to understand, the sample that follows—with an explanation of each of its parts—may help you better understand and use the descriptions.

Job Title →

Ambulance Drivers and Attendants, Except Emergency Medical Technicians

Data Elements →

- Annual Earnings: $18,790
- Growth: 28.0%
- Annual Job Openings: 5,000
- Education/Training Required: Moderate-term on-the-job training
- Self-Employed: 11.0%
- Part-Time: 15.8%

How the Job Improves the World →

How the Job Improves the World: Contributes to health.

Summary Description and Tasks →

Drive ambulance or assist ambulance driver in transporting sick, injured, or convalescent persons. Assist in lifting patients. Drive ambulances or assist ambulance drivers in transporting sick, injured, or convalescent persons. Remove and replace soiled linens and equipment to maintain sanitary conditions. Accompany and assist emergency medical technicians on calls. Place patients on stretchers and load stretchers into ambulances, usually with assistance from other attendants. Earn and maintain appropriate certifications. Replace supplies and disposable items on ambulances. Report facts concerning accidents or emergencies to hospital personnel or law enforcement officials. Administer first aid such as bandaging, splinting, and administering oxygen. Restrain or shackle violent patients.

Personality Type →

Personality Type: Social. Social occupations frequently involve working with, communicating with, and teaching people. These occupations often involve helping or providing service to others.

GOE Information →

GOE—Interest Area: 16. Transportation, Distribution, and Logistics. **Work Group:** 16.06. Other Services Requiring Driving. **Other Jobs in This Work Group:** Bus Drivers, School; Bus Drivers, Transit and Intercity; Couriers and Messengers; Driver/Sales Workers; Parking Lot Attendants; Postal Service Mail Carriers; Taxi Drivers and Chauffeurs.

Skills →

Skills—Equipment Maintenance: Performing routine maintenance on equipment and determining when and what kind of maintenance is needed. **Operation Monitoring:** Watching gauges, dials, or other indicators to make sure a machine is working properly. **Operation and Control:** Controlling operations of equipment or systems. **Repairing:** Repairing machines or systems by using the needed tools. **Technology Design:** Generating or adapting equipment and technology to serve user needs. **Service Orientation:** Actively looking for ways to help people. **Equipment Selection:** Determining the kind of tools and equipment needed to do a job. **Troubleshooting:** Determining causes of operating errors and deciding what to do about them.

Education and Training Program(s) →

Education and Training Program: Emergency Medical Technology/Technician (EMT Paramedic).

Related Knowledge/Courses →

Related Knowledge/Courses: Transportation: Principles and methods for moving people or goods by air, rail, sea, or road, including the relative costs and benefits. **Psychology:** Human behavior and performance; individual differences in ability, personality, and interests; learning and motivation; psychological research methods; and the assessment and treatment of behavioral and affective disorders. **Medicine and Dentistry:** The information and techniques needed to diagnose and treat human injuries, diseases, and deformities. This includes symptoms, treatment alternatives, drug properties and interactions, and preventive health-care measures.

Work Environment →

Work Environment: Outdoors; noisy; very hot or cold; disease or infections; sitting; using hands on objects, tools, or controls.

Here are some details on each of the major parts of the job descriptions you will find in Part II:

- **Job Title**—This is the job title for the job as defined by the U.S. Department of Labor and used in its O*NET database.

- **Data Elements**—The information comes from various U.S. Department of Labor and Census Bureau databases, as explained elsewhere in this introduction.

- **How the Job Improves the World**—This identifies the world-improving criteria that earned this job a place in this book.

- **Summary Description and Tasks**—The bold sentences provide a summary description of the occupation. It is followed by a listing of tasks that are generally performed by people who work in this job. This information comes from the O*NET database but where necessary has been edited to avoid exceeding 2,200 characters.

- **Personality Type**—This is the name of the related personality type from the Holland (RIASEC) classification. You can find more information on the personality types in the introduction to the lists of jobs based on personality types in Part I.

- **GOE Information**—This information cross-references the Guide for Occupational Exploration (or the GOE), a system developed by the U.S. Department of Labor that organizes jobs based on interests. We use the groups from the *New Guide for Occupational Exploration*, published by JIST. This book uses a set of interest areas based on the 16 career clusters developed by the U.S. Department of Education and used in a variety of career information systems. The description includes the major Interest Area the job fits into, its more-specific Work Group, and a list of related O*NET job titles that are in this same GOE Work Group. This information will help you identify other job titles that have similar interests or require similar skills. You can find more information on the GOE and its Interest Areas in the introduction to the lists of jobs based on interests in Part I, and you may peruse a full outline of the Interest Areas and Work Groups in Appendix B.

- **Skills**—The O*NET database provides data on many skills; we decided to list only those that were most important for each job rather than list pages of unhelpful details. For each job, we identified any skill that is rated at a level higher than the average rating for that skill for all jobs and that also is not rated as an unimportant skill. If there were more than eight, we included only those eight with the highest ratings, and we present them from highest to lowest score (that is, in terms of by how much its score exceeds the average score). We include up to 10 skills if scores were tied for eighth place. If no skill has a rating higher than the average for all jobs, we say "None met the criteria." Each listed skill is followed by a brief description of that skill.

◎ **Education and Training Program**(s)—This part of the job description provides the name of the educational or training program or programs for the job. It will help you identify sources of formal or informal training for a job that interests you. To get this information, we used a crosswalk created by the National Crosswalk Service Center to connect information in the Classification of Instructional Programs (CIP) to the O*NET job titles we use in this book. We made various changes to connect the O*NET job titles to the education or training programs related to them and also modified the names of some education and training programs so they would be more easily understood.

◎ **Related Knowledge/Courses**—This entry can help you understand the most important knowledge areas that are required for a job and the types of courses or programs you will likely need to take to prepare for it. We used information in the O*NET database for this entry. For each job, we identified any knowledge area with a rating that was higher than the average rating for that knowledge area for all jobs; then we listed them in descending order. If there were more than six, we included only the six with the highest ratings. Each listed knowledge area is followed by a brief definition.

◎ **Work Environment**—This entry in the job description, also derived from the O*NET, mentions aspects of the work setting that some people may want to avoid, such as exposure to loud noises or the necessity of standing for long periods of time. The ordering of the environmental factors is not significant.

Getting all the information we used in the job descriptions was not a simple process, and it is not always perfect. Even so, we used the best and most recent sources of data we could find, and we think that our efforts will be helpful to many people.

PART I

The Best Jobs Lists: Jobs for a Better World

This part contains a lot of interesting lists, and it's a good place for you to start using the book. Here are some suggestions for using the lists to explore career options that can improve the world:

- ◎ The table of contents at the beginning of this book presents a complete listing of the list titles in this section. You can browse the lists or use the table of contents to find those that interest you most.

- ◎ We gave the lists clear titles, so most require little explanation. We provide comments for each group of lists.

- ◎ As you review the lists of jobs, one or more of the jobs may appeal to you enough that you want to seek additional information. As this happens, mark that job (or, if someone else will be using this book, write it on a separate sheet of paper) so that you can look up the description of the job in Part II.

- ◎ Keep in mind that all jobs in these lists meet our basic criteria for being included in this book, as explained in the introduction. All lists, therefore, contain jobs that contribute to the betterment of the world, with emphasis on occupations that have high pay, high growth, or large numbers of openings. These measures are easily quantified and are often presented in lists of best jobs in the newspapers and other media. While earnings, growth, and openings are important, there are other factors to consider in your career planning. Obviously you are considering the contribution the job makes to society or nature; that's why you're reading this book. Other examples of factors to consider are location, liking the people you work with, and having opportunities to be creative. Many other factors that may help define the ideal job for you are difficult or impossible to quantify and thus are not used in this book, so you will need to consider the importance of these issues yourself.

- ◎ All data used to create these lists comes from the U.S. Department of Labor and the Census Bureau. The earnings figures are based on the average annual pay received by full-time workers. Because the earnings represent the national averages, actual pay rates can vary greatly by location, amount of previous work experience, and other factors.

Some Details on the Lists

The sources of the information we used in constructing these lists are presented in this book's introduction. Here are some additional details on how we created the lists:

◉ Some jobs have the same scores for one or more data elements. For example, in the category of fastest-growing, two jobs (Chiropractors and Kindergarten Teachers, Except Special Education) are expected to grow at the same rate, 22.4 percent. Therefore we ordered these two jobs alphabetically, and their order has no other significance. There was no way to avoid these ties, so simply understand that the difference of several positions on a list may not mean as much as it seems.

◉ Some jobs share certain data elements. For example, in Part II you will find separate descriptions of the jobs Radiologic Technologists and Radiologic Technicians—so you will also find these as two separate jobs on the lists here in Part I. However, the U.S. Department of Labor provides data on earnings, job growth, and job openings only for the *single combined* job called Radiologic Technologists and Technicians, which means that on these lists we have to print the same information for both jobs. That can be misleading if you don't understand that these jobs share data. The earnings figure of $45,950 represents the *average* for the two jobs; probably there are differences in their earnings, but we don't have separate data. The figure of 23.2 percent for their job growth is also an *average*. It's especially important to understand that the figure of 17,000 job openings represents the *total number of job openings for the two jobs*. They share this figure—each job is projected to have *some fraction* of 17,000 job openings, but we don't know exactly how many. To remind you about how to read these figures, we identify all the jobs that share data in footnotes after each list that contains such jobs.

◉ We collapsed some jobs that share certain data elements because as separate titles they would have overwhelmed the top of the list. In the following lists the job Physicians and Surgeons actually represents seven specific occupations, and Teachers, Postsecondary represents 35 specific occupations. The introduction to Part II identifies the specific jobs that we collapsed to create these more manageable job titles.

Best Jobs Overall for a Better World: Lists of Jobs with the Highest Pay, Fastest Growth, and Most Openings

The four lists that follow are the most important lists in this book. To create these lists, we ranked 160 major world-improving jobs according to a combination of their earnings, growth, and openings. We then selected the 150 jobs with the best combined scores for use in this book.

The first list presents all 150 best jobs according to these combined scores for pay, growth, and number of openings. Three additional lists present the 50 jobs with the best scores for each of three measures: annual earnings, projected percentage growth through 2014, and number of annual openings. Descriptions for all the jobs in these lists are included in Part II.

The 150 Best Jobs for a Better World—Jobs with the Best Combination of Pay, Growth, and Openings

This is the list that most people want to see first. It includes the 150 world-improving jobs that have the best overall combined ratings for earnings, projected growth, and number of openings. (The section in the introduction called "How the Best Jobs for a Better World Were Selected" explains in detail how we rated jobs to assemble this list.)

You'll notice a wide variety of jobs on the list. Among the top 20 are jobs in high technology, health care, and education.

Computer Security Specialists was the occupation with the best combined score, and it is on the top of the list. The other occupations follow in descending order based on their combined scores. Many jobs had tied scores and are simply listed one after another, so there are often only very small or even no differences between the scores of jobs that are near each other on the list. All other job lists in this book use this list as their source. You can find descriptions for each of these jobs in Part II, beginning on page 123.

The 150 Best Jobs Overall for a Better World

Job	Annual Earnings	Percent Growth	Annual Openings
1. Computer Security Specialists	$59,930	38.4%	34,000
2. Teachers, Postsecondary	$53,590	32.2%	329,000
3. Registered Nurses	$54,670	29.4%	229,000
4. Physicians and Surgeons	more than $145,600	24.0%	41,000
5. Dental Hygienists	$60,890	43.3%	17,000
6. Medical Scientists, Except Epidemiologists	$61,730	34.1%	15,000
7. Physician Assistants	$72,030	49.6%	10,000
8. Physical Therapists	$63,080	36.7%	13,000
9. Personal Financial Advisors	$63,500	25.9%	17,000
10. Pharmacists	$89,820	24.6%	16,000
11. Education Administrators, Postsecondary	$70,350	21.3%	18,000
12. Instructional Coordinators	$50,430	27.5%	15,000

(continued)

(continued)

The 150 Best Jobs Overall for a Better World

Job	Annual Earnings	Percent Growth	Annual Openings
13. Social and Community Service Managers	$49,500	25.5%	17,000
14. Occupational Therapists	$56,860	33.6%	7,000
15. Medical Assistants	$25,350	52.1%	93,000
16. Dental Assistants	$29,520	42.7%	45,000
17. Radiologic Technicians	$45,950	23.2%	17,000
18. Radiologic Technologists	$45,950	23.2%	17,000
19. Kindergarten Teachers, Except Special Education	$42,230	22.4%	28,000
20. Special Education Teachers, Preschool, Kindergarten, and Elementary School	$44,630	23.3%	18,000
21. Elementary School Teachers, Except Special Education	$44,040	18.2%	203,000
22. Home Health Aides	$18,800	56.0%	170,000
23. Clinical Psychologists	$57,170	19.1%	10,000
24. Counseling Psychologists	$57,170	19.1%	10,000
25. School Psychologists	$57,170	19.1%	10,000
26. Medical and Clinical Laboratory Technologists	$47,710	20.5%	14,000
27. Chiropractors	$67,200	22.4%	4,000
28. Personal and Home Care Aides	$17,340	41.0%	230,000
29. Forest Fire Fighters	$39,090	24.3%	21,000
30. Municipal Fire Fighters	$39,090	24.3%	21,000
31. Social and Human Service Assistants	$25,030	29.7%	61,000
32. Medical and Public Health Social Workers	$41,120	25.9%	14,000
33. Preschool Teachers, Except Special Education	$21,990	33.1%	77,000
34. Self-Enrichment Education Teachers	$32,360	25.3%	74,000
35. Education Administrators, Elementary and Secondary School	$75,400	10.4%	27,000
36. Veterinarians	$68,910	17.4%	8,000
37. Surgical Technologists	$34,830	29.5%	12,000
38. Forest Fire Fighting and Prevention Supervisors	$60,840	21.1%	4,000
39. Municipal Fire Fighting and Prevention Supervisors	$60,840	21.1%	4,000
40. Physical Therapist Assistants	$39,490	44.2%	7,000
41. Fitness Trainers and Aerobics Instructors	$25,840	27.1%	50,000
42. Respiratory Therapists	$45,140	28.4%	7,000
43. Mental Health and Substance Abuse Social Workers	$34,410	26.7%	15,000
44. Pharmacy Technicians	$24,390	28.6%	35,000
45. Secondary School Teachers, Except Special and Vocational Education	$46,060	14.4%	107,000
46. Mental Health Counselors	$34,010	27.2%	14,000

The 150 Best Jobs Overall for a Better World

Job	Annual Earnings	Percent Growth	Annual Openings
47. Police Patrol Officers	$46,290	15.5%	47,000
48. Sheriffs and Deputy Sheriffs	$46,290	15.5%	47,000
49. Directors—Stage, Motion Pictures, Television, and Radio	$53,860	16.6%	11,000
50. Talent Directors	$53,860	16.6%	11,000
51. Radiation Therapists	$62,340	26.3%	1,000
52. Architects, Except Landscape and Naval	$62,850	17.3%	7,000
53. Emergency Medical Technicians and Paramedics	$26,080	27.3%	21,000
54. First-Line Supervisors/Managers of Police and Detectives	$65,570	15.5%	9,000
55. Poets, Lyricists, and Creative Writers	$46,420	17.7%	14,000
56. Cardiovascular Technologists and Technicians	$40,420	32.6%	5,000
57. Optometrists	$88,040	19.7%	2,000
58. Educational, Vocational, and School Counselors	$46,440	14.8%	32,000
59. Education Administrators, Preschool and Child Care Center/ Program	$37,010	27.9%	9,000
60. Licensed Practical and Licensed Vocational Nurses	$35,230	17.1%	84,000
61. Nursing Aides, Orderlies, and Attendants	$21,440	22.3%	307,000
62. Residential Advisors	$21,850	28.9%	22,000
63. Child, Family, and School Social Workers	$35,350	19.0%	31,000
64. Substance Abuse and Behavioral Disorder Counselors	$32,580	28.7%	11,000
65. Criminal Investigators and Special Agents	$55,790	16.3%	9,000
66. Immigration and Customs Inspectors	$55,790	16.3%	9,000
67. Police Detectives	$55,790	16.3%	9,000
68. Medical Records and Health Information Technicians	$26,690	28.9%	14,000
69. Nuclear Medicine Technologists	$59,670	21.5%	2,000
70. Special Education Teachers, Secondary School	$46,820	17.9%	11,000
71. Middle School Teachers, Except Special and Vocational Education	$44,640	13.7%	83,000
72. Medical and Clinical Laboratory Technicians	$31,700	25.0%	14,000
73. Special Education Teachers, Middle School	$45,490	19.9%	8,000
74. Adult Literacy, Remedial Education, and GED Teachers and Instructors	$41,270	15.6%	27,000
75. Dentists, General	$125,300	13.5%	7,000
76. Environmental Scientists and Specialists, Including Health	$52,630	17.1%	8,000
77. Health Educators	$39,730	22.5%	8,000
78. Industrial-Organizational Psychologists	$84,690	20.4%	fewer than 500
79. Occupational Therapist Assistants	$39,750	34.1%	2,000

(continued)

(continued)

The 150 Best Jobs Overall for a Better World

Job	Annual Earnings	Percent Growth	Annual Openings
80. Epidemiologists	$52,170	26.2%	1,000
81. Coroners	$49,360	11.6%	17,000
82. Lifeguards, Ski Patrol, and Other Recreational Protective Service Workers	$16,910	20.4%	49,000
83. Air Traffic Controllers	$107,590	14.3%	2,000
84. Podiatrists	$100,550	16.2%	1,000
85. Flight Attendants	$46,680	16.3%	7,000
86. Landscape Architects	$54,220	19.4%	1,000
87. Speech-Language Pathologists	$54,880	14.6%	5,000
88. Crossing Guards	$20,050	19.7%	26,000
89. Film and Video Editors	$46,930	18.6%	3,000
90. Oral and Maxillofacial Surgeons	more than $145,600	16.2%	fewer than 500
91. Recreation Workers	$20,110	17.3%	69,000
92. Dietitians and Nutritionists	$44,940	18.3%	4,000
93. Physical Therapist Aides	$21,510	34.4%	5,000
94. Clergy	$38,540	12.4%	26,000
95. Urban and Regional Planners	$55,170	15.2%	3,000
96. Directors, Religious Activities and Education	$32,540	18.5%	10,000
97. Veterinary Assistants and Laboratory Animal Caretakers	$19,610	21.0%	14,000
98. Fire-Prevention and Protection Engineers	$65,210	13.4%	2,000
99. Industrial Safety and Health Engineers	$65,210	13.4%	2,000
100. Athletic Trainers	$34,260	29.3%	1,000
101. Probation Officers and Correctional Treatment Specialists	$40,210	12.8%	14,000
102. Orthodontists	more than $145,600	12.8%	1,000
103. Teacher Assistants	$20,090	14.1%	252,000
104. Vocational Education Teachers, Secondary School	$47,090	9.1%	10,000
105. Interpreters and Translators	$34,800	19.9%	4,000
106. Prosthodontists	more than $145,600	13.6%	fewer than 500
107. Orthotists and Prosthetists	$53,760	18.0%	fewer than 500
108. Bus Drivers, School	$24,070	13.6%	76,000
109. Child Care Workers	$17,050	13.8%	439,000
110. Nannies	$17,050	13.8%	439,000
111. Correctional Officers and Jailers	$34,090	6.7%	54,000
112. Medical Equipment Preparers	$24,880	20.0%	8,000
113. Ambulance Drivers and Attendants, Except Emergency Medical Technicians	$18,790	28.0%	5,000

The 150 Best Jobs Overall for a Better World

Job	Annual Earnings	Percent Growth	Annual Openings
114. Police, Fire, and Ambulance Dispatchers	$30,060	15.9%	12,000
115. Security Guards	$20,760	12.6%	230,000
116. Private Detectives and Investigators	$32,650	17.7%	7,000
117. Environmental Science and Protection Technicians, Including Health	$36,260	16.3%	6,000
118. Occupational Health and Safety Specialists	$53,710	12.4%	3,000
119. Funeral Attendants	$19,720	20.8%	8,000
120. Judges, Magistrate Judges, and Magistrates	$97,570	6.9%	1,000
121. Librarians	$47,400	4.9%	8,000
122. Sound Engineering Technicians	$38,390	18.4%	2,000
123. Audio-Visual Collections Specialists	$40,260	18.6%	1,000
124. City and Regional Planning Aides	$33,950	17.4%	4,000
125. Medical Equipment Repairers	$39,570	14.8%	4,000
126. Music Composers and Arrangers	$34,810	10.4%	11,000
127. Music Directors	$34,810	10.4%	11,000
128. Choreographers	$32,950	16.8%	4,000
129. Curators	$45,240	15.7%	1,000
130. Animal Trainers	$24,800	20.3%	3,000
131. Funeral Directors	$47,630	6.7%	3,000
132. Park Naturalists	$53,350	6.3%	2,000
133. Range Managers	$53,350	6.3%	2,000
134. Soil and Water Conservationists	$53,350	6.3%	2,000
135. Fine Artists, Including Painters, Sculptors, and Illustrators	$41,280	10.2%	4,000
136. Embalmers	$36,960	15.6%	2,000
137. Occupational Therapist Aides	$24,310	26.3%	fewer than 500
138. Dietetic Technicians	$23,470	19.1%	3,000
139. Audiologists	$53,490	9.1%	fewer than 500
140. Tour Guides and Escorts	$19,990	16.6%	5,000
141. Eligibility Interviewers, Government Programs	$33,740	–9.4%	10,000
142. Foresters	$48,670	6.7%	1,000
143. Opticians, Dispensing	$29,000	13.6%	6,000
144. Animal Control Workers	$26,780	14.4%	4,000
145. Museum Technicians and Conservators	$34,090	14.1%	2,000
146. Farm and Home Management Advisors	$41,890	7.7%	2,000
147. Transit and Railroad Police	$48,850	9.2%	fewer than 500

(continued)

(continued)

The 150 Best Jobs Overall for a Better World			
Job	Annual Earnings	Percent Growth	Annual Openings
148. Traffic Technicians	$37,070	14.1%	1,000
149. Fish and Game Wardens	$42,850	10.5%	1,000
150. Set and Exhibit Designers	$37,390	9.3%	2,000

Job 1 shares 34,000 openings with another job not included in this list. Jobs 17 and 18 share 17,000 openings. Jobs 23, 24, and 25 share 10,000 openings. Jobs 29 and 30 share 21,000 openings. Jobs 38 and 39 share 4,000 openings. Jobs 47 and 48 share 47,000 openings. Jobs 49 and 50 share 11,000 openings with each other and with three other jobs not included in this list. Job 55 shares 14,000 openings with another job not included in this list. Jobs 65, 66, and 67 share 9,000 openings with each other and with another job not included in this list. Job 81 shares 17,000 openings with four other jobs not included in this list. Jobs 98 and 99 share 2,000 openings with each other and with another job not included in this list. Jobs 109 and 110 share 439,000 openings. Job 124 shares 4,000 openings with another job not included in this list. Jobs 126 and 127 share 11,000 openings. Jobs 132, 133, and 134 share 2,000 openings.

The 50 Best-Paying Jobs for a Better World

Of the 150 jobs that met our criteria for this book, this list shows the 50 with the highest median earnings. (*Median earnings* means that half of all workers in these jobs earn more than that amount and half earn less. The median annual wage for all occupations in the workforce is $29,430.) This is a popular list for obvious reasons.

It's no accident that the top of this list is dominated by health-care jobs that require a college or professional degree. This industry is booming, so the jobs have lots of growth and job openings. You will find many other health-care jobs at various places on this list, but the jobs requiring a lot of education rank particularly high because they pay very well. Education tends to bring monetary rewards. Because you are interested in making a better world, keep in mind that in this field advanced education puts you at a level of skill where you can help people by performing critical procedures: doing surgery, prescribing drugs, or giving injections.

But you don't have to look very far down the list to find jobs that require considerably less education, and many good-paying jobs are open to people who gain experience in a related occupation.

As you look over this list, keep in mind that the earnings figures reflect the *national* median for *all* workers in the occupation. This is an important consideration, because starting pay in the job is usually a lot less than the pay that workers can earn with several years of experience. Earnings also vary significantly by region of the country, so actual pay in your area could be substantially different.

The 50 Best-Paying Jobs for a Better World

Job	Annual Earnings
1. Oral and Maxillofacial Surgeons	more than $145,600
2. Orthodontists	more than $145,600
3. Physicians and Surgeons	more than $145,600
4. Prosthodontists	more than $145,600
5. Dentists, General	$125,300
6. Air Traffic Controllers	$107,590
7. Podiatrists	$100,550
8. Judges, Magistrate Judges, and Magistrates	$97,570
9. Pharmacists	$89,820
10. Optometrists	$88,040
11. Industrial-Organizational Psychologists	$84,690
12. Education Administrators, Elementary and Secondary School	$75,400
13. Physician Assistants	$72,030
14. Education Administrators, Postsecondary	$70,350
15. Veterinarians	$68,910
16. Chiropractors	$67,200
17. First-Line Supervisors/Managers of Police and Detectives	$65,570
18. Fire-Prevention and Protection Engineers	$65,210
19. Industrial Safety and Health Engineers	$65,210
20. Personal Financial Advisors	$63,500
21. Physical Therapists	$63,080
22. Architects, Except Landscape and Naval	$62,850
23. Radiation Therapists	$62,340
24. Medical Scientists, Except Epidemiologists	$61,730
25. Dental Hygienists	$60,890
26. Forest Fire Fighting and Prevention Supervisors	$60,840
27. Municipal Fire Fighting and Prevention Supervisors	$60,840
28. Computer Security Specialists	$59,930
29. Nuclear Medicine Technologists	$59,670
30. Clinical Psychologists	$57,170
31. Counseling Psychologists	$57,170
32. School Psychologists	$57,170
33. Occupational Therapists	$56,860
34. Criminal Investigators and Special Agents	$55,790
35. Immigration and Customs Inspectors	$55,790
36. Police Detectives	$55,790
37. Urban and Regional Planners	$55,170

(continued)

(continued)

The 50 Best-Paying Jobs for a Better World

Job	Annual Earnings
38. Speech-Language Pathologists	$54,880
39. Registered Nurses	$54,670
40. Landscape Architects	$54,220
41. Directors—Stage, Motion Pictures, Television, and Radio	$53,860
42. Talent Directors	$53,860
43. Orthotists and Prosthetists	$53,760
44. Occupational Health and Safety Specialists	$53,710
45. Teachers, Postsecondary	$53,590
46. Audiologists	$53,490
47. Park Naturalists	$53,350
48. Range Managers	$53,350
49. Soil and Water Conservationists	$53,350
50. Environmental Scientists and Specialists, Including Health	$52,630

The 50 Fastest-Growing Jobs for a Better World

Of the 150 jobs that met our criteria for this book, this list shows the 50 that are projected to have the highest percentage increase in the number of people employed through 2014. (The average growth rate for *all* occupations in the workforce is 14.8 percent.) Fast-growing jobs are likely to offer a lot of opportunities to be hired and are less likely than most to be subject to layoffs.

Jobs in the health-care fields dominate the top of this list of the 50 fastest-growing jobs. Home Health Aides is the job with the highest growth rate; the number employed is projected to grow by more than half from 2004 to 2014.

The 50 Fastest-Growing Jobs for a Better World

Job	Percent Growth
1. Home Health Aides	56.0%
2. Medical Assistants	52.1%
3. Physician Assistants	49.6%
4. Physical Therapist Assistants	44.2%
5. Dental Hygienists	43.3%
6. Dental Assistants	42.7%
7. Personal and Home Care Aides	41.0%
8. Computer Security Specialists	38.4%

The 50 Fastest-Growing Jobs for a Better World

Job	Percent Growth
9. Physical Therapists	36.7%
10. Physical Therapist Aides	34.4%
11. Medical Scientists, Except Epidemiologists	34.1%
12. Occupational Therapist Assistants	34.1%
13. Occupational Therapists	33.6%
14. Preschool Teachers, Except Special Education	33.1%
15. Cardiovascular Technologists and Technicians	32.6%
16. Teachers, Postsecondary	32.2%
17. Social and Human Service Assistants	29.7%
18. Surgical Technologists	29.5%
19. Registered Nurses	29.4%
20. Athletic Trainers	29.3%
21. Medical Records and Health Information Technicians	28.9%
22. Residential Advisors	28.9%
23. Substance Abuse and Behavioral Disorder Counselors	28.7%
24. Pharmacy Technicians	28.6%
25. Respiratory Therapists	28.4%
26. Ambulance Drivers and Attendants, Except Emergency Medical Technicians	28.0%
27. Education Administrators, Preschool and Child Care Center/Program	27.9%
28. Instructional Coordinators	27.5%
29. Emergency Medical Technicians and Paramedics	27.3%
30. Mental Health Counselors	27.2%
31. Fitness Trainers and Aerobics Instructors	27.1%
32. Mental Health and Substance Abuse Social Workers	26.7%
33. Occupational Therapist Aides	26.3%
34. Radiation Therapists	26.3%
35. Epidemiologists	26.2%
36. Medical and Public Health Social Workers	25.9%
37. Personal Financial Advisors	25.9%
38. Social and Community Service Managers	25.5%
39. Self-Enrichment Education Teachers	25.3%
40. Medical and Clinical Laboratory Technicians	25.0%
41. Pharmacists	24.6%
42. Forest Fire Fighters	24.3%
43. Municipal Fire Fighters	24.3%
44. Physicians and Surgeons	24.0%
45. Special Education Teachers, Preschool, Kindergarten, and Elementary School	23.3%

(continued)

(continued)

The 50 Fastest-Growing Jobs for a Better World

Job	Percent Growth
46. Radiologic Technicians	23.2%
47. Radiologic Technologists	23.2%
48. Health Educators	22.5%
49. Chiropractors	22.4%
50. Kindergarten Teachers, Except Special Education	22.4%

The 50 Jobs for a Better World with the Most Openings

Of the 150 jobs that met our criteria for this book, this list shows the 50 jobs that are projected to have the largest number of job openings per year.

Jobs with many openings present several advantages that may be attractive to you. Because there are many openings, these jobs can be easier to obtain, particularly for those just entering the job market. These jobs may also offer more opportunities to move from one employer to another with relative ease. Though some of these jobs have average or below-average pay, some also pay quite well and can provide good long-term career opportunities or the ability to move up to more responsible roles.

Most of these jobs allow you to help people in person, rather than from behind the scenes. In fact, that is precisely why they have large numbers of openings: Because they require hands-on, on-site work, the work cannot easily be automated or exported overseas.

The 50 Jobs for a Better World with the Most Openings

Job	Annual Openings
1. Child Care Workers	439,000
2. Nannies	439,000
3. Teachers, Postsecondary	329,000
4. Nursing Aides, Orderlies, and Attendants	307,000
5. Teacher Assistants	252,000
6. Personal and Home Care Aides	230,000
7. Security Guards	230,000
8. Registered Nurses	229,000
9. Elementary School Teachers, Except Special Education	203,000
10. Home Health Aides	170,000
11. Secondary School Teachers, Except Special and Vocational Education	107,000

The 50 Jobs for a Better World with the Most Openings

Job	Annual Openings
12. Medical Assistants	93,000
13. Licensed Practical and Licensed Vocational Nurses	84,000
14. Middle School Teachers, Except Special and Vocational Education	83,000
15. Preschool Teachers, Except Special Education	77,000
16. Bus Drivers, School	76,000
17. Self-Enrichment Education Teachers	74,000
18. Recreation Workers	69,000
19. Social and Human Service Assistants	61,000
20. Correctional Officers and Jailers	54,000
21. Fitness Trainers and Aerobics Instructors	50,000
22. Lifeguards, Ski Patrol, and Other Recreational Protective Service Workers	49,000
23. Police Patrol Officers	47,000
24. Sheriffs and Deputy Sheriffs	47,000
25. Dental Assistants	45,000
26. Physicians and Surgeons	41,000
27. Pharmacy Technicians	35,000
28. Computer Security Specialists	34,000
29. Educational, Vocational, and School Counselors	32,000
30. Child, Family, and School Social Workers	31,000
31. Kindergarten Teachers, Except Special Education	28,000
32. Adult Literacy, Remedial Education, and GED Teachers and Instructors	27,000
33. Education Administrators, Elementary and Secondary School	27,000
34. Clergy	26,000
35. Crossing Guards	26,000
36. Residential Advisors	22,000
37. Emergency Medical Technicians and Paramedics	21,000
38. Forest Fire Fighters	21,000
39. Municipal Fire Fighters	21,000
40. Education Administrators, Postsecondary	18,000
41. Special Education Teachers, Preschool, Kindergarten, and Elementary School	18,000
42. Coroners	17,000
43. Dental Hygienists	17,000
44. Personal Financial Advisors	17,000
45. Radiologic Technicians	17,000
46. Radiologic Technologists	17,000
47. Social and Community Service Managers	17,000

(continued)

(continued)

The 50 Jobs for a Better World with the Most Openings	
Job	Annual Openings
48. Pharmacists	16,000
49. Instructional Coordinators	15,000
50. Medical Scientists, Except Epidemiologists	15,000

Jobs 1 and 2 share 439,000 openings. Jobs 23 and 24 share 47,000 openings. Job 28 shares 34,000 openings with another job not included in this list. Jobs 38 and 39 share 21,000 openings. Job 42 shares 17,000 openings with four other jobs not included in this list. Jobs 45 and 46 share 17,000 openings.

Best Jobs Rated High on Various World-Improving Criteria

As we explained in the introduction, we identified world-improving jobs in the O*NET database by flagging those that are rated high on certain criteria: the value Social Service, the knowledge Education and Training, the knowledge Fine Arts, the knowledge Medicine and Dentistry, the knowledge Public Safety and Security, and the knowledge Therapy and Counseling.

Although we threw all of these occupations into one combined list to determine which are the best 150 world-improving jobs, we thought it likely that you might be interested in bettering the world through *one* specific way. For example, you might want to contribute to a more beautiful world through Fine Arts and have no desire to get involved in Public Safety and Security or any of the other world-improving factors. So we created sets of lists showing the jobs that are rated highest on each of these different criteria. And, just for fun, we added a set of lists based on the ratings for all of the criteria *combined;* the jobs on that set of lists are not necessarily the most beneficial jobs, but they are beneficial in diverse ways.

In the following lists based on various world-improving criteria, the ratings for the criteria use a scale in which 100 is the highest possible rating and 0 is the lowest. The scale indicates the *level* of knowledge that is needed to perform the job, not a percentage of time spent using the knowledge. We included only jobs rated over 50 on each criterion, and this caused some lists to be smaller than others.

Each set offers five lists:

- ◎ The jobs rated highest on the criterion—as many as 50 jobs, but none rated less than 50 on the criterion
- ◎ The 20 jobs from this high-rated group with the best combined scores for earnings, growth, and number of openings
- ◎ The 20 jobs with the highest earnings

⊙ The 20 jobs with the highest growth rates

⊙ The 20 jobs with the largest number of openings

Best Jobs for a Better World Rated High on the Value Social Service

The value Social Service is defined as "having work where you do things for other people," so it is obviously of interest to many people who want to make a better world. At first glance the top of the list of highest-rated jobs does not seem to have a lot of variety because it is dominated by jobs in the health-care field. However, these jobs represent many levels of education and training, from short-term on-the-job training to first professional degree. And as you look further down the list you'll find jobs in education, religion, and mental health. Many of these jobs pay very well, so it's nice to discover that you can do well both for other people and for yourself.

Best Jobs for a Better World Rated Highest on the Value Social Service

Job	Rating on Social Service
1. Registered Nurses	100.0
2. Personal and Home Care Aides	100.0
3. Physicians and Surgeons	98.4
4. Audiologists	96.7
5. Clinical Psychologists	96.7
6. Counseling Psychologists	96.7
7. Emergency Medical Technicians and Paramedics	96.7
8. Licensed Practical and Licensed Vocational Nurses	96.7
9. Occupational Therapists	96.7
10. Oral and Maxillofacial Surgeons	96.7
11. Physical Therapists	96.7
12. Physician Assistants	96.7
13. Orthodontists	96.7
14. Speech-Language Pathologists	96.7
15. Child Care Workers	93.8
16. Chiropractors	93.8
17. Dentists, General	93.8
18. Home Health Aides	93.8
19. Optometrists	93.8
20. Podiatrists	93.8
21. Child, Family, and School Social Workers	90.5
22. Clergy	90.5

(continued)

(continued)

Best Jobs for a Better World Rated Highest on the Value Social Service

Job	Rating on Social Service
23. Medical and Public Health Social Workers	90.5
24. Mental Health and Substance Abuse Social Workers	90.5
25. Mental Health Counselors	90.5
26. Prosthodontists	90.5
27. Respiratory Therapists	90.5
28. Special Education Teachers, Middle School	90.5
29. Special Education Teachers, Preschool, Kindergarten, and Elementary School	90.5
30. Special Education Teachers, Secondary School	90.5
31. Substance Abuse and Behavioral Disorder Counselors	90.5
32. Ambulance Drivers and Attendants, Except Emergency Medical Technicians	87.5
33. Dental Hygienists	87.5
34. Middle School Teachers, Except Special and Vocational Education	87.5
35. Occupational Therapist Aides	87.5
36. Occupational Therapist Assistants	87.5
37. Opticians, Dispensing	87.5
38. Orthotists and Prosthetists	87.5
39. Physical Therapist Aides	87.5
40. Physical Therapist Assistants	87.5
41. Secondary School Teachers, Except Special and Vocational Education	87.5
42. Vocational Education Teachers, Secondary School	87.5
43. Athletic Trainers	84.2
44. Dietitians and Nutritionists	84.2
45. Directors, Religious Activities and Education	84.2
46. Elementary School Teachers, Except Special Education	84.2
47. Kindergarten Teachers, Except Special Education	84.2
48. Nursing Aides, Orderlies, and Attendants	84.2
49. Preschool Teachers, Except Special Education	84.2
50. Social and Community Service Managers	84.2

The jobs in the following four lists are derived from the preceding list of the jobs with the highest ratings on the value Social Service.

Best Jobs Overall Rated High on the Value Social Service

Job	Rating on Social Service	Annual Earnings	Percent Growth	Annual Openings
1. Registered Nurses	100.0	$54,670	29.4%	229,000
2. Dental Hygienists	87.5	$60,890	43.3%	17,000
3. Physicians and Surgeons	98.4	more than $145,600	24.0%	41,000
4. Physician Assistants	96.7	$72,030	49.6%	10,000
5. Physical Therapists	96.7	$63,080	36.7%	13,000
6. Home Health Aides	93.8	$18,800	56.0%	170,000
7. Occupational Therapists	96.7	$56,860	33.6%	7,000
8. Personal and Home Care Aides	100.0	$17,340	41.0%	230,000
9. Social and Community Service Managers	84.2	$49,500	25.5%	17,000
10. Preschool Teachers, Except Special Education	84.2	$21,990	33.1%	77,000
11. Clinical Psychologists	96.7	$57,170	19.1%	10,000
12. Counseling Psychologists	96.7	$57,170	19.1%	10,000
13. Kindergarten Teachers, Except Special Education	84.2	$42,230	22.4%	28,000
14. Physical Therapist Assistants	87.5	$39,490	44.2%	7,000
15. Special Education Teachers, Preschool, Kindergarten, and Elementary School	90.5	$44,630	23.3%	18,000
16. Elementary School Teachers, Except Special Education	84.2	$44,040	18.2%	203,000
17. Respiratory Therapists	90.5	$45,140	28.4%	7,000
18. Medical and Public Health Social Workers	90.5	$41,120	25.9%	14,000
19. Secondary School Teachers, Except Special and Vocational Education	87.5	$46,060	14.4%	107,000
20. Chiropractors	93.8	$67,200	22.4%	4,000

Jobs 11 and 12 share 10,000 openings with each other and with another job not included in this list.

Best-Paying Jobs Rated High on the Value Social Service

Job	Rating on Social Service	Annual Earnings
1. Oral and Maxillofacial Surgeons	96.7	more than $145,600
2. Orthodontists	96.7	more than $145,600
3. Physicians and Surgeons	98.4	more than $145,600
4. Prosthodontists	90.5	more than $145,600
5. Dentists, General	93.8	$125,300

(continued)

(continued)

Best-Paying Jobs Rated High on the Value Social Service

Job	Rating on Social Service	Annual Earnings
6. Podiatrists	93.8	$100,550
7. Optometrists	93.8	$88,040
8. Physician Assistants	96.7	$72,030
9. Chiropractors	93.8	$67,200
10. Physical Therapists	96.7	$63,080
11. Dental Hygienists	87.5	$60,890
12. Clinical Psychologists	96.7	$57,170
13. Counseling Psychologists	96.7	$57,170
14. Occupational Therapists	96.7	$56,860
15. Speech-Language Pathologists	96.7	$54,880
16. Registered Nurses	100.0	$54,670
17. Orthotists and Prosthetists	87.5	$53,760
18. Audiologists	96.7	$53,490
19. Social and Community Service Managers	84.2	$49,500
20. Vocational Education Teachers, Secondary School	87.5	$47,090

Fastest-Growing Jobs Rated High on the Value Social Service

Job	Rating on Social Service	Percent Growth
1. Home Health Aides	93.8	56.0%
2. Physician Assistants	96.7	49.6%
3. Physical Therapist Assistants	87.5	44.2%
4. Dental Hygienists	87.5	43.3%
5. Personal and Home Care Aides	100.0	41.0%
6. Physical Therapists	96.7	36.7%
7. Physical Therapist Aides	87.5	34.4%
8. Occupational Therapist Assistants	87.5	34.1%
9. Occupational Therapists	96.7	33.6%
10. Preschool Teachers, Except Special Education	84.2	33.1%
11. Registered Nurses	100.0	29.4%
12. Athletic Trainers	84.2	29.3%
13. Substance Abuse and Behavioral Disorder Counselors	90.5	28.7%
14. Respiratory Therapists	90.5	28.4%

Fastest-Growing Jobs Rated High on the Value Social Service

Job	Rating on Social Service	Percent Growth
15. Ambulance Drivers and Attendants, Except Emergency Medical Technicians	87.5	28.0%
16. Emergency Medical Technicians and Paramedics	96.7	27.3%
17. Mental Health Counselors	90.5	27.2%
18. Mental Health and Substance Abuse Social Workers	90.5	26.7%
19. Occupational Therapist Aides	87.5	26.3%
20. Medical and Public Health Social Workers	90.5	25.9%

Jobs with the Most Openings Rated High on the Value Social Service

Job	Rating on Social Service	Annual Openings
1. Child Care Workers	93.8	439,000
2. Nursing Aides, Orderlies, and Attendants	84.2	307,000
3. Personal and Home Care Aides	100.0	230,000
4. Registered Nurses	100.0	229,000
5. Elementary School Teachers, Except Special Education	84.2	203,000
6. Home Health Aides	93.8	170,000
7. Secondary School Teachers, Except Special and Vocational Education	87.5	107,000
8. Licensed Practical and Licensed Vocational Nurses	96.7	84,000
9. Middle School Teachers, Except Special and Vocational Education	87.5	83,000
10. Preschool Teachers, Except Special Education	84.2	77,000
11. Physicians and Surgeons	98.4	41,000
12. Child, Family, and School Social Workers	90.5	31,000
13. Kindergarten Teachers, Except Special Education	84.2	28,000
14. Clergy	90.5	26,000
15. Emergency Medical Technicians and Paramedics	96.7	21,000
16. Special Education Teachers, Preschool, Kindergarten, and Elementary School	90.5	18,000
17. Dental Hygienists	87.5	17,000
18. Social and Community Service Managers	84.2	17,000
19. Mental Health and Substance Abuse Social Workers	90.5	15,000
20. Medical and Public Health Social Workers	90.5	14,000

Job 1 shares 439,000 openings with another job not included in this list.

Best Jobs for a Better World Rated High on Knowledge of Education and Training

Everyone agrees that education improves the world. But not all the jobs in the following lists are classroom teaching jobs that require a teaching degree. Some of them involve training workers to do their jobs better. Others are concerned with educating individual clients about how to improve their lives—for example, when Dietitians and Nutritionists explain to patients how to eat better. Still others involve teaching the public about matters such as safety or conservation—for example, when Park Naturalists explain to visitors about the regulations and natural features of the park.

If you have been in the workforce for some years and want to move into a world-improving job, you may consider a job in teaching or training so you can share with other people some of the knowledge and skills that you have acquired.

Best Jobs for a Better World Rated Highest on Knowledge of Education and Training

Job	Rating on Education and Training
1. Instructional Coordinators	93.0
2. Education Administrators, Elementary and Secondary School	91.7
3. Industrial-Organizational Psychologists	88.0
4. Audio-Visual Collections Specialists	87.9
5. Farm and Home Management Advisors	86.6
6. Health Educators	85.6
7. Computer Security Specialists	84.4
8. Teachers, Postsecondary	84.3
9. Industrial Safety and Health Engineers	83.9
10. Vocational Education Teachers, Secondary School	83.6
11. Education Administrators, Preschool and Child Care Center/Program	83.4
12. Municipal Fire Fighting and Prevention Supervisors	83.0
13. Secondary School Teachers, Except Special and Vocational Education	82.4
14. Education Administrators, Postsecondary	81.9
15. School Psychologists	80.3
16. Educational, Vocational, and School Counselors	79.4
17. Middle School Teachers, Except Special and Vocational Education	79.0
18. First-Line Supervisors/Managers of Police and Detectives	76.6
19. Adult Literacy, Remedial Education, and GED Teachers and Instructors	76.4
20. Respiratory Therapists	76.3
21. Occupational Health and Safety Specialists	73.7
22. Speech-Language Pathologists	73.7
23. Dietitians and Nutritionists	73.6

Best Jobs for a Better World Rated Highest on Knowledge of Education and Training

Job	Rating on Education and Training
24. Special Education Teachers, Secondary School	73.4
25. Soil and Water Conservationists	73.3
26. Self-Enrichment Education Teachers	73.1
27. Social and Community Service Managers	72.3
28. Special Education Teachers, Middle School	72.0
29. Choreographers	71.4
30. Elementary School Teachers, Except Special Education	71.3
31. Environmental Science and Protection Technicians, Including Health	70.3
32. Forest Fire Fighters	69.9
33. Substance Abuse and Behavioral Disorder Counselors	69.1
34. Clinical Psychologists	69.0
35. Kindergarten Teachers, Except Special Education	69.0
36. Medical Scientists, Except Epidemiologists	68.6
37. Athletic Trainers	68.1
38. Park Naturalists	68.1
39. Physical Therapist Assistants	67.4
40. Oral and Maxillofacial Surgeons	67.1
41. Epidemiologists	66.7
42. Occupational Therapist Aides	66.1
43. Licensed Practical and Licensed Vocational Nurses	65.3
44. Police Detectives	65.1
45. Audiologists	64.7
46. Orthotists and Prosthetists	64.6
47. Special Education Teachers, Preschool, Kindergarten, and Elementary School	64.1
48. Sheriffs and Deputy Sheriffs	64.0
49. Physical Therapists	63.9
50. Surgical Technologists	63.4

The jobs in the following four lists are derived from the preceding list of the jobs with the highest ratings on knowledge of Education and Training.

Best Jobs Overall Rated High on Knowledge of Education and Training

Job	Rating on Education and Training	Annual Earnings	Percent Growth	Annual Openings
1. Computer Security Specialists	84.4	$59,930	38.4%	34,000
2. Physicians and Surgeons	70.5	more than $145,600	24.0%	41,000
3. Medical Scientists, Except Epidemiologists	68.6	$61,730	34.1%	15,000
4. Physical Therapists	63.9	$63,080	36.7%	13,000
5. Education Administrators, Postsecondary	81.9	$70,350	21.3%	18,000
6. Instructional Coordinators	93.0	$50,430	27.5%	15,000
7. Social and Community Service Managers	72.3	$49,500	25.5%	17,000
8. Clinical Psychologists	69.0	$57,170	19.1%	10,000
9. School Psychologists	80.3	$57,170	19.1%	10,000
10. Education Administrators, Elementary and Secondary School	91.7	$75,400	10.4%	27,000
11. Elementary School Teachers, Except Special Education	71.3	$44,040	18.2%	203,000
12. Kindergarten Teachers, Except Special Education	69.0	$42,230	22.4%	28,000
13. Special Education Teachers, Preschool, Kindergarten, and Elementary School	64.1	$44,630	23.3%	18,000
14. Municipal Fire Fighting and Prevention Supervisors	83.0	$60,840	21.1%	4,000
15. Self-Enrichment Education Teachers	73.1	$32,360	25.3%	74,000
16. First-Line Supervisors/Managers of Police and Detectives	76.6	$65,570	15.5%	9,000
17. Forest Fire Fighters	69.9	$39,090	24.3%	21,000
18. Respiratory Therapists	76.3	$45,140	28.4%	7,000
19. Sheriffs and Deputy Sheriffs	64.0	$46,290	15.5%	47,000
20. Surgical Technologists	63.4	$34,830	29.5%	12,000

Job 1 shares 34,000 openings with another job not included in this list. Jobs 8 and 9 share 10,000 openings. Job 14 shares 4,000 openings with another job not included in this list. Job 17 shares 21,000 openings with another job not included in this list. Job 19 shares 47,000 openings with another job not included in this list. Job 24 shares 9,000 openings with three other jobs not included in this list. Job 36 shares 2,000 openings with two other jobs not included in this list. Jobs 45 and 46 share 2,000 openings with each other and with another job not included in this list.

Best-Paying Jobs Rated High on Knowledge of Education and Training

Job	Rating on Education and Training	Annual Earnings
1. Oral and Maxillofacial Surgeons	67.1	more than $145,600
2. Industrial-Organizational Psychologists	88.0	$84,690
3. Education Administrators, Elementary and Secondary School	91.7	$75,400
4. Education Administrators, Postsecondary	81.9	$70,350
5. First-Line Supervisors/Managers of Police and Detectives	76.6	$65,570
6. Industrial Safety and Health Engineers	83.9	$65,210
7. Physical Therapists	63.9	$63,080
8. Medical Scientists, Except Epidemiologists	68.6	$61,730
9. Municipal Fire Fighting and Prevention Supervisors	83.0	$60,840
10. Computer Security Specialists	84.4	$59,930
11. Clinical Psychologists	69.0	$57,170
12. School Psychologists	80.3	$57,170
13. Police Detectives	65.1	$55,790
14. Speech-Language Pathologists	73.7	$54,880
15. Orthotists and Prosthetists	64.6	$53,760
16. Occupational Health and Safety Specialists	73.7	$53,710
17. Teachers, Postsecondary	84.3	$53,590
18. Audiologists	64.7	$53,490
19. Park Naturalists	68.1	$53,350
20. Soil and Water Conservationists	73.3	$53,350

Fastest-Growing Jobs Rated High on Knowledge of Education and Training

Job	Rating on Education and Training	Percent Growth
1. Physical Therapist Assistants	67.4	44.2%
2. Computer Security Specialists	84.4	38.4%
3. Physical Therapists	63.9	36.7%
4. Medical Scientists, Except Epidemiologists	68.6	34.1%
5. Teachers, Postsecondary	84.3	32.2%
6. Surgical Technologists	63.4	29.5%
7. Athletic Trainers	68.1	29.3%
8. Substance Abuse and Behavioral Disorder Counselors	69.1	28.7%

(continued)

(continued)

Fastest-Growing Jobs Rated High on Knowledge of Education and Training

Job	Rating on Education and Training	Percent Growth
9. Respiratory Therapists	76.3	28.4%
10. Education Administrators, Preschool and Child Care Center/Program	83.4	27.9%
11. Instructional Coordinators	93.0	27.5%
12. Occupational Therapist Aides	66.1	26.3%
13. Epidemiologists	66.7	26.2%
14. Social and Community Service Managers	72.3	25.5%
15. Self-Enrichment Education Teachers	73.1	25.3%
16. Forest Fire Fighters	69.9	24.3%
17. Special Education Teachers, Preschool, Kindergarten, and Elementary School	64.1	23.3%
18. Health Educators	85.6	22.5%
19. Kindergarten Teachers, Except Special Education	69.0	22.4%
20. Education Administrators, Postsecondary	81.9	21.3%

Jobs with the Most Openings Rated High on Knowledge of Education and Training

Job	Rating on Education and Training	Annual Openings
1. Teachers, Postsecondary	84.3	329,000
2. Elementary School Teachers, Except Special Education	71.3	203,000
3. Secondary School Teachers, Except Special and Vocational Education	82.4	107,000
4. Licensed Practical and Licensed Vocational Nurses	65.3	84,000
5. Middle School Teachers, Except Special and Vocational Education	79.0	83,000
6. Self-Enrichment Education Teachers	73.1	74,000
7. Sheriffs and Deputy Sheriffs	64.0	47,000
8. Computer Security Specialists	84.4	34,000
9. Educational, Vocational, and School Counselors	79.4	32,000
10. Kindergarten Teachers, Except Special Education	69.0	28,000
11. Adult Literacy, Remedial Education, and GED Teachers and Instructors	76.4	27,000
12. Education Administrators, Elementary and Secondary School	91.7	27,000

150 Best Jobs for a Better World © JIST Works

Jobs with the Most Openings Rated High on Knowledge of Education and Training

Job	Rating on Education and Training	Annual Openings
13. Forest Fire Fighters	69.9	21,000
14. Education Administrators, Postsecondary	81.9	18,000
15. Special Education Teachers, Preschool, Kindergarten, and Elementary School	64.1	18,000
16. Social and Community Service Managers	72.3	17,000
17. Instructional Coordinators	93.0	15,000
18. Medical Scientists, Except Epidemiologists	68.6	15,000
19. Physical Therapists	63.9	13,000
20. Surgical Technologists	63.4	12,000

Job 7 shares 47,000 openings with another job not included in this list. Job 8 shares 34,000 openings with another job not included in this list. Job 13 shares 21,000 openings with another job not included in this list.

Best Jobs for a Better World Rated High on Knowledge of Fine Arts

By itself, art probably cannot save the world. It does not save lives or protect the environment in the direct manner of medicine or law enforcement. But art greatly enriches people's lives. It inspires people, entertains them, and communicates moral messages. Even people who would never set foot in an art museum have artistic posters hanging on their walls. People who would never attend a ballet still enjoy highly choreographed music videos. Millions of people enjoy going to the movies and listening to popular music on the radio. A world without the arts would be a very impoverished and depressing place.

Of course, careers in the arts are notorious for their high level of competition and their usually low level of earnings. Fortunately for the world, creative people who are strongly committed to their art forms continue to fight the odds and produce artwork. They find great nonmonetary rewards in their work.

Not many occupations in the U.S. economy are rated high on knowledge of Fine Arts, and some of these (for example, Dancers) could not be included in this book because no data is available on annual earnings. As a result, the list of jobs rated highest on knowledge of Fine Arts contains only 10 entries, and each of the four lists that follow contains only 10 jobs instead of the usual 20.

Best Jobs for a Better World Rated Highest on Knowledge of Fine Arts

Job	Rating on Fine Arts
1. Choreographers	93.1
2. Music Composers and Arrangers	92.9
3. Fine Artists, Including Painters, Sculptors, and Illustrators	88.7
4. Set and Exhibit Designers	80.9
5. Sound Engineering Technicians	69.6
6. Music Directors	69.0
7. Poets, Lyricists, and Creative Writers	68.3
8. Talent Directors	67.0
9. Film and Video Editors	63.4
10. Curators	57.7

The jobs in the following four lists are derived from the preceding list of the jobs with the highest ratings on knowledge of Fine Arts.

Best Jobs Overall Rated High on Knowledge of Fine Arts

Job	Rating on Fine Arts	Annual Earnings	Percent Growth	Annual Openings
1. Poets, Lyricists, and Creative Writers	68.3	$46,420	17.7%	14,000
2. Talent Directors	67.0	$53,860	16.6%	11,000
3. Film and Video Editors	63.4	$46,930	18.6%	3,000
4. Sound Engineering Technicians	69.6	$38,390	18.4%	2,000
5. Music Composers and Arrangers	92.9	$34,810	10.4%	11,000
6. Music Directors	69.0	$34,810	10.4%	11,000
7. Choreographers	93.1	$32,950	16.8%	4,000
8. Fine Artists, Including Painters, Sculptors, and Illustrators	88.7	$41,280	10.2%	4,000
9. Curators	57.7	$45,240	15.7%	1,000
10. Set and Exhibit Designers	80.9	$37,390	9.3%	2,000

Job 1 shares 14,000 openings with another job not included in this list. Job 2 shares 11,000 openings with four other jobs not included in this list. Jobs 5 and 6 share 11,000 openings.

Best-Paying Jobs Rated High on Knowledge of Fine Arts

Job	Rating on Fine Arts	Annual Earnings
1. Talent Directors	67.0	$53,860
2. Film and Video Editors	63.4	$46,930
3. Poets, Lyricists, and Creative Writers	68.3	$46,420
4. Curators	57.7	$45,240
5. Fine Artists, Including Painters, Sculptors, and Illustrators	88.7	$41,280
6. Sound Engineering Technicians	69.6	$38,390
7. Set and Exhibit Designers	80.9	$37,390
8. Music Composers and Arrangers	92.9	$34,810
9. Music Directors	69.0	$34,810
10. Choreographers	93.1	$32,950

Fastest-Growing Jobs Rated High on Knowledge of Fine Arts

Job	Rating on Fine Arts	Percent Growth
1. Film and Video Editors	63.4	18.6%
2. Sound Engineering Technicians	69.6	18.4%
3. Poets, Lyricists, and Creative Writers	68.3	17.7%
4. Choreographers	93.1	16.8%
5. Talent Directors	67.0	16.6%
6. Curators	57.7	15.7%
7. Music Composers and Arrangers	92.9	10.4%
8. Music Directors	69.0	10.4%
9. Fine Artists, Including Painters, Sculptors, and Illustrators	88.7	10.2%
10. Set and Exhibit Designers	80.9	9.3%

Jobs with the Most Openings Rated High on Knowledge of Fine Arts

Job	Rating on Fine Arts	Annual Openings
1. Poets, Lyricists, and Creative Writers	68.3	14,000
2. Music Composers and Arrangers	92.9	11,000
3. Music Directors	69.0	11,000
4. Talent Directors	67.0	11,000

(continued)

(continued)

Jobs with the Most Openings Rated High on Knowledge of Fine Arts

Job	Rating on Fine Arts	Annual Openings
5. Choreographers	93.1	4,000
6. Fine Artists, Including Painters, Sculptors, and Illustrators	88.7	4,000
7. Film and Video Editors	63.4	3,000
8. Set and Exhibit Designers	80.9	2,000
9. Sound Engineering Technicians	69.6	2,000
10. Curators	57.7	1,000

Job 1 shares 14,000 openings with another job not included in this list. Jobs 2 and 3 share 11,000 openings. Job 4 shares 11,000 openings with four other jobs not included in this list.

Best Jobs for a Better World Rated High on Knowledge of Medicine and Dentistry

Helping improve people's health can be very rewarding work and is also part of one of the fastest-growing industries. Many of the hottest jobs in this field do not require a professional-level education, and many of the jobs do not involve the stress of life-or-death decisions. Some of the jobs offer lots of opportunities for part-time work.

Work in the health-care field is not for everybody. Some people are squeamish or simply have other interests. Nevertheless, this field is so big, fast-growing, and in many cases high-paying that you should at least consider some of the opportunities it offers.

Best Jobs for a Better World Rated Highest on Knowledge of Medicine and Dentistry

Job	Rating on Medicine and Dentistry
1. Oral and Maxillofacial Surgeons	91.4
2. Physicians and Surgeons	90.3
3. Dentists, General	90.1
4. Orthodontists	88.7
5. Physician Assistants	87.3
6. Coroners	86.4
7. Prosthodontists	85.9
8. Podiatrists	84.9
9. Veterinarians	77.0

Best Jobs for a Better World Rated Highest on Knowledge of Medicine and Dentistry

Job	Rating on Medicine and Dentistry
10. Surgical Technologists	76.9
11. Chiropractors	74.9
12. Respiratory Therapists	70.3
13. Optometrists	69.9
14. Dental Assistants	67.9
15. Medical Scientists, Except Epidemiologists	66.6
16. Registered Nurses	65.0
17. Radiation Therapists	64.1
18. Athletic Trainers	62.7
19. Municipal Fire Fighters	61.6
20. Cardiovascular Technologists and Technicians	60.6
21. Dental Hygienists	60.6
22. Nuclear Medicine Technologists	59.3
23. Municipal Fire Fighting and Prevention Supervisors	58.9
24. Orthotists and Prosthetists	58.9
25. Licensed Practical and Licensed Vocational Nurses	57.6
26. Pharmacists	57.6
27. Physical Therapists	57.4
28. Audiologists	56.9
29. Emergency Medical Technicians and Paramedics	56.1
30. Physical Therapist Assistants	54.4
31. Medical Assistants	54.1
32. Radiologic Technologists	53.1
33. Medical and Public Health Social Workers	52.9
34. Dietitians and Nutritionists	51.7

The jobs in the following four lists are derived from the preceding list of the jobs with the highest ratings on knowledge of Medicine and Dentistry.

Best Jobs Overall Rated High on Knowledge of Medicine and Dentistry

Job	Rating on Medicine and Dentistry	Annual Earnings	Percent Growth	Annual Openings
1. Physicians and Surgeons	90.3 more than	$145,600	24.0%	41,000
2. Dental Hygienists	60.6	$60,890	43.3%	17,000
3. Physician Assistants	87.3	$72,030	49.6%	10,000
4. Registered Nurses	65.0	$54,670	29.4%	229,000
5. Physical Therapists	57.4	$63,080	36.7%	13,000
6. Medical Scientists, Except Epidemiologists	66.6	$61,730	34.1%	15,000
7. Pharmacists	57.6	$89,820	24.6%	16,000
8. Medical Assistants	54.1	$25,350	52.1%	93,000
9. Dental Assistants	67.9	$29,520	42.7%	45,000
10. Physical Therapist Assistants	54.4	$39,490	44.2%	7,000
11. Radiologic Technologists	53.1	$45,950	23.2%	17,000
12. Municipal Fire Fighters	61.6	$39,090	24.3%	21,000
13. Emergency Medical Technicians and Paramedics	56.1	$26,080	27.3%	21,000
14. Chiropractors	74.9	$67,200	22.4%	4,000
15. Medical and Public Health Social Workers	52.9	$41,120	25.9%	14,000
16. Respiratory Therapists	70.3	$45,140	28.4%	7,000
17. Veterinarians	77.0	$68,910	17.4%	8,000
18. Dentists, General	90.1	$125,300	13.5%	7,000
19. Radiation Therapists	64.1	$62,340	26.3%	1,000
20. Surgical Technologists	76.9	$34,830	29.5%	12,000

Job 11 shares 17,000 openings with another job not included in this list. Job 12 shares 21,000 openings with another job not included in this list.

Best-Paying Jobs Rated High on Knowledge of Medicine and Dentistry

Job	Rating on Medicine and Dentistry	Annual Earnings
1. Oral and Maxillofacial Surgeons	91.4	more than $145,600
2. Orthodontists	88.7	more than $145,600
3. Physicians and Surgeons	90.3	more than $145,600
4. Prosthodontists	85.9	more than $145,600
5. Dentists, General	90.1	$125,300
6. Podiatrists	84.9	$100,550
7. Pharmacists	57.6	$89,820

Best-Paying Jobs Rated High on Knowledge of Medicine and Dentistry

Job	Rating on Medicine and Dentistry	Annual Earnings
8. Optometrists	69.9	$88,040
9. Physician Assistants	87.3	$72,030
10. Veterinarians	77.0	$68,910
11. Chiropractors	74.9	$67,200
12. Physical Therapists	57.4	$63,080
13. Radiation Therapists	64.1	$62,340
14. Medical Scientists, Except Epidemiologists	66.6	$61,730
15. Dental Hygienists	60.6	$60,890
16. Municipal Fire Fighting and Prevention Supervisors	58.9	$60,840
17. Nuclear Medicine Technologists	59.3	$59,670
18. Registered Nurses	65.0	$54,670
19. Orthotists and Prosthetists	58.9	$53,760
20. Audiologists	56.9	$53,490

Fastest-Growing Jobs Rated High on Knowledge of Medicine and Dentistry

Job	Rating on Medicine and Dentistry	Percent Growth
1. Medical Assistants	54.1	52.1%
2. Physician Assistants	87.3	49.6%
3. Physical Therapist Assistants	54.4	44.2%
4. Dental Hygienists	60.6	43.3%
5. Dental Assistants	67.9	42.7%
6. Physical Therapists	57.4	36.7%
7. Medical Scientists, Except Epidemiologists	66.6	34.1%
8. Cardiovascular Technologists and Technicians	60.6	32.6%
9. Surgical Technologists	76.9	29.5%
10. Registered Nurses	65.0	29.4%
11. Athletic Trainers	62.7	29.3%
12. Respiratory Therapists	70.3	28.4%
13. Emergency Medical Technicians and Paramedics	56.1	27.3%
14. Radiation Therapists	64.1	26.3%
15. Medical and Public Health Social Workers	52.9	25.9%

(continued)

(continued)

Fastest-Growing Jobs Rated High on Knowledge of Medicine and Dentistry

Job	Rating on Medicine and Dentistry	Percent Growth
16. Pharmacists	57.6	24.6%
17. Municipal Fire Fighters	61.6	24.3%
18. Physicians and Surgeons	90.3	24.0%
19. Radiologic Technologists	53.1	23.2%
20. Chiropractors	74.9	22.4%

Jobs with the Most Openings Rated High on Knowledge of Medicine and Dentistry

Job	Rating on Medicine and Dentistry	Annual Openings
1. Registered Nurses	65.0	229,000
2. Medical Assistants	54.1	93,000
3. Licensed Practical and Licensed Vocational Nurses	57.6	84,000
4. Dental Assistants	67.9	45,000
5. Physicians and Surgeons	90.3	41,000
6. Emergency Medical Technicians and Paramedics	56.1	21,000
7. Municipal Fire Fighters	61.6	21,000
8. Coroners	86.4	17,000
9. Dental Hygienists	60.6	17,000
10. Radiologic Technologists	53.1	17,000
11. Pharmacists	57.6	16,000
12. Medical Scientists, Except Epidemiologists	66.6	15,000
13. Medical and Public Health Social Workers	52.9	14,000
14. Physical Therapists	57.4	13,000
15. Surgical Technologists	76.9	12,000
16. Physician Assistants	87.3	10,000
17. Veterinarians	77.0	8,000
18. Dentists, General	90.1	7,000
19. Physical Therapist Assistants	54.4	7,000
20. Respiratory Therapists	70.3	7,000

Job 7 shares 21,000 openings with another job not included in this list. Job 8 shares 17,000 openings with four other jobs not included in this list. Job 10 shares 17,000 openings with another job not included in this list.

150 Best Jobs for a Better World © JIST Works

Best Jobs for a Better World Rated High on Knowledge of Public Safety and Security

The events of September 11, 2001, caused many people to realize for the first time how important safety and security are. Suddenly police and fire fighters were recognized as heroes whose daily job is to save lives and protect us from crime and disaster. The law touches on so many aspects of life that it is possible to work in law enforcement in a wide variety of fields, such as animal control, workplace safety, environmental protection, and parole management. Each new technology that emerges brings with it new safety and security concerns. For example, the computer industry has created a need for Computer Security Specialists. If you are a mid-life career changer, the security field may be an option for you to consider. After working in an industry long enough to know the major threats to safety and the laws, you may be able to work as an expert in security for the same industry.

Best Jobs for a Better World Rated Highest on Knowledge of Public Safety and Security

Job	Rating on Public Safety and Security
1. Sheriffs and Deputy Sheriffs	83.6
2. Municipal Fire Fighting and Prevention Supervisors	82.1
3. Forest Fire Fighting and Prevention Supervisors	78.9
4. Police Patrol Officers	77.4
5. Transit and Railroad Police	76.4
6. First-Line Supervisors/Managers of Police and Detectives	75.7
7. Police Detectives	73.9
8. Immigration and Customs Inspectors	71.7
9. Correctional Officers and Jailers	71.6
10. Traffic Technicians	70.1
11. Fish and Game Wardens	69.0
12. Industrial Safety and Health Engineers	68.4
13. Security Guards	68.0
14. Occupational Health and Safety Specialists	66.4
15. Judges, Magistrate Judges, and Magistrates	64.9
16. Municipal Fire Fighters	64.7
17. Fire-Prevention and Protection Engineers	64.3
18. Computer Security Specialists	63.0
19. Police, Fire, and Ambulance Dispatchers	61.9
20. Architects, Except Landscape and Naval	61.4

(continued)

(continued)

Best Jobs for a Better World Rated Highest on Knowledge of Public Safety and Security

Job	Rating on Public Safety and Security
21. Criminal Investigators and Special Agents	61.0
22. Probation Officers and Correctional Treatment Specialists	59.7
23. Animal Control Workers	59.0
24. Forest Fire Fighters	58.4
25. Environmental Science and Protection Technicians, Including Health	58.1
26. Education Administrators, Elementary and Secondary School	55.6
27. Emergency Medical Technicians and Paramedics	55.6
28. Soil and Water Conservationists	55.6
29. Flight Attendants	55.0
30. Licensed Practical and Licensed Vocational Nurses	53.9
31. Coroners	53.6
32. Environmental Scientists and Specialists, Including Health	52.1
33. Lifeguards, Ski Patrol, and Other Recreational Protective Service Workers	52.0
34. Park Naturalists	51.6
35. Private Detectives and Investigators	51.4
36. Vocational Education Teachers, Secondary School	51.1
37. Medical and Clinical Laboratory Technologists	50.6
38. Residential Advisors	50.6
39. Air Traffic Controllers	50.3

The jobs in the following four lists are derived from the preceding list of the jobs with the highest ratings on knowledge of Public Safety and Security.

Best Jobs Overall Rated High on Knowledge of Public Safety and Security

Job	Rating on Public Safety and Security	Annual Earnings	Percent Growth	Annual Openings
1. Computer Security Specialists	63.0	$59,930	38.4%	34,000
2. Architects, Except Landscape and Naval	61.4	$62,850	17.3%	7,000
3. Forest Fire Fighters	58.4	$39,090	24.3%	21,000
4. Municipal Fire Fighters	64.7	$39,090	24.3%	21,000
5. Forest Fire Fighting and Prevention Supervisors	78.9	$60,840	21.1%	4,000
6. Municipal Fire Fighting and Prevention Supervisors	82.1	$60,840	21.1%	4,000

Best Jobs Overall Rated High on Knowledge of Public Safety and Security

Job	Rating on Public Safety and Security	Annual Earnings	Percent Growth	Annual Openings
7. First-Line Supervisors/Managers of Police and Detectives	75.7	$65,570	15.5%	9,000
8. Medical and Clinical Laboratory Technologists	50.6	$47,710	20.5%	14,000
9. Criminal Investigators and Special Agents	61.0	$55,790	16.3%	9,000
10. Immigration and Customs Inspectors	71.7	$55,790	16.3%	9,000
11. Police Detectives	73.9	$55,790	16.3%	9,000
12. Education Administrators, Elementary and Secondary School	55.6	$75,400	10.4%	27,000
13. Licensed Practical and Licensed Vocational Nurses	53.9	$35,230	17.1%	84,000
14. Police Patrol Officers	77.4	$46,290	15.5%	47,000
15. Sheriffs and Deputy Sheriffs	83.6	$46,290	15.5%	47,000
16. Residential Advisors	50.6	$21,850	28.9%	22,000
17. Emergency Medical Technicians and Paramedics	55.6	$26,080	27.3%	21,000
18. Environmental Scientists and Specialists, Including Health	52.1	$52,630	17.1%	8,000
19. Lifeguards, Ski Patrol, and Other Recreational Protective Service Workers	52.0	$16,910	20.4%	49,000
20. Air Traffic Controllers	50.3	$107,590	14.3%	2,000

Job 1 shares 34,000 openings with another job not included in this list. Jobs 3 and 4 share 21,000 openings. Jobs 5 and 6 share 4,000 openings. Jobs 9, 10, and 11 share 9,000 openings with each other and with another job not included in this list. Jobs 14 and 15 share 47,000 openings.

Best-Paying Jobs Rated High on Knowledge of Public Safety and Security

Job	Rating on Public Safety and Security	Annual Earnings
1. Air Traffic Controllers	50.3	$107,590
2. Judges, Magistrate Judges, and Magistrates	64.9	$97,570
3. Education Administrators, Elementary and Secondary School	55.6	$75,400
4. First-Line Supervisors/Managers of Police and Detectives	75.7	$65,570
5. Fire-Prevention and Protection Engineers	64.3	$65,210
6. Industrial Safety and Health Engineers	68.4	$65,210
7. Architects, Except Landscape and Naval	61.4	$62,850
8. Forest Fire Fighting and Prevention Supervisors	78.9	$60,840
9. Municipal Fire Fighting and Prevention Supervisors	82.1	$60,840

(continued)

(continued)

Best-Paying Jobs Rated High on Knowledge of Public Safety and Security

Job	Rating on Public Safety and Security	Annual Earnings
10. Computer Security Specialists	63.0	$59,930
11. Criminal Investigators and Special Agents	61.0	$55,790
12. Immigration and Customs Inspectors	71.7	$55,790
13. Police Detectives	73.9	$55,790
14. Occupational Health and Safety Specialists	66.4	$53,710
15. Park Naturalists	51.6	$53,350
16. Soil and Water Conservationists	55.6	$53,350
17. Environmental Scientists and Specialists, Including Health	52.1	$52,630
18. Coroners	53.6	$49,360
19. Transit and Railroad Police	76.4	$48,850
20. Medical and Clinical Laboratory Technologists	50.6	$47,710

Fastest-Growing Jobs Rated High on Knowledge of Public Safety and Security

Job	Rating on Public Safety and Security	Percent Growth
1. Computer Security Specialists	63.0	38.4%
2. Residential Advisors	50.6	28.9%
3. Emergency Medical Technicians and Paramedics	55.6	27.3%
4. Forest Fire Fighters	58.4	24.3%
5. Municipal Fire Fighters	64.7	24.3%
6. Forest Fire Fighting and Prevention Supervisors	78.9	21.1%
7. Municipal Fire Fighting and Prevention Supervisors	82.1	21.1%
8. Medical and Clinical Laboratory Technologists	50.6	20.5%
9. Lifeguards, Ski Patrol, and Other Recreational Protective Service Workers	52.0	20.4%
10. Private Detectives and Investigators	51.4	17.7%
11. Architects, Except Landscape and Naval	61.4	17.3%
12. Environmental Scientists and Specialists, Including Health	52.1	17.1%
13. Licensed Practical and Licensed Vocational Nurses	53.9	17.1%
14. Criminal Investigators and Special Agents	61.0	16.3%
15. Environmental Science and Protection Technicians, Including Health	58.1	16.3%
16. Flight Attendants	55.0	16.3%

Fastest-Growing Jobs Rated High on Knowledge of Public Safety and Security

Job	Rating on Public Safety and Security	Percent Growth
17. Immigration and Customs Inspectors	71.7	16.3%
18. Police Detectives	73.9	16.3%
19. Police, Fire, and Ambulance Dispatchers	61.9	15.9%
20. First-Line Supervisors/Managers of Police and Detectives	75.7	15.5%

Jobs with the Most Openings Rated High on Knowledge of Public Safety and Security

Job	Rating on Public Safety and Security	Annual Openings
1. Security Guards	68.0	230,000
2. Licensed Practical and Licensed Vocational Nurses	53.9	84,000
3. Correctional Officers and Jailers	71.6	54,000
4. Lifeguards, Ski Patrol, and Other Recreational Protective Service Workers	52.0	49,000
5. Police Patrol Officers	77.4	47,000
6. Sheriffs and Deputy Sheriffs	83.6	47,000
7. Computer Security Specialists	63.0	34,000
8. Education Administrators, Elementary and Secondary School	55.6	27,000
9. Residential Advisors	50.6	22,000
10. Emergency Medical Technicians and Paramedics	55.6	21,000
11. Forest Fire Fighters	58.4	21,000
12. Municipal Fire Fighters	64.7	21,000
13. Coroners	53.6	17,000
14. Medical and Clinical Laboratory Technologists	50.6	14,000
15. Probation Officers and Correctional Treatment Specialists	59.7	14,000
16. Police, Fire, and Ambulance Dispatchers	61.9	12,000
17. Vocational Education Teachers, Secondary School	51.1	10,000
18. Criminal Investigators and Special Agents	61.0	9,000
19. Immigration and Customs Inspectors	71.7	9,000
20. Police Detectives	73.9	9,000

Jobs 5 and 6 share 47,000 openings. Job 7 shares 34,000 openings with another job not included in this list. Jobs 11 and 12 share 21,000 openings. Job 13 shares 17,000 openings with four other jobs not included in this list. Jobs 18, 19, and 20 share 9,000 openings with each other and with another job not included in this list.

Best Jobs for a Better World Rated High on Knowledge of Therapy and Counseling

Not all illnesses can be cured with pills and shots. Some physical illnesses require a lengthy process of rehabilitation in which patients strengthen their muscles, learn to use prosthetics, or relearn how to do everyday tasks. Mental illnesses and behavioral problems also benefit from appropriate therapies, and many people find counseling helpful for resolving problems of everyday life—including career choice. As a result, there are many career opportunities for people who want to work in a job that involves therapy and counseling. Some of these jobs require a lot of education and training, but others require much less. People skills are clearly necessary for all of these jobs, but those skills can be learned if you are really interested in working with people.

Best Jobs for a Better World Rated Highest on Knowledge of Therapy and Counseling

Job	Rating on Therapy and Counseling
1. Counseling Psychologists	99.0
2. Clinical Psychologists	97.4
3. School Psychologists	94.7
4. Substance Abuse and Behavioral Disorder Counselors	90.3
5. Child, Family, and School Social Workers	89.3
6. Mental Health Counselors	87.3
7. Occupational Therapists	83.3
8. Educational, Vocational, and School Counselors	82.3
9. Physicians and Surgeons	78.2
10. Probation Officers and Correctional Treatment Specialists	77.6
11. Speech-Language Pathologists	77.0
12. Physician Assistants	74.0
13. Athletic Trainers	70.0
14. Audiologists	69.6
15. Medical and Public Health Social Workers	69.4
16. Oral and Maxillofacial Surgeons	68.6
17. Licensed Practical and Licensed Vocational Nurses	68.4
18. Chiropractors	67.7
19. Special Education Teachers, Secondary School	67.4
20. Occupational Therapist Assistants	67.0
21. Mental Health and Substance Abuse Social Workers	65.9
22. Directors, Religious Activities and Education	65.7

Best Jobs for a Better World Rated Highest on Knowledge of Therapy and Counseling

Job	Rating on Therapy and Counseling
23. Physical Therapist Assistants	64.7
24. Social and Human Service Assistants	64.7
25. Physical Therapists	64.4
26. Education Administrators, Elementary and Secondary School	63.9
27. Dietitians and Nutritionists	62.1
28. Clergy	61.3
29. Residential Advisors	61.1
30. Judges, Magistrate Judges, and Magistrates	58.4
31. Orthotists and Prosthetists	57.4
32. Funeral Directors	56.1
33. Registered Nurses	56.0
34. Respiratory Therapists	55.7
35. Social and Community Service Managers	54.3
36. Podiatrists	53.6
37. Special Education Teachers, Middle School	53.4
38. Occupational Therapist Aides	53.1
39. Computer Security Specialists	52.7
40. Health Educators	50.7
41. Municipal Fire Fighting and Prevention Supervisors	50.7

The jobs in the following four lists are derived from the preceding list of the jobs with the highest ratings on knowledge of Therapy and Counseling.

Best Jobs Overall Rated High on Knowledge of Therapy and Counseling

Job	Rating on Therapy and Counseling	Annual Earnings	Percent Growth	Annual Openings
1. Computer Security Specialists	52.7	$59,930	38.4%	34,000
2. Physicians and Surgeons	78.2 more than	$145,600	24.0%	41,000
3. Registered Nurses	56.0	$54,670	29.4%	229,000
4. Physician Assistants	74.0	$72,030	49.6%	10,000
5. Physical Therapists	64.4	$63,080	36.7%	13,000
6. Occupational Therapists	83.3	$56,860	33.6%	7,000

(continued)

(continued)

Best Jobs Overall Rated High on Knowledge of Therapy and Counseling

Job	Rating on Therapy and Counseling	Annual Earnings	Percent Growth	Annual Openings
7. Social and Community Service Managers	54.3	$49,500	25.5%	17,000
8. Social and Human Service Assistants	64.7	$25,030	29.7%	61,000
9. Education Administrators, Elementary and Secondary School	63.9	$75,400	10.4%	27,000
10. Clinical Psychologists	97.4	$57,170	19.1%	10,000
11. Counseling Psychologists	99.0	$57,170	19.1%	10,000
12. School Psychologists	94.7	$57,170	19.1%	10,000
13. Medical and Public Health Social Workers	69.4	$41,120	25.9%	14,000
14. Chiropractors	67.7	$67,200	22.4%	4,000
15. Physical Therapist Assistants	64.7	$39,490	44.2%	7,000
16. Mental Health and Substance Abuse Social Workers	65.9	$34,410	26.7%	15,000
17. Municipal Fire Fighting and Prevention Supervisors	50.7	$60,840	21.1%	4,000
18. Residential Advisors	61.1	$21,850	28.9%	22,000
19. Educational, Vocational, and School Counselors	82.3	$46,440	14.8%	32,000
20. Mental Health Counselors	87.3	$34,010	27.2%	14,000

Job 1 shares 34,000 openings with another job not included in this list. Jobs 10, 11, and 12 share 10,000 openings. Job 17 shares 4,000 openings with another job not included in this list.

Best-Paying Jobs Rated High on Knowledge of Therapy and Counseling

Job	Rating on Therapy and Counseling	Annual Earnings
1. Oral and Maxillofacial Surgeons	68.6	more than $145,600
2. Physicians and Surgeons	78.2	more than $145,600
3. Podiatrists	53.6	$100,550
4. Judges, Magistrate Judges, and Magistrates	58.4	$97,570
5. Education Administrators, Elementary and Secondary School	63.9	$75,400
6. Physician Assistants	74.0	$72,030
7. Chiropractors	67.7	$67,200
8. Physical Therapists	64.4	$63,080
9. Municipal Fire Fighting and Prevention Supervisors	50.7	$60,840
10. Computer Security Specialists	52.7	$59,930
11. Clinical Psychologists	97.4	$57,170

Best-Paying Jobs Rated High on Knowledge of Therapy and Counseling

Job	Rating on Therapy and Counseling	Annual Earnings
12. Counseling Psychologists	99.0	$57,170
13. School Psychologists	94.7	$57,170
14. Occupational Therapists	83.3	$56,860
15. Speech-Language Pathologists	77.0	$54,880
16. Registered Nurses	56.0	$54,670
17. Orthotists and Prosthetists	57.4	$53,760
18. Audiologists	69.6	$53,490
19. Social and Community Service Managers	54.3	$49,500
20. Funeral Directors	56.1	$47,630

Fastest-Growing Jobs Rated High on Knowledge of Therapy and Counseling

Job	Rating on Therapy and Counseling	Percent Growth
1. Physician Assistants	74.0	49.6%
2. Physical Therapist Assistants	64.7	44.2%
3. Computer Security Specialists	52.7	38.4%
4. Physical Therapists	64.4	36.7%
5. Occupational Therapist Assistants	67.0	34.1%
6. Occupational Therapists	83.3	33.6%
7. Social and Human Service Assistants	64.7	29.7%
8. Registered Nurses	56.0	29.4%
9. Athletic Trainers	70.0	29.3%
10. Residential Advisors	61.1	28.9%
11. Substance Abuse and Behavioral Disorder Counselors	90.3	28.7%
12. Respiratory Therapists	55.7	28.4%
13. Mental Health Counselors	87.3	27.2%
14. Mental Health and Substance Abuse Social Workers	65.9	26.7%
15. Occupational Therapist Aides	53.1	26.3%
16. Medical and Public Health Social Workers	69.4	25.9%
17. Social and Community Service Managers	54.3	25.5%
18. Physicians and Surgeons	78.2	24.0%
19. Health Educators	50.7	22.5%
20. Chiropractors	67.7	22.4%

Jobs with the Most Openings Rated High on Knowledge of Therapy and Counseling

Job	Rating on Therapy and Counseling	Annual Openings
1. Registered Nurses	56.0	229,000
2. Licensed Practical and Licensed Vocational Nurses	68.4	84,000
3. Social and Human Service Assistants	64.7	61,000
4. Physicians and Surgeons	78.2	41,000
5. Computer Security Specialists	52.7	34,000
6. Educational, Vocational, and School Counselors	82.3	32,000
7. Child, Family, and School Social Workers	89.3	31,000
8. Education Administrators, Elementary and Secondary School	63.9	27,000
9. Clergy	61.3	26,000
10. Residential Advisors	61.1	22,000
11. Social and Community Service Managers	54.3	17,000
12. Mental Health and Substance Abuse Social Workers	65.9	15,000
13. Medical and Public Health Social Workers	69.4	14,000
14. Mental Health Counselors	87.3	14,000
15. Probation Officers and Correctional Treatment Specialists	77.6	14,000
16. Physical Therapists	64.4	13,000
17. Special Education Teachers, Secondary School	67.4	11,000
18. Substance Abuse and Behavioral Disorder Counselors	90.3	11,000
19. Clinical Psychologists	97.4	10,000
20. Counseling Psychologists	99.0	10,000

Job 4 shares 34,000 openings with another job not included in this list. Jobs 19 and 20 share 10,000 openings with each other and with another job not included in this list.

Best Jobs for a Better World Rated High on All Six World-Improving Criteria Combined

We thought it would be interesting to take the average of the ratings on *all six* criteria—Social Service, Education and Training, Fine Arts, Medicine and Dentistry, Public Safety and Security, and Therapy and Counseling—and identify the jobs that are rated highest on this combined score. The high-scoring jobs don't necessarily improve the world any better than do other jobs; they simply improve the world through a diverse variety of ways. For example, the highest-rated job, Physicians and Surgeons, gives you chances to do a lot of Social Service, work with knowledge of Medicine and Dentistry and Therapy and Counseling, and do a certain amount of Education and Training when you advise patients.

Best Jobs for a Better World Rated Highest on All Six World-Improving Criteria Combined

Job	Average Rating on All Six Criteria
1. Physicians and Surgeons	61.7
2. Oral and Maxillofacial Surgeons	60.0
3. Licensed Practical and Licensed Vocational Nurses	57.8
4. Clinical Psychologists	57.7
5. Physician Assistants	57.3
6. Athletic Trainers	57.2
7. Chiropractors	57.2
8. Municipal Fire Fighting and Prevention Supervisors	56.7
9. Dietitians and Nutritionists	56.0
10. Substance Abuse and Behavioral Disorder Counselors	56.0
11. School Psychologists	55.8
12. Speech-Language Pathologists	55.8
13. Podiatrists	55.7
14. Prosthodontists	55.5
15. Respiratory Therapists	55.0
16. Occupational Therapists	54.9
17. Dentists, General	54.3
18. Physical Therapists	54.1
19. Education Administrators, Elementary and Secondary School	54.0
20. Counseling Psychologists	53.5
21. Special Education Teachers, Secondary School	53.3
22. Physical Therapist Assistants	52.8
23. Vocational Education Teachers, Secondary School	52.8
24. Educational, Vocational, and School Counselors	52.7
25. Emergency Medical Technicians and Paramedics	52.4
26. Audiologists	52.2
27. Orthotists and Prosthetists	52.2
28. Registered Nurses	52.2
29. First-Line Supervisors/Managers of Police and Detectives	51.8
30. Mental Health Counselors	51.8
31. Secondary School Teachers, Except Special and Vocational Education	51.8
32. Orthodontists	50.8
33. Medical and Public Health Social Workers	50.7
34. Middle School Teachers, Except Special and Vocational Education	50.6
35. Clergy	50.2
36. Occupational Therapist Assistants	50.1

The jobs in the following four lists are derived from the preceding list of the jobs with the highest ratings on all six criteria combined.

Best Jobs Overall Rated High on All Six World-Improving Criteria Combined

Job	Average Rating on All Six Criteria	Annual Earnings	Percent Growth	Annual Openings
1. Physicians and Surgeons	61.7 more than	$145,600	24.0%	41,000
2. Physician Assistants	57.3	$72,030	49.6%	10,000
3. Registered Nurses	52.2	$54,670	29.4%	229,000
4. Physical Therapists	54.1	$63,080	36.7%	13,000
5. Occupational Therapists	54.9	$56,860	33.6%	7,000
6. Clinical Psychologists	57.7	$57,170	19.1%	10,000
7. Counseling Psychologists	53.5	$57,170	19.1%	10,000
8. School Psychologists	55.8	$57,170	19.1%	10,000
9. Education Administrators, Elementary and Secondary School	54.0	$75,400	10.4%	27,000
10. Chiropractors	57.2	$67,200	22.4%	4,000
11. Medical and Public Health Social Workers	50.7	$41,120	25.9%	14,000
12. Municipal Fire Fighting and Prevention Supervisors	56.7	$60,840	21.1%	4,000
13. Physical Therapist Assistants	52.8	$39,490	44.2%	7,000
14. Mental Health Counselors	51.8	$34,010	27.2%	14,000
15. Secondary School Teachers, Except Special and Vocational Education	51.8	$46,060	14.4%	107,000
16. Educational, Vocational, and School Counselors	52.7	$46,440	14.8%	32,000
17. Emergency Medical Technicians and Paramedics	52.4	$26,080	27.3%	21,000
18. First-Line Supervisors/Managers of Police and Detectives	51.8	$65,570	15.5%	9,000
19. Respiratory Therapists	55.0	$45,140	28.4%	7,000
20. Special Education Teachers, Secondary School	53.3	$46,820	17.9%	11,000

Jobs 6, 7, and 8 share 10,000 openings. Job 12 shares 4,000 openings with another job not included in this list.

Best-Paying Jobs Rated High on All Six World-Improving Criteria Combined

Job	Average Rating on All Six Criteria	Annual Earnings
1. Oral and Maxillofacial Surgeons	60.0	more than $145,600
2. Orthodontists	50.8	more than $145,600
3. Physicians and Surgeons	61.7	more than $145,600
4. Prosthodontists	55.5	more than $145,600
5. Dentists, General	54.3	$125,300
6. Podiatrists	55.7	$100,550
7. Education Administrators, Elementary and Secondary School	54.0	$75,400
8. Physician Assistants	57.3	$72,030
9. Chiropractors	57.2	$67,200
10. First-Line Supervisors/Managers of Police and Detectives	51.8	$65,570
11. Physical Therapists	54.1	$63,080
12. Municipal Fire Fighting and Prevention Supervisors	56.7	$60,840
13. Clinical Psychologists	57.7	$57,170
14. Counseling Psychologists	53.5	$57,170
15. School Psychologists	55.8	$57,170
16. Occupational Therapists	54.9	$56,860
17. Speech-Language Pathologists	55.8	$54,880
18. Registered Nurses	52.2	$54,670
19. Orthotists and Prosthetists	52.2	$53,760
20. Audiologists	52.2	$53,490

Fastest-Growing Jobs Rated High on All Six World-Improving Criteria Combined

Job	Average Rating on All Six Criteria	Percent Growth
1. Physician Assistants	57.3	49.6%
2. Physical Therapist Assistants	52.8	44.2%
3. Physical Therapists	54.1	36.7%
4. Occupational Therapist Assistants	50.1	34.1%
5. Occupational Therapists	54.9	33.6%

(continued)

(continued)

Fastest-Growing Jobs Rated High on All Six World-Improving Criteria Combined

Job	Average Rating on All Six Criteria	Percent Growth
6. Registered Nurses	52.2	29.4%
7. Athletic Trainers	57.2	29.3%
8. Substance Abuse and Behavioral Disorder Counselors	56.0	28.7%
9. Respiratory Therapists	55.0	28.4%
10. Emergency Medical Technicians and Paramedics	52.4	27.3%
11. Mental Health Counselors	51.8	27.2%
12. Medical and Public Health Social Workers	50.7	25.9%
13. Physicians and Surgeons	61.7	24.0%
14. Chiropractors	57.2	22.4%
15. Municipal Fire Fighting and Prevention Supervisors	56.7	21.1%
16. Clinical Psychologists	57.7	19.1%
17. Counseling Psychologists	53.5	19.1%
18. School Psychologists	55.8	19.1%
19. Dietitians and Nutritionists	56.0	18.3%
20. Orthotists and Prosthetists	52.2	18.0%

Jobs with the Most Openings Rated High on All Six World-Improving Criteria Combined

Job	Average Rating on All Six Criteria	Annual Openings
1. Registered Nurses	52.2	229,000
2. Secondary School Teachers, Except Special and Vocational Education	51.8	107,000
3. Licensed Practical and Licensed Vocational Nurses	57.8	84,000
4. Middle School Teachers, Except Special and Vocational Education	50.6	83,000
5. Physicians and Surgeons	61.7	41,000
6. Educational, Vocational, and School Counselors	52.7	32,000
7. Education Administrators, Elementary and Secondary School	54.0	27,000
8. Clergy	50.2	26,000
9. Emergency Medical Technicians and Paramedics	52.4	21,000
10. Medical and Public Health Social Workers	50.7	14,000

Jobs with the Most Openings Rated High on All Six World-Improving Criteria Combined

Job	Average Rating on All Six Criteria	Annual Openings
11. Mental Health Counselors	51.8	14,000
12. Physical Therapists	54.1	13,000
13. Special Education Teachers, Secondary School	53.3	11,000
14. Substance Abuse and Behavioral Disorder Counselors	56.0	11,000
15. Clinical Psychologists	57.7	10,000
16. Counseling Psychologists	53.5	10,000
17. School Psychologists	55.8	10,000
18. Physician Assistants	57.3	10,000
19. Vocational Education Teachers, Secondary School	52.8	10,000
20. First-Line Supervisors/Managers of Police and Detectives	51.8	9,000

Jobs 15, 16, and 17 share 10,000 openings.

Best Jobs Lists by Demographic

Demographic statistics can provide some useful insights into the 150 jobs in this book. So we included lists that highlight jobs with a high percentage of workers in various age brackets, people who work part-time or are self-employed, and male and female workers.

All of the lists in this section were created by using a similar process. We began with all 150 best jobs for a better world and sorted those jobs in order of the primary demographic criterion for each set of lists. Then, we selected the jobs with the highest percentage of workers fitting the primary criterion and listed them. (For example, we sorted all 150 jobs based on the percentage of part-time workers and then selected the jobs with more than 20 percent of these workers for inclusion in the first list for this group.) From the list of jobs with a high percentage of each type of worker, we created four more-specialized lists:

- 25 Best Jobs Overall (jobs with the best combined score for earnings, growth rate, and number of openings)
- 25 Best-Paying Jobs
- 25 Fastest-Growing Jobs
- 25 Jobs with the Most Openings

Again, each of these four lists includes only jobs from among those with the highest percentages of different types of workers. The same basic process was used to create all the lists in this section. The lists are interesting, and we hope you find them helpful.

Best Jobs with the Highest Percentage of Workers Age 16–24

From our list of 150 world-improving jobs used in this book, this list contains jobs with the highest percentage (more than 20 percent) of workers age 16 to 24, presented in order of the percentage of these young workers in each job. Younger workers are found in all jobs, but jobs with higher percentages of younger workers may present more opportunities for initial entry or upward mobility. Many jobs with the highest percentages of younger workers are those that don't require extensive training or education, and there is a wide variety of jobs in different fields among these jobs. You may also notice that several of these jobs have considerable physical demands that discourage older workers.

Best Jobs for a Better World with the Highest Percentage of Workers Age 16–24

Job	Percent Age 16–24
1. Lifeguards, Ski Patrol, and Other Recreational Protective Service Workers	71.5%
2. Choreographers	46.9%
3. Ambulance Drivers and Attendants, Except Emergency Medical Technicians	45.5%
4. Residential Advisors	34.1%
5. City and Regional Planning Aides	30.8%
6. Environmental Science and Protection Technicians, Including Health	30.8%
7. Fitness Trainers and Aerobics Instructors	29.1%
8. Recreation Workers	29.1%
9. Child Care Workers	27.9%
10. Nannies	27.9%
11. Dietetic Technicians	24.7%
12. Pharmacy Technicians	24.7%
13. Surgical Technologists	24.7%
14. Animal Control Workers	23.1%
15. Tour Guides and Escorts	22.6%
16. Medical Assistants	21.5%
17. Medical Equipment Preparers	21.5%
18. Veterinary Assistants and Laboratory Animal Caretakers	21.5%
19. Medical Records and Health Information Technicians	20.6%
20. Security Guards	20.6%

The jobs in the following four lists are derived from the preceding list of the jobs with the highest percentage of workers age 16–24.

Best Jobs Overall with a High Percentage of Workers Age 16–24

Job	Percent Age 16–24	Annual Earnings	Percent Growth	Annual Openings
1. Medical Assistants	21.5%	$25,350	52.1%	93,000
2. Surgical Technologists	24.7%	$34,830	29.5%	12,000
3. Medical Records and Health Information Technicians	20.6%	$26,690	28.9%	14,000
4. Fitness Trainers and Aerobics Instructors	29.1%	$25,840	27.1%	50,000
5. Pharmacy Technicians	24.7%	$24,390	28.6%	35,000
6. Residential Advisors	34.1%	$21,850	28.9%	22,000
7. Environmental Science and Protection Technicians, Including Health	30.8%	$36,260	16.3%	6,000
8. City and Regional Planning Aides	30.8%	$33,950	17.4%	4,000
9. Medical Equipment Preparers	21.5%	$24,880	20.0%	8,000
10. Recreation Workers	29.1%	$20,110	17.3%	69,000
11. Veterinary Assistants and Laboratory Animal Caretakers	21.5%	$19,610	21.0%	14,000
12. Choreographers	46.9%	$32,950	16.8%	4,000
13. Lifeguards, Ski Patrol, and Other Recreational Protective Service Workers	71.5%	$16,910	20.4%	49,000
14. Security Guards	20.6%	$20,760	12.6%	230,000
15. Child Care Workers	27.9%	$17,050	13.8%	439,000
16. Nannies	27.9%	$17,050	13.8%	439,000
17. Ambulance Drivers and Attendants, Except Emergency Medical Technicians	45.5%	$18,790	28.0%	5,000
18. Animal Control Workers	23.1%	$26,780	14.4%	4,000
19. Dietetic Technicians	24.7%	$23,470	19.1%	3,000
20. Tour Guides and Escorts	22.6%	$19,990	16.6%	5,000

Job 8 shares 4,000 openings with another job not included in this list. Jobs 15 and 16 share 439,000 openings.

Best-Paying Jobs with a High Percentage of Workers Age 16–24

Job	Percent Age 16–24	Annual Earnings
1. Environmental Science and Protection Technicians, Including Health	30.8%	$36,260
2. Surgical Technologists	24.7%	$34,830
3. City and Regional Planning Aides	30.8%	$33,950
4. Choreographers	46.9%	$32,950
5. Animal Control Workers	23.1%	$26,780

(continued)

(continued)

Best-Paying Jobs with a High Percentage of Workers Age 16–24

Job	Percent Age 16–24	Annual Earnings
6. Medical Records and Health Information Technicians	20.6%	$26,690
7. Fitness Trainers and Aerobics Instructors	29.1%	$25,840
8. Medical Assistants	21.5%	$25,350
9. Medical Equipment Preparers	21.5%	$24,880
10. Pharmacy Technicians	24.7%	$24,390
11. Dietetic Technicians	24.7%	$23,470
12. Residential Advisors	34.1%	$21,850
13. Security Guards	20.6%	$20,760
14. Recreation Workers	29.1%	$20,110
15. Tour Guides and Escorts	22.6%	$19,990
16. Veterinary Assistants and Laboratory Animal Caretakers	21.5%	$19,610
17. Ambulance Drivers and Attendants, Except Emergency Medical Technicians	45.5%	$18,790
18. Child Care Workers	27.9%	$17,050
19. Nannies	27.9%	$17,050
20. Lifeguards, Ski Patrol, and Other Recreational Protective Service Workers	71.5%	$16,910

Fastest-Growing Jobs with a High Percentage of Workers Age 16–24

Job	Percent Age 16–24	Percent Growth
1. Medical Assistants	21.5%	52.1%
2. Surgical Technologists	24.7%	29.5%
3. Medical Records and Health Information Technicians	20.6%	28.9%
4. Residential Advisors	34.1%	28.9%
5. Pharmacy Technicians	24.7%	28.6%
6. Ambulance Drivers and Attendants, Except Emergency Medical Technicians	45.5%	28.0%
7. Fitness Trainers and Aerobics Instructors	29.1%	27.1%
8. Veterinary Assistants and Laboratory Animal Caretakers	21.5%	21.0%
9. Lifeguards, Ski Patrol, and Other Recreational Protective Service Workers	71.5%	20.4%
10. Medical Equipment Preparers	21.5%	20.0%
11. Dietetic Technicians	24.7%	19.1%
12. City and Regional Planning Aides	30.8%	17.4%

Fastest-Growing Jobs with a High Percentage of Workers Age 16–24

Job	Percent Age 16–24	Percent Growth
13. Recreation Workers	29.1%	17.3%
14. Choreographers	46.9%	16.8%
15. Tour Guides and Escorts	22.6%	16.6%
16. Environmental Science and Protection Technicians, Including Health	30.8%	16.3%
17. Animal Control Workers	23.1%	14.4%
18. Child Care Workers	27.9%	13.8%
19. Nannies	27.9%	13.8%
20. Security Guards	20.6%	12.6%

Jobs with the Most Openings with a High Percentage of Workers Age 16–24

Job	Percent Age 16–24	Annual Openings
1. Child Care Workers	27.9%	439,000
2. Nannies	27.9%	439,000
3. Security Guards	20.6%	230,000
4. Medical Assistants	21.5%	93,000
5. Recreation Workers	29.1%	69,000
6. Fitness Trainers and Aerobics Instructors	29.1%	50,000
7. Lifeguards, Ski Patrol, and Other Recreational Protective Service Workers	71.5%	49,000
8. Pharmacy Technicians	24.7%	35,000
9. Residential Advisors	34.1%	22,000
10. Medical Records and Health Information Technicians	20.6%	14,000
11. Veterinary Assistants and Laboratory Animal Caretakers	21.5%	14,000
12. Surgical Technologists	24.7%	12,000
13. Medical Equipment Preparers	21.5%	8,000
14. Environmental Science and Protection Technicians, Including Health	30.8%	6,000
15. Ambulance Drivers and Attendants, Except Emergency Medical Technicians	45.5%	5,000
16. Tour Guides and Escorts	22.6%	5,000
17. City and Regional Planning Aides	30.8%	4,000
18. Choreographers	46.9%	4,000
19. Animal Control Workers	23.1%	4,000
20. Dietetic Technicians	24.7%	3,000

Jobs 1 and 2 share 439,000 openings. Job 17 shares 4,000 openings with another job not included in this list.

Best Jobs with a High Percentage of Workers Age 55 and Over

Older workers don't change careers as often as younger ones do, and on the average, they tend to have been in their jobs for quite some time. Many of the jobs with the highest percentages of workers age 55 and over—and those with the highest earnings—require considerable preparation, either through experience or through education and training. These are not the sort of jobs most younger workers could easily get. That should not come as a big surprise, as many of these folks have been in the workforce for a long time and therefore have lots of experience.

But go down the list of the jobs with the highest percentage (more than 20 percent) of older workers and you will find a variety of world-improving jobs that many older workers could more easily enter if they were changing careers. Some would make good "retirement" jobs, particularly if they allowed for part-time work or self-employment. Research indicates that many people planning to retire from one long-time occupation intend to work in a different occupation that can improve life in their community. If you are one of those people, this list is a good place to look for ideas.

Best Jobs for a Better World with the Highest Percentage of Workers Age 55 and Over

Job	Percent Age 55 and Over
1. Judges, Magistrate Judges, and Magistrates	42.4%
2. Tour Guides and Escorts	41.9%
3. Embalmers	41.7%
4. Funeral Attendants	41.7%
5. Funeral Directors	40.7%
6. Crossing Guards	38.6%
7. Clergy	32.7%
8. Clinical Psychologists	31.4%
9. Counseling Psychologists	31.4%
10. Industrial-Organizational Psychologists	31.4%
11. School Psychologists	31.4%
12. Bus Drivers, School	29.6%
13. Librarians	28.9%
14. Dentists, General	26.1%
15. Oral and Maxillofacial Surgeons	26.1%
16. Orthodontists	26.1%
17. Prosthodontists	26.1%

Best Jobs for a Better World with the Highest Percentage of Workers Age 55 and Over

Job	Percent Age 55 and Over
18. Education Administrators, Elementary and Secondary School	25.9%
19. Education Administrators, Postsecondary	25.9%
20. Education Administrators, Preschool and Child Care Center/Program	25.9%
21. Personal and Home Care Aides	25.4%
22. Teachers, Postsecondary	24.5%
23. Security Guards	24.3%
24. Directors, Religious Activities and Education	24.1%
25. Social and Community Service Managers	23.8%
26. Poets, Lyricists, and Creative Writers	23.7%
27. Private Detectives and Investigators	23.4%
28. Audiologists	23.1%
29. Urban and Regional Planners	22.7%
30. Fine Artists, Including Painters, Sculptors, and Illustrators	22.6%
31. Pharmacists	22.4%
32. Veterinarians	22.0%
33. Music Composers and Arrangers	21.8%
34. Music Directors	21.8%
35. Audio-Visual Collections Specialists	20.9%
36. Farm and Home Management Advisors	20.9%
37. Instructional Coordinators	20.9%

The jobs in the following four lists are derived from the preceding list of the jobs with the highest percentage of workers age 55 and over.

Best Jobs Overall with a High Percentage of Workers Age 55 and Over

Job	Percent Age 55 and Over	Annual Earnings	Percent Growth	Annual Openings
1. Teachers, Postsecondary	24.5%	$53,590	32.2%	329,000
2. Pharmacists	22.4%	$89,820	24.6%	16,000
3. Education Administrators, Postsecondary	25.9%	$70,350	21.3%	18,000
4. Instructional Coordinators	20.9%	$50,430	27.5%	15,000
5. Social and Community Service Managers	23.8%	$49,500	25.5%	17,000
6. Clinical Psychologists	31.4%	$57,170	19.1%	10,000

(continued)

(continued)

Best Jobs Overall with a High Percentage of Workers Age 55 and Over

Job	Percent Age 55 and Over	Annual Earnings	Percent Growth	Annual Openings
7. Counseling Psychologists	31.4%	$57,170	19.1%	10,000
8. School Psychologists	31.4%	$57,170	19.1%	10,000
9. Personal and Home Care Aides	25.4%	$17,340	41.0%	230,000
10. Education Administrators, Elementary and Secondary School	25.9%	$75,400	10.4%	27,000
11. Education Administrators, Preschool and Child Care Center/Program	25.9%	$37,010	27.9%	9,000
12. Veterinarians	22.0%	$68,910	17.4%	8,000
13. Poets, Lyricists, and Creative Writers	23.7%	$46,420	17.7%	14,000
14. Crossing Guards	38.6%	$20,050	19.7%	26,000
15. Industrial-Organizational Psychologists	31.4%	$84,690	20.4%	fewer than 500
16. Dentists, General	26.1%	$125,300	13.5%	7,000
17. Oral and Maxillofacial Surgeons	26.1%	more than $145,600	16.2%	fewer than 500
18. Orthodontists	26.1%	more than $145,600	12.8%	1,000
19. Prosthodontists	26.1%	more than $145,600	13.6%	fewer than 500
20. Bus Drivers, School	29.6%	$24,070	13.6%	76,000
21. Clergy	32.7%	$38,540	12.4%	26,000
22. Directors, Religious Activities and Education	24.1%	$32,540	18.5%	10,000
23. Security Guards	24.3%	$20,760	12.6%	230,000
24. Urban and Regional Planners	22.7%	$55,170	15.2%	3,000
25. Funeral Attendants	41.7%	$19,720	20.8%	8,000

Jobs 6, 7, and 8 share 10,000 openings. Job 13 shares 14,000 openings with another job not included in this list.

Best-Paying Jobs with a High Percentage of Workers Age 55 and Over

Job	Percent Age 55 and Over	Annual Earnings
1. Oral and Maxillofacial Surgeons	26.1%	more than $145,600
2. Orthodontists	26.1%	more than $145,600
3. Prosthodontists	26.1%	more than $145,600
4. Dentists, General	26.1%	$125,300
5. Judges, Magistrate Judges, and Magistrates	42.4%	$97,570
6. Pharmacists	22.4%	$89,820

Best-Paying Jobs with a High Percentage of Workers Age 55 and Over

Job	Percent Age 55 and Over	Annual Earnings
7. Industrial-Organizational Psychologists	31.4%	$84,690
8. Education Administrators, Elementary and Secondary School	25.9%	$75,400
9. Education Administrators, Postsecondary	25.9%	$70,350
10. Veterinarians	22.0%	$68,910
11. Clinical Psychologists	31.4%	$57,170
12. Counseling Psychologists	31.4%	$57,170
13. School Psychologists	31.4%	$57,170
14. Urban and Regional Planners	22.7%	$55,170
15. Teachers, Postsecondary	24.5%	$53,590
16. Audiologists	23.1%	$53,490
17. Instructional Coordinators	20.9%	$50,430
18. Social and Community Service Managers	23.8%	$49,500
19. Funeral Directors	40.7%	$47,630
20. Librarians	28.9%	$47,400
21. Poets, Lyricists, and Creative Writers	23.7%	$46,420
22. Farm and Home Management Advisors	20.9%	$41,890
23. Fine Artists, Including Painters, Sculptors, and Illustrators	22.6%	$41,280
24. Audio-Visual Collections Specialists	20.9%	$40,260
25. Clergy	32.7%	$38,540

Fastest-Growing Jobs with a High Percentage of Workers Age 55 and Over

Job	Percent Age 55 and Over	Annual Earnings
1. Personal and Home Care Aides	25.4%	41.0%
2. Teachers, Postsecondary	24.5%	32.2%
3. Education Administrators, Preschool and Child Care Center/Program	25.9%	27.9%
4. Instructional Coordinators	20.9%	27.5%
5. Social and Community Service Managers	23.8%	25.5%
6. Pharmacists	22.4%	24.6%
7. Education Administrators, Postsecondary	25.9%	21.3%
8. Funeral Attendants	41.7%	20.8%
9. Industrial-Organizational Psychologists	31.4%	20.4%

(continued)

(continued)

Fastest-Growing Jobs with a High Percentage of Workers Age 55 and Over

Job	Percent Age 55 and Over	Annual Earnings
10. Crossing Guards	38.6%	19.7%
11. Clinical Psychologists	31.4%	19.1%
12. Counseling Psychologists	31.4%	19.1%
13. School Psychologists	31.4%	19.1%
14. Audio-Visual Collections Specialists	20.9%	18.6%
15. Directors, Religious Activities and Education	24.1%	18.5%
16. Poets, Lyricists, and Creative Writers	23.7%	17.7%
17. Private Detectives and Investigators	23.4%	17.7%
18. Veterinarians	22.0%	17.4%
19. Tour Guides and Escorts	41.9%	16.6%
20. Oral and Maxillofacial Surgeons	26.1%	16.2%
21. Embalmers	41.7%	15.6%
22. Urban and Regional Planners	22.7%	15.2%
23. Prosthodontists	26.1%	13.6%
24. Bus Drivers, School	29.6%	13.6%
25. Dentists, General	26.1%	13.5%

Jobs with the Most Openings with a High Percentage of Workers Age 55 and Over

Job	Percent Age 55 and Over	Annual Earnings
1. Teachers, Postsecondary	24.5%	329,000
2. Personal and Home Care Aides	25.4%	230,000
3. Security Guards	24.3%	230,000
4. Bus Drivers, School	29.6%	76,000
5. Education Administrators, Elementary and Secondary School	25.9%	27,000
6. Crossing Guards	38.6%	26,000
7. Clergy	32.7%	26,000
8. Education Administrators, Postsecondary	25.9%	18,000
9. Social and Community Service Managers	23.8%	17,000
10. Pharmacists	22.4%	16,000

Jobs with the Most Openings with a High Percentage of Workers Age 55 and Over

Job	Percent Age 55 and Over	Annual Earnings
11. Instructional Coordinators	20.9%	15,000
12. Poets, Lyricists, and Creative Writers	23.7%	14,000
13. Music Composers and Arrangers	21.8%	11,000
14. Music Directors	21.8%	11,000
15. Clinical Psychologists	31.4%	10,000
16. Counseling Psychologists	31.4%	10,000
17. School Psychologists	31.4%	10,000
18. Directors, Religious Activities and Education	24.1%	10,000
19. Education Administrators, Preschool and Child Care Center/Program	25.9%	9,000
20. Funeral Attendants	41.7%	8,000
21. Veterinarians	22.0%	8,000
22. Librarians	28.9%	8,000
23. Private Detectives and Investigators	23.4%	7,000
24. Dentists, General	26.1%	7,000
25. Tour Guides and Escorts	41.9%	5,000

Job 12 shares 14,000 openings with another job not included in this list. Jobs 13 and 14 share 11,000 openings. Jobs 15, 16, and 17 share 10,000 openings.

Best Jobs for a Better World with a High Percentage of Part-Time Workers

Look over the list of the world-improving jobs with high percentages (more than 20 percent) of part-time workers and you will find a wide variety of fields represented: recreation, health care, education, the arts, and personal assistance.

In some cases, people work part time because they want the freedom of time this arrangement can provide, but others may do so because they can't find full-time employment in these jobs. These folks may work in other full- or part-time jobs to make ends meet. Still others work part time in night-shift positions that pay a higher hourly wage than full-time workers earn—an option available to many registered nurses and other skilled health-care workers. If you want to work part time now or in the future, these lists will help you identify world-improving jobs that are more likely to provide that opportunity. If you want full-time work, the lists may also help you identify jobs for which such opportunities are more difficult to find. In either case, it's good information to know in advance.

Best Jobs for a Better World with the Highest Percentage of Part-Time Workers

Job	Percent Part-Time Workers
1. Lifeguards, Ski Patrol, and Other Recreational Protective Service Workers	63.8%
2. Dental Hygienists	56.0%
3. Crossing Guards	53.9%
4. Choreographers	47.7%
5. Music Composers and Arrangers	46.1%
6. Music Directors	46.1%
7. Adult Literacy, Remedial Education, and GED Teachers and Instructors	45.6%
8. Self-Enrichment Education Teachers	45.6%
9. Embalmers	44.0%
10. Funeral Attendants	44.0%
11. Fitness Trainers and Aerobics Instructors	41.3%
12. Recreation Workers	41.3%
13. Dental Assistants	38.9%
14. Child Care Workers	38.8%
15. Nannies	38.8%
16. Teacher Assistants	38.5%
17. Bus Drivers, School	38.4%
18. Personal and Home Care Aides	36.6%
19. Fine Artists, Including Painters, Sculptors, and Illustrators	30.9%
20. Audiologists	30.8%
21. Poets, Lyricists, and Creative Writers	30.7%
22. Speech-Language Pathologists	30.2%
23. Tour Guides and Escorts	29.8%
24. Occupational Therapists	29.4%
25. Flight Attendants	28.8%
26. Physical Therapist Aides	28.6%
27. Physical Therapist Assistants	28.6%
28. Home Health Aides	28.0%
29. Nursing Aides, Orderlies, and Attendants	28.0%
30. Directors, Religious Activities and Education	27.9%
31. Film and Video Editors	27.6%
32. Medical Assistants	27.5%
33. Medical Equipment Preparers	27.5%
34. Veterinary Assistants and Laboratory Animal Caretakers	27.5%
35. Teachers, Postsecondary	27.3%
36. Kindergarten Teachers, Except Special Education	25.1%

Best Jobs for a Better World with the Highest Percentage of Part-Time Workers

Job	Percent Part-Time Workers
37. Preschool Teachers, Except Special Education	25.1%
38. Dietitians and Nutritionists	24.8%
39. Physical Therapists	24.7%
40. Registered Nurses	24.1%
41. Audio-Visual Collections Specialists	23.4%
42. Curators	23.4%
43. Farm and Home Management Advisors	23.4%
44. Instructional Coordinators	23.4%
45. Museum Technicians and Conservators	23.4%
46. Dietetic Technicians	23.2%
47. Pharmacy Technicians	23.2%
48. Surgical Technologists	23.2%
49. Animal Trainers	23.1%
50. Clinical Psychologists	22.8%
51. Counseling Psychologists	22.8%
52. Industrial-Organizational Psychologists	22.8%
53. School Psychologists	22.8%
54. City and Regional Planning Aides	22.7%
55. Environmental Science and Protection Technicians, Including Health	22.7%
56. Dentists, General	22.4%
57. Oral and Maxillofacial Surgeons	22.4%
58. Orthodontists	22.4%
59. Podiatrists	22.4%
60. Prosthodontists	22.4%
61. Librarians	22.3%
62. Licensed Practical and Licensed Vocational Nurses	21.9%
63. Animal Control Workers	21.3%
64. Set and Exhibit Designers	21.3%
65. Pharmacists	21.1%
66. Chiropractors	20.7%
67. Opticians, Dispensing	20.2%

The jobs in the following four lists are derived from the preceding list of the jobs with the highest percentage of part-time workers.

Best Jobs Overall with a High Percentage of Part-Time Workers

Job	Percent Part-Time Workers	Annual Earnings	Percent Growth	Annual Openings
1. Teachers, Postsecondary	27.3%	$53,590	32.2%	329,000
2. Dental Hygienists	56.0%	$60,890	43.3%	17,000
3. Registered Nurses	24.1%	$54,670	29.4%	229,000
4. Physical Therapists	24.7%	$63,080	36.7%	13,000
5. Pharmacists	21.1%	$89,820	24.6%	16,000
6. Instructional Coordinators	23.4%	$50,430	27.5%	15,000
7. Medical Assistants	27.5%	$25,350	52.1%	93,000
8. Occupational Therapists	29.4%	$56,860	33.6%	7,000
9. Kindergarten Teachers, Except Special Education	25.1%	$42,230	22.4%	28,000
10. Dental Assistants	38.9%	$29,520	42.7%	45,000
11. Clinical Psychologists	22.8%	$57,170	19.1%	10,000
12. Counseling Psychologists	22.8%	$57,170	19.1%	10,000
13. School Psychologists	22.8%	$57,170	19.1%	10,000
14. Home Health Aides	28.0%	$18,800	56.0%	170,000
15. Physical Therapist Assistants	28.6%	$39,490	44.2%	7,000
16. Self-Enrichment Education Teachers	45.6%	$32,360	25.3%	74,000
17. Chiropractors	20.7%	$67,200	22.4%	4,000
18. Preschool Teachers, Except Special Education	25.1%	$21,990	33.1%	77,000
19. Personal and Home Care Aides	36.6%	$17,340	41.0%	230,000
20. Surgical Technologists	23.2%	$34,830	29.5%	12,000
21. Fitness Trainers and Aerobics Instructors	41.3%	$25,840	27.1%	50,000
22. Nursing Aides, Orderlies, and Attendants	28.0%	$21,440	22.3%	307,000
23. Pharmacy Technicians	23.2%	$24,390	28.6%	35,000
24. Licensed Practical and Licensed Vocational Nurses	21.9%	$35,230	17.1%	84,000
25. Poets, Lyricists, and Creative Writers	30.7%	$46,420	17.7%	14,000

Jobs 11, 12, and 13 share 10,000 openings. Job 25 shares 14,000 openings with another job not included in this list.

Best-Paying Jobs with a High Percentage of Part-Time Workers

Job	Percent Part-Time Workers	Annual Earnings
1. Oral and Maxillofacial Surgeons	22.4%	more than $145,600
2. Orthodontists	22.4%	more than $145,600

Best-Paying Jobs with a High Percentage of Part-Time Workers

Job	Percent Part-Time Workers	Annual Earnings
3. Prosthodontists	22.4%	more than $145,600
4. Dentists, General	22.4%	$125,300
5. Podiatrists	22.4%	$100,550
6. Pharmacists	21.1%	$89,820
7. Industrial-Organizational Psychologists	22.8%	$84,690
8. Chiropractors	20.7%	$67,200
9. Physical Therapists	24.7%	$63,080
10. Dental Hygienists	56.0%	$60,890
11. Clinical Psychologists	22.8%	$57,170
12. Counseling Psychologists	22.8%	$57,170
13. School Psychologists	22.8%	$57,170
14. Occupational Therapists	29.4%	$56,860
15. Speech-Language Pathologists	30.2%	$54,880
16. Registered Nurses	24.1%	$54,670
17. Teachers, Postsecondary	27.3%	$53,590
18. Audiologists	30.8%	$53,490
19. Instructional Coordinators	23.4%	$50,430
20. Librarians	22.3%	$47,400
21. Film and Video Editors	27.6%	$46,930
22. Flight Attendants	28.8%	$46,680
23. Poets, Lyricists, and Creative Writers	30.7%	$46,420
24. Curators	23.4%	$45,240
25. Dietitians and Nutritionists	24.8%	$44,940

Fastest-Growing Jobs with a High Percentage of Part-Time Workers

Job	Percent Part-Time Workers	Percent Growth
1. Home Health Aides	28.0%	56.0%
2. Medical Assistants	27.5%	52.1%
3. Physical Therapist Assistants	28.6%	44.2%
4. Dental Hygienists	56.0%	43.3%
5. Dental Assistants	38.9%	42.7%
6. Personal and Home Care Aides	36.6%	41.0%

(continued)

(continued)

Fastest-Growing Jobs with a High Percentage of Part-Time Workers

Job	Percent Part-Time Workers	Percent Growth
7. Physical Therapists	24.7%	36.7%
8. Physical Therapist Aides	28.6%	34.4%
9. Occupational Therapists	29.4%	33.6%
10. Preschool Teachers, Except Special Education	25.1%	33.1%
11. Teachers, Postsecondary	27.3%	32.2%
12. Surgical Technologists	23.2%	29.5%
13. Registered Nurses	24.1%	29.4%
14. Pharmacy Technicians	23.2%	28.6%
15. Instructional Coordinators	23.4%	27.5%
16. Fitness Trainers and Aerobics Instructors	41.3%	27.1%
17. Self-Enrichment Education Teachers	45.6%	25.3%
18. Pharmacists	21.1%	24.6%
19. Chiropractors	20.7%	22.4%
20. Kindergarten Teachers, Except Special Education	25.1%	22.4%
21. Nursing Aides, Orderlies, and Attendants	28.0%	22.3%
22. Veterinary Assistants and Laboratory Animal Caretakers	27.5%	21.0%
23. Funeral Attendants	44.0%	20.8%
24. Industrial-Organizational Psychologists	22.8%	20.4%
25. Lifeguards, Ski Patrol, and Other Recreational Protective Service Workers	63.8%	20.4%

Jobs with a High Percentage of Part-Time Workers with the Most Openings

Job	Percent Part-Time Workers	Annual Openings
1. Child Care Workers	38.8%	439,000
2. Nannies	38.8%	439,000
3. Teachers, Postsecondary	27.3%	329,000
4. Nursing Aides, Orderlies, and Attendants	28.0%	307,000
5. Teacher Assistants	38.5%	252,000
6. Personal and Home Care Aides	36.6%	230,000
7. Registered Nurses	24.1%	229,000

Jobs with a High Percentage of Part-Time Workers with the Most Openings

Job	Percent Part-Time Workers	Annual Openings
8. Home Health Aides	28.0%	170,000
9. Medical Assistants	27.5%	93,000
10. Licensed Practical and Licensed Vocational Nurses	21.9%	84,000
11. Preschool Teachers, Except Special Education	25.1%	77,000
12. Bus Drivers, School	38.4%	76,000
13. Self-Enrichment Education Teachers	45.6%	74,000
14. Recreation Workers	41.3%	69,000
15. Fitness Trainers and Aerobics Instructors	41.3%	50,000
16. Lifeguards, Ski Patrol, and Other Recreational Protective Service Workers	63.8%	49,000
17. Dental Assistants	38.9%	45,000
18. Pharmacy Technicians	23.2%	35,000
19. Kindergarten Teachers, Except Special Education	25.1%	28,000
20. Adult Literacy, Remedial Education, and GED Teachers and Instructors	45.6%	27,000
21. Crossing Guards	53.9%	26,000
22. Dental Hygienists	56.0%	17,000
23. Pharmacists	21.1%	16,000
24. Instructional Coordinators	23.4%	15,000
25. Veterinary Assistants and Laboratory Animal Caretakers	27.5%	14,000

Jobs 1 and 2 share 439,000 openings.

Best Jobs for a Better World with a High Percentage of Self-Employed Workers

A bit more than 10 percent of the workforce is self-employed. Although you may think of the self-employed as having similar jobs, they actually work in an enormous range of situations, fields, and work environments that you may not have considered. Among the self-employed are people who own small or large businesses; professionals such as lawyers, psychologists, and medical doctors; part-time workers; people working on a contract basis for one or more employers; people running home consulting companies or other home-based businesses; and people in many other situations. They may go to the same office every day, as a chiropractor might; visit multiple employers during the course of a week; or do most of their work from home. Some work part time, others full time, some as a way to have fun, some so they can spend time with their children or go back to school.

The point is that there is an enormous range of situations, and one of them could make sense for you as a career that allows you to help your fellow humans.

The following list contains world-improving jobs in which more than 10 percent of the workers are self-employed.

Best Jobs for a Better World with the Highest Percentage of Self-Employed Workers

Job	Percent Self-Employed Workers
1. Poets, Lyricists, and Creative Writers	67.7%
2. Fine Artists, Including Painters, Sculptors, and Illustrators	61.9%
3. Animal Trainers	58.2%
4. Chiropractors	49.2%
5. Music Composers and Arrangers	44.8%
6. Music Directors	44.8%
7. Personal Financial Advisors	38.9%
8. Clinical Psychologists	38.2%
9. Counseling Psychologists	38.2%
10. Prosthodontists	38.2%
11. School Psychologists	38.2%
12. Industrial-Organizational Psychologists	37.6%
13. Orthodontists	35.9%
14. Child Care Workers	31.9%
15. Nannies	31.9%
16. Self-Enrichment Education Teachers	31.1%
17. Dentists, General	30.7%
18. Talent Directors	30.4%
19. Directors—Stage, Motion Pictures, Television, and Radio	30.4%
20. Adult Literacy, Remedial Education, and GED Teachers and Instructors	28.6%
21. Set and Exhibit Designers	27.6%
22. Optometrists	27.4%
23. Landscape Architects	23.7%
24. Private Detectives and Investigators	23.7%
25. Veterinarians	20.7%
26. Architects, Except Landscape and Naval	20.1%
27. Podiatrists	19.8%
28. Funeral Directors	19.7%
29. Film and Video Editors	18.2%
30. Choreographers	17.7%

Best Jobs for a Better World with the Highest Percentage of Self-Employed Workers

Job	Percent Self-Employed Workers
31. Medical Equipment Repairers	16.2%
32. Oral and Maxillofacial Surgeons	15.7%
33. Orthotists and Prosthetists	14.4%
34. Tour Guides and Escorts	14.4%
35. Interpreters and Translators	13.5%
36. Physicians and Surgeons	11.5%
37. Ambulance Drivers and Attendants, Except Emergency Medical Technicians	11.0%

The jobs in the following four lists are derived from the preceding list of the jobs with the highest percentage of self-employed workers. Where the following lists give earnings estimates, keep in mind that these figures are based on a survey that *does not include self-employed workers*. The median earnings for self-employed workers may be significantly higher or lower.

Best Jobs Overall with a High Percentage of Self-Employed Workers

Job	Percent Self-Employed Workers	Annual Earnings	Percent Growth	Annual Openings
1. Physicians and Surgeons	11.5%	more than $145,600	24.0%	41,000
2. Personal Financial Advisors	38.9%	$63,500	25.9%	17,000
3. Chiropractors	49.2%	$67,200	22.4%	4,000
4. Clinical Psychologists	38.2%	$57,170	19.1%	10,000
5. Counseling Psychologists	38.2%	$57,170	19.1%	10,000
6. School Psychologists	38.2%	$57,170	19.1%	10,000
7. Self-Enrichment Education Teachers	31.1%	$32,360	25.3%	74,000
8. Veterinarians	20.7%	$68,910	17.4%	8,000
9. Optometrists	27.4%	$88,040	19.7%	2,000
10. Poets, Lyricists, and Creative Writers	67.7%	$46,420	17.7%	14,000
11. Directors—Stage, Motion Pictures, Television, and Radio	30.4%	$53,860	16.6%	11,000
12. Talent Directors	30.4%	$53,860	16.6%	11,000
13. Architects, Except Landscape and Naval	20.1%	$62,850	17.3%	7,000
14. Industrial-Organizational Psychologists	37.6%	$84,690	20.4%	fewer than 500
15. Dentists, General	30.7%	$125,300	13.5%	7,000

150 Best Jobs for a Better World © JIST Works

(continued)

(continued)

Best Jobs Overall with a High Percentage of Self-Employed Workers

Job	Percent Self-Employed Workers	Annual Earnings	Percent Growth	Annual Openings
16. Adult Literacy, Remedial Education, and GED Teachers and Instructors	28.6%	$41,270	15.6%	27,000
17. Ambulance Drivers and Attendants, Except Emergency Medical Technicians	11.0%	$18,790	28.0%	5,000
18. Landscape Architects	23.7%	$54,220	19.4%	1,000
19. Interpreters and Translators	13.5%	$34,800	19.9%	4,000
20. Oral and Maxillofacial Surgeons	15.7%	more than $145,600	16.2%	fewer than 500
21. Film and Video Editors	18.2%	$46,930	18.6%	3,000
22. Podiatrists	19.8%	$100,550	16.2%	1,000
23. Private Detectives and Investigators	23.7%	$32,650	17.7%	7,000
24. Orthodontists	35.9%	more than $145,600	12.8%	1,000
25. Child Care Workers	31.9%	$17,050	13.8%	439,000

Jobs 4, 5, and 6 share 10,000 openings. Job 10 shares 14,000 openings with another job not included in this list. Jobs 11 and 12 share 11,000 openings with each other and with three other jobs not included in this list. Job 25 shares 439,000 openings with another job not included in this list.

Best-Paying Jobs with a High Percentage of Self-Employed Workers

Job	Percent Self-Employed Workers	Annual Earnings
1. Physicians and Surgeons	11.5%	more than $145,600
2. Oral and Maxillofacial Surgeons	15.7%	more than $145,600
3. Orthodontists	35.9%	more than $145,600
4. Prosthodontists	38.2%	more than $145,600
5. Dentists, General	30.7%	$125,300
6. Podiatrists	19.8%	$100,550
7. Optometrists	27.4%	$88,040
8. Industrial-Organizational Psychologists	37.6%	$84,690
9. Veterinarians	20.7%	$68,910
10. Chiropractors	49.2%	$67,200
11. Personal Financial Advisors	38.9%	$63,500
12. Architects, Except Landscape and Naval	20.1%	$62,850
13. Clinical Psychologists	38.2%	$57,170
14. Counseling Psychologists	38.2%	$57,170

Best-Paying Jobs with a High Percentage of Self-Employed Workers

Job	Percent Self-Employed Workers	Annual Earnings
15. School Psychologists	38.2%	$57,170
16. Landscape Architects	23.7%	$54,220
17. Directors—Stage, Motion Pictures, Television, and Radio	30.4%	$53,860
18. Talent Directors	30.4%	$53,860
19. Orthotists and Prosthetists	14.4%	$53,760
20. Funeral Directors	19.7%	$47,630
21. Film and Video Editors	18.2%	$46,930
22. Poets, Lyricists, and Creative Writers	67.7%	$46,420
23. Fine Artists, Including Painters, Sculptors, and Illustrators	61.9%	$41,280
24. Adult Literacy, Remedial Education, and GED Teachers and Instructors	28.6%	$41,270
25. Medical Equipment Repairers	16.2%	$39,570

Fastest-Growing Jobs with a High Percentage of Self-Employed Workers

Job	Percent Self-Employed Workers	Percent Growth
1. Ambulance Drivers and Attendants, Except Emergency Medical Technicians	11.0%	28.0%
2. Personal Financial Advisors	38.9%	25.9%
3. Self-Enrichment Education Teachers	31.1%	25.3%
4. Physicians and Surgeons	11.5%	24.0%
5. Chiropractors	49.2%	22.4%
6. Industrial-Organizational Psychologists	37.6%	20.4%
7. Animal Trainers	58.2%	20.3%
8. Interpreters and Translators	13.5%	19.9%
9. Optometrists	27.4%	19.7%
10. Landscape Architects	23.7%	19.4%
11. Clinical Psychologists	38.2%	19.1%
12. Counseling Psychologists	38.2%	19.1%
13. School Psychologists	38.2%	19.1%
14. Film and Video Editors	18.2%	18.6%
15. Orthotists and Prosthetists	14.4%	18.0%
16. Poets, Lyricists, and Creative Writers	67.7%	17.7%
17. Private Detectives and Investigators	23.7%	17.7%

(continued)

(continued)

Fastest-Growing Jobs with a High Percentage of Self-Employed Workers

Job	Percent Self-Employed Workers	Percent Growth
18. Veterinarians	20.7%	17.4%
19. Architects, Except Landscape and Naval	20.1%	17.3%
20. Choreographers	17.7%	16.8%
21. Directors—Stage, Motion Pictures, Television, and Radio	30.4%	16.6%
22. Talent Directors	30.4%	16.6%
23. Tour Guides and Escorts	14.4%	16.6%
24. Oral and Maxillofacial Surgeons	15.7%	16.2%
25. Podiatrists	19.8%	16.2%

Jobs with a High Percentage of Self-Employed Workers with the Most Openings

Job	Percent Self-Employed Workers	Annual Openings
1. Child Care Workers	31.9%	439,000
2. Nannies	31.9%	439,000
3. Self-Enrichment Education Teachers	31.1%	74,000
4. Physicians and Surgeons	11.5%	41,000
5. Adult Literacy, Remedial Education, and GED Teachers and Instructors	28.6%	27,000
6. Personal Financial Advisors	38.9%	17,000
7. Poets, Lyricists, and Creative Writers	67.7%	14,000
8. Directors—Stage, Motion Pictures, Television, and Radio	30.4%	11,000
9. Talent Directors	30.4%	11,000
10. Music Composers and Arrangers	44.8%	11,000
11. Music Directors	44.8%	11,000
12. Clinical Psychologists	38.2%	10,000
13. Counseling Psychologists	38.2%	10,000
14. School Psychologists	38.2%	10,000
15. Veterinarians	20.7%	8,000
16. Private Detectives and Investigators	23.7%	7,000
17. Architects, Except Landscape and Naval	20.1%	7,000
18. Dentists, General	30.7%	7,000

Jobs with a High Percentage of Self-Employed Workers with the Most Openings

Job	Percent Self-Employed Workers	Annual Openings
19. Ambulance Drivers and Attendants, Except Emergency Medical Technicians	11.0%	5,000
20. Tour Guides and Escorts	14.4%	5,000
21. Chiropractors	49.2%	4,000
22. Interpreters and Translators	13.5%	4,000
23. Choreographers	17.7%	4,000
24. Medical Equipment Repairers	16.2%	4,000
25. Fine Artists, Including Painters, Sculptors, and Illustrators	61.9%	4,000

Jobs 1 and 2 share 439,000 openings. Job 7 shares 14,000 openings with another job not included in this list. Jobs 8 and 9 share 11,000 openings with each other and with three other jobs not included in this list. Jobs 10 and 11 share 11,000 openings. Jobs 12, 13, and 14 share 10,000 openings.

Best Jobs for a Better World Employing a High Percentage of Women

Because men and women have different experiences in the workforce, we thought it would be interesting to look at what kinds of jobs have a high percentage of male or female workers. We're not saying that men or women workers should consider these jobs over others, but it is interesting to know what those jobs are and what their rewards are.

To create the two sets of four lists that follow, we sorted the 150 best jobs for a better world according to the percentages of women and men in the workforce and retained those that employ more than 70 percent of men or women. We knew we would create some controversy when we first included best jobs lists of this kind in an earlier book in this series. But these lists are not meant to restrict women or men from considering job options; one reason for including these lists is exactly the opposite. We hope the lists will help people see possibilities that they might not otherwise have considered. For example, perhaps women should consider some jobs that traditionally have high percentages of men in them.

An interesting and unfortunate tidbit to bring up at your next party is that in the jobs listed here with the highest percentage of women, the weighted average earnings are $35,337, compared to $42,297 in the jobs with the highest percentage of men. But earnings don't tell the whole story. We computed the average growth and job openings of the jobs with the highest percentage of women and found statistics of 24.8% growth and 78,677 openings, compared to 15.9% growth and 30,067 openings for the jobs with the highest percentage of men. This discrepancy reinforces the idea that men have had more problems than women in adapting to an economy dominated by service and information-based jobs. Many women may simply be better prepared for these jobs, possessing more appropriate skills for the jobs that are now growing rapidly and have more job openings.

The fact is that jobs with high percentages of women or high percentages of men offer good opportunities for both men and women if they want to do one of these jobs. So we suggest that women browse the lists of jobs that employ high percentages of men and that men browse the lists of jobs with high percentages of women. There are jobs among both lists that pay well, and women or men who are interested in them and who have or can obtain the necessary education and training should consider them.

Best Jobs for a Better World Employing the Highest Percentage of Women

Job	Percent Women
1. Kindergarten Teachers, Except Special Education	97.7%
2. Preschool Teachers, Except Special Education	97.7%
3. Dental Hygienists	97.1%
4. Dental Assistants	96.1%
5. Dietitians and Nutritionists	95.3%
6. Child Care Workers	94.8%
7. Nannies	94.8%
8. Licensed Practical and Licensed Vocational Nurses	93.4%
9. Occupational Therapists	92.9%
10. Registered Nurses	92.3%
11. Speech-Language Pathologists	92.0%
12. Teacher Assistants	90.9%
13. Athletic Trainers	89.0%
14. Medical Assistants	89.0%
15. Medical Equipment Preparers	89.0%
16. Occupational Health and Safety Specialists	89.0%
17. Opticians, Dispensing	89.0%
18. Orthotists and Prosthetists	89.0%
19. Veterinary Assistants and Laboratory Animal Caretakers	89.0%
20. Home Health Aides	88.7%
21. Nursing Aides, Orderlies, and Attendants	88.7%
22. Occupational Therapist Aides	88.7%
23. Occupational Therapist Assistants	88.7%
24. Physical Therapist Aides	88.7%
25. Physical Therapist Assistants	88.7%
26. Medical Records and Health Information Technicians	86.6%
27. Personal and Home Care Aides	85.9%

Best Jobs for a Better World Employing the Highest Percentage of Women

Job	Percent Women
28. Special Education Teachers, Middle School	85.3%
29. Special Education Teachers, Preschool, Kindergarten, and Elementary School	85.3%
30. Special Education Teachers, Secondary School	85.3%
31. Librarians	84.9%
32. Choreographers	84.2%
33. Eligibility Interviewers, Government Programs	82.7%
34. Elementary School Teachers, Except Special Education	82.2%
35. Middle School Teachers, Except Special and Vocational Education	82.2%
36. Dietetic Technicians	81.8%
37. Pharmacy Technicians	81.8%
38. Surgical Technologists	81.8%
39. Child, Family, and School Social Workers	80.1%
40. Medical and Public Health Social Workers	80.1%
41. Mental Health and Substance Abuse Social Workers	80.1%
42. Audiologists	76.7%
43. Flight Attendants	74.5%
44. Cardiovascular Technologists and Technicians	72.0%
45. Medical and Clinical Laboratory Technicians	72.0%
46. Medical and Clinical Laboratory Technologists	72.0%
47. Nuclear Medicine Technologists	72.0%
48. Radiologic Technicians	72.0%
49. Radiologic Technologists	72.0%

The jobs in the following four lists are derived from the preceding list of the jobs employing the highest percentage of women.

Best Jobs Overall Employing a High Percentage of Women

Job	Percent Women	Annual Earnings	Percent Growth	Annual Openings
1. Dental Hygienists	97.1%	$60,890	43.3%	17,000
2. Registered Nurses	92.3%	$54,670	29.4%	229,000
3. Occupational Therapists	92.9%	$56,860	33.6%	7,000
4. Medical Assistants	89.0%	$25,350	52.1%	93,000
5. Dental Assistants	96.1%	$29,520	42.7%	45,000
6. Radiologic Technicians	72.0%	$45,950	23.2%	17,000

(continued)

(continued)

Best Jobs Overall Employing a High Percentage of Women

Job	Percent Women	Annual Earnings	Percent Growth	Annual Openings
7. Radiologic Technologists	72.0%	$45,950	23.2%	17,000
8. Home Health Aides	88.7%	$18,800	56.0%	170,000
9. Special Education Teachers, Preschool, Kindergarten, and Elementary School	85.3%	$44,630	23.3%	18,000
10. Personal and Home Care Aides	85.9%	$17,340	41.0%	230,000
11. Medical and Clinical Laboratory Technologists	72.0%	$47,710	20.5%	14,000
12. Elementary School Teachers, Except Special Education	82.2%	$44,040	18.2%	203,000
13. Kindergarten Teachers, Except Special Education	97.7%	$42,230	22.4%	28,000
14. Physical Therapist Assistants	88.7%	$39,490	44.2%	7,000
15. Medical and Public Health Social Workers	80.1%	$41,120	25.9%	14,000
16. Preschool Teachers, Except Special Education	97.7%	$21,990	33.1%	77,000
17. Mental Health and Substance Abuse Social Workers	80.1%	$34,410	26.7%	15,000
18. Surgical Technologists	81.8%	$34,830	29.5%	12,000
19. Pharmacy Technicians	81.8%	$24,390	28.6%	35,000
20. Cardiovascular Technologists and Technicians	72.0%	$40,420	32.6%	5,000
21. Nursing Aides, Orderlies, and Attendants	88.7%	$21,440	22.3%	307,000
22. Child, Family, and School Social Workers	80.1%	$35,350	19.0%	31,000
23. Medical Records and Health Information Technicians	86.6%	$26,690	28.9%	14,000
24. Middle School Teachers, Except Special and Vocational Education	82.2%	$44,640	13.7%	83,000
25. Nuclear Medicine Technologists	72.0%	$59,670	21.5%	2,000

Jobs 6 and 7 share 17,000 openings.

Best-Paying Jobs Employing a High Percentage of Women

Job	Percent Women	Annual Earnings
1. Dental Hygienists	97.1%	$60,890
2. Nuclear Medicine Technologists	72.0%	$59,670
3. Occupational Therapists	92.9%	$56,860
4. Speech-Language Pathologists	92.0%	$54,880
5. Registered Nurses	92.3%	$54,670
6. Orthotists and Prosthetists	89.0%	$53,760

Best-Paying Jobs Employing a High Percentage of Women

Job	Percent Women	Annual Earnings
7. Occupational Health and Safety Specialists	89.0%	$53,710
8. Audiologists	76.7%	$53,490
9. Medical and Clinical Laboratory Technologists	72.0%	$47,710
10. Librarians	84.9%	$47,400
11. Special Education Teachers, Secondary School	85.3%	$46,820
12. Flight Attendants	74.5%	$46,680
13. Radiologic Technicians	72.0%	$45,950
14. Radiologic Technologists	72.0%	$45,950
15. Special Education Teachers, Middle School	85.3%	$45,490
16. Dietitians and Nutritionists	95.3%	$44,940
17. Middle School Teachers, Except Special and Vocational Education	82.2%	$44,640
18. Special Education Teachers, Preschool, Kindergarten, and Elementary School	85.3%	$44,630
19. Elementary School Teachers, Except Special Education	82.2%	$44,040
20. Kindergarten Teachers, Except Special Education	97.7%	$42,230
21. Medical and Public Health Social Workers	80.1%	$41,120
22. Cardiovascular Technologists and Technicians	72.0%	$40,420
23. Occupational Therapist Assistants	88.7%	$39,750
24. Physical Therapist Assistants	88.7%	$39,490
25. Child, Family, and School Social Workers	80.1%	$35,350

Fastest-Growing Jobs Employing a High Percentage of Women

Job	Percent Women	Annual Growth
1. Home Health Aides	88.7%	56.0%
2. Medical Assistants	89.0%	52.1%
3. Physical Therapist Assistants	88.7%	44.2%
4. Dental Hygienists	97.1%	43.3%
5. Dental Assistants	96.1%	42.7%
6. Personal and Home Care Aides	85.9%	41.0%
7. Physical Therapist Aides	88.7%	34.4%
8. Occupational Therapist Assistants	88.7%	34.1%
9. Occupational Therapists	92.9%	33.6%
10. Preschool Teachers, Except Special Education	97.7%	33.1%
11. Cardiovascular Technologists and Technicians	72.0%	32.6%

(continued)

(continued)

Fastest-Growing Jobs Employing a High Percentage of Women

Job	Percent Women	Percent Growth
12. Surgical Technologists	81.8%	29.5%
13. Registered Nurses	92.3%	29.4%
14. Athletic Trainers	89.0%	29.3%
15. Medical Records and Health Information Technicians	86.6%	28.9%
16. Pharmacy Technicians	81.8%	28.6%
17. Mental Health and Substance Abuse Social Workers	80.1%	26.7%
18. Occupational Therapist Aides	88.7%	26.3%
19. Medical and Public Health Social Workers	80.1%	25.9%
20. Medical and Clinical Laboratory Technicians	72.0%	25.0%
21. Special Education Teachers, Preschool, Kindergarten, and Elementary School	85.3%	23.3%
22. Radiologic Technicians	72.0%	23.2%
23. Radiologic Technologists	72.0%	23.2%
24. Kindergarten Teachers, Except Special Education	97.7%	22.4%
25. Nursing Aides, Orderlies, and Attendants	88.7%	22.3%

Jobs with the Most Openings Employing a High Percentage of Women

Job	Percent Women	Annual Openings
1. Child Care Workers	94.8%	439,000
2. Nannies	94.8%	439,000
3. Nursing Aides, Orderlies, and Attendants	88.7%	307,000
4. Teacher Assistants	90.9%	252,000
5. Personal and Home Care Aides	85.9%	230,000
6. Registered Nurses	92.3%	229,000
7. Elementary School Teachers, Except Special Education	82.2%	203,000
8. Home Health Aides	88.7%	170,000
9. Medical Assistants	89.0%	93,000
10. Licensed Practical and Licensed Vocational Nurses	93.4%	84,000
11. Middle School Teachers, Except Special and Vocational Education	82.2%	83,000
12. Preschool Teachers, Except Special Education	97.7%	77,000
13. Dental Assistants	96.1%	45,000
14. Pharmacy Technicians	81.8%	35,000

Jobs with the Most Openings Employing a High Percentage of Women

Job	Percent Women	Annual Openings
15. Child, Family, and School Social Workers	80.1%	31,000
16. Kindergarten Teachers, Except Special Education	97.7%	28,000
17. Special Education Teachers, Preschool, Kindergarten, and Elementary School	85.3%	18,000
18. Dental Hygienists	97.1%	17,000
19. Radiologic Technicians	72.0%	17,000
20. Radiologic Technologists	72.0%	17,000
21. Mental Health and Substance Abuse Social Workers	80.1%	15,000
22. Medical Records and Health Information Technicians	86.6%	14,000
23. Medical and Public Health Social Workers	80.1%	14,000
24. Medical and Clinical Laboratory Technicians	72.0%	14,000
25. Veterinary Assistants and Laboratory Animal Caretakers	89.0%	14,000

Jobs 1 and 2 share 439,000 openings. Jobs 19 and 20 share 17,000 openings.

Best Jobs for a Better World Employing a High Percentage of Men

If you have not already read the intro to the previous group of lists, best jobs for a better world employing a high percentage of women, consider doing so. Much of the content there applies to these lists as well.

It is significant that in all previous books in the *Best Jobs* series, the list of jobs employing more than 70 percent of men has consistently held more jobs than the list of jobs employing more than 70 percent of women—as many as three times the number of jobs. But this book features a larger number of female-dominated jobs. This says something about the kinds of jobs that have traditionally attracted female workers.

However, we did not include these groups of lists with the assumption that men should consider only jobs with high percentages of men or that women should consider only jobs with high percentages of women. Instead, these lists are here because we think they are interesting and perhaps helpful in considering nontraditional career options. For example, some men would do very well in and enjoy some of the jobs with high percentages of women but may not have considered them seriously. In a similar way, some women would very much enjoy and do well in some jobs that traditionally have been held by high percentages of men. We hope that these lists help you consider options that you simply did not seriously consider because of gender stereotypes.

In the jobs on the following lists, more than 70 percent of the workers are men.

Best Jobs for a Better World Employing the Highest Percentage of Men

Job	Percent Men
1. Forest Fire Fighters	96.7%
2. Municipal Fire Fighters	96.7%
3. Medical Equipment Repairers	92.3%
4. First-Line Supervisors/Managers of Police and Detectives	87.5%
5. Forest Fire Fighting and Prevention Supervisors	87.5%
6. Municipal Fire Fighting and Prevention Supervisors	87.5%
7. Sound Engineering Technicians	86.4%
8. Traffic Technicians	86.2%
9. Animal Control Workers	85.7%
10. Fish and Game Wardens	85.7%
11. Police Patrol Officers	85.7%
12. Sheriffs and Deputy Sheriffs	85.7%
13. Transit and Railroad Police	85.7%
14. Foresters	85.3%
15. Park Naturalists	85.3%
16. Range Managers	85.3%
17. Soil and Water Conservationists	85.3%
18. Fire-Prevention and Protection Engineers	85.1%
19. Industrial Safety and Health Engineers	85.1%
20. Clergy	84.5%
21. Podiatrists	84.3%
22. Ambulance Drivers and Attendants, Except Emergency Medical Technicians	83.9%
23. Air Traffic Controllers	81.6%
24. Computer Security Specialists	81.6%
25. Film and Video Editors	81.1%
26. Funeral Directors	78.5%
27. Chiropractors	78.2%
28. Embalmers	78.0%
29. Funeral Attendants	78.0%
30. Dentists, General	77.5%
31. Environmental Scientists and Specialists, Including Health	77.5%
32. Oral and Maxillofacial Surgeons	77.5%
33. Orthodontists	77.5%
34. Prosthodontists	77.5%
35. Criminal Investigators and Special Agents	76.0%
36. Immigration and Customs Inspectors	76.0%
37. Police Detectives	76.0%
38. Architects, Except Landscape and Naval	75.6%

Best Jobs for a Better World Employing the Highest Percentage of Men

Job	Percent Men
39. Landscape Architects	75.6%
40. Security Guards	75.3%
41. Optometrists	72.4%
42. Correctional Officers and Jailers	70.9%

The jobs in the following four lists are derived from the preceding list of the jobs employing the highest percentage of men.

Best Jobs Overall Employing a High Percentage of Men

Job	Percent Men	Annual Earnings	Percent Growth	Annual Openings
1. Computer Security Specialists	81.6%	$59,930	38.4%	34,000
2. Chiropractors	78.2%	$67,200	22.4%	4,000
3. Forest Fire Fighting and Prevention Supervisors	87.5%	$60,840	21.1%	4,000
4. Municipal Fire Fighting and Prevention Supervisors	87.5%	$60,840	21.1%	4,000
5. First-Line Supervisors/Managers of Police and Detectives	87.5%	$65,570	15.5%	9,000
6. Architects, Except Landscape and Naval	75.6%	$62,850	17.3%	7,000
7. Criminal Investigators and Special Agents	76.0%	$55,790	16.3%	9,000
8. Immigration and Customs Inspectors	76.0%	$55,790	16.3%	9,000
9. Police Detectives	76.0%	$55,790	16.3%	9,000
10. Optometrists	72.4%	$88,040	19.7%	2,000
11. Forest Fire Fighters	96.7%	$39,090	24.3%	21,000
12. Municipal Fire Fighters	96.7%	$39,090	24.3%	21,000
13. Dentists, General	77.5%	$125,300	13.5%	7,000
14. Environmental Scientists and Specialists, Including Health	77.5%	$52,630	17.1%	8,000
15. Police Patrol Officers	85.7%	$46,290	15.5%	47,000
16. Sheriffs and Deputy Sheriffs	85.7%	$46,290	15.5%	47,000
17. Air Traffic Controllers	81.6%	$107,590	14.3%	2,000
18. Podiatrists	84.3%	$100,550	16.2%	1,000
19. Oral and Maxillofacial Surgeons	77.5%	more than $145,600	16.2%	fewer than 500
20. Ambulance Drivers and Attendants, Except Emergency Medical Technicians	83.9%	$18,790	28.0%	5,000
21. Film and Video Editors	81.1%	$46,930	18.6%	3,000
22. Funeral Attendants	78.0%	$19,720	20.8%	8,000

(continued)

(continued)

Best Jobs Overall Employing a High Percentage of Men

Job	Percent Men	Annual Earnings	Percent Growth	Annual Openings
23. Landscape Architects	75.6%	$54,220	19.4%	1,000
24. Fire-Prevention and Protection Engineers	85.1%	$65,210	13.4%	2,000
25. Industrial Safety and Health Engineers	85.1%	$65,210	13.4%	2,000

Job 1 shares 34,000 openings with another job not included in this list. Jobs 3 and 4 share 4,000 openings. Jobs 7, 8, and 9 share 9,000 openings. Jobs 11 and 12 share 21,000 openings. Jobs 15 and 16 share 47,000 openings. Jobs 24 and 25 share 2,000 openings with each other and with another job not included in this list.

Best-Paying Jobs Employing a High Percentage of Men

Job	Percent Men	Annual Earnings
1. Oral and Maxillofacial Surgeons	77.5%	more than $145,600
2. Orthodontists	77.5%	more than $145,600
3. Prosthodontists	77.5%	more than $145,600
4. Dentists, General	77.5%	$125,300
5. Air Traffic Controllers	81.6%	$107,590
6. Podiatrists	84.3%	$100,550
7. Optometrists	72.4%	$88,040
8. Chiropractors	78.2%	$67,200
9. First-Line Supervisors/Managers of Police and Detectives	87.5%	$65,570
10. Fire-Prevention and Protection Engineers	85.1%	$65,210
11. Industrial Safety and Health Engineers	85.1%	$65,210
12. Architects, Except Landscape and Naval	75.6%	$62,850
13. Forest Fire Fighting and Prevention Supervisors	87.5%	$60,840
14. Municipal Fire Fighting and Prevention Supervisors	87.5%	$60,840
15. Computer Security Specialists	81.6%	$59,930
16. Criminal Investigators and Special Agents	76.0%	$55,790
17. Immigration and Customs Inspectors	76.0%	$55,790
18. Police Detectives	76.0%	$55,790
19. Landscape Architects	75.6%	$54,220
20. Park Naturalists	85.3%	$53,350
21. Range Managers	85.3%	$53,350
22. Soil and Water Conservationists	85.3%	$53,350
23. Environmental Scientists and Specialists, Including Health	77.5%	$52,630
24. Transit and Railroad Police	85.7%	$48,850
25. Foresters	85.3%	$48,670

Fastest-Growing Jobs Employing a High Percentage of Men

Job	Percent Men	Percent Growth
1. Computer Security Specialists	81.6%	38.4%
2. Ambulance Drivers and Attendants, Except Emergency Medical Technicians	83.9%	28.0%
3. Forest Fire Fighters	96.7%	24.3%
4. Municipal Fire Fighters	96.7%	24.3%
5. Chiropractors	78.2%	22.4%
6. Forest Fire Fighting and Prevention Supervisors	87.5%	21.1%
7. Municipal Fire Fighting and Prevention Supervisors	87.5%	21.1%
8. Funeral Attendants	78.0%	20.8%
9. Optometrists	72.4%	19.7%
10. Landscape Architects	75.6%	19.4%
11. Film and Video Editors	81.1%	18.6%
12. Sound Engineering Technicians	86.4%	18.4%
13. Architects, Except Landscape and Naval	75.6%	17.3%
14. Environmental Scientists and Specialists, Including Health	77.5%	17.1%
15. Criminal Investigators and Special Agents	76.0%	16.3%
16. Immigration and Customs Inspectors	76.0%	16.3%
17. Police Detectives	76.0%	16.3%
18. Oral and Maxillofacial Surgeons	77.5%	16.2%
19. Podiatrists	84.3%	16.2%
20. Embalmers	78.0%	15.6%
21. First-Line Supervisors/Managers of Police and Detectives	87.5%	15.5%
22. Police Patrol Officers	85.7%	15.5%
23. Sheriffs and Deputy Sheriffs	85.7%	15.5%
24. Medical Equipment Repairers	92.3%	14.8%
25. Animal Control Workers	85.7%	14.4%

Jobs with the Most Openings Employing a High Percentage of Men

Job	Percent Men	Annual Openings
1. Security Guards	75.3%	230,000
2. Correctional Officers and Jailers	70.9%	54,000
3. Police Patrol Officers	85.7%	47,000
4. Sheriffs and Deputy Sheriffs	85.7%	47,000

(continued)

(continued)

Jobs with the Most Openings Employing a High Percentage of Men

Job	Percent Men	Annual Openings
5. Computer Security Specialists	81.6%	34,000
6. Clergy	84.5%	26,000
7. Forest Fire Fighters	96.7%	21,000
8. Municipal Fire Fighters	96.7%	21,000
9. Criminal Investigators and Special Agents	76.0%	9,000
10. Immigration and Customs Inspectors	76.0%	9,000
11. Police Detectives	76.0%	9,000
12. First-Line Supervisors/Managers of Police and Detectives	87.5%	9,000
13. Funeral Attendants	78.0%	8,000
14. Environmental Scientists and Specialists, Including Health	77.5%	8,000
15. Architects, Except Landscape and Naval	75.6%	7,000
16. Dentists, General	77.5%	7,000
17. Ambulance Drivers and Attendants, Except Emergency Medical Technicians	83.9%	5,000
18. Chiropractors	78.2%	4,000
19. Forest Fire Fighting and Prevention Supervisors	87.5%	4,000
20. Municipal Fire Fighting and Prevention Supervisors	87.5%	4,000
21. Medical Equipment Repairers	92.3%	4,000
22. Animal Control Workers	85.7%	4,000
23. Film and Video Editors	81.1%	3,000
24. Funeral Directors	78.5%	3,000
25. Optometrists	72.4%	2,000

Jobs 3 and 4 share 47,000 openings. Job 5 shares 34,000 openings with another job not included in this list. Jobs 7 and 8 share 21,000 openings. Jobs 9, 10, and 11 share 9,000 openings. Jobs 19 and 20 share 4,000 openings.

Best Jobs Lists Based on Levels of Education and Experience

The lists in this section organize the 150 best world-improving jobs into groups based on the education or training typically required for entry. Unlike many of the previous sections, here we do not include separate lists for highest pay, growth, or number of openings. Instead, we provide one list that includes all the occupations in our database that fit into each of the education levels and ranks them by their total combined score for earnings, growth, and number of openings.

These lists can help you identify a job with higher earnings or better chances to be hired that requires a similar level of education to the job you now hold. For example, you will find jobs within the same level of education that require similar skills, yet one pays significantly better than the other, is projected to grow more rapidly, or has significantly more job openings per year. This information can help you leverage your present skills and experience into jobs that might provide better long-term career opportunities.

You can also use these lists to explore possible job options if you were to get additional training, education, or work experience. For example, you can use these lists to identify occupations that offer high potential and then (in Part II) identify the specific education or training programs required to get the jobs that interest you most.

The lists can also help you when you plan your education. For example, you might be thinking about a particular training program or college major because the pay is very good, but the lists may help you identify a job that interests you more and offers even better potential for the same general educational requirements.

The Education Levels

The following definitions are used by the federal government to classify jobs based on the minimum level of education or training typically required for entry into a job. We use these definitions to construct the lists in this section. Use the training and education level descriptions as guidelines that can help you understand what is generally required, but understand that you will need to learn more about specific requirements before you make a decision on one career over another.

- **Short-term on-the-job training:** It is possible to work in these occupations and achieve an average level of performance within a few days or weeks through on-the-job training.

- **Moderate-term on-the-job training:** Occupations that require this type of training can be performed adequately after a 1- to 12-month period of combined on-the-job and informal training. Typically, untrained workers begin by observing experienced workers performing tasks and are gradually moved into progressively more difficult assignments.

- **Long-term on-the-job training:** This type of training requires more than 12 months of on-the-job training or combined work experience and formal classroom instruction. This includes occupations that use formal apprenticeships for training workers that may take up to four years. It also includes intensive occupation-specific employer-sponsored training like police academies. Furthermore, it includes occupations that require natural talent that must be developed over many years.

- **Work experience in a related occupation:** This type of job requires a worker to have experience—usually several years of experience—in a related occupation (such as police detectives, who are selected based on their experience as police patrol officers).

- **Postsecondary vocational training:** This training requirement can vary in length; training usually lasts from a few months up to one year. In a few instances, there may be as many as four years of training.

- **Associate degree:** The associate degree usually requires 60 to 63 semester hours to complete. A normal course load for a full-time student each semester is 15 hours. This means that it typically takes two years to complete an associate degree.

- **Bachelor's degree:** A bachelor's degree usually requires 120 to 130 semester hours to complete. A full-time student usually takes four to five years to complete a bachelor's degree, depending on the complexity of courses. Traditionally, people have thought of the bachelor's degree as a four-year degree. There are some bachelor's degrees—like the Bachelor of Architecture—that are considered a first professional degree and take five or more years to complete.

- **Work experience plus degree:** Some jobs require work experience in a related job in addition to a degree. For example, almost all managers have worked in a related job before being promoted into a management position. Most of the jobs in this group require a four-year bachelor's degree, although some require an associate degree or a master's degree.

- **Master's degree:** This degree usually requires 33 to 60 semester hours beyond the bachelor's degree. The academic master's degrees—like a Master of Arts in Political Science—usually require 33 to 36 hours. A first professional degree at the master's level—like a Master of Social Work—requires almost two years of full-time work.

- **Doctoral degree:** The doctoral degree prepares students for careers that consist primarily of theory development, research, or college teaching. This type of degree is typically the Doctor of Philosophy (Ph.D.) or Doctor of Education (Ed.D.). Normally, a requirement for a doctoral degree is the completion of a master's degree plus an additional two to three years of full-time coursework and a one- to two-semester research project and paper called the dissertation. It usually takes four to five years beyond the bachelor's degree to complete a doctoral degree.

- **First professional degree:** Some professional degrees require three or more years of full-time academic study beyond the bachelor's degree. A professional degree prepares students for a specific profession. It uses theory and research to teach practical applications in a professional occupation. Examples of this type of degree are Doctor of Medicine (M.D.) for physicians, Doctor of Ministry (D.Min.) for clergy, and Juris Doctor (J.D.) for attorneys.

Another Warning About the Data

We warned you in the introduction to use caution in interpreting the data we use, and we want to do it again here. The occupational data we use is the most accurate available anywhere, but it has limitations. For example, a four-year degree in forestry, natural resources, or a related area is typically required for entry for Foresters. But about one-third of the people working as Foresters don't have a bachelor's degree, and others have much more education than the "minimum" required for entry.

In a similar way, people with a graduate degree will typically earn considerably more than someone with an associate or bachelor's degree. However, some people with an associate degree earn considerably more than the average for those with higher levels of education. Likewise, new entrants to any job will typically earn less than the average, and some areas of the country have lower wages overall (but may also have lower costs of living).

So as you browse the lists that follow, please use them as a way to be encouraged rather than discouraged. Education and training are very important for success in the labor market, but so are ability, drive, initiative, and, yes, luck.

Having said this, we encourage you to get as much education and training as you can. It used to be that you got your schooling and never went back, but this is not a good attitude to have now. You will probably need to continue learning new things throughout your working life. This can be done by going to school, which is a good thing for many people to do. But there are also many other ways to learn, such as workshops, adult education programs, certification programs, employer training, professional conferences, Internet training, reading related books and magazines, and many others. Upgrading your computer skills—and other technical skills—is particularly important in our rapidly changing workplace, and you avoid doing so at your peril.

Best Jobs for a Better World Requiring Short-Term On-the-Job Training

Job	Annual Earnings	Percent Growth	Annual Openings
1. Home Health Aides	$18,800	56.0%	170,000
2. Personal and Home Care Aides	$17,340	41.0%	230,000
3. Medical Equipment Preparers	$24,880	20.0%	8,000
4. Physical Therapist Aides	$21,510	34.4%	5,000
5. Teacher Assistants	$20,090	14.1%	252,000
6. Occupational Therapist Aides	$24,310	26.3%	fewer than 500
7. Recreation Workers	$20,110	17.3%	69,000
8. Bus Drivers, School	$24,070	13.6%	76,000
9. Security Guards	$20,760	12.6%	230,000
10. Traffic Technicians	$37,070	14.1%	1,000
11. Veterinary Assistants and Laboratory Animal Caretakers	$19,610	21.0%	14,000
12. Child Care Workers	$17,050	13.8%	439,000
13. Nannies	$17,050	13.8%	439,000
14. Crossing Guards	$20,050	19.7%	26,000
15. Funeral Attendants	$19,720	20.8%	8,000
16. Lifeguards, Ski Patrol, and Other Recreational Protective Service Workers	$16,910	20.4%	49,000

Jobs 12 and 13 share 439,000 openings.

Best Jobs for a Better World Requiring Moderate-Term On-the-Job Training

Job	Annual Earnings	Percent Growth	Annual Openings
1. Medical Assistants	$25,350	52.1%	93,000
2. Dental Assistants	$29,520	42.7%	45,000
3. Social and Human Service Assistants	$25,030	29.7%	61,000
4. Correctional Officers and Jailers	$34,090	6.7%	54,000
5. Pharmacy Technicians	$24,390	28.6%	35,000
6. Police, Fire, and Ambulance Dispatchers	$30,060	15.9%	12,000
7. Residential Advisors	$21,850	28.9%	22,000
8. Audio-Visual Collections Specialists	$40,260	18.6%	1,000
9. Eligibility Interviewers, Government Programs	$33,740	–9.4%	10,000
10. Animal Trainers	$24,800	20.3%	3,000
11. Ambulance Drivers and Attendants, Except Emergency Medical Technicians	$18,790	28.0%	5,000
12. Animal Control Workers	$26,780	14.4%	4,000
13. Dietetic Technicians	$23,470	19.1%	3,000
14. Tour Guides and Escorts	$19,990	16.6%	5,000

Best Jobs for a Better World Requiring Long-Term On-the-Job Training

Job	Annual Earnings	Percent Growth	Annual Openings
1. Talent Directors	$53,860	16.6%	11,000
2. Forest Fire Fighters	$39,090	24.3%	21,000
3. Municipal Fire Fighters	$39,090	24.3%	21,000
4. Police Patrol Officers	$46,290	15.5%	47,000
5. Sheriffs and Deputy Sheriffs	$46,290	15.5%	47,000
6. Flight Attendants	$46,680	16.3%	7,000
7. Air Traffic Controllers	$107,590	14.3%	2,000
8. Interpreters and Translators	$34,800	19.9%	4,000
9. Fine Artists, Including Painters, Sculptors, and Illustrators	$41,280	10.2%	4,000
10. Transit and Railroad Police	$48,850	9.2%	fewer than 500
12. Opticians, Dispensing	$29,000	13.6%	6,000

Job 1 shares 11,000 openings with four other jobs not included in this list. Jobs 2 and 3 share 47,000 openings. Jobs 4 and 5 share 21,000 openings.

Best Jobs for a Better World Requiring Work Experience in a Related Occupation

Job	Annual Earnings	Percent Growth	Annual Openings
1. Forest Fire Fighting and Prevention Supervisors	$60,840	21.1%	4,000
2. Municipal Fire Fighting and Prevention Supervisors	$60,840	21.1%	4,000
3. Self-Enrichment Education Teachers	$32,360	25.3%	74,000
4. Criminal Investigators and Special Agents	$55,790	16.3%	9,000
5. Immigration and Customs Inspectors	$55,790	16.3%	9,000
6. Police Detectives	$55,790	16.3%	9,000
7. First-Line Supervisors/Managers of Police and Detectives	$65,570	15.5%	9,000
8. Coroners	$49,360	11.6%	17,000
9. Private Detectives and Investigators	$32,650	17.7%	7,000
10. Choreographers	$32,950	16.8%	4,000

Jobs 1 and 2 share 4,000 openings. Jobs 4, 5, and 6 share 9,000 openings with each other and with another job not included in this list. Job 8 shares 17,000 openings with four other jobs not included in this list.

Best Jobs for a Better World Requiring Postsecondary Vocational Training

Job	Annual Earnings	Percent Growth	Annual Openings
1. Preschool Teachers, Except Special Education	$21,990	33.1%	77,000
2. Licensed Practical and Licensed Vocational Nurses	$35,230	17.1%	84,000
3. Surgical Technologists	$34,830	29.5%	12,000
4. Emergency Medical Technicians and Paramedics	$26,080	27.3%	21,000
5. Fitness Trainers and Aerobics Instructors	$25,840	27.1%	50,000
6. Nursing Aides, Orderlies, and Attendants	$21,440	22.3%	307,000
7. Sound Engineering Technicians	$38,390	18.4%	2,000
8. Embalmers	$36,960	15.6%	2,000

Best Jobs for a Better World Requiring an Associate Degree

Job	Annual Earnings	Percent Growth	Annual Openings
1. Dental Hygienists	$60,890	43.3%	17,000
2. Registered Nurses	$54,670	29.4%	229,000
3. Radiologic Technicians	$45,950	23.2%	17,000
4. Radiologic Technologists	$45,950	23.2%	17,000

(continued)

(continued)

Best Jobs for a Better World Requiring an Associate Degree

Job	Annual Earnings	Percent Growth	Annual Openings
5. Physical Therapist Assistants	$39,490	44.2%	7,000
6. Respiratory Therapists	$45,140	28.4%	7,000
7. Cardiovascular Technologists and Technicians	$40,420	32.6%	5,000
8. Radiation Therapists	$62,340	26.3%	1,000
9. Medical Records and Health Information Technicians	$26,690	28.9%	14,000
10. Occupational Therapist Assistants	$39,750	34.1%	2,000
11. Nuclear Medicine Technologists	$59,670	21.5%	2,000
12. Medical and Clinical Laboratory Technicians	$31,700	25.0%	14,000
13. Funeral Directors	$47,630	6.7%	3,000
14. Environmental Science and Protection Technicians, Including Health	$36,260	16.3%	6,000
15. Medical Equipment Repairers	$39,570	14.8%	4,000
16. City and Regional Planning Aides	$33,950	17.4%	4,000
17. Fish and Game Wardens	$42,850	10.5%	1,000

Jobs 3 and 4 share 17,000 openings. Job 16 shares 4,000 openings with another job not included in this list.

Best Jobs for a Better World Requiring a Bachelor's Degree

Job	Annual Earnings	Percent Growth	Annual Openings
1. Computer Security Specialists	$59,930	38.4%	34,000
2. Personal Financial Advisors	$63,500	25.9%	17,000
3. Physician Assistants	$72,030	49.6%	10,000
4. Social and Community Service Managers	$49,500	25.5%	17,000
5. Medical and Clinical Laboratory Technologists	$47,710	20.5%	14,000
6. Special Education Teachers, Preschool, Kindergarten, and Elementary School	$44,630	23.3%	18,000
7. Kindergarten Teachers, Except Special Education	$42,230	22.4%	28,000
8. Elementary School Teachers, Except Special Education	$44,040	18.2%	203,000
9. Medical and Public Health Social Workers	$41,120	25.9%	14,000
10. Secondary School Teachers, Except Special and Vocational Education	$46,060	14.4%	107,000
11. Architects, Except Landscape and Naval	$62,850	17.3%	7,000
12. Child, Family, and School Social Workers	$35,350	19.0%	31,000
13. Poets, Lyricists, and Creative Writers	$46,420	17.7%	14,000

Best Jobs for a Better World Requiring a Bachelor's Degree

Job	Annual Earnings	Percent Growth	Annual Openings
14. Special Education Teachers, Middle School	$45,490	19.9%	8,000
15. Landscape Architects	$54,220	19.4%	1,000
16. Middle School Teachers, Except Special and Vocational Education	$44,640	13.7%	83,000
17. Film and Video Editors	$46,930	18.6%	3,000
18. Fire-Prevention and Protection Engineers	$65,210	13.4%	2,000
19. Industrial Safety and Health Engineers	$65,210	13.4%	2,000
20. Special Education Teachers, Secondary School	$46,820	17.9%	11,000
21. Adult Literacy, Remedial Education, and GED Teachers and Instructors	$41,270	15.6%	27,000
22. Dietitians and Nutritionists	$44,940	18.3%	4,000
23. Occupational Health and Safety Specialists	$53,710	12.4%	3,000
24. Orthotists and Prosthetists	$53,760	18.0%	fewer than 500
25. Directors, Religious Activities and Education	$32,540	18.5%	10,000
26. Park Naturalists	$53,350	6.3%	2,000
27. Range Managers	$53,350	6.3%	2,000
28. Soil and Water Conservationists	$53,350	6.3%	2,000
29. Athletic Trainers	$34,260	29.3%	1,000
30. Probation Officers and Correctional Treatment Specialists	$40,210	12.8%	14,000
31. Foresters	$48,670	6.7%	1,000
32. Farm and Home Management Advisors	$41,890	7.7%	2,000
33. Museum Technicians and Conservators	$34,090	14.1%	2,000
34. Set and Exhibit Designers	$37,390	9.3%	2,000

Job 1 shares 34,000 openings with another job not included in this list. Job 13 shares 14,000 openings with another job not included in this list. Jobs 18 and 19 share 2,000 openings with each other and with another job not included in this list. Jobs 26, 27, and 28 share 2,000 openings.

Best Jobs for a Better World Requiring Work Experience Plus Degree

Job	Annual Earnings	Percent Growth	Annual Openings
1. Education Administrators, Elementary and Secondary School	$75,400	10.4%	27,000
2. Education Administrators, Postsecondary	$70,350	21.3%	18,000
3. Directors—Stage, Motion Pictures, Television, and Radio	$53,860	16.6%	11,000
4. Education Administrators, Preschool and Child Care Center/Program	$37,010	27.9%	9,000

(continued)

(continued)

Best Jobs for a Better World Requiring Work Experience Plus Degree

Job	Annual Earnings	Percent Growth	Annual Openings
5. Music Composers and Arrangers	$34,810	10.4%	11,000
6. Judges, Magistrate Judges, and Magistrates	$97,570	6.9%	1,000
7. Vocational Education Teachers, Secondary School	$47,090	9.1%	10,000

Job 3 shares 11,000 openings with four other jobs not included in this list. Job 5 shares 11,000 openings with another job not included in this list.

Best Jobs for a Better World Requiring a Master's Degree

Job	Annual Earnings	Percent Growth	Annual Openings
1. Physical Therapists	$63,080	36.7%	13,000
2. Teachers, Postsecondary	$53,590	32.2%	329,000
3. Instructional Coordinators	$50,430	27.5%	15,000
4. Occupational Therapists	$56,860	33.6%	7,000
5. Educational, Vocational, and School Counselors	$46,440	14.8%	32,000
6. Mental Health and Substance Abuse Social Workers	$34,410	26.7%	15,000
7. Environmental Scientists and Specialists, Including Health	$52,630	17.1%	8,000
8. Industrial-Organizational Psychologists	$84,690	20.4%	fewer than 500
9. Mental Health Counselors	$34,010	27.2%	14,000
10. Substance Abuse and Behavioral Disorder Counselors	$32,580	28.7%	11,000
11. Epidemiologists	$52,170	26.2%	1,000
12. Health Educators	$39,730	22.5%	8,000
13. Urban and Regional Planners	$55,170	15.2%	3,000
14. Clergy	$38,540	12.4%	26,000
15. Speech-Language Pathologists	$54,880	14.6%	5,000
16. Librarians	$47,400	4.9%	8,000
17. Curators	$45,240	15.7%	1,000
18. Music Directors	$34,810	10.4%	11,000

Job 18 shares 11,000 openings with another job not included in this list.

Best Jobs for a Better World Requiring a Doctoral Degree

Job	Annual Earnings	Percent Growth	Annual Openings
1. Medical Scientists, Except Epidemiologists	$61,730	34.1%	15,000
2. Clinical Psychologists	$57,170	19.1%	10,000
3. Counseling Psychologists	$57,170	19.1%	10,000
4. School Psychologists	$57,170	19.1%	10,000

Jobs 2, 3, and 4 share 10,000 openings.

Best Jobs for a Better World Requiring a First Professional Degree

Job	Annual Earnings	Percent Growth	Annual Openings
1. Physicians and Surgeons	more than $145,600	24.0%	41,000
2. Pharmacists	$89,820	24.6%	16,000
3. Oral and Maxillofacial Surgeons	more than $145,600	16.2%	fewer than 500
4. Veterinarians	$68,910	17.4%	8,000
5. Chiropractors	$67,200	22.4%	4,000
6. Dentists, General	$125,300	13.5%	7,000
7. Optometrists	$88,040	19.7%	2,000
8. Orthodontists	more than $145,600	12.8%	1,000
9. Prosthodontists	more than $145,600	13.6%	fewer than 500
10. Podiatrists	$100,550	16.2%	1,000
11. Audiologists	$53,490	9.1%	fewer than 500

Best Jobs Lists Based on Interests

This group of lists organizes the 150 best jobs for a better world into 15 interest areas. You can use these lists to quickly identify jobs based on your interests.

Find the interest area or areas that are most appealing to you. Then review the jobs in those areas to identify jobs you want to explore in more detail and look up their descriptions in Part II. You can also review interest areas where you have had past experience, education, or training to see if other jobs in those areas would meet your current requirements.

Within each interest area, jobs are listed in order of their combined scores based on earnings, growth, and number of openings.

Note: The interest areas used in these lists are 15 of the 16 used in the *New Guide for Occupational Exploration,* Fourth Edition, published by JIST. The original GOE was developed by the U.S. Department of Labor as an intuitive way to assist in career exploration.

The 16 interest areas used in the *New GOE* are based on the 16 career clusters that were developed by the U.S. Department of Education's Office of Vocational and Adult Education around 1999 and that presently are being used by many states to organize their career-oriented programs and career information.

Descriptions for the 16 Interest Areas

Brief descriptions for the 16 GOE interest areas follow. Some of them refer to jobs (as examples) that aren't included in this book.

Also note that we put each of the 150 best jobs into only one interest area list, the one it fit into best. However, many jobs could be included in more than one list, so consider reviewing a variety of these interest areas to find jobs that you might otherwise overlook.

One interest area defined in the following list, Business and Administration, accounts for *none* of the 150 jobs that met the criteria for this book and therefore is not represented by a list. The jobs belonging in this interest area are not rated high on any of the O*NET factors that we used for identifying jobs that improve people's lives. That does not mean that you cannot make the world a better place in a business career. As we explained in the introduction, you could work (for example) as a human resources manager in a charitable organization or as an accountant in a hospital and thus improve people's lives *indirectly* by contributing to the mission of your organization.

- Agriculture and Natural Resources: *An interest in working with plants, animals, forests, or mineral resources for agriculture, horticulture, conservation, extraction, and other purposes.* You can satisfy this interest by working in farming, landscaping, forestry, fishing, mining, and related fields. You may like doing physical work outdoors, such as on a farm or ranch, in a forest, or on a drilling rig. If you have scientific curiosity, you could study plants and animals or analyze biological or rock samples in a lab. If you have management ability, you could own, operate, or manage a fish hatchery, a landscaping business, or a greenhouse.

- Architecture and Construction: *An interest in designing, assembling, and maintaining components of buildings and other structures.* You may want to be part of the team of architects, drafters, and others who design buildings and render the plans. If construction interests you, you can find fulfillment in the many building projects that are being undertaken at all times. If you like to organize and plan, you can find careers in managing these projects. Or you can play a more direct role in putting up and finishing buildings by doing jobs such as plumbing, carpentry, masonry, painting, or roofing, either as a skilled craftsworker or as a helper. You can prepare the building site by operating heavy equipment or install, maintain, and repair vital building equipment and systems such as electricity and heating.

- Arts and Communication: *An interest in creatively expressing feelings or ideas, in communicating news or information, or in performing.* You can satisfy this interest in creative, verbal, or performing activities. For example, if you enjoy literature, perhaps writing or editing would appeal to you. Journalism and public relations are other fields for people who like to use their writing or speaking skills. Do you prefer to work in the performing arts? If so, you could direct or perform in drama, music, or dance. If you especially enjoy the visual arts, you could create paintings, sculpture, or ceramics or design products or visual displays. A flair for technology might lead you to specialize in photography, broadcast production, or dispatching.

◎ Business and Administration: *An interest in making a business organization or function run smoothly.* You can satisfy this interest by working in a position of leadership or by specializing in a function that contributes to the overall effort in a business, a nonprofit organization, or a government agency. If you especially enjoy working with people, you may find fulfillment from working in human resources. An interest in numbers may lead you to consider accounting, finance, budgeting, billing, or financial record-keeping. A job as an administrative assistant may interest you if you like a variety of work in a busy environment. If you are good with details and word processing, you may enjoy a job as a secretary or data entry keyer. Or perhaps you would do well as the manager of a business.

◎ Education and Training: *An interest in helping people learn.* You can satisfy this interest by teaching students, who may be preschoolers, retirees, or any age in between. You may specialize in a particular academic field or work with learners of a particular age, with a particular interest, or with a particular learning problem. Working in a library or museum may give you an opportunity to expand people's understanding of the world.

◎ Finance and Insurance: *An interest in helping businesses and people be assured of a financially secure future.* You can satisfy this interest by working in a financial or insurance business in a leadership or support role. If you like gathering and analyzing information, you may find fulfillment as an insurance adjuster or financial analyst. Or you may deal with information at the clerical level as a banking or insurance clerk or in person-to-person situations providing customer service. Another way to interact with people is to sell financial or insurance services that will meet their needs.

◎ Government and Public Administration: *An interest in helping a government agency serve the needs of the public.* You can satisfy this interest by working in a position of leadership or by specializing in a function that contributes to the role of government. You may help protect the public by working as an inspector or examiner to enforce standards. If you enjoy using clerical skills, you may work as a clerk in a law court or government office. Or perhaps you prefer the top-down perspective of a government executive or urban planner.

◎ Health Science: *An interest in helping people and animals be healthy.* You can satisfy this interest by working in a health care team as a doctor, therapist, or nurse. You might specialize in one of the many different parts of the body (such as the teeth or eyes) or in one of the many different types of care. Or you may wish to be a generalist who deals with the whole patient. If you like technology, you might find satisfaction working with X rays or new methods of diagnosis. You might work with healthy people, helping them eat right. If you enjoy working with animals, you might care for them and keep them healthy.

◎ Hospitality, Tourism, and Recreation: *An interest in catering to the personal wishes and needs of others so that they may enjoy a clean environment, good food and drink, comfortable lodging away from home, and recreation.* You can satisfy this interest by providing services for the convenience, care, and pampering of others in hotels, restaurants, airplanes, beauty parlors, and so on. You may wish to use your love of cooking as a chef. If you like working with people, you may wish to provide personal services by being a travel guide, a flight attendant, a concierge, a hairdresser, or a waiter. You may wish to work in cleaning and building services if you like a clean environment. If you enjoy sports or games, you may work for an athletic team or casino.

⊚ Human Service: *An interest in improving people's social, mental, emotional, or spiritual well-being.* You can satisfy this interest as a counselor, social worker, or religious worker who helps people sort out their complicated lives or solve personal problems. You may work as a caretaker for very young people or the elderly. Or you may interview people to help identify the social services they need.

⊚ Information Technology: *An interest in designing, developing, managing, and supporting information systems.* You can satisfy this interest by working with hardware, software, multimedia, or integrated systems. If you like to use your organizational skills, you might work as an administrator of a system or database. Or you can solve complex problems as a software engineer or systems analyst. If you enjoy getting your hands on the hardware, you might find work servicing computers, peripherals, and information-intense machines such as cash registers and ATMs.

⊚ Law and Public Safety: *An interest in upholding people's rights or in protecting people and property by using authority, inspecting, or investigating.* You can satisfy this interest by working in law, law enforcement, fire fighting, the military, and related fields. For example, if you enjoy mental challenge and intrigue, you could investigate crimes or fires for a living. If you enjoy working with verbal skills and research skills, you may want to defend citizens in court or research deeds, wills, and other legal documents. If you want to help people in critical situations, you may want to fight fires, work as a police officer, or become a paramedic. Or, if you want more routine work in public safety, perhaps a job in guarding, patrolling, or inspecting would appeal to you. If you have management ability, you could seek a leadership position in law enforcement and the protective services. Work in the military gives you a chance to use technical and leadership skills while serving your country.

⊚ Manufacturing: *An interest in processing materials into intermediate or final products or maintaining and repairing products by using machines or hand tools.* You can satisfy this interest by working in one of many industries that mass-produce goods or by working for a utility that distributes electric power or other resources. You may enjoy manual work, using your hands or hand tools in highly skilled jobs such as assembling engines or electronic equipment. If you enjoy making machines run efficiently or fixing them when they break down, you could seek a job installing or repairing such devices as copiers, aircraft engines, cars, or watches. Perhaps you prefer to set up or operate machines that are used to manufacture products made of food, glass, or paper. You may enjoy cutting and grinding metal and plastic parts to desired shapes and measurements. Or you may wish to operate equipment in systems that provide water and process wastewater. You may like inspecting, sorting, counting, or weighing products. Another option is to work with your hands and machinery to move boxes and freight in a warehouse. If leadership appeals to you, you could manage people engaged in production and repair.

- Retail and Wholesale Sales and Service: *An interest in bringing others to a particular point of view by personal persuasion and by sales and promotional techniques.* You can satisfy this interest in a variety of jobs that involve persuasion and selling. If you like using knowledge of science, you may enjoy selling pharmaceutical, medical, or electronic products or services. Real estate offers several kinds of sales jobs as well. If you like speaking on the phone, you could work as a telemarketer. Or you may enjoy selling apparel and other merchandise in a retail setting. If you prefer to help people, you may want a job in customer service.

- Scientific Research, Engineering, and Mathematics: *An interest in discovering, collecting, and analyzing information about the natural world; in applying scientific research findings to problems in medicine, the life sciences, human behavior, and the natural sciences; in imagining and manipulating quantitative data; and in applying technology to manufacturing, transportation, and other economic activities.* You can satisfy this interest by working with the knowledge and processes of the sciences. You may enjoy researching and developing new knowledge in mathematics, or perhaps solving problems in the physical, life, or social sciences would appeal to you. You may wish to study engineering and help create new machines, processes, and structures. If you want to work with scientific equipment and procedures, you could seek a job in a research or testing laboratory.

- Transportation, Distribution, and Logistics: *An interest in operations that move people or materials.* You can satisfy this interest by managing a transportation service, by helping vehicles keep on their assigned schedules and routes, or by driving or piloting a vehicle. If you enjoy taking responsibility, perhaps managing a rail line would appeal to you. Or would you rather get out on the highway, on the water, or up in the air? If so, then you could drive a truck from state to state, be employed on a ship, or fly a crop duster over a cornfield. If you prefer to stay closer to home, you could drive a delivery van, taxi, or school bus. You can use your physical strength to load freight and arrange it so it gets to its destination in one piece.

Best Jobs for a Better World for People Interested in Agriculture and Natural Resources

Job	Annual Earnings	Percent Growth	Annual Openings
1. Park Naturalists	$53,350	6.3%	2,000
2. Range Managers	$53,350	6.3%	2,000
3. Soil and Water Conservationists	$53,350	6.3%	2,000
4. Environmental Science and Protection Technicians, Including Health	$36,260	16.3%	6,000
5. Foresters	$48,670	6.7%	1,000

Jobs 1, 2, and 3 share 2,000 openings.

Best Jobs for a Better World for People Interested in Architecture and Construction

Job	Annual Earnings	Percent Growth	Annual Openings
1. Architects, Except Landscape and Naval	$62,850	17.3%	7,000
2. Landscape Architects	$54,220	19.4%	1,000

Best Jobs for a Better World for People Interested in Arts and Communication

Job	Annual Earnings	Percent Growth	Annual Openings
1. Poets, Lyricists, and Creative Writers	$46,420	17.7%	14,000
2. Directors—Stage, Motion Pictures, Television, and Radio	$53,860	16.6%	11,000
3. Talent Directors	$53,860	16.6%	11,000
4. Film and Video Editors	$46,930	18.6%	3,000
5. Interpreters and Translators	$34,800	19.9%	4,000
6. Air Traffic Controllers	$107,590	14.3%	2,000
7. Sound Engineering Technicians	$38,390	18.4%	2,000
8. Music Composers and Arrangers	$34,810	10.4%	11,000
9. Music Directors	$34,810	10.4%	11,000
10. Police, Fire, and Ambulance Dispatchers	$30,060	15.9%	12,000
11. Choreographers	$32,950	16.8%	4,000
12. Fine Artists, Including Painters, Sculptors, and Illustrators	$41,280	10.2%	4,000
13. Set and Exhibit Designers	$37,390	9.3%	2,000

Job 1 shares 14,000 openings with another job not included in this list. Jobs 2 and 3 share 11,000 openings. Jobs 8 and 9 share 11,000 openings.

Best Jobs for a Better World for People Interested in Education and Training

Job	Annual Earnings	Percent Growth	Annual Openings
1. Teachers, Postsecondary	$53,590	32.2%	329,000
2. Instructional Coordinators	$50,430	27.5%	15,000
3. Education Administrators, Postsecondary	$70,350	21.3%	18,000
4. Elementary School Teachers, Except Special Education	$44,040	18.2%	203,000
5. Preschool Teachers, Except Special Education	$21,990	33.1%	77,000

Best Jobs for a Better World for People Interested in Education and Training

Job	Annual Earnings	Percent Growth	Annual Openings
6. Secondary School Teachers, Except Special and Vocational Education	$46,060	14.4%	107,000
7. Special Education Teachers, Preschool, Kindergarten, and Elementary School	$44,630	23.3%	18,000
8. Education Administrators, Elementary and Secondary School	$75,400	10.4%	27,000
9. Educational, Vocational, and School Counselors	$46,440	14.8%	32,000
10. Kindergarten Teachers, Except Special Education	$42,230	22.4%	28,000
11. Self-Enrichment Education Teachers	$32,360	25.3%	74,000
12. Fitness Trainers and Aerobics Instructors	$25,840	27.1%	50,000
13. Special Education Teachers, Secondary School	$46,820	17.9%	11,000
14. Middle School Teachers, Except Special and Vocational Education	$44,640	13.7%	83,000
15. Special Education Teachers, Middle School	$45,490	19.9%	8,000
16. Education Administrators, Preschool and Child Care Center/Program	$37,010	27.9%	9,000
17. Adult Literacy, Remedial Education, and GED Teachers and Instructors	$41,270	15.6%	27,000
18. Health Educators	$39,730	22.5%	8,000
19. Teacher Assistants	$20,090	14.1%	252,000
20. Vocational Education Teachers, Secondary School	$47,090	9.1%	10,000
21. Librarians	$47,400	4.9%	8,000
22. Curators	$45,240	15.7%	1,000
23. Audio-Visual Collections Specialists	$40,260	18.6%	1,000
24. Farm and Home Management Advisors	$41,890	7.7%	2,000
25. Museum Technicians and Conservators	$34,090	14.1%	2,000

Best Jobs for a Better World for People Interested in Finance and Insurance

Job	Annual Earnings	Percent Growth	Annual Openings
1. Personal Financial Advisors	$63,500	25.9%	17,000

Best Jobs for a Better World for People Interested in Government and Public Administration

Job	Annual Earnings	Percent Growth	Annual Openings
1. Immigration and Customs Inspectors	$55,790	16.3%	9,000
2. Social and Community Service Managers	$49,500	25.5%	17,000
3. Urban and Regional Planners	$55,170	15.2%	3,000
4. City and Regional Planning Aides	$33,950	17.4%	4,000
5. Occupational Health and Safety Specialists	$53,710	12.4%	3,000
6. Fish and Game Wardens	$42,850	10.5%	1,000

Job 1 shares 9,000 openings with three other jobs not included in this list. Job 4 shares 4,000 openings with another job not included in this list.

Best Jobs for a Better World for People Interested in Health Science

Job	Annual Earnings	Percent Growth	Annual Openings
1. Dental Hygienists	$60,890	43.3%	17,000
2. Physicians and Surgeons	more than $145,600	24.0%	41,000
3. Physician Assistants	$72,030	49.6%	10,000
4. Registered Nurses	$54,670	29.4%	229,000
5. Physical Therapists	$63,080	36.7%	13,000
6. Pharmacists	$89,820	24.6%	16,000
7. Medical Assistants	$25,350	52.1%	93,000
8. Dental Assistants	$29,520	42.7%	45,000
9. Occupational Therapists	$56,860	33.6%	7,000
10. Home Health Aides	$18,800	56.0%	170,000
11. Radiologic Technicians	$45,950	23.2%	17,000
12. Radiologic Technologists	$45,950	23.2%	17,000
13. Physical Therapist Assistants	$39,490	44.2%	7,000
14. Surgical Technologists	$34,830	29.5%	12,000
15. Medical and Clinical Laboratory Technologists	$47,710	20.5%	14,000
16. Pharmacy Technicians	$24,390	28.6%	35,000
17. Respiratory Therapists	$45,140	28.4%	7,000
18. Cardiovascular Technologists and Technicians	$40,420	32.6%	5,000
19. Medical Records and Health Information Technicians	$26,690	28.9%	14,000
20. Chiropractors	$67,200	22.4%	4,000
21. Veterinarians	$68,910	17.4%	8,000
22. Medical and Clinical Laboratory Technicians	$31,700	25.0%	14,000

Best Jobs for a Better World for People Interested in Health Science

Job	Annual Earnings	Percent Growth	Annual Openings
23. Radiation Therapists	$62,340	26.3%	1,000
24. Dentists, General	$125,300	13.5%	7,000
25. Nursing Aides, Orderlies, and Attendants	$21,440	22.3%	307,000
26. Occupational Therapist Assistants	$39,750	34.1%	2,000
27. Licensed Practical and Licensed Vocational Nurses	$35,230	17.1%	84,000
28. Optometrists	$88,040	19.7%	2,000
29. Coroners	$49,360	11.6%	17,000
30. Nuclear Medicine Technologists	$59,670	21.5%	2,000
31. Physical Therapist Aides	$21,510	34.4%	5,000
32. Oral and Maxillofacial Surgeons	more than $145,600	16.2%	fewer than 500
33. Podiatrists	$100,550	16.2%	1,000
34. Orthodontists	more than $145,600	12.8%	1,000
35. Athletic Trainers	$34,260	29.3%	1,000
36. Prosthodontists	more than $145,600	13.6%	fewer than 500
37. Speech-Language Pathologists	$54,880	14.6%	5,000
38. Veterinary Assistants and Laboratory Animal Caretakers	$19,610	21.0%	14,000
39. Dietitians and Nutritionists	$44,940	18.3%	4,000
40. Medical Equipment Preparers	$24,880	20.0%	8,000
41. Orthotists and Prosthetists	$53,760	18.0%	fewer than 500
42. Animal Trainers	$24,800	20.3%	3,000
43. Occupational Therapist Aides	$24,310	26.3%	500
44. Embalmers	$36,960	15.6%	2,000
45. Opticians, Dispensing	$29,000	13.6%	6,000
46. Dietetic Technicians	$23,470	19.1%	3,000
47. Audiologists	$53,490	9.1%	fewer than 500

Jobs 11 and 12 share 17,000 openings. Job 29 shares 17,000 openings with four other jobs not included in this list.

Best Jobs for a Better World for People Interested in Hospitality, Tourism, and Recreation

Job	Annual Earnings	Percent Growth	Annual Openings
1. Recreation Workers	$20,110	17.3%	69,000
2. Flight Attendants	$46,680	16.3%	7,000
3. Tour Guides and Escorts	$19,990	16.6%	5,000

Best Jobs for a Better World for People Interested in Human Service

Job	Annual Earnings	Percent Growth	Annual Openings
1. Social and Human Service Assistants	$25,030	29.7%	61,000
2. Medical and Public Health Social Workers	$41,120	25.9%	14,000
3. Personal and Home Care Aides	$17,340	41.0%	230,000
4. Mental Health and Substance Abuse Social Workers	$34,410	26.7%	15,000
5. Child, Family, and School Social Workers	$35,350	19.0%	31,000
6. Mental Health Counselors	$34,010	27.2%	14,000
7. Clinical Psychologists	$57,170	19.1%	10,000
8. Counseling Psychologists	$57,170	19.1%	10,000
9. Residential Advisors	$21,850	28.9%	22,000
10. Substance Abuse and Behavioral Disorder Counselors	$32,580	28.7%	11,000
11. Clergy	$38,540	12.4%	26,000
12. Probation Officers and Correctional Treatment Specialists	$40,210	12.8%	14,000
13. Child Care Workers	$17,050	13.8%	439,000
14. Nannies	$17,050	13.8%	439,000
15. Directors, Religious Activities and Education	$32,540	18.5%	10,000
16. Eligibility Interviewers, Government Programs	$33,740	−9.4%	10,000
17. Funeral Attendants	$19,720	20.8%	8,000

Jobs 7 and 8 share 10,000 openings with each other and with another job not included in this list. Jobs 13 and 14 share 439,000 openings.

Best Jobs for a Better World for People Interested in Information Technology

Job	Annual Earnings	Percent Growth	Annual Openings
1. Computer Security Specialists	$59,930	38.4%	34,000

Job 1 shares 34,000 openings with another job not included in this list.

Best Jobs for a Better World for People Interested in Law and Public Safety

Job	Annual Earnings	Percent Growth	Annual Openings
1. Forest Fire Fighters	$39,090	24.3%	21,000
2. Municipal Fire Fighters	$39,090	24.3%	21,000

Best Jobs for a Better World for People Interested in Law and Public Safety

Job	Annual Earnings	Percent Growth	Annual Openings
3. Forest Fire Fighting and Prevention Supervisors	$60,840	21.1%	4,000
4. Municipal Fire Fighting and Prevention Supervisors	$60,840	21.1%	4,000
5. Emergency Medical Technicians and Paramedics	$26,080	27.3%	21,000
6. First-Line Supervisors/Managers of Police and Detectives	$65,570	15.5%	9,000
7. Police Patrol Officers	$46,290	15.5%	47,000
8. Sheriffs and Deputy Sheriffs	$46,290	15.5%	47,000
9. Criminal Investigators and Special Agents	$55,790	16.3%	9,000
10. Police Detectives	$55,790	16.3%	9,000
11. Lifeguards, Ski Patrol, and Other Recreational Protective Service Workers	$16,910	20.4%	49,000
12. Crossing Guards	$20,050	19.7%	26,000
13. Correctional Officers and Jailers	$34,090	6.7%	54,000
14. Security Guards	$20,760	12.6%	230,000
15. Private Detectives and Investigators	$32,650	17.7%	7,000
16. Judges, Magistrate Judges, and Magistrates	$97,570	6.9%	1,000
17. Transit and Railroad Police	$48,850	9.2%	fewer than 500
18. Animal Control Workers	$26,780	14.4%	4,000

Jobs 1 and 2 share 21,000 openings. Jobs 3 and 4 share 4,000 openings. Jobs 7 and 8 share 47,000 openings. Jobs 9 and 10 share 9,000 openings.

Best Jobs for a Better World for People Interested in Manufacturing

Job	Annual Earnings	Percent Growth	Annual Openings
1. Medical Equipment Repairers	$39,570	14.8%	4,000

Best Jobs for a Better World for People Interested in Retail and Wholesale Sales and Service

Job	Annual Earnings	Percent Growth	Annual Openings
1. Funeral Directors	$47,630	6.7%	3,000

Best Jobs for a Better World for People Interested in Scientific Research, Engineering, and Mathematics

Job	Annual Earnings	Percent Growth	Annual Openings
1. Medical Scientists, Except Epidemiologists	$61,730	34.1%	15,000
2. Industrial-Organizational Psychologists	$84,690	20.4%	fewer than 500
3. School Psychologists	$57,170	19.1%	10,000
4. Fire-Prevention and Protection Engineers	$65,210	13.4%	2,000
5. Industrial Safety and Health Engineers	$65,210	13.4%	2,000
6. Environmental Scientists and Specialists, Including Health	$52,630	17.1%	8,000
7. Epidemiologists	$52,170	26.2%	1,000

Job 3 shares 10,000 openings with two other jobs not included in this list. Jobs 4 and 5 share 2,000 openings with each other and with another job not included in this list.

Best Jobs for a Better World for People Interested in Transportation, Distribution, and Logistics

Job	Annual Earnings	Percent Growth	Annual Openings
1. Ambulance Drivers and Attendants, Except Emergency Medical Technicians	$18,790	28.0%	5,000
2. Bus Drivers, School	$24,070	13.6%	76,000
3. Traffic Technicians	$37,070	14.1%	1,000

Best Jobs Based on Personality Types

These lists organize the 150 best jobs into groups matching six personality types. The personality types are Realistic, Investigative, Artistic, Social, Enterprising, and Conventional. This system was developed by John L. Holland and is used in the *Self-Directed Search (SDS)* and other career assessment inventories and information systems.

If you have used one of these career inventories or systems, the lists will help you identify jobs that most closely match these personality types. Even if you have not used one of these systems, the concept of personality types and the jobs that are related to them can help you identify jobs that most closely match the type of person you are.

We've ranked the jobs within each personality type based on their combined scores for earnings, growth, and annual job openings. As in the job lists for interest areas, only one list for each personality type is given in the following pages. Note that each job is listed in the one personality type it most closely matches, even though it might also fit into others. Consider reviewing the jobs for more than one personality type so you don't overlook possible jobs that would interest you.

Following are brief descriptions for each of the six personality types used in the lists. Select the two or three descriptions that most closely describe you and then use the lists to identify jobs that best fit these personality types.

Descriptions of the Six Personality Types

- **Realistic:** These occupations frequently involve work activities that include practical, hands-on problems and solutions. They often deal with plants; animals; and real-world materials such as wood, tools, and machinery. Many of the occupations require working outside and do not involve a lot of paperwork or working closely with others.

- **Investigative:** These occupations frequently involve working with ideas and require an extensive amount of thinking. These occupations can involve searching for facts and figuring out problems mentally.

- **Artistic:** These occupations frequently involve working with forms, designs, and patterns. They often require self-expression, and the work can be done without following a clear set of rules.

- **Social:** These occupations frequently involve working with, communicating with, and teaching people. These occupations often involve helping or providing service to others.

- **Enterprising:** These occupations frequently involve starting up and carrying out projects. These occupations can involve leading people and making many decisions. They sometimes require risk taking and often deal with business.

- **Conventional:** These occupations frequently involve following set procedures and routines. These occupations can include working with data and details more than with ideas. Usually there is a clear line of authority to follow.

Best Jobs for a Better World for People with a Realistic Personality Type

Job	Annual Earnings	Percent Growth	Annual Openings
1. Forest Fire Fighters	$39,090	24.3%	21,000
2. Municipal Fire Fighters	$39,090	24.3%	21,000
3. Radiologic Technicians	$45,950	23.2%	17,000
4. Radiologic Technologists	$45,950	23.2%	17,000
5. Forest Fire Fighting and Prevention Supervisors	$60,840	21.1%	4,000
6. Municipal Fire Fighting and Prevention Supervisors	$60,840	21.1%	4,000
7. Surgical Technologists	$34,830	29.5%	12,000
8. Medical and Clinical Laboratory Technicians	$31,700	25.0%	14,000

(continued)

(continued)

Best Jobs for a Better World for People with a Realistic Personality Type

Job	Annual Earnings	Percent Growth	Annual Openings
9. Lifeguards, Ski Patrol, and Other Recreational Protective Service Workers	$16,910	20.4%	49,000
10. Medical Equipment Repairers	$39,570	14.8%	4,000
11. Bus Drivers, School	$24,070	13.6%	76,000
12. Correctional Officers and Jailers	$34,090	6.7%	54,000
13. Veterinary Assistants and Laboratory Animal Caretakers	$19,610	21.0%	14,000
14. Sound Engineering Technicians	$38,390	18.4%	2,000
15. Foresters	$48,670	6.7%	1,000
16. Medical Equipment Preparers	$24,880	20.0%	8,000
17. Embalmers	$36,960	15.6%	2,000
18. Fish and Game Wardens	$42,850	10.5%	1,000
19. Traffic Technicians	$37,070	14.1%	1,000

Jobs 1 and 2 share 21,000 openings. Jobs 3 and 4 share 17,000 openings. Jobs 5 and 6 share 4,000 openings.

Best Jobs for a Better World for People with an Investigative Personality Type

Job	Annual Earnings	Percent Growth	Annual Openings
1. Physicians and Surgeons	more than $145,600	24.0%	41,000
2. Pharmacists	$89,820	24.6%	16,000
3. Physician Assistants	$72,030	49.6%	10,000
4. Computer Security Specialists	$59,930	38.4%	34,000
5. Medical Scientists, Except Epidemiologists	$61,730	34.1%	15,000
6. Chiropractors	$67,200	22.4%	4,000
7. Veterinarians	$68,910	17.4%	8,000
8. Clinical Psychologists	$57,170	19.1%	10,000
9. School Psychologists	$57,170	19.1%	10,000
10. Optometrists	$88,040	19.7%	2,000
11. Dentists, General	$125,300	13.5%	7,000
12. Medical and Clinical Laboratory Technologists	$47,710	20.5%	14,000
13. Respiratory Therapists	$45,140	28.4%	7,000
14. Nuclear Medicine Technologists	$59,670	21.5%	2,000
15. Cardiovascular Technologists and Technicians	$40,420	32.6%	5,000

Best Jobs for a Better World for People with an Investigative Personality Type

Job	Annual Earnings	Percent Growth	Annual Openings
16. Industrial-Organizational Psychologists	$84,690	20.4%	fewer than 500
17. Oral and Maxillofacial Surgeons	more than $145,600	16.2%	fewer than 500
18. Environmental Scientists and Specialists, Including Health	$52,630	17.1%	8,000
19. Prosthodontists	more than $145,600	13.6%	fewer than 500
20. Orthodontists	more than $145,600	12.8%	1,000
21. Coroners	$49,360	11.6%	17,000
22. Epidemiologists	$52,170	26.2%	1,000
23. Fire-Prevention and Protection Engineers	$65,210	13.4%	2,000
24. Industrial Safety and Health Engineers	$65,210	13.4%	2,000
25. Urban and Regional Planners	$55,170	15.2%	3,000
26. Dietitians and Nutritionists	$44,940	18.3%	4,000
27. Environmental Science and Protection Technicians, Including Health	$36,260	16.3%	6,000
28. Range Managers	$53,350	6.3%	2,000
29. Soil and Water Conservationists	$53,350	6.3%	2,000

Job 4 shares 34,000 openings with another job not included in this list. Jobs 8 and 9 share 10,000 openings with each other and with another job not included in this list. Job 21 shares 17,000 openings with four other jobs not included in this list. Jobs 23 and 24 share 2,000 openings with each other and with another job not included in this list. Jobs 28 and 29 share 2,000 openings with each other and with another job not included in this list.

Best Jobs for a Better World for People with an Artistic Personality Type

Job	Annual Earnings	Percent Growth	Annual Openings
1. Directors—Stage, Motion Pictures, Television, and Radio	$53,860	16.6%	11,000
2. Talent Directors	$53,860	16.6%	11,000
3. Poets, Lyricists, and Creative Writers	$46,420	17.7%	14,000
4. Architects, Except Landscape and Naval	$62,850	17.3%	7,000
5. Landscape Architects	$54,220	19.4%	1,000
6. Film and Video Editors	$46,930	18.6%	3,000
7. Interpreters and Translators	$34,800	19.9%	4,000
8. Music Composers and Arrangers	$34,810	10.4%	11,000
9. Music Directors	$34,810	10.4%	11,000
10. Librarians	$47,400	4.9%	8,000
11. Choreographers	$32,950	16.8%	4,000

(continued)

(continued)

Best Jobs for a Better World for People with an Artistic Personality Type

Job	Annual Earnings	Percent Growth	Annual Openings
12. Fine Artists, Including Painters, Sculptors, and Illustrators	$41,280	10.2%	4,000
13. Curators	$45,240	15.7%	1,000
14. Museum Technicians and Conservators	$34,090	14.1%	2,000
15. Set and Exhibit Designers	$37,390	9.3%	2,000

Jobs 1 and 2 share 11,000 openings with each other and with three other jobs not included in this list. Job 3 shares 14,000 openings with another job not included in this list. Jobs 8 and 9 share 11,000 openings.

Best Jobs for a Better World for People with a Social Personality Type

Job	Annual Earnings	Percent Growth	Annual Openings
1. Teachers, Postsecondary	$53,590	32.2%	329,000
2. Registered Nurses	$54,670	29.4%	229,000
3. Dental Hygienists	$60,890	43.3%	17,000
4. Physical Therapists	$63,080	36.7%	13,000
5. Personal Financial Advisors	$63,500	25.9%	17,000
6. Medical Assistants	$25,350	52.1%	93,000
7. Occupational Therapists	$56,860	33.6%	7,000
8. Instructional Coordinators	$50,430	27.5%	15,000
9. Dental Assistants	$29,520	42.7%	45,000
10. Home Health Aides	$18,800	56.0%	170,000
11. Elementary School Teachers, Except Special Education	$44,040	18.2%	203,000
12. Social and Community Service Managers	$49,500	25.5%	17,000
13. Personal and Home Care Aides	$17,340	41.0%	230,000
14. Preschool Teachers, Except Special Education	$21,990	33.1%	77,000
15. Social and Human Service Assistants	$25,030	29.7%	61,000
16. Kindergarten Teachers, Except Special Education	$42,230	22.4%	28,000
17. Special Education Teachers, Preschool, Kindergarten, and Elementary School	$44,630	23.3%	18,000
18. Physical Therapist Assistants	$39,490	44.2%	7,000
19. Secondary School Teachers, Except Special and Vocational Education	$46,060	14.4%	107,000
20. Counseling Psychologists	$57,170	19.1%	10,000
21. Self-Enrichment Education Teachers	$32,360	25.3%	74,000
22. Fitness Trainers and Aerobics Instructors	$25,840	27.1%	50,000

Best Jobs for a Better World for People with a Social Personality Type

Job	Annual Earnings	Percent Growth	Annual Openings
23. Police Patrol Officers	$46,290	15.5%	47,000
24. Sheriffs and Deputy Sheriffs	$46,290	15.5%	47,000
25. Education Administrators, Elementary and Secondary School	$75,400	10.4%	27,000
26. Radiation Therapists	$62,340	26.3%	1,000
27. Medical and Public Health Social Workers	$41,120	25.9%	14,000
28. Educational, Vocational, and School Counselors	$46,440	14.8%	32,000
29. Nursing Aides, Orderlies, and Attendants	$21,440	22.3%	307,000
30. Licensed Practical and Licensed Vocational Nurses	$35,230	17.1%	84,000
31. Mental Health and Substance Abuse Social Workers	$34,410	26.7%	15,000
32. Middle School Teachers, Except Special and Vocational Education	$44,640	13.7%	83,000
33. Emergency Medical Technicians and Paramedics	$26,080	27.3%	21,000
34. Mental Health Counselors	$34,010	27.2%	14,000
35. Child, Family, and School Social Workers	$35,350	19.0%	31,000
36. Residential Advisors	$21,850	28.9%	22,000
37. Substance Abuse and Behavioral Disorder Counselors	$32,580	28.7%	11,000
38. Education Administrators, Preschool and Child Care Center/Program	$37,010	27.9%	9,000
39. Occupational Therapist Assistants	$39,750	34.1%	2,000
40. Adult Literacy, Remedial Education, and GED Teachers and Instructors	$41,270	15.6%	27,000
41. Special Education Teachers, Secondary School	$46,820	17.9%	11,000
42. Special Education Teachers, Middle School	$45,490	19.9%	8,000
43. Health Educators	$39,730	22.5%	8,000
44. Podiatrists	$100,550	16.2%	1,000
45. Speech-Language Pathologists	$54,880	14.6%	5,000
46. Physical Therapist Aides	$21,510	34.4%	5,000
47. Athletic Trainers	$34,260	29.3%	1,000
48. Orthotists and Prosthetists	$53,760	18.0%	fewer than 500
49. Recreation Workers	$20,110	17.3%	69,000
50. Teacher Assistants	$20,090	14.1%	252,000
51. Clergy	$38,540	12.4%	26,000
52. Child Care Workers	$17,050	13.8%	439,000
53. Nannies	$17,050	13.8%	439,000
54. Crossing Guards	$20,050	19.7%	26,000
55. Security Guards	$20,760	12.6%	230,000

(continued)

(continued)

Best Jobs for a Better World for People with a Social Personality Type

Job	Annual Earnings	Percent Growth	Annual Openings
56. Vocational Education Teachers, Secondary School	$47,090	9.1%	10,000
57. Directors, Religious Activities and Education	$32,540	18.5%	10,000
58. Probation Officers and Correctional Treatment Specialists	$40,210	12.8%	14,000
59. Occupational Health and Safety Specialists	$53,710	12.4%	3,000
60. Police, Fire, and Ambulance Dispatchers	$30,060	15.9%	12,000
61. Ambulance Drivers and Attendants, Except Emergency Medical Technicians	$18,790	28.0%	5,000
62. Occupational Therapist Aides	$24,310	26.3%	fewer than 500
63. Park Naturalists	$53,350	6.3%	2,000
64. Animal Trainers	$24,800	20.3%	3,000
65. Audiologists	$53,490	9.1%	fewer than 500
66. Funeral Attendants	$19,720	20.8%	8,000
67. Dietetic Technicians	$23,470	19.1%	3,000
68. Farm and Home Management Advisors	$41,890	7.7%	2,000
69. Animal Control Workers	$26,780	14.4%	4,000
70. Tour Guides and Escorts	$19,990	16.6%	5,000

Job 20 shares 10,000 openings with two other jobs not included in this list. Jobs 23 and 24 share 47,000 openings. Jobs 52 and 53 share 439,000 openings. Job 63 shares 2,000 openings with two other jobs not included in this list.

Best Jobs for a Better World for People with an Enterprising Personality Type

Job	Annual Earnings	Percent Growth	Annual Openings
1. Education Administrators, Postsecondary	$70,350	21.3%	18,000
2. Criminal Investigators and Special Agents	$55,790	16.3%	9,000
3. Police Detectives	$55,790	16.3%	9,000
4. First-Line Supervisors/Managers of Police and Detectives	$65,570	15.5%	9,000
5. Flight Attendants	$46,680	16.3%	7,000
6. Private Detectives and Investigators	$32,650	17.7%	7,000
7. Judges, Magistrate Judges, and Magistrates	$97,570	6.9%	1,000
8. Opticians, Dispensing	$29,000	13.6%	6,000
9. Transit and Railroad Police	$48,850	9.2%	fewer than 500
10. Funeral Directors	$47,630	6.7%	3,000

Jobs 2 and 3 share 9,000 openings.

Best Jobs for a Better World for People with a Conventional Personality Type

Job	Annual Earnings	Percent Growth	Annual Openings
1. Medical Records and Health Information Technicians	$26,690	28.9%	14,000
2. Pharmacy Technicians	$24,390	28.6%	35,000
3. Immigration and Customs Inspectors	$55,790	16.3%	9,000
4. Air Traffic Controllers	$107,590	14.3%	2,000
5. Audio-Visual Collections Specialists	$40,260	18.6%	1,000
6. City and Regional Planning Aides	$33,950	17.4%	4,000
7. Eligibility Interviewers, Government Programs	$33,740	–9.4%	10,000

Job 3 shares 9,000 openings with three other jobs not included in this list. Job 6 shares 4,000 openings with another job not included in this list.

PART II

Descriptions of the Best Jobs for a Better World

T his part provides descriptions for all the jobs included in one or more of the lists in Part I. The introduction gives more details on how to use and interpret the job descriptions, but here is some additional information:

◎ Job descriptions are arranged in alphabetical order by job title. This approach allows you to find a description quickly if you know its correct title from one of the lists in Part I.

◎ The job title Physicians and Surgeons, which is used in the Part I lists, represents seven jobs that are described here in Part II: Anesthesiologists; Family and General Practitioners; Internists, General; Obstetricians and Gynecologists; Pediatricians, General; Psychiatrists; and Surgeons. Likewise, the job title Teachers, Postsecondary, represents 36 occupational titles described here: Agricultural Sciences Teachers, Postsecondary; Anthropology and Archeology Teachers, Postsecondary; Architecture Teachers, Postsecondary; Area, Ethnic, and Cultural Studies Teachers, Postsecondary; Art, Drama, and Music Teachers, Postsecondary; Atmospheric, Earth, Marine, and Space Sciences Teachers, Postsecondary; Biological Science Teachers, Postsecondary; Business Teachers, Postsecondary; Chemistry Teachers, Postsecondary; Communications Teachers, Postsecondary; Computer Science Teachers, Postsecondary; Criminal Justice and Law Enforcement Teachers, Postsecondary; Economics Teachers, Postsecondary; Education Teachers, Postsecondary; Engineering Teachers, Postsecondary; English Language and Literature Teachers, Postsecondary; Environmental Science Teachers, Postsecondary; Foreign Language and Literature Teachers, Postsecondary; Forestry and Conservation Science Teachers, Postsecondary; Geography Teachers, Postsecondary; Graduate Teaching Assistants; Health Specialties Teachers, Postsecondary; History Teachers, Postsecondary; Home Economics Teachers, Postsecondary; Law Teachers, Postsecondary; Library Science Teachers, Postsecondary; Mathematical Science Teachers, Postsecondary; Nursing Instructors and Teachers, Postsecondary; Philosophy and Religion Teachers, Postsecondary; Physics Teachers, Postsecondary; Political Science Teachers, Postsecondary; Psychology Teachers, Postsecondary; Recreation and Fitness Studies Teachers, Postsecondary; Social Work Teachers, Postsecondary; Sociology Teachers, Postsecondary; and Vocational Education Teachers, Postsecondary.

- Consider the job descriptions in this section as a first step in career exploration. When you find a job that interests you, turn to Appendix A for suggestions about resources for further exploration.

- Appendix B can give you more context to understand the GOE work groups referred to in the descriptions; you'll find the complete outline of the GOE taxonomy there.

- If you are using this section to browse for interesting options, we suggest you begin with the table of contents. Part I features many interesting lists that will help you identify job titles to explore in more detail. If you have not browsed the lists in Part I, consider spending some time there. The lists are interesting and will help you identify job titles that interest you and that you can find described in the material that follows. The job titles in Part II are also listed in the table of contents.

Adult Literacy, Remedial Education, and GED Teachers and Instructors

◉ Annual Earnings: $41,270
◉ Growth: 15.6%
◉ Annual Job Openings: 27,000
◉ Education/Training Required: Bachelor's degree
◉ Self-Employed: 28.6%
◉ Part-Time: 45.6%

How the Job Improves the World: Contributes to education.

Teach or instruct out-of-school youths and adults in remedial education classes, preparatory classes for the General Educational Development test, literacy, or English as a Second Language. Teaching may or may not take place in a traditional educational institution. Adapt teaching methods and instructional materials to meet students' varying needs, abilities, and interests. Observe and evaluate students' work to determine progress and make suggestions for improvement. Instruct students individually and in groups, using various teaching methods such as lectures, discussions, and demonstrations. Plan and conduct activities for a balanced program of instruction, demonstration, and work time that provides students with opportunities to observe, question, and investigate. Maintain accurate and complete student records as required by laws or administrative policies. Prepare materials and classrooms for class activities. Establish clear objectives for all lessons, units, and projects and communicate those objectives to students. Conduct classes, workshops, and demonstrations to teach principles, techniques, or methods in subjects such as basic English language skills, life skills, and workforce entry skills. Prepare students for further education by encouraging them to explore learning opportunities and to persevere with challenging tasks. Establish and enforce rules for behavior and procedures for maintaining order among the students for whom they are responsible. Provide information, guidance, and preparation for the General Equivalency Diploma (GED) examination. Assign and grade classwork and homework. Observe students to determine qualifications, limitations, abilities, interests, and other individual characteristics. Register, orient, and assess new students according to standards and procedures. Prepare and implement remedial programs for students requiring extra help. Prepare and administer written, oral, and performance tests and issue grades in accordance with performance. Use computers, audiovisual aids, and other equipment and materials to supplement presentations. Prepare objectives and outlines for courses of study, following curriculum guidelines or requirements of states and schools. Guide and counsel students with adjustment or academic problems or special academic interests. Enforce administration policies and rules governing students.

Personality Type: Social. Social occupations frequently involve working with, communicating with, and teaching people. These occupations often involve helping or providing service to others.

GOE—Interest Area: 05. Education and Training. **Work Group:** 05.03. Postsecondary and Adult Teaching and Instructing. **Other Jobs in This Work Group:** Agricultural Sciences Teachers, Postsecondary; Anthropology and Archeology Teachers, Postsecondary; Architecture Teachers, Postsecondary; Area, Ethnic, and Cultural Studies Teachers, Postsecondary; Art, Drama, and Music Teachers, Postsecondary; Atmospheric, Earth, Marine, and Space Sciences Teachers, Postsecondary; Biological Science Teachers, Postsecondary; Business Teachers, Postsecondary; Chemistry Teachers, Postsecondary; Communications Teachers, Postsecondary; Computer Science Teachers, Postsecondary; Criminal Justice and Law Enforcement Teachers, Postsecondary; Economics Teachers, Postsecondary; Education Teachers,

Postsecondary; Engineering Teachers, Postsecondary; English Language and Literature Teachers, Postsecondary; Environmental Science Teachers, Postsecondary; Farm and Home Management Advisors; Foreign Language and Literature Teachers, Postsecondary; Forestry and Conservation Science Teachers, Postsecondary; Geography Teachers, Postsecondary; Graduate Teaching Assistants; Health Specialties Teachers, Postsecondary; History Teachers, Postsecondary; Home Economics Teachers, Postsecondary; Law Teachers, Postsecondary; Library Science Teachers, Postsecondary; Mathematical Science Teachers, Postsecondary; Nursing Instructors and Teachers, Postsecondary; Philosophy and Religion Teachers, Postsecondary; Physics Teachers, Postsecondary; Political Science Teachers, Postsecondary; Psychology Teachers, Postsecondary; Recreation and Fitness Studies Teachers, Postsecondary; Self-Enrichment Education Teachers; Social Work Teachers, Postsecondary; Sociology Teachers, Postsecondary; Vocational Education Teachers, Postsecondary.

Skills—Instructing: Teaching others how to do something. **Learning Strategies:** Selecting and using training/instructional methods and procedures appropriate for the situation when learning or teaching new things. **Social Perceptiveness:** Being aware of others' reactions and understanding why they react as they do. **Service Orientation:** Actively looking for ways to help people. **Persuasion:** Persuading others to change their minds or behavior. **Speaking:** Talking to others to convey information effectively. **Monitoring:** Monitoring/assessing your performance or that of other individuals or organizations to make improvements or take corrective action. **Writing:** Communicating effectively in writing as appropriate for the needs of the audience.

Education and Training Programs: Bilingual and Multilingual Education; Multicultural Education; Adult and Continuing Education and Teaching; Teaching English as a Second or Foreign Language/

ESL Language Instructor; Teaching French as a Second or Foreign Language; Adult Literacy Tutor/Instructor; Linguistics of ASL and Other Sign Languages. **Related Knowledge/Courses: Education and Training:** Principles and methods for curriculum and training design, teaching and instruction for individuals and groups, and the measurement of training effects. **History and Archeology:** Historical events and their causes, indicators, and effects on civilizations and cultures. **Sociology and Anthropology:** Group behavior and dynamics, societal trends and influences, human migrations, ethnicity, and cultures and their history and origins. **Therapy and Counseling:** Principles, methods, and procedures for diagnosis, treatment, and rehabilitation of physical and mental dysfunctions and for career counseling and guidance. **Geography:** Principles and methods for describing the features of land, sea, and air masses, including their physical characteristics; locations; interrelationships; and distribution of plant, animal, and human life. **English Language:** The structure and content of the English language, including the meaning and spelling of words, rules of composition, and grammar.

Work Environment: Indoors; more often standing than sitting.

Agricultural Sciences Teachers, Postsecondary

- Annual Earnings: $71,330
- Growth: 32.2%
- Annual Job Openings: 329,000
- Education/Training Required: Master's degree
- Self-Employed: 0.4%
- Part-Time: 27.3%

The job openings listed here are shared with 35 other postsecondary teaching occupations. For a complete list, see the beginning of this section.

How the Job Improves the World: Contributes to education and the food supply.

Teach courses in the agricultural sciences. Includes teachers of agronomy, dairy sciences, fisheries management, horticultural sciences, poultry sciences, range management, and agricultural soil conservation. Prepare course materials such as syllabi, homework assignments, and handouts. Evaluate and grade students' classwork, laboratory work, assignments, and papers. Keep abreast of developments in their field by reading current literature, talking with colleagues, and participating in professional conferences. Prepare and deliver lectures to undergraduate and/or graduate students on topics such as crop production, plant genetics, and soil chemistry. Initiate, facilitate, and moderate classroom discussions. Conduct research in a particular field of knowledge and publish findings in professional journals, books, and/or electronic media. Supervise laboratory sessions and fieldwork and coordinate laboratory operations. Supervise undergraduate and/or graduate teaching, internship, and research work. Compile, administer, and grade examinations or assign this work to others. Advise students on academic and vocational curricula and on career issues. Plan, evaluate, and revise curricula, course content, and course materials and methods of instruction. Maintain student attendance records, grades, and other required records. Write grant proposals to procure external research funding. Collaborate with colleagues to address teaching and research issues. Maintain regularly scheduled office hours in order to advise and assist students. Participate in student recruitment, registration, and placement activities. Select and obtain materials and supplies such as textbooks and laboratory equipment. Act as advisers to student organizations. Participate in campus and community events. Serve on academic or administrative committees that deal with institutional policies, departmental matters, and academic issues. Provide professional consulting services to government and/or industry. Perform administrative duties such as serving as department head. Compile bibliographies of specialized materials for outside reading assignments.

Personality Type: Investigative. Investigative occupations frequently involve working with ideas and require an extensive amount of thinking. These occupations can involve searching for facts and figuring out problems mentally.

GOE—Interest Area: 05. Education and Training. **Work Group:** 05.03. Postsecondary and Adult Teaching and Instructing. **Other Jobs in This Work Group:** Adult Literacy, Remedial Education, and GED Teachers and Instructors; Anthropology and Archeology Teachers, Postsecondary; Architecture Teachers, Postsecondary; Area, Ethnic, and Cultural Studies Teachers, Postsecondary; Art, Drama, and Music Teachers, Postsecondary; Atmospheric, Earth, Marine, and Space Sciences Teachers, Postsecondary; Biological Science Teachers, Postsecondary; Business Teachers, Postsecondary; Chemistry Teachers, Postsecondary; Communications Teachers, Postsecondary; Computer Science Teachers, Postsecondary; Criminal Justice and Law Enforcement Teachers, Postsecondary; Economics Teachers, Postsecondary; Education Teachers, Postsecondary; Engineering Teachers, Postsecondary; English Language and Literature Teachers, Postsecondary; Environmental Science Teachers, Postsecondary; Farm and Home Management Advisors; Foreign Language and Literature Teachers, Postsecondary; Forestry and Conservation Science Teachers, Postsecondary; Geography Teachers, Postsecondary; Graduate Teaching Assistants; Health Specialties Teachers, Postsecondary; History Teachers, Postsecondary; Home Economics Teachers, Postsecondary; Law Teachers, Postsecondary; Library Science Teachers, Postsecondary; Mathematical Science Teachers, Postsecondary; Nursing Instructors and Teachers, Postsecondary; Philosophy and Religion Teachers, Postsecondary; Physics Teachers, Postsecondary; Political Science Teachers, Postsecondary; Psychology Teachers, Postsecondary; Recreation and Fitness

Studies Teachers, Postsecondary; Self-Enrichment Education Teachers; Social Work Teachers, Postsecondary; Sociology Teachers, Postsecondary; Vocational Education Teachers, Postsecondary.

Skills—Science: Using scientific rules and methods to solve problems. **Management of Financial Resources:** Determining how money will be spent to get the work done and accounting for these expenditures. **Writing:** Communicating effectively in writing as appropriate for the needs of the audience. **Instructing:** Teaching others how to do something. **Reading Comprehension:** Understanding written sentences and paragraphs in work-related documents. **Active Learning:** Understanding the implications of new information for both current and future problem-solving and decision-making. **Complex Problem Solving:** Identifying complex problems and reviewing related information to develop and evaluate options and implement solutions. **Learning Strategies:** Selecting and using training/instructional methods and procedures appropriate for the situation when learning or teaching new things.

Education and Training Programs: Agriculture, General; Agricultural Business and Management, General; Agribusiness/Agricultural Business Operations; Agricultural Economics; Farm/Farm and Ranch Management; Agricultural/Farm Supplies Retailing and Wholesaling; Agricultural Business and Management, Other; Agricultural Mechanization, General; Agricultural Power Machinery Operation; Agricultural Mechanization, Other; others. **Related Knowledge/Courses: Biology:** Plant and animal organisms and their tissues, cells, functions, interdependencies, and interactions with each other and the environment. **Food Production:** Techniques and equipment for planting, growing, and harvesting food products (both plant and animal) for consumption, including storage/handling techniques. **Education and Training:** Principles and methods for curriculum and training design, teaching and instruction for individuals and groups, and the measurement of training

effects. **Geography:** Principles and methods for describing the features of land, sea, and air masses, including their physical characteristics; locations; interrelationships; and distribution of plant, animal, and human life. **Chemistry:** The chemical composition, structure, and properties of substances and of the chemical processes and transformations that they undergo. This includes uses of chemicals and their danger signs, production techniques, and disposal methods. **English Language:** The structure and content of the English language, including the meaning and spelling of words, rules of composition, and grammar.

Work Environment: Indoors; sitting.

Air Traffic Controllers

- Annual Earnings: $107,590
- Growth: 14.3%
- Annual Job Openings: 2,000
- Education/Training Required: Long-term on-the-job training
- Self-Employed: 1.8%
- Part-Time: 1.4%

How the Job Improves the World: Contributes to safety.

Control air traffic on and within vicinity of airport and movement of air traffic between altitude sectors and control centers according to established procedures and policies. Authorize, regulate, and control commercial airline flights according to government or company regulations to expedite and ensure flight safety. Issue landing and take-off authorizations and instructions. Monitor and direct the movement of aircraft within an assigned air space and on the ground at airports to minimize delays and maximize safety. Monitor aircraft within a specific airspace, using radar, computer equipment, and visual references. Inform pilots about nearby planes as well as potentially hazardous conditions such as weather, speed and direction of wind, and visibility problems. Provide flight path changes or directions to emergency landing fields for pilots traveling in bad weather or in emergency situations. Alert airport emergency services in cases of emergency and when aircraft are experiencing difficulties. Direct pilots to runways when space is available or direct them to maintain a traffic pattern until there is space for them to land. Transfer control of departing flights to traffic control centers and accept control of arriving flights. Direct ground traffic, including taxiing aircraft, maintenance and baggage vehicles, and airport workers. Determine the timing and procedures for flight vector changes. Maintain radio and telephone contact with adjacent control towers, terminal control units, and other area control centers to coordinate aircraft movement. Contact pilots by radio to provide meteorological, navigational, and other information. Initiate and coordinate searches for missing aircraft. Check conditions and traffic at different altitudes in response to pilots' requests for altitude changes. Relay to control centers such air traffic information as courses, altitudes, and expected arrival times. Compile information about flights from flight plans, pilot reports, radar, and observations. Inspect, adjust, and control radio equipment and airport lights. Conduct pre-flight briefings on weather conditions, suggested routes, altitudes, indications of turbulence, and other flight safety information. Analyze factors such as weather reports, fuel requirements, and maps to determine air routes. Organize flight plans and traffic management plans to prepare for planes about to enter assigned airspace.

Personality Type: Conventional. Conventional occupations frequently involve following set procedures and routines. These occupations can include working with data and details more than with ideas. Usually there is a clear line of authority to follow.

GOE—Interest Area: 03. Arts and Communication. **Work Group:** 03.10. Communications Technology. **Other Jobs in This Work Group:** Airfield Operations Specialists; Dispatchers, Except Police, Fire, and Ambulance; Police, Fire, and Ambulance Dispatchers; Telephone Operators.

Skills—Operation Monitoring: Watching gauges, dials, or other indicators to make sure a machine is working properly. **Operation and Control:** Controlling operations of equipment or systems. **Coordination:** Adjusting actions in relation to others' actions. **Complex Problem Solving:** Identifying complex problems and reviewing related information to develop and evaluate options and implement solutions. **Instructing:** Teaching others how to do something. **Active Listening:** Giving full attention to what other people are saying, taking time to understand the points being made, asking questions as appropriate, and not interrupting at inappropriate times. **Judgment and Decision Making:** Considering the relative costs and benefits of potential actions to choose the most appropriate one. **Monitoring:** Monitoring/assessing your performance or that of other individuals or organizations to make improvements or take corrective action.

Education and Training Program: Air Traffic Controller Training. **Related Knowledge/Courses: Transportation:** Principles and methods for moving people or goods by air, rail, sea, or road, including the relative costs and benefits. **Geography:** Principles and methods for describing the features of land, sea, and air masses, including their physical characteristics; locations; interrelationships; and distribution of plant, animal, and human life. **Telecommunications:** Transmission, broadcasting, switching, control, and operation of telecommunications systems. **Public Safety and Security:** Relevant equipment, policies, procedures, and strategies to promote effective local, state, or national security operations for the protection of people, data, property, and institutions. **Education and Training:** Principles and methods for curriculum and training design, teaching and instruction for individuals and groups, and the measurement of training effects. **Physics:** Physical principles and laws and their interrelationships and applications to understanding fluid, material, and atmospheric dynamics and mechanical, electrical, atomic, and subatomic structures and processes.

Work Environment: Indoors; noisy; sitting; using hands on objects, tools, or controls; repetitive motions.

Ambulance Drivers and Attendants, Except Emergency Medical Technicians

- Annual Earnings: $18,790
- Growth: 28.0%
- Annual Job Openings: 5,000
- Education/Training Required: Moderate-term on-the-job training
- Self-Employed: 11.0%
- Part-Time: 15.8%

How the Job Improves the World: Contributes to health.

Drive ambulance or assist ambulance driver in transporting sick, injured, or convalescent persons. Assist in lifting patients. Drive ambulances or assist ambulance drivers in transporting sick, injured, or convalescent persons. Remove and replace soiled linens and equipment to maintain sanitary conditions. Accompany and assist emergency medical technicians on calls. Place patients on stretchers and load stretchers into ambulances, usually with assistance from other attendants. Earn and maintain appropriate certifications. Replace supplies and disposable items on ambulances. Report facts concerning accidents or emergencies to hospital personnel or law enforcement officials. Administer first aid such as bandaging, splinting, and administering oxygen. Restrain or shackle violent patients.

Personality Type: Social. Social occupations frequently involve working with, communicating with, and teaching people. These occupations often involve helping or providing service to others.

GOE—Interest Area: 16. Transportation, Distribution, and Logistics. **Work Group:** 16.06. Other Services Requiring Driving. **Other Jobs in This Work Group:** Bus Drivers, School; Bus Drivers, Transit and Intercity; Couriers and Messengers; Driver/Sales Workers; Parking Lot Attendants; Postal Service Mail Carriers; Taxi Drivers and Chauffeurs.

Skills—Equipment Maintenance: Performing routine maintenance on equipment and determining when and what kind of maintenance is needed. **Operation Monitoring:** Watching gauges, dials, or other indicators to make sure a machine is working properly. **Operation and Control:** Controlling operations of equipment or systems. **Repairing:** Repairing machines or systems by using the needed tools. **Technology Design:** Generating or adapting equipment and technology to serve user needs. **Service Orientation:** Actively looking for ways to help people. **Equipment Selection:** Determining the kind of tools and equipment needed to do a job. **Troubleshooting:** Determining causes of operating errors and deciding what to do about them.

Education and Training Program: Emergency Medical Technology/Technician (EMT Paramedic). **Related Knowledge/Courses: Transportation:** Principles and methods for moving people or goods by air, rail, sea, or road, including the relative costs and benefits. **Psychology:** Human behavior and performance; individual differences in ability, personality, and interests; learning and motivation; psychological research methods; and the assessment and treatment of behavioral and affective disorders. **Medicine and Dentistry:** The information and techniques needed to diagnose and treat human injuries, diseases, and deformities. This includes symptoms, treatment alternatives, drug properties and interactions, and preventive health-care measures. **Customer and Personal Service:** Principles and processes for providing customer and personal services. This includes customer needs assessment, meeting quality standards for services, and evaluation of customer satisfaction. **Telecommunications:** Transmission, broadcasting, switching, control, and operation of telecommunications systems. **Public Safety and Security:** Relevant equipment, policies, procedures, and strategies to promote effective local, state, or national security operations for the protection of people, data, property, and institutions.

Work Environment: Outdoors; noisy; very hot or cold; disease or infections; sitting; using hands on objects, tools, or controls.

Anesthesiologists

- Annual Earnings: More than $145,600
- Growth: 24.0%
- Annual Job Openings: 41,000
- Education/Training Required: First professional degree
- Self-Employed: 11.5%
- Part-Time: 9.6%

The job openings listed here are shared with Family and General Practitioners; Internists, General; Obstetricians and Gynecologists; Pediatricians, General; Psychiatrists; and Surgeons.

How the Job Improves the World: Contributes to health.

Administer anesthetics during surgery or other medical procedures. Administer anesthetic or sedation during medical procedures, using local, intravenous, spinal, or caudal methods. Monitor patient before, during, and after anesthesia and counteract adverse reactions or complications. Provide and maintain life support and airway management and help prepare patients for emergency surgery. Record type and amount of anesthesia and patient condition throughout procedure. Examine patient; obtain medical history; and use diagnostic tests to determine risk during surgical, obstetrical, and other medical procedures. Position patient on operating table to maximize patient comfort and surgical accessibility. Decide when patients have recovered or stabilized enough to be sent to another room or ward or to be sent home following outpatient surgery. Coordinate administration of anesthetics with surgeons during operation. Confer with other medical professionals to determine type and method of anesthetic or sedation to render patient insensible to pain. Coordinate and direct work of nurses, medical technicians, and other health care providers. Order laboratory tests, X rays, and other diagnostic procedures. Diagnose illnesses, using examinations, tests, and reports. Manage anesthesiological services, coordinating them with other medical activities and formulating plans and procedures. Provide medical care and consultation in many settings, prescribing medication and treatment and referring patients for surgery. Inform students and staff of types and methods of anesthesia administration, signs of complications, and emergency methods to counteract reactions. Schedule and maintain use of surgical suite, including operating, wash-up, and waiting rooms and anesthetic and sterilizing equipment. Instruct individuals and groups on ways to preserve health and prevent disease. Conduct medical research to aid in controlling and curing disease, to investigate new medications, and to develop and test new medical techniques.

Personality Type: Investigative. Investigative occupations frequently involve working with ideas and require an extensive amount of thinking. These occupations can involve searching for facts and figuring out problems mentally.

GOE—Interest Area: 08. Health Science. **Work Group:** 08.02. Medicine and Surgery. **Other Jobs in**

This Work Group: Family and General Practitioners; Internists, General; Medical Assistants; Medical Transcriptionists; Obstetricians and Gynecologists; Pediatricians, General; Pharmacists; Pharmacy Aides; Pharmacy Technicians; Physician Assistants; Psychiatrists; Registered Nurses; Surgeons; Surgical Technologists.

Skills—Operation Monitoring: Watching gauges, dials, or other indicators to make sure a machine is working properly. **Science:** Using scientific rules and methods to solve problems. **Operation and Control:** Controlling operations of equipment or systems. **Judgment and Decision Making:** Considering the relative costs and benefits of potential actions to choose the most appropriate one. **Monitoring:** Monitoring/assessing your performance or that of other individuals or organizations to make improvements or take corrective action. **Complex Problem Solving:** Identifying complex problems and reviewing related information to develop and evaluate options and implement solutions. **Equipment Maintenance:** Performing routine maintenance on equipment and determining when and what kind of maintenance is needed. **Equipment Selection:** Determining the kind of tools and equipment needed to do a job.

Education and Training Programs: Anesthesiology; Critical Care Anesthesiology. **Related Knowledge/Courses: Medicine and Dentistry:** The information and techniques needed to diagnose and treat human injuries, diseases, and deformities. This includes symptoms, treatment alternatives, drug properties and interactions, and preventive health-care measures. **Biology:** Plant and animal organisms and their tissues, cells, functions, interdependencies, and interactions with each other and the environment. **Chemistry:** The chemical composition, structure, and properties of substances and of the chemical processes and transformations that they undergo. This includes uses of chemicals and their danger signs, production techniques, and disposal methods. **Psychology:**

Human behavior and performance; individual differences in ability, personality, and interests; learning and motivation; psychological research methods; and the assessment and treatment of behavioral and affective disorders. **Physics:** Physical principles and laws and their interrelationships and applications to understanding fluid, material, and atmospheric dynamics and mechanical, electrical, atomic, and subatomic structures and processes. **Therapy and Counseling:** Principles, methods, and procedures for diagnosis, treatment, and rehabilitation of physical and mental dysfunctions and for career counseling and guidance.

Work Environment: Indoors; contaminants; radiation; disease or infections; standing; using hands on objects, tools, or controls.

Animal Control Workers

- Annual Earnings: $26,780
- Growth: 14.4%
- Annual Job Openings: 4,000
- Education/Training Required: Moderate-term on-the-job training
- Self-Employed: 4.9%
- Part-Time: 21.3%

How the Job Improves the World: Contributes to animal and human health and safety.

Handle animals for the purpose of investigations of mistreatment or control of abandoned, dangerous, or unattended animals. Investigate reports of animal attacks or animal cruelty, interviewing witnesses, collecting evidence, and writing reports. Capture and remove stray, uncontrolled, or abused animals from undesirable conditions, using nets, nooses, or tranquilizer darts as necessary. Examine animals for injuries or malnutrition and arrange for any necessary medical treatment. Remove captured animals from animal-control service vehicles and place animals in shelter cages or other enclosures. Euthanize rabid, unclaimed, or severely injured animals. Supply animals with food, water, and personal care. Clean facilities and equipment such as dog pens and animal control trucks. Prepare for prosecutions related to animal treatment and give evidence in court. Contact animal owners to inform them that their pets are at animal holding facilities. Educate the public about animal welfare and animal control laws and regulations. Write reports of activities and maintain files of impoundments and dispositions of animals. Issue warnings or citations in connection with animal-related offenses or contact police to report violations and request arrests. Answer inquiries from the public concerning animal control operations. Examine animal licenses and inspect establishments housing animals for compliance with laws. Organize the adoption of unclaimed animals. Train police officers in dog handling and training techniques for tracking, crowd control, and narcotics and bomb detection.

Personality Type: Social. Social occupations frequently involve working with, communicating with, and teaching people. These occupations often involve helping or providing service to others.

GOE—Interest Area: 12. Law and Public Safety. **Work Group:** 12.05. Safety and Security. **Other Jobs in This Work Group:** Crossing Guards; Gaming Surveillance Officers and Gaming Investigators; Lifeguards, Ski Patrol, and Other Recreational Protective Service Workers; Private Detectives and Investigators; Security Guards; Transportation Security Screeners.

Skills—Negotiation: Bringing others together and trying to reconcile differences. **Active Listening:** Giving full attention to what other people are saying, taking time to understand the points being made, asking questions as appropriate, and not interrupting at inappropriate times. **Writing:** Communicating effectively in writing as appropriate for the needs of the audience. **Reading Comprehension:** Understanding written sentences and paragraphs in work-related documents. **Equipment Maintenance:** Performing routine maintenance on equipment and determining when and what kind of maintenance is needed. **Social Perceptiveness:** Being aware of others' reactions and understanding why they react as they do. **Equipment Selection:** Determining the kind of tools and equipment needed to do a job. **Service Orientation:** Actively looking for ways to help people.

Education and Training Program: Security and Protective Services, Other. **Related Knowledge/Courses: Public Safety and Security:** Relevant equipment, policies, procedures, and strategies to promote effective local, state, or national security operations for the protection of people, data, property, and institutions. **Law and Government:** Laws, legal codes, court procedures, precedents, government regulations, executive orders, agency rules, and the democratic political process. **Biology:** Plant and animal organisms and their tissues, cells, functions, interdependencies, and interactions with each other and the environment. **Customer and Personal Service:** Principles and processes for providing customer and personal services. This includes customer needs assessment, meeting quality standards for services, and evaluation of customer satisfaction. **Telecommunications:** Transmission, broadcasting, switching, control, and operation of telecommunications systems. **Education and Training:** Principles and methods for curriculum and training design, teaching and instruction for individuals and groups, and the measurement of training effects.

Work Environment: More often outdoors than indoors; contaminants; disease or infections; minor burns, cuts, bites, or stings; using hands on objects, tools, or controls.

Animal Trainers

- Annual Earnings: $24,800
- Growth: 20.3%
- Annual Job Openings: 3,000
- Education/Training Required: Moderate-term on-the-job training
- Self-Employed: 58.2%
- Part-Time: 23.1%

How the Job Improves the World: Contributes to safety.

Train animals for riding, harness, security, performance, or obedience or assisting persons with disabilities. Accustom animals to human voice and contact and condition animals to respond to commands. Train animals according to prescribed standards for show or competition. May train animals to carry pack loads or work as part of pack team. Observe animals' physical conditions to detect illness or unhealthy conditions requiring medical care. Cue or signal animals during performances. Administer prescribed medications to animals. Evaluate animals to determine their temperaments, abilities, and aptitude for training. Feed and exercise animals and provide other general care such as cleaning and maintaining holding and performance areas. Talk to and interact with animals in order to familiarize them to human voices and contact. Conduct training programs to develop and maintain desired animal behaviors for competition, entertainment, obedience, security, riding, and related areas. Keep records documenting animal health, diet, and behavior. Advise animal owners regarding the purchase of specific animals. Instruct jockeys in handling specific horses during races. Train horses or other equines for riding, harness, show, racing, or other work, using knowledge of breed characteristics, training methods, performance standards, and the peculiarities of each animal. Use oral, spur, rein, and hand commands to condition horses to carry riders or to pull horse-drawn equipment. Place tack or harnesses on horses to accustom horses to the feel of equipment. Train dogs in human-assistance or property protection duties. Retrain horses to break bad habits, such as kicking, bolting, and resisting bridling and grooming. Train and rehearse animals, according to scripts, for motion picture, television, film, stage, or circus performances. Organize and conduct animal shows. Arrange for mating of stallions and mares and assist mares during foaling.

Personality Type: Social. Social occupations frequently involve working with, communicating with, and teaching people. These occupations often involve helping or providing service to others.

GOE—Interest Area: 08. Health Science. **Work Group:** 08.05. Animal Care. **Other Jobs in This Work Group:** Animal Breeders; Nonfarm Animal Caretakers; Veterinarians; Veterinary Assistants and Laboratory Animal Caretakers; Veterinary Technologists and Technicians.

Skills—Management of Financial Resources: Determining how money will be spent to get the work done and accounting for these expenditures. **Persuasion:** Persuading others to change their minds or behavior. **Instructing:** Teaching others how to do something. **Service Orientation:** Actively looking for ways to help people. **Learning Strategies:** Selecting and using training/instructional methods and procedures appropriate for the situation when learning or teaching new things. **Monitoring:** Monitoring/assessing your performance or that of other individuals or organizations to make improvements or take corrective action. **Social Perceptiveness:** Being aware of others' reactions and understanding why they react as they do. **Management of Material Resources:** Obtaining and seeing to the appropriate use of equipment, facilities, and materials needed to do certain work.

Education and Training Programs: Animal Training; Equestrian/Equine Studies. **Related Knowledge/**

Courses: **Sales and Marketing:** Principles and methods for showing, promoting, and selling products or services. This includes marketing strategy and tactics, product demonstration, sales techniques, and sales control systems. **Biology:** Plant and animal organisms and their tissues, cells, functions, interdependencies, and interactions with each other and the environment. **Customer and Personal Service:** Principles and processes for providing customer and personal services. This includes customer needs assessment, meeting quality standards for services, and evaluation of customer satisfaction. **Economics and Accounting:** Economic and accounting principles and practices, the financial markets, banking, and the analysis and reporting of financial data. **Communications and Media:** Media production, communication, and dissemination techniques and methods. This includes alternative ways to inform and entertain via written, oral, and visual media. **Clerical Practices:** Administrative and clerical procedures and systems such as word processing, managing files and records, stenography and transcription, designing forms, and other office procedures and terminology.

Work Environment: Outdoors; noisy; standing; walking and running; using hands on objects, tools, or controls; repetitive motions.

Anthropology and Archeology Teachers, Postsecondary

- ◎ Annual Earnings: $60,710
- ◎ Growth: 32.2%
- ◎ Annual Job Openings: 329,000
- ◎ Education/Training Required: Master's degree
- ◎ Self-Employed: 0.4%
- ◎ Part-Time: 27.3%

The job openings listed here are shared with 35 other postsecondary teaching occupations. For a complete list, see the beginning of this section.

How the Job Improves the World: Contributes to education.

Teach courses in anthropology or archeology. Conduct research in a particular field of knowledge and publish findings in professional journals, books, and electronic media. Keep abreast of developments in their field by reading current literature, talking with colleagues, and participating in professional conferences. Prepare and deliver lectures to undergraduate and graduate students on topics such as research methods, urban anthropology, and language and culture. Evaluate and grade students' classwork, assignments, and papers. Initiate, facilitate, and moderate classroom discussions. Write grant proposals to procure external research funding. Supervise undergraduate and/or graduate teaching, internship, and research work. Prepare course materials such as syllabi, homework assignments, and handouts. Compile, administer, and grade examinations or assign this work to others. Supervise students' laboratory work or fieldwork. Plan, evaluate, and revise curricula, course content, and course materials and methods of instruction. Advise students on academic and vocational curricula, career issues, and laboratory and field research. Maintain student attendance records, grades, and other required records. Maintain regularly scheduled office hours in order to advise and assist students. Collaborate with colleagues to address teaching and research issues. Compile bibliographies of specialized materials for outside reading assignments. Perform administrative duties such as serving as department head. Select and obtain materials and supplies such as textbooks and laboratory equipment. Serve on academic or administrative committees that deal with institutional policies, departmental matters, and academic issues. Participate in student recruitment, registration, and placement activities. Participate in campus and community events. Provide professional consulting services to government and industry. Act as advisers to student organizations.

Personality Type: Social. Social occupations frequently involve working with, communicating with, and teaching people. These occupations often involve helping or providing service to others.

GOE—Interest Area: 05. Education and Training. **Work Group:** 05.03. Postsecondary and Adult Teaching and Instructing. **Other Jobs in This Work Group:** Adult Literacy, Remedial Education, and GED Teachers and Instructors; Agricultural Sciences Teachers, Postsecondary; Architecture Teachers, Postsecondary; Area, Ethnic, and Cultural Studies Teachers, Postsecondary; Art, Drama, and Music Teachers, Postsecondary; Atmospheric, Earth, Marine, and Space Sciences Teachers, Postsecondary; Biological Science Teachers, Postsecondary; Business Teachers, Postsecondary; Chemistry Teachers, Postsecondary; Communications Teachers, Postsecondary; Computer Science Teachers, Postsecondary; Criminal Justice and Law Enforcement Teachers, Postsecondary; Economics Teachers, Postsecondary; Education Teachers, Postsecondary; Engineering Teachers, Postsecondary; English Language and Literature Teachers, Postsecondary; Environmental Science Teachers, Postsecondary; Farm and Home Management Advisors; Foreign Language and Literature Teachers, Postsecondary; Forestry and Conservation Science Teachers, Postsecondary; Geography Teachers, Postsecondary; Graduate Teaching Assistants; Health Specialties Teachers, Postsecondary; History Teachers, Postsecondary; Home Economics Teachers, Postsecondary; Law Teachers, Postsecondary; Library Science Teachers, Postsecondary; Mathematical Science Teachers, Postsecondary; Nursing Instructors and Teachers, Postsecondary; Philosophy and Religion Teachers, Postsecondary; Physics Teachers, Postsecondary; Political Science Teachers, Postsecondary; Psychology Teachers, Postsecondary; Recreation and Fitness

Studies Teachers, Postsecondary; Self-Enrichment Education Teachers; Social Work Teachers, Postsecondary; Sociology Teachers, Postsecondary; Vocational Education Teachers, Postsecondary.

Skills—Science: Using scientific rules and methods to solve problems. **Writing:** Communicating effectively in writing as appropriate for the needs of the audience. **Critical Thinking:** Using logic and reasoning to identify the strengths and weaknesses of alternative solutions, conclusions, or approaches to problems. **Instructing:** Teaching others how to do something. **Active Learning:** Understanding the implications of new information for both current and future problem-solving and decision-making. **Reading Comprehension:** Understanding written sentences and paragraphs in work-related documents. **Management of Financial Resources:** Determining how money will be spent to get the work done and accounting for these expenditures. **Learning Strategies:** Selecting and using training/instructional methods and procedures appropriate for the situation when learning or teaching new things.

Education and Training Programs: Social Science Teacher Education; Anthropology; Physical Anthropology; Archeology. **Related Knowledge/Courses: Sociology and Anthropology:** Group behavior and dynamics, societal trends and influences, human migrations, ethnicity, and cultures and their history and origins. **History and Archeology:** Historical events and their causes, indicators, and effects on civilizations and cultures. **Geography:** Principles and methods for describing the features of land, sea, and air masses, including their physical characteristics; locations; interrelationships; and distribution of plant, animal, and human life. **Foreign Language:** The structure and content of a foreign (non-English) language, including the meaning and spelling of words, rules of composition and grammar, and pronunciation. **Philosophy and Theology:** Different philosophical systems and religions. This includes their basic principles, values, ethics, ways of thinking, customs, and practices and their impact on human culture. **English Language:** The structure and content of the English language, including the meaning and spelling of words, rules of composition, and grammar.

Work Environment: Indoors; sitting.

Architects, Except Landscape and Naval

- ◉ Annual Earnings: $62,850
- ◉ Growth: 17.3%
- ◉ Annual Job Openings: 7,000
- ◉ Education/Training Required: Bachelor's degree
- ◉ Self-Employed: 20.1%
- ◉ Part-Time: 9.1%

How the Job Improves the World: Contributes to physical environment.

Plan and design structures, such as private residences, office buildings, theaters, factories, and other structural property. Prepare information regarding design, structure specifications, materials, color, equipment, estimated costs, or construction time. Consult with client to determine functional and spatial requirements of structure. Direct activities of workers engaged in preparing drawings and specification documents. Plan layout of project. Prepare contract documents for building contractors. Prepare scale drawings. Integrate engineering element into unified design. Conduct periodic on-site observation of work during construction to monitor compliance with plans. Administer construction contracts. Represent client in obtaining bids and awarding construction contracts. Prepare operating and maintenance manuals, studies, and reports.

Personality Type: Artistic. Artistic occupations frequently involve working with forms, designs, and patterns. They often require self-expression, and the work can be done without following a clear set of rules.

GOE—Interest Area: 02. Architecture and Construction. **Work Group:** 02.02. Architectural Design. **Other Jobs in This Work Group:** Landscape Architects.

Skills—Operations Analysis: Analyzing needs and product requirements to create a design. **Management of Financial Resources:** Determining how money will be spent to get the work done and accounting for these expenditures. **Complex Problem Solving:** Identifying complex problems and reviewing related information to develop and evaluate options and implement solutions. **Management of Personnel Resources:** Motivating, developing, and directing people as they work; identifying the best people for the job. **Coordination:** Adjusting actions in relation to others' actions. **Negotiation:** Bringing others together and trying to reconcile differences. **Persuasion:** Persuading others to change their minds or behavior. **Writing:** Communicating effectively in writing as appropriate for the needs of the audience.

Education and Training Programs: Architecture (BArch, BA/BS, MArch, MA/MS, PhD); Environmental Design/Architecture; Architectural History and Criticism, General; Architecture and Related Services, Other. **Related Knowledge/Courses: Building and Construction:** The materials, methods, and tools involved in the construction or repair of houses, buildings, or other structures such as highways and roads. **Design:** Design techniques, tools, and principles involved in production of precision technical plans, blueprints, drawings, and models. **Engineering and Technology:** The practical application of engineering science and technology. This includes applying principles, techniques, procedures, and equipment to the design and production of various goods and services. **Fine Arts:** The theory and techniques required to compose, produce, and perform works of music, dance, visual art, drama, and sculpture. **Law and Government:** Laws, legal codes, court procedures, precedents, government regulations, executive orders, agency rules, and the democratic political process. **Physics:** Physical principles and laws and their interrelationships and applications to understanding fluid, material, and atmospheric dynamics and mechanical, electrical, atomic, and subatomic structures and processes.

Work Environment: Indoors; sitting.

Architecture Teachers, Postsecondary

- ◎ Annual Earnings: $62,270
- ◎ Growth: 32.2%
- ◎ Annual Job Openings: 329,000
- ◎ Education/Training Required: Master's degree
- ◎ Self-Employed: 0.4%
- ◎ Part-Time: 27.3%

The job openings listed here are shared with 35 other postsecondary teaching occupations. For a complete list, see the beginning of this section.

How the Job Improves the World: Contributes to education and the physical environment.

Teach courses in architecture and architectural design, such as architectural environmental design, interior architecture/design, and landscape architecture. Evaluate and grade students' work, including work performed in design studios. Prepare and deliver lectures to undergraduate and/or graduate students on topics such as architectural design methods, aesthetics and design, and structures and materials.

Prepare course materials such as syllabi, homework assignments, and handouts. Initiate, facilitate, and moderate classroom discussions. Plan, evaluate, and revise curricula, course content, and course materials and methods of instruction. Keep abreast of developments in their field by reading current literature, talking with colleagues, and participating in professional conferences. Maintain student attendance records, grades, and other required records. Maintain regularly scheduled office hours to advise and assist students. Compile, administer, and grade examinations or assign this work to others. Conduct research in a particular field of knowledge and publish findings in professional journals, books, and/or electronic media. Supervise undergraduate and/or graduate teaching, internship, and research work. Advise students on academic and vocational curricula and on career issues. Collaborate with colleagues to address teaching and research issues. Compile bibliographies of specialized materials for outside reading assignments. Serve on academic or administrative committees that deal with institutional policies, departmental matters, and academic issues. Participate in student recruitment, registration, and placement activities. Select and obtain materials and supplies such as textbooks and laboratory equipment. Write grant proposals to procure external research funding. Provide professional consulting services to government and/or industry. Perform administrative duties such as serving as department head. Act as advisers to student organizations. Participate in campus and community events.

Personality Type: No data available.

GOE—Interest Area: 05. Education and Training. **Work Group:** 05.03. Postsecondary and Adult Teaching and Instructing. **Other Jobs in This Work Group:** Adult Literacy, Remedial Education, and GED Teachers and Instructors; Agricultural Sciences Teachers, Postsecondary; Anthropology and Archeology Teachers, Postsecondary; Area, Ethnic, and Cultural Studies Teachers, Postsecondary; Art,

Drama, and Music Teachers, Postsecondary; Atmospheric, Earth, Marine, and Space Sciences Teachers, Postsecondary; Biological Science Teachers, Postsecondary; Business Teachers, Postsecondary; Chemistry Teachers, Postsecondary; Communications Teachers, Postsecondary; Computer Science Teachers, Postsecondary; Criminal Justice and Law Enforcement Teachers, Postsecondary; Economics Teachers, Postsecondary; Education Teachers, Postsecondary; Engineering Teachers, Postsecondary; English Language and Literature Teachers, Postsecondary; Environmental Science Teachers, Postsecondary; Farm and Home Management Advisors; Foreign Language and Literature Teachers, Postsecondary; Forestry and Conservation Science Teachers, Postsecondary; Geography Teachers, Postsecondary; Graduate Teaching Assistants; Health Specialties Teachers, Postsecondary; History Teachers, Postsecondary; Home Economics Teachers, Postsecondary; Law Teachers, Postsecondary; Library Science Teachers, Postsecondary; Mathematical Science Teachers, Postsecondary; Nursing Instructors and Teachers, Postsecondary; Philosophy and Religion Teachers, Postsecondary; Physics Teachers, Postsecondary; Political Science Teachers, Postsecondary; Psychology Teachers, Postsecondary; Recreation and Fitness Studies Teachers, Postsecondary; Self-Enrichment Education Teachers; Social Work Teachers, Postsecondary; Sociology Teachers, Postsecondary; Vocational Education Teachers, Postsecondary.

Skills—Instructing: Teaching others how to do something. **Technology Design:** Generating or adapting equipment and technology to serve user needs. **Operations Analysis:** Analyzing needs and product requirements to create a design. **Writing:** Communicating effectively in writing as appropriate for the needs of the audience. **Complex Problem Solving:** Identifying complex problems and reviewing related information to develop and evaluate options and implement solutions. **Learning Strategies:** Selecting and using training/instructional methods and procedures appropriate for the situation when learning or teaching new things. **Speaking:** Talking to others to convey information effectively. **Critical Thinking:** Using logic and reasoning to identify the strengths and weaknesses of alternative solutions, conclusions, or approaches to problems.

Education and Training Programs: Architecture (BArch, BA/BS, MArch, MA/MS, PhD); City/Urban, Community, and Regional Planning; Environmental Design/Architecture; Interior Architecture; Landscape Architecture (BS, BSLA, BLA, MSLA, MLA, PhD); Teacher Education and Professional Development, Specific Subject Areas, Other; Architectural Engineering. **Related Knowledge/Courses: Fine Arts:** The theory and techniques required to compose, produce, and perform works of music, dance, visual art, drama, and sculpture. **Design:** Design techniques, tools, and principles involved in production of precision technical plans, blueprints, drawings, and models. **Building and Construction:** The materials, methods, and tools involved in the construction or repair of houses, buildings, or other structures such as highways and roads. **History and Archeology:** Historical events and their causes, indicators, and effects on civilizations and cultures. **Philosophy and Theology:** Different philosophical systems and religions. This includes their basic principles, values, ethics, ways of thinking, customs, and practices and their impact on human culture. **Geography:** Principles and methods for describing the features of land, sea, and air masses, including their physical characteristics; locations; interrelationships; and distribution of plant, animal, and human life.

Work Environment: Indoors; sitting.

Area, Ethnic, and Cultural Studies Teachers, Postsecondary

- Annual Earnings: $55,610
- Growth: 32.2%
- Annual Job Openings: 329,000
- Education/Training Required: Master's degree
- Self-Employed: 0.4%
- Part-Time: 27.3%

The job openings listed here are shared with 35 other postsecondary teaching occupations. For a complete list, see the beginning of this section.

How the Job Improves the World: Contributes to education and intercultural understanding.

Teach courses pertaining to the culture and development of an area (e.g., Latin America), an ethnic group, or any other group (e.g., women's studies, urban affairs). Keep abreast of developments in their field by reading current literature, talking with colleagues, and participating in professional conferences. Conduct research in a particular field of knowledge and publish findings in professional journals, books, and/or electronic media. Evaluate and grade students' classwork, assignments, and papers. Prepare course materials such as syllabi, homework assignments, and handouts. Prepare and deliver lectures to undergraduate and/or graduate students on topics such as race and ethnic relations, gender studies, and cross-cultural perspectives. Initiate, facilitate, and moderate classroom discussions. Compile, administer, and grade examinations or assign this work to others. Maintain regularly scheduled office hours in order to advise and assist students. Plan, evaluate, and revise curricula, course content, and course materials and methods of instruction. Maintain student attendance records, grades, and other required records. Advise students on academic and vocational curricula and on career issues. Supervise undergraduate and/or graduate teaching, internship, and research work. Select and obtain materials and supplies such as textbooks. Collaborate with colleagues to address teaching and research issues. Serve on academic or administrative committees that deal with institutional policies, departmental matters, and academic issues. Compile bibliographies of specialized materials for outside reading assignments. Write grant proposals to procure external research funding. Participate in campus and community events. Participate in student recruitment, registration, and placement activities. Act as advisers to student organizations. Incorporate experiential/site visit components into courses. Perform administrative duties such as serving as department head. Provide professional consulting services to government and/or industry.

Personality Type: Social. Social occupations frequently involve working with, communicating with, and teaching people. These occupations often involve helping or providing service to others.

GOE—Interest Area: 05. Education and Training. **Work Group:** 05.03. Postsecondary and Adult Teaching and Instructing. **Other Jobs in This Work Group:** Adult Literacy, Remedial Education, and GED Teachers and Instructors; Agricultural Sciences Teachers, Postsecondary; Anthropology and Archeology Teachers, Postsecondary; Architecture Teachers, Postsecondary; Art, Drama, and Music Teachers, Postsecondary; Atmospheric, Earth, Marine, and Space Sciences Teachers, Postsecondary; Biological Science Teachers, Postsecondary; Business Teachers, Postsecondary; Chemistry Teachers, Postsecondary; Communications Teachers, Postsecondary; Computer Science Teachers, Postsecondary; Criminal Justice and Law Enforcement Teachers, Postsecondary; Economics Teachers, Postsecondary; Education Teachers, Postsecondary; Engineering Teachers, Postsecondary; English Language and Literature Teachers, Postsecondary; Environmental Science Teachers, Postsecondary; Farm and Home

Management Advisors; Foreign Language and Literature Teachers, Postsecondary; Forestry and Conservation Science Teachers, Postsecondary; Geography Teachers, Postsecondary; Graduate Teaching Assistants; Health Specialties Teachers, Postsecondary; History Teachers, Postsecondary; Home Economics Teachers, Postsecondary; Law Teachers, Postsecondary; Library Science Teachers, Postsecondary; Mathematical Science Teachers, Postsecondary; Nursing Instructors and Teachers, Postsecondary; Philosophy and Religion Teachers, Postsecondary; Physics Teachers, Postsecondary; Political Science Teachers, Postsecondary; Psychology Teachers, Postsecondary; Recreation and Fitness Studies Teachers, Postsecondary; Self-Enrichment Education Teachers; Social Work Teachers, Postsecondary; Sociology Teachers, Postsecondary; Vocational Education Teachers, Postsecondary.

Skills—Writing: Communicating effectively in writing as appropriate for the needs of the audience. **Critical Thinking:** Using logic and reasoning to identify the strengths and weaknesses of alternative solutions, conclusions, or approaches to problems. **Instructing:** Teaching others how to do something. **Persuasion:** Persuading others to change their minds or behavior. **Active Learning:** Understanding the implications of new information for both current and future problem-solving and decision-making. **Learning Strategies:** Selecting and using training/instructional methods and procedures appropriate for the situation when learning or teaching new things. **Speaking:** Talking to others to convey information effectively. **Management of Financial Resources:** Determining how money will be spent to get the work done and accounting for these expenditures.

Education and Training Programs: African Studies; American/United States Studies/Civilization; Asian Studies/Civilization; East Asian Studies; Central/Middle and Eastern European Studies; European Studies/Civilization; Latin American Studies; Near and Middle Eastern Studies; Pacific Area/Pacific Rim Studies; Russian Studies; Scandinavian Studies; South Asian Studies; Southeast Asian Studies; Western European Studies; others. **Related Knowledge/Courses: History and Archeology:** Historical events and their causes, indicators, and effects on civilizations and cultures. **Sociology and Anthropology:** Group behavior and dynamics, societal trends and influences, human migrations, ethnicity, and cultures and their history and origins. **Foreign Language:** The structure and content of a foreign (non-English) language, including the meaning and spelling of words, rules of composition and grammar, and pronunciation. **Philosophy and Theology:** Different philosophical systems and religions. This includes their basic principles, values, ethics, ways of thinking, customs, and practices and their impact on human culture. **Geography:** Principles and methods for describing the features of land, sea, and air masses, including their physical characteristics; locations; interrelationships; and distribution of plant, animal, and human life. **Education and Training:** Principles and methods for curriculum and training design, teaching and instruction for individuals and groups, and the measurement of training effects.

Work Environment: Indoors; sitting.

Art, Drama, and Music Teachers, Postsecondary

- Annual Earnings: $51,240
- Growth: 32.2%
- Annual Job Openings: 329,000
- Education/Training Required: Master's degree
- Self-Employed: 0.4%
- Part-Time: 27.3%

The job openings listed here are shared with 35 other postsecondary teaching occupations. For a complete list, see the beginning of this section.

How the Job Improves the World: Contributes to education and the arts.

Teach courses in drama; music; and the arts, including fine and applied art, such as painting and sculpture, or design and crafts. Evaluate and grade students' classwork, performances, projects, assignments, and papers. Explain and demonstrate artistic techniques. Prepare students for performances, exams, or assessments. Prepare and deliver lectures to undergraduate or graduate students on topics such as acting techniques, fundamentals of music, and art history. Organize performance groups and direct their rehearsals. Prepare course materials such as syllabi, homework assignments, and handouts. Initiate, facilitate, and moderate classroom discussions. Keep abreast of developments in their field by reading current literature, talking with colleagues, and participating in professional conferences. Advise students on academic and vocational curricula and on career issues. Maintain student attendance records, grades, and other required records. Conduct research in a particular field of knowledge and publish findings in professional journals, books, or electronic media. Supervise undergraduate and/or graduate teaching, internship, and research work. Plan, evaluate, and revise curricula, course content, and course materials and methods of instruction. Maintain regularly scheduled office hours to advise and assist students. Compile, administer, and grade examinations or assign this work to others. Participate in student recruitment, registration, and placement activities. Select and obtain materials and supplies such as textbooks and performance pieces. Collaborate with colleagues to address teaching and research issues. Serve on academic or administrative committees that deal with institutional policies, departmental matters, and academic issues. Participate in campus and community events. Keep students informed of community events such as plays and concerts. Compile bibliographies of specialized materials for outside reading assignments. Display students' work in schools, galleries, and exhibitions. Perform administrative duties such as serving as department head. Act as advisers to student organizations. Write grant proposals to procure external research funding. Provide professional consulting services to government or industry.

Personality Type: Artistic. Artistic occupations frequently involve working with forms, designs, and patterns. They often require self-expression, and the work can be done without following a clear set of rules.

GOE—Interest Area: 05. Education and Training. **Work Group:** 05.03. Postsecondary and Adult Teaching and Instructing. **Other Jobs in This Work Group:** Adult Literacy, Remedial Education, and GED Teachers and Instructors; Agricultural Sciences Teachers, Postsecondary; Anthropology and Archeology Teachers, Postsecondary; Architecture Teachers, Postsecondary; Area, Ethnic, and Cultural Studies Teachers, Postsecondary; Atmospheric, Earth, Marine, and Space Sciences Teachers, Postsecondary; Biological Science Teachers, Postsecondary; Business Teachers, Postsecondary; Chemistry Teachers, Postsecondary; Communications Teachers, Postsecondary; Computer Science Teachers, Postsecondary; Criminal Justice and Law Enforcement Teachers, Postsecondary; Economics Teachers, Postsecondary; Education Teachers, Postsecondary; Engineering Teachers, Postsecondary; English Language and Literature Teachers, Postsecondary; Environmental Science Teachers, Postsecondary; Farm and Home Management Advisors; Foreign Language and Literature Teachers, Postsecondary; Forestry and Conservation Science Teachers, Postsecondary; Geography Teachers, Postsecondary; Graduate Teaching Assistants; Health Specialties Teachers, Postsecondary; History Teachers, Postsecondary; Home Economics Teachers, Postsecondary; Law Teachers, Postsecondary; Library Science Teachers, Postsecondary; Mathematical Science Teachers, Postsecondary; Nursing Instructors and Teachers, Postsecondary; Philosophy and Religion Teachers, Postsecondary; Physics Teachers, Postsecondary;

Political Science Teachers, Postsecondary; Psychology Teachers, Postsecondary; Recreation and Fitness Studies Teachers, Postsecondary; Self-Enrichment Education Teachers; Social Work Teachers, Postsecondary; Sociology Teachers, Postsecondary; Vocational Education Teachers, Postsecondary.

Skills—Instructing: Teaching others how to do something. **Social Perceptiveness:** Being aware of others' reactions and understanding why they react as they do. **Speaking:** Talking to others to convey information effectively. **Persuasion:** Persuading others to change their minds or behavior. **Active Listening:** Giving full attention to what other people are saying, taking time to understand the points being made, asking questions as appropriate, and not interrupting at inappropriate times. **Learning Strategies:** Selecting and using training/instructional methods and procedures appropriate for the situation when learning or teaching new things. **Critical Thinking:** Using logic and reasoning to identify the strengths and weaknesses of alternative solutions, conclusions, or approaches to problems. **Monitoring:** Monitoring/assessing your performance or that of other individuals or organizations to make improvements or take corrective action.

Education and Training Programs: Visual and Performing Arts, General; Crafts/Craft Design, Folk Art, and Artisanry; Dance, General; Design and Visual Communications, General; Industrial Design; Commercial Photography; Fashion/Apparel Design; Interior Design; Graphic Design; Design and Applied Arts, Other; Drama and Dramatics/Theatre Arts, General; Technical Theatre/Theatre Design and Technology; Playwriting and Screenwriting; others. **Related Knowledge/Courses: Fine Arts:** The theory and techniques required to compose, produce, and perform works of music, dance, visual art, drama, and sculpture. **History and Archeology:** Historical events and their causes, indicators, and effects on civilizations and cultures. **Philosophy and Theology:** Different philosophical systems and religions. This includes their basic principles, values, ethics, ways of thinking,

customs, and practices and their impact on human culture. **Education and Training:** Principles and methods for curriculum and training design, teaching and instruction for individuals and groups, and the measurement of training effects. **Communications and Media:** Media production, communication, and dissemination techniques and methods. This includes alternative ways to inform and entertain via written, oral, and visual media. **Sociology and Anthropology:** Group behavior and dynamics, societal trends and influences, human migrations, ethnicity, and cultures and their history and origins.

Work Environment: Indoors; noisy; sitting.

Athletic Trainers

- Annual Earnings: $34,260
- Growth: 29.3%
- Annual Job Openings: 1,000
- Education/Training Required: Bachelor's degree
- Self-Employed: 4.0%
- Part-Time: 6.5%

How the Job Improves the World: Contributes to health and well-being.

Evaluate, advise, and treat athletes to assist recovery from injury, avoid injury, or maintain peak physical fitness. Conduct an initial assessment of an athlete's injury or illness to provide emergency or continued care and to determine whether they should be referred to physicians for definitive diagnosis and treatment. Care for athletic injuries, using physical therapy equipment, techniques, and medication. Evaluate athletes' readiness to play and provide participation clearances when necessary and warranted. Apply protective or injury preventive devices such as tape, bandages, or braces to body parts such as ankles, fingers, or wrists. Assess and report the progress of recovering athletes to coaches and physicians. Collaborate with physicians to develop and implement comprehensive rehabilitation programs for athletic injuries. Advise athletes on the proper use of equipment. Plan and implement comprehensive athletic injury and illness prevention programs. Develop training programs and routines designed to improve athletic performance. Travel with athletic teams to be available at sporting events. Instruct coaches, athletes, parents, medical personnel, and community members in the care and prevention of athletic injuries. Inspect playing fields to locate any items that could injure players. Conduct research and provide instruction on subject matter related to athletic training or sports medicine. Recommend special diets to improve athletes' health, increase their stamina, or alter their weight. Massage body parts to relieve soreness, strains, and bruises. Confer with coaches to select protective equipment. Accompany injured athletes to hospitals. Perform team-support duties such as running errands, maintaining equipment, and stocking supplies. Lead stretching exercises for team members prior to games and practices.

Personality Type: Social. Social occupations frequently involve working with, communicating with, and teaching people. These occupations often involve helping or providing service to others.

GOE—Interest Area: 08. Health Science. **Work Group:** 08.09. Health Protection and Promotion. **Other Jobs in This Work Group:** Dietetic Technicians; Dietitians and Nutritionists; Embalmers.

Skills—Social Perceptiveness: Being aware of others' reactions and understanding why they react as they do. **Science:** Using scientific rules and methods to solve problems. **Management of Material Resources:** Obtaining and seeing to the appropriate use of equipment, facilities, and materials needed to do certain work. **Management of Financial Resources:** Determining how money will be spent to get the work done and accounting for these expenditures. **Time Management:** Managing one's own time and the time of others. **Management of Personnel Resources:** Motivating, developing, and directing people as they work; identifying the best people for the job. **Writing:** Communicating effectively in writing as appropriate for the needs of the audience. **Service Orientation:** Actively looking for ways to help people.

Education and Training Program: Athletic Training/Trainer. **Related Knowledge/Courses: Therapy and Counseling:** Principles, methods, and procedures for diagnosis, treatment, and rehabilitation of physical and mental dysfunctions and for career counseling and guidance. **Medicine and Dentistry:** The information and techniques needed to diagnose and treat human injuries, diseases, and deformities. This includes symptoms, treatment alternatives, drug properties and interactions, and preventive health-care measures. **Biology:** Plant and animal organisms and their tissues, cells, functions, interdependencies, and interactions with each other and the environment. **Psychology:** Human behavior and performance; individual differences in ability, personality, and interests; learning and motivation; psychological research methods; and the assessment and treatment of behavioral and affective disorders. **Sociology and Anthropology:** Group behavior and dynamics, societal trends and influences, human migrations, ethnicity, and cultures and their history and origins. **Education and Training:** Principles and methods for curriculum and training design, teaching and instruction for individuals and groups, and the measurement of training effects.

Work Environment: More often indoors than outdoors; very hot or cold; contaminants; disease or infections; standing.

Atmospheric, Earth, Marine, and Space Sciences Teachers, Postsecondary

- Annual Earnings: $65,720
- Growth: 32.2%
- Annual Job Openings: 329,000
- Education/Training Required: Master's degree
- Self-Employed: 0.4%
- Part-Time: 27.3%

The job openings listed here are shared with 35 other postsecondary teaching occupations. For a complete list, see the beginning of this section.

How the Job Improves the World: Contributes to education and the natural environment.

Teach courses in the physical sciences, except chemistry and physics. Conduct research in a particular field of knowledge and publish findings in professional journals, books, and/or electronic media. Write grant proposals to procure external research funding. Keep abreast of developments in their field by reading current literature, talking with colleagues, and participating in professional conferences. Supervise undergraduate and/or graduate teaching, internship, and research work. Prepare and deliver lectures to undergraduate and/or graduate students on topics such as structural geology, micrometeorology, and atmospheric thermodynamics. Supervise laboratory work and fieldwork. Evaluate and grade students' classwork, assignments, and papers. Prepare course materials such as syllabi, homework assignments, and handouts. Collaborate with colleagues to address teaching and research issues. Compile, administer, and grade examinations or assign this work to others. Plan, evaluate, and revise curricula, course content, and course materials and methods of instruction. Initiate, facilitate, and moderate classroom discussions. Maintain regularly scheduled office hours in order to advise and assist students. Advise students on academic and vocational curricula and on career issues. Maintain student attendance records, grades, and other required records. Participate in student recruitment, registration, and placement activities. Perform administrative duties such as serving as department head. Select and obtain materials and supplies such as textbooks and laboratory equipment. Serve on academic or administrative committees that deal with institutional policies, departmental matters, and academic issues. Compile bibliographies of specialized materials for outside reading assignments. Provide professional consulting services to government and/or industry. Act as advisers to student organizations. Participate in campus and community events.

Personality Type: No data available.

GOE—Interest Area: 05. Education and Training. **Work Group:** 05.03. Postsecondary and Adult Teaching and Instructing. **Other Jobs in This Work Group:** Adult Literacy, Remedial Education, and GED Teachers and Instructors; Agricultural Sciences Teachers, Postsecondary; Anthropology and Archeology Teachers, Postsecondary; Architecture Teachers, Postsecondary; Area, Ethnic, and Cultural Studies Teachers, Postsecondary; Art, Drama, and Music Teachers, Postsecondary; Biological Science Teachers, Postsecondary; Business Teachers, Postsecondary; Chemistry Teachers, Postsecondary; Communications Teachers, Postsecondary; Computer Science Teachers, Postsecondary; Criminal Justice and Law Enforcement Teachers, Postsecondary; Economics Teachers, Postsecondary; Education Teachers, Postsecondary; Engineering Teachers, Postsecondary; English Language and Literature Teachers, Postsecondary; Environmental Science Teachers, Postsecondary; Farm and Home Management Advisors; Foreign Language and Literature Teachers, Postsecondary; Forestry and

Conservation Science Teachers, Postsecondary; Geography Teachers, Postsecondary; Graduate Teaching Assistants; Health Specialties Teachers, Postsecondary; History Teachers, Postsecondary; Home Economics Teachers, Postsecondary; Law Teachers, Postsecondary; Library Science Teachers, Postsecondary; Mathematical Science Teachers, Postsecondary; Nursing Instructors and Teachers, Postsecondary; Philosophy and Religion Teachers, Postsecondary; Physics Teachers, Postsecondary; Political Science Teachers, Postsecondary; Psychology Teachers, Postsecondary; Recreation and Fitness Studies Teachers, Postsecondary; Self-Enrichment Education Teachers; Social Work Teachers, Postsecondary; Sociology Teachers, Postsecondary; Vocational Education Teachers, Postsecondary.

Skills—Science: Using scientific rules and methods to solve problems. **Programming:** Writing computer programs for various purposes. **Management of Financial Resources:** Determining how money will be spent to get the work done and accounting for these expenditures. **Mathematics:** Using mathematics to solve problems. **Complex Problem Solving:** Identifying complex problems and reviewing related information to develop and evaluate options and implement solutions. **Instructing:** Teaching others how to do something. **Writing:** Communicating effectively in writing as appropriate for the needs of the audience. **Active Learning:** Understanding the implications of new information for both current and future problem-solving and decision-making.

Education and Training Programs: Science Teacher Education/General Science Teacher Education; Physics Teacher Education; Astronomy; Astrophysics; Planetary Astronomy and Science; Atmospheric Sciences and Meteorology, General; Atmospheric Chemistry and Climatology; Atmospheric Physics and Dynamics; Meteorology; Atmospheric Sciences and Meteorology, Other; Geology/Earth Science, General; Geochemistry; Geophysics and Seismology; others. **Related Knowledge/Courses: Physics:**

Physical principles and laws and their interrelationships and applications to understanding fluid, material, and atmospheric dynamics and mechanical, electrical, atomic, and subatomic structures and processes. **Geography:** Principles and methods for describing the features of land, sea, and air masses, including their physical characteristics; locations; interrelationships; and distribution of plant, animal, and human life. **Chemistry:** The chemical composition, structure, and properties of substances and of the chemical processes and transformations that they undergo. This includes uses of chemicals and their danger signs, production techniques, and disposal methods. **Biology:** Plant and animal organisms and their tissues, cells, functions, interdependencies, and interactions with each other and the environment. **Mathematics:** Arithmetic, algebra, geometry, calculus, and statistics and their applications. **Education and Training:** Principles and methods for curriculum and training design, teaching and instruction for individuals and groups, and the measurement of training effects.

Work Environment: Indoors; sitting.

Audiologists

- Annual Earnings: $53,490
- Growth: 9.1%
- Annual Job Openings: Fewer than 500
- Education/Training Required: First professional degree
- Self-Employed: 1.4%
- Part-Time: 30.8%

How the Job Improves the World: Contributes to health and well-being.

Assess and treat persons with hearing and related disorders. May fit hearing aids and provide auditory training. May perform research related to hearing problems. Evaluate hearing and speech/language disorders to determine diagnoses and courses of treatment. Administer hearing or speech/language evaluations, tests, or examinations to patients to collect information on type and degree of impairment, using specialized instruments and electronic equipment. Fit and dispense assistive devices, such as hearing aids. Maintain client records at all stages, including initial evaluation and discharge. Refer clients to additional medical or educational services if needed. Counsel and instruct clients in techniques to improve hearing or speech impairment, including sign language or lip-reading. Monitor clients' progress and discharge them from treatment when goals have been attained. Plan and conduct treatment programs for clients' hearing or speech problems, consulting with physicians, nurses, psychologists, and other health care personnel as necessary. Recommend assistive devices according to clients' needs or nature of impairments. Participate in conferences or training to update or share knowledge of new hearing or speech disorder treatment methods or technologies. Instruct clients, parents, teachers, or employers in how to avoid behavior patterns that lead to miscommunication. Examine and clean patients' ear canals. Advise educators or other medical staff on speech or hearing topics. Educate and supervise audiology students and health care personnel. Fit and tune cochlear implants, providing rehabilitation for adjustment to listening with implant amplification systems. Work with multi-disciplinary teams to assess and rehabilitate recipients of implanted hearing devices. Develop and supervise hearing screening programs. Conduct or direct research on hearing or speech topics and report findings to help in the development of procedures, technology, or treatments. Measure noise levels in workplaces and conduct hearing protection programs in industry, schools, and communities.

Personality Type: Social. Social occupations frequently involve working with, communicating with, and teaching people. These occupations often involve helping or providing service to others.

GOE—Interest Area: 08. Health Science. **Work Group:** 08.07. Medical Therapy. **Other Jobs in This Work Group:** Massage Therapists; Occupational Therapist Aides; Occupational Therapist Assistants; Occupational Therapists; Physical Therapist Aides; Physical Therapist Assistants; Physical Therapists; Radiation Therapists; Recreational Therapists; Respiratory Therapists; Respiratory Therapy Technicians; Speech-Language Pathologists.

Skills—Social Perceptiveness: Being aware of others' reactions and understanding why they react as they do. **Science:** Using scientific rules and methods to solve problems. **Service Orientation:** Actively looking for ways to help people. **Persuasion:** Persuading others to change their minds or behavior. **Equipment Selection:** Determining the kind of tools and equipment needed to do a job. **Reading Comprehension:** Understanding written sentences and paragraphs in work-related documents. **Active Learning:** Understanding the implications of new information for both current and future problem-solving and decision-making. **Technology Design:** Generating or adapting equipment and technology to serve user needs.

Education and Training Programs: Communication Disorders, General; Audiology/Audiologist and Hearing Sciences; Audiology/Audiologist and Speech-Language Pathology/Pathologist; Communication Disorders Sciences and Services, Other. **Related Knowledge/Courses: Therapy and Counseling:** Principles, methods, and procedures for diagnosis, treatment, and rehabilitation of physical and mental dysfunctions and for career counseling and guidance. **Medicine and Dentistry:** The information and techniques needed to diagnose and treat human injuries, diseases, and deformities. This includes symptoms, treatment alternatives, drug properties and interactions, and preventive health-care measures. **Psychology:** Human behavior and performance; individual differences in ability, personality, and interests; learning and motivation; psychological research methods;

and the assessment and treatment of behavioral and affective disorders. **Customer and Personal Service:** Principles and processes for providing customer and personal services. This includes customer needs assessment, meeting quality standards for services, and evaluation of customer satisfaction. **Sales and Marketing:** Principles and methods for showing, promoting, and selling products or services. This includes marketing strategy and tactics, product demonstration, sales techniques, and sales control systems. **English Language:** The structure and content of the English language, including the meaning and spelling of words, rules of composition, and grammar.

Work Environment: Indoors; disease or infections; sitting; using hands on objects, tools, or controls.

Audio-Visual Collections Specialists

- Annual Earnings: $40,260
- Growth: 18.6%
- Annual Job Openings: 1,000
- Education/Training Required: Moderate-term on-the-job training
- Self-Employed: 3.8%
- Part-Time: 23.4%

How the Job Improves the World: Contributes to education.

Prepare, plan, and operate audiovisual teaching aids for use in education. May record, catalogue, and file audio-visual materials. Set up, adjust, and operate audiovisual equipment such as cameras, film and slide projectors, and recording equipment for meetings, events, classes, seminars, and videoconferences. Offer presentations and workshops on the role of multimedia in effective presentations. Attend conventions and conferences, read trade journals, and communicate with industry insiders to keep abreast of industry developments. Instruct users in the selection, use, and design of audiovisual materials and assist them in the preparation of instructional materials and the rehearsal of presentations. Maintain hardware and software, including computers, scanners, color copiers, and color laser printers. Confer with teachers to select course materials and to determine which training aids are best suited to particular grade levels. Perform simple maintenance tasks such as cleaning monitors and lenses and changing batteries and light bulbs. Develop manuals, texts, workbooks, or related materials for use in conjunction with production materials. Determine formats, approaches, content, levels, and mediums necessary to meet production objectives effectively and within budgetary constraints. Direct and coordinate activities of assistants and other personnel during production. Acquire, catalog, and maintain collections of audiovisual material such as films, videotapes and audiotapes, photographs, and software programs. Narrate presentations and productions. Construct and position properties, sets, lighting equipment, and other equipment. Develop preproduction ideas and incorporate them into outlines, scripts, storyboards, and graphics. Plan and prepare audiovisual teaching aids and methods for use in school systems. Produce rough and finished graphics and graphic designs. Locate and secure settings, properties, effects, and other production necessities.

Personality Type: Conventional. Conventional occupations frequently involve following set procedures and routines. These occupations can include working with data and details more than with ideas. Usually there is a clear line of authority to follow.

GOE—Interest Area: 05. Education and Training. **Work Group:** 05.05. Archival and Museum Services. **Other Jobs in This Work Group:** Archivists; Curators; Museum Technicians and Conservators.

Skills—Troubleshooting: Determining causes of operating errors and deciding what to do about them.

Installation: Installing equipment, machines, wiring, or programs to meet specifications. **Technology Design:** Generating or adapting equipment and technology to serve user needs. **Instructing:** Teaching others how to do something. **Equipment Selection:** Determining the kind of tools and equipment needed to do a job. **Operations Analysis:** Analyzing needs and product requirements to create a design. **Writing:** Communicating effectively in writing as appropriate for the needs of the audience. **Equipment Maintenance:** Performing routine maintenance on equipment and determining when and what kind of maintenance is needed.

Education and Training Program: Educational/Instructional Media Design. **Related Knowledge/Courses: Education and Training:** Principles and methods for curriculum and training design, teaching and instruction for individuals and groups, and the measurement of training effects. **Communications and Media:** Media production, communication, and dissemination techniques and methods. This includes alternative ways to inform and entertain via written, oral, and visual media. **Computers and Electronics:** Circuit boards; processors; chips; electronic equipment; and computer hardware and software, including applications and programming. **Telecommunications:** Transmission, broadcasting, switching, control, and operation of telecommunications systems. **Customer and Personal Service:** Principles and processes for providing customer and personal services. This includes customer needs assessment, meeting quality standards for services, and evaluation of customer satisfaction. **Clerical Practices:** Administrative and clerical procedures and systems such as word processing, managing files and records, stenography and transcription, designing forms, and other office procedures and terminology.

Work Environment: Indoors; sitting; using hands on objects, tools, or controls.

Biological Science Teachers, Postsecondary

- Annual Earnings: $63,570
- Growth: 32.2%
- Annual Job Openings: 329,000
- Education/Training Required: Master's degree
- Self-Employed: 0.4%
- Part-Time: 27.3%

The job openings listed here are shared with 35 other postsecondary teaching occupations. For a complete list, see the beginning of this section.

How the Job Improves the World: Contributes to education, health, and the natural environment.

Teach courses in biological sciences. Prepare and deliver lectures to undergraduate and/or graduate students on topics such as molecular biology, marine biology, and botany. Evaluate and grade students' classwork, laboratory work, assignments, and papers. Prepare course materials such as syllabi, homework assignments, and handouts. Compile, administer, and grade examinations or assign this work to others. Supervise students' laboratory work. Keep abreast of developments in their field by reading current literature, talking with colleagues, and participating in professional conferences. Maintain student attendance records, grades, and other required records. Initiate, facilitate, and moderate classroom discussions. Plan, evaluate, and revise curricula, course content, and course materials and methods of instruction. Advise students on academic and vocational curricula and on career issues. Maintain regularly scheduled office hours to advise and assist students. Supervise undergraduate and/or graduate teaching, internship, and research work. Select and obtain materials and supplies such as textbooks and laboratory equipment. Collaborate with colleagues to address teaching and

B

research issues. Conduct research in a particular field of knowledge and publish findings in professional journals, books, and/or electronic media. Serve on academic or administrative committees that deal with institutional policies, departmental matters, and academic issues. Participate in student recruitment, registration, and placement activities. Write grant proposals to procure external research funding. Perform administrative duties such as serving as department head. Act as advisers to student organizations. Compile bibliographies of specialized materials for outside reading assignments. Participate in campus and community events. Provide professional consulting services to government and/or industry.

Personality Type: Investigative. Investigative occupations frequently involve working with ideas and require an extensive amount of thinking. These occupations can involve searching for facts and figuring out problems mentally.

GOE—Interest Area: 05. Education and Training. **Work Group:** 05.03. Postsecondary and Adult Teaching and Instructing. **Other Jobs in This Work Group:** Adult Literacy, Remedial Education, and GED Teachers and Instructors; Agricultural Sciences Teachers, Postsecondary; Anthropology and Archeology Teachers, Postsecondary; Architecture Teachers, Postsecondary; Area, Ethnic, and Cultural Studies Teachers, Postsecondary; Art, Drama, and Music Teachers, Postsecondary; Atmospheric, Earth, Marine, and Space Sciences Teachers, Postsecondary; Business Teachers, Postsecondary; Chemistry Teachers, Postsecondary; Communications Teachers, Postsecondary; Computer Science Teachers, Postsecondary; Criminal Justice and Law Enforcement Teachers, Postsecondary; Economics Teachers, Postsecondary; Education Teachers, Postsecondary; Engineering Teachers, Postsecondary; English Language and Literature Teachers, Postsecondary; Environmental Science Teachers, Postsecondary; Farm and Home Management Advisors; Foreign Language and Literature Teachers, Postsecondary; Forestry and Conservation Science Teachers, Postsecondary; Geography Teachers, Postsecondary; Graduate Teaching Assistants; Health Specialties Teachers, Postsecondary; History Teachers, Postsecondary; Home Economics Teachers, Postsecondary; Law Teachers, Postsecondary; Library Science Teachers, Postsecondary; Mathematical Science Teachers, Postsecondary; Nursing Instructors and Teachers, Postsecondary; Philosophy and Religion Teachers, Postsecondary; Physics Teachers, Postsecondary; Political Science Teachers, Postsecondary; Psychology Teachers, Postsecondary; Recreation and Fitness Studies Teachers, Postsecondary; Self-Enrichment Education Teachers; Social Work Teachers, Postsecondary; Sociology Teachers, Postsecondary; Vocational Education Teachers, Postsecondary.

Skills—Science: Using scientific rules and methods to solve problems. **Instructing:** Teaching others how to do something. **Writing:** Communicating effectively in writing as appropriate for the needs of the audience. **Learning Strategies:** Selecting and using training/instructional methods and procedures appropriate for the situation when learning or teaching new things. **Reading Comprehension:** Understanding written sentences and paragraphs in work-related documents. **Speaking:** Talking to others to convey information effectively. **Active Learning:** Understanding the implications of new information for both current and future problem-solving and decision-making. **Critical Thinking:** Using logic and reasoning to identify the strengths and weaknesses of alternative solutions, conclusions, or approaches to problems.

Education and Training Programs: Biology/Biological Sciences, General; Biochemistry; Biophysics; Molecular Biology; Radiation Biology/Radiobiology; Botany/Plant Biology; Plant Pathology/Phytopathology; Plant Physiology; Cell/Cellular Biology and Histology; Anatomy; Microbiology, General; Virology; Parasitology; Immunology; Zoology/Animal Biology; Entomology;

Animal Physiology; others. **Related Knowledge/ Courses: Biology:** Plant and animal organisms and their tissues, cells, functions, interdependencies, and interactions with each other and the environment. **Chemistry:** The chemical composition, structure, and properties of substances and of the chemical processes and transformations that they undergo. This includes uses of chemicals and their danger signs, production techniques, and disposal methods. **Education and Training:** Principles and methods for curriculum and training design, teaching and instruction for individuals and groups, and the measurement of training effects. **Medicine and Dentistry:** The information and techniques needed to diagnose and treat human injuries, diseases, and deformities. This includes symptoms, treatment alternatives, drug properties and interactions, and preventive health-care measures. **English Language:** The structure and content of the English language, including the meaning and spelling of words, rules of composition, and grammar. **Physics:** Physical principles and laws and their interrelationships and applications to understanding fluid, material, and atmospheric dynamics and mechanical, electrical, atomic, and subatomic structures and processes.

Work Environment: Indoors; more often sitting than standing.

Bus Drivers, School

- Annual Earnings: $24,070
- Growth: 13.6%
- Annual Job Openings: 76,000
- Education/Training Required: Short-term on-the-job training
- Self-Employed: 0.5%
- Part-Time: 38.4%

How the Job Improves the World: Contributes to safety and education.

Transport students or special clients, such as the elderly or persons with disabilities. Ensure adherence to safety rules. May assist passengers in boarding or exiting. Follow safety rules as students are boarding and exiting buses and as they cross streets near bus stops. Comply with traffic regulations to operate vehicles in a safe and courteous manner. Check the condition of a vehicle's tires, brakes, windshield wipers, lights, oil, fuel, water, and safety equipment to ensure that everything is in working order. Maintain order among pupils during trips to ensure safety. Pick up and drop off students at regularly scheduled neighborhood locations, following strict time schedules. Report any bus malfunctions or needed repairs. Drive gasoline, diesel, or electrically powered multi-passenger vehicles to transport students between neighborhoods, schools, and school activities. Prepare and submit reports that may include the number of passengers or trips, hours worked, mileage, fuel consumption, and fares received. Maintain knowledge of first-aid procedures. Keep bus interiors clean for passengers. Read maps and follow written and verbal geographic directions. Report delays, accidents, or other traffic and transportation situations, using telephones or mobile two-way radios. Regulate heating, lighting, and ventilation systems for passenger comfort. Escort small children across roads and highways. Make minor repairs to vehicles.

Personality Type: Realistic. Realistic occupations frequently involve work activities that include practical, hands-on problems and solutions. They often deal with plants; animals; and real-world materials such as wood, tools, and machinery. Many of the occupations require working outside and do not involve a lot of paperwork or working closely with others.

GOE—Interest Area: 16. Transportation, Distribution, and Logistics. **Work Group:** 16.06. Other Services Requiring Driving. **Other Jobs in This Work Group:** Ambulance Drivers and Attendants, Except Emergency Medical Technicians; Bus Drivers, Transit and Intercity; Couriers and Messengers;

Driver/Sales Workers; Parking Lot Attendants; Postal Service Mail Carriers; Taxi Drivers and Chauffeurs.

Skills—No data available.

Education and Training Program: Truck and Bus Driver/Commercial Vehicle Operation. **Related Knowledge/Courses: Transportation:** Principles and methods for moving people or goods by air, rail, sea, or road, including the relative costs and benefits. **Psychology:** Human behavior and performance; individual differences in ability, personality, and interests; learning and motivation; psychological research methods; and the assessment and treatment of behavioral and affective disorders. **Public Safety and Security:** Relevant equipment, policies, procedures, and strategies to promote effective local, state, or national security operations for the protection of people, data, property, and institutions. **Law and Government:** Laws, legal codes, court procedures, precedents, government regulations, executive orders, agency rules, and the democratic political process.

Work Environment: Noisy; contaminants; disease or infections; sitting; using hands on objects, tools, or controls; repetitive motions.

Business Teachers, Postsecondary

- ◎ Annual Earnings: $59,210
- ◎ Growth: 32.2%
- ◎ Annual Job Openings: 329,000
- ◎ Education/Training Required: Master's degree
- ◎ Self-Employed: 0.4%
- ◎ Part-Time: 27.3%

The job openings listed here are shared with 35 other postsecondary teaching occupations. For a complete list, see the beginning of this section.

How the Job Improves the World: Contributes to education.

Teach courses in business administration and management, such as accounting, finance, human resources, labor relations, marketing, and operations research. Prepare and deliver lectures to undergraduate and/or graduate students on topics such as financial accounting, principles of marketing, and operations management. Evaluate and grade students' classwork, assignments, and papers. Compile, administer, and grade examinations or assign this work to others. Prepare course materials such as syllabi, homework assignments, and handouts. Maintain student attendance records, grades, and other required records. Initiate, facilitate, and moderate classroom discussions. Plan, evaluate, and revise curricula, course content, and course materials and methods of instruction. Keep abreast of developments in their field by reading current literature, talking with colleagues, and participating in professional organizations and conferences. Maintain regularly scheduled office hours to advise and assist students. Advise students on academic and vocational curricula and on career issues. Select and obtain materials and supplies such as textbooks. Collaborate with colleagues to address teaching and research issues. Collaborate with members of the business community to improve programs, to develop new programs, and to provide student access to learning opportunities such as internships. Participate in student recruitment, registration, and placement activities. Serve on academic or administrative committees that deal with institutional policies, departmental matters, and academic issues. Participate in campus and community events. Compile bibliographies of specialized materials for outside reading assignments. Perform administrative duties such as serving as department head. Supervise undergraduate and/or graduate teaching, internship, and research work. Conduct research in a particular field of knowledge and publish findings in professional journals, books, and/or electronic media. Act as advisers to student organizations.

Provide professional consulting services to government and/or industry. Write grant proposals to procure external research funding.

Personality Type: No data available.

GOE—Interest Area: 05. Education and Training. **Work Group:** 05.03. Postsecondary and Adult Teaching and Instructing. **Other Jobs in This Work Group:** Adult Literacy, Remedial Education, and GED Teachers and Instructors; Agricultural Sciences Teachers, Postsecondary; Anthropology and Archeology Teachers, Postsecondary; Architecture Teachers, Postsecondary; Area, Ethnic, and Cultural Studies Teachers, Postsecondary; Art, Drama, and Music Teachers, Postsecondary; Atmospheric, Earth, Marine, and Space Sciences Teachers, Postsecondary; Biological Science Teachers, Postsecondary; Chemistry Teachers, Postsecondary; Communications Teachers, Postsecondary; Computer Science Teachers, Postsecondary; Criminal Justice and Law Enforcement Teachers, Postsecondary; Economics Teachers, Postsecondary; Education Teachers, Postsecondary; Engineering Teachers, Postsecondary; English Language and Literature Teachers, Postsecondary; Environmental Science Teachers, Postsecondary; Farm and Home Management Advisors; Foreign Language and Literature Teachers, Postsecondary; Forestry and Conservation Science Teachers, Postsecondary; Geography Teachers, Postsecondary; Graduate Teaching Assistants; Health Specialties Teachers, Postsecondary; History Teachers, Postsecondary; Home Economics Teachers, Postsecondary; Law Teachers, Postsecondary; Library Science Teachers, Postsecondary; Mathematical Science Teachers, Postsecondary; Nursing Instructors and Teachers, Postsecondary; Philosophy and Religion Teachers, Postsecondary; Physics Teachers, Postsecondary; Political Science Teachers, Postsecondary; Psychology Teachers, Postsecondary; Recreation and Fitness Studies Teachers, Postsecondary; Self-Enrichment Education Teachers; Social Work Teachers, Postsecondary; Sociology Teachers, Postsecondary; Vocational Education Teachers, Postsecondary.

Skills—Instructing: Teaching others how to do something. **Learning Strategies:** Selecting and using training/instructional methods and procedures appropriate for the situation when learning or teaching new things. **Writing:** Communicating effectively in writing as appropriate for the needs of the audience. **Monitoring:** Monitoring/assessing your performance or that of other individuals or organizations to make improvements or take corrective action. **Active Learning:** Understanding the implications of new information for both current and future problem-solving and decision-making. **Speaking:** Talking to others to convey information effectively. **Persuasion:** Persuading others to change their minds or behavior. **Time Management:** Managing one's own time and the time of others.

Education and Training Programs: Business Teacher Education; Business/Commerce, General; Business Administration and Management, General; Purchasing, Procurement/Acquisitions, and Contracts Management; Logistics and Materials Management; Operations Management and Supervision; Accounting; Business/Corporate Communications; Entrepreneurship/Entrepreneurial Studies; Franchising and Franchise Operations; Finance, General; others. **Related Knowledge/Courses: Economics and Accounting:** Economic and accounting principles and practices, the financial markets, banking, and the analysis and reporting of financial data. **Education and Training:** Principles and methods for curriculum and training design, teaching and instruction for individuals and groups, and the measurement of training effects. **Sales and Marketing:** Principles and methods for showing, promoting, and selling products or services. This includes marketing strategy and tactics, product demonstration, sales techniques, and sales control systems. **Sociology and Anthropology:** Group behavior and dynamics, societal trends and influences, human migrations, ethnicity, and cultures and their history and origins. **English Language:** The structure and content of the English language, including the meaning and spelling of words, rules of composition, and grammar. **Personnel and Human Resources:** Principles and procedures for personnel recruitment, selection, training, compensation and benefits, labor relations and negotiation, and personnel information systems.

Work Environment: Indoors; sitting.

Cardiovascular Technologists and Technicians

- Annual Earnings: $40,420
- Growth: 32.6%
- Annual Job Openings: 5,000
- Education/Training Required: Associate degree
- Self-Employed: 0.4%
- Part-Time: 17.2%

How the Job Improves the World: Contributes to health.

Conduct tests on pulmonary or cardiovascular systems of patients for diagnostic purposes. May conduct or assist in electrocardiograms, cardiac catheterizations, pulmonary-functions, lung capacity, and similar tests. Monitor patients' blood pressure and heart rate, using electrocardiogram (EKG) equipment, during diagnostic and therapeutic procedures to notify the physician if something appears wrong. Monitor patients' comfort and safety during tests, alerting physicians to abnormalities or changes in patient responses. Explain testing procedures to patient to obtain cooperation and reduce anxiety. Prepare reports of diagnostic procedures for interpretation by physician. Observe gauges, recorder, and video screens of data analysis system during imaging of cardiovascular system. Conduct electrocardiogram (EKG), phonocardiogram, echocardiogram, stress testing, or other cardiovascular tests to record patients' cardiac activity, using specialized electronic test equipment, recording devices, and laboratory instruments. Obtain and record patient identification, medical history, or test results. Prepare and position patients for testing. Attach electrodes to the patients' chests, arms, and legs; connect electrodes to leads from the electrocardiogram (EKG) machine; and operate the EKG machine to obtain a reading. Adjust equipment and controls according to physicians' orders or established protocol. Check, test, and maintain cardiology equipment, making minor repairs when necessary, to ensure proper operation. Supervise and train other cardiology technologists and students. Assist physicians in diagnosis and treatment of cardiac and peripheral vascular treatments, for example, assisting with balloon angioplasties to treat blood vessel blockages. Operate diagnostic imaging equipment to produce contrast-enhanced radiographs of heart and cardiovascular system. Inject contrast medium into patients' blood vessels. Observe ultrasound display screen and listen to signals to record vascular information such as blood pressure, limb volume changes, oxygen saturation, and cerebral circulation. Assess cardiac physiology and calculate valve areas from blood flow velocity measurements. Compare measurements of heart wall thickness and chamber sizes to standard norms to identify abnormalities. Activate fluoroscope and camera to produce images used to guide catheter through cardiovascular system.

Personality Type: Investigative. Investigative occupations frequently involve working with ideas and require an extensive amount of thinking. These occupations can involve searching for facts and figuring out problems mentally.

GOE—Interest Area: 08. Health Science. **Work Group:** 08.06. Medical Technology. **Other Jobs in This Work Group:** Biological Technicians; Diagnostic Medical Sonographers; Medical and Clinical

Laboratory Technicians; Medical and Clinical Laboratory Technologists; Medical Equipment Preparers; Medical Records and Health Information Technicians; Nuclear Medicine Technologists; Opticians, Dispensing; Orthotists and Prosthetists; Radiologic Technicians; Radiologic Technologists; Radiologic Technologists and Technicians.

Skills—Operation Monitoring: Watching gauges, dials, or other indicators to make sure a machine is working properly. Science: Using scientific rules and methods to solve problems. Equipment Maintenance: Performing routine maintenance on equipment and determining when and what kind of maintenance is needed. Instructing: Teaching others how to do something. Service Orientation: Actively looking for ways to help people. Operation and Control: Controlling operations of equipment or systems. Management of Material Resources: Obtaining and seeing to the appropriate use of equipment, facilities, and materials needed to do certain work. Equipment Selection: Determining the kind of tools and equipment needed to do a job.

Education and Training Programs: Cardiovascular Technology/Technologist; Electrocardiograph Technology/Technician; Perfusion Technology/Perfusionist; Cardiopulmonary Technology/Technologist. Related Knowledge/Courses: Medicine and Dentistry: The information and techniques needed to diagnose and treat human injuries, diseases, and deformities. This includes symptoms, treatment alternatives, drug properties and interactions, and preventive health-care measures. Customer and Personal Service: Principles and processes for providing customer and personal services. This includes customer needs assessment, meeting quality standards for services, and evaluation of customer satisfaction. Psychology: Human behavior and performance; individual differences in ability, personality, and interests; learning and motivation; psychological research methods; and the assessment and treatment of behavioral and affective disorders. Physics: Physical principles and laws and

their interrelationships and applications to understanding fluid, material, and atmospheric dynamics and mechanical, electrical, atomic, and subatomic structures and processes. Biology: Plant and animal organisms and their tissues, cells, functions, interdependencies, and interactions with each other and the environment. Therapy and Counseling: Principles, methods, and procedures for diagnosis, treatment, and rehabilitation of physical and mental dysfunctions and for career counseling and guidance.

Work Environment: Indoors; radiation; disease or infections; standing; walking and running; using hands on objects, tools, or controls.

Chemistry Teachers, Postsecondary

- Annual Earnings: $58,060
- Growth: 32.2%
- Annual Job Openings: 329,000
- Education/Training Required: Master's degree
- Self-Employed: 0.4%
- Part-Time: 27.3%

The job openings listed here are shared with 35 other postsecondary teaching occupations. For a complete list, see the beginning of this section.

How the Job Improves the World: Contributes to education, health, and the natural environment.

Teach courses pertaining to the chemical and physical properties and compositional changes of substances. Work may include instruction in the methods of qualitative and quantitative chemical analysis. Includes both teachers primarily engaged in teaching and those who do a combination of both teaching and research. Prepare and deliver lectures to undergraduate and/or graduate students on topics such as organic chemistry, analytical chemistry, and chemical separation. Supervise students' laboratory work. Evaluate and grade students' classwork, laboratory performance, assignments, and papers. Compile, administer, and grade examinations or assign this work to others. Maintain student attendance records, grades, and other required records. Prepare course materials such as syllabi, homework assignments, and handouts. Maintain regularly scheduled office hours in order to advise and assist students. Plan, evaluate, and revise curricula, course content, and course materials and methods of instruction. Supervise undergraduate and/or graduate teaching, internship, and research work. Keep abreast of developments in their field by reading current literature, talking with colleagues, and participating in professional conferences. Initiate, facilitate, and moderate classroom discussions. Select and obtain materials and supplies such as textbooks and laboratory equipment. Conduct research in a particular field of knowledge and publish findings in professional journals, books, and/or electronic media. Advise students on academic and vocational curricula and on career issues. Collaborate with colleagues to address teaching and research issues. Serve on academic or administrative committees that deal with institutional policies, departmental matters, and academic issues. Write grant proposals to procure external research funding. Participate in student recruitment, registration, and placement activities. Prepare and submit required reports related to instruction. Perform administrative duties such as serving as a department head. Act as advisers to student organizations. Compile bibliographies of specialized materials for outside reading assignments. Participate in campus and community events. Provide professional consulting services to government and/or industry.

Personality Type: Investigative. Investigative occupations frequently involve working with ideas and require an extensive amount of thinking. These occupations can involve searching for facts and figuring out problems mentally.

GOE—Interest Area: 05. Education and Training. **Work Group:** 05.03. Postsecondary and Adult Teaching and Instructing. **Other Jobs in This Work Group:** Adult Literacy, Remedial Education, and GED Teachers and Instructors; Agricultural Sciences Teachers, Postsecondary; Anthropology and Archeology Teachers, Postsecondary; Architecture Teachers, Postsecondary; Area, Ethnic, and Cultural Studies Teachers, Postsecondary; Art, Drama, and Music Teachers, Postsecondary; Atmospheric, Earth, Marine, and Space Sciences Teachers, Postsecondary; Biological Science Teachers, Postsecondary; Business Teachers, Postsecondary; Communications Teachers, Postsecondary; Computer Science Teachers, Postsecondary; Criminal Justice and Law Enforcement Teachers, Postsecondary; Economics Teachers, Postsecondary; Education Teachers, Postsecondary; Engineering Teachers, Postsecondary; English Language and Literature Teachers, Postsecondary; Environmental Science Teachers, Postsecondary; Farm and Home Management Advisors; Foreign Language and Literature Teachers, Postsecondary; Forestry and Conservation Science Teachers, Postsecondary; Geography Teachers, Postsecondary; Graduate Teaching Assistants; Health Specialties Teachers, Postsecondary; History Teachers, Postsecondary; Home Economics Teachers, Postsecondary; Law Teachers, Postsecondary; Library Science Teachers, Postsecondary; Mathematical Science Teachers, Postsecondary; Nursing Instructors and Teachers, Postsecondary; Philosophy and Religion Teachers, Postsecondary; Physics Teachers, Postsecondary; Political Science Teachers, Postsecondary; Psychology Teachers, Postsecondary; Recreation and Fitness Studies Teachers, Postsecondary; Self-Enrichment Education Teachers; Social Work Teachers, Postsecondary; Sociology Teachers, Postsecondary; Vocational Education Teachers, Postsecondary.

Skills—Science: Using scientific rules and methods to solve problems. **Mathematics:** Using mathematics to solve problems. **Instructing:** Teaching others how to do something. **Active Learning:** Understanding the implications of new information for both current and future problem-solving and decision-making. **Writing:** Communicating effectively in writing as appropriate for the needs of the audience. **Reading Comprehension:** Understanding written sentences and paragraphs in work-related documents. **Technology Design:** Generating or adapting equipment and technology to serve user needs. **Complex Problem Solving:** Identifying complex problems and reviewing related information to develop and evaluate options and implement solutions.

Education and Training Programs: Chemistry, General; Analytical Chemistry; Inorganic Chemistry; Organic Chemistry; Physical and Theoretical Chemistry; Polymer Chemistry; Chemical Physics; Chemistry, Other; Geochemistry. **Related Knowledge/Courses: Chemistry:** The chemical composition, structure, and properties of substances and of the chemical processes and transformations that they undergo. This includes uses of chemicals and their danger signs, production techniques, and disposal methods. **Biology:** Plant and animal organisms and their tissues, cells, functions, interdependencies, and interactions with each other and the environment. **Physics:** Physical principles and laws and their interrelationships and applications to understanding fluid, material, and atmospheric dynamics and mechanical, electrical, atomic, and subatomic structures and processes. **Education and Training:** Principles and methods for curriculum and training design, teaching and instruction for individuals and groups, and the measurement of training effects. **Mathematics:** Arithmetic, algebra, geometry, calculus, and statistics and their applications. **English Language:** The structure and content of the English language, including the meaning and spelling of words, rules of composition, and grammar.

Work Environment: Indoors; contaminants; hazardous conditions; sitting.

Child Care Workers

◎ Annual Earnings: $17,050

◎ Growth: 13.8%

◎ Annual Job Openings: 439,000

◎ Education/Training Required: Short-term on-the-job training

◎ Self-Employed: 31.9%

◎ Part-Time: 38.8%

The job openings listed here are shared with Nannies.

How the Job Improves the World: Contributes to health, safety, and education.

Attend to children at schools, businesses, private households, and child care institutions. Perform a variety of tasks, such as dressing, feeding, bathing, and overseeing play. Support children's emotional and social development, encouraging understanding of others and positive self-concepts. Care for children in institutional setting, such as group homes, nursery schools, private businesses, or schools for the handicapped. Sanitize toys and play equipment. Discipline children and recommend or initiate other measures to control behavior, such as caring for own clothing and picking up toys and books. Identify signs of emotional or developmental problems in children and bring them to parents' or guardians' attention. Observe and monitor children's play activities. Keep records on individual children, including daily observations and information about activities, meals served, and medications administered. Instruct children in health and personal habits such as eating, resting, and toilet habits. Read to children and teach them simple painting, drawing, handicrafts, and songs. Organize and participate in recreational activities, such as games. Assist in preparing food for children, serve meals and refreshments to children, and regulate rest periods. Organize and store toys and materials to ensure order in activity areas. Operate in-house daycare centers within businesses. Sterilize bottles and prepare formulas. Provide counseling or therapy to mentally disturbed, delinquent, or handicapped children. Dress children and change diapers. Help children with homework and school work. Perform housekeeping duties such as laundry, cleaning, dishwashing, and changing of linens. Accompany children to and from school, on outings, and to medical appointments. Place or hoist children into baths or pools.

Personality Type: Social. Social occupations frequently involve working with, communicating with, and teaching people. These occupations often involve helping or providing service to others.

GOE—Interest Area: 10. Human Service. **Work Group:** 10.03. Child/Personal Care and Services. **Other Jobs in This Work Group:** Funeral Attendants; Nannies; Personal and Home Care Aides.

Skills—Negotiation: Bringing others together and trying to reconcile differences. **Social Perceptiveness:** Being aware of others' reactions and understanding why they react as they do. **Learning Strategies:** Selecting and using training/instructional methods and procedures appropriate for the situation when learning or teaching new things. **Service Orientation:** Actively looking for ways to help people. **Persuasion:** Persuading others to change their minds or behavior. **Monitoring:** Monitoring/assessing your performance or that of other individuals or organizations to make improvements or take corrective action. **Writing:** Communicating effectively in writing as appropriate for the needs of the audience. **Time Management:** Managing one's own time and the time of others.

Education and Training Program: Child Care Provider/Assistant. **Related Knowledge/Courses: Sociology and Anthropology:** Group behavior and dynamics, societal trends and influences, human migrations, ethnicity, and cultures and their history and origins. **Psychology:** Human behavior and performance; individual differences in ability, personality, and interests; learning and motivation; psychological research methods; and the assessment and treatment of

behavioral and affective disorders. **Public Safety and Security:** Relevant equipment, policies, procedures, and strategies to promote effective local, state, or national security operations for the protection of people, data, property, and institutions.

Work Environment: Indoors; noisy; disease or infections; standing.

Child, Family, and School Social Workers

- Annual Earnings: $35,350
- Growth: 19.0%
- Annual Job Openings: 31,000
- Education/Training Required: Bachelor's degree
- Self-Employed: 3.3%
- Part-Time: 11.5%

How the Job Improves the World: Contributes to mental health and social well-being.

Provide social services and assistance to improve the social and psychological functioning of children and their families and to maximize the family well-being and the academic functioning of children. May assist single parents, arrange adoptions, and find foster homes for abandoned or abused children. In schools, they address such problems as teenage pregnancy, misbehavior, and truancy. May also advise teachers on how to deal with problem children. Interview clients individually, in families, or in groups, assessing their situations, capabilities, and problems, to determine what services are required to meet their needs. Counsel individuals, groups, families, or communities regarding issues including mental health, poverty, unemployment, substance abuse, physical abuse, rehabilitation, social adjustment, child care, or medical care. Maintain case history records and prepare reports. Counsel students whose behavior, school progress, or mental or physical impairment indicate a need for assistance, diagnosing students' problems and arranging for needed services. Consult with parents, teachers, and other school personnel to determine causes of problems such as truancy and misbehavior and to implement solutions. Counsel parents with child rearing problems, interviewing the child and family to determine whether further action is required. Develop and review service plans in consultation with clients and perform follow-ups assessing the quantity and quality of services provided. Collect supplementary information needed to assist clients, such as employment records, medical records, or school reports. Address legal issues, such as child abuse and discipline, assisting with hearings and providing testimony to inform custody arrangements. Provide, find, or arrange for support services, such as child care, homemaker service, prenatal care, substance abuse treatment, job training, counseling, or parenting classes, to prevent more serious problems from developing. Refer clients to community resources for services such as job placement, debt counseling, legal aid, housing, medical treatment, or financial assistance and provide concrete information, such as where to go and how to apply. Arrange for medical, psychiatric, and other tests that may disclose causes of difficulties and indicate remedial measures. Work in child and adolescent residential institutions. Administer welfare programs. Evaluate personal characteristics and home conditions of foster home or adoption applicants. Serve as liaisons between students, homes, schools, family services, child guidance clinics, courts, protective services, doctors, and other contacts to help children who face problems such as disabilities, abuse, or poverty.

Personality Type: Social. Social occupations frequently involve working with, communicating with, and teaching people. These occupations often involve helping or providing service to others.

GOE—Interest Area: 10. Human Service. **Work Group:** 10.01. Counseling and Social Work. **Other Jobs in This Work Group:** Clinical Psychologists; Clinical, Counseling, and School Psychologists; Counseling Psychologists; Marriage and Family Therapists; Medical and Public Health Social Workers; Mental Health and Substance Abuse Social Workers; Mental Health Counselors; Probation Officers and Correctional Treatment Specialists; Rehabilitation Counselors; Residential Advisors; Social and Human Service Assistants; Substance Abuse and Behavioral Disorder Counselors.

Skills—Social Perceptiveness: Being aware of others' reactions and understanding why they react as they do. **Service Orientation:** Actively looking for ways to help people. **Speaking:** Talking to others to convey information effectively. **Monitoring:** Monitoring/assessing your performance or that of other individuals or organizations to make improvements or take corrective action. **Negotiation:** Bringing others together and trying to reconcile differences. **Learning Strategies:** Selecting and using training/instructional methods and procedures appropriate for the situation when learning or teaching new things. **Writing:** Communicating effectively in writing as appropriate for the needs of the audience. **Active Listening:** Giving full attention to what other people are saying, taking time to understand the points being made, asking questions as appropriate, and not interrupting at inappropriate times.

Education and Training Programs: Juvenile Corrections; Social Work; Youth Services/Administration. **Related Knowledge/Courses: Therapy and Counseling:** Principles, methods, and procedures for diagnosis, treatment, and rehabilitation of physical and mental dysfunctions and for career counseling and guidance. **Psychology:** Human behavior and performance; individual differences in ability, personality, and interests; learning and motivation; psychological research methods; and the assessment and treatment of behavioral and affective disorders. **Sociology and Anthropology:** Group behavior and dynamics, societal trends and influences, human migrations, ethnicity, and cultures and their history and origins. **Customer and Personal Service:** Principles and processes for providing customer and personal services. This includes customer needs assessment, meeting quality standards for services, and evaluation of customer satisfaction. **Philosophy and Theology:** Different philosophical systems and religions. This includes their basic principles, values, ethics, ways of thinking, customs, and practices and their impact on human culture. **Law and Government:** Laws, legal codes, court procedures, precedents, government regulations, executive orders, agency rules, and the democratic political process.

Work Environment: Indoors; sitting.

Chiropractors

- Annual Earnings: $67,200
- Growth: 22.4%
- Annual Job Openings: 4,000
- Education/Training Required: First professional degree
- Self-Employed: 49.2%
- Part-Time: 20.7%

How the Job Improves the World: Contributes to health.

Adjust spinal column and other articulations of the body to correct abnormalities of the human body believed to be caused by interference with the nervous system. Examine patient to determine nature and extent of disorder. Manipulate spine or other involved area. May utilize supplementary measures, such as exercise, rest, water, light, heat, and nutritional therapy. Perform a series of manual adjustments to the spine, or other articulations of the body, to correct the musculoskeletal system. Evaluate the functioning of the neuromuscularskeletal system and the spine, using systems of chiropractic diagnosis. Diagnose health problems by reviewing patients' health and medical histories; questioning, observing, and examining pa-

tients; and interpreting X rays. Maintain accurate case histories of patients. Advise patients about recommended courses of treatment. Obtain and record patients' medical histories. Analyze X rays to locate the sources of patients' difficulties and to rule out fractures or diseases as sources of problems. Counsel patients about nutrition, exercise, sleeping habits, stress management, and other matters. Arrange for diagnostic X rays to be taken. Consult with and refer patients to appropriate health practitioners when necessary. Suggest and apply the use of supports such as straps, tapes, bandages, and braces if necessary.

Personality Type: Investigative. Investigative occupations frequently involve working with ideas and require an extensive amount of thinking. These occupations can involve searching for facts and figuring out problems mentally.

GOE—Interest Area: 08. Health Science. **Work Group:** 08.04. Health Specialties. **Other Jobs in This Work Group:** Optometrists; Podiatrists.

Skills—Science: Using scientific rules and methods to solve problems. **Social Perceptiveness:** Being aware of others' reactions and understanding why they react as they do. **Management of Financial Resources:** Determining how money will be spent to get the work done and accounting for these expenditures. **Persuasion:** Persuading others to change their minds or behavior. **Service Orientation:** Actively looking for ways to help people. **Reading Comprehension:** Understanding written sentences and paragraphs in work-related documents. **Monitoring:** Monitoring/ assessing your performance or that of other individuals or organizations to make improvements or take corrective action. **Management of Personnel Resources:** Motivating, developing, and directing people as they work; identifying the best people for the job.

Education and Training Program: Chiropractic (DC). **Related Knowledge/Courses: Medicine and Dentistry:** The information and techniques needed to diagnose and treat human injuries, diseases, and deformities. This includes symptoms, treatment alternatives, drug properties and interactions, and preventive health-care measures. **Therapy and Counseling:** Principles, methods, and procedures for diagnosis, treatment, and rehabilitation of physical and mental dysfunctions and for career counseling and guidance. **Biology:** Plant and animal organisms and their tissues, cells, functions, interdependencies, and interactions with each other and the environment. **Psychology:** Human behavior and performance; individual differences in ability, personality, and interests; learning and motivation; psychological research methods; and the assessment and treatment of behavioral and affective disorders. **Sales and Marketing:** Principles and methods for showing, promoting, and selling products or services. This includes marketing strategy and tactics, product demonstration, sales techniques, and sales control systems. **Customer and Personal Service:** Principles and processes for providing customer and personal services. This includes customer needs assessment, meeting quality standards for services, and evaluation of customer satisfaction.

Work Environment: Indoors; disease or infections; standing; using hands on objects, tools, or controls; bending or twisting the body; repetitive motions.

Choreographers

- Annual Earnings: $32,950
- Growth: 16.8%
- Annual Job Openings: 4,000
- Education/Training Required: Work experience in a related occupation
- Self-Employed: 17.7%
- Part-Time: 47.7%

How the Job Improves the World: Contributes to the arts.

Create and teach dance. May direct and stage presentations. Direct rehearsals to instruct dancers in how to use dance steps and in techniques to achieve desired effects. Read and study storylines and musical scores to determine how to translate ideas and moods into dance movements. Design dances for individual dancers, dance companies, musical theatre, opera, fashion shows, film, television productions, and special events and for dancers ranging from beginners to professionals. Choose the music, sound effects, or spoken narrative to accompany a dance. Advise dancers on how to stand and move properly, teaching correct dance techniques to help prevent injuries. Coordinate production music with music directors. Audition performers for one or more dance parts. Direct and stage dance presentations for various forms of entertainment. Develop ideas for creating dances, keeping notes and sketches to record influences. Train, exercise, and attend dance classes to maintain high levels of technical proficiency, physical ability, and physical fitness. Teach students, dancers, and other performers about rhythm and interpretive movement. Assess students' dancing abilities to determine where improvement or change is needed. Experiment with different types of dancers, steps, dances, and placements, testing ideas informally to get feedback from dancers. Seek influences from other art forms such as theatre, the visual arts, and architecture. Design sets, lighting, costumes, and other artistic elements of productions in collaboration with cast members. Record dance movements and their technical aspects, using a technical understanding of the patterns and formations of choreography. Re-stage traditional dances and works in dance companies' repertoires, developing new interpretations. Manage dance schools or assist in their management.

Personality Type: Artistic. Artistic occupations frequently involve working with forms, designs, and patterns. They often require self-expression, and the work can be done without following a clear set of rules.

GOE—Interest Area: 03. Arts and Communication. Work Group: 03.08. Dance. Other Jobs in This Work Group: Dancers.

Skills—Management of Personnel Resources: Motivating, developing, and directing people as they work; identifying the best people for the job. Instructing: Teaching others how to do something. Time Management: Managing one's own time and the time of others. Persuasion: Persuading others to change their minds or behavior. Negotiation: Bringing others together and trying to reconcile differences. Speaking: Talking to others to convey information effectively. Social Perceptiveness: Being aware of others' reactions and understanding why they react as they do. Coordination: Adjusting actions in relation to others' actions.

Education and Training Programs: Dance, General; Dance, Other. Related Knowledge/Courses: Fine Arts: The theory and techniques required to compose, produce, and perform works of music, dance, visual art, drama, and sculpture. History and Archeology: Historical events and their causes, indicators, and effects on civilizations and cultures. Philosophy and Theology: Different philosophical systems and religions. This includes their basic principles, values, ethics, ways of thinking, customs, and practices and their impact on human culture. Sociology and Anthropology: Group behavior and dynamics, societal trends and influences, human migrations, ethnicity, and cultures and their history and origins. Communications and Media: Media production, communication, and dissemination techniques and methods. This includes alternative ways to inform and entertain via written, oral, and visual media. Education and Training: Principles and methods for curriculum and training design, teaching and instruction for individuals and groups, and the measurement of training effects.

Work Environment: Indoors; standing; walking and running; keeping or regaining balance; bending or . twisting the body; repetitive motions.

City and Regional Planning Aides

- ◉ Annual Earnings: $33,950
- ◉ Growth: 17.4%
- ◉ Annual Job Openings: 4,000
- ◉ Education/Training Required: Associate degree
- ◉ Self-Employed: 1.2%
- ◉ Part-Time: 22.7%

The job openings listed here are shared with Social Science Research Assistants.

How the Job Improves the World: Contributes to physical and natural environment.

Compile data from various sources, such as maps, reports, and field and file investigations, for use by city planner in making planning studies. Prepare, maintain, and update files and records, including land use data and statistics. Respond to public inquiries and complaints. Research, compile, analyze, and organize information from maps, reports, investigations, and books for use in reports and special projects. Prepare, develop, and maintain maps and databases. Serve as liaison between planning department and other departments and agencies. Prepare reports, using statistics, charts, and graphs, to illustrate planning studies in areas such as population, land use, or zoning. Participate in and support team planning efforts. Provide and process zoning and project permits and applications. Perform clerical duties such as composing, typing, and proofreading documents; scheduling appointments and meetings; handling mail; and posting public notices. Conduct interviews, surveys, and site inspections concerning factors that affect land usage, such as zoning, traffic flow, and housing. Perform code enforcement tasks. Inspect sites and review plans for minor development permit applications.

Personality Type: Conventional. Conventional occupations frequently involve following set procedures and routines. These occupations can include working with data and details more than with ideas. Usually there is a clear line of authority to follow.

GOE—Interest Area: 07. Government and Public Administration. **Work Group:** 07.02. Public Planning. **Other Jobs in This Work Group:** Urban and Regional Planners.

Skills—Service Orientation: Actively looking for ways to help people. **Coordination:** Adjusting actions in relation to others' actions. **Writing:** Communicating effectively in writing as appropriate for the needs of the audience. **Social Perceptiveness:** Being aware of others' reactions and understanding why they react as they do. **Persuasion:** Persuading others to change their minds or behavior. **Complex Problem Solving:** Identifying complex problems and reviewing related information to develop and evaluate options and implement solutions. **Active Learning:** Understanding the implications of new information for both current and future problem-solving and decision-making. **Negotiation:** Bringing others together and trying to reconcile differences.

Education and Training Program: Social Sciences, General. **Related Knowledge/Courses: Geography:** Principles and methods for describing the features of land, sea, and air masses, including their physical characteristics; locations; interrelationships; and distribution of plant, animal, and human life. **Design:** Design techniques, tools, and principles involved in production of precision technical plans, blueprints, drawings, and models. **Law and Government:** Laws, legal codes, court procedures, precedents, government regulations, executive orders, agency rules, and the democratic political process. **Clerical Practices:** Administrative and clerical procedures and systems such as word processing, managing files and records, stenography and transcription, designing forms, and other office procedures and terminology. **English Language:** The structure and content of the English language, including the meaning and spelling of words, rules of composition, and grammar. **Building and Construction:** The materials, methods, and tools involved in the construction or repair of houses, buildings, or other structures such as highways and roads.

Work Environment: Indoors; noisy; sitting.

Clergy

- Annual Earnings: $38,540
- Growth: 12.4%
- Annual Job Openings: 26,000
- Education/Training Required: Master's degree
- Self-Employed: 0.3%
- Part-Time: 10.9%

How the Job Improves the World: Contributes to spiritual well-being.

Conduct religious worship and perform other spiritual functions associated with beliefs and practices of religious faith or denomination. Provide spiritual and moral guidance and assistance to members. Pray and promote spirituality. Read from sacred texts such as the Bible, Torah, or Koran. Prepare and deliver sermons and other talks. Organize and lead regular religious services. Share information about religious issues by writing articles, giving speeches, or teaching. Instruct people who seek conversion to a particular faith. Visit people in homes, hospitals, and prisons to provide them with comfort and support. Counsel individuals and groups concerning their spiritual, emotional, and personal needs. Train leaders of church, community, and youth groups. Administer religious rites or ordinances. Study and interpret religious laws, doctrines, or traditions. Conduct special ceremonies such as weddings, funerals, and confirmations. Plan and lead religious education programs for their congregations. Respond to requests for assistance during emergencies or crises. Devise ways in which congregation membership can be expanded. Collaborate with committees and individuals to address financial and administrative issues pertaining to congregations. Prepare people for participation in religious ceremonies. Perform administrative duties such as overseeing building management, ordering supplies, contracting for services and repairs, and supervising the work of staff members and volunteers. Refer people to community support services, psychologists, and doctors as necessary. Participate in fundraising activities to support congregation activities and facilities. Organize and engage in interfaith, community, civic, educational, and recreational activities sponsored by or related to their religion.

Personality Type: Social. Social occupations frequently involve working with, communicating with, and teaching people. These occupations often involve helping or providing service to others.

GOE—Interest Area: 10. Human Service. **Work Group:** 10.02. Religious Work. **Other Jobs in This Work Group:** Directors, Religious Activities and Education.

Skills—Management of Personnel Resources: Motivating, developing, and directing people as they work; identifying the best people for the job. **Management of Financial Resources:** Determining how money will be spent to get the work done and accounting for these expenditures. **Service Orientation:** Actively looking for ways to help people. **Negotiation:** Bringing others together and trying to reconcile differences. **Persuasion:** Persuading others to change their minds or behavior. **Judgment and Decision Making:** Considering the relative costs and benefits of potential actions to choose the most appropriate one. **Social Perceptiveness:** Being aware of others' reactions

and understanding why they react as they do. **Coordination:** Adjusting actions in relation to others' actions.

Education and Training Programs: Theology/Theological Studies; Divinity/Ministry (BD, MDiv.); Pre-Theology/Pre-Ministerial Studies; Rabbinical Studies; Theological and Ministerial Studies, Other; Pastoral Studies/Counseling; Youth Ministry; Pastoral Counseling and Specialized Ministries, Other; Theology and Religious Vocations, Other; Clinical Pastoral Counseling/Patient Counseling. **Related Knowledge/Courses: Philosophy and Theology:** Different philosophical systems and religions. This includes their basic principles, values, ethics, ways of thinking, customs, and practices and their impact on human culture. **Therapy and Counseling:** Principles, methods, and procedures for diagnosis, treatment, and rehabilitation of physical and mental dysfunctions and for career counseling and guidance. **Sociology and Anthropology:** Group behavior and dynamics, societal trends and influences, human migrations, ethnicity, and cultures and their history and origins. **Psychology:** Human behavior and performance; individual differences in ability, personality, and interests; learning and motivation; psychological research methods; and the assessment and treatment of behavioral and affective disorders. **Customer and Personal Service:** Principles and processes for providing customer and personal services. This includes customer needs assessment, meeting quality standards for services, and evaluation of customer satisfaction. **Public Safety and Security:** Relevant equipment, policies, procedures, and strategies to promote effective local, state, or national security operations for the protection of people, data, property, and institutions.

Work Environment: Indoors; sitting.

Clinical Psychologists

- ◉ Annual Earnings: $57,170
- ◉ Growth: 19.1%
- ◉ Annual Job Openings: 10,000
- ◉ Education/Training Required: Doctoral degree
- ◉ Self-Employed: 38.2%
- ◉ Part-Time: 22.8%

The job openings listed here are shared with Counseling Psychologists and with School Psychologists.

How the Job Improves the World: Contributes to mental health.

Diagnose or evaluate mental and emotional disorders of individuals through observation, interview, and psychological tests and formulate and administer programs of treatment. Identify psychological, emotional, or behavioral issues and diagnose disorders, using information obtained from interviews, tests, records, and reference materials. Develop and implement individual treatment plans, specifying type, frequency, intensity, and duration of therapy. Interact with clients to assist them in gaining insight, defining goals, and planning action to achieve effective personal, social, educational, and vocational development and adjustment. Discuss the treatment of problems with clients. Utilize a variety of treatment methods such as psychotherapy, hypnosis, behavior modification, stress reduction therapy, psychodrama, and play therapy. Counsel individuals and groups regarding problems such as stress, substance abuse, and family situations to modify behavior or to improve personal, social, and vocational adjustment. Write reports on clients and maintain required paperwork. Evaluate the effectiveness of counseling or treatments and the accuracy and completeness of diagnoses; then modify plans and diagnoses as necessary. Obtain and study medical, psychological, social, and family histories by interviewing individuals, couples, or families

and by reviewing records. Consult reference material such as textbooks, manuals, and journals to identify symptoms, make diagnoses, and develop approaches to treatment. Maintain current knowledge of relevant research. Observe individuals at play, in group interactions, or in other contexts to detect indications of mental deficiency, abnormal behavior, or maladjustment. Select, administer, score, and interpret psychological tests to obtain information on individuals' intelligence, achievements, interests, and personalities. Refer clients to other specialists, institutions, or support services as necessary. Develop, direct, and participate in training programs for staff and students. Provide psychological or administrative services and advice to private firms and community agencies regarding mental health programs or individual cases. Provide occupational, educational, and other information to individuals so that they can make educational and vocational plans.

Personality Type: Investigative. Investigative occupations frequently involve working with ideas and require an extensive amount of thinking. These occupations can involve searching for facts and figuring out problems mentally.

GOE—Interest Area: 10. Human Service. **Work Group:** 10.01. Counseling and Social Work. **Other Jobs in This Work Group:** Child, Family, and School Social Workers; Clinical, Counseling, and School Psychologists; Counseling Psychologists; Marriage and Family Therapists; Medical and Public Health Social Workers; Mental Health and Substance Abuse Social Workers; Mental Health Counselors; Probation Officers and Correctional Treatment Specialists; Rehabilitation Counselors; Residential Advisors; Social and Human Service Assistants; Substance Abuse and Behavioral Disorder Counselors.

Skills—Social Perceptiveness: Being aware of others' reactions and understanding why they react as they do. **Service Orientation:** Actively looking for ways to help people. **Complex Problem Solving:** Identifying

C

complex problems and reviewing related information to develop and evaluate options and implement solutions. **Learning Strategies:** Selecting and using training/instructional methods and procedures appropriate for the situation when learning or teaching new things. **Negotiation:** Bringing others together and trying to reconcile differences. **Active Listening:** Giving full attention to what other people are saying, taking time to understand the points being made, asking questions as appropriate, and not interrupting at inappropriate times. **Active Learning:** Understanding the implications of new information for both current and future problem-solving and decision-making. **Critical Thinking:** Using logic and reasoning to identify the strengths and weaknesses of alternative solutions, conclusions, or approaches to problems.

Education and Training Programs: Psychology, General; Clinical Psychology; Counseling Psychology; Developmental and Child Psychology; School Psychology; Clinical Child Psychology; Psychoanalysis and Psychotherapy. **Related Knowledge/Courses: Therapy and Counseling:** Principles, methods, and procedures for diagnosis, treatment, and rehabilitation of physical and mental dysfunctions and for career counseling and guidance. **Psychology:** Human behavior and performance; individual differences in ability, personality, and interests; learning and motivation; psychological research methods; and the assessment and treatment of behavioral and affective disorders. **Sociology and Anthropology:** Group behavior and dynamics, societal trends and influences, human migrations, ethnicity, and cultures and their history and origins. **Philosophy and Theology:** Different philosophical systems and religions. This includes their basic principles, values, ethics, ways of thinking, customs, and practices and their impact on human culture. **Customer and Personal Service:** Principles and processes for providing customer and personal services. This includes customer needs assessment, meeting quality standards for services, and evaluation of customer satisfaction. **Medicine and**

Dentistry: The information and techniques needed to diagnose and treat human injuries, diseases, and deformities. This includes symptoms, treatment alternatives, drug properties and interactions, and preventive health-care measures.

Work Environment: Indoors; sitting.

Communications Teachers, Postsecondary

- Annual Earnings: $50,890
- Growth: 32.2%
- Annual Job Openings: 329,000
- Education/Training Required: Master's degree
- Self-Employed: 0.4%
- Part-Time: 27.3%

The job openings listed here are shared with 35 other postsecondary teaching occupations. For a complete list, see the beginning of this section.

How the Job Improves the World: Contributes to education.

Teach courses in communications, such as organizational communications, public relations, radio/television broadcasting, and journalism. Evaluate and grade students' classwork, assignments, and papers. Prepare course materials such as syllabi, homework assignments, and handouts. Initiate, facilitate, and moderate classroom discussions. Prepare and deliver lectures to undergraduate or graduate students on topics such as public speaking, media criticism, and oral traditions. Compile, administer, and grade examinations or assign this work to others. Maintain student attendance records, grades, and other required records. Plan, evaluate, and revise curricula, course content, and course materials and methods of instruction. Maintain regularly scheduled office hours to advise and assist students. Keep abreast of developments in their field by reading current literature, talking with colleagues, and participating in professional conferences. Advise students on academic and vocational curricula and on career issues. Supervise undergraduate or graduate teaching, internship, and research work. Select and obtain materials and supplies such as textbooks. Collaborate with colleagues to address teaching and research issues. Conduct research in a particular field of knowledge and publish findings in professional journals, books, or electronic media. Participate in student recruitment, registration, and placement activities. Serve on academic or administrative committees that deal with institutional policies, departmental matters, and academic issues. Compile bibliographies of specialized materials for outside reading assignments. Act as advisers to student organizations. Participate in campus and community events. Perform administrative duties such as serving as department head. Write grant proposals to procure external research funding. Provide professional consulting services to government or industry.

Personality Type: No data available.

GOE—Interest Area: 05. Education and Training. **Work Group:** 05.03. Postsecondary and Adult Teaching and Instructing. **Other Jobs in This Work Group:** Adult Literacy, Remedial Education, and GED Teachers and Instructors; Agricultural Sciences Teachers, Postsecondary; Anthropology and Archeology Teachers, Postsecondary; Architecture Teachers, Postsecondary; Area, Ethnic, and Cultural Studies Teachers, Postsecondary; Art, Drama, and Music Teachers, Postsecondary; Atmospheric, Earth, Marine, and Space Sciences Teachers, Postsecondary; Biological Science Teachers, Postsecondary; Business Teachers, Postsecondary; Chemistry Teachers, Postsecondary; Computer Science Teachers, Postsecondary; Criminal Justice and Law Enforcement Teachers, Postsecondary; Economics Teachers, Postsecondary; Education Teachers, Postsecondary; Engineering Teachers, Postsecondary;

English Language and Literature Teachers, Postsecondary; Environmental Science Teachers, Postsecondary; Farm and Home Management Advisors; Foreign Language and Literature Teachers, Postsecondary; Forestry and Conservation Science Teachers, Postsecondary; Geography Teachers, Postsecondary; Graduate Teaching Assistants; Health Specialties Teachers, Postsecondary; History Teachers, Postsecondary; Home Economics Teachers, Postsecondary; Law Teachers, Postsecondary; Library Science Teachers, Postsecondary; Mathematical Science Teachers, Postsecondary; Nursing Instructors and Teachers, Postsecondary; Philosophy and Religion Teachers, Postsecondary; Physics Teachers, Postsecondary; Political Science Teachers, Postsecondary; Psychology Teachers, Postsecondary; Recreation and Fitness Studies Teachers, Postsecondary; Self-Enrichment Education Teachers; Social Work Teachers, Postsecondary; Sociology Teachers, Postsecondary; Vocational Education Teachers, Postsecondary.

Skills—Instructing: Teaching others how to do something. **Writing:** Communicating effectively in writing as appropriate for the needs of the audience. **Persuasion:** Persuading others to change their minds or behavior. **Learning Strategies:** Selecting and using training/instructional methods and procedures appropriate for the situation when learning or teaching new things. **Monitoring:** Monitoring/assessing your performance or that of other individuals or organizations to make improvements or take corrective action. **Speaking:** Talking to others to convey information effectively. **Social Perceptiveness:** Being aware of others' reactions and understanding why they react as they do. **Critical Thinking:** Using logic and reasoning to identify the strengths and weaknesses of alternative solutions, conclusions, or approaches to problems.

Education and Training Programs: Communication Studies/Speech Communication and Rhetoric; Mass Communication/Media Studies; Journalism; Broadcast Journalism; Journalism, Other; Radio and

Television; Digital Communication and Media/Multimedia; Public Relations/Image Management; Advertising; Political Communication; Health Communication; Communication, Journalism, and Related Programs, Other. **Related Knowledge/Courses: Communications and Media:** Media production, communication, and dissemination techniques and methods. This includes alternative ways to inform and entertain via written, oral, and visual media. **Education and Training:** Principles and methods for curriculum and training design, teaching and instruction for individuals and groups, and the measurement of training effects. **Philosophy and Theology:** Different philosophical systems and religions. This includes their basic principles, values, ethics, ways of thinking, customs, and practices and their impact on human culture. **English Language:** The structure and content of the English language, including the meaning and spelling of words, rules of composition, and grammar. **Sociology and Anthropology:** Group behavior and dynamics, societal trends and influences, human migrations, ethnicity, and cultures and their history and origins. **History and Archeology:** Historical events and their causes, indicators, and effects on civilizations and cultures.

Work Environment: Indoors; sitting.

Computer Science Teachers, Postsecondary

- Annual Earnings: $54,270
- Growth: 32.2%
- Annual Job Openings: 329,000
- Education/Training Required: Master's degree
- Self-Employed: 0.4%
- Part-Time: 27.3%

The job openings listed here are shared with 35 other postsecondary teaching occupations. For a complete list, see the beginning of this section.

How the Job Improves the World: Contributes to education.

Teach courses in computer science. May specialize in a field of computer science, such as the design and function of computers or operations and research analysis. Evaluate and grade students' classwork, laboratory work, assignments, and papers. Maintain student attendance records, grades, and other required records. Prepare and deliver lectures to undergraduate and/or graduate students on topics such as programming, data structures, and software design. Prepare course materials such as syllabi, homework assignments, and handouts. Compile, administer, and grade examinations or assign this work to others. Keep abreast of developments in their field by reading current literature, talking with colleagues, and participating in professional conferences. Initiate, facilitate, and moderate classroom discussions. Plan, evaluate, and revise curricula, course content, and course materials and methods of instruction. Supervise students' laboratory work. Maintain regularly scheduled office hours to advise and assist students. Select and obtain materials and supplies such as textbooks and laboratory equipment. Advise students on academic and vocational curricula and on career issues. Participate in student recruitment, registration, and placement activities. Collaborate with colleagues to address teaching and research issues. Serve on academic or administrative committees that deal with institutional policies, departmental matters, and academic issues. Act as advisers to student organizations. Supervise undergraduate and/or graduate teaching, internship, and research work. Perform administrative duties such as serving as department head. Conduct research in a particular field of knowledge and publish findings in professional journals, books, and/or electronic media.

Direct research of other teachers or of graduate students working for advanced academic degrees. Provide professional consulting services to government and/or industry. Participate in campus and community events. Compile bibliographies of specialized materials for outside reading assignments. Write grant proposals to procure external research funding.

Personality Type: Investigative. Investigative occupations frequently involve working with ideas and require an extensive amount of thinking. These occupations can involve searching for facts and figuring out problems mentally.

GOE—Interest Area: 05. Education and Training. **Work Group:** 05.03. Postsecondary and Adult Teaching and Instructing. **Other Jobs in This Work Group:** Adult Literacy, Remedial Education, and GED Teachers and Instructors; Agricultural Sciences Teachers, Postsecondary; Anthropology and Archeology Teachers, Postsecondary; Architecture Teachers, Postsecondary; Area, Ethnic, and Cultural Studies Teachers, Postsecondary; Art, Drama, and Music Teachers, Postsecondary; Atmospheric, Earth, Marine, and Space Sciences Teachers, Postsecondary; Biological Science Teachers, Postsecondary; Business Teachers, Postsecondary; Chemistry Teachers, Postsecondary; Communications Teachers, Postsecondary; Criminal Justice and Law Enforcement Teachers, Postsecondary; Economics Teachers, Postsecondary; Education Teachers, Postsecondary; Engineering Teachers, Postsecondary; English Language and Literature Teachers, Postsecondary; Environmental Science Teachers, Postsecondary; Farm and Home Management Advisors; Foreign Language and Literature Teachers, Postsecondary; Forestry and Conservation Science Teachers, Postsecondary; Geography Teachers, Postsecondary; Graduate Teaching Assistants; Health Specialties Teachers, Postsecondary; History Teachers, Postsecondary; Home Economics Teachers, Postsecondary; Law Teachers, Postsecondary; Library Science Teachers, Postsecondary; Mathematical Science Teachers, Postsecondary; Nursing Instructors and Teachers, Postsecondary; Philosophy and Religion Teachers, Postsecondary; Physics Teachers, Postsecondary; Political Science Teachers, Postsecondary; Psychology Teachers, Postsecondary; Recreation and Fitness Studies Teachers, Postsecondary; Self-Enrichment Education Teachers; Social Work Teachers, Postsecondary; Sociology Teachers, Postsecondary; Vocational Education Teachers, Postsecondary.

Skills—Programming: Writing computer programs for various purposes. **Instructing:** Teaching others how to do something. **Technology Design:** Generating or adapting equipment and technology to serve user needs. **Operations Analysis:** Analyzing needs and product requirements to create a design. **Learning Strategies:** Selecting and using training/instructional methods and procedures appropriate for the situation when learning or teaching new things. **Mathematics:** Using mathematics to solve problems. **Complex Problem Solving:** Identifying complex problems and reviewing related information to develop and evaluate options and implement solutions. **Science:** Using scientific rules and methods to solve problems.

Education and Training Programs: Computer and Information Sciences, General; Computer Programming/Programmer, General; Information Science/Studies; Computer Systems Analysis/Analyst; Computer Science. **Related Knowledge/Courses: Computers and Electronics:** Circuit boards; processors; chips; electronic equipment; and computer hardware and software, including applications and programming. **Education and Training:** Principles and methods for curriculum and training design, teaching and instruction for individuals and groups, and the measurement of training effects. **Telecommunications:** Transmission, broadcasting, switching, control, and operation of telecommunications systems. **Mathematics:** Arithmetic, algebra, geometry, calculus, and statistics and their applications. **English Language:** The structure and content of the English language, including the meaning and spelling of words, rules of composition, and grammar. **Engineering and Technology:** The practical application of engineering science and technology. This includes applying principles, techniques, procedures, and equipment to the design and production of various goods and services.

Work Environment: Indoors; sitting.

Computer Security Specialists

- Annual Earnings: $59,930
- Growth: 38.4%
- Annual Job Openings: 34,000
- Education/Training Required: Bachelor's degree
- Self-Employed: 0.6%
- Part-Time: 4.2%

The job openings listed here are shared with Network and Computer Systems Administrators.

How the Job Improves the World: Contributes to law enforcement.

Plan, coordinate, and implement security measures for information systems to regulate access to computer data files and prevent unauthorized modification, destruction, or disclosure of information. Train users and promote security awareness to ensure system security and to improve server and network efficiency. Develop plans to safeguard computer files against accidental or unauthorized modification, destruction, or disclosure and to meet emergency data processing needs. Confer with users to discuss issues such as computer data access needs, security violations, and programming changes. Monitor current reports of computer viruses to determine when to update virus

protection systems. Modify computer security files to incorporate new software, correct errors, or change individual access status. Coordinate implementation of computer system plan with establishment personnel and outside vendors. Monitor use of data files and regulate access to safeguard information in computer files. Perform risk assessments and execute tests of data-processing system to ensure functioning of data-processing activities and security measures. Encrypt data transmissions and erect firewalls to conceal confidential information as it is being transmitted and to keep out tainted digital transfers. Document computer security and emergency measures policies, procedures, and tests. Review violations of computer security procedures and discuss procedures with violators to ensure violations are not repeated. Maintain permanent fleet cryptologic and carry-on direct support systems required in special land, sea surface, and subsurface operations.

Personality Type: Investigative. Investigative occupations frequently involve working with ideas and require an extensive amount of thinking. These occupations can involve searching for facts and figuring out problems mentally.

GOE—Interest Area: 11. Information Technology. **Work Group:** 11.02. Information Technology Specialties. **Other Jobs in This Work Group:** Computer and Information Scientists, Research; Computer Operators; Computer Programmers; Computer Software Engineers, Applications; Computer Software Engineers, Systems Software; Computer Support Specialists; Computer Systems Analysts; Computer Systems Engineers/Architects; Database Administrators; Network Designers; Network Systems and Data Communications Analysts; Software Quality Assurance Engineers and Testers; Web Administrators; Web Developers.

Skills—Systems Evaluation: Identifying measures or indicators of system performance and the actions needed to improve or correct performance relative to the goals of the system. **Systems Analysis:** Determining how a system should work and how changes in conditions, operations, and the environment will affect outcomes. **Programming:** Writing computer programs for various purposes. **Installation:** Installing equipment, machines, wiring, or programs to meet specifications. **Management of Material Resources:** Obtaining and seeing to the appropriate use of equipment, facilities, and materials needed to do certain work. **Operations Analysis:** Analyzing needs and product requirements to create a design. **Troubleshooting:** Determining causes of operating errors and deciding what to do about them. **Management of Financial Resources:** Determining how money will be spent to get the work done and accounting for these expenditures.

Education and Training Programs: Computer and Information Sciences, General; Information Science/Studies; Computer Systems Analysis/Analyst; Computer Systems Networking and Telecommunications; System Administration/Administrator; System, Networking, and LAN/WAN Management/Manager; Computer and Information Systems Security; Computer and Information Sciences and Support Services, Other. **Related Knowledge/Courses: Computers and Electronics:** Circuit boards; processors; chips; electronic equipment; and computer hardware and software, including applications and programming. **Telecommunications:** Transmission, broadcasting, switching, control, and operation of telecommunications systems. **Design:** Design techniques, tools, and principles involved in production of precision technical plans, blueprints, drawings, and models. **Engineering and Technology:** The practical application of engineering science and technology. This includes applying principles, techniques, procedures, and equipment to the design and production of various goods and services. **Education and Training:** Principles and methods for curriculum and training design, teaching and instruction for individuals and

groups, and the measurement of training effects. **Therapy and Counseling:** Principles, methods, and procedures for diagnosis, treatment, and rehabilitation of physical and mental dysfunctions and for career counseling and guidance.

Work Environment: Indoors; sitting.

Coroners

- Annual Earnings: $49,360
- Growth: 11.6%
- Annual Job Openings: 17,000
- Education/Training Required: Work experience in a related occupation
- Self-Employed: 0.0%
- Part-Time: 5.1%

The job openings listed here are shared with Environmental Compliance Inspectors; Equal Opportunity Representatives and Officers; Government Property Inspectors and Investigators; and Licensing Examiners and Inspectors.

How the Job Improves the World: Contributes to justice and law enforcement.

Direct activities such as autopsies, pathological and toxicological analyses, and inquests relating to the investigation of deaths occurring within a legal jurisdiction to determine cause of death or to fix responsibility for accidental, violent, or unexplained deaths. Perform medico-legal examinations and autopsies, conducting preliminary examinations of the body in order to identify victims, to locate signs of trauma, and to identify factors that would indicate time of death. Inquire into the cause, manner, and circumstances of human deaths and establish the identities of deceased persons. Direct activities of workers who conduct autopsies, perform pathological and toxicological analyses, and prepare documents for permanent records. Complete death certificates, including the assignment of a cause and manner of death. Observe and record the positions and conditions of bodies and of related evidence. Collect and document any pertinent medical history information. Observe, record, and preserve any objects or personal property related to deaths, including objects such as medication containers and suicide notes. Complete reports and forms required to finalize cases. Remove or supervise removal of bodies from death scenes, using the proper equipment and supplies, and arrange for transportation to morgues. Testify at inquests, hearings, and court trials. Interview persons present at death scenes to obtain information useful in determining the manner of death. Provide information concerning the circumstances of death to relatives of the deceased. Locate and document information regarding the next of kin, including their relationship to the deceased and the status of notification attempts. Confer with officials of public health and law enforcement agencies in order to coordinate interdepartmental activities. Inventory personal effects, such as jewelry or wallets, that are recovered from bodies. Coordinate the release of personal effects to authorized persons and facilitate the disposition of unclaimed corpses and personal effects. Arrange for the next of kin to be notified of deaths. Record the disposition of minor children, as well as details of arrangements made for their care. Collect wills, burial instructions, and other documentation needed for investigations and for handling of the remains. Witness and certify deaths that are the result of a judicial order.

Personality Type: Investigative. Investigative occupations frequently involve working with ideas and require an extensive amount of thinking. These occupations can involve searching for facts and figuring out problems mentally.

GOE—Interest Area: 08. Health Science. **Work Group:** 08.01. Managerial Work in Medical and Health Services. **Other Jobs in This Work Group:** Medical and Health Services Managers.

Skills—Science: Using scientific rules and methods to solve problems. **Management of Financial Resources:** Determining how money will be spent to get the work done and accounting for these expenditures. **Management of Personnel Resources:** Motivating, developing, and directing people as they work; identifying the best people for the job. **Reading Comprehension:** Understanding written sentences and paragraphs in work-related documents. **Critical Thinking:** Using logic and reasoning to identify the strengths and weaknesses of alternative solutions, conclusions, or approaches to problems. **Speaking:** Talking to others to convey information effectively. **Management of Material Resources:** Obtaining and seeing to the appropriate use of equipment, facilities, and materials needed to do certain work. **Instructing:** Teaching others how to do something.

Education and Training Program: Public Administration. **Related Knowledge/Courses: Medicine and Dentistry:** The information and techniques needed to diagnose and treat human injuries, diseases, and deformities. This includes symptoms, treatment alternatives, drug properties and interactions, and preventive health-care measures. **Biology:** Plant and animal organisms and their tissues, cells, functions, interdependencies, and interactions with each other and the environment. **Psychology:** Human behavior and performance; individual differences in ability, personality, and interests; learning and motivation; psychological research methods; and the assessment and treatment of behavioral and affective disorders. **Therapy and Counseling:** Principles, methods, and procedures for diagnosis, treatment, and rehabilitation of physical and mental dysfunctions and for career counseling and guidance. **Chemistry:** The chemical composition, structure, and properties of substances and of the chemical processes and transformations that they undergo. This includes uses of chemicals and their danger signs, production techniques, and disposal methods. **Law and Government:** Laws, legal codes, court procedures, precedents, government regulations, executive orders, agency rules, and the democratic political process.

Work Environment: More often indoors than outdoors; contaminants; disease or infections; hazardous equipment; using hands on objects, tools, or controls.

Correctional Officers and Jailers

- ◎ Annual Earnings: $34,090
- ◎ Growth: 6.7%
- ◎ Annual Job Openings: 54,000
- ◎ Education/Training Required: Moderate-term on-the-job training
- ◎ Self-Employed: 0.0%
- ◎ Part-Time: 2.1%

How the Job Improves the World: Contributes to justice and law enforcement.

Guard inmates in penal or rehabilitative institution in accordance with established regulations and procedures. May guard prisoners in transit between jail, courtroom, prison, or other point. Includes deputy sheriffs and police who spend the majority of their time guarding prisoners in correctional institutions. Monitor conduct of prisoners according to established policies, regulations, and procedures to prevent escape or violence. Inspect conditions of locks, window bars, grills, doors, and gates at correctional facilities to ensure that they will prevent escapes. Search prisoners, cells, and vehicles for weapons, valuables, or drugs. Guard facility entrances to screen visitors. Search for and recapture escapees. Inspect mail for the presence of contraband. Take prisoners into custody and escort to locations within and outside of facility, such as visiting room, courtroom, or airport. Record information such as prisoner identification, charges, and incidences of inmate disturbance. Use weapons, handcuffs, and physical force to maintain discipline and or-

der among prisoners. Conduct fire, safety, and sanitation inspections. Provide to supervisors oral and written reports of the quality and quantity of work performed by inmates, inmate disturbances and rule violations, and unusual occurrences. Settle disputes between inmates. Drive passenger vehicles and trucks used to transport inmates to other institutions, courtrooms, hospitals, and work sites. Arrange daily schedules for prisoners, including library visits, work assignments, family visits, and counseling appointments. Assign duties to inmates, providing instructions as needed. Issue clothing, tools, and other authorized items to inmates. Serve meals and distribute commissary items to prisoners. Investigate crimes that have occurred within an institution or assist police in their investigations of crimes and inmates. Maintain records of prisoners' identification and charges. Supervise and coordinate work of other correctional service officers. Sponsor inmate recreational activities such as newspapers and self-help groups.

Personality Type: Realistic. Realistic occupations frequently involve work activities that include practical, hands-on problems and solutions. They often deal with plants; animals; and real-world materials such as wood, tools, and machinery. Many of the occupations require working outside and do not involve a lot of paperwork or working closely with others.

GOE—Interest Area: 12. Law and Public Safety. **Work Group:** 12.04. Law Enforcement and Public Safety. **Other Jobs in This Work Group:** Bailiffs; Criminal Investigators and Special Agents; Detectives and Criminal Investigators; Fire Investigators; Forensic Science Technicians; Parking Enforcement Workers; Police and Sheriff's Patrol Officers; Police Detectives; Police Identification and Records Officers; Police Patrol Officers; Sheriffs and Deputy Sheriffs; Transit and Railroad Police.

Skills—Social Perceptiveness: Being aware of others' reactions and understanding why they react as they do. **Persuasion:** Persuading others to change their minds or behavior. **Negotiation:** Bringing others together and trying to reconcile differences. **Writing:** Communicating effectively in writing as appropriate for the needs of the audience. **Speaking:** Talking to others to convey information effectively. **Monitoring:** Monitoring/assessing your performance or that of other individuals or organizations to make improvements or take corrective action. **Active Listening:** Giving full attention to what other people are saying, taking time to understand the points being made, asking questions as appropriate, and not interrupting at inappropriate times. **Critical Thinking:** Using logic and reasoning to identify the strengths and weaknesses of alternative solutions, conclusions, or approaches to problems.

Education and Training Programs: Corrections; Juvenile Corrections; Corrections and Criminal Justice, Other. **Related Knowledge/Courses: Psychology:** Human behavior and performance; individual differences in ability, personality, and interests; learning and motivation; psychological research methods; and the assessment and treatment of behavioral and affective disorders. **Public Safety and Security:** Relevant equipment, policies, procedures, and strategies to promote effective local, state, or national security operations for the protection of people, data, property, and institutions. **Law and Government:** Laws, legal codes, court procedures, precedents, government regulations, executive orders, agency rules, and the democratic political process. **Philosophy and Theology:** Different philosophical systems and religions. This includes their basic principles, values, ethics, ways of thinking, customs, and practices and their impact on human culture. **Sociology and Anthropology:** Group behavior and dynamics, societal trends and influences, human migrations, ethnicity, and cultures and their history and origins. **Therapy and Counseling:** Principles, methods, and procedures for diagnosis, treatment, and rehabilitation of physical and mental dysfunctions and for career counseling and guidance.

Work Environment: More often indoors than outdoors; noisy; contaminants; disease or infections; standing.

Counseling Psychologists

- Annual Earnings: $57,170
- Growth: 19.1%
- Annual Job Openings: 10,000
- Education/Training Required: Doctoral degree
- Self-Employed: 38.2%
- Part-Time: 22.8%

The job openings listed here are shared with Clinical Psychologists and with School Psychologists.

How the Job Improves the World: Contributes to mental health.

Assess and evaluate individuals' problems through the use of case history, interview, and observation and provide individual or group counseling services to assist individuals in achieving more effective personal, social, educational, and vocational development and adjustment. Collect information about individuals or clients, using interviews, case histories, observational techniques, and other assessment methods. Counsel individuals, groups, or families to help them understand problems, define goals, and develop realistic action plans. Develop therapeutic and treatment plans based on clients' interests, abilities, and needs. Consult with other professionals to discuss therapies, treatments, counseling resources, or techniques and to share occupational information. Analyze data such as interview notes, test results, and reference manuals in order to identify symptoms and to diagnose the nature of clients' problems. Advise clients on how they could be helped by counseling. Evaluate the results of counseling methods to determine the reliability and validity of treatments. Provide consulting services to schools, social service agencies, and businesses. Refer clients to specialists or to other institutions for non-counseling treatment of problems. Select, administer, and interpret psychological tests to assess intelligence, aptitudes, abilities, or interests. Conduct research to develop or improve diagnostic or therapeutic counseling techniques.

Personality Type: Social. Social occupations frequently involve working with, communicating with, and teaching people. These occupations often involve helping or providing service to others.

GOE—Interest Area: 10. Human Service. **Work Group:** 10.01. Counseling and Social Work. **Other Jobs in This Work Group:** Child, Family, and School Social Workers; Clinical Psychologists; Clinical, Counseling, and School Psychologists; Marriage and Family Therapists; Medical and Public Health Social Workers; Mental Health and Substance Abuse Social Workers; Mental Health Counselors; Probation Officers and Correctional Treatment Specialists; Rehabilitation Counselors; Residential Advisors; Social and Human Service Assistants; Substance Abuse and Behavioral Disorder Counselors.

Skills—Social Perceptiveness: Being aware of others' reactions and understanding why they react as they do. **Active Listening:** Giving full attention to what other people are saying, taking time to understand the points being made, asking questions as appropriate, and not interrupting at inappropriate times. **Persuasion:** Persuading others to change their minds or behavior. **Service Orientation:** Actively looking for ways to help people. **Negotiation:** Bringing others together and trying to reconcile differences. **Coordination:** Adjusting actions in relation to others' actions. **Learning Strategies:** Selecting and using training/instructional methods and procedures appropriate for the situation when learning or teaching new things. **Monitoring:** Monitoring/assessing your performance or that of other individuals or organizations to make improvements or take corrective action.

Education and Training Programs: Psychology, General; Clinical Psychology; Counseling Psychology; Developmental and Child Psychology; School Psychology; Clinical Child Psychology; Psychoanalysis and Psychotherapy. **Related Knowledge/Courses: Therapy and Counseling:** Principles, methods, and procedures for diagnosis, treatment, and rehabilitation of physical and mental dysfunctions and for career counseling and guidance. **Philosophy and Theology:** Different philosophical systems and religions. This includes their basic principles, values, ethics, ways of thinking, customs, and practices and their impact on human culture. **Sociology and Anthropology:** Group behavior and dynamics, societal trends and influences, human migrations, ethnicity, and cultures and their history and origins. **Psychology:** Human behavior and performance; individual differences in ability, personality, and interests; learning and motivation; psychological research methods; and the assessment and treatment of behavioral and affective disorders. **English Language:** The structure and content of the English language, including the meaning and spelling of words, rules of composition, and grammar. **Customer and Personal Service:** Principles and processes for providing customer and personal services. This includes customer needs assessment, meeting quality standards for services, and evaluation of customer satisfaction.

Work Environment: Indoors; sitting.

Criminal Investigators and Special Agents

- Annual Earnings: $55,790
- Growth: 16.3%
- Annual Job Openings: 9,000
- Education/Training Required: Work experience in a related occupation
- Self-Employed: 0.0%
- Part-Time: 2.5%

The job openings listed here are shared with Immigration and Customs Inspectors; Police Detectives; and Police Identification and Records Officers.

How the Job Improves the World: Contributes to justice and law enforcement.

Investigate alleged or suspected criminal violations of federal, state, or local laws to determine if evidence is sufficient to recommend prosecution. Record evidence and documents, using equipment such as cameras and photocopy machines. Obtain and verify evidence by interviewing and observing suspects and witnesses or by analyzing records. Examine records to locate links in chains of evidence or information. Prepare reports that detail investigation findings. Determine scope, timing, and direction of investigations. Collaborate with other offices and agencies to exchange information and coordinate activities. Testify before grand juries concerning criminal activity investigations. Analyze evidence in laboratories or in the field. Investigate organized crime, public corruption, financial crime, copyright infringement, civil rights violations, bank robbery, extortion, kidnapping, and other violations of federal or state statutes. Identify case issues and evidence needed, based on analysis of charges, complaints, or allegations of law violations. Obtain and use search and arrest warrants. Serve subpoenas or other official papers. Collaborate with other authorities on activities such as surveillance, transcription, and research. Develop relationships with informants to obtain information related to cases. Search for and collect evidence such as fingerprints, using investigative equipment. Collect and record physical information about arrested suspects, including fingerprints, height and weight measurements, and photographs. Compare crime scene fingerprints with those from suspects or fingerprint files to identify perpetrators, using computers. Administer counter-terrorism and counter-narcotics reward programs. Provide protection for individuals such as government leaders, political candidates, and visiting foreign dignitaries. Perform undercover assignments and maintain surveillance, including monitoring authorized wiretaps. Manage security programs designed to protect personnel, facilities, and information. Issue security clearances.

Personality Type: Enterprising. Enterprising occupations frequently involve starting up and carrying out projects. These occupations can involve leading people and making many decisions. They sometimes require risk taking and often deal with business.

GOE—Interest Area: 12. Law and Public Safety. **Work Group:** 12.04. Law Enforcement and Public Safety. **Other Jobs in This Work Group:** Bailiffs; Correctional Officers and Jailers; Detectives and Criminal Investigators; Fire Investigators; Forensic Science Technicians; Parking Enforcement Workers; Police and Sheriff's Patrol Officers; Police Detectives; Police Identification and Records Officers; Police Patrol Officers; Sheriffs and Deputy Sheriffs; Transit and Railroad Police.

Skills—Negotiation: Bringing others together and trying to reconcile differences. **Programming:** Writing computer programs for various purposes. **Judgment and Decision Making:** Considering the relative costs and benefits of potential actions to choose the most appropriate one. **Operations Analysis:** Analyzing needs and product requirements to create a design. **Service Orientation:** Actively looking for ways to help people. **Persuasion:** Persuading others to change their minds or behavior. **Complex Problem Solving:** Identifying complex problems and reviewing related information to develop and evaluate options and implement solutions. **Equipment Selection:** Determining the kind of tools and equipment needed to do a job.

Education and Training Programs: Criminal Justice/Police Science; Criminalistics and Criminal Science. **Related Knowledge/Courses: Law and Government:** Laws, legal codes, court procedures, precedents, government regulations, executive orders, agency rules, and the democratic political process. **Psychology:** Human behavior and performance; individual differences in ability, personality, and interests; learning and motivation; psychological research methods; and the assessment and treatment of behavioral and affective disorders. **Geography:** Principles and methods for describing the features of land, sea, and air masses, including their physical characteristics; locations; interrelationships; and distribution of plant, animal, and human life. **Public Safety and Security:** Relevant equipment, policies, procedures, and strategies to promote effective local, state, or national security operations for the protection of people, data, property, and institutions. **Clerical Practices:** Administrative and clerical procedures and systems such as word processing, managing files and records, stenography and transcription, designing forms, and other office procedures and terminology. **Telecommunications:** Transmission, broadcasting, switching, control, and operation of telecommunications systems.

Work Environment: More often outdoors than indoors; noisy; very hot or cold; standing.

Criminal Justice and Law Enforcement Teachers, Postsecondary

- Annual Earnings: $49,240
- Growth: 32.2%
- Annual Job Openings: 329,000
- Education/Training Required: Master's degree
- Self-Employed: 0.4%
- Part-Time: 27.3%

The job openings listed here are shared with 35 other postsecondary teaching occupations. For a complete list, see the beginning of this section.

How the Job Improves the World: Contributes to education, justice, and law enforcement.

Teach courses in criminal justice, corrections, and law enforcement administration. Initiate, facilitate, and moderate classroom discussions. Keep abreast of developments in their field by reading current literature, talking with colleagues, and participating in professional conferences. Evaluate and grade students' classwork, assignments, and papers. Compile, administer, and grade examinations or assign this work to others. Prepare and deliver lectures to undergraduate or graduate students on topics such as criminal law, defensive policing, and investigation techniques. Prepare course materials such as syllabi, homework assignments, and handouts. Conduct research in a particular field of knowledge and publish findings in professional journals, books, and/or electronic media. Plan, evaluate, and revise curricula, course content, and course materials and methods of instruction. Supervise undergraduate and/or graduate teaching, internship, and research work. Maintain student attendance records, grades, and other required records. Select and obtain materials and supplies such as textbooks. Advise students on academic and vocational curricula and on career issues. Maintain regularly scheduled office hours to advise and assist students. Collaborate with colleagues to address teaching and research issues. Write grant proposals to procure external research funding. Serve on academic or administrative committees that deal with institutional policies, departmental matters, and academic issues. Compile bibliographies of specialized materials for outside reading assignments. Participate in student recruitment, registration, and placement activities. Provide professional consulting services to government and/or industry. Perform administrative duties such as serving as department head. Participate in campus and community events. Act as advisers to student organizations.

Personality Type: No data available.

GOE—Interest Area: 05. Education and Training. **Work Group:** 05.03. Postsecondary and Adult Teaching and Instructing. **Other Jobs in This Work Group:** Adult Literacy, Remedial Education, and GED Teachers and Instructors; Agricultural Sciences Teachers, Postsecondary; Anthropology and Archeology Teachers, Postsecondary; Architecture Teachers, Postsecondary; Area, Ethnic, and Cultural Studies Teachers, Postsecondary; Art, Drama, and Music Teachers, Postsecondary; Atmospheric, Earth, Marine, and Space Sciences Teachers, Postsecondary; Biological Science Teachers, Postsecondary; Business Teachers, Postsecondary; Chemistry Teachers, Postsecondary; Communications Teachers, Postsecondary; Computer Science Teachers, Postsecondary; Economics Teachers, Postsecondary; Education Teachers, Postsecondary; Engineering Teachers, Postsecondary; English Language and Literature Teachers, Postsecondary; Environmental Science Teachers, Postsecondary; Farm and Home Management Advisors; Foreign Language and Literature Teachers, Postsecondary; Forestry and Conservation Science Teachers, Postsecondary; Geography Teachers, Postsecondary; Graduate Teaching Assistants; Health Specialties Teachers, Postsecondary; History Teachers, Postsecondary; Home Economics Teachers, Postsecondary; Law Teachers, Postsecondary; Library Science Teachers, Postsecondary; Mathematical Science Teachers, Postsecondary; Nursing Instructors and Teachers, Postsecondary; Philosophy and Religion Teachers, Postsecondary; Physics Teachers, Postsecondary; Political Science Teachers, Postsecondary; Psychology Teachers, Postsecondary; Recreation and Fitness Studies Teachers, Postsecondary; Self-Enrichment Education Teachers; Social Work Teachers, Postsecondary; Sociology Teachers, Postsecondary; Vocational Education Teachers, Postsecondary.

Skills—Writing: Communicating effectively in writing as appropriate for the needs of the audience. **Critical Thinking:** Using logic and reasoning to identify the strengths and weaknesses of alternative solutions, conclusions, or approaches to problems. **Instructing:** Teaching others how to do something. **Active Learning:** Understanding the implications of new information for both current and future problem-solving and decision-making. **Persuasion:** Persuading others to change their minds or behavior. **Reading Comprehension:** Understanding written sentences and paragraphs in work-related documents. **Speaking:** Talking to others to convey information effectively. **Learning Strategies:** Selecting and using training/instructional methods and procedures appropriate for the situation when learning or teaching new things.

Education and Training Programs: Teacher Education and Professional Development, Specific Subject Areas, Other; Corrections; Criminal Justice/Law Enforcement Administration; Criminal Justice/Safety Studies; Forensic Science and Technology; Criminal Justice/Police Science; Security and Loss Prevention Services; Juvenile Corrections; Criminalistics and Criminal Science; Corrections Administration; Corrections and Criminal Justice, Other. **Related Knowledge/Courses: Sociology and Anthropology:** Group behavior and dynamics, societal trends and influences, human migrations, ethnicity, and cultures and their history and origins. **Philosophy and Theology:** Different philosophical systems and religions. This includes their basic principles, values, ethics, ways of thinking, customs, and practices and their impact on human culture. **History and Archeology:** Historical events and their causes, indicators, and effects on civilizations and cultures. **Law and Government:** Laws, legal codes, court procedures, precedents, government regulations, executive orders, agency rules, and the democratic political process. **English Language:** The structure and content of the English language, including the meaning and spelling of words, rules of composition, and grammar. **Education and Training:** Principles and methods for curriculum and training design, teaching and instruction for individuals and groups, and the measurement of training effects.

Work Environment: Indoors; sitting.

Crossing Guards

- ◎ Annual Earnings: $20,050
- ◎ Growth: 19.7%
- ◎ Annual Job Openings: 26,000
- ◎ Education/Training Required: Short-term on-the-job training
- ◎ Self-Employed: 0.0%
- ◎ Part-Time: 53.9%

How the Job Improves the World: Contributes to safety.

Guide or control vehicular or pedestrian traffic at such places as streets, schools, railroad crossings, or construction sites. Monitor traffic flow to locate safe gaps through which pedestrians can cross streets. Direct or escort pedestrians across streets, stopping traffic as necessary. Guide or control vehicular or pedestrian traffic at such places as street and railroad crossings and construction sites. Communicate traffic and crossing rules and other information to students and adults. Report unsafe behavior of children to school officials. Record license numbers of vehicles disregarding traffic signals and report infractions to appropriate authorities. Direct traffic movement or warn of hazards, using signs, flags, lanterns, and hand signals. Learn the location and purpose of street traffic signs within assigned patrol areas. Stop speeding vehicles to warn drivers of traffic laws. Distribute traffic control signs and markers at designated points. Discuss traffic routing plans and control point locations with superiors. Inform drivers of detour routes through construction sites.

Personality Type: Social. Social occupations frequently involve working with, communicating with, and teaching people. These occupations often involve helping or providing service to others.

GOE—Interest Area: 12. Law and Public Safety. **Work Group:** 12.05. Safety and Security. **Other Jobs in This Work Group:** Animal Control Workers; Gaming Surveillance Officers and Gaming Investigators; Lifeguards, Ski Patrol, and Other Recreational Protective Service Workers; Private Detectives and Investigators; Security Guards; Transportation Security Screeners.

Skills—No data available.

Education and Training Program: Security and Protective Services, Other. **Related Knowledge/Courses: Public Safety and Security:** Relevant equipment, policies, procedures, and strategies to promote effective local, state, or national security operations for the protection of people, data, property, and institutions.

Work Environment: Outdoors; contaminants; hazardous equipment; standing; walking and running; using hands on objects, tools, or controls.

Curators

- Annual Earnings: $45,240
- Growth: 15.7%
- Annual Job Openings: 1,000
- Education/Training Required: Master's degree
- Self-Employed: 6.4%
- Part-Time: 23.4%

How the Job Improves the World: Contributes to education.

Administer affairs of museum and conduct research programs. Direct instructional, research, and public service activities of institution. Plan and organize the acquisition, storage, and exhibition of collections and related materials, including the selection of exhibition themes and designs. Develop and maintain an institution's registration, cataloging, and basic recordkeeping systems, using computer databases. Provide information from the institution's holdings to other curators and to the public. Inspect premises to assess the need for repairs and to ensure that climate and pest-control issues are addressed. Train and supervise curatorial, fiscal, technical, research, and clerical staff, as well as volunteers or interns. Negotiate and authorize purchase, sale, exchange, or loan of collections. Plan and conduct special research projects in area of interest or expertise. Conduct or organize tours, workshops, and instructional sessions to acquaint individuals with an institution's facilities and materials. Confer with the board of directors to formulate and interpret policies, to determine budget requirements, and to plan overall operations. Attend meetings, conventions, and civic events to promote use of institution's services, to seek financing, and to maintain community alliances. Schedule events and organize details, including refreshment, entertainment, decorations, and the collection of any fees. Write and review grant proposals, journal articles, institutional reports, and publicity

materials. Study, examine, and test acquisitions to authenticate their origin, composition, and history and to assess their current value. Arrange insurance coverage for objects on loan or for special exhibits and recommend changes in coverage for the entire collection. Establish specifications for reproductions and oversee their manufacture or select items from commercially available replica sources.

Personality Type: Artistic. Artistic occupations frequently involve working with forms, designs, and patterns. They often require self-expression, and the work can be done without following a clear set of rules.

GOE—Interest Area: 05. Education and Training. **Work Group:** 05.05. Archival and Museum Services. **Other Jobs in This Work Group:** Archivists; Audio-Visual Collections Specialists; Museum Technicians and Conservators.

Skills—Management of Financial Resources: Determining how money will be spent to get the work done and accounting for these expenditures. **Management of Personnel Resources:** Motivating, developing, and directing people as they work; identifying the best people for the job. **Writing:** Communicating effectively in writing as appropriate for the needs of the audience. **Time Management:** Managing one's own time and the time of others. **Speaking:** Talking to others to convey information effectively. **Persuasion:** Persuading others to change their minds or behavior. **Monitoring:** Monitoring/assessing your performance or that of other individuals or organizations to make improvements or take corrective action. **Negotiation:** Bringing others together and trying to reconcile differences.

Education and Training Programs: Museology/Museum Studies; Art History, Criticism, and Conservation; Public/Applied History and Archival Administration. **Related Knowledge/Courses: Fine Arts:** The theory and techniques required to compose, produce, and perform works of music, dance, visual art, drama, and sculpture. **History and Archeology:**

Historical events and their causes, indicators, and effects on civilizations and cultures. **Clerical Practices:** Administrative and clerical procedures and systems such as word processing, managing files and records, stenography and transcription, designing forms, and other office procedures and terminology. **Philosophy and Theology:** Different philosophical systems and religions. This includes their basic principles, values, ethics, ways of thinking, customs, and practices and their impact on human culture. **Sociology and Anthropology:** Group behavior and dynamics, societal trends and influences, human migrations, ethnicity, and cultures and their history and origins. **Geography:** Principles and methods for describing the features of land, sea, and air masses, including their physical characteristics; locations; interrelationships; and distribution of plant, animal, and human life.

Work Environment: Indoors; sitting.

Dental Assistants

- Annual Earnings: $29,520
- Growth: 42.7%
- Annual Job Openings: 45,000
- Education/Training Required: Moderate-term on-the-job training
- Self-Employed: 0.0%
- Part-Time: 38.9%

How the Job Improves the World: Contributes to health.

Assist dentist, set up patient and equipment, and keep records. Prepare patient, sterilize and disinfect instruments, set up instrument trays, prepare materials, and assist dentist during dental procedures. Expose dental diagnostic X rays. Record treatment information in patient records. Take and record medical and dental histories and vital signs of patients. Provide postoperative instructions prescribed by dentist. Assist dentist in management of medical and dental emergencies. Pour, trim, and polish study casts. Instruct patients in oral hygiene and plaque control programs. Make preliminary impressions for study casts and occlusal registrations for mounting study casts. Clean and polish removable appliances. Clean teeth, using dental instruments. Apply protective coating of fluoride to teeth. Fabricate temporary restorations and custom impressions from preliminary impressions. Schedule appointments, prepare bills, and receive payment for dental services; complete insurance forms; and maintain records, manually or using computer.

Personality Type: Social. Social occupations frequently involve working with, communicating with, and teaching people. These occupations often involve helping or providing service to others.

GOE—Interest Area: 08. Health Science. **Work Group:** 08.03. Dentistry. **Other Jobs in This Work Group:** Dental Hygienists; Dentists, General; Oral and Maxillofacial Surgeons; Orthodontists; Prosthodontists.

Skills—Equipment Maintenance: Performing routine maintenance on equipment and determining when and what kind of maintenance is needed. **Social Perceptiveness:** Being aware of others' reactions and understanding why they react as they do. **Operation and Control:** Controlling operations of equipment or systems. **Management of Material Resources:** Obtaining and seeing to the appropriate use of equipment, facilities, and materials needed to do certain work. **Operation Monitoring:** Watching gauges, dials, or other indicators to make sure a machine is working properly. **Equipment Selection:** Determining the kind of tools and equipment needed to do a job. **Installation:** Installing equipment, machines, wiring, or programs to meet specifications. **Troubleshooting:** Determining causes of operating errors and deciding what to do about them.

Education and Training Program: Dental Assisting/Assistant. **Related Knowledge/Courses: Medicine and Dentistry:** The information and techniques needed to diagnose and treat human injuries, diseases, and deformities. This includes symptoms, treatment alternatives, drug properties and interactions, and preventive health-care measures. **Chemistry:** The chemical composition, structure, and properties of substances and of the chemical processes and transformations that they undergo. This includes uses of chemicals and their danger signs, production techniques, and disposal methods. **Clerical Practices:** Administrative and clerical procedures and systems such as word processing, managing files and records, stenography and transcription, designing forms, and other office procedures and terminology. **Customer and Personal Service:** Principles and processes for providing customer and personal services. This includes customer needs assessment, meeting quality standards for services, and evaluation of customer satisfaction. **Psychology:** Human behavior and performance; individual differences in ability, personality, and interests; learning and motivation; psychological research methods; and the assessment and treatment of behavioral and affective disorders. **Computers and Electronics:** Circuit boards; processors; chips; electronic equipment; and computer hardware and software, including applications and programming.

Work Environment: Indoors; contaminants; disease or infections; using hands on objects, tools, or controls; bending or twisting the body; repetitive motions.

Dental Hygienists

- Annual Earnings: $60,890
- Growth: 43.3%
- Annual Job Openings: 17,000
- Education/Training Required: Associate degree
- Self-Employed: 0.3%
- Part-Time: 56.0%

How the Job Improves the World: Contributes to health.

Clean teeth and examine oral areas, head, and neck for signs of oral disease. May educate patients on oral hygiene, take and develop X rays, or apply fluoride or sealants. Clean calcareous deposits, accretions, and stains from teeth and beneath margins of gums, using dental instruments. Feel and visually examine gums for sores and signs of disease. Chart conditions of decay and disease for diagnosis and treatment by dentist. Feel lymph nodes under patient's chin to detect swelling or tenderness that could indicate presence of oral cancer. Apply fluorides and other cavity-preventing agents to arrest dental decay. Examine gums, using probes, to locate periodontal recessed gums and signs of gum disease. Expose and develop X-ray film. Provide clinical services and health education to improve and maintain oral health of schoolchildren. Remove excess cement from coronal surfaces of teeth. Make impressions for study casts. Place, carve, and finish amalgam restorations. Administer local anesthetic agents. Conduct dental health clinics for community groups to augment services of dentist. Remove sutures and dressings. Place and remove rubber dams, matrices, and temporary restorations.

Personality Type: Social. Social occupations frequently involve working with, communicating with, and teaching people. These occupations often involve helping or providing service to others.

GOE—Interest Area: 08. Health Science. Work Group: 08.03. Dentistry. Other Jobs in This Work Group: Dental Assistants; Dentists, General; Oral and Maxillofacial Surgeons; Orthodontists; Prosthodontists.

Skills—Active Learning: Understanding the implications of new information for both current and future problem-solving and decision-making. Time Management: Managing one's own time and the time of others. Persuasion: Persuading others to change their minds or behavior. Reading Comprehension: Understanding written sentences and paragraphs in work-related documents. Science: Using scientific rules and methods to solve problems. Social Perceptiveness: Being aware of others' reactions and understanding why they react as they do. Writing: Communicating effectively in writing as appropriate for the needs of the audience. Equipment Selection: Determining the kind of tools and equipment needed to do a job.

Education and Training Program: Dental Hygiene/Hygienist. Related Knowledge/Courses: Biology: Plant and animal organisms and their tissues, cells, functions, interdependencies, and interactions with each other and the environment. Medicine and Dentistry: The information and techniques needed to diagnose and treat human injuries, diseases, and deformities. This includes symptoms, treatment alternatives, drug properties and interactions, and preventive health-care measures. Chemistry: The chemical composition, structure, and properties of substances and of the chemical processes and transformations that they undergo. This includes uses of chemicals and their danger signs, production techniques, and disposal methods. Psychology: Human behavior and performance; individual differences in ability, personality, and interests; learning and motivation; psychological research methods; and the assessment and treatment of behavioral and affective disorders. Sales and Marketing: Principles and methods for showing, promoting, and selling products or services. This includes

marketing strategy and tactics, product demonstration, sales techniques, and sales control systems. Therapy and Counseling: Principles, methods, and procedures for diagnosis, treatment, and rehabilitation of physical and mental dysfunctions and for career counseling and guidance.

Work Environment: Indoors; radiation; disease or infections; sitting; using hands on objects, tools, or controls; repetitive motions.

Dentists, General

- Annual Earnings: $125,300
- Growth: 13.5%
- Annual Job Openings: 7,000
- Education/Training Required: First professional degree
- Self-Employed: 30.7%
- Part-Time: 22.4%

How the Job Improves the World: Contributes to health.

Diagnose and treat diseases, injuries, and malformations of teeth and gums and related oral structures. May treat diseases of nerve, pulp, and other dental tissues affecting vitality of teeth. Use masks, gloves, and safety glasses to protect themselves and their patients from infectious diseases. Administer anesthetics to limit the amount of pain experienced by patients during procedures. Examine teeth, gums, and related tissues, using dental instruments, X rays, and other diagnostic equipment, to evaluate dental health, diagnose diseases or abnormalities, and plan appropriate treatments. Formulate plan of treatment for patient's teeth and mouth tissue. Use air turbine and hand instruments, dental appliances, and surgical implements. Advise and instruct patients regarding preventive dental care, the causes and treatment of dental problems, and oral health care services. Design, make, and fit prosthodontic appliances such as space maintainers, bridges, and dentures or write fabrication instructions or prescriptions for denturists and dental technicians. Diagnose and treat diseases, injuries, and malformations of teeth, gums, and related oral structures and provide preventive and corrective services. Fill pulp chamber and canal with endodontic materials. Write prescriptions for antibiotics and other medications. Analyze and evaluate dental needs to determine changes and trends in patterns of dental disease. Treat exposure of pulp by pulp capping, removal of pulp from pulp chamber, or root canal, using dental instruments. Eliminate irritating margins of fillings and correct occlusions, using dental instruments. Perform oral and periodontal surgery on the jaw or mouth. Remove diseased tissue, using surgical instruments. Apply fluoride and sealants to teeth. Manage business, employing and supervising staff and handling paperwork and insurance claims. Bleach, clean, or polish teeth to restore natural color. Plan, organize, and maintain dental health programs. Produce and evaluate dental health educational materials.

Personality Type: Investigative. Investigative occupations frequently involve working with ideas and require an extensive amount of thinking. These occupations can involve searching for facts and figuring out problems mentally.

GOE—Interest Area: 08. Health Science. **Work Group:** 08.03. Dentistry. **Other Jobs in This Work Group:** Dental Assistants; Dental Hygienists; Oral and Maxillofacial Surgeons; Orthodontists; Prosthodontists.

Skills—Science: Using scientific rules and methods to solve problems. **Management of Financial Resources:** Determining how money will be spent to get the work done and accounting for these expenditures. **Management of Material Resources:** Obtaining and seeing to the appropriate use of equipment, facilities, and materials needed to do certain work. **Complex Problem Solving:** Identifying complex problems and reviewing related information to develop and evaluate

options and implement solutions. **Equipment Selection:** Determining the kind of tools and equipment needed to do a job. **Management of Personnel Resources:** Motivating, developing, and directing people as they work; identifying the best people for the job. **Service Orientation:** Actively looking for ways to help people. **Reading Comprehension:** Understanding written sentences and paragraphs in work-related documents.

Education and Training Programs: Dentistry (DDS, DMD); Dental Clinical Sciences, General (MS, PhD); Advanced General Dentistry (Cert, MS, PhD); Oral Biology and Oral Pathology (MS, PhD); Dental Public Health and Education (Cert, MS/MPH, PhD/DPH); Dental Materials (MS, PhD); Pediatric Dentistry/Pedodontics (Cert, MS, PhD); Dental Public Health Specialty; Pedodontics Specialty. **Related Knowledge/Courses: Medicine and Dentistry:** The information and techniques needed to diagnose and treat human injuries, diseases, and deformities. This includes symptoms, treatment alternatives, drug properties and interactions, and preventive health-care measures. **Biology:** Plant and animal organisms and their tissues, cells, functions, interdependencies, and interactions with each other and the environment. **Psychology:** Human behavior and performance; individual differences in ability, personality, and interests; learning and motivation; psychological research methods; and the assessment and treatment of behavioral and affective disorders. **Personnel and Human Resources:** Principles and procedures for personnel recruitment, selection, training, compensation and benefits, labor relations and negotiation, and personnel information systems. **Chemistry:** The chemical composition, structure, and properties of substances and of the chemical processes and transformations that they undergo. This includes uses of chemicals and their danger signs, production techniques, and disposal methods. **Economics and Accounting:** Economic and accounting principles and practices, the financial markets, banking, and the analysis and reporting of financial data.

Work Environment: Indoors; contaminants; radiation; disease or infections; sitting; using hands on objects, tools, or controls.

Dietetic Technicians

- Annual Earnings: $23,470
- Growth: 19.1%
- Annual Job Openings: 3,000
- Education/Training Required: Moderate-term on-the-job training
- Self-Employed: 0.4%
- Part-Time: 23.2%

How the Job Improves the World: Contributes to health.

Assist dietitians in the provision of food service and nutritional programs. Under the supervision of dietitians, may plan and produce meals based on established guidelines, teach principles of food and nutrition, or counsel individuals. Observe patient food intake and report progress and dietary problems to dietician. Prepare a major meal, following recipes and determining group food quantities. Analyze menus and recipes, standardize recipes, and test new products. Supervise food production and service or assist dietitians and nutritionists in food service supervision and planning. Obtain and evaluate dietary histories of individuals to plan nutritional programs. Plan menus and diets or guide individuals and families in food selection, preparation, and menu planning based upon nutritional needs and established guidelines. Determine food and beverage costs and assist in implementing cost control procedures. Develop job specifications, job descriptions, and work schedules. Select, schedule, and conduct orientation and in-service education programs. Provide dietitians with assistance researching food, nutrition, and food service systems. Deliver speeches on diet, nutrition, and health to promote healthy eating habits and illness prevention and treatment. Refer patients to other relevant services to provide continuity of care.

Personality Type: Social. Social occupations frequently involve working with, communicating with, and teaching people. These occupations often involve helping or providing service to others.

GOE—Interest Area: 08. Health Science. **Work Group:** 08.09. Health Protection and Promotion. **Other Jobs in This Work Group:** Athletic Trainers; Dietitians and Nutritionists; Embalmers.

Skills—No data available.

Education and Training Programs: Foods, Nutrition, and Wellness Studies, General; Nutrition Sciences; Dietetics/Dietitian (RD); Dietetic Technician (DTR); Dietitian Assistant. **Related Knowledge/Courses: Food Production:** Techniques and equipment for planting, growing, and harvesting food products (both plant and animal) for consumption, including storage/handling techniques. **Medicine and Dentistry:** The information and techniques needed to diagnose and treat human injuries, diseases, and deformities. This includes symptoms, treatment alternatives, drug properties and interactions, and preventive health-care measures.

Work Environment: Indoors; disease or infections; minor burns, cuts, bites, or stings; standing; walking and running; repetitive motions.

Dietitians and Nutritionists

- Annual Earnings: $44,940
- Growth: 18.3%
- Annual Job Openings: 4,000
- Education/Training Required: Bachelor's degree
- Self-Employed: 3.6%
- Part-Time: 24.8%

How the Job Improves the World: Contributes to health.

Plan and conduct food service or nutritional programs to assist in the promotion of health and control of disease. May supervise activities of a department providing quantity food services, counsel individuals, or conduct nutritional research. Assess nutritional needs, diet restrictions, and current health plans to develop and implement dietary-care plans and provide nutritional counseling. Consult with physicians and health care personnel to determine nutritional needs and diet restrictions of patient or client. Advise patients and their families on nutritional principles, dietary plans and diet modifications, and food selection and preparation. Counsel individuals and groups on basic rules of good nutrition, healthy eating habits, and nutrition monitoring to improve their quality of life. Monitor food service operations to ensure conformance to nutritional, safety, sanitation, and quality standards. Coordinate recipe development and standardization and develop new menus for independent food service operations. Develop policies for food service or nutritional programs to assist in health promotion and disease control. Inspect meals served for conformance to prescribed diets and standards of palatability and appearance. Develop curriculum and prepare manuals, visual aids, course outlines, and other materials used in teaching. Prepare and administer budgets for food, equipment, and supplies. Purchase food in accordance with health and safety codes. Select, train, and supervise workers who plan, prepare, and serve meals. Manage quantity food service departments or clinical and community nutrition services. Coordinate diet counseling services. Advise food service managers and organizations on sanitation, safety procedures, menu development, budgeting, and planning to assist with the establishment, operation, and evaluation of food service facilities and nutrition programs. Organize, develop, analyze, test, and prepare special meals such as low-fat, low-cholesterol, and chemical-free meals.

Plan, conduct, and evaluate dietary, nutritional, and epidemiological research. Plan and conduct training programs in dietetics, nutrition, and institutional management and administration for medical students, health-care personnel, and the general public. Make recommendations regarding public policy, such as nutrition labeling, food fortification, and nutrition standards for school programs.

Personality Type: Investigative. Investigative occupations frequently involve working with ideas and require an extensive amount of thinking. These occupations can involve searching for facts and figuring out problems mentally.

GOE—Interest Area: 08. Health Science. **Work Group:** 08.09. Health Protection and Promotion. **Other Jobs in This Work Group:** Athletic Trainers; Dietetic Technicians; Embalmers.

Skills—Science: Using scientific rules and methods to solve problems. **Social Perceptiveness:** Being aware of others' reactions and understanding why they react as they do. **Writing:** Communicating effectively in writing as appropriate for the needs of the audience. **Instructing:** Teaching others how to do something. **Speaking:** Talking to others to convey information effectively. **Reading Comprehension:** Understanding written sentences and paragraphs in work-related documents. **Learning Strategies:** Selecting and using training/instructional methods and procedures appropriate for the situation when learning or teaching new things. **Persuasion:** Persuading others to change their minds or behavior.

Education and Training Programs: Foods, Nutrition, and Wellness Studies, General; Human Nutrition; Foodservice Systems Administration/Management; Foods, Nutrition, and Related Services, Other; Nutrition Sciences; Dietetics/Dietitian (RD); Clinical Nutrition/Nutritionist; Dietetics and Clinical Nutrition Services, Other. **Related Knowledge/Courses: Food Production:** Techniques and equipment for planting, growing, and harvesting food products (both plant and animal) for consumption, including storage/handling techniques. **Therapy and Counseling:** Principles, methods, and procedures for diagnosis, treatment, and rehabilitation of physical and mental dysfunctions and for career counseling and guidance. **Sociology and Anthropology:** Group behavior and dynamics, societal trends and influences, human migrations, ethnicity, and cultures and their history and origins. **Medicine and Dentistry:** The information and techniques needed to diagnose and treat human injuries, diseases, and deformities. This includes symptoms, treatment alternatives, drug properties and interactions, and preventive health-care measures. **Philosophy and Theology:** Different philosophical systems and religions. This includes their basic principles, values, ethics, ways of thinking, customs, and practices and their impact on human culture. **Psychology:** Human behavior and performance; individual differences in ability, personality, and interests; learning and motivation; psychological research methods; and the assessment and treatment of behavioral and affective disorders.

Work Environment: Indoors; more often sitting than standing.

Directors—Stage, Motion Pictures, Television, and Radio

◉ Annual Earnings: $53,860
◉ Growth: 16.6%
◉ Annual Job Openings: 11,000
◉ Education/Training Required: Work experience plus degree
◉ Self-Employed: 30.4%
◉ Part-Time: 8.1%

The job openings listed here are shared with Producers, Program Directors, Talent Directors, and Technical Directors/Managers.

How the Job Improves the World: Contributes to the arts.

Interpret script, conduct rehearsals, and direct activities of cast and technical crew for stage, motion pictures, television, or radio programs. Direct live broadcasts, films and recordings, or non-broadcast programming for public entertainment or education. Supervise and coordinate the work of camera, lighting, design, and sound crew members. Study and research scripts to determine how they should be directed. Cut and edit film or tape to integrate component parts into desired sequences. Collaborate with film and sound editors during the post-production process as films are edited and soundtracks are added. Confer with technical directors, managers, crew members, and writers to discuss details of production, such as photography, script, music, sets, and costumes. Plan details such as framing, composition, camera movement, sound, and actor movement for each shot or scene. Communicate to actors the approach, characterization, and movement needed for each scene in such a way that rehearsals and takes are minimized. Establish pace of programs and sequences of scenes according to time requirements and cast and set accessibility. Choose settings and locations for films and determine how scenes will be shot in these settings. Identify and approve equipment and elements required for productions, such as scenery, lights, props, costumes, choreography, and music. Compile scripts, program notes, and other material related to productions. Perform producers' duties such as securing financial backing, establishing and administering budgets, and recruiting cast and crew. Select plays or scripts for production and determine how material should be interpreted and performed. Compile cue words and phrases; cue announcers, cast members, and technicians during performances. Consult with writers, producers, or actors about script changes or "workshop" scripts, through rehearsal with writers and actors, to create final drafts. Collaborate with producers to hire crew members such as art directors, cinematographers, and costumer designers. Review film daily to check on work in progress and to plan for future filming. Interpret stage-set diagrams to determine stage layouts and supervise placement of equipment and scenery. Hold auditions for parts or negotiate contracts with actors determined suitable for specific roles, working in conjunction with producers.

Personality Type: Artistic. Artistic occupations frequently involve working with forms, designs, and patterns. They often require self-expression, and the work can be done without following a clear set of rules.

GOE—Interest Area: 03. Arts and Communication. **Work Group:** 03.06. Drama. **Other Jobs in This Work Group:** Actors; Costume Attendants; Makeup Artists, Theatrical and Performance; Public Address System and Other Announcers; Radio and Television Announcers.

Skills—Management of Personnel Resources: Motivating, developing, and directing people as they work; identifying the best people for the job. **Time Management:** Managing one's own time and the time of others. **Judgment and Decision Making:** Considering the relative costs and benefits of potential actions to choose the most appropriate one. **Operations Analysis:** Analyzing needs and product requirements to create a design. **Active Listening:** Giving full attention to what other people are saying, taking time to understand the points being made, asking questions as appropriate, and not interrupting at inappropriate times. **Speaking:** Talking to others to convey information effectively. **Critical Thinking:** Using logic and reasoning to identify the strengths and weaknesses of alternative solutions, conclusions, or approaches to problems. **Equipment Selection:** Determining the kind of tools and equipment needed to do a job.

Education and Training Programs: Radio and Television; Drama and Dramatics/Theatre Arts, General; Directing and Theatrical Production; Theatre/Theatre Arts Management; Dramatic/Theatre Arts and Stagecraft, Other; Film/Cinema Studies; Cinematography and Film/Video Production. **Related Knowledge/Courses: Communications and Media:** Media production, communication, and dissemination techniques and methods. This includes alternative ways to inform and entertain via written, oral, and visual media. **Telecommunications:** Transmission, broadcasting, switching, control, and operation of telecommunications systems. **Fine Arts:** The theory and techniques required to compose, produce, and perform works of music, dance, visual art, drama, and sculpture. **Geography:** Principles and methods for describing the features of land, sea, and air masses, including their physical characteristics; locations; interrelationships; and distribution of plant, animal, and human life. **Computers and Electronics:** Circuit boards; processors; chips; electronic equipment; and computer hardware and software, including applications and programming. **Education and Training:** Principles and methods for curriculum and training design, teaching and instruction for individuals and groups, and the measurement of training effects.

Work Environment: More often indoors than outdoors; noisy; sitting; using hands on objects, tools, or controls.

Directors, Religious Activities and Education

- ◎ Annual Earnings: $32,540
- ◎ Growth: 18.5%
- ◎ Annual Job Openings: 10,000
- ◎ Education/Training Required: Bachelor's degree
- ◎ Self-Employed: 0.0%
- ◎ Part-Time: 27.9%

How the Job Improves the World: Contributes to spiritual well-being and education.

Direct and coordinate activities of a denominational group to meet religious needs of students. Plan, direct, or coordinate church school programs designed to promote religious education among church membership. May provide counseling and guidance relative to marital, health, financial, and religious problems. Select appropriate curricula and class structures for educational programs. Attend workshops, seminars, and conferences to obtain program ideas, information, and resources. Train and supervise religious education instructional staff. Analyze revenue and program cost data to determine budget priorities. Counsel individuals regarding interpersonal, health, financial, and religious problems. Participate in denominational activities aimed at goals such as promoting interfaith understanding or providing aid to new or small congregations. Plan and conduct conferences dealing with the interpretation of religious ideas and convictions. Visit congregation members' homes, or arrange for pastoral visits, to provide information and resources regarding religious education programs. Locate and distribute resources such as periodicals and curricula to enhance the effectiveness of educational programs. Schedule special events such as camps, conferences, meetings, seminars, and retreats. Interpret religious education activities to the public through speaking, leading discussions, and writing articles for local and national publications. Publicize programs through sources such as newsletters, bulletins, and mailings. Implement program plans by ordering needed materials, scheduling speakers, reserving space, and handling other administrative details. Identify and recruit potential volunteer workers. Develop and direct study courses and religious education programs within congregations. Confer with clergy members, congregation officials, and congregation organizations to encourage support of and participation in religious education activities. Collaborate with other ministry members to establish goals and objectives for religious education programs and to develop ways to encourage program participation. Analyze member participation and changes in congregation emphasis to determine needs for religious education.

Personality Type: Social. Social occupations frequently involve working with, communicating with, and teaching people. These occupations often involve helping or providing service to others.

GOE—Interest Area: 10. Human Service. **Work Group:** 10.02. Religious Work. **Other Jobs in This Work Group:** Clergy.

Skills—Management of Financial Resources: Determining how money will be spent to get the work done and accounting for these expenditures. **Management of Personnel Resources:** Motivating, developing, and directing people as they work; identifying the best people for the job. **Social Perceptiveness:** Being aware of others' reactions and understanding why they react as they do. **Systems Analysis:** Determining how a system should work and how changes in conditions, operations, and the environment will affect outcomes. **Management of Material Resources:** Obtaining and seeing to the appropriate use of equipment, facilities, and materials needed to do certain work. **Service Orientation:** Actively looking for ways to help people. **Systems Evaluation:** Identifying measures or indicators of system performance and the actions needed to improve or correct performance relative to the goals of the system. **Writing:** Communicating effectively in writing as appropriate for the needs of the audience.

Education and Training Programs: Bible/Biblical Studies; Missions/Missionary Studies and Missiology; Religious Education; Youth Ministry. **Related Knowledge/Courses: Therapy and Counseling:** Principles, methods, and procedures for diagnosis, treatment, and rehabilitation of physical and mental dysfunctions and for career counseling and guidance. **Philosophy and Theology:** Different philosophical systems and religions. This includes their basic principles, values, ethics, ways of thinking, customs, and practices and their impact on human culture. **Sociology and Anthropology:** Group behavior and dynamics, societal trends and influences, human migrations, ethnicity, and cultures and their history and origins. **Economics and Accounting:** Economic and accounting principles and practices, the financial markets, banking, and the analysis and reporting of financial data. **Administration and Management:** Business and management principles involved in strategic planning, resource allocation, human resources modeling, leadership techniques, production methods, and coordination of people and resources. **Psychology:** Human behavior and performance; individual differences in ability, personality, and interests; learning and motivation; psychological research methods; and the assessment and treatment of behavioral and affective disorders.

Work Environment: Indoors; sitting.

Economics Teachers, Postsecondary

- Annual Earnings: $68,910
- Growth: 32.2%
- Annual Job Openings: 329,000
- Education/Training Required: Master's degree
- Self-Employed: 0.4%
- Part-Time: 27.3%

The job openings listed here are shared with 35 other postsecondary teaching occupations. For a complete list, see the beginning of this section.

How the Job Improves the World: Contributes to education.

Teach courses in economics. Prepare and deliver lectures to undergraduate and/or graduate students on topics such as econometrics, price theory, and macroeconomics. Prepare course materials such as syllabi, homework assignments, and handouts. Evaluate and grade students' classwork, assignments, and papers. Compile, administer, and grade examinations or assign this work to others. Keep abreast of developments in their field by reading current literature, talking with colleagues, and participating in professional conferences. Maintain student attendance records, grades, and other required records. Initiate, facilitate, and moderate classroom discussions. Maintain regularly scheduled office hours in order to advise and assist students. Select and obtain materials and supplies such as textbooks. Plan, evaluate, and revise curricula, course content, and course materials and methods of instruction. Conduct research in a particular field of knowledge and publish findings in professional journals, books, and/or electronic media. Supervise undergraduate and/or graduate teaching, internship, and research work. Advise students on academic and vocational curricula and on career issues. Serve on academic or administrative committees that deal with institutional policies, departmental matters, and academic issues. Collaborate with colleagues to address teaching and research issues. Compile bibliographies of specialized materials for outside reading assignments. Participate in student recruitment, registration, and placement activities. Perform administrative duties such as serving as department head. Write grant proposals to procure external research funding. Participate in campus and community events. Provide professional consulting services to government and/or industry. Act as advisers to student organizations.

Personality Type: Social. Social occupations frequently involve working with, communicating with, and teaching people. These occupations often involve helping or providing service to others.

GOE—Interest Area: 05. Education and Training. **Work Group:** 05.03. Postsecondary and Adult Teaching and Instructing. **Other Jobs in This Work Group:** Adult Literacy, Remedial Education, and GED Teachers and Instructors; Agricultural Sciences Teachers, Postsecondary; Anthropology and Archeology Teachers, Postsecondary; Architecture Teachers, Postsecondary; Area, Ethnic, and Cultural Studies Teachers, Postsecondary; Art, Drama, and Music Teachers, Postsecondary; Atmospheric, Earth, Marine, and Space Sciences Teachers, Postsecondary; Biological Science Teachers, Postsecondary; Business Teachers, Postsecondary; Chemistry Teachers, Postsecondary; Communications Teachers, Postsecondary; Computer Science Teachers, Postsecondary; Criminal Justice and Law Enforcement Teachers, Postsecondary; Education Teachers, Postsecondary; Engineering Teachers, Postsecondary; English Language and Literature Teachers, Postsecondary; Environmental Science Teachers, Postsecondary; Farm and Home Management Advisors; Foreign Language and Literature Teachers, Postsecondary; Forestry and Conservation Science Teachers, Postsecondary; Geography Teachers, Postsecondary; Graduate Teaching Assistants; Health Specialties Teachers,

Postsecondary; History Teachers, Postsecondary; Home Economics Teachers, Postsecondary; Law Teachers, Postsecondary; Library Science Teachers, Postsecondary; Mathematical Science Teachers, Postsecondary; Nursing Instructors and Teachers, Postsecondary; Philosophy and Religion Teachers, Postsecondary; Physics Teachers, Postsecondary; Political Science Teachers, Postsecondary; Psychology Teachers, Postsecondary; Recreation and Fitness Studies Teachers, Postsecondary; Self-Enrichment Education Teachers; Social Work Teachers, Postsecondary; Sociology Teachers, Postsecondary; Vocational Education Teachers, Postsecondary.

Skills—Mathematics: Using mathematics to solve problems. **Writing:** Communicating effectively in writing as appropriate for the needs of the audience. **Instructing:** Teaching others how to do something. **Speaking:** Talking to others to convey information effectively. **Reading Comprehension:** Understanding written sentences and paragraphs in work-related documents. **Critical Thinking:** Using logic and reasoning to identify the strengths and weaknesses of alternative solutions, conclusions, or approaches to problems. **Learning Strategies:** Selecting and using training/instructional methods and procedures appropriate for the situation when learning or teaching new things. **Active Learning:** Understanding the implications of new information for both current and future problem-solving and decision-making.

Education and Training Programs: Social Science Teacher Education; Economics, General; Applied Economics; Econometrics and Quantitative Economics; Development Economics and International Development; International Economics; Economics, Other; Business/Managerial Economics. **Related Knowledge/Courses: Economics and Accounting:** Economic and accounting principles and practices, the financial markets, banking, and the analysis and reporting of financial data. **History and Archeology:** Historical events and their causes, indicators, and effects on civilizations and cultures. **Mathematics:**

Arithmetic, algebra, geometry, calculus, and statistics and their applications. **Education and Training:** Principles and methods for curriculum and training design, teaching and instruction for individuals and groups, and the measurement of training effects. **Philosophy and Theology:** Different philosophical systems and religions. This includes their basic principles, values, ethics, ways of thinking, customs, and practices and their impact on human culture. **English Language:** The structure and content of the English language, including the meaning and spelling of words, rules of composition, and grammar.

Work Environment: Indoors; sitting.

Education Administrators, Elementary and Secondary School

- Annual Earnings: $75,400
- Growth: 10.4%
- Annual Job Openings: 27,000
- Education/Training Required: Work experience plus degree
- Self-Employed: 3.6%
- Part-Time: 9.3%

How the Job Improves the World: Contributes to education.

Plan, direct, or coordinate the academic, clerical, or auxiliary activities of public or private elementary or secondary-level schools. Review and approve new programs or recommend modifications to existing programs, submitting program proposals for school board approval as necessary. Prepare, maintain, or oversee the preparation and maintenance of attendance, activity, planning, or personnel reports and records. Confer with parents and staff to discuss educational activities, policies, and student behavioral or learning problems. Prepare and submit budget requests and recommendations or grant proposals to solicit program funding. Direct and coordinate school maintenance services and the use of school facilities. Counsel and provide guidance to students regarding personal, academic, vocational, or behavioral issues. Organize and direct committees of specialists, volunteers, and staff to provide technical and advisory assistance for programs. Teach classes or courses to students. Advocate for new schools to be built or for existing facilities to be repaired or remodeled. Plan and develop instructional methods and content for educational, vocational, or student activity programs. Develop partnerships with businesses, communities, and other organizations to help meet identified educational needs and to provide school-to-work programs. Direct and coordinate activities of teachers, administrators, and support staff at schools, public agencies, and institutions. Evaluate curricula, teaching methods, and programs to determine their effectiveness, efficiency, and utilization and to ensure that school activities comply with federal, state, and local regulations. Set educational standards and goals and help establish policies and procedures to carry them out. Recruit, hire, train, and evaluate primary and supplemental staff. Enforce discipline and attendance rules. Observe teaching methods and examine learning materials to evaluate and standardize curricula and teaching techniques and to determine areas where improvement is needed. Establish, coordinate, and oversee particular programs across school districts, such as programs to evaluate student academic achievement. Review and interpret government codes and develop programs to ensure adherence to codes and facility safety, security, and maintenance.

Personality Type: Social. Social occupations frequently involve working with, communicating with, and teaching people. These occupations often involve helping or providing service to others.

GOE—Interest Area: 05. Education and Training.

Work Group: 05.01. Managerial Work in Education. **Other Jobs in This Work Group:** Education Administrators, Postsecondary; Education Administrators, Preschool and Child Care Center/Program; Instructional Coordinators.

Skills—Management of Personnel Resources: Motivating, developing, and directing people as they work; identifying the best people for the job. **Management of Financial Resources:** Determining how money will be spent to get the work done and accounting for these expenditures. **Negotiation:** Bringing others together and trying to reconcile differences. **Learning Strategies:** Selecting and using training/instructional methods and procedures appropriate for the situation when learning or teaching new things. **Social Perceptiveness:** Being aware of others' reactions and understanding why they react as they do. **Monitoring:** Monitoring/assessing your performance or that of other individuals or organizations to make improvements or take corrective action. **Management of Material Resources:** Obtaining and seeing to the appropriate use of equipment, facilities, and materials needed to do certain work. **Systems Evaluation:** Identifying measures or indicators of system performance and the actions needed to improve or correct performance relative to the goals of the system.

Education and Training Programs: Educational Leadership and Administration, General; Educational, Instructional, and Curriculum Supervision; Elementary and Middle School Administration/Principalship; Secondary School Administration/Principalship; Educational Administration and Supervision, Other. **Related Knowledge/Courses: Education and Training:** Principles and methods for curriculum and training design, teaching and instruction for individuals and groups, and the measurement of training effects. **Therapy and Counseling:** Principles, methods, and procedures for diagnosis, treatment, and rehabilitation of physical and mental dysfunctions and for career counseling and guidance.

Personnel and Human Resources: Principles and procedures for personnel recruitment, selection, training, compensation and benefits, labor relations and negotiation, and personnel information systems. **Psychology:** Human behavior and performance; individual differences in ability, personality, and interests; learning and motivation; psychological research methods; and the assessment and treatment of behavioral and affective disorders. **Sociology and Anthropology:** Group behavior and dynamics, societal trends and influences, human migrations, ethnicity, and cultures and their history and origins. **History and Archeology:** Historical events and their causes, indicators, and effects on civilizations and cultures.

Work Environment: Indoors; standing.

Education Administrators, Postsecondary

- Annual Earnings: $70,350
- Growth: 21.3%
- Annual Job Openings: 18,000
- Education/Training Required: Work experience plus degree
- Self-Employed: 3.3%
- Part-Time: 9.3%

How the Job Improves the World: Contributes to education.

Plan, direct, or coordinate research, instructional, student administration and services, and other educational activities at postsecondary institutions, including universities, colleges, and junior and community colleges. Recruit, hire, train, and terminate departmental personnel. Plan, administer, and control budgets; maintain financial records; and produce financial reports. Represent institutions at community and campus events, in meetings with other institution personnel, and during accreditation

processes. Participate in faculty and college committee activities. Provide assistance to faculty and staff in duties such as teaching classes, conducting orientation programs, issuing transcripts, and scheduling events. Establish operational policies and procedures and make any necessary modifications, based on analysis of operations, demographics, and other research information. Confer with other academic staff to explain and formulate admission requirements and course credit policies. Appoint individuals to faculty positions and evaluate their performance. Direct activities of administrative departments such as admissions, registration, and career services. Develop curricula and recommend curricula revisions and additions. Determine course schedules and coordinate teaching assignments and room assignments to ensure optimum use of buildings and equipment. Consult with government regulatory and licensing agencies to ensure the institution's conformance with applicable standards. Direct, coordinate, and evaluate the activities of personnel engaged in administering academic institutions, departments, and/or alumni organizations. Teach courses within their department. Participate in student recruitment, selection, and admission, making admissions recommendations when required to do so. Review student misconduct reports requiring disciplinary action and counsel students regarding such reports. Supervise coaches. Assess and collect tuition and fees. Direct scholarship, fellowship, and loan programs, performing activities such as selecting recipients and distributing aid. Coordinate the production and dissemination of university publications such as course catalogs and class schedules. Review registration statistics and consult with faculty officials to develop registration policies. Audit the financial status of student organizations and facility accounts.

Personality Type: Enterprising. Enterprising occupations frequently involve starting up and carrying out projects. These occupations can involve leading people and making many decisions. They sometimes require risk taking and often deal with business.

GOE—Interest Area: 05. Education and Training. **Work Group:** 05.01. Managerial Work in Education. **Other Jobs in This Work Group:** Education Administrators, Elementary and Secondary School; Education Administrators, Preschool and Child Care Center/Program; Instructional Coordinators.

Skills—Management of Financial Resources: Determining how money will be spent to get the work done and accounting for these expenditures. **Management of Personnel Resources:** Motivating, developing, and directing people as they work; identifying the best people for the job. **Systems Evaluation:** Identifying measures or indicators of system performance and the actions needed to improve or correct performance relative to the goals of the system. **Persuasion:** Persuading others to change their minds or behavior. **Monitoring:** Monitoring/assessing your performance or that of other individuals or organizations to make improvements or take corrective action. **Judgment and Decision Making:** Considering the relative costs and benefits of potential actions to choose the most appropriate one. **Management of Material Resources:** Obtaining and seeing to the appropriate use of equipment, facilities, and materials needed to do certain work. **Social Perceptiveness:** Being aware of others' reactions and understanding why they react as they do.

Education and Training Programs: Educational Leadership and Administration, General; Educational, Instructional, and Curriculum Supervision; Higher Education/Higher Education Administration; Community College Education; Educational Administration and Supervision, Other. **Related Knowledge/Courses: Education and Training:** Principles and methods for curriculum and training design, teaching and instruction for individuals and groups, and the measurement of training effects. **Personnel and Human Resources:** Principles and procedures for personnel recruitment, selection, training, compensation and benefits, labor relations and negotiation, and personnel information systems.

Sociology and Anthropology: Group behavior and dynamics, societal trends and influences, human migrations, ethnicity, and cultures and their history and origins. **Administration and Management:** Business and management principles involved in strategic planning, resource allocation, human resources modeling, leadership techniques, production methods, and coordination of people and resources. **Sales and Marketing:** Principles and methods for showing, promoting, and selling products or services. This includes marketing strategy and tactics, product demonstration, sales techniques, and sales control systems. **English Language:** The structure and content of the English language, including the meaning and spelling of words, rules of composition, and grammar.

Work Environment: Indoors; sitting.

Education Administrators, Preschool and Child Care Center/Program

- ◎ Annual Earnings: $37,010
- ◎ Growth: 27.9%
- ◎ Annual Job Openings: 9,000
- ◎ Education/Training Required: Work experience plus degree
- ◎ Self-Employed: 3.2%
- ◎ Part-Time: 9.3%

How the Job Improves the World: Contributes to education.

Plan, direct, or coordinate the academic and nonacademic activities of preschool and child care centers or programs. Confer with parents and staff to discuss educational activities and policies and students' behavioral or learning problems. Prepare and maintain attendance, activity, planning, accounting, or personnel reports and records for officials and agencies or direct preparation and maintenance activities. Set educational standards and goals and help establish policies, procedures, and programs to carry them out. Monitor students' progress and provide students and teachers with assistance in resolving any problems. Determine allocations of funds for staff, supplies, materials, and equipment and authorize purchases. Recruit, hire, train, and evaluate primary and supplemental staff and recommend personnel actions for programs and services. Direct and coordinate activities of teachers or administrators at daycare centers, schools, public agencies, or institutions. Plan, direct, and monitor instructional methods and content of educational, vocational, or student activity programs. Review and interpret government codes and develop procedures to meet codes and to ensure facility safety, security, and maintenance. Determine the scope of educational program offerings and prepare drafts of program schedules and descriptions to estimate staffing and facility requirements. Review and evaluate new and current programs to determine their efficiency; effectiveness; and compliance with state, local, and federal regulations, and recommend any necessary modifications. Teach classes or courses or provide direct care to children. Prepare and submit budget requests or grant proposals to solicit program funding. Write articles, manuals, and other publications and assist in the distribution of promotional literature about programs and facilities. Collect and analyze survey data, regulatory information, and demographic and employment trends to forecast enrollment patterns and the need for curriculum changes. Inform businesses, community groups, and governmental agencies about educational needs, available programs, and program policies. Organize and direct committees of specialists, volunteers, and staff to provide technical and advisory assistance for programs.

Personality Type: Social. Social occupations frequently involve working with, communicating with, and teaching people. These occupations often involve helping or providing service to others.

GOE—Interest Area: 05. Education and Training. **Work Group:** 05.01. Managerial Work in Education. **Other Jobs in This Work Group:** Education Administrators, Elementary and Secondary School; Education Administrators, Postsecondary; Instructional Coordinators.

Skills—Management of Financial Resources: Determining how money will be spent to get the work done and accounting for these expenditures. **Management of Personnel Resources:** Motivating, developing, and directing people as they work; identifying the best people for the job. **Learning Strategies:** Selecting and using training/instructional methods and procedures appropriate for the situation when learning or teaching new things. **Management of Material Resources:** Obtaining and seeing to the appropriate use of equipment, facilities, and materials needed to do certain work. **Social Perceptiveness:** Being aware of others' reactions and understanding why they react as they do. **Monitoring:** Monitoring/assessing your performance or that of other individuals or organizations to make improvements or take corrective action. **Negotiation:** Bringing others together and trying to reconcile differences. **Persuasion:** Persuading others to change their minds or behavior.

Education and Training Programs: Educational Leadership and Administration, General; Educational, Instructional, and Curriculum Supervision; Elementary and Middle School Administration/Principalship; Educational Administration and Supervision, Other. **Related Knowledge/Courses: Personnel and Human Resources:** Principles and procedures for personnel recruitment, selection, training, compensation and benefits, labor relations and negotiation, and personnel information systems. **Education and Training:** Principles and methods for curriculum and training design, teaching and instruction for individuals and groups, and the measurement of training effects. **Clerical Practices:** Administrative and clerical procedures and systems such as word processing, managing files and records, stenography and transcription, designing forms, and other office procedures and terminology. **Philosophy and Theology:** Different philosophical systems and religions. This includes their basic principles, values, ethics, ways of thinking, customs, and practices and their impact on human culture. **Therapy and Counseling:** Principles, methods, and procedures for diagnosis, treatment, and rehabilitation of physical and mental dysfunctions and for career counseling and guidance. **Sociology and Anthropology:** Group behavior and dynamics, societal trends and influences, human migrations, ethnicity, and cultures and their history and origins.

Work Environment: Indoors; standing.

Education Teachers, Postsecondary

- Annual Earnings: $50,380
- Growth: 32.2%
- Annual Job Openings: 329,000
- Education/Training Required: Master's degree
- Self-Employed: 0.4%
- Part-Time: 27.3%

The job openings listed here are shared with 35 other postsecondary teaching occupations. For a complete list, see the beginning of this section.

How the Job Improves the World: Contributes to education.

Teach courses pertaining to education, such as counseling, curriculum, guidance, instruction, teacher education, and teaching English as a second language. Prepare course materials such as syllabi, homework assignments, and handouts. Prepare and deliver lectures to undergraduate and/or graduate students on topics such as children's literature, learning and development, and reading instruction. Initiate, facilitate, and moderate classroom discussions. Evaluate and grade students' classwork, assignments, and papers. Plan, evaluate, and revise curricula, course content, and course materials and methods of instruction. Supervise students' fieldwork, internship, and research work. Keep abreast of developments in their field by reading current literature, talking with colleagues, and participating in professional conferences. Advise students on academic and vocational curricula and on career issues. Maintain regularly scheduled office hours to advise and assist students. Maintain student attendance records, grades, and other required records. Collaborate with colleagues to address teaching and research issues. Compile, administer, and grade examinations or assign this work to others. Conduct research in a particular field of knowledge and publish findings in professional journals, books, or electronic media. Select and obtain materials and supplies such as textbooks. Participate in student recruitment, registration, and placement activities. Advise and instruct teachers employed in school systems by providing activities such as in-service seminars. Serve on academic or administrative committees that deal with institutional policies, departmental matters, and academic issues. Compile bibliographies of specialized materials for outside reading assignments. Write grant proposals to procure external research funding. Participate in campus and community events. Perform administrative duties such as serving as department head. Act as advisers to student organizations. Provide professional consulting services to government and/or industry.

Personality Type: No data available.

GOE—Interest Area: 05. Education and Training. **Work Group:** 05.03. Postsecondary and Adult Teaching and Instructing. **Other Jobs in This Work Group:** Adult Literacy, Remedial Education, and GED Teachers and Instructors; Agricultural Sciences Teachers, Postsecondary; Anthropology and Archeology Teachers, Postsecondary; Architecture Teachers, Postsecondary; Area, Ethnic, and Cultural Studies Teachers, Postsecondary; Art, Drama, and Music Teachers, Postsecondary; Atmospheric, Earth, Marine, and Space Sciences Teachers, Postsecondary; Biological Science Teachers, Postsecondary; Business Teachers, Postsecondary; Chemistry Teachers, Postsecondary; Communications Teachers, Postsecondary; Computer Science Teachers, Postsecondary; Criminal Justice and Law Enforcement Teachers, Postsecondary; Economics Teachers, Postsecondary; Engineering Teachers, Postsecondary; English Language and Literature Teachers, Postsecondary; Environmental Science Teachers, Postsecondary; Farm and Home Management Advisors; Foreign Language and Literature Teachers, Postsecondary; Forestry and Conservation Science Teachers, Postsecondary; Geography Teachers, Postsecondary; Graduate Teaching Assistants; Health Specialties Teachers, Postsecondary; History Teachers, Postsecondary; Home Economics Teachers, Postsecondary; Law Teachers, Postsecondary; Library Science Teachers, Postsecondary; Mathematical Science Teachers, Postsecondary; Nursing Instructors and Teachers, Postsecondary; Philosophy and Religion Teachers, Postsecondary; Physics Teachers, Postsecondary; Political Science Teachers, Postsecondary; Psychology Teachers, Postsecondary; Recreation and Fitness Studies Teachers, Postsecondary; Self-Enrichment Education Teachers; Social Work Teachers, Postsecondary; Sociology Teachers, Postsecondary; Vocational Education Teachers, Postsecondary.

Skills—Instructing: Teaching others how to do something. **Learning Strategies:** Selecting and using training/instructional methods and procedures appropriate for the situation when learning or teaching new things. **Writing:** Communicating effectively in writing as appropriate for the needs of the audience. **Social Perceptiveness:** Being aware of others' reactions and understanding why they react as they do. **Persuasion:** Persuading others to change their minds or behavior.

Speaking: Talking to others to convey information effectively. **Monitoring:** Monitoring/assessing your performance or that of other individuals or organizations to make improvements or take corrective action. **Active Learning:** Understanding the implications of new information for both current and future problem-solving and decision-making.

Education and Training Programs: Education, General; Indian/Native American Education; Social and Philosophical Foundations of Education; Agricultural Teacher Education; Art Teacher Education; Business Teacher Education; Driver and Safety Teacher Education; English/Language Arts Teacher Education; Foreign Language Teacher Education; Health Teacher Education; Family and Consumer Sciences/Home Economics Teacher Education; others. **Related Knowledge/Courses: Education and Training:** Principles and methods for curriculum and training design, teaching and instruction for individuals and groups, and the measurement of training effects. **Therapy and Counseling:** Principles, methods, and procedures for diagnosis, treatment, and rehabilitation of physical and mental dysfunctions and for career counseling and guidance. **Sociology and Anthropology:** Group behavior and dynamics, societal trends and influences, human migrations, ethnicity, and cultures and their history and origins. **Philosophy and Theology:** Different philosophical systems and religions. This includes their basic principles, values, ethics, ways of thinking, customs, and practices and their impact on human culture. **Psychology:** Human behavior and performance; individual differences in ability, personality, and interests; learning and motivation; psychological research methods; and the assessment and treatment of behavioral and affective disorders. **English Language:** The structure and content of the English language, including the meaning and spelling of words, rules of composition, and grammar.

Work Environment: Indoors; sitting.

Educational, Vocational, and School Counselors

- Annual Earnings: $46,440
- Growth: 14.8%
- Annual Job Openings: 32,000
- Education/Training Required: Master's degree
- Self-Employed: 5.8%
- Part-Time: 16.7%

How the Job Improves the World: Contributes to education and mental health.

Counsel individuals and provide group educational and vocational guidance services. Counsel students regarding educational issues such as course and program selection, class scheduling, school adjustment, truancy, study habits, and career planning. Counsel individuals to help them understand and overcome personal, social, or behavioral problems affecting their educational or vocational situations. Maintain accurate and complete student records as required by laws, district policies, and administrative regulations. Confer with parents or guardians, teachers, other counselors, and administrators to resolve students' behavioral, academic, and other problems. Provide crisis intervention to students when difficult situations occur at schools. Identify cases involving domestic abuse or other family problems affecting students' development. Meet with parents and guardians to discuss their children's progress and to determine their priorities for their children and their resource needs. Prepare students for later educational experiences by encouraging them to explore learning opportunities and to persevere with challenging tasks. Encourage students and/or parents to seek additional assistance from mental health professionals when necessary. Observe and evaluate students' performance, behavior, social development, and physical health. Enforce all administration policies and rules governing students. Meet with other professionals to discuss individual students' needs and progress. Provide students with information on such topics as college degree programs and admission requirements, financial aid opportunities, trade and technical schools, and apprenticeship programs. Evaluate individuals' abilities, interests, and personality characteristics, using tests, records, interviews, and professional sources. Collaborate with teachers and administrators in the development, evaluation, and revision of school programs. Establish and enforce behavioral rules and procedures to maintain order among students. Teach classes and present self-help or information sessions on subjects related to education and career planning. Attend professional meetings, educational conferences, and teacher training workshops to maintain and improve professional competence.

Personality Type: Social. Social occupations frequently involve working with, communicating with, and teaching people. These occupations often involve helping or providing service to others.

GOE—Interest Area: 05. Education and Training. **Work Group:** 05.06. Counseling, Health, and Fitness Education. **Other Jobs in This Work Group:** Fitness Trainers and Aerobics Instructors; Health Educators.

Skills—Social Perceptiveness: Being aware of others' reactions and understanding why they react as they do. **Service Orientation:** Actively looking for ways to help people. **Negotiation:** Bringing others together and trying to reconcile differences. **Persuasion:** Persuading others to change their minds or behavior. **Active Listening:** Giving full attention to what other people are saying, taking time to understand the points being made, asking questions as appropriate, and not interrupting at inappropriate times. **Learning Strategies:** Selecting and using training/instructional methods and procedures appropriate for the situation when learning or teaching new things. **Monitoring:** Monitoring/assessing your performance or that of other individuals or organizations to make improvements or take corrective action. **Writing:** Communicating effectively in writing as appropriate for the needs of the audience.

Education and Training Programs: Counselor Education/School Counseling and Guidance Services; College Student Counseling and Personnel Services. **Related Knowledge/Courses: Therapy and Counseling:** Principles, methods, and procedures for diagnosis, treatment, and rehabilitation of physical and mental dysfunctions and for career counseling and guidance. **Psychology:** Human behavior and performance; individual differences in ability, personality, and interests; learning and motivation; psychological research methods; and the assessment and treatment of behavioral and affective disorders. **Sociology and Anthropology:** Group behavior and dynamics, societal trends and influences, human migrations, ethnicity, and cultures and their history and origins. **Education and Training:** Principles and methods for curriculum and training design, teaching and instruction for individuals and groups, and the measurement of training effects. **Philosophy and Theology:** Different philosophical systems and religions. This includes their basic principles, values, ethics, ways of thinking, customs, and practices and their impact on human culture. **Clerical Practices:** Administrative and clerical procedures and systems such as word processing, managing files and records, stenography and transcription, designing forms, and other office procedures and terminology.

Work Environment: Indoors; sitting.

Elementary School Teachers, Except Special Education

- Annual Earnings: $44,040
- Growth: 18.2%
- Annual Job Openings: 203,000
- Education/Training Required: Bachelor's degree
- Self-Employed: 0.0%
- Part-Time: 12.6%

How the Job Improves the World: Contributes to education.

Teach pupils in public or private schools at the elementary level basic academic, social, and other formative skills. Establish and enforce rules for behavior and procedures for maintaining order among the students for whom they are responsible. Observe and evaluate students' performance, behavior, social development, and physical health. Prepare materials and classrooms for class activities. Adapt teaching methods and instructional materials to meet students' varying needs and interests. Plan and conduct activities for a balanced program of instruction, demonstration, and work time that provides students with opportunities to observe, question, and investigate. Instruct students individually and in groups, using various teaching methods such as lectures, discussions, and demonstrations. Establish clear objectives for all lessons, units, and projects and communicate those objectives to students. Assign and grade classwork and homework. Read books to entire classes or small groups. Prepare, administer, and grade tests and assignments in order to evaluate students' progress. Confer with parents or guardians, teachers, counselors, and administrators to resolve students' behavioral and academic problems. Meet with parents and guardians to discuss their children's progress and to determine their priorities for their children and their resource needs. Prepare students for later grades by encouraging them to explore learning opportunities and to persevere with challenging tasks. Maintain accurate and complete student records as required by laws, district policies, and administrative regulations. Guide and counsel students with adjustment or academic problems or special academic interests. Prepare and implement remedial programs for students requiring extra help. Prepare objectives and outlines for courses of study, following curriculum guidelines or requirements of states and schools. Provide a variety of materials and resources for children to explore, manipulate, and use, both in learning activities and in imaginative play. Enforce administration policies and rules governing students. Confer with other staff members to plan and schedule lessons promoting learning, following approved curricula.

Personality Type: Social. Social occupations frequently involve working with, communicating with, and teaching people. These occupations often involve helping or providing service to others.

GOE—Interest Area: 05. Education and Training. **Work Group:** 05.02. Preschool, Elementary, and Secondary Teaching and Instructing. **Other Jobs in This Work Group:** Kindergarten Teachers, Except Special Education; Middle School Teachers, Except Special and Vocational Education; Preschool Teachers, Except Special Education; Secondary School Teachers, Except Special and Vocational Education; Special Education Teachers, Middle School; Special Education Teachers, Preschool, Kindergarten, and Elementary School; Special Education Teachers, Secondary School; Teacher Assistants; Vocational Education Teachers, Middle School; Vocational Education Teachers, Secondary School.

Skills—Instructing: Teaching others how to do something. **Learning Strategies:** Selecting and using training/instructional methods and procedures appropriate for the situation when learning or teaching new things. **Monitoring:** Monitoring/assessing your performance or that of other individuals or organizations to make improvements or take corrective action. **Social Perceptiveness:** Being aware of others' reactions and understanding why they react as they do. **Persuasion:** Persuading others to change their minds or behavior. **Speaking:** Talking to others to convey information effectively. **Service Orientation:** Actively looking for ways to help people. **Time Management:** Managing one's own time and the time of others.

Education and Training Programs: Elementary Education and Teaching; Teacher Education, Multiple Levels; Montessori Teacher Education. **Related Knowledge/Courses: Geography:** Principles and methods for describing the features of land, sea, and air masses, including their physical characteristics; locations; interrelationships; and distribution of plant, animal, and human life. **History and Archeology:** Historical events and their causes, indicators, and effects on civilizations and cultures. **Sociology and Anthropology:** Group behavior and dynamics, societal trends and influences, human migrations, ethnicity, and cultures and their history and origins. **Education and Training:** Principles and methods for curriculum and training design, teaching and instruction for individuals and groups, and the measurement of training effects. **Therapy and Counseling:** Principles, methods, and procedures for diagnosis, treatment, and rehabilitation of physical and mental dysfunctions and for career counseling and guidance. **Philosophy and Theology:** Different philosophical systems and religions. This includes their basic principles, values, ethics, ways of thinking, customs, and practices and their impact on human culture.

Work Environment: Indoors; noisy; disease or infections; standing.

Eligibility Interviewers, Government Programs

- Annual Earnings: $33,740
- Growth: –9.4%
- Annual Job Openings: 10,000
- Education/Training Required: Moderate-term on-the-job training
- Self-Employed: 0.2%
- Part-Time: 5.4%

How the Job Improves the World: Contributes to social well-being.

Determine eligibility of persons applying to receive assistance from government programs and agency resources, such as welfare, unemployment benefits, social security, and public housing. Answer applicants' questions about benefits and claim procedures. Interview benefits recipients at specified intervals to certify their eligibility for continuing benefits. Interpret and explain information such as eligibility requirements, application details, payment methods, and applicants' legal rights. Initiate procedures to grant, modify, deny, or terminate assistance or refer applicants to other agencies for assistance. Compile, record, and evaluate personal and financial data to verify completeness and accuracy and to determine eligibility status. Interview and investigate applicants for public assistance to gather information pertinent to their applications. Check with employers or other references to verify answers and obtain further information. Keep records of assigned cases and prepare required reports. Schedule benefits claimants for adjudication interviews to address questions of eligibility. Prepare applications and forms for applicants for such purposes as school enrollment, employment, and medical services. Refer applicants to job openings or to interviews with other staff in accordance with administrative guidelines or office procedures. Provide social workers with pertinent information gathered during applicant interviews. Compute and authorize amounts of assistance for programs such as grants, monetary payments, and food stamps. Monitor the payments of benefits throughout the duration of a claim. Provide applicants with assistance in completing application forms such as those for job referrals or unemployment compensation claims. Investigate claimants for the possibility of fraud or abuse. Conduct annual, interim, and special housing reviews and home visits to ensure conformance to regulations.

Personality Type: Conventional. Conventional occupations frequently involve following set procedures and routines. These occupations can include working with data and details more than with ideas. Usually there is a clear line of authority to follow.

GOE—Interest Area: 10. Human Service. **Work Group:** 10.04. Client Interviewing. **Other Jobs in This Work Group:** Interviewers, Except Eligibility and Loan.

Skills—Service Orientation: Actively looking for ways to help people. **Speaking:** Talking to others to convey information effectively. **Active Listening:** Giving full attention to what other people are saying, taking time to understand the points being made, asking questions as appropriate, and not interrupting at inappropriate times. **Social Perceptiveness:** Being aware of others' reactions and understanding why they react as they do. **Writing:** Communicating effectively in writing as appropriate for the needs of the audience. **Active Learning:** Understanding the implications of new information for both current and future problem-solving and decision-making. **Time Management:** Managing one's own time and the time of others. **Learning Strategies:** Selecting and using training/instructional methods and procedures appropriate for the situation when learning or teaching new things.

Education and Training Program: Community Organization and Advocacy. **Related Knowledge/**

Courses: Clerical Practices: Administrative and clerical procedures and systems such as word processing, managing files and records, stenography and transcription, designing forms, and other office procedures and terminology. **Customer and Personal Service:** Principles and processes for providing customer and personal services. This includes customer needs assessment, meeting quality standards for services, and evaluation of customer satisfaction. **Law and Government:** Laws, legal codes, court procedures, precedents, government regulations, executive orders, agency rules, and the democratic political process. **Psychology:** Human behavior and performance; individual differences in ability, personality, and interests; learning and motivation; psychological research methods; and the assessment and treatment of behavioral and affective disorders. **Sociology and Anthropology:** Group behavior and dynamics, societal trends and influences, human migrations, ethnicity, and cultures and their history and origins. **Computers and Electronics:** Circuit boards; processors; chips; electronic equipment; and computer hardware and software, including applications and programming.

Work Environment: Indoors; contaminants; sitting; using hands on objects, tools, or controls; repetitive motions.

Embalmers

- Annual Earnings: $36,960
- Growth: 15.6%
- Annual Job Openings: 2,000
- Education/Training Required: Postsecondary vocational training
- Self-Employed: 0.0%
- Part-Time: 44.0%

How the Job Improves the World: Contributes to consolation of mourners.

Prepare bodies for interment in conformity with legal requirements. Conform to laws of health and sanitation and ensure that legal requirements concerning embalming are met. Apply cosmetics to impart lifelike appearance to the deceased. Incise stomach and abdominal walls and probe internal organs, using trocar, to withdraw blood and waste matter from organs. Close incisions, using needles and sutures. Reshape or reconstruct disfigured or maimed bodies when necessary, using derma-surgery techniques and materials such as clay, cotton, plaster of paris, and wax. Make incisions in arms or thighs and drain blood from circulatory system and replace it with embalming fluid, using pump. Dress bodies and place them in caskets. Join lips, using needles and thread or wire. Conduct interviews to arrange for the preparation of obituary notices, to assist with the selection of caskets or urns, and to determine the location and time of burials or cremations. Perform the duties of funeral directors, including coordinating funeral activities. Attach trocar to pump-tube, start pump, and repeat probing to force embalming fluid into organs. Perform special procedures necessary for remains that are to be transported to other states or overseas or where death was caused by infectious disease. Maintain records such as itemized lists of clothing or valuables delivered with body and names of persons embalmed. Insert convex celluloid or cotton between eyeballs and eyelids to prevent slipping and sinking of eyelids. Wash and dry bodies, using germicidal soap and towels or hot air dryers. Arrange for transporting the deceased to another state for interment. Supervise funeral attendants and other funeral home staff. Pack body orifices with cotton saturated with embalming fluid to prevent escape of gases or waste matter. Assist with placing caskets in hearses and organize cemetery processions. Serve as pallbearers, attend visiting rooms, and provide other assistance to the bereaved. Direct casket and floral display placement and arrange guest seating. Arrange funeral home equipment and perform general maintenance. Assist coroners at death scenes or at autopsies, file police reports, and testify at inquests or in court if employed by a coroner.

Personality Type: Realistic. Realistic occupations frequently involve work activities that include practical, hands-on problems and solutions. They often deal with plants; animals; and real-world materials such as wood, tools, and machinery. Many of the occupations require working outside and do not involve a lot of paperwork or working closely with others.

GOE—Interest Area: 08. Health Science. **Work Group:** 08.09. Health Protection and Promotion. **Other Jobs in This Work Group:** Athletic Trainers; Dietetic Technicians; Dietitians and Nutritionists.

Skills—Service Orientation: Actively looking for ways to help people. **Science:** Using scientific rules and methods to solve problems. **Management of Financial Resources:** Determining how money will be spent to get the work done and accounting for these expenditures. **Management of Material Resources:** Obtaining and seeing to the appropriate use of equipment, facilities, and materials needed to do certain work. **Social Perceptiveness:** Being aware of others' reactions and understanding why they react as they do. **Equipment Maintenance:** Performing routine maintenance on equipment and determining when and what kind of maintenance is needed. **Operation Monitoring:** Watching gauges, dials, or other indicators to make sure a machine is working properly. **Management of Personnel Resources:** Motivating, developing, and directing people as they work; identifying the best people for the job.

Education and Training Programs: Funeral Service and Mortuary Science, General; Mortuary Science and Embalming/Embalmer. **Related Knowledge/Courses: Chemistry:** The chemical composition, structure, and properties of substances and of the chemical processes and transformations that they undergo. This includes uses of chemicals and their danger signs, production techniques, and disposal methods. **Biology:** Plant and animal organisms and their tissues, cells, functions, interdependencies, and interactions with each other and the environment. **Customer and Personal Service:** Principles and processes for providing customer and personal services. This includes customer needs assessment, meeting quality standards for services, and evaluation of customer satisfaction. **Philosophy and Theology:** Different philosophical systems and religions. This includes their basic principles, values, ethics, ways of thinking, customs, and practices and their impact on human culture. **Therapy and Counseling:** Principles, methods, and procedures for diagnosis, treatment, and rehabilitation of physical and mental dysfunctions and for career counseling and guidance. **Medicine and Dentistry:** The information and techniques needed to diagnose and treat human injuries, diseases, and deformities. This includes symptoms, treatment alternatives, drug properties and interactions, and preventive health-care measures.

Work Environment: Indoors; contaminants; disease or infections; hazardous conditions; standing; using hands on objects, tools, or controls.

Emergency Medical Technicians and Paramedics

- Annual Earnings: $26,080
- Growth: 27.3%
- Annual Job Openings: 21,000
- Education/Training Required: Postsecondary vocational training
- Self-Employed: 0.1%
- Part-Time: 10.6%

How the Job Improves the World: Contributes to health.

Assess injuries, administer emergency medical care, and extricate trapped individuals. Transport injured or sick persons to medical facilities. Administer first-aid treatment and life-support care to sick or injured persons in prehospital setting. Operate equipment such as electrocardiograms (EKGs), external defibrillators, and bag-valve mask resuscitators in advanced life-support environments. Assess nature and extent of illness or injury to establish and prioritize medical procedures. Maintain vehicles and medical and communication equipment and replenish first-aid equipment and supplies. Observe, record, and report to physician the patient's condition or injury, the treatment provided, and reactions to drugs and treatment. Perform emergency diagnostic and treatment procedures, such as stomach suction, airway management, or heart monitoring, during ambulance ride. Administer drugs, orally or by injection, and perform intravenous procedures under a physician's direction. Comfort and reassure patients. Coordinate work with other emergency medical team members and police and fire department personnel. Communicate with dispatchers and treatment center personnel to provide information about situation, to arrange reception of victims, and to receive instructions for further treatment. Immobilize patient for placement on stretcher and ambulance transport, using backboard or other spinal immobilization device. Decontaminate ambulance interior following treatment of patient with infectious disease and report case to proper authorities. Drive mobile intensive care unit to specified location, following instructions from emergency medical dispatcher. Coordinate with treatment center personnel to obtain patients' vital statistics and medical history, to determine the circumstances of the emergency, and to administer emergency treatment.

Personality Type: Social. Social occupations frequently involve working with, communicating with, and teaching people. These occupations often involve helping or providing service to others.

GOE—Interest Area: 12. Law and Public Safety. Work Group: 12.06. Emergency Responding. Other Jobs in This Work Group: Fire Fighters; Forest Fire Fighters; Municipal Fire Fighters.

Skills—Equipment Maintenance: Performing routine maintenance on equipment and determining when and what kind of maintenance is needed. Operation Monitoring: Watching gauges, dials, or other indicators to make sure a machine is working properly. Service Orientation: Actively looking for ways to help people. Social Perceptiveness: Being aware of others' reactions and understanding why they react as they do. Operation and Control: Controlling operations of equipment or systems. Coordination: Adjusting actions in relation to others' actions. Equipment Selection: Determining the kind of tools and equipment needed to do a job. Speaking: Talking to others to convey information effectively.

Education and Training Programs: Emergency Care Attendant (EMT Ambulance); Emergency Medical Technology/Technician (EMT Paramedic). Related Knowledge/Courses: Medicine and Dentistry: The information and techniques needed to diagnose and treat human injuries, diseases, and deformities. This includes symptoms, treatment alternatives, drug properties and interactions, and preventive health-care measures. Therapy and Counseling: Principles, methods, and procedures for diagnosis, treatment, and rehabilitation of physical and mental dysfunctions and for career counseling and guidance. Customer and Personal Service: Principles and processes for providing customer and personal services. This includes customer needs assessment, meeting quality standards for services, and evaluation of customer satisfaction. Chemistry: The chemical composition, structure, and properties of substances and of the chemical processes and transformations that they undergo. This includes uses of chemicals and their danger signs, production techniques, and disposal methods. Psychology: Human behavior and performance; individual differences in ability, personality, and interests; learning and

motivation; psychological research methods; and the assessment and treatment of behavioral and affective disorders. Biology: Plant and animal organisms and their tissues, cells, functions, interdependencies, and interactions with each other and the environment.

Work Environment: Outdoors; noisy; very bright or dim lighting; contaminants; cramped work space, awkward positions; disease or infections.

Engineering Teachers, Postsecondary

- Annual Earnings: $74,540
- Growth: 32.2%
- Annual Job Openings: 329,000
- Education/Training Required: Master's degree
- Self-Employed: 0.4%
- Part-Time: 27.3%

The job openings listed here are shared with 35 other postsecondary teaching occupations. For a complete list, see the beginning of this section.

How the Job Improves the World: Contributes to education.

Teach courses pertaining to the application of physical laws and principles of engineering for the development of machines, materials, instruments, processes, and services. Includes teachers of subjects such as chemical, civil, electrical, industrial, mechanical, mineral, and petroleum engineering. Includes both teachers primarily engaged in teaching and those who do a combination of both teaching and research. Prepare and deliver lectures to undergraduate and/or graduate students on topics such as mechanics, hydraulics, and robotics. Keep abreast of developments in their field by reading current literature, talking with colleagues, and participating in professional

E

conferences. Supervise undergraduate and/or graduate teaching, internship, and research work. Evaluate and grade students' classwork, laboratory work, assignments, and papers. Conduct research in a particular field of knowledge and publish findings in professional journals, books, and/or electronic media. Prepare course materials such as syllabi, homework assignments, and handouts. Compile, administer, and grade examinations or assign this work to others. Write grant proposals to procure external research funding. Supervise students' laboratory work. Initiate, facilitate, and moderate class discussions. Maintain regularly scheduled office hours to advise and assist students. Plan, evaluate, and revise curricula, course content, and course materials and methods of instruction. Advise students on academic and vocational curricula and on career issues. Maintain student attendance records, grades, and other required records. Collaborate with colleagues to address teaching and research issues. Select and obtain materials and supplies such as textbooks and laboratory equipment. Participate in student recruitment, registration, and placement activities. Serve on academic or administrative committees that deal with institutional policies, departmental matters, and academic issues. Perform administrative duties such as serving as department head. Provide professional consulting services to government and/or industry. Compile bibliographies of specialized materials for outside reading assignments. Act as advisers to student organizations. Participate in campus and community events.

Personality Type: Investigative. Investigative occupations frequently involve working with ideas and require an extensive amount of thinking. These occupations can involve searching for facts and figuring out problems mentally.

GOE—Interest Area: 05. Education and Training. **Work Group:** 05.03. Postsecondary and Adult Teaching and Instructing. **Other Jobs in This Work Group:** Adult Literacy, Remedial Education, and GED Teachers and Instructors; Agricultural Sciences Teachers, Postsecondary; Anthropology and Archeology Teachers, Postsecondary; Architecture Teachers, Postsecondary; Area, Ethnic, and Cultural Studies Teachers, Postsecondary; Art, Drama, and Music Teachers, Postsecondary; Atmospheric, Earth, Marine, and Space Sciences Teachers, Postsecondary; Biological Science Teachers, Postsecondary; Business Teachers, Postsecondary; Chemistry Teachers, Postsecondary; Communications Teachers, Postsecondary; Computer Science Teachers, Postsecondary; Criminal Justice and Law Enforcement Teachers, Postsecondary; Economics Teachers, Postsecondary; Education Teachers, Postsecondary; English Language and Literature Teachers, Postsecondary; Environmental Science Teachers, Postsecondary; Farm and Home Management Advisors; Foreign Language and Literature Teachers, Postsecondary; Forestry and Conservation Science Teachers, Postsecondary; Geography Teachers, Postsecondary; Graduate Teaching Assistants; Health Specialties Teachers, Postsecondary; History Teachers, Postsecondary; Home Economics Teachers, Postsecondary; Law Teachers, Postsecondary; Library Science Teachers, Postsecondary; Mathematical Science Teachers, Postsecondary; Nursing Instructors and Teachers, Postsecondary; Philosophy and Religion Teachers, Postsecondary; Physics Teachers, Postsecondary; Political Science Teachers, Postsecondary; Psychology Teachers, Postsecondary; Recreation and Fitness Studies Teachers, Postsecondary; Self-Enrichment Education Teachers; Social Work Teachers, Postsecondary; Sociology Teachers, Postsecondary; Vocational Education Teachers, Postsecondary.

Skills—Science: Using scientific rules and methods to solve problems. **Programming:** Writing computer programs for various purposes. **Mathematics:** Using mathematics to solve problems. **Technology Design:** Generating or adapting equipment and technology to serve user needs. **Complex Problem Solving:** Identifying complex problems and reviewing related information to develop and evaluate options and implement solutions. **Management of Financial Resources:** Determining how money will be spent to get the work done and accounting for these expenditures. **Critical Thinking:** Using logic and reasoning to identify the strengths and weaknesses of alternative solutions, conclusions, or approaches to problems. **Active Learning:** Understanding the implications of new information for both current and future problem-solving and decision-making.

Education and Training Programs: Teacher Education and Professional Development, Specific Subject Areas, Other; Engineering, General; Aerospace, Aeronautical, and Astronautical Engineering; Agricultural/Biological Engineering and Bioengineering; Architectural Engineering; Biomedical/Medical Engineering; Ceramic Sciences and Engineering; Chemical Engineering; Civil Engineering, General; Geotechnical Engineering; Structural Engineering; others. **Related Knowledge/Courses: Engineering and Technology:** The practical application of engineering science and technology. This includes applying principles, techniques, procedures, and equipment to the design and production of various goods and services. **Design:** Design techniques, tools, and principles involved in production of precision technical plans, blueprints, drawings, and models. **Physics:** Physical principles and laws and their interrelationships and applications to understanding fluid, material, and atmospheric dynamics and mechanical, electrical, atomic, and subatomic structures and processes. **Mathematics:** Arithmetic, algebra, geometry, calculus, and statistics and their applications. **Education and Training:** Principles and methods for curriculum and training design, teaching and instruction for individuals and groups, and the measurement of training effects. **Telecommunications:** Transmission, broadcasting, switching, control, and operation of telecommunications systems.

Work Environment: Indoors; sitting.

English Language and Literature Teachers, Postsecondary

- Annual Earnings: $49,480
- Growth: 32.2%
- Annual Job Openings: 329,000
- Education/Training Required: Master's degree
- Self-Employed: 0.4%
- Part-Time: 27.3%

The job openings listed here are shared with 35 other postsecondary teaching occupations. For a complete list, see the beginning of this section.

How the Job Improves the World: Contributes to education and the arts.

Teach courses in English language and literature, including linguistics and comparative literature. Initiate, facilitate, and moderate classroom discussions. Evaluate and grade students' classwork, assignments, and papers. Prepare course materials such as syllabi, homework assignments, and handouts. Prepare and deliver lectures to undergraduate and graduate students on topics such as poetry, novel structure, and translation and adaptation. Maintain student attendance records, grades, and other required records. Plan, evaluate, and revise curricula, course content, and course materials and methods of instruction. Compile, administer, and grade examinations or assign this work to others. Maintain regularly scheduled office hours in order to advise and assist students. Keep abreast of developments in their field by reading current literature, talking with colleagues, and participating in professional conferences. Select and obtain materials and supplies such as textbooks. Advise students on academic and vocational curricula and on career issues. Conduct research in a particular field of knowledge and publish findings in professional journals, books, or electronic media. Collaborate with colleagues to address teaching and research issues. Serve on academic or administrative committees that deal with institutional policies, departmental matters, and academic issues. Participate in campus and community events. Participate in student recruitment, registration, and placement activities. Compile bibliographies of specialized materials for outside reading assignments. Supervise undergraduate and/or graduate teaching, internship, and research work. Provide assistance to students in college writing centers. Perform administrative duties such as serving as department head. Recruit, train, and supervise student writing instructors. Act as advisers to student organizations. Write grant proposals to procure external research funding. Provide professional consulting services to government or industry.

Personality Type: Artistic. Artistic occupations frequently involve working with forms, designs, and patterns. They often require self-expression, and the work can be done without following a clear set of rules.

GOE—Interest Area: 05. Education and Training. **Work Group:** 05.03. Postsecondary and Adult Teaching and Instructing. **Other Jobs in This Work Group:** Adult Literacy, Remedial Education, and GED Teachers and Instructors; Agricultural Sciences Teachers, Postsecondary; Anthropology and Archeology Teachers, Postsecondary; Architecture Teachers, Postsecondary; Area, Ethnic, and Cultural Studies Teachers, Postsecondary; Art, Drama, and Music Teachers, Postsecondary; Atmospheric, Earth, Marine, and Space Sciences Teachers, Postsecondary; Biological Science Teachers, Postsecondary; Business Teachers, Postsecondary; Chemistry Teachers, Postsecondary; Communications Teachers, Postsecondary; Computer Science Teachers, Postsecondary; Criminal Justice and Law Enforcement Teachers, Postsecondary; Economics Teachers, Postsecondary; Education Teachers, Postsecondary; Engineering Teachers, Postsecondary; Environmental Science Teachers, Postsecondary; Farm and Home Management Advisors; Foreign Language and Literature Teachers, Postsecondary; Forestry and Conservation Science Teachers, Postsecondary; Geography Teachers, Postsecondary; Graduate Teaching Assistants; Health Specialties Teachers, Postsecondary; History Teachers, Postsecondary; Home Economics Teachers, Postsecondary; Law Teachers, Postsecondary; Library Science Teachers, Postsecondary; Mathematical Science Teachers, Postsecondary; Nursing Instructors and Teachers, Postsecondary; Philosophy and Religion Teachers, Postsecondary; Physics Teachers, Postsecondary; Political Science Teachers, Postsecondary; Psychology Teachers, Postsecondary; Recreation and Fitness Studies Teachers, Postsecondary; Self-Enrichment Education Teachers; Social Work Teachers, Postsecondary; Sociology Teachers, Postsecondary; Vocational Education Teachers, Postsecondary.

Skills—Instructing: Teaching others how to do something. **Learning Strategies:** Selecting and using training/instructional methods and procedures appropriate for the situation when learning or teaching new things. **Writing:** Communicating effectively in writing as appropriate for the needs of the audience. **Social Perceptiveness:** Being aware of others' reactions and understanding why they react as they do. **Persuasion:** Persuading others to change their minds or behavior. **Reading Comprehension:** Understanding written sentences and paragraphs in work-related documents. **Critical Thinking:** Using logic and reasoning to identify the strengths and weaknesses of alternative solutions, conclusions, or approaches to problems. **Active Learning:** Understanding the implications of new information for both current and future problem-solving and decision-making.

Education and Training Programs: Comparative Literature; English Language and Literature, General; English Composition; Creative Writing; American Literature (United States); American Literature (Canadian); English Literature (British and

Commonwealth); Technical and Business Writing; English Language and Literature/Letters, Other. **Related Knowledge/Courses: Philosophy and Theology:** Different philosophical systems and religions. This includes their basic principles, values, ethics, ways of thinking, customs, and practices and their impact on human culture. **English Language:** The structure and content of the English language, including the meaning and spelling of words, rules of composition, and grammar. **History and Archeology:** Historical events and their causes, indicators, and effects on civilizations and cultures. **Education and Training:** Principles and methods for curriculum and training design, teaching and instruction for individuals and groups, and the measurement of training effects. **Sociology and Anthropology:** Group behavior and dynamics, societal trends and influences, human migrations, ethnicity, and cultures and their history and origins. **Fine Arts:** The theory and techniques required to compose, produce, and perform works of music, dance, visual art, drama, and sculpture.

Work Environment: Indoors; sitting.

Environmental Science and Protection Technicians, Including Health

- Annual Earnings: $36,260
- Growth: 16.3%
- Annual Job Openings: 6,000
- Education/Training Required: Associate degree
- Self-Employed: 1.4%
- Part-Time: 22.7%

How the Job Improves the World: Contributes to natural environment.

Perform laboratory and field tests to monitor the environment and investigate sources of pollution, including those that affect health. Under direction of an environmental scientist or specialist, may collect samples of gases, soil, water, and other materials for testing and take corrective actions as assigned. Record test data and prepare reports, summaries, and charts that interpret test results. Collect samples of gases, soils, water, industrial wastewater, and asbestos products to conduct tests on pollutant levels and identify sources of pollution. Respond to and investigate hazardous conditions or spills or outbreaks of disease or food poisoning, collecting samples for analysis. Provide information and technical and program assistance to government representatives, employers, and the general public on the issues of public health, environmental protection, or workplace safety. Calibrate microscopes and test instruments. Make recommendations to control or eliminate unsafe conditions at workplaces or public facilities. Inspect sanitary conditions at public facilities. Prepare samples or photomicrographs for testing and analysis. Calculate amount of pollutant in samples or compute air pollution or gas flow in industrial processes, using chemical and mathematical formulas. Initiate procedures to close down or fine establishments violating environmental or health regulations. Determine amounts and kinds of chemicals to use in destroying harmful organisms and removing impurities from purification systems. Discuss test results and analyses with customers. Maintain files such as hazardous waste databases, chemical usage data, personnel exposure information, and diagrams showing equipment locations. Perform statistical analysis of environmental data. Set up equipment or stations to monitor and collect pollutants from sites such as smokestacks, manufacturing plants, or mechanical equipment. Distribute permits, closure plans, and cleanup plans. Inspect workplaces to ensure the absence of health and safety hazards such as high noise levels, radiation, or potential lighting hazards. Weigh, analyze, and measure collected sample

E

particles, such as lead, coal dust, or rock, to determine concentration of pollutants. Examine and analyze material for presence and concentration of contaminants such as asbestos, using variety of microscopes. Develop testing procedures or direct activities of workers in laboratory.

Personality Type: Investigative. Investigative occupations frequently involve working with ideas and require an extensive amount of thinking. These occupations can involve searching for facts and figuring out problems mentally.

GOE—Interest Area: 01. Agriculture and Natural Resources. **Work Group:** 01.03. Resource Technologies for Plants, Animals, and the Environment. **Other Jobs in This Work Group:** Agricultural and Food Science Technicians; Agricultural Technicians; Food Science Technicians; Food Scientists and Technologists; Geological and Petroleum Technicians; Geological Sample Test Technicians; Geophysical Data Technicians.

Skills—Science: Using scientific rules and methods to solve problems. **Persuasion:** Persuading others to change their minds or behavior. **Active Learning:** Understanding the implications of new information for both current and future problem-solving and decision-making. **Mathematics:** Using mathematics to solve problems. **Reading Comprehension:** Understanding written sentences and paragraphs in work-related documents. **Quality Control Analysis:** Conducting tests and inspections of products, services, or processes to evaluate quality or performance. **Troubleshooting:** Determining causes of operating errors and deciding what to do about them. **Operation Monitoring:** Watching gauges, dials, or other indicators to make sure a machine is working properly.

Education and Training Programs: Environmental Studies; Environmental Science; Physical Science Technologies/Technicians, Other; Science Technologies/Technicians, Other. **Related Knowledge/ Courses: Biology:** Plant and animal organisms and their tissues, cells, functions, interdependencies, and interactions with each other and the environment. **Engineering and Technology:** The practical application of engineering science and technology. This includes applying principles, techniques, procedures, and equipment to the design and production of various goods and services. **Chemistry:** The chemical composition, structure, and properties of substances and of the chemical processes and transformations that they undergo. This includes uses of chemicals and their danger signs, production techniques, and disposal methods. **Physics:** Physical principles and laws and their interrelationships and applications to understanding fluid, material, and atmospheric dynamics and mechanical, electrical, atomic, and subatomic structures and processes. **Building and Construction:** The materials, methods, and tools involved in the construction or repair of houses, buildings, or other structures such as highways and roads. **Design:** Design techniques, tools, and principles involved in production of precision technical plans, blueprints, drawings, and models.

Work Environment: More often indoors than outdoors; noisy; very hot or cold; contaminants; sitting.

Environmental Science Teachers, Postsecondary

- Annual Earnings: $60,880
- Growth: 32.2%
- Annual Job Openings: 329,000
- Education/Training Required: Master's degree
- Self-Employed: 0.4%
- Part-Time: 27.3%

The job openings listed here are shared with 35 other postsecondary teaching occupations. For a complete list, see the beginning of this section.

How the Job Improves the World: Contributes to education and the natural environment.

Teach courses in environmental science. Supervise undergraduate and/or graduate teaching, internship, and research work. Conduct research in a particular field of knowledge and publish findings in professional journals, books, and/or electronic media. Keep abreast of developments in their field by reading current literature, talking with colleagues, and participating in professional conferences. Evaluate and grade students' classwork, laboratory work, assignments, and papers. Write grant proposals to procure external research funding. Supervise students' laboratory work and fieldwork. Prepare course materials such as syllabi, homework assignments, and handouts. Plan, evaluate, and revise curricula, course content, and course materials and methods of instruction. Compile, administer, and grade examinations or assign this work to others. Initiate, facilitate, and moderate classroom discussions. Advise students on academic and vocational curricula and on career issues. Prepare and deliver lectures to undergraduate and/or graduate students on topics such as hazardous waste management, industrial safety, and environmental toxicology. Maintain student attendance records, grades, and other required records. Select and obtain materials and supplies such as textbooks and laboratory equipment. Maintain regularly scheduled office hours in order to advise and assist students. Collaborate with colleagues to address teaching and research issues. Perform administrative duties such as serving as department head. Participate in student recruitment, registration, and placement activities. Provide professional consulting services to government and/or industry. Serve on academic or administrative committees that deal with institutional policies, departmental matters, and academic issues. Compile bibliographies of specialized materials for outside reading assignments. Participate in campus and community events. Act as advisers to student organizations.

Personality Type: No data available.

GOE—Interest Area: 05. Education and Training. **Work Group:** 05.03. Postsecondary and Adult Teaching and Instructing. **Other Jobs in This Work Group:** Adult Literacy, Remedial Education, and GED Teachers and Instructors; Agricultural Sciences Teachers, Postsecondary; Anthropology and Archeology Teachers, Postsecondary; Architecture Teachers, Postsecondary; Area, Ethnic, and Cultural Studies Teachers, Postsecondary; Art, Drama, and Music Teachers, Postsecondary; Atmospheric, Earth, Marine, and Space Sciences Teachers, Postsecondary; Biological Science Teachers, Postsecondary; Business Teachers, Postsecondary; Chemistry Teachers, Postsecondary; Communications Teachers, Postsecondary; Computer Science Teachers, Postsecondary; Criminal Justice and Law Enforcement Teachers, Postsecondary; Economics Teachers, Postsecondary; Education Teachers, Postsecondary; Engineering Teachers, Postsecondary; English Language and Literature Teachers, Postsecondary; Farm and Home Management Advisors; Foreign Language and Literature Teachers, Postsecondary; Forestry and Conservation Science Teachers, Postsecondary; Geography Teachers, Postsecondary; Graduate Teaching Assistants; Health Specialties Teachers, Postsecondary; History Teachers, Postsecondary; Home Economics Teachers, Postsecondary; Law Teachers, Postsecondary; Library Science Teachers, Postsecondary; Mathematical Science Teachers, Postsecondary; Nursing Instructors and Teachers, Postsecondary; Philosophy and Religion Teachers, Postsecondary; Physics Teachers, Postsecondary; Political Science Teachers, Postsecondary; Psychology Teachers, Postsecondary; Recreation and Fitness Studies Teachers, Postsecondary; Self-Enrichment Education Teachers; Social Work Teachers, Postsecondary; Sociology Teachers, Postsecondary; Vocational Education Teachers, Postsecondary.

E

Skills—Science: Using scientific rules and methods to solve problems. **Writing:** Communicating effectively in writing as appropriate for the needs of the audience. **Instructing:** Teaching others how to do something. **Reading Comprehension:** Understanding written sentences and paragraphs in work-related documents. **Management of Financial Resources:** Determining how money will be spent to get the work done and accounting for these expenditures. **Critical Thinking:** Using logic and reasoning to identify the strengths and weaknesses of alternative solutions, conclusions, or approaches to problems. **Programming:** Writing computer programs for various purposes. **Mathematics:** Using mathematics to solve problems.

Education and Training Programs: Environmental Studies; Environmental Science; Science Teacher Education/General Science Teacher Education. **Related Knowledge/Courses: Biology:** Plant and animal organisms and their tissues, cells, functions, interdependencies, and interactions with each other and the environment. **Geography:** Principles and methods for describing the features of land, sea, and air masses, including their physical characteristics; locations; interrelationships; and distribution of plant, animal, and human life. **Chemistry:** The chemical composition, structure, and properties of substances and of the chemical processes and transformations that they undergo. This includes uses of chemicals and their danger signs, production techniques, and disposal methods. **Education and Training:** Principles and methods for curriculum and training design, teaching and instruction for individuals and groups, and the measurement of training effects. **Physics:** Physical principles and laws and their interrelationships and applications to understanding fluid, material, and atmospheric dynamics and mechanical, electrical, atomic, and subatomic structures and processes. **History and Archeology:** Historical events and their causes, indicators, and effects on civilizations and cultures.

Work Environment: Indoors; sitting.

Environmental Scientists and Specialists, Including Health

- Annual Earnings: $52,630
- Growth: 17.1%
- Annual Job Openings: 8,000
- Education/Training Required: Master's degree
- Self-Employed: 4.2%
- Part-Time: 5.7%

How the Job Improves the World: Contributes to natural environment.

Conduct research or perform investigation for the purpose of identifying, abating, or eliminating sources of pollutants or hazards that affect either the environment or the health of the population. Utilizing knowledge of various scientific disciplines, may collect, synthesize, study, report, and take action based on data derived from measurements or observations of air, food, soil, water, and other sources. Conduct environmental audits and inspections and investigations of violations. Evaluate violations or problems discovered during inspections to determine appropriate regulatory actions or to provide advice on the development and prosecution of regulatory cases. Communicate scientific and technical information through oral briefings, written documents, workshops, conferences, and public hearings. Review and implement environmental technical standards, guidelines, policies, and formal regulations that meet all appropriate requirements. Provide technical guidance, support, and oversight to environmental programs, industry, and the public. Provide advice on proper standards and regulations or the development of policies, strategies, and codes of practice for environmental management. Analyze data to determine validity, quality, and scientific significance and to interpret correlations between human activities and environmental effects. Collect, synthesize, and analyze data derived from pollution emission measurements, atmospheric monitoring, meteorological and mineralogical information, and soil or water samples. Determine data collection methods to be employed in research projects and surveys. Prepare charts or graphs from data samples, providing summary information on the environmental relevance of the data. Develop the technical portions of legal documents, administrative orders, or consent decrees. Investigate and report on accidents affecting the environment. Monitor environmental impacts of development activities. Supervise environmental technologists and technicians. Develop programs designed to obtain the most productive, non-damaging use of land. Research sources of pollution to determine their effects on the environment and to develop theories or methods of pollution abatement or control. Monitor effects of pollution and land degradation and recommend means of prevention or control. Design and direct studies to obtain technical environmental information about planned projects. Conduct applied research on topics such as waste control and treatment and pollution control methods.

Personality Type: Investigative. Investigative occupations frequently involve working with ideas and require an extensive amount of thinking. These occupations can involve searching for facts and figuring out problems mentally.

GOE—Interest Area: 15. Scientific Research, Engineering, and Mathematics. **Work Group:** 15.03. Life Sciences. **Other Jobs in This Work Group:** Biochemists and Biophysicists; Biologists; Epidemiologists; Medical Scientists, Except Epidemiologists; Microbiologists.

Skills—Science: Using scientific rules and methods to solve problems. **Service Orientation:** Actively looking for ways to help people. **Negotiation:** Bringing others together and trying to reconcile differences. **Coordination:** Adjusting actions in relation to others' actions. **Reading Comprehension:** Understanding written sentences and paragraphs in work-related documents. **Complex Problem Solving:** Identifying complex problems and reviewing related information to develop and evaluate options and implement solutions. **Operations Analysis:** Analyzing needs and product requirements to create a design. **Mathematics:** Using mathematics to solve problems.

Education and Training Programs: Environmental Studies; Environmental Science. **Related Knowledge/Courses: Biology:** Plant and animal organisms and their tissues, cells, functions, interdependencies, and interactions with each other and the environment. **Geography:** Principles and methods for describing the features of land, sea, and air masses, including their physical characteristics; locations; interrelationships; and distribution of plant, animal, and human life. **Chemistry:** The chemical composition, structure, and properties of substances and of the chemical processes and transformations that they undergo. This includes uses of chemicals and their danger signs, production techniques, and disposal methods. **Law and Government:** Laws, legal codes, court procedures, precedents, government regulations, executive orders, agency rules, and the democratic political process. **Engineering and Technology:** The practical application of engineering science and technology. This includes applying principles, techniques, procedures, and equipment to the design and production of various goods and services. **Physics:** Physical principles and laws and their interrelationships and applications to understanding fluid, material, and atmospheric dynamics and mechanical, electrical, atomic, and subatomic structures and processes.

Work Environment: More often indoors than outdoors; noisy; sitting.

E

Epidemiologists

- Annual Earnings: $52,170
- Growth: 26.2%
- Annual Job Openings: 1,000
- Education/Training Required: Master's degree
- Self-Employed: 0.4%
- Part-Time: 5.5%

How the Job Improves the World: Contributes to health.

Investigate and describe the determinants and distribution of disease, disability, and other health outcomes and develop the means for prevention and control. Oversee public health programs, including statistical analysis, health care planning, surveillance systems, and public health improvement. Investigate diseases or parasites to determine cause and risk factors, progress, life cycle, or mode of transmission. Plan and direct studies to investigate human or animal disease, preventive methods, and treatments for disease. Plan, administer, and evaluate health safety standards and programs to improve public health, conferring with health department, industry personnel, physicians, and others. Provide expertise in the design, management, and evaluation of study protocols and health status questionnaires, sample selection, and analysis. Conduct research to develop methodologies, instrumentation, and procedures for medical application, analyzing data and presenting findings. Consult with and advise physicians, educators, researchers, government health officials, and others regarding medical applications of sciences such as physics, biology, and chemistry. Supervise professional, technical, and clerical personnel. Identify and analyze public health issues related to foodborne parasitic diseases and their impact on public policies or scientific studies or surveys. Teach principles of medicine and medical and laboratory procedures to physicians, residents, students, and technicians. Standardize drug dosages, methods of immunization, and procedures for manufacture of drugs and medicinal compounds. Prepare and analyze samples to study effects of drugs, gases, pesticides, or microorganisms on cell structure and tissue.

Personality Type: Investigative. Investigative occupations frequently involve working with ideas and require an extensive amount of thinking. These occupations can involve searching for facts and figuring out problems mentally.

GOE—Interest Area: 15. Scientific Research, Engineering, and Mathematics. **Work Group:** 15.03. Life Sciences. **Other Jobs in This Work Group:** Biochemists and Biophysicists; Biologists; Environmental Scientists and Specialists, Including Health; Medical Scientists, Except Epidemiologists; Microbiologists.

Skills—Science: Using scientific rules and methods to solve problems. **Programming:** Writing computer programs for various purposes. **Reading Comprehension:** Understanding written sentences and paragraphs in work-related documents. **Mathematics:** Using mathematics to solve problems. **Writing:** Communicating effectively in writing as appropriate for the needs of the audience. **Complex Problem Solving:** Identifying complex problems and reviewing related information to develop and evaluate options and implement solutions. **Active Learning:** Understanding the implications of new information for both current and future problem-solving and decision-making. **Persuasion:** Persuading others to change their minds or behavior. **Operations Analysis:** Analyzing needs and product requirements to create a design.

Education and Training Programs: Biophysics; Cell/Cellular Biology and Histology; Epidemiology; Medical Scientist (MS, PhD). **Related Knowledge/Courses: Biology:** Plant and animal organisms and their tissues, cells, functions, interdependencies, and interactions with each other and the environment.

Sociology and Anthropology: Group behavior and dynamics, societal trends and influences, human migrations, ethnicity, and cultures and their history and origins. **Medicine and Dentistry:** The information and techniques needed to diagnose and treat human injuries, diseases, and deformities. This includes symptoms, treatment alternatives, drug properties and interactions, and preventive health-care measures. **English Language:** The structure and content of the English language, including the meaning and spelling of words, rules of composition, and grammar. **Mathematics:** Arithmetic, algebra, geometry, calculus, and statistics and their applications. **Computers and Electronics:** Circuit boards; processors; chips; electronic equipment; and computer hardware and software, including applications and programming.

Work Environment: Indoors; noisy; sitting; repetitive motions.

Family and General Practitioners

- Annual Earnings: $140,400
- Growth: 24.0%
- Annual Job Openings: 41,000
- Education/Training Required: First professional degree
- Self-Employed: 11.5%
- Part-Time: 9.6%

The job openings listed here are shared with Anesthesiologists; Internists, General; Obstetricians and Gynecologists; Pediatricians, General; Psychiatrists; and Surgeons.

How the Job Improves the World: Contributes to health.

Diagnose, treat, and help prevent diseases and injuries that commonly occur in the general popula-tion. Prescribe or administer treatment, therapy, medication, vaccination, and other specialized medical care to treat or prevent illness, disease, or injury. Order, perform, and interpret tests and analyze records, reports, and examination information to diagnose patients' condition. Monitor the patients' conditions and progress and re-evaluate treatments as necessary. Explain procedures and discuss test results or prescribed treatments with patients. Collect, record, and maintain patient information, such as medical history, reports, and examination results. Advise patients and community members concerning diet, activity, hygiene, and disease prevention. Refer patients to medical specialists or other practitioners when necessary. Direct and coordinate activities of nurses, students, assistants, specialists, therapists, and other medical staff. Coordinate work with nurses, social workers, rehabilitation therapists, pharmacists, psychologists, and other health care providers. Deliver babies. Operate on patients to remove, repair, or improve functioning of diseased or injured body parts and systems. Plan, implement, or administer health programs or standards in hospital, business, or community for information, prevention, or treatment of injury or illness. Prepare reports for government or management of birth, death, and disease statistics; workforce evaluations; or medical status of individuals. Conduct research to study anatomy and develop or test medications, treatments, or procedures to prevent or control disease or injury.

Personality Type: Investigative. Investigative occupations frequently involve working with ideas and require an extensive amount of thinking. These occupations can involve searching for facts and figuring out problems mentally.

GOE—Interest Area: 08. Health Science. **Work Group:** 08.02. Medicine and Surgery. **Other Jobs in This Work Group:** Anesthesiologists; Internists, General; Medical Assistants; Medical Transcriptionists; Obstetricians and Gynecologists; Pediatricians, General; Pharmacists; Pharmacy Aides; Pharmacy

Technicians; Physician Assistants; Psychiatrists; Registered Nurses; Surgeons; Surgical Technologists.

Skills—Science: Using scientific rules and methods to solve problems. **Social Perceptiveness:** Being aware of others' reactions and understanding why they react as they do. **Reading Comprehension:** Understanding written sentences and paragraphs in work-related documents. **Complex Problem Solving:** Identifying complex problems and reviewing related information to develop and evaluate options and implement solutions. **Persuasion:** Persuading others to change their minds or behavior. **Service Orientation:** Actively looking for ways to help people. **Instructing:** Teaching others how to do something. **Management of Financial Resources:** Determining how money will be spent to get the work done and accounting for these expenditures.

Education and Training Programs: Medicine (MD); Osteopathic Medicine/Osteopathy (DO); Family Medicine. **Related Knowledge/Courses: Medicine and Dentistry:** The information and techniques needed to diagnose and treat human injuries, diseases, and deformities. This includes symptoms, treatment alternatives, drug properties and interactions, and preventive health-care measures. **Therapy and Counseling:** Principles, methods, and procedures for diagnosis, treatment, and rehabilitation of physical and mental dysfunctions and for career counseling and guidance. **Biology:** Plant and animal organisms and their tissues, cells, functions, interdependencies, and interactions with each other and the environment. **Psychology:** Human behavior and performance; individual differences in ability, personality, and interests; learning and motivation; psychological research methods; and the assessment and treatment of behavioral and affective disorders. **Sociology and Anthropology:** Group behavior and dynamics, societal trends and influences, human migrations, ethnicity, and cultures and their history and origins. **Chemistry:** The chemical composition, structure, and properties of substances and of the chemical processes and transformations that they

undergo. This includes uses of chemicals and their danger signs, production techniques, and disposal methods.

Work Environment: Indoors; disease or infections; standing; using hands on objects, tools, or controls.

Farm and Home Management Advisors

- Annual Earnings: $41,890
- Growth: 7.7%
- Annual Job Openings: 2,000
- Education/Training Required: Bachelor's degree
- Self-Employed: 3.8%
- Part-Time: 23.4%

How the Job Improves the World: Contributes to education.

Advise, instruct, and assist individuals and families engaged in agriculture, agricultural-related processes, or home economics activities. Demonstrate procedures and apply research findings to solve problems; instruct and train in product development, sales, and the utilization of machinery and equipment to promote general welfare. Includes county agricultural agents, feed and farm management advisers, home economists, and extension service advisors. Collaborate with producers to diagnose and prevent management and production problems. Conduct classes or deliver lectures on subjects such as nutrition, home management, and farming techniques. Advise farmers and demonstrate techniques in areas such as feeding and health maintenance of livestock, growing and harvesting practices, and financial planning. Research information requested by farmers. Prepare and distribute leaflets, pamphlets, and visual aids for educational and informational purposes. Collect and evaluate data to determine community program needs. Maintain records of services provided and the effects of advice given. Schedule and make regular visits to farmers. Collaborate with social service and health care professionals to advise individuals and families on home management practices such as budget planning, meal preparation, and time management. Organize, advise, and participate in community activities and organizations such as county and state fair events and 4-H clubs. Conduct field demonstrations of new products, techniques, or services. Conduct agricultural research, analyze data, and prepare research reports. Act as an advocate for farmers or farmers' groups. Provide direct assistance to farmers by performing activities such as purchasing or selling products and supplies, supervising properties, and collecting soil and herbage samples for testing. Set and monitor production targets.

Personality Type: Social. Social occupations frequently involve working with, communicating with, and teaching people. These occupations often involve helping or providing service to others.

GOE—Interest Area: 05. Education and Training. **Work Group:** 05.03. Postsecondary and Adult Teaching and Instructing. **Other Jobs in This Work Group:** Adult Literacy, Remedial Education, and GED Teachers and Instructors; Agricultural Sciences Teachers, Postsecondary; Anthropology and Archeology Teachers, Postsecondary; Architecture Teachers, Postsecondary; Area, Ethnic, and Cultural Studies Teachers, Postsecondary; Art, Drama, and Music Teachers, Postsecondary; Atmospheric, Earth, Marine, and Space Sciences Teachers, Postsecondary; Biological Science Teachers, Postsecondary; Business Teachers, Postsecondary; Chemistry Teachers, Postsecondary; Communications Teachers, Postsecondary; Computer Science Teachers, Postsecondary; Criminal Justice and Law Enforcement Teachers, Postsecondary; Economics Teachers, Postsecondary; Education Teachers, Postsecondary; Engineering Teachers, Postsecondary; English Language and Literature Teachers, Postsecondary; Environmental Science Teachers, Postsecondary; Foreign Language and Literature Teachers, Postsecondary; Forestry and Conservation Science Teachers, Postsecondary; Geography Teachers, Postsecondary; Graduate Teaching Assistants; Health Specialties Teachers, Postsecondary; History Teachers, Postsecondary; Home Economics Teachers, Postsecondary; Law Teachers, Postsecondary; Library Science Teachers, Postsecondary; Mathematical Science Teachers, Postsecondary; Nursing Instructors and Teachers, Postsecondary; Philosophy and Religion Teachers, Postsecondary; Physics Teachers, Postsecondary; Political Science Teachers, Postsecondary; Psychology Teachers, Postsecondary; Recreation and Fitness Studies Teachers, Postsecondary; Self-Enrichment Education Teachers; Social Work Teachers, Postsecondary; Sociology Teachers, Postsecondary; Vocational Education Teachers, Postsecondary.

Skills—Management of Financial Resources: Determining how money will be spent to get the work done and accounting for these expenditures. **Science:** Using scientific rules and methods to solve problems. **Service Orientation:** Actively looking for ways to help people. **Learning Strategies:** Selecting and using training/instructional methods and procedures appropriate for the situation when learning or teaching new things. **Management of Personnel Resources:** Motivating, developing, and directing people as they work; identifying the best people for the job. **Writing:** Communicating effectively in writing as appropriate for the needs of the audience. **Persuasion:** Persuading others to change their minds or behavior. **Instructing:** Teaching others how to do something.

Education and Training Programs: Farm/Farm and Ranch Management; Animal/Livestock Husbandry and Production; Crop Production; Agricultural and Extension Education Services; Animal Nutrition; Work and Family Studies; Family and Consumer Sciences/Human Sciences, General; Business Family and Consumer Sciences/Human Sciences; Consumer Merchandising/Retailing Management; Family

Resource Management Studies, General; Consumer Economics; others. **Related Knowledge/Courses: Food Production:** Techniques and equipment for planting, growing, and harvesting food products (both plant and animal) for consumption, including storage/handling techniques. **Education and Training:** Principles and methods for curriculum and training design, teaching and instruction for individuals and groups, and the measurement of training effects. **Biology:** Plant and animal organisms and their tissues, cells, functions, interdependencies, and interactions with each other and the environment. **Sociology and Anthropology:** Group behavior and dynamics, societal trends and influences, human migrations, ethnicity, and cultures and their history and origins. **Customer and Personal Service:** Principles and processes for providing customer and personal services. This includes customer needs assessment, meeting quality standards for services, and evaluation of customer satisfaction. **Psychology:** Human behavior and performance; individual differences in ability, personality, and interests; learning and motivation; psychological research methods; and the assessment and treatment of behavioral and affective disorders.

Work Environment: Indoors; sitting.

Film and Video Editors

- Annual Earnings: $46,930
- Growth: 18.6%
- Annual Job Openings: 3,000
- Education/Training Required: Bachelor's degree
- Self-Employed: 18.2%
- Part-Time: 27.6%

How the Job Improves the World: Contributes to the arts.

Edit motion picture soundtracks, film, and video. Cut shot sequences to different angles at specific points in scenes, making each individual cut as fluid and seamless as possible. Study scripts to become familiar with production concepts and requirements. Edit films and videotapes to insert music, dialogue, and sound effects; to arrange films into sequences; and to correct errors, using editing equipment. Select and combine the most effective shots of each scene to form a logical and smoothly running story. Mark frames where a particular shot or piece of sound is to begin or end. Determine the specific audio and visual effects and music necessary to complete films. Verify key numbers and time codes on materials. Organize and string together raw footage into a continuous whole according to scripts or the instructions of directors and producers. Review assembled films or edited videotapes on screens or monitors to determine if corrections are necessary. Program computerized graphic effects. Review footage sequence by sequence to become familiar with it before assembling it into a final product. Set up and operate computer editing systems, electronic titling systems, video switching equipment, and digital video effects units to produce a final product. Record needed sounds or obtain them from sound effects libraries. Confer with producers and directors concerning layout or editing approaches needed to increase dramatic or entertainment value of productions. Manipulate plot, score, sound, and graphics to make the parts into a continuous whole, working closely with people in audio, visual, music, optical, or special effects departments. Supervise and coordinate activities of workers engaged in film editing, assembling, and recording activities. Trim film segments to specified lengths and reassemble segments in sequences that present stories with maximum effect. Develop post-production models for films. Piece sounds together to develop film soundtracks. Conduct film screenings for directors and members of production staffs. Collaborate with music editors to select appropriate passages of music and develop production scores. Discuss the sound requirements of pictures with sound effects editors.

Personality Type: Artistic. Artistic occupations frequently involve working with forms, designs, and patterns. They often require self-expression, and the work can be done without following a clear set of rules.

GOE—Interest Area: 03. Arts and Communication. **Work Group:** 03.09. Media Technology. **Other Jobs in This Work Group:** Audio and Video Equipment Technicians; Broadcast Technicians; Camera Operators, Television, Video, and Motion Picture; Multi-Media Artists and Animators; Photographers; Radio Operators; Sound Engineering Technicians.

Skills—Operation and Control: Controlling operations of equipment or systems. **Equipment Selection:** Determining the kind of tools and equipment needed to do a job. **Equipment Maintenance:** Performing routine maintenance on equipment and determining when and what kind of maintenance is needed. **Operations Analysis:** Analyzing needs and product requirements to create a design. **Installation:** Installing equipment, machines, wiring, or programs to meet specifications. **Troubleshooting:** Determining causes of operating errors and deciding what to do about them. **Operation Monitoring:** Watching gauges, dials, or other indicators to make sure a machine is working properly. **Active Learning:** Understanding the implications of new information for both current and future problem-solving and decision-making.

Education and Training Programs: Photojournalism; Radio and Television; Communications Technology/Technician; Radio and Television Broadcasting Technology/Technician; Audiovisual Communications Technologies/Technicians, Other; Cinematography and Film/Video Production. **Related Knowledge/Courses: Fine Arts:** The theory and techniques required to compose, produce, and perform works of music, dance, visual art, drama, and sculpture. **Communications and Media:** Media production, communication, and dissemination techniques and methods. This includes alternative ways to inform and entertain via written, oral, and visual media.

Design: Design techniques, tools, and principles involved in production of precision technical plans, blueprints, drawings, and models. **Computers and Electronics:** Circuit boards; processors; chips; electronic equipment; and computer hardware and software, including applications and programming. **Education and Training:** Principles and methods for curriculum and training design, teaching and instruction for individuals and groups, and the measurement of training effects. **Telecommunications:** Transmission, broadcasting, switching, control, and operation of telecommunications systems.

Work Environment: Indoors; sitting; using hands on objects, tools, or controls; repetitive motions.

Fine Artists, Including Painters, Sculptors, and Illustrators

- Annual Earnings: $41,280
- Growth: 10.2%
- Annual Job Openings: 4,000
- Education/Training Required: Long-term on-the-job training
- Self-Employed: 61.9%
- Part-Time: 30.9%

How the Job Improves the World: Contributes to the arts.

Create original artwork, using any of a wide variety of mediums and techniques such as painting and sculpture. Use materials such as pens and ink, watercolors, charcoal, oil, or computer software to create artwork. Integrate and develop visual elements, such as line, space, mass, color, and perspective, to produce desired effects such as the illustration of ideas, emotions, or moods. Confer with clients, editors, writers, art directors, and other interested parties regarding the nature and content of artwork to be produced. Submit preliminary or finished artwork or project plans to clients for approval, incorporating changes as necessary. Maintain portfolios of artistic work to demonstrate styles, interests, and abilities. Create finished artwork as decoration or to elucidate or substitute for spoken or written messages. Cut, bend, laminate, arrange, and fasten individual or mixed raw and manufactured materials and products to form works of art. Monitor events, trends, and other circumstances; research specific subject areas; attend art exhibitions; and read art publications to develop ideas and keep current on art world activities. Study different techniques to learn how to apply them to artistic endeavors. Render drawings, illustrations, and sketches of buildings, manufactured products, or models, working from sketches, blueprints, memory, models, or reference materials. Create sculptures, statues, and other three-dimensional artwork by using abrasives and tools to shape, carve, and fabricate materials such as clay, stone, wood, or metal. Create sketches, profiles, or likenesses of posed subjects or photographs, using any combination of freehand drawing, mechanical assembly kits, and computer imaging. Study styles, techniques, colors, textures, and materials used in works undergoing restoration to ensure consistency during the restoration process. Develop project budgets for approval, estimating timelines and material costs. Shade and fill in sketch outlines and backgrounds, using a variety of media such as watercolors, markers, and transparent washes, labeling designated colors when necessary. Collaborate with engineers, mechanics, and other technical experts as necessary to build and install creations.

Personality Type: Artistic. Artistic occupations frequently involve working with forms, designs, and patterns. They often require self-expression, and the work can be done without following a clear set of rules.

GOE—Interest Area: 03. Arts and Communication. **Work Group:** 03.04. Studio Art. **Other Jobs in This Work Group:** Craft Artists; Potters, Manufacturing.

Skills—Management of Financial Resources: Determining how money will be spent to get the work done and accounting for these expenditures. **Equipment Selection:** Determining the kind of tools and equipment needed to do a job. **Operations Analysis:** Analyzing needs and product requirements to create a design. **Repairing:** Repairing machines or systems by using the needed tools. **Equipment Maintenance:** Performing routine maintenance on equipment and determining when and what kind of maintenance is needed. **Complex Problem Solving:** Identifying complex problems and reviewing related information to develop and evaluate options and implement solutions. **Installation:** Installing equipment, machines, wiring, or programs to meet specifications. **Mathematics:** Using mathematics to solve problems.

Education and Training Programs: Visual and Performing Arts, General; Art/Art Studies, General; Fine/Studio Arts, General; Drawing; Painting; Fine Arts and Art Studies, Other. **Related Knowledge/Courses: Fine Arts:** The theory and techniques required to compose, produce, and perform works of music, dance, visual art, drama, and sculpture. **Design:** Design techniques, tools, and principles involved in production of precision technical plans, blueprints, drawings, and models. **Sales and Marketing:** Principles and methods for showing, promoting, and selling products or services. This includes marketing strategy and tactics, product demonstration, sales techniques, and sales control systems. **Production and Processing:** Raw materials, production processes, quality control, costs, and other techniques for maximizing the effective manufacture and distribution of goods. **Economics and Accounting:** Economic and accounting principles and practices, the financial markets, banking, and the analysis and reporting of financial data. **Communications and Media:** Media production, communication, and dissemination techniques and methods. This includes alternative ways to inform and entertain via written, oral, and visual media.

Work Environment: Indoors; contaminants; standing; using hands on objects, tools, or controls; repetitive motions.

Fire-Prevention and Protection Engineers

- Annual Earnings: $65,210
- Growth: 13.4%
- Annual Job Openings: 2,000
- Education/Training Required: Bachelor's degree
- Self-Employed: 0.5%
- Part-Time: 2.6%

The job openings listed here are shared with Industrial Safety and Health Engineers and with Product Safety Engineers.

How the Job Improves the World: Contributes to safety.

Research causes of fires, determine fire protection methods, and design or recommend materials or equipment such as structural components or fire-detection equipment to assist organizations in safeguarding life and property against fire, explosion, and related hazards. Design fire detection equipment, alarm systems, and fire extinguishing devices and systems. Inspect buildings or building designs to determine fire protection system requirements and potential problems in areas such as water supplies, exit locations, and construction materials. Advise architects, builders, and other construction personnel on fire prevention equipment and techniques and on fire code and standard interpretation and compliance. Prepare and write reports detailing specific fire prevention and protection issues, such as work performed and proposed review schedules. Determine causes of fires and ways in which they could have been prevented. Direct the purchase, modification, installation, maintenance, and operation of fire protection systems. Consult with authorities to discuss safety regulations and to recommend changes as necessary. Develop plans for the prevention of destruction by fire, wind, and water. Study the relationships between ignition sources and materials to determine how fires start. Attend workshops, seminars, or conferences to present or obtain information regarding fire prevention and protection. Develop training materials and conduct training sessions on fire protection. Evaluate fire department performance and the laws and regulations affecting fire prevention or fire safety. Conduct research on fire retardants and the fire safety of materials and devices.

Personality Type: Investigative. Investigative occupations frequently involve working with ideas and require an extensive amount of thinking. These occupations can involve searching for facts and figuring out problems mentally.

GOE—Interest Area: 15. Scientific Research, Engineering, and Mathematics. **Work Group:** 15.08. Industrial and Safety Engineering. **Other Jobs in This Work Group:** Health and Safety Engineers, Except Mining Safety Engineers and Inspectors; Industrial Engineers; Industrial Safety and Health Engineers; Product Safety Engineers.

Skills—Science: Using scientific rules and methods to solve problems. **Management of Financial Resources:** Determining how money will be spent to get the work done and accounting for these expenditures. **Operations Analysis:** Analyzing needs and product requirements to create a design. **Mathematics:** Using mathematics to solve problems. **Systems Analysis:** Determining how a system should work and how changes in conditions, operations, and the environment will affect outcomes. **Negotiation:** Bringing others together and trying to reconcile differences. **Management of Personnel Resources:** Motivating, developing, and directing people as they work; identifying the best people for the job. **Complex Problem**

Solving: Identifying complex problems and reviewing related information to develop and evaluate options and implement solutions.

Education and Training Program: Environmental/ Environmental Health Engineering. **Related Knowledge/Courses: Design:** Design techniques, tools, and principles involved in production of precision technical plans, blueprints, drawings, and models. **Engineering and Technology:** The practical application of engineering science and technology. This includes applying principles, techniques, procedures, and equipment to the design and production of various goods and services. **Building and Construction:** The materials, methods, and tools involved in the construction or repair of houses, buildings, or other structures such as highways and roads. **Physics:** Physical principles and laws and their interrelationships and applications to understanding fluid, material, and atmospheric dynamics and mechanical, electrical, atomic, and subatomic structures and processes. **Chemistry:** The chemical composition, structure, and properties of substances and of the chemical processes and transformations that they undergo. This includes uses of chemicals and their danger signs, production techniques, and disposal methods. **Public Safety and Security:** Relevant equipment, policies, procedures, and strategies to promote effective local, state, or national security operations for the protection of people, data, property, and institutions.

Work Environment: Indoors; sitting.

First-Line Supervisors/Managers of Police and Detectives

- Annual Earnings: $65,570
- Growth: 15.5%
- Annual Job Openings: 9,000
- Education/Training Required: Work experience in a related occupation
- Self-Employed: 0.0%
- Part-Time: 0.9%

How the Job Improves the World: Contributes to justice and law enforcement.

Supervise and coordinate activities of members of police force. Explain police operations to subordinates to assist them in performing their job duties. Inform personnel of changes in regulations and policies, implications of new or amended laws, and new techniques of police work. Supervise and coordinate the investigation of criminal cases, offering guidance and expertise to investigators and ensuring that procedures are conducted in accordance with laws and regulations. Investigate and resolve personnel problems within organization and charges of misconduct against staff. Train staff in proper police work procedures. Maintain logs; prepare reports; and direct the preparation, handling, and maintenance of departmental records. Monitor and evaluate the job performance of subordinates and authorize promotions and transfers. Direct collection, preparation, and handling of evidence and personal property of prisoners. Develop, implement, and revise departmental policies and procedures. Conduct raids and order detention of witnesses and suspects for questioning. Prepare work schedules and assign duties to subordinates. Discipline staff for violation of department rules and regulations. Cooperate with court personnel and officials from other law enforcement agencies and testify in court as necessary. Review contents of written orders to ensure adherence to legal requirements. Inspect facilities, supplies, vehicles, and equipment to ensure conformance to standards. Prepare news releases and respond to police correspondence. Requisition and issue equipment and supplies. Meet with civic, educational, and community groups to develop community programs and events and to discuss law enforcement subjects. Direct release or transfer of prisoners. Prepare budgets and manage expenditures of department funds.

Personality Type: Enterprising. Enterprising occupations frequently involve starting up and carrying out projects. These occupations can involve leading people and making many decisions. They sometimes require risk taking and often deal with business.

GOE—Interest Area: 12. Law and Public Safety. **Work Group:** 12.01. Managerial Work in Law and Public Safety. **Other Jobs in This Work Group:** Emergency Management Specialists; First-Line Supervisors/Managers of Correctional Officers; First-Line Supervisors/Managers of Fire Fighting and Prevention Workers; Forest Fire Fighting and Prevention Supervisors; Municipal Fire Fighting and Prevention Supervisors.

Skills—Management of Personnel Resources: Motivating, developing, and directing people as they work; identifying the best people for the job. **Persuasion:** Persuading others to change their minds or behavior. **Negotiation:** Bringing others together and trying to reconcile differences. **Social Perceptiveness:** Being aware of others' reactions and understanding why they react as they do. **Service Orientation:** Actively looking for ways to help people. **Monitoring:** Monitoring/assessing your performance or that of other individuals or organizations to make improvements or take corrective action. **Judgment and Decision Making:** Considering the relative costs and benefits of potential actions to choose the most appropriate one. **Management of Material Resources:** Obtaining and seeing to the appropriate use of equipment, facilities, and materials needed to do certain work.

Education and Training Programs: Corrections; Criminal Justice/Law Enforcement Administration; Criminal Justice/Safety Studies. **Related Knowledge/Courses: Public Safety and Security:** Relevant equipment, policies, procedures, and strategies to promote effective local, state, or national security operations for the protection of people, data, property, and institutions. **Psychology:** Human behavior and performance; individual differences in ability, personality, and interests; learning and motivation; psychological research methods; and the assessment and treatment of behavioral and affective disorders. **Law and Government:** Laws, legal codes, court procedures, precedents, government regulations, executive orders, agency rules, and the democratic political process. **Personnel and Human Resources:** Principles and procedures for personnel recruitment, selection, training, compensation and benefits, labor relations and negotiation, and personnel information systems. **Education and Training:** Principles and methods for curriculum and training design, teaching and instruction for individuals and groups, and the measurement of training effects. **Telecommunications:** Transmission, broadcasting, switching, control, and operation of telecommunications systems.

Work Environment: More often outdoors than indoors; very hot or cold; very bright or dim lighting; hazardous equipment; sitting.

Fish and Game Wardens

- Annual Earnings: $42,850
- Growth: 10.5%
- Annual Job Openings: 1,000
- Education/Training Required: Associate degree
- Self-Employed: 0.0%
- Part-Time: No data available

How the Job Improves the World: Contributes to safety and the natural environment.

Patrol assigned area to prevent fish and game law violations. Investigate reports of damage to crops or property by wildlife. Compile biological data. Patrol assigned areas by car, boat, airplane, or horse or on foot to enforce game, fish, or boating laws and to manage wildlife programs, lakes, or land. Investigate hunting accidents and reports of fish and game law violations and issue warnings or citations and file reports as necessary. Serve warrants, make arrests, and compile and present evidence for court actions. Protect and preserve native wildlife, plants, and ecosystems. Promote and provide hunter and trapper safety training. Seize equipment used in fish and game law violations and arrange for disposition of fish or game illegally taken or possessed. Provide assistance to other local law enforcement agencies as required. Address schools, civic groups, sporting clubs, and the media to disseminate information concerning wildlife conservation and regulations. Recommend revisions or changes in hunting and trapping regulations or seasons and in animal management programs so that wildlife balances and habitats can be maintained. Inspect commercial operations relating to fish and wildlife, recreation, and protected areas. Collect and report information on populations and conditions of fish and wildlife in their habitats, availability of game food and cover, and suspected pollution. Survey areas and compile figures of bag counts of hunters to determine the effectiveness of control measures. Participate in search-and-rescue operations and in firefighting efforts. Investigate crop, property, or habitat damage or destruction or instances of water pollution to determine causes and to advise property owners of preventive measures. Design and implement control measures to prevent or counteract damage caused by wildlife or people. Document and detail the extent of crop, property, or habitat damage and make financial loss estimates and compensation recommendations.

Supervise the activities of seasonal workers. Issue licenses, permits, and other documentation. Provide advice and information to park and reserve visitors. Perform facilities maintenance work such as constructing or repairing structures and controlling weeds and pests.

Personality Type: Realistic. Realistic occupations frequently involve work activities that include practical, hands-on problems and solutions. They often deal with plants; animals; and real-world materials such as wood, tools, and machinery. Many of the occupations require working outside and do not involve a lot of paperwork or working closely with others.

GOE—Interest Area: 07. Government and Public Administration. **Work Group:** 07.03. Regulations Enforcement. **Other Jobs in This Work Group:** Agricultural Inspectors; Aviation Inspectors; Compliance Officers, Except Agriculture, Construction, Health and Safety, and Transportation; Construction and Building Inspectors; Environmental Compliance Inspectors; Equal Opportunity Representatives and Officers; Financial Examiners; Fire Inspectors; Forest Fire Inspectors and Prevention Specialists; Freight and Cargo Inspectors; Government Property Inspectors and Investigators; Immigration and Customs Inspectors; Licensing Examiners and Inspectors; Nuclear Monitoring Technicians; Occupational Health and Safety Specialists; Occupational Health and Safety Technicians; Tax Examiners, Collectors, and Revenue Agents; Transportation Vehicle, Equipment, and Systems Inspectors, Except Aviation.

Skills—Persuasion: Persuading others to change their minds or behavior. **Equipment Maintenance:** Performing routine maintenance on equipment and determining when and what kind of maintenance is needed. **Social Perceptiveness:** Being aware of others' reactions and understanding why they react as they do. **Speaking:** Talking to others to convey information effectively. **Science:** Using scientific rules and methods to solve problems. **Writing:** Communicating effectively in writing as appropriate for the needs of the audience. **Negotiation:** Bringing others together and trying to reconcile differences. **Repairing:** Repairing machines or systems by using the needed tools.

Education and Training Programs: Natural Resource Economics; Fishing and Fisheries Sciences and Management; Wildlife and Wildlands Science and Management. **Related Knowledge/Courses: Biology:** Plant and animal organisms and their tissues, cells, functions, interdependencies, and interactions with each other and the environment. **Law and Government:** Laws, legal codes, court procedures, precedents, government regulations, executive orders, agency rules, and the democratic political process. **Public Safety and Security:** Relevant equipment, policies, procedures, and strategies to promote effective local, state, or national security operations for the protection of people, data, property, and institutions. **Geography:** Principles and methods for describing the features of land, sea, and air masses, including their physical characteristics; locations; interrelationships; and distribution of plant, animal, and human life. **Psychology:** Human behavior and performance; individual differences in ability, personality, and interests; learning and motivation; psychological research methods; and the assessment and treatment of behavioral and affective disorders. **Sociology and Anthropology:** Group behavior and dynamics, societal trends and influences, human migrations, ethnicity, and cultures and their history and origins.

Work Environment: Outdoors; very hot or cold; very bright or dim lighting; contaminants; hazardous equipment; minor burns, cuts, bites, or stings.

Fitness Trainers and Aerobics Instructors

- Annual Earnings: $25,840
- Growth: 27.1%
- Annual Job Openings: 50,000
- Education/Training Required: Postsecondary vocational training
- Self-Employed: 6.6%
- Part-Time: 41.3%

How the Job Improves the World: Contributes to health and fitness.

Instruct or coach groups or individuals in exercise activities and the fundamentals of sports. Demonstrate techniques and methods of participation. Observe participants and inform them of corrective measures necessary to improve their skills. Explain and enforce safety rules and regulations governing sports, recreational activities, and the use of exercise equipment. Offer alternatives during classes to accommodate different levels of fitness. Plan routines, choose appropriate music, and choose different movements for each set of muscles, depending on participants' capabilities and limitations. Observe participants and inform them of corrective measures necessary for skill improvement. Teach proper breathing techniques used during physical exertion. Teach and demonstrate use of gymnastic and training equipment such as trampolines and weights. Instruct participants in maintaining exertion levels to maximize benefits from exercise routines. Maintain fitness equipment. Conduct therapeutic, recreational, or athletic activities. Monitor participants' progress and adapt programs as needed. Evaluate individuals' abilities, needs, and physical conditions and develop suitable training programs to meet any special requirements. Plan physical education programs to promote development of participants' physical attributes and social skills. Provide students with information and resources regarding nutrition, weight control, and lifestyle issues. Administer emergency first aid, wrap injuries, treat minor chronic disabilities, or refer injured persons to physicians. Advise clients about proper clothing and shoes. Wrap ankles, fingers, wrists, or other body parts with synthetic skin, gauze, or adhesive tape to support muscles and ligaments. Teach individual and team sports to participants through instruction and demonstration, utilizing knowledge of sports techniques and of participants' physical capabilities. Promote health clubs through membership sales and record member information. Organize, lead, and referee indoor and outdoor games such as volleyball, baseball, and basketball. Maintain equipment inventories and select, store, or issue equipment as needed. Organize and conduct competitions and tournaments. Advise participants in use of heat or ultraviolet treatments and hot baths. Massage body parts to relieve soreness, strains, and bruises.

Personality Type: Social. Social occupations frequently involve working with, communicating with, and teaching people. These occupations often involve helping or providing service to others.

GOE—Interest Area: 05. Education and Training. **Work Group:** 05.06. Counseling, Health, and Fitness Education. **Other Jobs in This Work Group:** Educational, Vocational, and School Counselors; Health Educators.

Skills—Instructing: Teaching others how to do something. **Equipment Selection:** Determining the kind of tools and equipment needed to do a job. **Monitoring:** Monitoring/assessing your performance or that of other individuals or organizations to make improvements or take corrective action. **Service Orientation:** Actively looking for ways to help people. **Coordination:** Adjusting actions in relation to others' actions. **Social Perceptiveness:** Being aware of others'

reactions and understanding why they react as they do. **Time Management:** Managing one's own time and the time of others. **Speaking:** Talking to others to convey information effectively.

Education and Training Programs: Physical Education Teaching and Coaching; Health and Physical Education, General; Sport and Fitness Administration/Management. **Related Knowledge/Courses: Customer and Personal Service:** Principles and processes for providing customer and personal services. This includes customer needs assessment, meeting quality standards for services, and evaluation of customer satisfaction. **Psychology:** Human behavior and performance; individual differences in ability, personality, and interests; learning and motivation; psychological research methods; and the assessment and treatment of behavioral and affective disorders. **Education and Training:** Principles and methods for curriculum and training design, teaching and instruction for individuals and groups, and the measurement of training effects. **Sociology and Anthropology:** Group behavior and dynamics, societal trends and influences, human migrations, ethnicity, and cultures and their history and origins. **Sales and Marketing:** Principles and methods for showing, promoting, and selling products or services. This includes marketing strategy and tactics, product demonstration, sales techniques, and sales control systems. **Personnel and Human Resources:** Principles and procedures for personnel recruitment, selection, training, compensation and benefits, labor relations and negotiation, and personnel information systems.

Work Environment: Indoors; standing; walking and running; repetitive motions.

Flight Attendants

- Annual Earnings: $46,680
- Growth: 16.3%
- Annual Job Openings: 7,000
- Education/Training Required: Long-term on-the-job training
- Self-Employed: 0.2%
- Part-Time: 28.8%

How the Job Improves the World: Contributes to health and safety.

Provide personal services to ensure the safety and comfort of airline passengers during flight. Greet passengers, verify tickets, explain use of safety equipment, and serve food or beverages. Direct and assist passengers in the event of an emergency, such as directing passengers to evacuate a plane following an emergency landing. Announce and demonstrate safety and emergency procedures such as the use of oxygen masks, seat belts, and life jackets. Walk aisles of planes to verify that passengers have complied with federal regulations prior to takeoffs and landings. Verify that first aid kits and other emergency equipment, including fire extinguishers and oxygen bottles, are in working order. Administer first aid to passengers in distress. Attend preflight briefings concerning weather, altitudes, routes, emergency procedures, crew coordination, lengths of flights, food and beverage services offered, and numbers of passengers. Prepare passengers and aircraft for landing, following procedures. Determine special assistance needs of passengers such as small children, the elderly, or disabled persons. Check to ensure that food, beverages, blankets, reading material, emergency equipment, and other supplies are aboard and are in adequate supply. Reassure passengers when situations such as turbulence are encountered. Announce flight delays and descent preparations. Inspect passenger tickets to verify information and to obtain destination information.

Answer passengers' questions about flights, aircraft, weather, travel routes and services, arrival times, and schedules. Assist passengers while entering or disembarking the aircraft. Inspect and clean cabins, checking for any problems and making sure that cabins are in order. Greet passengers boarding aircraft and direct them to assigned seats. Conduct periodic trips through the cabin to ensure passenger comfort and to distribute reading material, headphones, pillows, playing cards, and blankets. Take inventory of headsets, alcoholic beverages, and money collected. Operate audio and video systems. Assist passengers in placing carry-on luggage in overhead, garment, or underseat storage. Prepare reports showing places of departure and destination, passenger ticket numbers, meal and beverage inventories, the conditions of cabin equipment, and any problems encountered by passengers.

Personality Type: Enterprising. Enterprising occupations frequently involve starting up and carrying out projects. These occupations can involve leading people and making many decisions. They sometimes require risk taking and often deal with business.

GOE—Interest Area: 09. Hospitality, Tourism, and Recreation. **Work Group:** 09.03. Hospitality and Travel Services. **Other Jobs in This Work Group:** Baggage Porters and Bellhops; Concierges; Hotel, Motel, and Resort Desk Clerks; Janitors and Cleaners, Except Maids and Housekeeping Cleaners; Maids and Housekeeping Cleaners; Reservation and Transportation Ticket Agents and Travel Clerks; Tour Guides and Escorts; Transportation Attendants, Except Flight Attendants and Baggage Porters; Travel Agents; Travel Guides.

Skills—No data available.

Education and Training Program: Airline Flight Attendant. **Related Knowledge/Courses: Customer and Personal Service:** Principles and processes for providing customer and personal services. This includes customer needs assessment, meeting quality standards for services, and evaluation of customer satisfaction.

Psychology: Human behavior and performance; individual differences in ability, personality, and interests; learning and motivation; psychological research methods; and the assessment and treatment of behavioral and affective disorders. **Transportation:** Principles and methods for moving people or goods by air, rail, sea, or road, including the relative costs and benefits. **Geography:** Principles and methods for describing the features of land, sea, and air masses, including their physical characteristics; locations; interrelationships; and distribution of plant, animal, and human life. **Philosophy and Theology:** Different philosophical systems and religions. This includes their basic principles, values, ethics, ways of thinking, customs, and practices and their impact on human culture. **Public Safety and Security:** Relevant equipment, policies, procedures, and strategies to promote effective local, state, or national security operations for the protection of people, data, property, and institutions.

Work Environment: Indoors; noisy; contaminants; disease or infections; high places; standing.

Foreign Language and Literature Teachers, Postsecondary

- Annual Earnings: $49,570
- Growth: 32.2%
- Annual Job Openings: 329,000
- Education/Training Required: Master's degree
- Self-Employed: 0.4%
- Part-Time: 27.3%

The job openings listed here are shared with 35 other postsecondary teaching occupations. For a complete list, see the beginning of this section.

How the Job Improves the World: Contributes to education, intercultural understanding, and the arts.

Teach courses in foreign (i.e., other than English) languages and literature. Evaluate and grade students' classwork, assignments, and papers. Prepare course materials such as syllabi, homework assignments, and handouts. Initiate, facilitate, and moderate classroom discussions. Maintain student attendance records, grades, and other required records. Compile, administer, and grade examinations or assign this work to others. Plan, evaluate, and revise curricula, course content, and course materials and methods of instruction. Prepare and deliver lectures to undergraduate and graduate students on topics such as how to speak and write a foreign language and the cultural aspects of areas where a particular language is used. Maintain regularly scheduled office hours to advise and assist students. Select and obtain materials and supplies such as textbooks. Keep abreast of developments in their field by reading current literature, talking with colleagues, and participating in professional organizations and activities. Advise students on academic and vocational curricula and on career issues. Conduct research in a particular field of knowledge and publish findings in scholarly journals, books, and/or electronic media. Collaborate with colleagues to address teaching and research issues. Serve on academic or administrative committees that deal with institutional policies, departmental matters, and academic issues. Participate in student recruitment, registration, and placement activities. Compile bibliographies of specialized materials for outside reading assignments. Participate in campus and community events. Act as advisers to student organizations. Perform administrative duties such as serving as department head. Supervise undergraduate and graduate teaching, internship, and research work. Write grant proposals to procure external research funding. Provide professional consulting services to government or industry.

Personality Type: Artistic. Artistic occupations frequently involve working with forms, designs, and patterns. They often require self-expression, and the work can be done without following a clear set of rules.

GOE—Interest Area: 05. Education and Training. **Work Group:** 05.03. Postsecondary and Adult Teaching and Instructing. **Other Jobs in This Work Group:** Adult Literacy, Remedial Education, and GED Teachers and Instructors; Agricultural Sciences Teachers, Postsecondary; Anthropology and Archeology Teachers, Postsecondary; Architecture Teachers, Postsecondary; Area, Ethnic, and Cultural Studies Teachers, Postsecondary; Art, Drama, and Music Teachers, Postsecondary; Atmospheric, Earth, Marine, and Space Sciences Teachers, Postsecondary; Biological Science Teachers, Postsecondary; Business Teachers, Postsecondary; Chemistry Teachers, Postsecondary; Communications Teachers, Postsecondary; Computer Science Teachers, Postsecondary; Criminal Justice and Law Enforcement Teachers, Postsecondary; Economics Teachers, Postsecondary; Education Teachers, Postsecondary; Engineering Teachers, Postsecondary; English Language and Literature Teachers, Postsecondary; Environmental Science Teachers, Postsecondary; Farm and Home Management Advisors; Forestry and Conservation Science Teachers, Postsecondary; Geography Teachers, Postsecondary; Graduate Teaching Assistants; Health Specialties Teachers, Postsecondary; History Teachers, Postsecondary; Home Economics Teachers, Postsecondary; Law Teachers, Postsecondary; Library Science Teachers, Postsecondary; Mathematical Science Teachers, Postsecondary; Nursing Instructors and Teachers, Postsecondary; Philosophy and Religion Teachers, Postsecondary; Physics Teachers, Postsecondary; Political Science Teachers, Postsecondary; Psychology Teachers, Postsecondary; Recreation and Fitness Studies Teachers, Postsecondary; Self-Enrichment Education Teachers; Social Work Teachers, Postsecondary; Sociology Teachers, Postsecondary; Vocational Education Teachers, Postsecondary.

Skills—Instructing: Teaching others how to do something. **Learning Strategies:** Selecting and using training/instructional methods and procedures appropriate for the situation when learning or teaching new things. **Writing:** Communicating effectively in writing as appropriate for the needs of the audience. **Persuasion:** Persuading others to change their minds or behavior. **Speaking:** Talking to others to convey information effectively. **Reading Comprehension:** Understanding written sentences and paragraphs in work-related documents. **Social Perceptiveness:** Being aware of others' reactions and understanding why they react as they do. **Critical Thinking:** Using logic and reasoning to identify the strengths and weaknesses of alternative solutions, conclusions, or approaches to problems.

Education and Training Programs: Latin Teacher Education; Foreign Languages and Literatures, General; Linguistics; Language Interpretation and Translation; African Languages, Literatures, and Linguistics; East Asian Languages, Literatures, and Linguistics, General; Chinese Language and Literature; Japanese Language and Literature; Korean Language and Literature; Tibetan Language and Literature; others. **Related Knowledge/Courses: Foreign Language:** The structure and content of a foreign (non-English) language, including the meaning and spelling of words, rules of composition and grammar, and pronunciation. **Philosophy and Theology:** Different philosophical systems and religions. This includes their basic principles, values, ethics, ways of thinking, customs, and practices and their impact on human culture. **History and Archeology:** Historical events and their causes, indicators, and effects on civilizations and cultures. **Sociology and Anthropology:** Group behavior and dynamics, societal trends and influences, human migrations, ethnicity, and cultures and their history and origins. **Geography:** Principles and methods for describing the features of land, sea, and air masses, including their physical characteristics; locations; interrelationships; and distribution of plant, animal, and human life. **English Language:** The structure and content of the English language, including the meaning and spelling of words, rules of composition, and grammar.

Work Environment: Indoors; sitting.

Forest Fire Fighters

- ◎ Annual Earnings: $39,090
- ◎ Growth: 24.3%
- ◎ Annual Job Openings: 21,000
- ◎ Education/Training Required: Long-term on-the-job training
- ◎ Self-Employed: 0.1%
- ◎ Part-Time: 1.5%

The job openings listed here are shared with Municipal Fire Fighters.

How the Job Improves the World: Contributes to safety and the natural environment.

Control and suppress fires in forests or vacant public land. Maintain contact with fire dispatchers at all times to notify them of the need for additional firefighters and supplies or to detail any difficulties encountered. Rescue fire victims and administer emergency medical aid. Collaborate with other firefighters as a member of a firefighting crew. Patrol burned areas after fires to locate and eliminate hot spots that may restart fires. Extinguish flames and embers to suppress fires, using shovels or engine- or hand-driven water or chemical pumps. Fell trees, cut and clear brush, and dig trenches to create firelines, using axes, chainsaws, or shovels. Maintain knowledge of current firefighting practices by participating in drills and by attending seminars, conventions, and conferences. Operate pumps connected to high-pressure hoses. Participate in physical training to maintain high levels of physical fitness. Establish water supplies, connect hoses, and direct water onto fires. Maintain fire

equipment and firehouse living quarters. Inform and educate the public about fire prevention. Take action to contain any hazardous chemicals that could catch fire, leak, or spill. Organize fire caches, positioning equipment for the most effective response. Transport personnel and cargo to and from fire areas. Participate in fire prevention and inspection programs. Perform forest maintenance and improvement tasks such as cutting brush, planting trees, building trails, and marking timber. Test and maintain tools, equipment, jump gear, and parachutes to ensure readiness for fire-suppression activities. Observe forest areas from fire lookout towers to spot potential problems. Orient self in relation to fire, using compass and map, and collect supplies and equipment dropped by parachute. Serve as fully trained lead helicopter crewmember and as helispot manager. Drop weighted paper streamers from aircraft to determine the speed and direction of the wind at fire sites.

Personality Type: Realistic. Realistic occupations frequently involve work activities that include practical, hands-on problems and solutions. They often deal with plants; animals; and real-world materials such as wood, tools, and machinery. Many of the occupations require working outside and do not involve a lot of paperwork or working closely with others.

GOE—Interest Area: 12. Law and Public Safety. **Work Group:** 12.06. Emergency Responding. **Other Jobs in This Work Group:** Emergency Medical Technicians and Paramedics; Fire Fighters; Municipal Fire Fighters.

Skills—Management of Personnel Resources: Motivating, developing, and directing people as they work; identifying the best people for the job. **Repairing:** Repairing machines or systems by using the needed tools. **Equipment Maintenance:** Performing routine maintenance on equipment and determining when and what kind of maintenance is needed. **Operation Monitoring:** Watching gauges, dials, or other indicators to make sure a machine is working properly. **Systems Analysis:** Determining how a system should work and how changes in conditions, operations, and the environment will affect outcomes. **Operation and Control:** Controlling operations of equipment or systems. **Equipment Selection:** Determining the kind of tools and equipment needed to do a job. **Management of Material Resources:** Obtaining and seeing to the appropriate use of equipment, facilities, and materials needed to do certain work.

Education and Training Programs: Fire Science/Firefighting; Fire Protection, Other. **Related Knowledge/Courses: Geography:** Principles and methods for describing the features of land, sea, and air masses, including their physical characteristics; locations; interrelationships; and distribution of plant, animal, and human life. **Customer and Personal Service:** Principles and processes for providing customer and personal services. This includes customer needs assessment, meeting quality standards for services, and evaluation of customer satisfaction. **Mechanical Devices:** Machines and tools, including their designs, uses, repair, and maintenance. **Education and Training:** Principles and methods for curriculum and training design, teaching and instruction for individuals and groups, and the measurement of training effects. **Public Safety and Security:** Relevant equipment, policies, procedures, and strategies to promote effective local, state, or national security operations for the protection of people, data, property, and institutions. **Psychology:** Human behavior and performance; individual differences in ability, personality, and interests; learning and motivation; psychological research methods; and the assessment and treatment of behavioral and affective disorders.

Work Environment: Outdoors; very hot or cold; contaminants; hazardous conditions; minor burns, cuts, bites, or stings; using hands on objects, tools, or controls.

Forest Fire Fighting and Prevention Supervisors

- Annual Earnings: $60,840
- Growth: 21.1%
- Annual Job Openings: 4,000
- Education/Training Required: Work experience in a related occupation
- Self-Employed: 0.0%
- Part-Time: 0.4%

The job openings listed here are shared with Municipal Fire Fighting and Prevention Supervisors.

How the Job Improves the World: Contributes to safety and the natural environment.

Supervise fire fighters who control and suppress fires in forests or vacant public land. Communicate fire details to superiors, subordinates, and interagency dispatch centers, using two-way radios. Serve as working leader of an engine, hand, helicopter, or prescribed fire crew of three or more firefighters. Maintain fire suppression equipment in good condition, checking equipment periodically to ensure that it is ready for use. Evaluate size, location, and condition of forest fires in order to request and dispatch crews and position equipment so fires can be contained safely and effectively. Operate wildland fire engines and hoselays. Direct and supervise prescribed burn projects and prepare post-burn reports analyzing burn conditions and results. Monitor prescribed burns to ensure that they are conducted safely and effectively. Identify staff training and development needs to ensure that appropriate training can be arranged. Maintain knowledge of forest fire laws and fire prevention techniques and tactics. Recommend equipment modifications or new equipment purchases. Perform administrative duties such as compiling and maintaining records, completing forms, preparing reports, and composing correspondence. Recruit and hire forest fire-fighting personnel. Train workers in such skills as parachute jumping, fire suppression, aerial observation, and radio communication, both in the classroom and on the job. Review and evaluate employee performance. Observe fires and crews from air to determine fire-fighting force requirements and to note changing conditions that will affect fire-fighting efforts. Inspect all stations, uniforms, equipment, and recreation areas to ensure compliance with safety standards, taking corrective action as necessary. Schedule employee work assignments and set work priorities. Regulate open burning by issuing burning permits, inspecting problem sites, issuing citations for violations of laws and ordinances, and educating the public in proper burning practices. Direct investigations of suspected arsons in wildfires, working closely with other investigating agencies. Monitor fire suppression expenditures to ensure that they are necessary and reasonable.

Personality Type: Realistic. Realistic occupations frequently involve work activities that include practical, hands-on problems and solutions. They often deal with plants; animals; and real-world materials such as wood, tools, and machinery. Many of the occupations require working outside and do not involve a lot of paperwork or working closely with others.

GOE—Interest Area: 12. Law and Public Safety. **Work Group:** 12.01. Managerial Work in Law and Public Safety. **Other Jobs in This Work Group:** Emergency Management Specialists; First-Line Supervisors/Managers of Correctional Officers; First-Line Supervisors/Managers of Fire Fighting and Prevention Workers; First-Line Supervisors/Managers of Police and Detectives; Municipal Fire Fighting and Prevention Supervisors.

Skills—Equipment Maintenance: Performing routine maintenance on equipment and determining when and what kind of maintenance is needed. **Repairing:** Repairing machines or systems by using the needed tools. **Operation Monitoring:** Watching gauges, dials, or other indicators to make sure a machine is working properly. **Management of Personnel Resources:** Motivating, developing, and directing people as they work; identifying the best people for the job. **Operation and Control:** Controlling operations of equipment or systems. **Management of Material Resources:** Obtaining and seeing to the appropriate use of equipment, facilities, and materials needed to do certain work. **Management of Financial Resources:** Determining how money will be spent to get the work done and accounting for these expenditures. **Science:** Using scientific rules and methods to solve problems.

Education and Training Programs: Fire Protection and Safety Technology/Technician; Fire Services Administration. **Related Knowledge/Courses: Public Safety and Security:** Relevant equipment, policies, procedures, and strategies to promote effective local, state, or national security operations for the protection of people, data, property, and institutions. **Building and Construction:** The materials, methods, and tools involved in the construction or repair of houses, buildings, or other structures such as highways and roads. **Customer and Personal Service:** Principles and processes for providing customer and personal services. This includes customer needs assessment, meeting quality standards for services, and evaluation of customer satisfaction. **Personnel and Human Resources:** Principles and procedures for personnel recruitment, selection, training, compensation and benefits, labor relations and negotiation, and personnel information systems. **Mechanical Devices:** Machines and tools, including their designs, uses, repair, and maintenance. **Transportation:** Principles and methods for moving people or goods by air, rail, sea, or road, including the relative costs and benefits.

Work Environment: Outdoors; noisy; very hot or cold; hazardous equipment; minor burns, cuts, bites, or stings; standing.

Foresters

- Annual Earnings: $48,670
- Growth: 6.7%
- Annual Job Openings: 1,000
- Education/Training Required: Bachelor's degree
- Self-Employed: 9.1%
- Part-Time: 6.7%

How the Job Improves the World: Contributes to natural environment.

Manage forested lands for economic, recreational, and conservation purposes. May inventory the type, amount, and location of standing timber; appraise the timber's worth; negotiate the purchase; and draw up contracts for procurement. May determine how to conserve wildlife habitats, creek beds, water quality, and soil stability and how best to comply with environmental regulations. May devise plans for planting and growing new trees, monitor trees for healthy growth, and determine the best time for harvesting. Develop forest management plans for public and privately owned forested lands. Monitor contract compliance and results of forestry activities to assure adherence to government regulations. Establish short- and long-term plans for management of forest lands and forest resources. Supervise activities of other forestry workers. Choose and prepare sites for new trees, using controlled burning, bulldozers, or herbicides to clear weeds, brush, and logging debris. Plan and supervise forestry projects, such as determining the type, number, and placement of trees to be planted; managing tree nurseries; thinning forest; and monitoring growth of new seedlings. Negotiate terms and conditions of agreements and contracts for forest harvesting, forest management, and leasing of forest lands. Direct and participate in forest-fire suppression. Determine methods of cutting and removing timber with minimum waste and environmental damage.

Analyze effect of forest conditions on tree growth rates and tree species prevalence and the yield, duration, seed production, growth viability, and germination of different species. Monitor forest-cleared lands to ensure that they are reclaimed to their most suitable end use. Plan and implement projects for conservation of wildlife habitats and soil and water quality. Plan and direct forest surveys and related studies and prepare reports and recommendations. Perform inspections of forests or forest nurseries. Map forest area soils and vegetation to estimate the amount of standing timber and future value and growth. Conduct public educational programs on forest care and conservation. Procure timber from private landowners. Subcontract with loggers or pulpwood cutters for tree removal and to aid in road layout. Plan cutting programs and manage timber sales from harvested areas, helping companies to achieve production goals. Monitor wildlife populations and assess the impacts of forest operations on population and habitats. Plan and direct construction and maintenance of recreation facilities, fire towers, trails, roads, and bridges, ensuring that they comply with guidelines and regulations set for forested public lands. Contact local forest owners and gain permission to take inventory of the type, amount, and location of all standing timber on the property.

Personality Type: Realistic. Realistic occupations frequently involve work activities that include practical, hands-on problems and solutions. They often deal with plants; animals; and real-world materials such as wood, tools, and machinery. Many of the occupations require working outside and do not involve a lot of paperwork or working closely with others.

GOE—Interest Area: 01. Agriculture and Natural Resources. **Work Group:** 01.02. Resource Science/ Engineering for Plants, Animals, and the Environment. **Other Jobs in This Work Group:** Agricultural Engineers; Animal Scientists; Conservation Scientists; Environmental Engineers; Mining and Geological Engineers, Including Mining Safety Engineers; Petroleum Engineers; Range

Managers; Soil and Plant Scientists; Soil and Water Conservationists; Zoologists and Wildlife Biologists.

Skills—Management of Financial Resources: Determining how money will be spent to get the work done and accounting for these expenditures. **Science:** Using scientific rules and methods to solve problems. **Programming:** Writing computer programs for various purposes. **Quality Control Analysis:** Conducting tests and inspections of products, services, or processes to evaluate quality or performance. **Mathematics:** Using mathematics to solve problems. **Operations Analysis:** Analyzing needs and product requirements to create a design. **Coordination:** Adjusting actions in relation to others' actions. **Time Management:** Managing one's own time and the time of others.

Education and Training Programs: Natural Resources/Conservation, General; Natural Resources Management and Policy; Natural Resources Management and Policy, Other; Forestry, General; Forest Sciences and Biology; Forest Management/Forest Resources Management; Urban Forestry; Wood Science and Wood Products/Pulp and Paper Technology; Forest Resources Production and Management; Forestry, Other; Natural Resources and Conservation, Other. **Related Knowledge/Courses: Biology:** Plant and animal organisms and their tissues, cells, functions, interdependencies, and interactions with each other and the environment. **Geography:** Principles and methods for describing the features of land, sea, and air masses, including their physical characteristics; locations; interrelationships; and distribution of plant, animal, and human life. **Mathematics:** Arithmetic, algebra, geometry, calculus, and statistics and their applications. **Law and Government:** Laws, legal codes, court procedures, precedents, government regulations, executive orders, agency rules, and the democratic political process. **Computers and Electronics:** Circuit boards; processors; chips; electronic equipment; and computer hardware and software, including applications and programming. **English Language:** The structure and content of the English language, including the meaning and spelling of words, rules of composition, and grammar.

Work Environment: More often indoors than outdoors; noisy; sitting.

Forestry and Conservation Science Teachers, Postsecondary

- Annual Earnings: $64,870
- Growth: 32.2%
- Annual Job Openings: 329,000
- Education/Training Required: Master's degree
- Self-Employed: 0.4%
- Part-Time: 27.3%

The job openings listed here are shared with 35 other postsecondary teaching occupations. For a complete list, see the beginning of this section.

How the Job Improves the World: Contributes to education and the natural environment.

Teach courses in environmental and conservation science. Conduct research in a particular field of knowledge and publish findings in books, professional journals, and/or electronic media. Keep abreast of developments in their field by reading current literature, talking with colleagues, and participating in professional conferences. Prepare and deliver lectures to undergraduate and/or graduate students on topics such as forest resource policy, forest pathology, and mapping. Evaluate and grade students' classwork, assignments, and papers. Write grant proposals to procure external research funding. Supervise undergraduate and/or graduate teaching, internship, and research work. Plan, evaluate, and revise curricula, course content, and course materials and methods of instruction. Prepare course materials such as syllabi, homework assignments, and handouts. Compile, administer, and grade examinations or assign this work to others. Advise students on academic and vocational curricula and on career issues. Initiate, facilitate, and moderate classroom discussions. Supervise students' laboratory work and fieldwork. Maintain student attendance records, grades, and other required records. Collaborate with colleagues to address teaching and research issues. Maintain regularly scheduled office hours in order to advise and assist students. Select and obtain materials and supplies such as textbooks and laboratory equipment. Participate in student recruitment, registration, and placement activities. Serve on academic or administrative committees that deal with institutional policies, departmental matters, and academic issues. Provide professional consulting services to government and/or industry. Perform administrative duties such as serving as department head. Compile bibliographies of specialized materials for outside reading assignments. Act as advisers to student organizations. Participate in campus and community events.

Personality Type: Investigative. Investigative occupations frequently involve working with ideas and require an extensive amount of thinking. These occupations can involve searching for facts and figuring out problems mentally.

GOE—Interest Area: 05. Education and Training. **Work Group:** 05.03. Postsecondary and Adult Teaching and Instructing. **Other Jobs in This Work Group:** Adult Literacy, Remedial Education, and GED Teachers and Instructors; Agricultural Sciences Teachers, Postsecondary; Anthropology and Archeology Teachers, Postsecondary; Architecture Teachers, Postsecondary; Area, Ethnic, and Cultural Studies Teachers, Postsecondary; Art, Drama, and Music Teachers, Postsecondary; Atmospheric, Earth, Marine, and Space Sciences Teachers, Postsecondary; Biological Science Teachers, Postsecondary; Business Teachers, Postsecondary; Chemistry Teachers, Postsecondary; Communications Teachers, Postsecondary; Computer Science Teachers, Postsecondary; Criminal Justice and Law Enforcement Teachers, Postsecondary; Economics Teachers, Postsecondary; Education Teachers, Postsecondary; Engineering Teachers, Postsecondary; English Language and Literature Teachers, Postsecondary; Environmental Science Teachers, Postsecondary; Farm and Home Management Advisors; Foreign Language and Literature Teachers, Postsecondary; Geography Teachers, Postsecondary; Graduate Teaching Assistants; Health Specialties Teachers, Postsecondary; History Teachers, Postsecondary; Home Economics Teachers, Postsecondary; Law Teachers, Postsecondary; Library Science Teachers, Postsecondary; Mathematical Science Teachers, Postsecondary; Nursing Instructors and Teachers, Postsecondary; Philosophy and Religion Teachers, Postsecondary; Physics Teachers, Postsecondary; Political Science Teachers, Postsecondary; Psychology Teachers, Postsecondary; Recreation and Fitness Studies Teachers, Postsecondary; Self-Enrichment Education Teachers; Social Work Teachers, Postsecondary; Sociology Teachers, Postsecondary; Vocational Education Teachers, Postsecondary.

Skills—Science: Using scientific rules and methods to solve problems. **Management of Financial Resources:** Determining how money will be spent to get the work done and accounting for these expenditures. **Instructing:** Teaching others how to do something. **Writing:** Communicating effectively in writing as appropriate for the needs of the audience. **Management of Personnel Resources:** Motivating, developing, and directing people as they work; identifying the best people for the job. **Mathematics:** Using mathematics to solve problems. **Active Learning:** Understanding the implications of new information for both current and future problem-solving and decision-making. **Complex Problem Solving:** Identifying complex problems and reviewing related information to develop and evaluate options and implement solutions.

Education and Training Program: Science Teacher Education/General Science Teacher Education. **Related Knowledge/Courses: Biology:** Plant and animal organisms and their tissues, cells, functions, interdependencies, and interactions with each other and the environment. **Geography:** Principles and methods for describing the features of land, sea, and air masses, including their physical characteristics; locations; interrelationships; and distribution of plant, animal, and human life. **Education and Training:** Principles and methods for curriculum and training design, teaching and instruction for individuals and groups, and the measurement of training effects. **Mathematics:** Arithmetic, algebra, geometry, calculus, and statistics and their applications. **English Language:** The structure and content of the English language, including the meaning and spelling of words, rules of composition, and grammar. **Chemistry:** The chemical composition, structure, and properties of substances and of the chemical processes and transformations that they undergo. This includes uses of chemicals and their danger signs, production techniques, and disposal methods.

Work Environment: Indoors; sitting.

Funeral Attendants

- Annual Earnings: $19,720
- Growth: 20.8%
- Annual Job Openings: 8,000
- Education/Training Required: Short-term on-the-job training
- Self-Employed: 0.0%
- Part-Time: 44.0%

How the Job Improves the World: Contributes to consolation of mourners.

Perform variety of tasks during funeral, such as placing casket in parlor or chapel prior to service, arranging floral offerings or lights around casket, directing or escorting mourners, closing casket, and issuing and storing funeral equipment. Perform a variety of tasks during funerals to assist funeral directors and to ensure that services run smoothly and as planned. Greet people at the funeral home. Offer assistance to mourners as they enter or exit limousines. Close caskets at appropriate point in services. Transfer the deceased to funeral homes. Obtain burial permits and register deaths. Direct or escort mourners to parlors or chapels in which wakes or funerals are being held. Place caskets in parlors or chapels prior to wakes or funerals. Clean and drive funeral vehicles such as cars or hearses in funeral processions. Carry flowers to hearses or limousines for transportation to places of interment. Clean funeral parlors and chapels. Arrange floral offerings or lights around caskets. Provide advice to mourners on how to make charitable donations in honor of the deceased. Perform general maintenance duties for funeral homes. Issue and store funeral equipment. Assist with cremations and with the processing and packaging of cremated remains. Act as pallbearers.

Personality Type: Social. Social occupations frequently involve working with, communicating with, and teaching people. These occupations often involve helping or providing service to others.

GOE—Interest Area: 10. Human Service. **Work Group:** 10.03. Child/Personal Care and Services. **Other Jobs in This Work Group:** Child Care Workers; Nannies; Personal and Home Care Aides.

Skills—No data available.

Education and Training Program: Funeral Service and Mortuary Science, General. **Related Knowledge/Courses: Philosophy and Theology:** Different philosophical systems and religions. This includes their basic principles, values, ethics, ways of thinking, customs, and practices and their impact on human culture. **Customer and Personal Service:** Principles and processes for providing customer and personal services. This includes customer needs assessment, meeting quality standards for services, and evaluation of customer satisfaction. **Transportation:** Principles and methods for moving people or goods by air, rail, sea, or road, including the relative costs and benefits. **Psychology:** Human behavior and performance; individual differences in ability, personality, and interests; learning and motivation; psychological research methods; and the assessment and treatment of behavioral and affective disorders. **Law and Government:** Laws, legal codes, court procedures, precedents, government regulations, executive orders, agency rules, and the democratic political process. **Clerical Practices:** Administrative and clerical procedures and systems such as word processing, managing files and records, stenography and transcription, designing forms, and other office procedures and terminology.

Work Environment: More often indoors than outdoors; standing.

Funeral Directors

◎ Annual Earnings: $47,630

◎ Growth: 6.7%

◎ Annual Job Openings: 3,000

◎ Education/Training Required: Associate degree

◎ Self-Employed: 19.7%

◎ Part-Time: 9.0%

How the Job Improves the World: Contributes to consolation of mourners.

Perform various tasks to arrange and direct funeral services, such as coordinating transportation of body to mortuary for embalming, interviewing family or other authorized person to arrange details, selecting pallbearers, procuring official for religious rites, and providing transportation for mourners. Consult with families or friends of the deceased to arrange funeral details such as obituary notice wording, casket selection, and plans for services. Plan, schedule, and coordinate funerals, burials, and cremations, arranging such details as the time and place of services. Obtain information needed to complete legal documents such as death certificates and burial permits. Oversee the preparation and care of the remains of people who have died. Contact cemeteries to schedule the opening and closing of graves. Provide information on funeral service options, products, and merchandise and maintain a casket display area. Manage funeral home operations, including hiring and supervising embalmers, funeral attendants, and other staff. Offer counsel and comfort to bereaved families and friends. Close caskets and lead funeral corteges to churches or burial sites. Arrange for clergy members to perform needed services. Provide or arrange transportation between sites for the remains, mourners, pallbearers, clergy, and flowers. Perform embalming duties as necessary. Direct preparations and shipment of bodies for out-of-state burial. Discuss and negotiate prearranged funerals with clients. Inform survivors of benefits for which they may be eligible. Maintain financial records, order merchandise, and prepare accounts. Plan placement of caskets at funeral sites and place and adjust lights, fixtures, and floral displays. Arrange for pallbearers and inform pallbearers and honorary groups of their duties. Receive people and usher them to their seats for services.

Personality Type: Enterprising. Enterprising occupations frequently involve starting up and carrying out projects. These occupations can involve leading people and making many decisions. They sometimes require risk taking and often deal with business.

GOE—Interest Area: 14. Retail and Wholesale Sales and Service. **Work Group:** 14.01. Managerial Work in Retail/Wholesale Sales and Service. **Other Jobs in This Work Group:** Advertising and Promotions Managers; First-Line Supervisors/Managers of Non-Retail Sales Workers; First-Line Supervisors/Managers of Retail Sales Workers; Marketing Managers; Property, Real Estate, and Community Association Managers; Purchasing Managers; Sales Managers.

Skills—Service Orientation: Actively looking for ways to help people. **Management of Financial Resources:** Determining how money will be spent to get the work done and accounting for these expenditures. **Social Perceptiveness:** Being aware of others' reactions and understanding why they react as they do. **Management of Personnel Resources:** Motivating, developing, and directing people as they work; identifying the best people for the job. **Management of Material Resources:** Obtaining and seeing to the appropriate use of equipment, facilities, and materials needed to do certain work. **Coordination:** Adjusting actions in relation to others' actions. **Negotiation:** Bringing others together and trying to reconcile differences. **Science:** Using scientific rules and methods to solve problems.

Education and Training Programs: Funeral Service and Mortuary Science, General; Funeral Direction/Service. **Related Knowledge/Courses: Therapy and Counseling:** Principles, methods, and procedures for diagnosis, treatment, and rehabilitation of physical and mental dysfunctions and for career counseling and guidance. **Philosophy and Theology:** Different philosophical systems and religions. This includes their basic principles, values, ethics, ways of thinking, customs, and practices and their impact on human culture. **Customer and Personal Service:** Principles and processes for providing customer and personal services. This includes customer needs assessment, meeting quality standards for services, and evaluation of customer satisfaction. **Sales and Marketing:** Principles and methods for showing, promoting, and selling products or services. This includes marketing strategy and tactics, product demonstration, sales techniques, and sales control systems. **Clerical Practices:** Administrative and clerical procedures and systems such as word processing, managing files and records, stenography and transcription, designing

forms, and other office procedures and terminology. **Psychology:** Human behavior and performance; individual differences in ability, personality, and interests; learning and motivation; psychological research methods; and the assessment and treatment of behavioral and affective disorders.

Work Environment: More often indoors than outdoors; contaminants; disease or infections; standing.

Geography Teachers, Postsecondary

- Annual Earnings: $57,870
- Growth: 32.2%
- Annual Job Openings: 329,000
- Education/Training Required: Master's degree
- Self-Employed: 0.4%
- Part-Time: 27.3%

The job openings listed here are shared with 35 other postsecondary teaching occupations. For a complete list, see the beginning of this section.

How the Job Improves the World: Contributes to education.

Teach courses in geography. Prepare and deliver lectures to undergraduate and/or graduate students on topics such as urbanization, environmental systems, and cultural geography. Evaluate and grade students' classwork, assignments, and papers. Compile, administer, and grade examinations or assign this work to others. Initiate, facilitate, and moderate classroom discussions. Maintain student attendance records, grades, and other required records. Prepare course materials such as syllabi, homework assignments, and handouts. Keep abreast of developments in their field by reading current literature, talking with colleagues, and participating in professional conferences. Supervise undergraduate and/or graduate teaching, internship, and research work. Plan, evaluate, and revise curricula, course content, and course materials and methods of instruction. Maintain regularly scheduled office hours to advise and assist students. Supervise students' laboratory work and fieldwork. Conduct research in a particular field of knowledge and publish findings in professional journals, books, and electronic media. Collaborate with colleagues to address teaching and research issues. Select and obtain materials and supplies such as textbooks. Advise students on academic and vocational curricula and on career issues. Serve on academic or administrative committees that deal with institutional policies, departmental matters, and academic issues. Participate in student recruitment, registration, and placement activities. Participate in campus and community events. Compile bibliographies of specialized materials for outside reading assignments. Perform administrative duties such as serving as department head. Write grant proposals to procure external research funding. Maintain geographic information systems laboratories, performing duties such as updating software. Perform spatial analysis and modeling, using geographic information system techniques. Act as advisers to student organizations. Provide professional consulting services to government and industry.

Personality Type: No data available.

GOE—Interest Area: 05. Education and Training. **Work Group:** 05.03. Postsecondary and Adult Teaching and Instructing. **Other Jobs in This Work Group:** Adult Literacy, Remedial Education, and GED Teachers and Instructors; Agricultural Sciences Teachers, Postsecondary; Anthropology and Archeology Teachers, Postsecondary; Architecture Teachers, Postsecondary; Area, Ethnic, and Cultural Studies Teachers, Postsecondary; Art, Drama, and Music Teachers, Postsecondary; Atmospheric, Earth, Marine, and Space Sciences Teachers, Postsecondary; Biological Science Teachers, Postsecondary; Business Teachers, Postsecondary; Chemistry Teachers, Postsecondary; Communications Teachers, Postsecondary; Computer Science Teachers, Postsecondary; Criminal Justice and Law Enforcement Teachers, Postsecondary; Economics Teachers, Postsecondary; Education Teachers, Postsecondary; Engineering Teachers, Postsecondary; English Language and Literature Teachers, Postsecondary; Environmental Science Teachers, Postsecondary; Farm and Home Management Advisors; Foreign Language and Literature Teachers, Postsecondary; Forestry and Conservation Science Teachers, Postsecondary; Graduate Teaching Assistants; Health Specialties Teachers, Postsecondary; History Teachers, Postsecondary; Home Economics Teachers, Postsecondary; Law Teachers, Postsecondary; Library Science Teachers, Postsecondary; Mathematical Science Teachers, Postsecondary; Nursing Instructors and Teachers, Postsecondary; Philosophy and Religion Teachers, Postsecondary; Physics Teachers, Postsecondary; Political Science Teachers, Postsecondary; Psychology Teachers, Postsecondary; Recreation and Fitness Studies Teachers, Postsecondary; Self-Enrichment Education Teachers; Social Work Teachers, Postsecondary; Sociology Teachers, Postsecondary; Vocational Education Teachers, Postsecondary.

Skills—Science: Using scientific rules and methods to solve problems. **Writing:** Communicating effectively in writing as appropriate for the needs of the audience. **Instructing:** Teaching others how to do something. **Learning Strategies:** Selecting and using training/instructional methods and procedures appropriate for the situation when learning or teaching new things. **Reading Comprehension:** Understanding written sentences and paragraphs in work-related documents. **Critical Thinking:** Using logic and reasoning to identify the strengths and weaknesses of alternative solutions, conclusions, or approaches to problems. **Speaking:** Talking to others to convey information effectively. **Active Learning:** Understanding the implications of new information for both current and future problem-solving and decision-making.

Education and Training Programs: Geography Teacher Education; Geography. **Related Knowledge/Courses: Geography:** Principles and methods for describing the features of land, sea, and air masses, including their physical characteristics; locations; interrelationships; and distribution of plant, animal, and human life. **Sociology and Anthropology:** Group behavior and dynamics, societal trends and influences, human migrations, ethnicity, and cultures and their history and origins. **History and Archeology:** Historical events and their causes, indicators, and effects on civilizations and cultures. **Philosophy and Theology:** Different philosophical systems and religions. This includes their basic principles, values, ethics, ways of thinking, customs, and practices and their impact on human culture. **Education and Training:** Principles and methods for curriculum and training design, teaching and instruction for individuals and groups, and the measurement of training effects. **Communications and Media:** Media production, communication, and dissemination techniques and methods. This includes alternative ways to inform and entertain via written, oral, and visual media.

Work Environment: Indoors; sitting.

Graduate Teaching Assistants

- Annual Earnings: $27,340
- Growth: 32.2%
- Annual Job Openings: 329,000
- Education/Training Required: Master's degree
- Self-Employed: 0.4%
- Part-Time: 27.3%

The job openings listed here are shared with 35 other postsecondary teaching occupations. For a complete list, see the beginning of this section.

How the Job Improves the World: Contributes to education.

Assist department chairperson, faculty members, or other professional staff members in college or university by performing teaching or teaching-related duties, such as teaching lower-level courses, developing teaching materials, preparing and giving examinations, and grading examinations or papers. Graduate assistants must be enrolled in a graduate school program. Graduate assistants who primarily perform non-teaching duties, such as laboratory research, should be reported in the occupational category related to the work performed. Lead discussion sections, tutorials, and laboratory sections. Evaluate and grade examinations, assignments, and papers and record grades. Return assignments to students in accordance with established deadlines. Schedule and maintain regular office hours to meet with students. Inform students of the procedures for completing and submitting class work such as lab reports. Prepare and proctor examinations. Notify instructors of errors or problems with assignments. Meet with supervisors to discuss students' grades and to complete required grade-related paperwork. Copy and distribute classroom materials. Demonstrate use of laboratory equipment and enforce laboratory rules. Teach undergraduate-level courses. Complete laboratory projects prior to assigning them to students so that any needed modifications can be made. Develop teaching materials such as syllabi, visual aids, answer keys, supplementary notes, and course Web sites. Provide assistance to faculty members or staff with laboratory or field research. Arrange for supervisors to conduct teaching observations; meet with supervisors to receive feedback about teaching performance. Attend lectures given by the instructor whom they are assisting. Order or obtain materials needed for classes. Provide instructors with assistance in the use of audiovisual equipment. Assist faculty members or staff with student conferences.

Personality Type: Social. Social occupations frequently involve working with, communicating with, and teaching people. These occupations often involve helping or providing service to others.

GOE—Interest Area: 05. Education and Training. **Work Group:** 05.03. Postsecondary and Adult Teaching and Instructing. **Other Jobs in This Work Group:** Adult Literacy, Remedial Education, and GED Teachers and Instructors; Agricultural Sciences Teachers, Postsecondary; Anthropology and Archeology Teachers, Postsecondary; Architecture Teachers, Postsecondary; Area, Ethnic, and Cultural Studies Teachers, Postsecondary; Art, Drama, and Music Teachers, Postsecondary; Atmospheric, Earth, Marine, and Space Sciences Teachers, Postsecondary; Biological Science Teachers, Postsecondary; Business Teachers, Postsecondary; Chemistry Teachers, Postsecondary; Communications Teachers, Postsecondary; Computer Science Teachers, Postsecondary; Criminal Justice and Law Enforcement Teachers, Postsecondary; Economics Teachers, Postsecondary; Education Teachers, Postsecondary; Engineering Teachers, Postsecondary; English Language and Literature Teachers, Postsecondary; Environmental Science Teachers, Postsecondary; Farm and Home Management Advisors; Foreign Language and Literature Teachers, Postsecondary; Forestry and Conservation Science Teachers, Postsecondary; Geography Teachers, Postsecondary; Health Specialties Teachers, Postsecondary; History Teachers, Postsecondary; Home Economics Teachers, Postsecondary; Law Teachers, Postsecondary; Library Science Teachers, Postsecondary; Mathematical Science Teachers, Postsecondary; Nursing Instructors and Teachers, Postsecondary; Philosophy and Religion Teachers, Postsecondary; Physics Teachers, Postsecondary; Political Science Teachers, Postsecondary; Psychology Teachers, Postsecondary;

Recreation and Fitness Studies Teachers, Postsecondary; Self-Enrichment Education Teachers; Social Work Teachers, Postsecondary; Sociology Teachers, Postsecondary; Vocational Education Teachers, Postsecondary.

Skills—Learning Strategies: Selecting and using training/instructional methods and procedures appropriate for the situation when learning or teaching new things. **Instructing:** Teaching others how to do something. **Social Perceptiveness:** Being aware of others' reactions and understanding why they react as they do. **Reading Comprehension:** Understanding written sentences and paragraphs in work-related documents. **Time Management:** Managing one's own time and the time of others. **Writing:** Communicating effectively in writing as appropriate for the needs of the audience. **Speaking:** Talking to others to convey information effectively. **Active Learning:** Understanding the implications of new information for both current and future problem-solving and decision-making.

Education and Training Program: Education, General. **Related Knowledge/Courses: Education and Training:** Principles and methods for curriculum and training design, teaching and instruction for individuals and groups, and the measurement of training effects. **Sociology and Anthropology:** Group behavior and dynamics, societal trends and influences, human migrations, ethnicity, and cultures and their history and origins. **English Language:** The structure and content of the English language, including the meaning and spelling of words, rules of composition, and grammar. **Psychology:** Human behavior and performance; individual differences in ability, personality, and interests; learning and motivation; psychological research methods; and the assessment and treatment of behavioral and affective disorders. **Philosophy and Theology:** Different philosophical systems and religions. This includes their basic principles, values, ethics, ways of thinking, customs, and practices and their impact on human culture. **Computers and**

Electronics: Circuit boards; processors; chips; electronic equipment; and computer hardware and software, including applications and programming.

Work Environment: Indoors; sitting.

Health Educators

- Annual Earnings: $39,730
- Growth: 22.5%
- Annual Job Openings: 8,000
- Education/Training Required: Master's degree
- Self-Employed: 0.1%
- Part-Time: 16.0%

How the Job Improves the World: Contributes to education and mental health.

Promote, maintain, and improve individual and community health by assisting individuals and communities to adopt healthy behaviors. Collect and analyze data to identify community needs prior to planning, implementing, monitoring, and evaluating programs designed to encourage healthy lifestyles, policies, and environments. May also serve as a resource to assist individuals, other professionals, or the community and may administer fiscal resources for health education programs. Document activities, recording information such as the numbers of applications completed, presentations conducted, and persons assisted. Develop and present health education and promotion programs such as training workshops, conferences, and school or community presentations. Develop and maintain cooperative working relationships with agencies and organizations interested in public health care. Prepare and distribute health education materials, including reports; bulletins; and visual aids such as films, videotapes, photographs, and posters. Develop operational plans and policies necessary to achieve health education objectives and services. Collaborate with health specialists and civic groups to determine community health needs and the availability of services and to develop goals for meeting needs. Maintain databases, mailing lists, telephone networks, and other information to facilitate the functioning of health education programs. Supervise professional and technical staff in implementing health programs, objectives, and goals. Design and conduct evaluations and diagnostic studies to assess the quality and performance of health education programs. Provide program information to the public by preparing and presenting press releases, conducting media campaigns, and/or maintaining program-related Web sites. Develop, prepare, and coordinate grant applications and grant-related activities to obtain funding for health education programs and related work. Provide guidance to agencies and organizations in the assessment of health education needs and in the development and delivery of health education programs. Develop and maintain health education libraries to provide resources for staff and community agencies. Develop, conduct, or coordinate health needs assessments and other public health surveys.

Personality Type: Social. Social occupations frequently involve working with, communicating with, and teaching people. These occupations often involve helping or providing service to others.

GOE—Interest Area: 05. Education and Training. **Work Group:** 05.06. Counseling, Health, and Fitness Education. **Other Jobs in This Work Group:** Educational, Vocational, and School Counselors; Fitness Trainers and Aerobics Instructors.

Skills—Service Orientation: Actively looking for ways to help people. **Social Perceptiveness:** Being aware of others' reactions and understanding why they react as they do. **Monitoring:** Monitoring/assessing your performance or that of other individuals or organizations to make improvements or take corrective action. **Learning Strategies:** Selecting and using training/instructional methods and procedures appropriate for the situation when learning or teaching new things. **Instructing:** Teaching others how to do something. **Speaking:** Talking to others to convey information effectively. **Coordination:** Adjusting actions in relation to others' actions. **Active Learning:** Understanding the implications of new information for both current and future problem-solving and decision-making.

Education and Training Programs: Health Communication; Community Health Services/Liaison/Counseling; Public Health Education and Promotion; Maternal and Child Health; International Public Health/International Health; Bioethics/Medical Ethics. **Related Knowledge/Courses: Sociology and Anthropology:** Group behavior and dynamics, societal trends and influences, human migrations, ethnicity, and cultures and their history and origins. **Customer and Personal Service:** Principles and processes for providing customer and personal services. This includes customer needs assessment, meeting quality standards for services, and evaluation of customer satisfaction. **Education and Training:** Principles and methods for curriculum and training design, teaching and instruction for individuals and groups, and the measurement of training effects. **Personnel and Human Resources:** Principles and procedures for personnel recruitment, selection, training, compensation and benefits, labor relations and negotiation, and personnel information systems. **Psychology:** Human behavior and performance; individual differences in ability, personality, and interests; learning and motivation; psychological research methods; and the assessment and treatment of behavioral and affective disorders. **Therapy and Counseling:** Principles, methods, and procedures for diagnosis, treatment, and rehabilitation of physical and mental dysfunctions and for career counseling and guidance.

Work Environment: Indoors; disease or infections; sitting; using hands on objects, tools, or controls.

Health Specialties Teachers, Postsecondary

- Annual Earnings: $70,890
- Growth: 32.2%
- Annual Job Openings: 329,000
- Education/Training Required: Master's degree
- Self-Employed: 0.4%
- Part-Time: 27.3%

The job openings listed here are shared with 35 other postsecondary teaching occupations. For a complete list, see the beginning of this section.

How the Job Improves the World: Contributes to education and health.

Teach courses in health specialties, such as veterinary medicine, dentistry, pharmacy, therapy, laboratory technology, and public health. Initiate, facilitate, and moderate classroom discussions. Keep abreast of developments in their field by reading current literature, talking with colleagues, and participating in professional conferences. Compile, administer, and grade examinations or assign this work to others. Evaluate and grade students' classwork, assignments, and papers. Prepare course materials such as syllabi, homework assignments, and handouts. Prepare and deliver lectures to undergraduate or graduate students on topics such as public health, stress management, and worksite health promotion. Plan, evaluate, and revise curricula, course content, and course materials and methods of instruction. Supervise undergraduate or graduate teaching, internship, and research work. Conduct research in a particular field of knowledge and publish findings in professional journals, books, or electronic media. Collaborate with colleagues to address teaching and research issues. Supervise laboratory sessions. Maintain student attendance records, grades, and other required records. Maintain regularly scheduled office hours in order to advise and assist students. Advise students on academic and vocational curricula and on career issues. Participate in student recruitment, registration, and placement activities. Write grant proposals to procure external research funding. Serve on academic or administrative committees that deal with institutional policies, departmental matters, and academic issues. Select and obtain materials and supplies such as textbooks and laboratory equipment. Act as advisers to student organizations. Perform administrative duties such as serving as department head. Compile bibliographies of specialized materials for outside reading assignments. Provide professional consulting services to government and industry. Participate in campus and community events.

Personality Type: Investigative. Investigative occupations frequently involve working with ideas and require an extensive amount of thinking. These occupations can involve searching for facts and figuring out problems mentally.

GOE—Interest Area: 05. Education and Training. **Work Group:** 05.03. Postsecondary and Adult Teaching and Instructing. **Other Jobs in This Work Group:** Adult Literacy, Remedial Education, and GED Teachers and Instructors; Agricultural Sciences Teachers, Postsecondary; Anthropology and Archeology Teachers, Postsecondary; Architecture Teachers, Postsecondary; Area, Ethnic, and Cultural Studies Teachers, Postsecondary; Art, Drama, and Music Teachers, Postsecondary; Atmospheric, Earth, Marine, and Space Sciences Teachers, Postsecondary; Biological Science Teachers, Postsecondary; Business Teachers, Postsecondary; Chemistry Teachers, Postsecondary; Communications Teachers, Postsecondary; Computer Science Teachers, Postsecondary; Criminal Justice and Law Enforcement Teachers, Postsecondary; Economics Teachers, Postsecondary; Education Teachers, Postsecondary; Engineering Teachers, Postsecondary; English Language and Literature Teachers, Postsecondary; Environmental Science Teachers, Postsecondary; Farm and Home Management Advisors; Foreign Language and Literature Teachers, Postsecondary; Forestry and Conservation Science Teachers, Postsecondary; Geography Teachers, Postsecondary; Graduate Teaching Assistants; History Teachers, Postsecondary; Home Economics Teachers, Postsecondary; Law Teachers, Postsecondary; Library Science Teachers, Postsecondary; Mathematical Science Teachers, Postsecondary; Nursing Instructors and Teachers, Postsecondary; Philosophy and Religion Teachers, Postsecondary; Physics Teachers, Postsecondary; Political Science Teachers, Postsecondary; Psychology Teachers, Postsecondary; Recreation and Fitness Studies Teachers, Postsecondary; Self-Enrichment Education Teachers; Social Work Teachers, Postsecondary; Sociology Teachers, Postsecondary; Vocational Education Teachers, Postsecondary.

Skills—Science: Using scientific rules and methods to solve problems. **Instructing:** Teaching others how to do something. **Writing:** Communicating effectively in writing as appropriate for the needs of the audience. **Learning Strategies:** Selecting and using training/instructional methods and procedures appropriate for the situation when learning or teaching new things. **Reading Comprehension:** Understanding written sentences and paragraphs in work-related documents. **Critical Thinking:** Using logic and reasoning to identify the strengths and weaknesses of alternative solutions, conclusions, or approaches to problems. **Complex Problem Solving:** Identifying complex problems and reviewing related information to develop and evaluate options and implement solutions. **Speaking:** Talking to others to convey information effectively.

Education and Training Programs: Health Occupations Teacher Education; Biostatistics; Epidemiology; Chiropractic (DC); Communication Disorders, General; Audiology/Audiologist and Hearing Sciences; Speech-Language Pathology/Pathologist; Audiology/Audiologist and Speech-Language Pathology/Pathologist; Dentistry (DDS, DMD); Dental Clinical Sciences, General (MS, PhD); Dental Assisting/Assistant; Dental Hygiene/Hygienist; others. Related Knowledge/Courses: Biology: Plant and animal organisms and their tissues, cells, functions, interdependencies, and interactions with each other and the environment. Medicine and Dentistry: The information and techniques needed to diagnose and treat human injuries, diseases, and deformities. This includes symptoms, treatment alternatives, drug properties and interactions, and preventive health-care measures. Education and Training: Principles and methods for curriculum and training design, teaching and instruction for individuals and groups, and the measurement of training effects. Therapy and Counseling: Principles, methods, and procedures for diagnosis, treatment, and rehabilitation of physical and mental dysfunctions and for career counseling and guidance. Sociology and Anthropology: Group behavior and dynamics, societal trends and influences, human migrations, ethnicity, and cultures and their history and origins. Psychology: Human behavior and performance; individual differences in ability, personality, and interests; learning and motivation; psychological research methods; and the assessment and treatment of behavioral and affective disorders.

Work Environment: Indoors; sitting.

History Teachers, Postsecondary

- Annual Earnings: $54,780
- Growth: 32.2%
- Annual Job Openings: 329,000
- Education/Training Required: Master's degree
- Self-Employed: 0.4%
- Part-Time: 27.3%

The job openings listed here are shared with 35 other postsecondary teaching occupations. For a complete list, see the beginning of this section.

How the Job Improves the World: Contributes to education and intercultural understanding.

Teach courses in human history and historiography. Prepare and deliver lectures to undergraduate and/or graduate students on topics such as ancient history, postwar civilizations, and the history of third-world countries. Evaluate and grade students' classwork, assignments, and papers. Prepare course materials such as syllabi, homework assignments, and handouts. Compile, administer, and grade examinations or assign this work to others. Initiate, facilitate, and moderate classroom discussions. Keep abreast of developments in their field by reading current literature, talking with colleagues, and participating in professional conferences. Plan, evaluate, and revise curricula, course content, and course materials and methods of instruction. Maintain student attendance records, grades, and other required records. Maintain regularly scheduled office hours to advise and assist students. Conduct research in a particular field of knowledge and publish findings in professional journals, books, or electronic media. Select and obtain materials and supplies such as textbooks. Advise students on academic and vocational curricula and on career issues. Collaborate with colleagues to address teaching and research issues. Serve on academic or administrative committees that deal with institutional policies, departmental matters, and academic issues. Participate in campus and community events. Act as advisers to student organizations. Participate in student recruitment, registration, and placement activities. Compile bibliographies of specialized materials for outside reading assignments. Supervise undergraduate and graduate teaching, internship, and research work. Perform administrative duties such as serving as department head. Write grant proposals to procure external research funding. Provide professional consulting services to government, educational institutions, and industry.

Personality Type: Social. Social occupations frequently involve working with, communicating with, and teaching people. These occupations often involve helping or providing service to others.

GOE—Interest Area: 05. Education and Training. **Work Group:** 05.03. Postsecondary and Adult Teaching and Instructing. **Other Jobs in This Work Group:** Adult Literacy, Remedial Education, and GED Teachers and Instructors; Agricultural Sciences Teachers, Postsecondary; Anthropology and Archeology Teachers, Postsecondary; Architecture Teachers, Postsecondary; Area, Ethnic, and Cultural Studies Teachers, Postsecondary; Art, Drama, and Music Teachers, Postsecondary; Atmospheric, Earth, Marine, and Space Sciences Teachers, Postsecondary; Biological Science Teachers, Postsecondary; Business Teachers, Postsecondary; Chemistry Teachers, Postsecondary; Communications Teachers, Postsecondary; Computer Science Teachers, Postsecondary; Criminal Justice and Law Enforcement Teachers, Postsecondary; Economics Teachers, Postsecondary; Education Teachers, Postsecondary; Engineering Teachers, Postsecondary; English Language and Literature Teachers, Postsecondary; Environmental Science Teachers, Postsecondary; Farm and Home Management Advisors; Foreign Language and Literature Teachers, Postsecondary; Forestry and Conservation Science Teachers, Postsecondary; Geography Teachers, Postsecondary; Graduate Teaching Assistants; Health Specialties Teachers, Postsecondary; Home Economics Teachers, Postsecondary; Law Teachers, Postsecondary; Library Science Teachers, Postsecondary; Mathematical Science Teachers, Postsecondary; Nursing Instructors and Teachers, Postsecondary; Philosophy and Religion Teachers, Postsecondary; Physics Teachers, Postsecondary; Political Science Teachers, Postsecondary; Psychology Teachers, Postsecondary; Recreation and Fitness Studies Teachers, Postsecondary; Self-Enrichment Education Teachers; Social Work Teachers, Postsecondary; Sociology Teachers, Postsecondary; Vocational Education Teachers, Postsecondary.

Skills—Writing: Communicating effectively in writing as appropriate for the needs of the audience. **Instructing:** Teaching others how to do something. **Learning Strategies:** Selecting and using training/instructional methods and procedures appropriate for the situation when learning or teaching new things. **Speaking:** Talking to others to convey information effectively. **Persuasion:** Persuading others to change their minds or behavior. **Reading Comprehension:** Understanding written sentences and paragraphs in work-related documents. **Critical Thinking:** Using logic and reasoning to identify the strengths and weaknesses of alternative solutions, conclusions, or approaches to problems. **Active Learning:** Understanding the implications of new information for both current and future problem-solving and decision-making.

Education and Training Programs: History, General; American History (United States); European History; History and Philosophy of Science and Technology; Public/Applied History and Archival Administration; Asian History; Canadian History; History, Other. **Related Knowledge/Courses:** History and

Archeology: Historical events and their causes, indicators, and effects on civilizations and cultures. **Philosophy and Theology:** Different philosophical systems and religions. This includes their basic principles, values, ethics, ways of thinking, customs, and practices and their impact on human culture. **Geography:** Principles and methods for describing the features of land, sea, and air masses, including their physical characteristics; locations; interrelationships; and distribution of plant, animal, and human life. **Sociology and Anthropology:** Group behavior and dynamics, societal trends and influences, human migrations, ethnicity, and cultures and their history and origins. **Education and Training:** Principles and methods for curriculum and training design, teaching and instruction for individuals and groups, and the measurement of training effects. **English Language:** The structure and content of the English language, including the meaning and spelling of words, rules of composition, and grammar.

Work Environment: Indoors; sitting.

Home Economics Teachers, Postsecondary

- Annual Earnings: $48,720
- Growth: 32.2%
- Annual Job Openings: 329,000
- Education/Training Required: Master's degree
- Self-Employed: 0.4%
- Part-Time: 27.3%

The job openings listed here are shared with 35 other postsecondary teaching occupations. For a complete list, see the beginning of this section.

How the Job Improves the World: Contributes to education.

Teach courses in child care, family relations, finance, nutrition, and related subjects as pertaining to home management. Evaluate and grade students' classwork, laboratory work, projects, assignments, and papers. Initiate, facilitate, and moderate classroom discussions. Prepare and deliver lectures to undergraduate or graduate students on topics such as food science, nutrition, and child care. Prepare course materials such as syllabi, homework assignments, and handouts. Keep abreast of developments in their field by reading current literature, talking with colleagues, and participating in professional conferences. Maintain student attendance records, grades, and other required records. Plan, evaluate, and revise curricula, course content, and course materials and methods of instruction. Compile, administer, and grade examinations or assign this work to others. Advise students on academic and vocational curricula and on career issues. Maintain regularly scheduled office hours to advise and assist students. Supervise undergraduate or graduate teaching, internship, and research work. Select and obtain materials and supplies such as textbooks. Conduct research in a particular field of knowledge and publish findings in professional journals, books, and/or electronic media. Collaborate with colleagues to address teaching and research issues. Act as advisers to student organizations. Participate in student recruitment, registration, and placement activities. Serve on academic or administrative committees that deal with institutional policies, departmental matters, and academic issues. Participate in campus and community events. Compile bibliographies of specialized materials for outside reading assignments. Perform administrative duties such as serving as department head. Write grant proposals to procure external research funding. Provide professional consulting services to government and industry.

Personality Type: No data available.

GOE—Interest Area: 05. Education and Training. **Work Group:** 05.03. Postsecondary and Adult Teaching and Instructing. **Other Jobs in This Work**

Group: Adult Literacy, Remedial Education, and GED Teachers and Instructors; Agricultural Sciences Teachers, Postsecondary; Anthropology and Archeology Teachers, Postsecondary; Architecture Teachers, Postsecondary; Area, Ethnic, and Cultural Studies Teachers, Postsecondary; Art, Drama, and Music Teachers, Postsecondary; Atmospheric, Earth, Marine, and Space Sciences Teachers, Postsecondary; Biological Science Teachers, Postsecondary; Business Teachers, Postsecondary; Chemistry Teachers, Postsecondary; Communications Teachers, Postsecondary; Computer Science Teachers, Postsecondary; Criminal Justice and Law Enforcement Teachers, Postsecondary; Economics Teachers, Postsecondary; Education Teachers, Postsecondary; Engineering Teachers, Postsecondary; English Language and Literature Teachers, Postsecondary; Environmental Science Teachers, Postsecondary; Farm and Home Management Advisors; Foreign Language and Literature Teachers, Postsecondary; Forestry and Conservation Science Teachers, Postsecondary; Geography Teachers, Postsecondary; Graduate Teaching Assistants; Health Specialties Teachers, Postsecondary; History Teachers, Postsecondary; Law Teachers, Postsecondary; Library Science Teachers, Postsecondary; Mathematical Science Teachers, Postsecondary; Nursing Instructors and Teachers, Postsecondary; Philosophy and Religion Teachers, Postsecondary; Physics Teachers, Postsecondary; Political Science Teachers, Postsecondary; Psychology Teachers, Postsecondary; Recreation and Fitness Studies Teachers, Postsecondary; Self-Enrichment Education Teachers; Social Work Teachers, Postsecondary; Sociology Teachers, Postsecondary; Vocational Education Teachers, Postsecondary.

Skills—Writing: Communicating effectively in writing as appropriate for the needs of the audience. **Instructing:** Teaching others how to do something. **Learning Strategies:** Selecting and using training/instructional methods and procedures appropriate for the situation when learning or teaching new things.

Service Orientation: Actively looking for ways to help people. **Active Learning:** Understanding the implications of new information for both current and future problem-solving and decision-making. **Social Perceptiveness:** Being aware of others' reactions and understanding why they react as they do. **Persuasion:** Persuading others to change their minds or behavior. **Negotiation:** Bringing others together and trying to reconcile differences.

Education and Training Programs: Family and Consumer Sciences/Human Sciences, General; Business Family and Consumer Sciences/Human Sciences; Foodservice Systems Administration/Management; Human Development and Family Studies, General; Child Care and Support Services Management. **Related Knowledge/Courses: Sociology and Anthropology:** Group behavior and dynamics, societal trends and influences, human migrations, ethnicity, and cultures and their history and origins. **Philosophy and Theology:** Different philosophical systems and religions. This includes their basic principles, values, ethics, ways of thinking, customs, and practices and their impact on human culture. **Education and Training:** Principles and methods for curriculum and training design, teaching and instruction for individuals and groups, and the measurement of training effects. **Therapy and Counseling:** Principles, methods, and procedures for diagnosis, treatment, and rehabilitation of physical and mental dysfunctions and for career counseling and guidance. **Psychology:** Human behavior and performance; individual differences in ability, personality, and interests; learning and motivation; psychological research methods; and the assessment and treatment of behavioral and affective disorders. **English Language:** The structure and content of the English language, including the meaning and spelling of words, rules of composition, and grammar.

Work Environment: Indoors; sitting.

Home Health Aides

- Annual Earnings: $18,800
- Growth: 56.0%
- Annual Job Openings: 170,000
- Education/Training Required: Short-term on-the-job training
- Self-Employed: 1.4%
- Part-Time: 28.0%

How the Job Improves the World: Contributes to health.

Provide routine, personal healthcare, such as bathing, dressing, or grooming, to elderly, convalescent, or disabled persons in the home of patients or in a residential care facility. Maintain records of patient care, condition, progress, or problems to report and discuss observations with supervisor or case manager. Provide patients with help moving in and out of beds, baths, wheelchairs, or automobiles and with dressing and grooming. Provide patients and families with emotional support and instruction in areas such as caring for infants, preparing healthy meals, living independently, or adapting to disability or illness. Change bed linens, wash and iron patients' laundry, and clean patients' quarters. Entertain, converse with, or read aloud to patients to keep them mentally healthy and alert. Plan, purchase, prepare, or serve meals to patients or other family members according to prescribed diets. Direct patients in simple prescribed exercises or in the use of braces or artificial limbs. Check patients' pulse, temperature, and respiration. Change dressings. Perform a variety of duties as requested by client, such as obtaining household supplies or running errands. Accompany clients to doctors' offices and on other trips outside the home, providing transportation, assistance, and companionship. Administer prescribed oral medications under written direction of physician or as directed by home care nurse and aide. Care for children who are disabled or who have sick or disabled parents. Massage patients and apply preparations and treatments such as liniment, alcohol rubs, and heat-lamp stimulation.

Personality Type: Social. Social occupations frequently involve working with, communicating with, and teaching people. These occupations often involve helping or providing service to others.

GOE—Interest Area: 08. Health Science. **Work Group:** 08.08. Patient Care and Assistance. **Other Jobs in This Work Group:** Licensed Practical and Licensed Vocational Nurses; Nursing Aides, Orderlies, and Attendants; Psychiatric Aides; Psychiatric Technicians.

Skills—No data available.

Education and Training Program: Home Health Aide/Home Attendant. **Related Knowledge/ Courses: Medicine and Dentistry:** The information and techniques needed to diagnose and treat human injuries, diseases, and deformities. This includes symptoms, treatment alternatives, drug properties and interactions, and preventive health-care measures. **Therapy and Counseling:** Principles, methods, and procedures for diagnosis, treatment, and rehabilitation of physical and mental dysfunctions and for career counseling and guidance. **Psychology:** Human behavior and performance; individual differences in ability, personality, and interests; learning and motivation; psychological research methods; and the assessment and treatment of behavioral and affective disorders.

Work Environment: Indoors; disease or infections; standing; walking and running; repetitive motions.

Immigration and Customs Inspectors

- Annual Earnings: $55,790
- Growth: 16.3%
- Annual Job Openings: 9,000
- Education/Training Required: Work experience in a related occupation
- Self-Employed: 0.0%
- Part-Time: 2.5%

The job openings listed here are shared with Criminal Investigators and Special Agents; Police Detectives; and Police Identification and Records Officers.

How the Job Improves the World: Contributes to justice, law enforcement, and homeland security.

Investigate and inspect persons, common carriers, goods, and merchandise arriving in or departing from the United States or moving between states to detect violations of immigration and customs laws and regulations. Examine immigration applications, visas, and passports and interview persons to determine eligibility for admission, residence, and travel in U.S. Detain persons found to be in violation of customs or immigration laws and arrange for legal action such as deportation. Locate and seize contraband or undeclared merchandise and vehicles, aircraft, or boats that contain such merchandise. Interpret and explain laws and regulations to travelers, prospective immigrants, shippers, and manufacturers. Inspect cargo, baggage, and personal articles entering or leaving U.S. for compliance with revenue laws and U.S. Customs Service regulations. Record and report job-related activities, findings, transactions, violations, discrepancies, and decisions. Institute civil and criminal prosecutions and cooperate with other law enforcement agencies in the investigation and prosecution of those in violation of immigration or customs laws. Testify regarding decisions at immigration appeals or in federal court. Determine duty and taxes to be paid on goods. Collect samples of merchandise for examination, appraisal, or testing. Investigate applications for duty refunds and petition for remission or mitigation of penalties when warranted.

Personality Type: Conventional. Conventional occupations frequently involve following set procedures and routines. These occupations can include working with data and details more than with ideas. Usually there is a clear line of authority to follow.

GOE—Interest Area: 07. Government and Public Administration. **Work Group:** 07.03. Regulations Enforcement. **Other Jobs in This Work Group:** Agricultural Inspectors; Aviation Inspectors; Compliance Officers, Except Agriculture, Construction, Health and Safety, and Transportation; Construction and Building Inspectors; Environmental Compliance Inspectors; Equal Opportunity Representatives and Officers; Financial Examiners; Fire Inspectors; Fish and Game Wardens; Forest Fire Inspectors and Prevention Specialists; Freight and Cargo Inspectors; Government Property Inspectors and Investigators; Licensing Examiners and Inspectors; Nuclear Monitoring Technicians; Occupational Health and Safety Specialists; Occupational Health and Safety Technicians; Tax Examiners, Collectors, and Revenue Agents; Transportation Vehicle, Equipment, and Systems Inspectors, Except Aviation.

Skills—Persuasion: Persuading others to change their minds or behavior. **Negotiation:** Bringing others together and trying to reconcile differences. **Speaking:** Talking to others to convey information effectively. **Social Perceptiveness:** Being aware of others' reactions and understanding why they react as they do. **Operations Analysis:** Analyzing needs and product requirements to create a design. **Equipment Selection:** Determining the kind of tools and equipment needed to do a job. **Active Listening:** Giving full attention to what other people are saying, taking time to understand the points being made, asking questions as appropriate, and not interrupting at inappropriate times. **Instructing:** Teaching others how to do something.

Education and Training Programs: Criminal Justice/Police Science; Criminalistics and Criminal Science. **Related Knowledge/Courses: Public Safety and Security:** Relevant equipment, policies, procedures, and strategies to promote effective local, state, or national security operations for the protection of people, data, property, and institutions. **Law and Government:** Laws, legal codes, court procedures, precedents, government regulations, executive orders, agency rules, and the democratic political process. **Foreign Language:** The structure and content of a foreign (non-English) language, including the meaning and spelling of words, rules of composition and grammar, and pronunciation. **Geography:** Principles and methods for describing the features of land, sea, and air masses, including their physical characteristics; locations; interrelationships; and distribution of plant, animal, and human life. **Customer and Personal Service:** Principles and processes for providing customer and personal services. This includes customer needs assessment, meeting quality standards for services, and evaluation of customer satisfaction. **Philosophy and Theology:** Different philosophical systems and religions. This includes their basic principles, values, ethics, ways of thinking, customs, and practices and their impact on human culture.

Work Environment: More often outdoors than indoors; noisy; contaminants; radiation; hazardous equipment.

Industrial Safety and Health Engineers

- Annual Earnings: $65,210
- Growth: 13.4%
- Annual Job Openings: 2,000
- Education/Training Required: Bachelor's degree
- Self-Employed: 0.5%
- Part-Time: 2.6%

The job openings listed here are shared with Fire-Prevention and Protection Engineers and with Product Safety Engineers.

How the Job Improves the World: Contributes to health and safety.

Plan, implement, and coordinate safety programs, requiring application of engineering principles and technology to prevent or correct unsafe environmental working conditions. Investigate industrial accidents, injuries, or occupational diseases to determine causes and preventive measures. Report or review findings from accident investigations, facilities inspections, or environmental testing. Maintain and apply knowledge of current policies, regulations, and industrial processes. Inspect facilities, machinery, and safety equipment to identify and correct potential hazards and to ensure safety regulation compliance. Conduct or coordinate worker training in areas such as safety laws and regulations, hazardous condition monitoring, and use of safety equipment. Review employee safety programs to determine their adequacy. Interview employers and employees to obtain information about work environments and workplace incidents. Review plans and specifications for construction of new machinery or equipment to determine whether all safety requirements have been met. Compile, analyze, and interpret statistical data related to occupational illnesses and accidents. Interpret safety regulations for others interested in industrial safety, such as safety engineers, labor representatives, and safety inspectors. Recommend process and product safety features that will reduce employees' exposure to chemical, physical, and biological work hazards. Conduct or direct testing of air quality, noise, temperature, or radiation levels to verify compliance with health and safety regulations. Provide technical advice and guidance to organizations on how to handle health-related problems and make needed changes. Confer with medical professionals to assess health risks and to develop ways to manage health issues and concerns. Install safety devices on machinery or direct device installation. Maintain liaisons with outside organizations such as fire departments, mutual aid societies, and rescue teams so that emergency responses can be facilitated. Evaluate adequacy of actions taken to correct health inspection violations. Write and revise safety regulations and codes. Check floors of plants to ensure that they are strong enough to support heavy machinery. Plan and conduct industrial hygiene research.

Personality Type: Investigative. Investigative occupations frequently involve working with ideas and require an extensive amount of thinking. These occupations can involve searching for facts and figuring out problems mentally.

GOE—Interest Area: 15. Scientific Research, Engineering, and Mathematics. **Work Group:** 15.08. Industrial and Safety Engineering. **Other Jobs in This Work Group:** Fire-Prevention and Protection Engineers; Health and Safety Engineers, Except Mining Safety Engineers and Inspectors; Industrial Engineers; Product Safety Engineers.

Skills—Management of Financial Resources: Determining how money will be spent to get the work done and accounting for these expenditures. **Science:** Using scientific rules and methods to solve problems. **Systems Analysis:** Determining how a system should work and how changes in conditions, operations, and

the environment will affect outcomes. **Persuasion:** Persuading others to change their minds or behavior. **Systems Evaluation:** Identifying measures or indicators of system performance and the actions needed to improve or correct performance relative to the goals of the system. **Management of Personnel Resources:** Motivating, developing, and directing people as they work; identifying the best people for the job. **Management of Material Resources:** Obtaining and seeing to the appropriate use of equipment, facilities, and materials needed to do certain work. **Negotiation:** Bringing others together and trying to reconcile differences.

Education and Training Program: Environmental/ Environmental Health Engineering. **Related Knowledge/Courses: Building and Construction:** The materials, methods, and tools involved in the construction or repair of houses, buildings, or other structures such as highways and roads. **Education and Training:** Principles and methods for curriculum and training design, teaching and instruction for individuals and groups, and the measurement of training effects. **Chemistry:** The chemical composition, structure, and properties of substances and of the chemical processes and transformations that they undergo. This includes uses of chemicals and their danger signs, production techniques, and disposal methods. **Physics:** Physical principles and laws and their interrelationships and applications to understanding fluid, material, and atmospheric dynamics and mechanical, electrical, atomic, and subatomic structures and processes. **Engineering and Technology:** The practical application of engineering science and technology. This includes applying principles, techniques, procedures, and equipment to the design and production of various goods and services. **Biology:** Plant and animal organisms and their tissues, cells, functions, interdependencies, and interactions with each other and the environment.

Work Environment: More often indoors than outdoors; noisy; sitting.

Industrial-Organizational Psychologists

- Annual Earnings: $84,690
- Growth: 20.4%
- Annual Job Openings: Fewer than 500
- Education/Training Required: Master's degree
- Self-Employed: 37.6%
- Part-Time: 22.8%

How the Job Improves the World: Contributes to mental health.

Apply principles of psychology to personnel, administration, management, sales, and marketing problems. Activities may include policy planning; employee screening, training, and development; and organizational development and analysis. May work with management to reorganize the work setting to improve worker productivity. Develop and implement employee selection and placement programs. Analyze job requirements and content in order to establish criteria for classification, selection, training, and other related personnel functions. Observe and interview workers in order to obtain information about the physical, mental, and educational requirements of jobs as well as information about aspects such as job satisfaction. Write reports on research findings and implications in order to contribute to general knowledge and to suggest potential changes in organizational functioning. Advise management concerning personnel, managerial, and marketing policies and practices and their potential effects on organizational effectiveness and efficiency. Identify training and development needs. Conduct research studies of physical work environments, organizational structures, communication systems, group interactions, morale, and motivation in order to assess organizational functioning. Formulate and implement training programs, applying principles of learning and individual differences. Develop interview techniques, rating scales, and psychological tests used to assess skills, abilities, and interests for the purpose of employee selection, placement, and promotion. Assess employee performance. Study organizational effectiveness, productivity, and efficiency, including the nature of workplace supervision and leadership. Facilitate organizational development and change. Analyze data, using statistical methods and applications, to evaluate the outcomes and effectiveness of workplace programs. Counsel workers about job and career-related issues. Study consumers' reactions to new products and package designs and to advertising efforts, using surveys and tests. Participate in mediation and dispute resolution.

Personality Type: Investigative. Investigative occupations frequently involve working with ideas and require an extensive amount of thinking. These occupations can involve searching for facts and figuring out problems mentally.

GOE—Interest Area: 15. Scientific Research, Engineering, and Mathematics. **Work Group:** 15.04. Social Sciences. **Other Jobs in This Work Group:** Anthropologists; Anthropologists and Archeologists; Archeologists; Economists; Historians; Political Scientists; School Psychologists; Sociologists.

Skills—Science: Using scientific rules and methods to solve problems. **Management of Personnel Resources:** Motivating, developing, and directing people as they work; identifying the best people for the job. **Systems Evaluation:** Identifying measures or indicators of system performance and the actions needed to improve or correct performance relative to the goals of the system. **Judgment and Decision Making:** Considering the relative costs and benefits of potential actions to choose the most appropriate one. **Complex Problem Solving:** Identifying complex problems and reviewing related information to develop and evaluate options and implement solutions.

Writing: Communicating effectively in writing as appropriate for the needs of the audience. **Service Orientation:** Actively looking for ways to help people. **Management of Financial Resources:** Determining how money will be spent to get the work done and accounting for these expenditures.

Education and Training Programs: Psychology, General; Industrial and Organizational Psychology. **Related Knowledge/Courses: Personnel and Human Resources:** Principles and procedures for personnel recruitment, selection, training, compensation and benefits, labor relations and negotiation, and personnel information systems. **Psychology:** Human behavior and performance; individual differences in ability, personality, and interests; learning and motivation; psychological research methods; and the assessment and treatment of behavioral and affective disorders. **Education and Training:** Principles and methods for curriculum and training design, teaching and instruction for individuals and groups, and the measurement of training effects. **Sales and Marketing:** Principles and methods for showing, promoting, and selling products or services. This includes marketing strategy and tactics, product demonstration, sales techniques, and sales control systems. **Sociology and Anthropology:** Group behavior and dynamics, societal trends and influences, human migrations, ethnicity, and cultures and their history and origins. **Therapy and Counseling:** Principles, methods, and procedures for diagnosis, treatment, and rehabilitation of physical and mental dysfunctions and for career counseling and guidance.

Work Environment: Indoors; sitting.

Instructional Coordinators

- Annual Earnings: $50,430
- Growth: 27.5%
- Annual Job Openings: 15,000
- Education/Training Required: Master's degree
- Self-Employed: 3.1%
- Part-Time: 23.4%

How the Job Improves the World: Contributes to education.

Develop instructional material, coordinate educational content, and incorporate current technology in specialized fields that provide guidelines to educators and instructors for developing curricula and conducting courses. Conduct or participate in workshops, committees, and conferences designed to promote the intellectual, social, and physical welfare of students. Plan and conduct teacher training programs and conferences dealing with new classroom procedures, instructional materials and equipment, and teaching aids. Advise teaching and administrative staff in curriculum development, use of materials and equipment, and implementation of state and federal programs and procedures. Recommend, order, or authorize purchase of instructional materials, supplies, equipment, and visual aids designed to meet student educational needs and district standards. Interpret and enforce provisions of state education codes and rules and regulations of state education boards. Confer with members of educational committees and advisory groups to obtain knowledge of subject areas and to relate curriculum materials to specific subjects, individual student needs, and occupational areas. Organize production and design of curriculum materials. Research, evaluate, and prepare recommendations on curricula, instructional methods, and materials for school systems. Observe work of teaching staff to evaluate performance and to recommend changes that could strengthen teaching skills. Develop instructional materials to be used by educators and instructors. Prepare grant proposals, budgets, and program policies and goals or assist in their preparation. Develop tests, questionnaires, and procedures that measure the effectiveness of curricula and use these tools to determine whether program objectives are being met. Update the content of educational programs to ensure that students are being trained with equipment and processes that are technologically current. Address public audiences to explain program objectives and to elicit support. Advise and teach students. Prepare or approve manuals, guidelines, and reports on state educational policies and practices for distribution to school districts. Develop classroom-based and distance-learning training courses, using needs assessments and skill level analyses. Inspect instructional equipment to determine if repairs are needed and authorize necessary repairs.

Personality Type: Social. Social occupations frequently involve working with, communicating with, and teaching people. These occupations often involve helping or providing service to others.

GOE—Interest Area: 05. Education and Training. **Work Group:** 05.01. Managerial Work in Education. **Other Jobs in This Work Group:** Education Administrators, Elementary and Secondary School; Education Administrators, Postsecondary; Education Administrators, Preschool and Child Care Center/ Program.

Skills—Management of Financial Resources: Determining how money will be spent to get the work done and accounting for these expenditures. **Learning Strategies:** Selecting and using training/instructional methods and procedures appropriate for the situation when learning or teaching new things. **Social Perceptiveness:** Being aware of others' reactions and understanding why they react as they do. **Monitoring:** Monitoring/assessing your performance or that of

other individuals or organizations to make improvements or take corrective action. **Coordination:** Adjusting actions in relation to others' actions. **Time Management:** Managing one's own time and the time of others. **Management of Personnel Resources:** Motivating, developing, and directing people as they work; identifying the best people for the job. **Persuasion:** Persuading others to change their minds or behavior.

Education and Training Programs: Curriculum and Instruction; Educational/Instructional Media Design; International and Comparative Education. **Related Knowledge/Courses: Education and Training:** Principles and methods for curriculum and training design, teaching and instruction for individuals and groups, and the measurement of training effects. **Personnel and Human Resources:** Principles and procedures for personnel recruitment, selection, training, compensation and benefits, labor relations and negotiation, and personnel information systems. **English Language:** The structure and content of the English language, including the meaning and spelling of words, rules of composition, and grammar. **Sociology and Anthropology:** Group behavior and dynamics, societal trends and influences, human migrations, ethnicity, and cultures and their history and origins. **Communications and Media:** Media production, communication, and dissemination techniques and methods. This includes alternative ways to inform and entertain via written, oral, and visual media. **Psychology:** Human behavior and performance; individual differences in ability, personality, and interests; learning and motivation; psychological research methods; and the assessment and treatment of behavioral and affective disorders.

Work Environment: Indoors; sitting.

Internists, General

- Annual Earnings: More than $145,600
- Growth: 24.0%
- Annual Job Openings: 41,000
- Education/Training Required: First professional degree
- Self-Employed: 11.5%
- Part-Time: 9.6%

The job openings listed here are shared with Anesthesiologists; Family and General Practitioners; Obstetricians and Gynecologists; Pediatricians, General; Psychiatrists; and Surgeons.

How the Job Improves the World: Contributes to health.

Diagnose and provide non-surgical treatment of diseases and injuries of internal organ systems. Provide care mainly for adults who have a wide range of problems associated with the internal organs. Treat internal disorders, such as hypertension; heart disease; diabetes; and problems of the lung, brain, kidney, and gastrointestinal tract. Analyze records, reports, test results, or examination information to diagnose medical condition of patient. Prescribe or administer medication, therapy, and other specialized medical care to treat or prevent illness, disease, or injury. Provide and manage long-term, comprehensive medical care, including diagnosis and non-surgical treatment of diseases, for adult patients in an office or hospital. Manage and treat common health problems, such as infections, influenza and pneumonia, as well as serious, chronic, and complex illnesses, in adolescents, adults, and the elderly. Monitor patients' conditions and progress and re-evaluate treatments as necessary. Collect, record, and maintain patient information, such as medical history, reports, and examination results. Make diagnoses when different illnesses occur together or in situations where the diagnosis may be obscure. Explain procedures and discuss test results or prescribed treatments with patients. Advise patients and community members concerning diet, activity, hygiene, and disease prevention. Refer patient to medical specialist or other practitioner when necessary. Immunize patients to protect them from preventable diseases. Advise surgeon of a patient's risk status and recommend appropriate intervention to minimize risk. Direct and coordinate activities of nurses, students, assistants, specialists, therapists, and other medical staff. Provide consulting services to other doctors caring for patients with special or difficult problems. Operate on patients to remove, repair, or improve functioning of diseased or injured body parts and systems. Plan, implement, or administer health programs in hospitals, businesses, or communities for prevention and treatment of injuries or illnesses. Conduct research to develop or test medications, treatments, or procedures to prevent or control disease or injury. Prepare government or organizational reports on birth, death, and disease statistics; workforce evaluations; or the medical status of individuals.

Personality Type: Investigative. Investigative occupations frequently involve working with ideas and require an extensive amount of thinking. These occupations can involve searching for facts and figuring out problems mentally.

GOE—Interest Area: 08. Health Science. **Work Group:** 08.02. Medicine and Surgery. **Other Jobs in This Work Group:** Anesthesiologists; Family and General Practitioners; Medical Assistants; Medical Transcriptionists; Obstetricians and Gynecologists; Pediatricians, General; Pharmacists; Pharmacy Aides; Pharmacy Technicians; Physician Assistants; Psychiatrists; Registered Nurses; Surgeons; Surgical Technologists.

Skills—Science: Using scientific rules and methods to solve problems. **Judgment and Decision Making:** Considering the relative costs and benefits of potential actions to choose the most appropriate one. **Complex Problem Solving:** Identifying complex problems and reviewing related information to develop and evaluate options and implement solutions. **Social Perceptiveness:** Being aware of others' reactions and understanding why they react as they do. **Persuasion:** Persuading others to change their minds or behavior. **Service Orientation:** Actively looking for ways to help people. **Management of Financial Resources:** Determining how money will be spent to get the work done and accounting for these expenditures. **Reading Comprehension:** Understanding written sentences and paragraphs in work-related documents.

Education and Training Programs: Cardiology; Critical Care Medicine; Endocrinology and Metabolism; Gastroenterology; Geriatric Medicine; Hematology; Infectious Disease; Internal Medicine; Nephrology; Neurology; Nuclear Medicine; Oncology; Pulmonary Disease; Rheumatology. **Related Knowledge/Courses: Medicine and Dentistry:** The information and techniques needed to diagnose and treat human injuries, diseases, and deformities. This includes symptoms, treatment alternatives, drug properties and interactions, and preventive health-care measures. **Biology:** Plant and animal organisms and their tissues, cells, functions, interdependencies, and interactions with each other and the environment. **Therapy and Counseling:** Principles, methods, and procedures for diagnosis, treatment, and rehabilitation of physical and mental dysfunctions and for career counseling and guidance. **Psychology:** Human behavior and performance; individual differences in ability, personality, and interests; learning and motivation; psychological research methods; and the assessment and treatment of behavioral and affective disorders. **Chemistry:** The chemical composition, structure, and properties of substances and of the chemical processes and transformations that they undergo. This includes uses of chemicals and their danger signs, production techniques, and disposal methods. **Education and Training:** Principles and methods for curriculum and training design, teaching and instruction for individuals and groups, and the measurement of training effects.

Work Environment: Indoors; disease or infections; standing.

Interpreters and Translators

- Annual Earnings: $34,800
- Growth: 19.9%
- Annual Job Openings: 4,000
- Education/Training Required: Long-term on-the-job training
- Self-Employed: 13.5%
- Part-Time: No data available

How the Job Improves the World: Contributes to the arts and intercultural understanding.

Translate or interpret written, oral, or sign language text into another language for others. Follow ethical codes that protect the confidentiality of information. Identify and resolve conflicts related to the meanings of words, concepts, practices, or behaviors. Proofread, edit, and revise translated materials. Translate messages simultaneously or consecutively into specified languages orally or by using hand signs, maintaining message content, context, and style as much as possible. Check translations of technical terms and terminology to ensure that they are accurate and remain consistent throughout translation revisions. Read written materials such as legal documents, scientific works, or news reports and rewrite material into specified languages. Refer to reference materials such as dictionaries, lexicons, encyclopedias, and computerized terminology banks as needed to ensure translation accuracy. Compile terminology and information to be used in translations, including technical terms such as those for legal or medical material. Adapt translations to students' cognitive and grade levels, collaborating with educational team members as necessary. Listen to speakers' statements to determine meanings and to prepare translations, using electronic listening systems as necessary. Check original texts or confer with authors to ensure that translations retain the content, meaning, and feeling of the original material. Compile information about the content and context of information to be translated, as well as details of the groups for whom translation or interpretation is being performed. Discuss translation requirements with clients and determine any fees to be charged for services provided. Adapt software and accompanying technical documents to another language and culture. Educate students, parents, staff, and teachers about the roles and functions of educational interpreters. Train and supervise other translators/interpreters. Travel with or guide tourists who speak another language.

Personality Type: Artistic. Artistic occupations frequently involve working with forms, designs, and patterns. They often require self-expression, and the work can be done without following a clear set of rules.

GOE—Interest Area: 03. Arts and Communication. **Work Group:** 03.03. News, Broadcasting, and Public Relations. **Other Jobs in This Work Group:** Broadcast News Analysts; Public Relations Specialists; Reporters and Correspondents.

Skills—No data available.

Education and Training Programs: Education/ Teaching of Individuals with Hearing Impairments, Including Deafness; Foreign Languages and Literatures, General; Linguistics; Language Interpretation and Translation; African Languages, Literatures, and Linguistics; East Asian Languages, Literatures, and Linguistics, General; Chinese Language and Literature; Japanese Language and Literature; Korean Language and Literature; Tibetan Language and Literature; others. **Related Knowledge/Courses: Foreign Language:** The structure and content of a foreign (non-English) language, including the meaning and spelling of words, rules of composition and grammar, and pronunciation. **English Language:** The structure and content of the English language, including the meaning and spelling of words, rules of composition, and grammar. **Geography:** Principles and methods for describing the features of land, sea, and air masses, including their physical characteristics; locations; interrelationships; and distribution of plant, animal, and human life. **Sociology and Anthropology:** Group behavior and dynamics, societal trends and influences, human migrations, ethnicity, and cultures and their history and origins. **Computers and Electronics:** Circuit boards; processors; chips; electronic equipment; and computer hardware and software, including applications and programming. **Communications and Media:** Media production, communication, and dissemination techniques and methods. This includes alternative ways to inform and entertain via written, oral, and visual media.

Work Environment: Indoors; sitting; repetitive motions.

Judges, Magistrate Judges, and Magistrates

- Annual Earnings: $97,570
- Growth: 6.9%
- Annual Job Openings: 1,000
- Education/Training Required: Work experience plus degree
- Self-Employed: 0.0%
- Part-Time: No data available

How the Job Improves the World: Contributes to justice and law enforcement.

Arbitrate, advise, adjudicate, or administer justice in a court of law. May sentence defendant in criminal cases according to government statutes. May determine liability of defendant in civil cases. May issue marriage licenses and perform wedding ceremonies. Instruct juries on applicable laws, direct juries to deduce the facts from the evidence presented, and hear their verdicts. Sentence defendants in criminal cases on conviction by jury according to applicable government statutes. Rule on admissibility of evidence and methods of conducting testimony. Preside over hearings and listen to allegations made by plaintiffs to determine whether the evidence supports the charges. Read documents on pleadings and motions to ascertain facts and issues. Interpret and enforce rules of procedure or establish new rules in situations where there are no procedures already established by law. Monitor proceedings to ensure that all applicable rules and procedures are followed. Advise attorneys, juries, litigants, and court personnel regarding conduct, issues, and proceedings. Research legal issues and write opinions on the issues. Conduct preliminary hearings to decide issues such as whether there is reasonable and probable cause to hold defendants in felony cases. Write decisions on cases. Award compensation for damages to litigants in civil cases in relation to findings by juries or by the court. Settle disputes between opposing attorneys. Supervise other judges, court officers, and the court's administrative staff. Impose restrictions upon parties in civil cases until trials can be held. Rule on custody and access disputes and enforce court orders regarding custody and support of children. Grant divorces and divide assets between spouses. Participate in judicial tribunals to help resolve disputes. Perform wedding ceremonies.

Personality Type: Enterprising. Enterprising occupations frequently involve starting up and carrying out projects. These occupations can involve leading people and making many decisions. They sometimes require risk taking and often deal with business.

GOE—Interest Area: 12. Law and Public Safety. **Work Group:** 12.02. Legal Practice and Justice Administration. **Other Jobs in This Work Group:** Administrative Law Judges, Adjudicators, and Hearing Officers; Arbitrators, Mediators, and Conciliators; Lawyers.

Skills—Judgment and Decision Making: Considering the relative costs and benefits of potential actions to choose the most appropriate one. **Persuasion:** Persuading others to change their minds or behavior. **Negotiation:** Bringing others together and trying to reconcile differences. **Critical Thinking:** Using logic and reasoning to identify the strengths and weaknesses of alternative solutions, conclusions, or approaches to problems. **Active Listening:** Giving full attention to what other people are saying, taking time to understand the points being made, asking questions as appropriate, and not interrupting at inappropriate times. **Reading Comprehension:** Understanding written sentences and paragraphs in work-related documents. **Social Perceptiveness:** Being aware of others' reactions and understanding why they react as they do. **Management of Personnel Resources:** Motivating, developing, and directing people as they work; identifying the best people for the job.

Education and Training Programs: Law (LL.B., J.D.); Legal Professions and Studies, Other. **Related Knowledge/Courses: Law and Government:** Laws, legal codes, court procedures, precedents, government regulations, executive orders, agency rules, and the democratic political process. **English Language:** The structure and content of the English language, including the meaning and spelling of words, rules of composition, and grammar. **Philosophy and Theology:** Different philosophical systems and religions. This includes their basic principles, values, ethics, ways of thinking, customs, and practices and their impact on human culture. **Therapy and Counseling:** Principles, methods, and procedures for diagnosis, treatment, and rehabilitation of physical and mental dysfunctions and for career counseling and guidance. **Psychology:** Human behavior and performance; individual differences in ability, personality, and interests; learning and motivation; psychological research methods; and the assessment and treatment of behavioral and affective disorders. **Sociology and Anthropology:** Group behavior and dynamics, societal trends and influences, human migrations, ethnicity, and cultures and their history and origins.

Work Environment: Indoors; sitting.

Kindergarten Teachers, Except Special Education

- Annual Earnings: $42,230
- Growth: 22.4%
- Annual Job Openings: 28,000
- Education/Training Required: Bachelor's degree
- Self-Employed: 1.5%
- Part-Time: 25.1%

How the Job Improves the World: Contributes to education.

Teach elemental natural and social science, personal hygiene, music, art, and literature to children from 4 to 6 years old. Promote physical, mental, and social development. May be required to hold state certification. Teach basic skills such as color, shape, number, and letter recognition; personal hygiene; and social skills. Establish and enforce rules for behavior and policies and procedures to maintain order among students. Observe and evaluate children's performance, behavior, social development, and physical health. Instruct students individually and in groups, adapting teaching methods to meet students' varying needs and interests. Read books to entire classes or to small groups. Demonstrate activities to children. Provide a variety of materials and resources for children to explore, manipulate, and use, both in learning activities and in imaginative play. Plan and conduct activities for a balanced program of instruction, demonstration, and work time that provides students with opportunities to observe, question, and investigate. Confer with parents or guardians, other teachers, counselors, and administrators to resolve students' behavioral and aca-

demic problems. Prepare children for later grades by encouraging them to explore learning opportunities and to persevere with challenging tasks. Establish clear objectives for all lessons, units, and projects and communicate those objectives to children. Prepare and implement remedial programs for students requiring extra help. Meet with parents and guardians to discuss their children's progress and to determine their priorities for their children and their resource needs. Prepare objectives and outlines for courses of study, following curriculum guidelines or requirements of states and schools. Organize and lead activities designed to promote physical, mental, and social development such as games, arts and crafts, music, and storytelling. Guide and counsel students with adjustment or academic problems or special academic interests. Identify children showing signs of emotional, developmental, or health-related problems and discuss them with supervisors, parents or guardians, and child development specialists. Instruct and monitor students in the use and care of equipment and materials to prevent injuries and damage. Assimilate arriving children to the school environment by greeting them, helping them remove outerwear, and selecting activities of interest to them.

Personality Type: Social. Social occupations frequently involve working with, communicating with, and teaching people. These occupations often involve helping or providing service to others.

GOE—Interest Area: 05. Education and Training. **Work Group:** 05.02. Preschool, Elementary, and Secondary Teaching and Instructing. **Other Jobs in This Work Group:** Elementary School Teachers, Except Special Education; Middle School Teachers, Except Special and Vocational Education; Preschool Teachers, Except Special Education; Secondary School Teachers, Except Special and Vocational Education; Special Education Teachers, Middle School; Special Education Teachers, Preschool, Kindergarten, and Elementary School; Special Education Teachers, Secondary School; Teacher Assistants; Vocational

Education Teachers, Middle School; Vocational Education Teachers, Secondary School.

Skills—Instructing: Teaching others how to do something. **Learning Strategies:** Selecting and using training/instructional methods and procedures appropriate for the situation when learning or teaching new things. **Social Perceptiveness:** Being aware of others' reactions and understanding why they react as they do. **Monitoring:** Monitoring/assessing your performance or that of other individuals or organizations to make improvements or take corrective action. **Time Management:** Managing one's own time and the time of others. **Writing:** Communicating effectively in writing as appropriate for the needs of the audience. **Coordination:** Adjusting actions in relation to others' actions. **Persuasion:** Persuading others to change their minds or behavior.

Education and Training Programs: Montessori Teacher Education; Waldorf/Steiner Teacher Education; Kindergarten/Preschool Education and Teaching; Early Childhood Education and Teaching. **Related Knowledge/Courses: History and Archeology:** Historical events and their causes, indicators, and effects on civilizations and cultures. **Geography:** Principles and methods for describing the features of land, sea, and air masses, including their physical characteristics; locations; interrelationships; and distribution of plant, animal, and human life. **Sociology and Anthropology:** Group behavior and dynamics, societal trends and influences, human migrations, ethnicity, and cultures and their history and origins. **Philosophy and Theology:** Different philosophical systems and religions. This includes their basic principles, values, ethics, ways of thinking, customs, and practices and their impact on human culture. **Education and Training:** Principles and methods for curriculum and training design, teaching and instruction for individuals and groups, and the measurement of training effects. **Psychology:** Human behavior and performance; individual differences in ability, personality, and interests; learning and motiva-

tion; psychological research methods; and the assessment and treatment of behavioral and affective disorders.

Work Environment: Indoors; disease or infections; standing.

Landscape Architects

- Annual Earnings: $54,220
- Growth: 19.4%
- Annual Job Openings: 1,000
- Education/Training Required: Bachelor's degree
- Self-Employed: 23.7%
- Part-Time: No data available

How the Job Improves the World: Contributes to physical and natural environment.

Plan and design land areas for such projects as parks and other recreational facilities; airports; highways; hospitals; schools; land subdivisions; and commercial, industrial, and residential sites. Prepare site plans, specifications, and cost estimates for land development, coordinating arrangement of existing and proposed land features and structures. Confer with clients, engineering personnel, and architects on overall program. Compile and analyze data on conditions such as location, drainage, and location of structures for environmental reports and landscaping plans. Inspect landscape work to ensure compliance with specifications, approve quality of materials and work, and advise client and construction personnel.

Personality Type: Artistic. Artistic occupations frequently involve working with forms, designs, and patterns. They often require self-expression, and the work can be done without following a clear set of rules.

GOE—Interest Area: 02. Architecture and Construction. **Work Group:** 02.02. Architectural

Design. **Other Jobs in This Work Group:** Architects, Except Landscape and Naval.

Skills—Operations Analysis: Analyzing needs and product requirements to create a design. **Management of Financial Resources:** Determining how money will be spent to get the work done and accounting for these expenditures. **Coordination:** Adjusting actions in relation to others' actions. **Mathematics:** Using mathematics to solve problems. **Social Perceptiveness:** Being aware of others' reactions and understanding why they react as they do. **Persuasion:** Persuading others to change their minds or behavior. **Complex Problem Solving:** Identifying complex problems and reviewing related information to develop and evaluate options and implement solutions. **Systems Evaluation:** Identifying measures or indicators of system performance and the actions needed to improve or correct performance relative to the goals of the system.

Education and Training Programs: Environmental Design/Architecture; Landscape Architecture (BS, BSLA, BLA, MSLA, MLA, PhD). **Related Knowledge/Courses: Design:** Design techniques, tools, and principles involved in production of precision technical plans, blueprints, drawings, and models. **Building and Construction:** The materials, methods, and tools involved in the construction or repair of houses, buildings, or other structures such as highways and roads. **Geography:** Principles and methods for describing the features of land, sea, and air masses, including their physical characteristics; locations; interrelationships; and distribution of plant, animal, and human life. **Engineering and Technology:** The practical application of engineering science and technology. This includes applying principles, techniques, procedures, and equipment to the design and production of various goods and services. **Biology:** Plant and animal organisms and their tissues, cells, functions, interdependencies, and interactions with each other and the environment. **Fine Arts:** The theory and techniques required to compose, produce, and perform works of music, dance, visual art, drama, and sculpture.

Work Environment: More often indoors than outdoors; very hot or cold; hazardous equipment; minor burns, cuts, bites, or stings; sitting.

Law Teachers, Postsecondary

- Annual Earnings: $89,790
- Growth: 32.2%
- Annual Job Openings: 329,000
- Education/Training Required: First professional degree
- Self-Employed: 0.4%
- Part-Time: 27.3%

The job openings listed here are shared with 35 other postsecondary teaching occupations. For a complete list, see the beginning of this section.

How the Job Improves the World: Contributes to education, justice, and law enforcement.

Teach courses in law. Evaluate and grade students' classwork, assignments, papers, and oral presentations. Compile, administer, and grade examinations or assign this work to others. Prepare and deliver lectures to undergraduate or graduate students on topics such as civil procedure, contracts, and torts. Initiate, facilitate, and moderate classroom discussions. Prepare course materials such as syllabi, homework assignments, and handouts. Keep abreast of developments in their field by reading current literature, talking with colleagues, and participating in professional conferences. Plan, evaluate, and revise curricula, course content, and course materials and methods of instruction. Maintain regularly scheduled office hours to advise and assist students. Conduct research in a particular field of knowledge and publish findings in professional journals, books, or electronic media. Advise students on academic and vocational curricula and on career issues. Supervise undergraduate and/or graduate teaching, internship, and research work. Select and obtain materials and supplies such as textbooks. Maintain student attendance records, grades, and other required records. Serve on academic or administrative committees that deal with institutional policies, departmental matters, and academic issues. Perform administrative duties such as serving as department head. Collaborate with colleagues to address teaching and research issues. Participate in student recruitment, registration, and placement activities. Compile bibliographies of specialized materials for outside reading assignments. Participate in campus and community events. Act as advisers to student organizations. Assign cases for students to hear and try. Provide professional consulting services to government or industry. Write grant proposals to procure external research funding.

Personality Type: No data available.

GOE—Interest Area: 05. Education and Training. **Work Group:** 05.03. Postsecondary and Adult Teaching and Instructing. **Other Jobs in This Work Group:** Adult Literacy, Remedial Education, and GED Teachers and Instructors; Agricultural Sciences Teachers, Postsecondary; Anthropology and Archeology Teachers, Postsecondary; Architecture Teachers, Postsecondary; Area, Ethnic, and Cultural Studies Teachers, Postsecondary; Art, Drama, and Music Teachers, Postsecondary; Atmospheric, Earth, Marine, and Space Sciences Teachers, Postsecondary; Biological Science Teachers, Postsecondary; Business Teachers, Postsecondary; Chemistry Teachers, Postsecondary; Communications Teachers, Postsecondary; Computer Science Teachers, Postsecondary; Criminal Justice and Law Enforcement Teachers, Postsecondary; Economics Teachers, Postsecondary; Education Teachers, Postsecondary; Engineering Teachers, Postsecondary; English Language and Literature Teachers, Postsecondary; Environmental

Science Teachers, Postsecondary; Farm and Home Management Advisors; Foreign Language and Literature Teachers, Postsecondary; Forestry and Conservation Science Teachers, Postsecondary; Geography Teachers, Postsecondary; Graduate Teaching Assistants; Health Specialties Teachers, Postsecondary; History Teachers, Postsecondary; Home Economics Teachers, Postsecondary; Library Science Teachers, Postsecondary; Mathematical Science Teachers, Postsecondary; Nursing Instructors and Teachers, Postsecondary; Philosophy and Religion Teachers, Postsecondary; Physics Teachers, Postsecondary; Political Science Teachers, Postsecondary; Psychology Teachers, Postsecondary; Recreation and Fitness Studies Teachers, Postsecondary; Self-Enrichment Education Teachers; Social Work Teachers, Postsecondary; Sociology Teachers, Postsecondary; Vocational Education Teachers, Postsecondary.

Skills—Instructing: Teaching others how to do something. **Critical Thinking:** Using logic and reasoning to identify the strengths and weaknesses of alternative solutions, conclusions, or approaches to problems. **Writing:** Communicating effectively in writing as appropriate for the needs of the audience. **Reading Comprehension:** Understanding written sentences and paragraphs in work-related documents. **Persuasion:** Persuading others to change their minds or behavior. **Speaking:** Talking to others to convey information effectively. **Active Listening:** Giving full attention to what other people are saying, taking time to understand the points being made, asking questions as appropriate, and not interrupting at inappropriate times. **Learning Strategies:** Selecting and using training/instructional methods and procedures appropriate for the situation when learning or teaching new things.

Education and Training Programs: Legal Studies, General; Law (LL.B., J.D.). **Related Knowledge/Courses: Law and Government:** Laws, legal codes, court procedures, precedents, government regulations, executive orders, agency rules, and the democratic political process. **English Language:** The structure and content of the English language, including the meaning and spelling of words, rules of composition, and grammar. **Education and Training:** Principles and methods for curriculum and training design, teaching and instruction for individuals and groups, and the measurement of training effects. **History and Archeology:** Historical events and their causes, indicators, and effects on civilizations and cultures. **Philosophy and Theology:** Different philosophical systems and religions. This includes their basic principles, values, ethics, ways of thinking, customs, and practices and their impact on human culture. **Communications and Media:** Media production, communication, and dissemination techniques and methods. This includes alternative ways to inform and entertain via written, oral, and visual media.

Work Environment: Indoors; sitting.

Librarians

- Annual Earnings: $47,400
- Growth: 4.9%
- Annual Job Openings: 8,000
- Education/Training Required: Master's degree
- Self-Employed: 0.0%
- Part-Time: 22.3%

How the Job Improves the World: Contributes to education.

Administer libraries and perform related library services. Work in a variety of settings, including public libraries, schools, colleges and universities, museums, corporations, government agencies, law firms, nonprofit organizations, and health-care providers. Tasks may include selecting, acquiring, cataloguing, classifying, circulating, and maintaining library materials and furnishing reference, bibliographical, and read-

ers' advisory services. **May perform in-depth, strategic research and synthesize, analyze, edit, and filter information. May set up or work with databases and information systems to catalogue and access information.** Search standard reference materials, including online sources and the Internet, to answer patrons' reference questions. Analyze patrons' requests to determine needed information and assist in furnishing or locating that information. Teach library patrons to search for information by using databases. Keep records of circulation and materials. Supervise budgeting, planning, and personnel activities. Check books in and out of the library. Explain use of library facilities, resources, equipment, and services and provide information about library policies. Review and evaluate resource material, such as book reviews and catalogs, to select and order print, audiovisual, and electronic resources. Code, classify, and catalog books, publications, films, audiovisual aids, and other library materials based on subject matter or standard library classification systems. Locate unusual or unique information in response to specific requests. Direct and train library staff in duties such as receiving, shelving, researching, cataloging, and equipment use. Respond to customer complaints, taking action as necessary. Organize collections of books, publications, documents, audiovisual aids, and other reference materials for convenient access. Develop library policies and procedures. Evaluate materials to determine outdated or unused items to be discarded. Develop information access aids such as indexes and annotated bibliographies, Web pages, electronic pathfinders, and online tutorials. Plan and deliver client-centered programs and services such as special services for corporate clients, storytelling for children, newsletters, or programs for special groups. Compile lists of books, periodicals, articles, and audiovisual materials on particular subjects. Arrange for interlibrary loans of materials not available in a particular library. Assemble and arrange display materials. Confer with teachers, parents, and community organizations to develop, plan, and conduct programs in reading, viewing, and communication skills. Compile lists of overdue materials and notify borrowers that their materials are overdue.

Personality Type: Artistic. Artistic occupations frequently involve working with forms, designs, and patterns. They often require self-expression, and the work can be done without following a clear set of rules.

GOE—Interest Area: 05. Education and Training. **Work Group:** 05.04. Library Services. **Other Jobs in This Work Group:** Library Assistants, Clerical; Library Technicians.

Skills—Management of Financial Resources: Determining how money will be spent to get the work done and accounting for these expenditures. **Management of Material Resources:** Obtaining and seeing to the appropriate use of equipment, facilities, and materials needed to do certain work. **Learning Strategies:** Selecting and using training/instructional methods and procedures appropriate for the situation when learning or teaching new things. **Persuasion:** Persuading others to change their minds or behavior. **Service Orientation:** Actively looking for ways to help people. **Systems Evaluation:** Identifying measures or indicators of system performance and the actions needed to improve or correct performance relative to the goals of the system. **Monitoring:** Monitoring/assessing your performance or that of other individuals or organizations to make improvements or take corrective action. **Equipment Selection:** Determining the kind of tools and equipment needed to do a job.

Education and Training Programs: School Librarian/School Library Media Specialist; Library Science/Librarianship; Library Science, Other. **Related Knowledge/Courses: Customer and Personal Service:** Principles and processes for providing customer and personal services. This includes customer needs assessment, meeting quality standards for services, and evaluation of customer satisfaction. **Communications and Media:** Media production, communication, and dissemination techniques and methods. This includes alternative ways to inform and entertain via written, oral, and visual media. **Clerical Practices:** Administrative and clerical procedures and systems such as word processing, managing files and records, stenography and transcription, designing forms, and other office procedures and terminology. **Personnel and Human Resources:** Principles and procedures for personnel recruitment, selection, training, compensation and benefits, labor relations and negotiation, and personnel information systems. **English Language:** The structure and content of the English language, including the meaning and spelling of words, rules of composition, and grammar. **Computers and Electronics:** Circuit boards; processors; chips; electronic equipment; and computer hardware and software, including applications and programming.

Work Environment: Indoors; sitting; using hands on objects, tools, or controls; repetitive motions.

Library Science Teachers, Postsecondary

- Annual Earnings: $53,810
- Growth: 32.2%
- Annual Job Openings: 329,000
- Education/Training Required: Master's degree
- Self-Employed: 0.4%
- Part-Time: 27.3%

The job openings listed here are shared with 35 other postsecondary teaching occupations. For a complete list, see the beginning of this section.

How the Job Improves the World: Contributes to education.

Teach courses in library science. Prepare course materials such as syllabi, homework assignments, and handouts. Prepare and deliver lectures to undergraduate or graduate students on topics such as collection development, archival methods, and indexing and abstracting. Evaluate and grade students' classwork, assignments, and papers. Keep abreast of developments in their field by reading current literature, talking with colleagues, and participating in professional conferences. Initiate, facilitate, and moderate classroom discussions. Plan, evaluate, and revise curricula, course content, and course materials and methods of instruction. Conduct research in a particular field of knowledge and publish findings in professional journals, books, and/or electronic media. Maintain student attendance records, grades, and other required records. Collaborate with colleagues to address teaching and research issues. Advise students on academic and vocational curricula and on career issues. Compile, administer, and grade examinations or assign this work to others. Supervise undergraduate or graduate teaching, internship, and research work. Maintain regularly scheduled office hours in order to advise and assist students. Write grant proposals to procure external research funding. Select and obtain materials and supplies such as textbooks. Serve on academic or administrative committees that deal with institutional policies, departmental matters, and academic issues. Compile bibliographies of specialized materials for outside reading assignments. Participate in student recruitment, registration, and placement activities. Perform administrative duties such as serving as department head. Participate in campus and community events. Act as advisers to student organizations. Provide professional consulting services to government and/or industry.

Personality Type: No data available.

GOE—Interest Area: 05. Education and Training. **Work Group:** 05.03. Postsecondary and Adult Teaching and Instructing. **Other Jobs in This Work Group:** Adult Literacy, Remedial Education, and GED Teachers and Instructors; Agricultural Sciences Teachers, Postsecondary; Anthropology and Archeology Teachers, Postsecondary; Architecture Teachers, Postsecondary; Area, Ethnic, and Cultural Studies Teachers, Postsecondary; Art, Drama, and Music Teachers, Postsecondary; Atmospheric, Earth, Marine, and Space Sciences Teachers, Postsecondary; Biological Science Teachers, Postsecondary; Business Teachers, Postsecondary; Chemistry Teachers, Postsecondary; Communications Teachers, Postsecondary; Computer Science Teachers, Postsecondary; Criminal Justice and Law Enforcement Teachers, Postsecondary; Economics Teachers, Postsecondary; Education Teachers, Postsecondary; Engineering Teachers, Postsecondary; English Language and Literature Teachers, Postsecondary; Environmental Science Teachers, Postsecondary; Farm and Home Management Advisors; Foreign Language and Literature Teachers, Postsecondary; Forestry and Conservation Science Teachers, Postsecondary; Geography Teachers, Postsecondary; Graduate Teaching Assistants; Health Specialties Teachers, Postsecondary; History Teachers, Postsecondary; Home Economics Teachers, Postsecondary; Law Teachers, Postsecondary; Mathematical Science Teachers, Postsecondary; Nursing Instructors and Teachers, Postsecondary; Philosophy and Religion Teachers, Postsecondary; Physics Teachers, Postsecondary; Political Science Teachers, Postsecondary; Psychology Teachers, Postsecondary; Recreation and Fitness Studies Teachers, Postsecondary; Self-Enrichment Education Teachers; Social Work Teachers, Postsecondary; Sociology Teachers, Postsecondary; Vocational Education Teachers, Postsecondary.

Skills—Writing: Communicating effectively in writing as appropriate for the needs of the audience. **Instructing:** Teaching others how to do something.

Learning Strategies: Selecting and using training/instructional methods and procedures appropriate for the situation when learning or teaching new things. **Active Learning:** Understanding the implications of new information for both current and future problem-solving and decision-making. **Reading Comprehension:** Understanding written sentences and paragraphs in work-related documents. **Monitoring:** Monitoring/assessing your performance or that of other individuals or organizations to make improvements or take corrective action. **Speaking:** Talking to others to convey information effectively. **Critical Thinking:** Using logic and reasoning to identify the strengths and weaknesses of alternative solutions, conclusions, or approaches to problems.

Education and Training Programs: Teacher Education and Professional Development, Specific Subject Areas, Other; Library Science/Librarianship. **Related Knowledge/Courses: Education and Training:** Principles and methods for curriculum and training design, teaching and instruction for individuals and groups, and the measurement of training effects. **Sociology and Anthropology:** Group behavior and dynamics, societal trends and influences, human migrations, ethnicity, and cultures and their history and origins. **English Language:** The structure and content of the English language, including the meaning and spelling of words, rules of composition, and grammar. **Communications and Media:** Media production, communication, and dissemination techniques and methods. This includes alternative ways to inform and entertain via written, oral, and visual media. **History and Archeology:** Historical events and their causes, indicators, and effects on civilizations and cultures. **Philosophy and Theology:** Different philosophical systems and religions. This includes their basic principles, values, ethics, ways of thinking, customs, and practices and their impact on human culture.

Work Environment: Indoors; sitting.

Licensed Practical and Licensed Vocational Nurses

- Annual Earnings: $35,230
- Growth: 17.1%
- Annual Job Openings: 84,000
- Education/Training Required: Postsecondary vocational training
- Self-Employed: 0.6%
- Part-Time: 21.9%

How the Job Improves the World: Contributes to health.

Care for ill, injured, convalescent, or disabled persons in hospitals, nursing homes, clinics, private homes, group homes, and similar institutions. May work under the supervision of a registered nurse. Licensing required. Observe patients, charting and reporting changes in patients' conditions, such as adverse reactions to medication or treatment, and taking any necessary action. Administer prescribed medications or start intravenous fluids and note times and amounts on patients' charts. Answer patients' calls and determine how to assist them. Measure and record patients' vital signs, such as height, weight, temperature, blood pressure, pulse, and respiration. Provide basic patient care and treatments, such as taking temperatures or blood pressures, dressing wounds, treating bedsores, giving enemas or douches, rubbing with alcohol, massaging, or performing catheterizations. Help patients with bathing, dressing, maintaining personal hygiene, moving in bed, or standing and walking. Supervise nurses' aides and assistants. Work as part of a health care team to assess patient needs, plan and modify care, and implement interventions. Record food and fluid intake and output. Evaluate nursing intervention outcomes, conferring with other health care team members as necessary. Assemble and use equipment such as catheters, tracheotomy tubes, and oxygen suppliers. Collect samples such as blood, urine, and sputum from patients and perform routine laboratory tests on samples. Prepare patients for examinations, tests, or treatments and explain procedures. Prepare food trays and examine them for conformance to prescribed diet. Apply compresses, ice bags, and hot water bottles. Clean rooms and make beds. Inventory and requisition supplies and instruments. Provide medical treatment and personal care to patients in private home settings, such as cooking, keeping rooms orderly, seeing that patients are comfortable and in good spirits, and instructing family members in simple nursing tasks. Sterilize equipment and supplies, using germicides, sterilizer, or autoclave. Assist in delivery, care, and feeding of infants. Wash and dress bodies of deceased persons. Make appointments, keep records, and perform other clerical duties in doctors' offices and clinics. Set up equipment and prepare medical treatment rooms.

Personality Type: Social. Social occupations frequently involve working with, communicating with, and teaching people. These occupations often involve helping or providing service to others.

GOE—Interest Area: 08. Health Science. **Work Group:** 08.08. Patient Care and Assistance. **Other Jobs in This Work Group:** Home Health Aides; Nursing Aides, Orderlies, and Attendants; Psychiatric Aides; Psychiatric Technicians.

Skills—Science: Using scientific rules and methods to solve problems. **Operation Monitoring:** Watching gauges, dials, or other indicators to make sure a machine is working properly. **Service Orientation:** Actively looking for ways to help people. **Judgment and Decision Making:** Considering the relative costs and benefits of potential actions to choose the most appropriate one. **Active Listening:** Giving full attention to what other people are saying, taking time to understand the points being made, asking questions as

appropriate, and not interrupting at inappropriate times. **Management of Personnel Resources:** Motivating, developing, and directing people as they work; identifying the best people for the job. **Writing:** Communicating effectively in writing as appropriate for the needs of the audience. **Time Management:** Managing one's own time and the time of others.

Education and Training Program: Licensed Practical/Vocational Nurse Training (LPN, LVN, Cert, Dipl, AAS). **Related Knowledge/Courses: Psychology:** Human behavior and performance; individual differences in ability, personality, and interests; learning and motivation; psychological research methods; and the assessment and treatment of behavioral and affective disorders. **Therapy and Counseling:** Principles, methods, and procedures for diagnosis, treatment, and rehabilitation of physical and mental dysfunctions and for career counseling and guidance. **Medicine and Dentistry:** The information and techniques needed to diagnose and treat human injuries, diseases, and deformities. This includes symptoms, treatment alternatives, drug properties and interactions, and preventive health-care measures. **Customer and Personal Service:** Principles and processes for providing customer and personal services. This includes customer needs assessment, meeting quality standards for services, and evaluation of customer satisfaction. **Philosophy and Theology:** Different philosophical systems and religions. This includes their basic principles, values, ethics, ways of thinking, customs, and practices and their impact on human culture. **Sociology and Anthropology:** Group behavior and dynamics, societal trends and influences, human migrations, ethnicity, and cultures and their history and origins.

Work Environment: Indoors; disease or infections; standing; walking and running.

Lifeguards, Ski Patrol, and Other Recreational Protective Service Workers

- Annual Earnings: $16,910
- Growth: 20.4%
- Annual Job Openings: 49,000
- Education/Training Required: Short-term on-the-job training
- Self-Employed: 0.2%
- Part-Time: 63.8%

How the Job Improves the World: Contributes to safety.

Monitor recreational areas, such as pools, beaches, or ski slopes, to provide assistance and protection to participants. Rescue distressed persons, using rescue techniques and equipment. Contact emergency medical personnel in case of serious injury. Patrol or monitor recreational areas such as trails, slopes, and swimming areas on foot, in vehicles, or from towers. Examine injured persons and administer first aid or cardiopulmonary resuscitation if necessary, utilizing training and medical supplies and equipment. Instruct participants in skiing, swimming, or other recreational activities and provide safety precaution information. Warn recreational participants of inclement weather, unsafe areas, or illegal conduct. Complete and maintain records of weather and beach conditions, emergency medical treatments performed, and other relevant incident information. Inspect recreational equipment, such as rope tows, T-bars, J-bars, and chair lifts, for safety hazards and damage or wear. Provide assistance with staff selection, training, and supervision. Inspect recreational facilities for cleanliness. Observe activities in assigned areas, using binoculars to detect hazards, disturbances, or safety infractions. Provide assistance in the safe use of equipment such as ski lifts.

Operate underwater recovery units. Participate in recreational demonstrations to entertain resort guests.

Personality Type: Realistic. Realistic occupations frequently involve work activities that include practical, hands-on problems and solutions. They often deal with plants; animals; and real-world materials such as wood, tools, and machinery. Many of the occupations require working outside and do not involve a lot of paperwork or working closely with others.

GOE—Interest Area: 12. Law and Public Safety. **Work Group:** 12.05. Safety and Security. **Other Jobs in This Work Group:** Animal Control Workers; Crossing Guards; Gaming Surveillance Officers and Gaming Investigators; Private Detectives and Investigators; Security Guards; Transportation Security Screeners.

Skills—No data available.

Education and Training Program: Security and Protective Services, Other. **Related Knowledge/Courses: Medicine and Dentistry:** The information and techniques needed to diagnose and treat human injuries, diseases, and deformities. This includes symptoms, treatment alternatives, drug properties and interactions, and preventive health-care measures. **Chemistry:** The chemical composition, structure, and properties of substances and of the chemical processes and transformations that they undergo. This includes uses of chemicals and their danger signs, production techniques, and disposal methods. **Customer and Personal Service:** Principles and processes for providing customer and personal services. This includes customer needs assessment, meeting quality standards for services, and evaluation of customer satisfaction. **Psychology:** Human behavior and performance; individual differences in ability, personality, and interests; learning and motivation; psychological research methods; and the assessment and treatment of behavioral and affective disorders. **Public Safety and Security:**

Relevant equipment, policies, procedures, and strategies to promote effective local, state, or national security operations for the protection of people, data, property, and institutions. **Education and Training:** Principles and methods for curriculum and training design, teaching and instruction for individuals and groups, and the measurement of training effects.

Work Environment: Indoors; noisy; sitting.

Mathematical Science Teachers, Postsecondary

- Annual Earnings: $53,820
- Growth: 32.2%
- Annual Job Openings: 329,000
- Education/Training Required: Master's degree
- Self-Employed: 0.4%
- Part-Time: 27.3%

The job openings listed here are shared with 35 other postsecondary teaching occupations. For a complete list, see the beginning of this section.

How the Job Improves the World: Contributes to education.

Teach courses pertaining to mathematical concepts, statistics, and actuarial science and to the application of original and standardized mathematical techniques in solving specific problems and situations. Evaluate and grade students' classwork, assignments, and papers. Compile, administer, and grade examinations or assign this work to others. Prepare and deliver lectures to undergraduate and/or graduate students on topics such as linear algebra, differential equations, and discrete mathematics. Prepare course materials such as syllabi, homework assignments, and handouts. Maintain student attendance records, grades, and other required records. Maintain regularly scheduled of-

fice hours to advise and assist students. Plan, evaluate, and revise curricula, course content, and course materials and methods of instruction. Initiate, facilitate, and moderate classroom discussions. Select and obtain materials and supplies such as textbooks. Keep abreast of developments in their field by reading current literature, talking with colleagues, and participating in professional conferences. Advise students on academic and vocational curricula and on career issues. Collaborate with colleagues to address teaching and research issues. Serve on academic or administrative committees that deal with institutional policies, departmental matters, and academic issues. Participate in student recruitment, registration, and placement activities. Perform administrative duties such as serving as department head. Conduct research in a particular field of knowledge and publish findings in books, professional journals, and/or electronic media. Supervise undergraduate and/or graduate teaching, internship, and research work. Act as advisers to student organizations. Participate in campus and community events. Write grant proposals to procure external research funding. Compile bibliographies of specialized materials for outside reading assignments. Provide professional consulting services to government and/or industry.

Personality Type: Investigative. Investigative occupations frequently involve working with ideas and require an extensive amount of thinking. These occupations can involve searching for facts and figuring out problems mentally.

GOE—Interest Area: 05. Education and Training. **Work Group:** 05.03. Postsecondary and Adult Teaching and Instructing. **Other Jobs in This Work Group:** Adult Literacy, Remedial Education, and GED Teachers and Instructors; Agricultural Sciences Teachers, Postsecondary; Anthropology and Archeology Teachers, Postsecondary; Architecture Teachers, Postsecondary; Area, Ethnic, and Cultural Studies Teachers, Postsecondary; Art, Drama, and Music Teachers, Postsecondary; Atmospheric, Earth,

Marine, and Space Sciences Teachers, Postsecondary; Biological Science Teachers, Postsecondary; Business Teachers, Postsecondary; Chemistry Teachers, Postsecondary; Communications Teachers, Postsecondary; Computer Science Teachers, Postsecondary; Criminal Justice and Law Enforcement Teachers, Postsecondary; Economics Teachers, Postsecondary; Education Teachers, Postsecondary; Engineering Teachers, Postsecondary; English Language and Literature Teachers, Postsecondary; Environmental Science Teachers, Postsecondary; Farm and Home Management Advisors; Foreign Language and Literature Teachers, Postsecondary; Forestry and Conservation Science Teachers, Postsecondary; Geography Teachers, Postsecondary; Graduate Teaching Assistants; Health Specialties Teachers, Postsecondary; History Teachers, Postsecondary; Home Economics Teachers, Postsecondary; Law Teachers, Postsecondary; Library Science Teachers, Postsecondary; Nursing Instructors and Teachers, Postsecondary; Philosophy and Religion Teachers, Postsecondary; Physics Teachers, Postsecondary; Political Science Teachers, Postsecondary; Psychology Teachers, Postsecondary; Recreation and Fitness Studies Teachers, Postsecondary; Self-Enrichment Education Teachers; Social Work Teachers, Postsecondary; Sociology Teachers, Postsecondary; Vocational Education Teachers, Postsecondary.

Skills—Mathematics: Using mathematics to solve problems. **Instructing:** Teaching others how to do something. **Learning Strategies:** Selecting and using training/instructional methods and procedures appropriate for the situation when learning or teaching new things. **Critical Thinking:** Using logic and reasoning to identify the strengths and weaknesses of alternative solutions, conclusions, or approaches to problems. **Complex Problem Solving:** Identifying complex problems and reviewing related information to develop and evaluate options and implement solutions. **Speaking:** Talking to others to convey information

effectively. **Science:** Using scientific rules and methods to solve problems. **Active Learning:** Understanding the implications of new information for both current and future problem-solving and decision-making.

Education and Training Programs: Mathematics, General; Algebra and Number Theory; Analysis and Functional Analysis; Geometry/Geometric Analysis; Topology and Foundations; Mathematics, Other; Applied Mathematics; Statistics, General; Mathematical Statistics and Probability; Mathematics and Statistics, Other; Logic; Business Statistics. **Related Knowledge/Courses: Mathematics:** Arithmetic, algebra, geometry, calculus, and statistics and their applications. **Education and Training:** Principles and methods for curriculum and training design, teaching and instruction for individuals and groups, and the measurement of training effects. **Physics:** Physical principles and laws and their interrelationships and applications to understanding fluid, material, and atmospheric dynamics and mechanical, electrical, atomic, and subatomic structures and processes. **Computers and Electronics:** Circuit boards; processors; chips; electronic equipment; and computer hardware and software, including applications and programming. **English Language:** The structure and content of the English language, including the meaning and spelling of words, rules of composition, and grammar. **Psychology:** Human behavior and performance; individual differences in ability, personality, and interests; learning and motivation; psychological research methods; and the assessment and treatment of behavioral and affective disorders.

Work Environment: Indoors; more often standing than sitting.

Medical and Clinical Laboratory Technicians

- Annual Earnings: $31,700
- Growth: 25.0%
- Annual Job Openings: 14,000
- Education/Training Required: Associate degree
- Self-Employed: 0.1%
- Part-Time: 17.3%

How the Job Improves the World: Contributes to health.

Perform routine medical laboratory tests for the diagnosis, treatment, and prevention of disease. May work under the supervision of a medical technologist. Conduct chemical analyses of body fluids, such as blood and urine, using microscope or automatic analyzer to detect abnormalities or diseases, and enter findings into computer. Set up, adjust, maintain, and clean medical laboratory equipment. Analyze the results of tests and experiments to ensure conformity to specifications, using special mechanical and electrical devices. Analyze and record test data to issue reports that use charts, graphs and narratives. Conduct blood tests for transfusion purposes and perform blood counts. Perform medical research to further control and cure disease. Obtain specimens, cultivating, isolating, and identifying microorganisms for analysis. Examine cells stained with dye to locate abnormalities. Collect blood or tissue samples from patients, observing principles of asepsis to obtain blood sample. Consult with a pathologist to determine a final diagnosis when abnormal cells are found. Inoculate fertilized eggs, broths, or other bacteriological media with organisms. Cut, stain, and mount tissue samples for examination by pathologists. Supervise and instruct other technicians and laboratory assistants. Prepare standard volumetric solutions and reagents to be combined with samples, following standardized formulas or experimental procedures. Prepare vaccines and serums by standard laboratory methods, testing for virus inactivity and sterility. Test raw materials, processes, and finished products to determine quality and quantity of materials or characteristics of a substance.

Personality Type: Realistic. Realistic occupations frequently involve work activities that include practical, hands-on problems and solutions. They often deal with plants; animals; and real-world materials such as wood, tools, and machinery. Many of the occupations require working outside and do not involve a lot of paperwork or working closely with others.

GOE—Interest Area: 08. Health Science. **Work Group:** 08.06. Medical Technology. **Other Jobs in This Work Group:** Biological Technicians; Cardiovascular Technologists and Technicians; Diagnostic Medical Sonographers; Medical and Clinical Laboratory Technologists; Medical Equipment Preparers; Medical Records and Health Information Technicians; Nuclear Medicine Technologists; Opticians, Dispensing; Orthotists and Prosthetists; Radiologic Technicians; Radiologic Technologists; Radiologic Technologists and Technicians.

Skills—Science: Using scientific rules and methods to solve problems. **Equipment Maintenance:** Performing routine maintenance on equipment and determining when and what kind of maintenance is needed. **Troubleshooting:** Determining causes of operating errors and deciding what to do about them. **Operation Monitoring:** Watching gauges, dials, or other indicators to make sure a machine is working properly. **Quality Control Analysis:** Conducting tests and inspections of products, services, or processes to evaluate quality or performance. **Operation and Control:** Controlling operations of equipment or systems. **Monitoring:** Monitoring/assessing your performance or that of other individuals or organizations to make improvements or take corrective action. **Instructing:** Teaching others how to do something.

Education and Training Programs: Clinical/ Medical Laboratory Assistant; Blood Bank Technology Specialist; Hematology Technology/ Technician; Clinical/Medical Laboratory Technician; Histologic Technician. Related Knowledge/Courses: Medicine and Dentistry: The information and techniques needed to diagnose and treat human injuries, diseases, and deformities. This includes symptoms, treatment alternatives, drug properties and interactions, and preventive health-care measures. Therapy and Counseling: Principles, methods, and procedures for diagnosis, treatment, and rehabilitation of physical and mental dysfunctions and for career counseling and guidance. Biology: Plant and animal organisms and their tissues, cells, functions, interdependencies, and interactions with each other and the environment. Clerical Practices: Administrative and clerical procedures and systems such as word processing, managing files and records, stenography and transcription, designing forms, and other office procedures and terminology.

Work Environment: Indoors; disease or infections; standing; walking and running; using hands on objects, tools, or controls.

Medical and Clinical Laboratory Technologists

- Annual Earnings: $47,710
- Growth: 20.5%
- Annual Job Openings: 14,000
- Education/Training Required: Bachelor's degree
- Self-Employed: 0.1%
- Part-Time: 17.3%

How the Job Improves the World: Contributes to health.

Perform complex medical laboratory tests for diagnosis, treatment, and prevention of disease. May train or supervise staff. Analyze laboratory findings to check the accuracy of the results. Conduct chemical analysis of body fluids, including blood, urine, and spinal fluid, to determine presence of normal and abnormal components. Operate, calibrate, and maintain equipment used in quantitative and qualitative analysis, such as spectrophotometers, calorimeters, flame photometers, and computer-controlled analyzers. Enter data from analysis of medical tests and clinical results into computer for storage. Analyze samples of biological material for chemical content or reaction. Establish and monitor programs to ensure the accuracy of laboratory results. Set up, clean, and maintain laboratory equipment. Provide technical information about test results to physicians, family members, and researchers. Supervise, train, and direct lab assistants, medical and clinical laboratory technicians and technologists, and other medical laboratory workers engaged in laboratory testing. Develop, standardize, evaluate, and modify procedures, techniques, and tests used in the analysis of specimens and in medical laboratory experiments. Cultivate, isolate, and assist in identifying microbial organisms and perform various tests on these microorganisms. Study blood samples to determine the number of cells and their morphology, as well as the blood group, type, and compatibility for transfusion purposes, using microscopic technique. Obtain, cut, stain, and mount biological material on slides for microscopic study and diagnosis, following standard laboratory procedures. Select and prepare specimen and media for cell culture, using aseptic technique and knowledge of medium components and cell requirements. Conduct medical research under direction of microbiologist or biochemist. Harvest cell cultures at optimum time based on knowledge of cell cycle differences and culture conditions.

Personality Type: Investigative. Investigative occupations frequently involve working with ideas and require an extensive amount of thinking. These occupations can involve searching for facts and figuring out problems mentally.

GOE—Interest Area: 08. Health Science. Work Group: 08.06. Medical Technology. Other Jobs in This Work Group: Biological Technicians; Cardiovascular Technologists and Technicians; Diagnostic Medical Sonographers; Medical and Clinical Laboratory Technicians; Medical Equipment Preparers; Medical Records and Health Information Technicians; Nuclear Medicine Technologists; Opticians, Dispensing; Orthotists and Prosthetists; Radiologic Technicians; Radiologic Technologists; Radiologic Technologists and Technicians.

Skills—Equipment Maintenance: Performing routine maintenance on equipment and determining when and what kind of maintenance is needed. Operation Monitoring: Watching gauges, dials, or other indicators to make sure a machine is working properly. Quality Control Analysis: Conducting tests and inspections of products, services, or processes to evaluate quality or performance. Science: Using scientific rules and methods to solve problems. Operation and Control: Controlling operations of equipment or systems. Repairing: Repairing machines or systems by using the needed tools. Troubleshooting: Determining causes of operating errors and deciding what to do about them. Equipment Selection: Determining the kind of tools and equipment needed to do a job.

Education and Training Programs: Cytotechnology/Cytotechnologist; Clinical Laboratory Science/Medical Technology/Technologist; Histologic Technology/Histotechnologist; Cytogenetics/Genetics/Clinical Genetics Technology/Technologist; Renal/Dialysis Technologist/Technician; Clinical/Medical Laboratory Science and Allied Professions, Other. Related Knowledge/Courses: Biology: Plant and animal organisms and their tissues, cells, functions, interdependencies, and interactions with each other and the environment. Chemistry: The chemical composition, structure, and properties of substances and of the chemical processes and transformations that they undergo. This includes uses of chemicals and their danger signs, production techniques, and disposal methods. Mechanical Devices: Machines and tools, including their designs, uses, repair, and maintenance. Public Safety and Security: Relevant equipment, policies, procedures, and strategies to promote effective local, state, or national security operations for the protection of people, data, property, and institutions. Computers and Electronics: Circuit boards; processors; chips; electronic equipment; and computer hardware and software, including applications and programming. Medicine and Dentistry: The information and techniques needed to diagnose and treat human injuries, diseases, and deformities. This includes symptoms, treatment alternatives, drug properties and interactions, and preventive health-care measures.

Work Environment: Indoors; contaminants; disease or infections; hazardous conditions; using hands on objects, tools, or controls; repetitive motions.

Medical and Public Health Social Workers

- Annual Earnings: $41,120
- Growth: 25.9%
- Annual Job Openings: 14,000
- Education/Training Required: Bachelor's degree
- Self-Employed: 3.0%
- Part-Time: 11.5%

How the Job Improves the World: Contributes to mental health and social well-being.

Provide persons, families, or vulnerable populations with the psychosocial support needed to cope with chronic, acute, or terminal illnesses, such as Alzheimer's, cancer, or AIDS. Services include advising family caregivers, providing patient education and counseling, and making necessary referrals for other social services. Collaborate with other professionals to evaluate patients' medical or physical condition and to assess client needs. Investigate child abuse or neglect cases and take authorized protective action when necessary. Refer patient, client, or family to community resources to assist in recovery from mental or physical illness and to provide access to services such as financial assistance, legal aid, housing, job placement, or education. Counsel clients and patients in individual and group sessions to help them overcome dependencies, recover from illness, and adjust to life. Organize support groups or counsel family members to assist them in understanding, dealing with, and supporting the client or patient. Advocate for clients or patients to resolve crises. Identify environmental impediments to client or patient progress through interviews and review of patient records. Utilize consultation data and social work experience to plan and coordinate client or patient care and rehabilitation, following through to ensure service efficacy. Modify treatment plans to comply with changes in clients' status. Monitor, evaluate, and record client progress according to measurable goals described in treatment and care plan. Supervise and direct other workers providing services to clients or patients. Develop or advise on social policy and assist in community development. Oversee Medicaid- and Medicare-related paperwork and recordkeeping in hospitals. Conduct social research to advance knowledge in the social work field. Plan and conduct programs to combat social problems, prevent substance abuse, or improve community health and counseling services.

Personality Type: Social. Social occupations frequently involve working with, communicating with, and teaching people. These occupations often involve helping or providing service to others.

GOE—Interest Area: 10. Human Service. **Work Group:** 10.01. Counseling and Social Work. **Other Jobs in This Work Group:** Child, Family, and School

Social Workers; Clinical Psychologists; Clinical, Counseling, and School Psychologists; Counseling Psychologists; Marriage and Family Therapists; Mental Health and Substance Abuse Social Workers; Mental Health Counselors; Probation Officers and Correctional Treatment Specialists; Rehabilitation Counselors; Residential Advisors; Social and Human Service Assistants; Substance Abuse and Behavioral Disorder Counselors.

Skills—Social Perceptiveness: Being aware of others' reactions and understanding why they react as they do. **Service Orientation:** Actively looking for ways to help people. **Negotiation:** Bringing others together and trying to reconcile differences. **Coordination:** Adjusting actions in relation to others' actions. **Active Listening:** Giving full attention to what other people are saying, taking time to understand the points being made, asking questions as appropriate, and not interrupting at inappropriate times. **Speaking:** Talking to others to convey information effectively. **Writing:** Communicating effectively in writing as appropriate for the needs of the audience. **Critical Thinking:** Using logic and reasoning to identify the strengths and weaknesses of alternative solutions, conclusions, or approaches to problems.

Education and Training Program: Clinical/Medical Social Work. **Related Knowledge/Courses: Therapy and Counseling:** Principles, methods, and procedures for diagnosis, treatment, and rehabilitation of physical and mental dysfunctions and for career counseling and guidance. **Psychology:** Human behavior and performance; individual differences in ability, personality, and interests; learning and motivation; psychological research methods; and the assessment and treatment of behavioral and affective disorders. **Philosophy and Theology:** Different philosophical systems and religions. This includes their basic principles, values, ethics, ways of thinking, customs, and practices and their impact on human culture. **Sociology and Anthropology:** Group behavior and dynamics, societal trends and influences, human migrations, ethnicity, and cultures and their history and origins. **Medicine and Dentistry:** The information and techniques needed to diagnose and treat human injuries, diseases, and deformities. This includes symptoms, treatment alternatives, drug properties and interactions, and preventive health-care measures. **Customer and Personal Service:** Principles and processes for providing customer and personal services. This includes customer needs assessment, meeting quality standards for services, and evaluation of customer satisfaction.

Work Environment: Indoors; noisy; disease or infections; sitting.

Medical Assistants

- Annual Earnings: $25,350
- Growth: 52.1%
- Annual Job Openings: 93,000
- Education/Training Required: Moderate-term on-the-job training
- Self-Employed: 0.0%
- Part-Time: 27.5%

How the Job Improves the World: Contributes to health.

Perform administrative and certain clinical duties under the direction of physician. Administrative duties may include scheduling appointments, maintaining medical records, billing, and coding for insurance purposes. Clinical duties may include taking and recording vital signs and medical histories, preparing patients for examination, drawing blood, and administering medications as directed by physician. Interview patients to obtain medical information and measure their vital signs, weight, and height. Show patients to examination rooms and prepare them for the physician. Record patients' medical history, vital statistics, and information such as test results in medical records. Prepare and administer medica-

tions as directed by a physician. Collect blood, tissue, or other laboratory specimens; log the specimens; and prepare them for testing. Explain treatment procedures, medications, diets, and physicians' instructions to patients. Help physicians examine and treat patients, handing them instruments and materials or performing such tasks as giving injections or removing sutures. Authorize drug refills and provide prescription information to pharmacies. Prepare treatment rooms for patient examinations, keeping the rooms neat and clean. Clean and sterilize instruments and dispose of contaminated supplies. Schedule appointments for patients. Change dressings on wounds. Greet and log in patients arriving at office or clinic. Contact medical facilities or departments to schedule patients for tests or admission. Perform general office duties such as answering telephones, taking dictation, or completing insurance forms. Inventory and order medical, lab, or office supplies and equipment. Perform routine laboratory tests and sample analyses. Set up medical laboratory equipment. Keep financial records and perform other bookkeeping duties, such as handling credit and collections and mailing monthly statements to patients. Operate X-ray, electrocardiogram (EKG), and other equipment to administer routine diagnostic tests. Give physiotherapy treatments such as diathermy, galvanics, and hydrotherapy.

Personality Type: Social. Social occupations frequently involve working with, communicating with, and teaching people. These occupations often involve helping or providing service to others.

GOE—Interest Area: 08. Health Science. **Work Group:** 08.02. Medicine and Surgery. **Other Jobs in This Work Group:** Anesthesiologists; Family and General Practitioners; Internists, General; Medical Transcriptionists; Obstetricians and Gynecologists; Pediatricians, General; Pharmacists; Pharmacy Aides; Pharmacy Technicians; Physician Assistants; Psychiatrists; Registered Nurses; Surgeons; Surgical Technologists.

Skills—Social Perceptiveness: Being aware of others' reactions and understanding why they react as they do. Service Orientation: Actively looking for ways to help people. Instructing: Teaching others how to do something. Operation Monitoring: Watching gauges, dials, or other indicators to make sure a machine is working properly. Active Listening: Giving full attention to what other people are saying, taking time to understand the points being made, asking questions as appropriate, and not interrupting at inappropriate times. Operation and Control: Controlling operations of equipment or systems. Learning Strategies: Selecting and using training/instructional methods and procedures appropriate for the situation when learning or teaching new things. Mathematics: Using mathematics to solve problems.

Education and Training Programs: Medical Office Management/Administration; Medical Office Assistant/Specialist; Medical Reception/Receptionist; Medical Insurance Coding Specialist/Coder; Medical Administrative/Executive Assistant and Medical Secretary; Medical/Clinical Assistant; Anesthesiologist Assistant; Chiropractic Assistant/Technician; Allied Health and Medical Assisting Services, Other; Optomeric Technician/Assistant; others. Related Knowledge/Courses: Medicine and Dentistry: The information and techniques needed to diagnose and treat human injuries, diseases, and deformities. This includes symptoms, treatment alternatives, drug properties and interactions, and preventive health-care measures. Therapy and Counseling: Principles, methods, and procedures for diagnosis, treatment, and rehabilitation of physical and mental dysfunctions and for career counseling and guidance. Customer and Personal Service: Principles and processes for providing customer and personal services. This includes customer needs assessment, meeting quality standards for services, and evaluation of customer satisfaction. Clerical Practices: Administrative and clerical procedures and systems such as word processing, managing files and records, stenography and transcription, de-

signing forms, and other office procedures and terminology. Psychology: Human behavior and performance; individual differences in ability, personality, and interests; learning and motivation; psychological research methods; and the assessment and treatment of behavioral and affective disorders. English Language: The structure and content of the English language, including the meaning and spelling of words, rules of composition, and grammar.

Work Environment: Indoors; disease or infections; standing; walking and running; using hands on objects, tools, or controls.

Medical Equipment Preparers

- Annual Earnings: $24,880
- Growth: 20.0%
- Annual Job Openings: 8,000
- Education/Training Required: Short-term on-the-job training
- Self-Employed: 2.7%
- Part-Time: 27.5%

How the Job Improves the World: Contributes to health.

Prepare, sterilize, install, or clean laboratory or healthcare equipment. May perform routine laboratory tasks and operate or inspect equipment. Organize and assemble routine and specialty surgical instrument trays and other sterilized supplies, filling special requests as needed. Clean instruments to prepare them for sterilization. Operate and maintain steam autoclaves, keeping records of loads completed, items in loads, and maintenance procedures performed. Record sterilizer test results. Disinfect and sterilize equipment such as respirators, hospital beds, and oxygen and dialysis equipment, using sterilizers, aerators, and washers. Start equipment and observe gauges and equipment operation to detect malfunctions and to ensure equipment is operating to prescribed standards. Examine equipment to detect leaks, worn or loose parts, or other indications of disrepair. Report defective equipment to appropriate supervisors or staff. Check sterile supplies to ensure that they are not outdated. Maintain records of inventory and equipment usage. Attend hospital in-service programs related to areas of work specialization. Purge wastes from equipment by connecting equipment to water sources and flushing water through systems. Deliver equipment to specified hospital locations or to patients' residences. Assist hospital staff with patient care duties such as providing transportation or setting up traction. Install and set up medical equipment, using hand tools.

Personality Type: Realistic. Realistic occupations frequently involve work activities that include practical, hands-on problems and solutions. They often deal with plants; animals; and real-world materials such as wood, tools, and machinery. Many of the occupations require working outside and do not involve a lot of paperwork or working closely with others.

GOE—Interest Area: 08. Health Science. **Work Group:** 08.06. Medical Technology. **Other Jobs in This Work Group:** Biological Technicians; Cardiovascular Technologists and Technicians; Diagnostic Medical Sonographers; Medical and Clinical Laboratory Technicians; Medical and Clinical Laboratory Technologists; Medical Records and Health Information Technicians; Nuclear Medicine Technologists; Opticians, Dispensing; Orthotists and Prosthetists; Radiologic Technicians; Radiologic Technologists; Radiologic Technologists and Technicians.

Skills—Operation Monitoring: Watching gauges, dials, or other indicators to make sure a machine is working properly. **Management of Material Resources:** Obtaining and seeing to the appropriate use of equipment, facilities, and materials needed to do certain work. **Equipment Maintenance:** Performing routine maintenance on equipment and determining when and what kind of maintenance is needed. **Quality Control Analysis:** Conducting tests and inspections of products, services, or processes to evaluate quality or performance. **Service Orientation:** Actively looking for ways to help people. **Operation and Control:** Controlling operations of equipment or systems. **Management of Personnel Resources:** Motivating, developing, and directing people as they work; identifying the best people for the job. **Monitoring:** Monitoring/assessing your performance or that of other individuals or organizations to make improvements or take corrective action.

Education and Training Programs: Medical/Clinical Assistant; Allied Health and Medical Assisting Services, Other. **Related Knowledge/Courses: Chemistry:** The chemical composition, structure, and properties of substances and of the chemical processes and transformations that they undergo. This includes uses of chemicals and their danger signs, production techniques, and disposal methods. **Biology:** Plant and animal organisms and their tissues, cells, functions, interdependencies, and interactions with each other and the environment. **Medicine and Dentistry:** The information and techniques needed to diagnose and treat human injuries, diseases, and deformities. This includes symptoms, treatment alternatives, drug properties and interactions, and preventive health-care measures. **Production and Processing:** Raw materials, production processes, quality control, costs, and other techniques for maximizing the effective manufacture and distribution of goods. **Education and Training:** Principles and methods for curriculum and training design, teaching and instruction for individuals and groups, and the measurement of training effects. **Customer and Personal Service:** Principles and processes for providing customer and personal services. This includes customer needs assessment, meeting quality standards for services, and evaluation of customer satisfaction.

Work Environment: Indoors; contaminants; disease or infections; standing; using hands on objects, tools, or controls; repetitive motions.

Medical Equipment Repairers

- Annual Earnings: $39,570
- Growth: 14.8%
- Annual Job Openings: 4,000
- Education/Training Required: Associate degree
- Self-Employed: 16.2%
- Part-Time: 12.1%

How the Job Improves the World: Contributes to health.

Test, adjust, or repair biomedical or electromedical equipment. Inspect and test malfunctioning medical and related equipment following manufacturers' specifications, using test and analysis instruments. Examine medical equipment and facility's structural environment and check for proper use of equipment to protect patients and staff from electrical or mechanical hazards and to ensure compliance with safety regulations. Disassemble malfunctioning equipment and remove, repair, and replace defective parts such as motors, clutches, or transformers. Keep records of maintenance, repair, and required updates of equipment. Perform preventive maintenance or service such as cleaning, lubricating, and adjusting equipment. Test and calibrate components and equipment, following manufacturers' manuals and troubleshooting techniques and using hand tools, power tools, and measuring devices. Explain and demonstrate correct operation and preventive maintenance of medical equipment to personnel. Study technical manuals and attend training sessions provided by equipment manufacturers to maintain current knowledge. Plan and carry out work assignments, using blueprints, schematic drawings, technical manuals, wiring diagrams, and liquid and air flow sheets, following prescribed regulations, directives, and other instructions as required. Solder loose connections, using soldering iron. Test, evaluate, and classify excess or in-use medical equipment and determine serviceability, condition, and disposition in accordance with regulations. Research catalogs and repair part lists to locate sources for repair parts, requisitioning parts and recording their receipt. Evaluate technical specifications to identify equipment and systems best suited for intended use and possible purchase based on specifications, user needs, and technical requirements. Contribute expertise to develop medical maintenance standard operating procedures. Compute power and space requirements for installing medical, dental, or related equipment and install units to manufacturers' specifications. Supervise and advise subordinate personnel. Repair shop equipment, metal furniture, and hospital equipment, including welding broken parts and replacing missing parts, or bring item into local shop for major repairs.

Personality Type: Realistic. Realistic occupations frequently involve work activities that include practical, hands-on problems and solutions. They often deal with plants; animals; and real-world materials such as wood, tools, and machinery. Many of the occupations require working outside and do not involve a lot of paperwork or working closely with others.

GOE—Interest Area: 13. Manufacturing. **Work Group:** 13.15. Medical and Technical Equipment Repair. **Other Jobs in This Work Group:** Camera and Photographic Equipment Repairers; Watch Repairers.

Skills—Repairing: Repairing machines or systems by using the needed tools. **Installation:** Installing equipment, machines, wiring, or programs to meet specifications. **Equipment Maintenance:** Performing routine maintenance on equipment and determining when and what kind of maintenance is needed.

Troubleshooting: Determining causes of operating errors and deciding what to do about them. **Systems Analysis:** Determining how a system should work and how changes in conditions, operations, and the environment will affect outcomes. **Operation Monitoring:** Watching gauges, dials, or other indicators to make sure a machine is working properly. **Quality Control Analysis:** Conducting tests and inspections of products, services, or processes to evaluate quality or performance. **Science:** Using scientific rules and methods to solve problems.

Education and Training Program: Biomedical Technology/Technician. **Related Knowledge/ Courses: Mechanical Devices:** Machines and tools, including their designs, uses, repair, and maintenance. **Computers and Electronics:** Circuit boards; processors; chips; electronic equipment; and computer hardware and software, including applications and programming. **Engineering and Technology:** The practical application of engineering science and technology. This includes applying principles, techniques, procedures, and equipment to the design and production of various goods and services. **Physics:** Physical principles and laws and their interrelationships and applications to understanding fluid, material, and atmospheric dynamics and mechanical, electrical, atomic, and subatomic structures and processes. **Telecommunications:** Transmission, broadcasting, switching, control, and operation of telecommunications systems. **Medicine and Dentistry:** The information and techniques needed to diagnose and treat human injuries, diseases, and deformities. This includes symptoms, treatment alternatives, drug properties and interactions, and preventive health-care measures.

Work Environment: Indoors; contaminants; disease or infections; standing; using hands on objects, tools, or controls.

Medical Records and Health Information Technicians

- Annual Earnings: $26,690
- Growth: 28.9%
- Annual Job Openings: 14,000
- Education/Training Required: Associate degree
- Self-Employed: 0.1%
- Part-Time: 17.6%

How the Job Improves the World: Contributes to health.

Compile, process, and maintain medical records of hospital and clinic patients in a manner consistent with medical, administrative, ethical, legal, and regulatory requirements of the health-care system. Process, maintain, compile, and report patient information for health requirements and standards. Protect the security of medical records to ensure that confidentiality is maintained. Process patient admission and discharge documents. Review records for completeness, accuracy, and compliance with regulations. Compile and maintain patients' medical records to document condition and treatment and to provide data for research or cost control and care improvement efforts. Enter data such as demographic characteristics, history and extent of disease, diagnostic procedures, and treatment into computer. Release information to persons and agencies according to regulations. Plan, develop, maintain, and operate a variety of health record indexes and storage and retrieval systems to collect, classify, store, and analyze information. Manage the department and supervise clerical workers, directing and controlling activities of personnel in the medical records department. Transcribe medical reports. Identify, compile, abstract, and code patient data, using standard classification systems. Resolve or clarify codes and diagnoses with conflicting, missing, or unclear information by consulting with doctors or others or by participating in the coding team's regular meetings. Train medical records staff. Assign the patient to diagnosis-related groups (DRGs), using appropriate computer software. Post medical insurance billings. Process and prepare business and government forms. Contact discharged patients, their families, and physicians to maintain registry with follow-up information, such as quality of life and length of survival of cancer patients. Prepare statistical reports, narrative reports, and graphic presentations of information such as tumor registry data for use by hospital staff, researchers, or other users. Consult classification manuals to locate information about disease processes. Compile medical care and census data for statistical reports on diseases treated, surgery performed, or use of hospital beds. Develop in-service educational materials.

Personality Type: Conventional. Conventional occupations frequently involve following set procedures and routines. These occupations can include working with data and details more than with ideas. Usually there is a clear line of authority to follow.

GOE—Interest Area: 08. Health Science. **Work Group:** 08.06. Medical Technology. **Other Jobs in This Work Group:** Biological Technicians; Cardiovascular Technologists and Technicians; Diagnostic Medical Sonographers; Medical and Clinical Laboratory Technicians; Medical and Clinical Laboratory Technologists; Medical Equipment Preparers; Nuclear Medicine Technologists; Opticians, Dispensing; Orthotists and Prosthetists; Radiologic Technicians; Radiologic Technologists; Radiologic Technologists and Technicians.

Skills—Systems Evaluation: Identifying measures or indicators of system performance and the actions needed to improve or correct performance relative to the goals of the system. **Active Listening:** Giving full attention to what other people are saying, taking time to understand the points being made, asking questions as appropriate, and not interrupting at inappropriate times. **Reading Comprehension:** Understanding written sentences and paragraphs in work-related documents. **Instructing:** Teaching others how to do something. **Critical Thinking:** Using logic and reasoning to identify the strengths and weaknesses of alternative solutions, conclusions, or approaches to problems. **Time Management:** Managing one's own time and the time of others. **Service Orientation:** Actively looking for ways to help people. **Learning Strategies:** Selecting and using training/instructional methods and procedures appropriate for the situation when learning or teaching new things.

Education and Training Programs: Health Information/Medical Records Technology/Technician; Medical Insurance Coding Specialist/Coder. **Related Knowledge/Courses: Clerical Practices:** Administrative and clerical procedures and systems such as word processing, managing files and records, stenography and transcription, designing forms, and other office procedures and terminology. **Personnel and Human Resources:** Principles and procedures for personnel recruitment, selection, training, compensation and benefits, labor relations and negotiation, and personnel information systems. **Administration and Management:** Business and management principles involved in strategic planning, resource allocation, human resources modeling, leadership techniques, production methods, and coordination of people and resources. **Computers and Electronics:** Circuit boards; processors; chips; electronic equipment; and computer hardware and software, including applications and programming.

Work Environment: Indoors; noisy; sitting; using hands on objects, tools, or controls; repetitive motions.

M

Medical Scientists, Except Epidemiologists

- Annual Earnings: $61,730
- Growth: 34.1%
- Annual Job Openings: 15,000
- Education/Training Required: Doctoral degree
- Self-Employed: 0.4%
- Part-Time: 5.5%

How the Job Improves the World: Contributes to health.

Conduct research dealing with the understanding of human diseases and the improvement of human health. Engage in clinical investigation or other research, production, technical writing, or related activities. Conduct research to develop methodologies, instrumentation, and procedures for medical application, analyzing data and presenting findings. Plan and direct studies to investigate human or animal disease, preventive methods, and treatments for disease. Follow strict safety procedures when handling toxic materials to avoid contamination. Evaluate effects of drugs, gases, pesticides, parasites, and microorganisms at various levels. Teach principles of medicine and medical and laboratory procedures to physicians, residents, students, and technicians. Prepare and analyze organ, tissue, and cell samples to identify toxicity, bacteria, or microorganisms or to study cell structure. Standardize drug dosages, methods of immunization, and procedures for manufacture of drugs and medicinal compounds. Investigate cause, progress, life cycle, or mode of transmission of diseases or parasites. Confer with health department, industry personnel, physicians, and others to develop health safety standards and public health improvement programs. Study animal and human health and physiological processes. Consult with and advise physicians, educators, researchers, and others regarding medical applications of physics, biology, and chemistry. Use equipment such as atomic absorption spectrometers, electron microscopes, flow cytometers, and chromatography systems.

Personality Type: Investigative. Investigative occupations frequently involve working with ideas and require an extensive amount of thinking. These occupations can involve searching for facts and figuring out problems mentally.

GOE—Interest Area: 15. Scientific Research, Engineering, and Mathematics. **Work Group:** 15.03. Life Sciences. **Other Jobs in This Work Group:** Biochemists and Biophysicists; Biologists; Environmental Scientists and Specialists, Including Health; Epidemiologists; Microbiologists.

Skills—Science: Using scientific rules and methods to solve problems. **Management of Financial Resources:** Determining how money will be spent to get the work done and accounting for these expenditures. **Judgment and Decision Making:** Considering the relative costs and benefits of potential actions to choose the most appropriate one. **Reading Comprehension:** Understanding written sentences and paragraphs in work-related documents. **Writing:** Communicating effectively in writing as appropriate for the needs of the audience. **Time Management:** Managing one's own time and the time of others. **Instructing:** Teaching others how to do something. **Complex Problem Solving:** Identifying complex problems and reviewing related information to develop and evaluate options and implement solutions.

Education and Training Programs: Biomedical Sciences, General; Biochemistry; Biophysics; Molecular Biology; Cell/Cellular Biology and Histology; Anatomy; Medical Microbiology and Bacteriology; Immunology; Human/Medical Genetics; Physiology, General; Molecular Physiology; Cell Physiology; Endocrinology; Reproductive Biology; Neurobiology and Neurophysiology; Cardiovascular Science; others. **Related Knowledge/Courses: Biology:** Plant and animal organisms and their tissues, cells, functions, interdependencies, and interactions with each other and the environment. **Medicine and Dentistry:** The information and techniques needed to diagnose and treat human injuries, diseases, and deformities. This includes symptoms, treatment alternatives, drug properties and interactions, and preventive health-care measures. **Chemistry:** The chemical composition, structure, and properties of substances and of the chemical processes and transformations that they undergo. This includes uses of chemicals and their danger signs, production techniques, and disposal methods. **Communications and Media:** Media production, communication, and dissemination techniques and methods. This includes alternative ways to inform and entertain via written, oral, and visual media. **Personnel and Human Resources:** Principles and procedures for personnel recruitment, selection, training, compensation and benefits, labor relations and negotiation, and personnel information systems. **Mathematics:** Arithmetic, algebra, geometry, calculus, and statistics and their applications.

Work Environment: Indoors; sitting; using hands on objects, tools, or controls.

Mental Health and Substance Abuse Social Workers

- Annual Earnings: $34,410
- Growth: 26.7%
- Annual Job Openings: 15,000
- Education/Training Required: Master's degree
- Self-Employed: 2.5%
- Part-Time: 11.5%

How the Job Improves the World: Contributes to mental health and social well-being.

Assess and treat individuals with mental, emotional, or substance abuse problems, including abuse of alcohol, tobacco, and/or other drugs. Activities may include individual and group therapy, crisis intervention, case management, client advocacy, prevention, and education. Counsel clients in individual and group sessions to assist them in dealing with substance abuse, mental and physical illness, poverty, unemployment, or physical abuse. Interview clients, review records, and confer with other professionals to evaluate mental or physical condition of client or patient. Collaborate with counselors, physicians, and nurses to plan and coordinate treatment, drawing on social work experience and patient needs. Monitor, evaluate, and record client progress with respect to treatment goals. Refer patient, client, or family to community resources for housing or treatment to assist in recovery from mental or physical illness, following through to ensure service efficacy. Counsel and aid family members to assist them in understanding, dealing with, and supporting the client or patient. Modify treatment plans according to changes in client status. Plan and conduct programs to prevent substance abuse, to combat social problems, or to improve health and counseling services in community. Supervise and direct other workers who provide services to clients or patients. Develop or advise on social policy and assist in community development. Conduct social research to advance knowledge in the social work field.

Personality Type: Social. Social occupations frequently involve working with, communicating with, and teaching people. These occupations often involve helping or providing service to others.

GOE—Interest Area: 10. Human Service. **Work Group:** 10.01. Counseling and Social Work. **Other Jobs in This Work Group:** Child, Family, and School Social Workers; Clinical Psychologists; Clinical, Counseling, and School Psychologists; Counseling Psychologists; Marriage and Family Therapists; Medical and Public Health Social Workers; Mental Health Counselors; Probation Officers and

Correctional Treatment Specialists; Rehabilitation Counselors; Residential Advisors; Social and Human Service Assistants; Substance Abuse and Behavioral Disorder Counselors.

Skills—Social Perceptiveness: Being aware of others' reactions and understanding why they react as they do. **Service Orientation:** Actively looking for ways to help people. **Negotiation:** Bringing others together and trying to reconcile differences. **Persuasion:** Persuading others to change their minds or behavior. **Active Listening:** Giving full attention to what other people are saying, taking time to understand the points being made, asking questions as appropriate, and not interrupting at inappropriate times. **Judgment and Decision Making:** Considering the relative costs and benefits of potential actions to choose the most appropriate one. **Complex Problem Solving:** Identifying complex problems and reviewing related information to develop and evaluate options and implement solutions. **Active Learning:** Understanding the implications of new information for both current and future problem-solving and decision-making.

Education and Training Program: Clinical/Medical Social Work. **Related Knowledge/Courses: Psychology:** Human behavior and performance; individual differences in ability, personality, and interests; learning and motivation; psychological research methods; and the assessment and treatment of behavioral and affective disorders. **Therapy and Counseling:** Principles, methods, and procedures for diagnosis, treatment, and rehabilitation of physical and mental dysfunctions and for career counseling and guidance. **Customer and Personal Service:** Principles and processes for providing customer and personal services. This includes customer needs assessment, meeting quality standards for services, and evaluation of customer satisfaction. **Sociology and Anthropology:** Group behavior and dynamics, societal trends and influences, human migrations, ethnicity, and cultures and their history and origins.

Work Environment: Indoors; noisy; sitting.

Mental Health Counselors

- Annual Earnings: $34,010
- Growth: 27.2%
- Annual Job Openings: 14,000
- Education/Training Required: Master's degree
- Self-Employed: 5.0%
- Part-Time: 16.7%

How the Job Improves the World: Contributes to education and mental health.

Counsel with emphasis on prevention. Work with individuals and groups to promote optimum mental health. May help individuals deal with addictions and substance abuse; family, parenting, and marital problems; suicide; stress management; problems with self-esteem; and issues associated with aging and mental and emotional health. Maintain confidentiality of records relating to clients' treatment. Guide clients in the development of skills and strategies for dealing with their problems. Encourage clients to express their feelings and discuss what is happening in their lives and help them to develop insight into themselves and their relationships. Prepare and maintain all required treatment records and reports. Counsel clients and patients, individually and in group sessions, to assist in overcoming dependencies, adjusting to life, and making changes. Collect information about clients through interviews, observation, and tests. Act as client advocates to coordinate required services or to resolve emergency problems in crisis situations. Develop and implement treatment plans based on clinical experience and knowledge. Collaborate with other staff members to perform clinical assessments and develop treatment plans. Evaluate clients' physical or mental condition based on review of client information. Meet with families, probation officers, police, and other interested parties to exchange necessary information during the treatment process. Refer patients, clients, or family members to community resources or to specialists as necessary. Evaluate the effectiveness of counseling programs and clients' progress in resolving identified problems and moving towards defined objectives. Counsel family members to assist them in understanding, dealing with, and supporting clients or patients. Plan, organize, and lead structured programs of counseling, work, study, recreation, and social activities for clients. Modify treatment activities and approaches as needed to comply with changes in clients' status. Learn about new developments in their field by reading professional literature, attending courses and seminars, and establishing and maintaining contact with other social service agencies. Discuss with individual patients their plans for life after leaving therapy. Gather information about community mental health needs and resources that could be used in conjunction with therapy. Monitor clients' use of medications. Supervise other counselors, social service staff, and assistants.

Personality Type: Social. Social occupations frequently involve working with, communicating with, and teaching people. These occupations often involve helping or providing service to others.

GOE—Interest Area: 10. Human Service. **Work Group:** 10.01. Counseling and Social Work. **Other Jobs in This Work Group:** Child, Family, and School Social Workers; Clinical Psychologists; Clinical, Counseling, and School Psychologists; Counseling Psychologists; Marriage and Family Therapists; Medical and Public Health Social Workers; Mental Health and Substance Abuse Social Workers; Probation Officers and Correctional Treatment Specialists; Rehabilitation Counselors; Residential Advisors; Social and Human Service Assistants; Substance Abuse and Behavioral Disorder Counselors.

Skills—Social Perceptiveness: Being aware of others' reactions and understanding why they react as they do. **Service Orientation:** Actively looking for ways to help people. **Negotiation:** Bringing others together and trying to reconcile differences. **Persuasion:** Persuading others to change their minds or behavior. **Learning Strategies:** Selecting and using training/instructional methods and procedures appropriate for the situation when learning or teaching new things. **Active Listening:** Giving full attention to what other people are saying, taking time to understand the points being made, asking questions as appropriate, and not interrupting at inappropriate times. **Speaking:** Talking to others to convey information effectively. **Critical Thinking:** Using logic and reasoning to identify the strengths and weaknesses of alternative solutions, conclusions, or approaches to problems.

Education and Training Programs: Substance Abuse/Addiction Counseling; Clinical/Medical Social Work; Mental Health Counseling/Counselor; Mental and Social Health Services and Allied Professions, Other. **Related Knowledge/Courses: Therapy and Counseling:** Principles, methods, and procedures for diagnosis, treatment, and rehabilitation of physical and mental dysfunctions and for career counseling and guidance. **Psychology:** Human behavior and performance; individual differences in ability, personality, and interests; learning and motivation; psychological research methods; and the assessment and treatment of behavioral and affective disorders. **Sociology and Anthropology:** Group behavior and dynamics, societal trends and influences, human migrations, ethnicity, and cultures and their history and origins. **Philosophy and Theology:** Different philosophical systems and religions. This includes their basic principles, values, ethics, ways of thinking, customs, and practices and their impact on human culture. **Medicine and Dentistry:** The information and techniques needed to diagnose and treat human injuries, diseases, and deformities. This includes symptoms, treatment alternatives, drug properties and interactions, and preventive health-care measures. **Education**

M

and Training: Principles and methods for curriculum and training design, teaching and instruction for individuals and groups, and the measurement of training effects.

Work Environment: Indoors; noisy; sitting.

Middle School Teachers, Except Special and Vocational Education

- ◎ Annual Earnings: $44,640
- ◎ Growth: 13.7%
- ◎ Annual Job Openings: 83,000
- ◎ Education/Training Required: Bachelor's degree
- ◎ Self-Employed: 0.0%
- ◎ Part-Time: 12.6%

How the Job Improves the World: Contributes to education.

Teach students in public or private schools in one or more subjects at the middle, intermediate, or junior high level, which falls between elementary and senior high school as defined by applicable state laws and regulations. Establish and enforce rules for behavior and procedures for maintaining order among the students for whom they are responsible. Adapt teaching methods and instructional materials to meet students' varying needs and interests. Instruct through lectures, discussions, and demonstrations in one or more subjects such as English, mathematics, or social studies. Prepare, administer, and grade tests and assignments to evaluate students' progress. Establish clear objectives for all lessons, units, and projects and communicate these objectives to students. Plan and conduct activities for a balanced program of instruction, demonstration, and work time that provides students with opportunities to observe, question, and investigate. Maintain accurate, complete, and correct student records as required by laws, district policies, and administrative regulations. Observe and evaluate students' performance, behavior, social development, and physical health. Assign lessons and correct homework. Prepare materials and classrooms for class activities. Enforce all administration policies and rules governing students. Confer with parents or guardians, other teachers, counselors, and administrators to resolve students' behavioral and academic problems. Prepare students for later grades by encouraging them to explore learning opportunities and to persevere with challenging tasks. Prepare objectives and outlines for courses of study, following curriculum guidelines or requirements of states and schools. Guide and counsel students with adjustment or academic problems or special academic interests. Meet with parents and guardians to discuss their children's progress and to determine their priorities for their children and their resource needs. Meet with other professionals to discuss individual students' needs and progress. Prepare and implement remedial programs for students requiring extra help. Prepare for assigned classes and show written evidence of preparation upon request of immediate supervisors. Instruct and monitor students in the use and care of equipment and materials to prevent injury and damage.

Personality Type: Social. Social occupations frequently involve working with, communicating with, and teaching people. These occupations often involve helping or providing service to others.

GOE—Interest Area: 05. Education and Training. Work Group: 05.02. Preschool, Elementary, and Secondary Teaching and Instructing. Other Jobs in This Work Group: Elementary School Teachers, Except Special Education; Kindergarten Teachers, Except Special Education; Preschool Teachers, Except Special Education; Secondary School Teachers, Except Special and Vocational Education; Special Education Teachers, Middle School; Special Education Teachers, Preschool, Kindergarten, and Elementary School;

Special Education Teachers, Secondary School; Teacher Assistants; Vocational Education Teachers, Middle School; Vocational Education Teachers, Secondary School.

Skills—Learning Strategies: Selecting and using training/instructional methods and procedures appropriate for the situation when learning or teaching new things. **Instructing:** Teaching others how to do something. **Social Perceptiveness:** Being aware of others' reactions and understanding why they react as they do. **Monitoring:** Monitoring/assessing your performance or that of other individuals or organizations to make improvements or take corrective action. **Time Management:** Managing one's own time and the time of others. **Persuasion:** Persuading others to change their minds or behavior. **Negotiation:** Bringing others together and trying to reconcile differences. **Speaking:** Talking to others to convey information effectively.

Education and Training Programs: Junior High/Intermediate/Middle School Education and Teaching; Montessori Teacher Education; Waldorf/Steiner Teacher Education; Art Teacher Education; English/Language Arts Teacher Education; Foreign Language Teacher Education; Health Teacher Education; Family and Consumer Sciences/Home Economics Teacher Education; Technology Teacher Education/Industrial Arts Teacher Education; Mathematics Teacher Education; others. **Related Knowledge/Courses: Sociology and Anthropology:** Group behavior and dynamics, societal trends and influences, human migrations, ethnicity, and cultures and their history and origins. **Education and Training:** Principles and methods for curriculum and training design, teaching and instruction for individuals and groups, and the measurement of training effects. **History and Archeology:** Historical events and their causes, indicators, and effects on civilizations and cultures. **Philosophy and Theology:** Different philosophical systems and religions. This includes their basic principles, values, ethics, ways of thinking,

customs, and practices and their impact on human culture. **Geography:** Principles and methods for describing the features of land, sea, and air masses, including their physical characteristics; locations; interrelationships; and distribution of plant, animal, and human life. **Therapy and Counseling:** Principles, methods, and procedures for diagnosis, treatment, and rehabilitation of physical and mental dysfunctions and for career counseling and guidance.

Work Environment: Indoors; noisy; standing.

Municipal Fire Fighters

- Annual Earnings: $39,090
- Growth: 24.3%
- Annual Job Openings: 21,000
- Education/Training Required: Long-term on-the-job training
- Self-Employed: 0.1%
- Part-Time: 1.5%

The job openings listed here are shared with Forest Fire Fighters.

How the Job Improves the World: Contributes to safety.

Control and extinguish municipal fires, protect life and property, and conduct rescue efforts. Administer first aid and cardiopulmonary resuscitation to injured persons. Rescue victims from burning buildings and accident sites. Search burning buildings to locate fire victims. Drive and operate fire fighting vehicles and equipment. Move toward the source of a fire, using knowledge of types of fires, construction design, building materials, and physical layout of properties. Dress with equipment such as fire-resistant clothing and breathing apparatus. Position and climb ladders to gain access to upper levels of buildings or to rescue individuals from burning structures. Take action to contain hazardous chemicals that might catch fire, leak, or spill. Assess fires and situations and report conditions to superiors to receive instructions, using two-way radios. Respond to fire alarms and other calls for assistance, such as automobile and industrial accidents. Operate pumps connected to high-pressure hoses. Select and attach hose nozzles, depending on fire type, and direct streams of water or chemicals onto fires. Create openings in buildings for ventilation or entrance, using axes, chisels, crowbars, electric saws, or core cutters. Inspect fire sites after flames have been extinguished to ensure that there is no further danger. Lay hose lines and connect them to water supplies. Protect property from water and smoke, using waterproof salvage covers, smoke ejectors, and deodorants. Participate in physical training activities to maintain a high level of physical fitness. Salvage property by removing broken glass, pumping out water, and ventilating buildings to remove smoke. Participate in fire drills and demonstrations of fire fighting techniques. Clean and maintain fire stations and fire fighting equipment and apparatus. Collaborate with police to respond to accidents, disasters, and arson investigation calls. Establish firelines to prevent unauthorized persons from entering areas near fires. Inform and educate the public on fire prevention. Inspect buildings for fire hazards and compliance with fire prevention ordinances, testing and checking smoke alarms and fire suppression equipment as necessary.

Personality Type: Realistic. Realistic occupations frequently involve work activities that include practical, hands-on problems and solutions. They often deal with plants; animals; and real-world materials such as wood, tools, and machinery. Many of the occupations require working outside and do not involve a lot of paperwork or working closely with others.

GOE—Interest Area: 12. Law and Public Safety. **Work Group:** 12.06. Emergency Responding. **Other Jobs in This Work Group:** Emergency Medical Technicians and Paramedics; Fire Fighters; Forest Fire Fighters.

Skills—Equipment Maintenance: Performing routine maintenance on equipment and determining when and what kind of maintenance is needed. **Service Orientation:** Actively looking for ways to help people. **Equipment Selection:** Determining the kind of tools and equipment needed to do a job. **Operation Monitoring:** Watching gauges, dials, or other indicators to make sure a machine is working properly. **Social Perceptiveness:** Being aware of others' reactions and understanding why they react as they do. **Coordination:** Adjusting actions in relation to others' actions. **Complex Problem Solving:** Identifying complex problems and reviewing related information to develop and evaluate options and implement solutions. **Learning Strategies:** Selecting and using training/instructional methods and procedures appropriate for the situation when learning or teaching new things.

Education and Training Programs: Fire Science/Firefighting; Fire Protection, Other. **Related Knowledge/Courses: Medicine and Dentistry:** The information and techniques needed to diagnose and treat human injuries, diseases, and deformities. This includes symptoms, treatment alternatives, drug properties and interactions, and preventive health-care measures. **Customer and Personal Service:** Principles and processes for providing customer and personal services. This includes customer needs assessment, meeting quality standards for services, and evaluation of customer satisfaction. **Physics:** Physical principles and laws and their interrelationships and applications to understanding fluid, material, and atmospheric dynamics and mechanical, electrical, atomic, and subatomic structures and processes. **Building and Construction:** The materials, methods, and tools involved in the construction or repair of houses, buildings, or other structures such as highways and roads. **Chemistry:** The chemical composition, structure, and properties of substances and of the chemical processes and transformations that they undergo. This includes uses of chemicals and their danger signs, production techniques, and disposal methods. **Public Safety and Security:** Relevant equipment, policies, procedures, and strategies to promote effective local, state, or national security operations for the protection of people, data, property, and institutions.

Work Environment: More often outdoors than indoors; noisy; contaminants; disease or infections; hazardous equipment.

Municipal Fire Fighting and Prevention Supervisors

- ◎ Annual Earnings: $60,840
- ◎ Growth: 21.1%
- ◎ Annual Job Openings: 4,000
- ◎ Education/Training Required: Work experience in a related occupation
- ◎ Self-Employed: 0.0%
- ◎ Part-Time: 0.4%

The job openings listed here are shared with Forest Fire Fighting and Prevention Supervisors.

How the Job Improves the World: Contributes to safety.

Supervise fire fighters who control and extinguish municipal fires, protect life and property, and conduct rescue efforts. Assign firefighters to jobs at strategic locations to facilitate rescue of persons and maximize application of extinguishing agents. Provide emergency medical services as required and perform light to heavy rescue functions at emergencies. Assess nature and extent of fire, condition of building, danger to adjacent buildings, and water supply status to determine crew or company requirements. Instruct and drill fire department personnel in assigned duties, including firefighting, medical care, hazardous materials response, fire prevention, and related subjects.

Evaluate the performance of assigned firefighting personnel. Direct the training of firefighters, assigning of instructors to training classes, and providing of supervisors with reports on training progress and status. Prepare activity reports listing fire call locations, actions taken, fire types and probable causes, damage estimates, and situation dispositions. Maintain required maps and records. Attend in-service training classes to remain current in knowledge of codes, laws, ordinances, and regulations. Evaluate fire station procedures to ensure efficiency and enforcement of departmental regulations. Direct firefighters in station maintenance duties and participate in these duties. Compile and maintain equipment and personnel records, including accident reports. Direct investigation of cases of suspected arson, hazards, and false alarms and submit reports outlining findings. Recommend personnel actions related to disciplinary procedures, performance, leaves of absence, and grievances. Supervise and participate in the inspection of properties to ensure that they are in compliance with applicable fire codes, ordinances, laws, regulations, and standards. Write and submit proposals for repair, modification, or replacement of firefighting equipment. Coordinate the distribution of fire prevention promotional materials. Identify corrective actions needed to bring properties into compliance with applicable fire codes and ordinances and conduct follow-up inspections to see if corrective actions have been taken. Participate in creating fire safety guidelines and evacuation schemes for non-residential buildings.

Personality Type: Realistic. Realistic occupations frequently involve work activities that include practical, hands-on problems and solutions. They often deal with plants; animals; and real-world materials such as wood, tools, and machinery. Many of the occupations require working outside and do not involve a lot of paperwork or working closely with others.

GOE—Interest Area: 12. Law and Public Safety. **Work Group:** 12.01. Managerial Work in Law and Public Safety. **Other Jobs in This Work Group:**

Emergency Management Specialists; First-Line Supervisors/Managers of Correctional Officers; First-Line Supervisors/Managers of Fire Fighting and Prevention Workers; First-Line Supervisors/Managers of Police and Detectives; Forest Fire Fighting and Prevention Supervisors.

Skills—Equipment Maintenance: Performing routine maintenance on equipment and determining when and what kind of maintenance is needed. **Management of Personnel Resources:** Motivating, developing, and directing people as they work; identifying the best people for the job. **Service Orientation:** Actively looking for ways to help people. **Operation Monitoring:** Watching gauges, dials, or other indicators to make sure a machine is working properly. **Management of Material Resources:** Obtaining and seeing to the appropriate use of equipment, facilities, and materials needed to do certain work. **Coordination:** Adjusting actions in relation to others' actions. **Judgment and Decision Making:** Considering the relative costs and benefits of potential actions to choose the most appropriate one. **Operation and Control:** Controlling operations of equipment or systems.

Education and Training Programs: Fire Protection and Safety Technology/Technician; Fire Services Administration. **Related Knowledge/Courses: Public Safety and Security:** Relevant equipment, policies, procedures, and strategies to promote effective local, state, or national security operations for the protection of people, data, property, and institutions. **Building and Construction:** The materials, methods, and tools involved in the construction or repair of houses, buildings, or other structures such as highways and roads. **Medicine and Dentistry:** The information and techniques needed to diagnose and treat human injuries, diseases, and deformities. This includes symptoms, treatment alternatives, drug properties and interactions, and preventive health-care measures. **Education and Training:** Principles and methods for curriculum and training design, teaching and instruction for indi-

viduals and groups, and the measurement of training effects. **Customer and Personal Service:** Principles and processes for providing customer and personal services. This includes customer needs assessment, meeting quality standards for services, and evaluation of customer satisfaction. **Mechanical Devices:** Machines and tools, including their designs, uses, repair, and maintenance.

Work Environment: More often outdoors than indoors; noisy; contaminants; disease or infections; hazardous equipment.

Museum Technicians and Conservators

- Annual Earnings: $34,090
- Growth: 14.1%
- Annual Job Openings: 2,000
- Education/Training Required: Bachelor's degree
- Self-Employed: 9.4%
- Part-Time: 23.4%

How the Job Improves the World: Contributes to education.

Prepare specimens, such as fossils, skeletal parts, lace, and textiles, for museum collection and exhibits. May restore documents or install, arrange, and exhibit materials. Install, arrange, assemble, and prepare artifacts for exhibition, ensuring the artifacts' safety, reporting their status and condition, and identifying and correcting any problems with the setup. Coordinate exhibit installations, assisting with design; constructing displays, dioramas, display cases, and models; and ensuring the availability of necessary materials. Determine whether objects need repair and choose the safest and most effective method of repair. Clean objects, such as paper, textiles, wood, metal, glass, rock, pottery, and furniture, using cleansers, solvents, soap solutions, and polishes. Prepare artifacts for storage and shipping. Supervise and work with volunteers. Present public programs and tours. Specialize in particular materials or types of object, such as documents and books, paintings, decorative arts, textiles, metals, or architectural materials. Recommend preservation procedures, such as control of temperature and humidity, to curatorial and building staff. Classify and assign registration numbers to artifacts and supervise inventory control. Direct and supervise curatorial and technical staff in the handling, mounting, care, and storage of art objects. Perform on-site fieldwork, which may involve interviewing people, inspecting and identifying artifacts, note-taking, viewing sites and collections, and repainting exhibition spaces. Repair, restore, and reassemble artifacts, designing and fabricating missing or broken parts, to restore them to their original appearance and prevent deterioration. Prepare reports on the operation of conservation laboratories, documenting the condition of artifacts, treatment options, and the methods of preservation and repair used. Study object documentation or conduct standard chemical and physical tests to ascertain the object's age, composition, original appearance, need for treatment or restoration, and appropriate preservation method. Cut and weld metal sections in reconstruction or renovation of exterior structural sections and accessories of exhibits. Perform tests and examinations to establish storage and conservation requirements, policies, and procedures.

Personality Type: Artistic. Artistic occupations frequently involve working with forms, designs, and patterns. They often require self-expression, and the work can be done without following a clear set of rules.

GOE—Interest Area: 05. Education and Training. **Work Group:** 05.05. Archival and Museum Services. **Other Jobs in This Work Group:** Archivists; Audio-Visual Collections Specialists; Curators.

Skills—Management of Material Resources: Obtaining and seeing to the appropriate use of equip-

ment, facilities, and materials needed to do certain work. **Repairing:** Repairing machines or systems by using the needed tools. **Installation:** Installing equipment, machines, wiring, or programs to meet specifications. **Technology Design:** Generating or adapting equipment and technology to serve user needs. **Equipment Maintenance:** Performing routine maintenance on equipment and determining when and what kind of maintenance is needed. **Time Management:** Managing one's own time and the time of others. **Operations Analysis:** Analyzing needs and product requirements to create a design. **Equipment Selection:** Determining the kind of tools and equipment needed to do a job.

Education and Training Programs: Museology/Museum Studies; Art History, Criticism, and Conservation; Public/Applied History and Archival Administration. **Related Knowledge/Courses: History and Archeology:** Historical events and their causes, indicators, and effects on civilizations and cultures. **Fine Arts:** The theory and techniques required to compose, produce, and perform works of music, dance, visual art, drama, and sculpture. **Sociology and Anthropology:** Group behavior and dynamics, societal trends and influences, human migrations, ethnicity, and cultures and their history and origins. **Design:** Design techniques, tools, and principles involved in production of precision technical plans, blueprints, drawings, and models. **Clerical Practices:** Administrative and clerical procedures and systems such as word processing, managing files and records, stenography and transcription, designing forms, and other office procedures and terminology. **Education and Training:** Principles and methods for curriculum and training design, teaching and instruction for individuals and groups, and the measurement of training effects.

Work Environment: Indoors; standing; using hands on objects, tools, or controls.

Music Composers and Arrangers

- ◎ Annual Earnings: $34,810
- ◎ Growth: 10.4%
- ◎ Annual Job Openings: 11,000
- ◎ Education/Training Required: Work experience plus degree
- ◎ Self-Employed: 44.8%
- ◎ Part-Time: 46.1%

The job openings listed here are shared with Music Directors.

How the Job Improves the World: Contributes to the arts.

Write and transcribe musical scores. Determine voices, instruments, harmonic structures, rhythms, tempos, and tone balances required to achieve the effects desired in a musical composition. Experiment with different sounds and types and pieces of music, using synthesizers and computers as necessary to test and evaluate ideas. Explore and develop musical ideas based on sources such as imagination or sounds in the environment. Fill in details of orchestral sketches, such as adding vocal parts to scores. Rewrite original musical scores in different musical styles by changing rhythms, harmonies, or tempos. Create original musical forms or write within circumscribed musical forms such as sonatas, symphonies, or operas. Use computers and synthesizers to compose, orchestrate, and arrange music. Score compositions so that they are consistent with instrumental and vocal capabilities such as ranges and keys, using knowledge of music theory. Write changes directly into compositions or use computer software to make changes. Transcribe ideas for musical compositions into musical notation, using instruments, pen and paper, or computers. Write music for commercial media, including advertising jingles or film soundtracks. Transpose music from one voice or instrument to another to accommodate particular musicians. Collaborate with other colleagues, such as copyists, to complete final scores. Study films or scripts to determine how musical scores can be used to create desired effects or moods. Accept commissions to create music for special occasions. Write musical scores for orchestras, bands, choral groups, or individual instrumentalists or vocalists, using knowledge of music theory and of instrumental and vocal capabilities. Study original pieces of music to become familiar with them prior to making any changes. Guide musicians during rehearsals, performances, or recording sessions. Copy parts from scores for individual performers. Confer with producers and directors to define the nature and placement of film or television music. Apply elements of music theory to create musical and tonal structures, including harmonies and melodies.

Personality Type: Artistic. Artistic occupations frequently involve working with forms, designs, and patterns. They often require self-expression, and the work can be done without following a clear set of rules.

GOE—Interest Area: 03. Arts and Communication. **Work Group:** 03.07. Music. **Other Jobs in This Work Group:** Music Directors; Music Directors and Composers; Musicians and Singers; Musicians, Instrumental; Singers; Talent Directors.

Skills—No data available.

Education and Training Programs: Religious/Sacred Music; Music Performance, General; Music Theory and Composition; Musicology and Ethnomusicology; Conducting; Voice and Opera; Music Management and Merchandising; Music, Other. **Related Knowledge/Courses: Fine Arts:** The theory and techniques required to compose, produce, and perform works of music, dance, visual art, drama, and sculpture.

Work Environment: Indoors; sitting.

Music Directors

- ◎ Annual Earnings: $34,810
- ◎ Growth: 10.4%
- ◎ Annual Job Openings: 11,000
- ◎ Education/Training Required: Master's degree
- ◎ Self-Employed: 44.8%
- ◎ Part-Time: 46.1%

The job openings listed here are shared with Music Composers and Arrangers.

How the Job Improves the World: Contributes to the arts.

Direct and conduct instrumental or vocal performances by musical groups such as orchestras or choirs. Coordinate and organize tours or hire touring companies to arrange concert dates, venues, accommodations, and transportation for longer tours. Position members within groups to obtain balance among instrumental or vocal sections. Study scores to learn the music in detail and to develop interpretations. Use gestures to shape the music being played, communicating desired tempo, phrasing, tone, color, pitch, volume, and other performance aspects. Collaborate with music librarians to ensure availability of scores. Meet with composers to discuss interpretations of their work. Perform administrative tasks such as applying for grants, developing budgets, negotiating contracts, and designing and printing programs and other promotional materials. Confer with clergy to select music for church services. Plan and implement fundraising and promotional activities. Assign and review staff work in such areas as scoring, arranging, and copying music and vocal coaching. Plan and schedule rehearsals and performances and arrange details such as locations, accompanists, and instrumentalists. Transcribe musical compositions and melodic lines to adapt them to a particular group or to create a particular musical style. Engage services of composers to write scores. Direct groups at rehearsals and live or recorded performances to achieve desired effects such as tonal and harmonic balance dynamics, rhythm, and tempo. Consider such factors as ensemble size and abilities, availability of scores, and the need for musical variety to select music to be performed. Conduct guest soloists in addition to ensemble members. Audition and select performers for musical presentations. Meet with soloists and concertmasters to discuss and prepare for performances.

Personality Type: Artistic. Artistic occupations frequently involve working with forms, designs, and patterns. They often require self-expression, and the work can be done without following a clear set of rules.

GOE—Interest Area: 03. Arts and Communication. **Work Group:** 03.07. Music. **Other Jobs in This Work Group:** Music Composers and Arrangers; Music Directors and Composers; Musicians and Singers; Musicians, Instrumental; Singers; Talent Directors.

Skills—No data available.

Education and Training Programs: Religious/Sacred Music; Music Performance, General; Music Theory and Composition; Musicology and Ethnomusicology; Conducting; Voice and Opera; Music Management and Merchandising; Music, Other. **Related Knowledge/Courses: Fine Arts:** The theory and techniques required to compose, produce, and perform works of music, dance, visual art, drama, and sculpture. **Personnel and Human Resources:** Principles and procedures for personnel recruitment, selection, training, compensation and benefits, labor relations and negotiation, and personnel information systems. **Administration and Management:** Business and management principles involved in strategic planning, resource allocation, human resources modeling, leadership techniques, production methods, and coordination of people and resources.

Work Environment: Indoors; more often standing than sitting.

Nannies

- Annual Earnings: $17,050
- Growth: 13.8%
- Annual Job Openings: 439,000
- Education/Training Required: Short-term on-the-job training
- Self-Employed: 31.9%
- Part-Time: 38.8%

The job openings listed here are shared with Child Care Workers.

How the Job Improves the World: Contributes to health, safety, and education.

Care for children in private households and provide support and expertise to parents in satisfying children's physical, emotional, intellectual, and social needs. Duties may include meal planning and preparation, laundry and clothing care, organization of play activities and outings, discipline, intellectual stimulation, language activities, and transportation. Perform first aid or CPR when required. Regulate children's rest periods and nap schedules. Meet regularly with parents to discuss children's activities and development. Help prepare and serve nutritionally balanced meals and snacks for children. Instruct children in safe behavior, such as seeking adult assistance when crossing the street and avoiding contact or play with unsafe objects. Organize and conduct age-appropriate recreational activities, such as games, arts and crafts, sports, walks, and play dates. Observe children's behavior for irregularities, take temperature, transport children to doctor, or administer medications as directed to maintain children's health. Model appropriate social behaviors and encourage concern for others to cultivate development of interpersonal relationships and communication skills. Work with parents to develop and implement discipline programs to promote desirable child behavior. Help develop or monitor family schedule. Supervise and assist with homework. Assign appropriate chores and praise targeted behaviors to encourage development of self-control, self-confidence, and responsibility. Transport children to schools, social outings, and medical appointments. Perform housekeeping and cleaning duties related to children's care. Instruct and assist children in the development of health and personal habits, such as eating, resting, and toilet behavior. Keep records of play, meal schedules, and bill payment. Teach and perform age-appropriate activities such as lap play, reading, and arts and crafts to encourage intellectual development of children. Remove hazards and develop appropriate boundaries and rules to create a safe environment for children.

Personality Type: Social. Social occupations frequently involve working with, communicating with, and teaching people. These occupations often involve helping or providing service to others.

GOE—Interest Area: 10. Human Service. **Work Group:** 10.03. Child/Personal Care and Services. **Other Jobs in This Work Group:** Child Care Workers; Funeral Attendants; Personal and Home Care Aides.

Skills—No data available.

Education and Training Program: Child Care Provider/Assistant. **Related Knowledge/Courses: Philosophy and Theology:** Different philosophical systems and religions. This includes their basic principles, values, ethics, ways of thinking, customs, and practices and their impact on human culture. **Medicine and Dentistry:** The information and techniques needed to diagnose and treat human injuries, diseases, and deformities. This includes symptoms, treatment alternatives, drug properties and interactions, and preventive health-care measures. **Geography:** Principles and methods for describing the features of land, sea, and air masses, including their physical characteristics; locations; interrelationships;

and distribution of plant, animal, and human life. **Therapy and Counseling:** Principles, methods, and procedures for diagnosis, treatment, and rehabilitation of physical and mental dysfunctions and for career counseling and guidance. **Sociology and Anthropology:** Group behavior and dynamics, societal trends and influences, human migrations, ethnicity, and cultures and their history and origins. **Psychology:** Human behavior and performance; individual differences in ability, personality, and interests; learning and motivation; psychological research methods; and the assessment and treatment of behavioral and affective disorders.

Work Environment: More often indoors than outdoors; disease or infections; standing; using hands on objects, tools, or controls.

Nuclear Medicine Technologists

- Annual Earnings: $59,670
- Growth: 21.5%
- Annual Job Openings: 2,000
- Education/Training Required: Associate degree
- Self-Employed: 0.5%
- Part-Time: 17.2%

How the Job Improves the World: Contributes to health.

Prepare, administer, and measure radioactive isotopes in therapeutic, diagnostic, and tracer studies, utilizing a variety of radioisotope equipment. Prepare stock solutions of radioactive materials and calculate doses to be administered by radiologists. Subject patients to radiation. Execute blood volume, red cell survival, and fat absorption studies, following standard laboratory techniques. Calculate, measure, and record radiation dosage or radiopharmaceuticals re-

ceived, used, and disposed, using computer and following physician's prescription. Detect and map radiopharmaceuticals in patients' bodies, using a camera to produce photographic or computer images. Explain test procedures and safety precautions to patients and provide them with assistance during test procedures. Administer radiopharmaceuticals or radiation to patients to detect or treat diseases, using radioisotope equipment, under direction of physician. Produce a computer-generated or film image for interpretation by a physician. Process cardiac function studies, using computer. Dispose of radioactive materials and store radiopharmaceuticals, following radiation safety procedures. Record and process results of procedures. Prepare stock radiopharmaceuticals, adhering to safety standards that minimize radiation exposure to workers and patients. Maintain and calibrate radioisotope and laboratory equipment. Gather information on patients' illnesses and medical history to guide the choice of diagnostic procedures for therapy. Measure glandular activity, blood volume, red cell survival, and radioactivity of patient, using scanners, Geiger counters, scintillometers, and other laboratory equipment. Train and supervise student or subordinate nuclear medicine technologists. Position radiation fields, radiation beams, and patient to allow for most effective treatment of patient's disease, using computer. Add radioactive substances to biological specimens, such as blood, urine, and feces, to determine therapeutic drug or hormone levels. Develop treatment procedures for nuclear medicine treatment programs.

Personality Type: Investigative. Investigative occupations frequently involve working with ideas and require an extensive amount of thinking. These occupations can involve searching for facts and figuring out problems mentally.

GOE—Interest Area: 08. Health Science. **Work Group:** 08.06. Medical Technology. **Other Jobs in This Work Group:** Biological Technicians; Cardiovascular Technologists and Technicians; Diagnostic Medical Sonographers; Medical and

Clinical Laboratory Technicians; Medical and Clinical Laboratory Technologists; Medical Equipment Preparers; Medical Records and Health Information Technicians; Opticians, Dispensing; Orthotists and Prosthetists; Radiologic Technicians; Radiologic Technologists; Radiologic Technologists and Technicians.

Skills—Science: Using scientific rules and methods to solve problems. **Operation Monitoring:** Watching gauges, dials, or other indicators to make sure a machine is working properly. **Operation and Control:** Controlling operations of equipment or systems. **Quality Control Analysis:** Conducting tests and inspections of products, services, or processes to evaluate quality or performance. **Social Perceptiveness:** Being aware of others' reactions and understanding why they react as they do. **Service Orientation:** Actively looking for ways to help people. **Troubleshooting:** Determining causes of operating errors and deciding what to do about them. **Reading Comprehension:** Understanding written sentences and paragraphs in work-related documents.

Education and Training Programs: Nuclear Medical Technology/Technologist; Radiation Protection/Health Physics Technician. **Related Knowledge/Courses: Medicine and Dentistry:** The information and techniques needed to diagnose and treat human injuries, diseases, and deformities. This includes symptoms, treatment alternatives, drug properties and interactions, and preventive health-care measures. **Biology:** Plant and animal organisms and their tissues, cells, functions, interdependencies, and interactions with each other and the environment. **Physics:** Physical principles and laws and their interrelationships and applications to understanding fluid, material, and atmospheric dynamics and mechanical, electrical, atomic, and subatomic structures and processes. **Chemistry:** The chemical composition, structure, and properties of substances and of the chemical processes and transformations that they un-

dergo. This includes uses of chemicals and their danger signs, production techniques, and disposal methods. **Customer and Personal Service:** Principles and processes for providing customer and personal services. This includes customer needs assessment, meeting quality standards for services, and evaluation of customer satisfaction. **Computers and Electronics:** Circuit boards; processors; chips; electronic equipment; and computer hardware and software, including applications and programming.

Work Environment: Indoors; contaminants; radiation; disease or infections; standing; using hands on objects, tools, or controls.

Nursing Aides, Orderlies, and Attendants

- Annual Earnings: $21,440
- Growth: 22.3%
- Annual Job Openings: 307,000
- Education/Training Required: Postsecondary vocational training
- Self-Employed: 1.9%
- Part-Time: 28.0%

How the Job Improves the World: Contributes to health.

Provide basic patient care under direction of nursing staff. Perform duties such as feeding, bathing, dressing, grooming, or moving patients or changing linens. Turn and reposition bedridden patients, alone or with assistance, to prevent bedsores. Answer patients' call signals. Feed patients who are unable to feed themselves. Observe patients' conditions, measuring and recording food and liquid intake and output and vital signs, and report changes to professional staff. Provide patient care by supplying and emptying bedpans, applying dressings, and supervising exercise routines. Provide patients with help walking, exercising, and moving in and out of bed. Bathe, groom, shave, dress, or drape patients to prepare them for surgery, treatment, or examination. Collect specimens such as urine, feces, or sputum. Prepare, serve, and collect food trays. Clean rooms and change linens. Transport patients to treatment units, using a wheelchair or stretcher. Deliver messages, documents, and specimens. Answer phones and direct visitors. Administer medications and treatments, such as catheterizations, suppositories, irrigations, enemas, massages, and douches, as directed by a physician or nurse. Restrain patients if necessary. Maintain inventory by storing, preparing, sterilizing, and issuing supplies such as dressing packs and treatment trays. Explain medical instructions to patients and family members. Perform clerical duties such as processing documents and scheduling appointments. Work as part of a medical team that examines and treats clinic outpatients. Set up equipment such as oxygen tents, portable X-ray machines, and overhead irrigation bottles.

Personality Type: Social. Social occupations frequently involve working with, communicating with, and teaching people. These occupations often involve helping or providing service to others.

GOE—Interest Area: 08. Health Science. **Work Group:** 08.08. Patient Care and Assistance. **Other Jobs in This Work Group:** Home Health Aides; Licensed Practical and Licensed Vocational Nurses; Psychiatric Aides; Psychiatric Technicians.

Skills—Social Perceptiveness: Being aware of others' reactions and understanding why they react as they do. **Operation Monitoring:** Watching gauges, dials, or other indicators to make sure a machine is working properly. **Time Management:** Managing one's own time and the time of others. **Service Orientation:** Actively looking for ways to help people. **Monitoring:** Monitoring/assessing your performance or that of other individuals or organizations to make improve-

ments or take corrective action. **Instructing:** Teaching others how to do something. **Technology Design:** Generating or adapting equipment and technology to serve user needs. **Systems Evaluation:** Identifying measures or indicators of system performance and the actions needed to improve or correct performance relative to the goals of the system.

Education and Training Programs: Nurse/Nursing Assistant/Aide and Patient Care Assistant; Health Aide. **Related Knowledge/Courses: Psychology:** Human behavior and performance; individual differences in ability, personality, and interests; learning and motivation; psychological research methods; and the assessment and treatment of behavioral and affective disorders. **Medicine and Dentistry:** The information and techniques needed to diagnose and treat human injuries, diseases, and deformities. This includes symptoms, treatment alternatives, drug properties and interactions, and preventive health-care measures. **Customer and Personal Service:** Principles and processes for providing customer and personal services. This includes customer needs assessment, meeting quality standards for services, and evaluation of customer satisfaction. **Chemistry:** The chemical composition, structure, and properties of substances and of the chemical processes and transformations that they undergo. This includes uses of chemicals and their danger signs, production techniques, and disposal methods. **English Language:** The structure and content of the English language, including the meaning and spelling of words, rules of composition, and grammar. **Education and Training:** Principles and methods for curriculum and training design, teaching and instruction for individuals and groups, and the measurement of training effects.

Work Environment: Indoors; disease or infections; standing; walking and running; using hands on objects, tools, or controls; bending or twisting the body.

Nursing Instructors and Teachers, Postsecondary

- Annual Earnings: $53,160
- Growth: 32.2%
- Annual Job Openings: 329,000
- Education/Training Required: Master's degree
- Self-Employed: 0.4%
- Part-Time: 27.3%

The job openings listed here are shared with 35 other postsecondary teaching occupations. For a complete list, see the beginning of this section.

How the Job Improves the World: Contributes to education and health.

Demonstrate and teach patient care in classroom and clinical units to nursing students. Includes both teachers primarily engaged in teaching and those who do a combination of both teaching and research. Initiate, facilitate, and moderate classroom discussions. Prepare and deliver lectures to undergraduate or graduate students on topics such as pharmacology, mental health nursing, and community health care practices. Keep abreast of developments in their field by reading current literature, talking with colleagues, and participating in professional conferences. Prepare course materials such as syllabi, homework assignments, and handouts. Supervise students' laboratory and clinical work. Evaluate and grade students' classwork, laboratory and clinic work, assignments, and papers. Collaborate with colleagues to address teaching and research issues. Plan, evaluate, and revise curricula, course content, and course materials and methods of instruction. Assess clinical education needs and patient and client teaching needs, utilizing a variety of methods. Compile, administer, and grade examinations or assign this work to others. Advise students on academic and vocational curricula and on career issues. Maintain student attendance records, grades, and other required records. Maintain regularly scheduled office hours to advise and assist students. Supervise undergraduate or graduate teaching, internship, and research work. Conduct research in a particular field of knowledge and publish findings in professional journals, books, and/or electronic media. Participate in student recruitment, registration, and placement activities. Serve on academic or administrative committees that deal with institutional policies, departmental matters, and academic issues. Coordinate training programs with area universities, clinics, hospitals, health agencies, and/or vocational schools. Compile bibliographies of specialized materials for outside reading assignments. Select and obtain materials and supplies such as textbooks and laboratory equipment. Participate in campus and community events. Write grant proposals to procure external research funding. Act as advisers to student organizations. Demonstrate patient care in clinical units of hospitals. Perform administrative duties such as serving as department head.

Personality Type: Social. Social occupations frequently involve working with, communicating with, and teaching people. These occupations often involve helping or providing service to others.

GOE—Interest Area: 05. Education and Training. **Work Group:** 05.03. Postsecondary and Adult Teaching and Instructing. **Other Jobs in This Work Group:** Adult Literacy, Remedial Education, and GED Teachers and Instructors; Agricultural Sciences Teachers, Postsecondary; Anthropology and Archeology Teachers, Postsecondary; Architecture Teachers, Postsecondary; Area, Ethnic, and Cultural Studies Teachers, Postsecondary; Art, Drama, and Music Teachers, Postsecondary; Atmospheric, Earth, Marine, and Space Sciences Teachers, Postsecondary; Biological Science Teachers, Postsecondary; Business Teachers, Postsecondary; Chemistry Teachers, Postsecondary; Communications Teachers,

Postsecondary; Computer Science Teachers, Postsecondary; Criminal Justice and Law Enforcement Teachers, Postsecondary; Economics Teachers, Postsecondary; Education Teachers, Postsecondary; Engineering Teachers, Postsecondary; English Language and Literature Teachers, Postsecondary; Environmental Science Teachers, Postsecondary; Farm and Home Management Advisors; Foreign Language and Literature Teachers, Postsecondary; Forestry and Conservation Science Teachers, Postsecondary; Geography Teachers, Postsecondary; Graduate Teaching Assistants; Health Specialties Teachers, Postsecondary; History Teachers, Postsecondary; Home Economics Teachers, Postsecondary; Law Teachers, Postsecondary; Library Science Teachers, Postsecondary; Mathematical Science Teachers, Postsecondary; Philosophy and Religion Teachers, Postsecondary; Physics Teachers, Postsecondary; Political Science Teachers, Postsecondary; Psychology Teachers, Postsecondary; Recreation and Fitness Studies Teachers, Postsecondary; Self-Enrichment Education Teachers; Social Work Teachers, Postsecondary; Sociology Teachers, Postsecondary; Vocational Education Teachers, Postsecondary.

Skills—Science: Using scientific rules and methods to solve problems. **Instructing:** Teaching others how to do something. **Social Perceptiveness:** Being aware of others' reactions and understanding why they react as they do. **Writing:** Communicating effectively in writing as appropriate for the needs of the audience. **Learning Strategies:** Selecting and using training/instructional methods and procedures appropriate for the situation when learning or teaching new things. **Reading Comprehension:** Understanding written sentences and paragraphs in work-related documents. **Service Orientation:** Actively looking for ways to help people. **Persuasion:** Persuading others to change their minds or behavior.

Education and Training Programs: Pre-Nursing Studies; Nursing—Registered Nurse Training (RN, ASN, BSN, MSN); Adult Health Nurse/Nursing; Nurse Anesthetist; Family Practice Nurse/Nurse Practitioner; Maternal/Child Health and Neonatal Nurse/Nursing; Nurse Midwife/Nursing Midwifery; Nursing Science (MS, PhD); Pediatric Nurse/Nursing; Psychiatric/Mental Health Nurse/Nursing; Public Health/Community Nurse/Nursing; others. **Related Knowledge/Courses: Therapy and Counseling:** Principles, methods, and procedures for diagnosis, treatment, and rehabilitation of physical and mental dysfunctions and for career counseling and guidance. **Sociology and Anthropology:** Group behavior and dynamics, societal trends and influences, human migrations, ethnicity, and cultures and their history and origins. **Biology:** Plant and animal organisms and their tissues, cells, functions, interdependencies, and interactions with each other and the environment. **Medicine and Dentistry:** The information and techniques needed to diagnose and treat human injuries, diseases, and deformities. This includes symptoms, treatment alternatives, drug properties and interactions, and preventive health-care measures. **Philosophy and Theology:** Different philosophical systems and religions. This includes their basic principles, values, ethics, ways of thinking, customs, and practices and their impact on human culture. **Psychology:** Human behavior and performance; individual differences in ability, personality, and interests; learning and motivation; psychological research methods; and the assessment and treatment of behavioral and affective disorders.

Work Environment: Indoors; disease or infections; sitting.

Obstetricians and Gynecologists

- Annual Earnings: More than $145,600
- Growth: 24.0%
- Annual Job Openings: 41,000
- Education/Training Required: First professional degree
- Self-Employed: 11.5%
- Part-Time: 9.6%

The job openings listed here are shared with Anesthesiologists; Family and General Practitioners; Internists, General; Pediatricians, General; Psychiatrists; and Surgeons.

How the Job Improves the World: Contributes to health.

Diagnose, treat, and help prevent diseases of women, especially those affecting the reproductive system and the process of childbirth. Care for and treat women during prenatal, natal, and post-natal periods. Explain procedures and discuss test results or prescribed treatments with patients. Treat diseases of female organs. Monitor patients' condition and progress and re-evaluate treatments as necessary. Perform cesarean sections or other surgical procedures as needed to preserve patients' health and deliver babies safely. Prescribe or administer therapy, medication, and other specialized medical care to treat or prevent illness, disease, or injury. Analyze records, reports, test results, or examination information to diagnose medical condition of patient. Collect, record, and maintain patient information, such as medical histories, reports, and examination results. Advise patients and community members concerning diet, activity, hygiene, and disease prevention. Refer patient to medical specialist or other practitioner when necessary. Consult with, or provide consulting services to, other physicians. Direct and coordinate activities of nurses, students, assistants, specialists, therapists, and other medical staff. Plan, implement, or administer health programs in hospitals, businesses, or communities for prevention and treatment of injuries or illnesses. Prepare government and organizational reports on birth, death, and disease statistics; workforce evaluations; or the medical status of individuals. Conduct research to develop or test medications, treatments, or procedures to prevent or control disease or injury.

Personality Type: Investigative. Investigative occupations frequently involve working with ideas and require an extensive amount of thinking. These occupations can involve searching for facts and figuring out problems mentally.

GOE—Interest Area: 08. Health Science. **Work Group:** 08.02. Medicine and Surgery. **Other Jobs in This Work Group:** Anesthesiologists; Family and General Practitioners; Internists, General; Medical Assistants; Medical Transcriptionists; Pediatricians, General; Pharmacists; Pharmacy Aides; Pharmacy Technicians; Physician Assistants; Psychiatrists; Registered Nurses; Surgeons; Surgical Technologists.

Skills—Science: Using scientific rules and methods to solve problems. **Judgment and Decision Making:** Considering the relative costs and benefits of potential actions to choose the most appropriate one. **Reading Comprehension:** Understanding written sentences and paragraphs in work-related documents. **Active Learning:** Understanding the implications of new information for both current and future problem-solving and decision-making. **Complex Problem Solving:** Identifying complex problems and reviewing related information to develop and evaluate options and implement solutions. **Social Perceptiveness:** Being aware of others' reactions and understanding why they react as they do. **Instructing:** Teaching others how to do something. **Critical Thinking:** Using logic and reasoning to identify the strengths and weaknesses of alternative solutions, conclusions, or approaches to problems.

Education and Training Programs: Neonatal-Perinatal Medicine; Obstetrics and Gynecology. **Related Knowledge/Courses: Medicine and Dentistry:** The information and techniques needed to diagnose and treat human injuries, diseases, and deformities. This includes symptoms, treatment alternatives, drug properties and interactions, and preventive health-care measures. **Therapy and Counseling:** Principles, methods, and procedures for diagnosis, treatment, and rehabilitation of physical and mental dysfunctions and for career counseling and guidance. **Biology:** Plant and animal organisms and their tissues, cells, functions, interdependencies, and interactions with each other and the environment. **Psychology:** Human behavior and performance; individual differences in ability, personality, and interests; learning and motivation; psychological research methods; and the assessment and treatment of behavioral and affective disorders. **Sociology and Anthropology:** Group behavior and dynamics, societal trends and influences, human migrations, ethnicity, and cultures and their history and origins. **Chemistry:** The chemical composition, structure, and properties of substances and of the chemical processes and transformations that they undergo. This includes uses of chemicals and their danger signs, production techniques, and disposal methods.

Work Environment: Indoors; disease or infections; standing; using hands on objects, tools, or controls.

Occupational Health and Safety Specialists

- Annual Earnings: $53,710
- Growth: 12.4%
- Annual Job Openings: 3,000
- Education/Training Required: Bachelor's degree
- Self-Employed: 5.0%
- Part-Time: 6.5%

How the Job Improves the World: Contributes to health and safety.

Review, evaluate, and analyze work environments and design programs and procedures to control, eliminate, and prevent disease or injury caused by chemical, physical, and biological agents or ergonomic factors. May conduct inspections and enforce adherence to laws and regulations governing the health and safety of individuals. May be employed in the public or private sector. Order suspension of activities that pose threats to workers' health and safety. Recommend measures to help protect workers from potentially hazardous work methods, processes, or materials. Investigate accidents to identify causes and to determine how such accidents might be prevented in the future. Investigate the adequacy of ventilation, exhaust equipment, lighting, and other conditions that could affect employee health, comfort, or performance. Develop and maintain hygiene programs such as noise surveys, continuous atmosphere monitoring, ventilation surveys, and asbestos management plans. Inspect and evaluate workplace environments, equipment, and practices to ensure compliance with safety standards and government regulations. Collaborate with engineers and physicians to institute control and remedial measures for hazardous and potentially hazardous conditions or equipment. Conduct safety training and education programs and demonstrate the use of safety equipment. Provide new-employee health and safety orientations and develop materials for these presentations. Collect samples of dust, gases, vapors, and other potentially toxic materials for analysis. Investigate health-related complaints and inspect facilities to ensure that they comply with public health legislation and regulations. Coordinate "right-to-know" programs regarding hazardous chemicals and other substances. Maintain and update emergency response plans and procedures. Develop and maintain medical monitoring programs for employees. Conduct audits at hazardous waste sites or industrial sites and participate in hazardous waste site investigations. Inspect specified areas to ensure the presence of fire prevention equipment, safety equipment, and first-aid supplies. Collect samples of hazardous materials or arrange for sample collection. Maintain inventories of hazardous materials and hazardous wastes, using waste tracking systems to ensure that materials are handled properly. Prepare hazardous, radioactive, and mixed waste samples for transportation and storage by treating, compacting, packaging, and labeling them.

Personality Type: Social. Social occupations frequently involve working with, communicating with, and teaching people. These occupations often involve helping or providing service to others.

GOE—Interest Area: 07. Government and Public Administration. **Work Group:** 07.03. Regulations Enforcement. **Other Jobs in This Work Group:** Agricultural Inspectors; Aviation Inspectors; Compliance Officers, Except Agriculture, Construction, Health and Safety, and Transportation; Construction and Building Inspectors; Environmental Compliance Inspectors; Equal Opportunity Representatives and Officers; Financial Examiners; Fire Inspectors; Fish and Game Wardens; Forest Fire Inspectors and Prevention Specialists; Freight and Cargo Inspectors; Government Property Inspectors and Investigators; Immigration and Customs Inspectors; Licensing Examiners and Inspectors; Nuclear Monitoring Technicians; Occupational Health and Safety Technicians; Tax Examiners, Collectors, and Revenue Agents; Transportation Vehicle, Equipment, and Systems Inspectors, Except Aviation.

Skills—Science: Using scientific rules and methods to solve problems. **Management of Financial Resources:** Determining how money will be spent to get the work done and accounting for these expenditures. **Technology Design:** Generating or adapting equipment and technology to serve user needs. **Persuasion:** Persuading others to change their minds or behavior. **Systems Analysis:** Determining how a system should work and how changes in conditions, operations, and the environment will affect outcomes. **Management of Material Resources:** Obtaining and seeing to the appropriate use of equipment, facilities, and materials needed to do certain work. **Management of Personnel Resources:** Motivating, developing, and directing people as they work; identifying the best people for the job. **Systems Evaluation:** Identifying measures or indicators of system performance and the actions needed to improve or correct performance relative to the goals of the system.

Education and Training Programs: Occupational Safety and Health Technology/Technician; Industrial Safety Technology/Technician; Quality Control and Safety Technologies/Technicians, Other; Environmental Health; Occupational Health and Industrial Hygiene. **Related Knowledge/Courses: Chemistry:** The chemical composition, structure, and properties of substances and of the chemical processes and transformations that they undergo. This includes uses of chemicals and their danger signs, production techniques, and disposal methods. **Biology:** Plant and animal organisms and their tissues, cells, functions, interdependencies, and interactions with each other and the environment. **Physics:** Physical principles and laws and their interrelationships and applications to understanding fluid, material, and atmospheric dynamics and mechanical, electrical, atomic, and subatomic structures and processes. **Engineering and**

Technology: The practical application of engineering science and technology. This includes applying principles, techniques, procedures, and equipment to the design and production of various goods and services. Public Safety and Security: Relevant equipment, policies, procedures, and strategies to promote effective local, state, or national security operations for the protection of people, data, property, and institutions. Education and Training: Principles and methods for curriculum and training design, teaching and instruction for individuals and groups, and the measurement of training effects.

Work Environment: More often indoors than outdoors; noisy; contaminants; sitting.

Occupational Therapist Aides

- Annual Earnings: $24,310
- Growth: 26.3%
- Annual Job Openings: Fewer than 500
- Education/Training Required: Short-term on-the-job training
- Self-Employed: 0.0%
- Part-Time: 18.6%

How the Job Improves the World: Contributes to health and well-being.

Under close supervision of an occupational therapist or occupational therapy assistant, perform only delegated, selected, or routine tasks in specific situations. These duties include preparing patient and treatment room. Encourage patients and attend to their physical needs to facilitate the attainment of therapeutic goals. Report to supervisors or therapists, verbally or in writing, on patients' progress, attitudes, attendance, and accomplishments. Observe patients' attendance, progress, attitudes, and accomplishments and record and maintain information in client records.

Manage intra-departmental infection control and equipment security. Evaluate the living skills and capacities of physically, developmentally, or emotionally disabled clients. Prepare and maintain work area, materials, and equipment and maintain inventory of treatment and educational supplies. Instruct patients and families in work, social, and living skills; the care and use of adaptive equipment; and other skills to facilitate home and work adjustment to disability. Supervise patients in choosing and completing work details or arts and crafts projects. Assist occupational therapists in planning, implementing, and administering therapy programs to restore, reinforce, and enhance performance, using selected activities and special equipment. Perform clerical, administrative, and secretarial duties such as answering phones, restocking and ordering supplies, filling out paperwork, and scheduling appointments. Demonstrate therapy techniques, such as manual and creative arts and games. Transport patients to and from the occupational therapy work area. Adjust and repair assistive devices and make adaptive changes to other equipment and to environments. Assist educational specialists or clinical psychologists in administering situational or diagnostic tests to measure client's abilities or progress. Accompany patients on outings, providing transportation when necessary.

Personality Type: Social. Social occupations frequently involve working with, communicating with, and teaching people. These occupations often involve helping or providing service to others.

GOE—Interest Area: 08. Health Science. Work Group: 08.07. Medical Therapy. Other Jobs in This Work Group: Audiologists; Massage Therapists; Occupational Therapist Assistants; Occupational Therapists; Physical Therapist Aides; Physical Therapist Assistants; Physical Therapists; Radiation Therapists; Recreational Therapists; Respiratory Therapists; Respiratory Therapy Technicians; Speech-Language Pathologists.

Skills—Service Orientation: Actively looking for ways to help people. Learning Strategies: Selecting and using training/instructional methods and procedures appropriate for the situation when learning or teaching new things. Social Perceptiveness: Being aware of others' reactions and understanding why they react as they do. Coordination: Adjusting actions in relation to others' actions. Equipment Maintenance: Performing routine maintenance on equipment and determining when and what kind of maintenance is needed. Technology Design: Generating or adapting equipment and technology to serve user needs. Management of Material Resources: Obtaining and seeing to the appropriate use of equipment, facilities, and materials needed to do certain work. Operation Monitoring: Watching gauges, dials, or other indicators to make sure a machine is working properly.

Education and Training Program: Occupational Therapist Assistant. Related Knowledge/Courses: Therapy and Counseling: Principles, methods, and procedures for diagnosis, treatment, and rehabilitation of physical and mental dysfunctions and for career counseling and guidance. Medicine and Dentistry: The information and techniques needed to diagnose and treat human injuries, diseases, and deformities. This includes symptoms, treatment alternatives, drug properties and interactions, and preventive health-care measures. Psychology: Human behavior and performance; individual differences in ability, personality, and interests; learning and motivation; psychological research methods; and the assessment and treatment of behavioral and affective disorders. Biology: Plant and animal organisms and their tissues, cells, functions, interdependencies, and interactions with each other and the environment. Education and Training: Principles and methods for curriculum and training design, teaching and instruction for individuals and groups, and the measurement of training effects. Customer and Personal Service: Principles and processes for providing customer and personal services. This includes customer needs assessment, meeting

quality standards for services, and evaluation of customer satisfaction.

Work Environment: Indoors; noisy; contaminants; disease or infections; standing; walking and running.

Occupational Therapist Assistants

- ◎ Annual Earnings: $39,750
- ◎ Growth: 34.1%
- ◎ Annual Job Openings: 2,000
- ◎ Education/Training Required: Associate degree
- ◎ Self-Employed: 0.0%
- ◎ Part-Time: 18.6%

How the Job Improves the World: Contributes to health and well-being.

Assist occupational therapists in providing occupational therapy treatments and procedures. May, in accordance with state laws, assist in development of treatment plans, carry out routine functions, direct activity programs, and document the progress of treatments. Generally requires formal training. Observe and record patients' progress, attitudes, and behavior and maintain this information in client records. Maintain and promote a positive attitude toward clients and their treatment programs. Monitor patients' performance in therapy activities, providing encouragement. Select therapy activities to fit patients' needs and capabilities. Instruct, or assist in instructing, patients and families in home programs, basic living skills, and the care and use of adaptive equipment. Evaluate the daily living skills and capacities of physically, developmentally, or emotionally disabled clients. Aid patients in dressing and grooming themselves. Implement, or assist occupational therapists with implementing, treatment plans designed to help clients function independently. Report to supervisors, verbally or in writing, on patients' progress, attitudes, and behavior. Alter treatment programs to obtain better results if treatment is not having the intended effect. Work under the direction of occupational therapists to plan, implement, and administer educational, vocational, and recreational programs that restore and enhance performance in individuals with functional impairments. Design, fabricate, and repair assistive devices and make adaptive changes to equipment and environments. Assemble, clean, and maintain equipment and materials for patient use. Teach patients how to deal constructively with their emotions. Perform clerical duties such as scheduling appointments, collecting data, and documenting health insurance billings. Transport patients to and from the occupational therapy work area. Demonstrate therapy techniques such as manual and creative arts or games. Order any needed educational or treatment supplies. Assist educational specialists or clinical psychologists in administering situational or diagnostic tests to measure client's abilities or progress.

Personality Type: Social. Social occupations frequently involve working with, communicating with, and teaching people. These occupations often involve helping or providing service to others.

GOE—Interest Area: 08. Health Science. **Work Group:** 08.07. Medical Therapy. **Other Jobs in This Work Group:** Audiologists; Massage Therapists; Occupational Therapist Aides; Occupational Therapists; Physical Therapist Aides; Physical Therapist Assistants; Physical Therapists; Radiation Therapists; Recreational Therapists; Respiratory Therapists; Respiratory Therapy Technicians; Speech-Language Pathologists.

Skills—Social Perceptiveness: Being aware of others' reactions and understanding why they react as they do. **Operations Analysis:** Analyzing needs and product requirements to create a design. **Persuasion:** Persuading others to change their minds or behavior. **Service Orientation:** Actively looking for ways to help

people. **Writing:** Communicating effectively in writing as appropriate for the needs of the audience. **Time Management:** Managing one's own time and the time of others. **Monitoring:** Monitoring/assessing your performance or that of other individuals or organizations to make improvements or take corrective action. **Learning Strategies:** Selecting and using training/instructional methods and procedures appropriate for the situation when learning or teaching new things.

Education and Training Program: Occupational Therapist Assistant. **Related Knowledge/Courses: Therapy and Counseling:** Principles, methods, and procedures for diagnosis, treatment, and rehabilitation of physical and mental dysfunctions and for career counseling and guidance. **Psychology:** Human behavior and performance; individual differences in ability, personality, and interests; learning and motivation; psychological research methods; and the assessment and treatment of behavioral and affective disorders. **Sociology and Anthropology:** Group behavior and dynamics, societal trends and influences, human migrations, ethnicity, and cultures and their history and origins. **Philosophy and Theology:** Different philosophical systems and religions. This includes their basic principles, values, ethics, ways of thinking, customs, and practices and their impact on human culture. **Medicine and Dentistry:** The information and techniques needed to diagnose and treat human injuries, diseases, and deformities. This includes symptoms, treatment alternatives, drug properties and interactions, and preventive health-care measures. **Biology:** Plant and animal organisms and their tissues, cells, functions, interdependencies, and interactions with each other and the environment.

Work Environment: Indoors; disease or infections; standing; walking and running; using hands on objects, tools, or controls; bending or twisting the body.

Occupational Therapists

- ⊚ Annual Earnings: $56,860
- ⊚ Growth: 33.6%
- ⊚ Annual Job Openings: 7,000
- ⊚ Education/Training Required: Master's degree
- ⊚ Self-Employed: 6.0%
- ⊚ Part-Time: 29.4%

How the Job Improves the World: Contributes to health and well-being.

Assess, plan, organize, and participate in rehabilitative programs that help restore vocational, homemaking, and daily living skills, as well as general independence, to disabled persons. Complete and maintain necessary records. Evaluate patients' progress and prepare reports that detail progress. Test and evaluate patients' physical and mental abilities and analyze medical data to determine realistic rehabilitation goals for patients. Select activities that will help individuals learn work and life-management skills within limits of their mental and physical capabilities. Plan, organize, and conduct occupational therapy programs in hospital, institutional, or community settings to help rehabilitate those impaired because of illness, injury or psychological or developmental problems. Recommend changes in patients' work or living environments consistent with their needs and capabilities. Consult with rehabilitation team to select activity programs and coordinate occupational therapy with other therapeutic activities. Help clients improve decisionmaking, abstract reasoning, memory, sequencing, coordination, and perceptual skills, using computer programs. Develop and participate in health promotion programs, group activities, or discussions to promote client health, facilitate social adjustment, alleviate stress, and prevent physical or mental disability. Provide training and supervision in therapy techniques and objectives for students and nurses and other medical staff. Design and create, or requisition, special supplies and equipment, such as splints, braces, and computer-aided adaptive equipment. Plan and implement programs and social activities to help patients learn work and school skills and adjust to handicaps. Lay out materials such as puzzles, scissors, and eating utensils for use in therapy; clean and repair these tools after therapy sessions. Advise on health risks in the workplace and on health-related transition to retirement. Conduct research in occupational therapy. Provide patients with assistance in locating and holding jobs.

Personality Type: Social. Social occupations frequently involve working with, communicating with, and teaching people. These occupations often involve helping or providing service to others.

GOE—Interest Area: 08. Health Science. **Work Group:** 08.07. Medical Therapy. **Other Jobs in This Work Group:** Audiologists; Massage Therapists; Occupational Therapist Aides; Occupational Therapist Assistants; Physical Therapist Aides; Physical Therapist Assistants; Physical Therapists; Radiation Therapists; Recreational Therapists; Respiratory Therapists; Respiratory Therapy Technicians; Speech-Language Pathologists.

Skills—Social Perceptiveness: Being aware of others' reactions and understanding why they react as they do. **Service Orientation:** Actively looking for ways to help people. **Science:** Using scientific rules and methods to solve problems. **Technology Design:** Generating or adapting equipment and technology to serve user needs. **Reading Comprehension:** Understanding written sentences and paragraphs in work-related documents. **Coordination:** Adjusting actions in relation to others' actions. **Writing:** Communicating effectively in writing as appropriate for the needs of the audience. **Active Learning:** Understanding the implications of new information for both current and future problem-solving and decision-making.

Education and Training Program: Occupational Therapy/Therapist. **Related Knowledge/Courses: Therapy and Counseling:** Principles, methods, and procedures for diagnosis, treatment, and rehabilitation of physical and mental dysfunctions and for career counseling and guidance. **Psychology:** Human behavior and performance; individual differences in ability, personality, and interests; learning and motivation; psychological research methods; and the assessment and treatment of behavioral and affective disorders. **Medicine and Dentistry:** The information and techniques needed to diagnose and treat human injuries, diseases, and deformities. This includes symptoms, treatment alternatives, drug properties and interactions, and preventive health-care measures. **Customer and Personal Service:** Principles and processes for providing customer and personal services. This includes customer needs assessment, meeting quality standards for services, and evaluation of customer satisfaction. **Biology:** Plant and animal organisms and their tissues, cells, functions, interdependencies, and interactions with each other and the environment. **Sociology and Anthropology:** Group behavior and dynamics, societal trends and influences, human migrations, ethnicity, and cultures and their history and origins.

Work Environment: Indoors; disease or infections; standing.

Opticians, Dispensing

- Annual Earnings: $29,000
- Growth: 13.6%
- Annual Job Openings: 6,000
- Education/Training Required: Long-term on-the-job training
- Self-Employed: 4.5%
- Part-Time: 20.2%

How the Job Improves the World: Contributes to health and well-being.

Design, measure, fit, and adapt lenses and frames for client according to written optical prescription or specification. Assist client with selecting frames. Measure customer for size of eyeglasses and coordinate frames with facial and eye measurements and optical prescription. Prepare work order for optical laboratory containing instructions for grinding and mounting lenses in frames. Verify exactness of finished lens spectacles. Adjust frame and lens position to fit client. May shape or reshape frames. Measure clients' bridge and eye size, temple length, vertex distance, pupillary distance, and optical centers of eyes, using measuring devices. Verify that finished lenses are ground to specifications. Prepare work orders and instructions for grinding lenses and fabricating eyeglasses. Assist clients in selecting frames according to style and color and ensure that frames are coordinated with facial and eye measurements and optical prescriptions. Maintain records of customer prescriptions, work orders, and payments. Perform administrative duties such as tracking inventory and sales, submitting patient insurance information, and performing simple bookkeeping. Recommend specific lenses, lens coatings, and frames to suit client needs. Sell goods such as contact lenses, spectacles, sunglasses, and other goods related to eyes in general. Heat, shape, or bend plastic or metal frames to adjust eyeglasses to fit clients, using pliers and hands. Evaluate prescriptions in conjunction with clients' vocational and avocational visual requirements. Instruct clients in how to wear and care for eyeglasses. Determine clients' current lens prescriptions, when necessary, using lensometers or lens analyzers and clients' eyeglasses. Show customers how to insert, remove, and care for their contact lenses. Repair damaged frames. Obtain a customer's previous record or verify a prescription with the examining optometrist or ophthalmologist. Arrange and maintain displays of optical merchandise. Fabricate lenses to meet prescription specifications. Grind lens edges or apply coatings to lenses. Assemble eyeglasses by cutting and edging lenses and fitting the lenses into frames. Supervise the training of student opticians.

Personality Type: Enterprising. Enterprising occupations frequently involve starting up and carrying out projects. These occupations can involve leading people and making many decisions. They sometimes require risk taking and often deal with business.

GOE—Interest Area: 08. Health Science. **Work Group:** 08.06. Medical Technology. **Other Jobs in This Work Group:** Biological Technicians; Cardiovascular Technologists and Technicians; Diagnostic Medical Sonographers; Medical and Clinical Laboratory Technicians; Medical and Clinical Laboratory Technologists; Medical Equipment Preparers; Medical Records and Health Information Technicians; Nuclear Medicine Technologists; Orthotists and Prosthetists; Radiologic Technicians; Radiologic Technologists; Radiologic Technologists and Technicians.

Skills—Persuasion: Persuading others to change their minds or behavior. **Service Orientation:** Actively looking for ways to help people. **Technology Design:** Generating or adapting equipment and technology to serve user needs. **Speaking:** Talking to others to convey information effectively. **Equipment Selection:** Determining the kind of tools and equipment needed to do a job. **Mathematics:** Using mathematics to solve problems. **Management of Financial Resources:** Determining how money will be spent to get the work done and accounting for these expenditures. **Science:** Using scientific rules and methods to solve problems.

Education and Training Program: Opticianry/Ophthalmic Dispensing Optician. **Related Knowledge/Courses: Sales and Marketing:** Principles and methods for showing, promoting, and selling products or services. This includes marketing strategy and tactics, product demonstration, sales techniques, and sales control systems. **Customer and Personal Service:** Principles and processes for providing customer and personal services. This includes customer needs assessment, meeting quality standards for services, and evaluation of customer satisfaction. **Production and Processing:** Raw materials, production processes,

quality control, costs, and other techniques for maximizing the effective manufacture and distribution of goods. **Clerical Practices:** Administrative and clerical procedures and systems such as word processing, managing files and records, stenography and transcription, designing forms, and other office procedures and terminology. **Economics and Accounting:** Economic and accounting principles and practices, the financial markets, banking, and the analysis and reporting of financial data. **Psychology:** Human behavior and performance; individual differences in ability, personality, and interests; learning and motivation; psychological research methods; and the assessment and treatment of behavioral and affective disorders.

Work Environment: Indoors; standing; using hands on objects, tools, or controls.

Optometrists

- Annual Earnings: $88,040
- Growth: 19.7%
- Annual Job Openings: 2,000
- Education/Training Required: First professional degree
- Self-Employed: 27.4%
- Part-Time: 16.5%

How the Job Improves the World: Contributes to health and well-being.

Diagnose, manage, and treat conditions and diseases of the human eye and visual system. Examine eyes and visual system, diagnose problems or impairments, prescribe corrective lenses, and provide treatment. May prescribe therapeutic drugs to treat specific eye conditions. Examine eyes, using observation, instruments, and pharmaceutical agents, to determine visual acuity and perception, focus, and coordination and to diagnose diseases and other abnormalities such as glaucoma or color-blindness. Analyze test results and develop a treatment plan.

Prescribe, supply, fit, and adjust eyeglasses, contact lenses, and other vision aids. Prescribe medications to treat eye diseases if state laws permit. Educate and counsel patients on contact lens care, visual hygiene, lighting arrangements, and safety factors. Consult with and refer patients to ophthalmologist or other health care practitioner if additional medical treatment is determined necessary. Remove foreign bodies from the eye. Provide patients undergoing eye surgeries, such as cataract and laser vision correction, with pre- and post-operative care. Prescribe therapeutic procedures to correct or conserve vision. Provide vision therapy and low vision rehabilitation.

Personality Type: Investigative. Investigative occupations frequently involve working with ideas and require an extensive amount of thinking. These occupations can involve searching for facts and figuring out problems mentally.

GOE—Interest Area: 08. Health Science. **Work Group:** 08.04. Health Specialties. **Other Jobs in This Work Group:** Chiropractors; Podiatrists.

Skills—Science: Using scientific rules and methods to solve problems. **Judgment and Decision Making:** Considering the relative costs and benefits of potential actions to choose the most appropriate one. **Management of Personnel Resources:** Motivating, developing, and directing people as they work; identifying the best people for the job. **Active Listening:** Giving full attention to what other people are saying, taking time to understand the points being made, asking questions as appropriate, and not interrupting at inappropriate times. **Reading Comprehension:** Understanding written sentences and paragraphs in work-related documents. **Persuasion:** Persuading others to change their minds or behavior. **Management of Material Resources:** Obtaining and seeing to the appropriate use of equipment, facilities, and materials needed to do certain work. **Service Orientation:** Actively looking for ways to help people.

Education and Training Program: Optometry (OD). **Related Knowledge/Courses: Medicine and Dentistry:** The information and techniques needed to diagnose and treat human injuries, diseases, and deformities. This includes symptoms, treatment alternatives, drug properties and interactions, and preventive health-care measures. **Biology:** Plant and animal organisms and their tissues, cells, functions, interdependencies, and interactions with each other and the environment. **Psychology:** Human behavior and performance; individual differences in ability, personality, and interests; learning and motivation; psychological research methods; and the assessment and treatment of behavioral and affective disorders. **Sales and Marketing:** Principles and methods for showing, promoting, and selling products or services. This includes marketing strategy and tactics, product demonstration, sales techniques, and sales control systems. **Economics and Accounting:** Economic and accounting principles and practices, the financial markets, banking, and the analysis and reporting of financial data. **Personnel and Human Resources:** Principles and procedures for personnel recruitment, selection, training, compensation and benefits, labor relations and negotiation, and personnel information systems.

Work Environment: Indoors; disease or infections; sitting; using hands on objects, tools, or controls; repetitive motions.

Oral and Maxillofacial Surgeons

- Annual Earnings: More than $145,600
- Growth: 16.2%
- Annual Job Openings: Fewer than 500
- Education/Training Required: First professional degree
- Self-Employed: 15.7%
- Part-Time: 22.4%

How the Job Improves the World: Contributes to health.

Perform surgery on mouth, jaws, and related head and neck structure to execute difficult and multiple extractions of teeth, to remove tumors and other abnormal growths, to correct abnormal jaw relations by mandibular or maxillary revision, to prepare mouth for insertion of dental prosthesis, or to treat fractured jaws. Administer general and local anesthetics. Remove impacted, damaged, and non-restorable teeth. Evaluate the position of the wisdom teeth in order to determine whether problems exist currently or might occur in the future. Collaborate with other professionals such as restorative dentists and orthodontists in order to plan treatment. Perform surgery to prepare the mouth for dental implants and to aid in the regeneration of deficient bone and gum tissues. Remove tumors and other abnormal growths of the oral and facial regions, using surgical instruments. Treat infections of the oral cavity, salivary glands, jaws, and neck. Treat problems affecting the oral mucosa such as mouth ulcers and infections. Provide emergency treatment of facial injuries, including facial lacerations, intra-oral lacerations, and fractured facial bones. Perform surgery on the mouth and jaws in order to treat conditions such as cleft lip and palate and jaw growth problems. Restore form and function by moving skin, bone, nerves, and other tissues from other parts of the body in order to reconstruct the jaws and face. Perform minor cosmetic procedures such as chin and cheekbone enhancements and minor facial rejuvenation procedures, including the use of Botox and laser technology. Treat snoring problems, using laser surgery.

Personality Type: Investigative. Investigative occupations frequently involve working with ideas and require an extensive amount of thinking. These occupations can involve searching for facts and figuring out problems mentally.

GOE—Interest Area: 08. Health Science. **Work Group:** 08.03. Dentistry. **Other Jobs in This Work Group:** Dental Assistants; Dental Hygienists; Dentists, General; Orthodontists; Prosthodontists.

Skills—Science: Using scientific rules and methods to solve problems. **Management of Financial Resources:** Determining how money will be spent to get the work done and accounting for these expenditures. **Equipment Selection:** Determining the kind of tools and equipment needed to do a job. **Management of Personnel Resources:** Motivating, developing, and directing people as they work; identifying the best people for the job. **Service Orientation:** Actively looking for ways to help people. **Complex Problem Solving:** Identifying complex problems and reviewing related information to develop and evaluate options and implement solutions. **Active Learning:** Understanding the implications of new information for both current and future problem-solving and decision-making. **Reading Comprehension:** Understanding written sentences and paragraphs in work-related documents.

Education and Training Programs: Oral/Maxillofacial Surgery (Cert, MS, PhD); Dental/Oral Surgery Specialty. **Related Knowledge/Courses: Medicine and Dentistry:** The information and techniques needed to diagnose and treat human injuries, diseases, and deformities. This includes symptoms, treatment alternatives, drug properties and interactions, and preventive health-care measures. **Biology:** Plant and animal organisms and their tissues, cells, functions, interdependencies, and interactions with each other and the environment. **Therapy and Counseling:** Principles, methods, and procedures for diagnosis, treatment, and rehabilitation of physical and mental dysfunctions and for career counseling and guidance. **Chemistry:** The chemical composition, structure, and properties of substances and of the chemical processes and transformations that they undergo. This includes uses of chemicals and their danger signs, production techniques, and disposal methods. **Psychology:** Human behavior and performance; individual differences in ability, personality, and interests; learning and motivation; psychological research methods; and the assessment and treatment of behavioral and affective disorders. **Personnel and Human Resources:** Principles and procedures for personnel recruitment, selection, training, compensation and benefits, labor relations and negotiation, and personnel information systems.

Work Environment: Indoors; disease or infections; standing; using hands on objects, tools, or controls; bending or twisting the body; repetitive motions.

Orthodontists

- Annual Earnings: More than $145,600
- Growth: 12.8%
- Annual Job Openings: 1,000
- Education/Training Required: First professional degree
- Self-Employed: 35.9%
- Part-Time: 22.4%

How the Job Improves the World: Contributes to health.

Examine, diagnose, and treat dental malocclusions and oral cavity anomalies. Design and fabricate appliances to realign teeth and jaws to produce and maintain normal function and to improve appearance. Fit dental appliances in patients' mouths to alter the position and relationship of teeth and jaws and to realign teeth. Study diagnostic records such as medical/dental histories, plaster models of the teeth, photos of a patient's face and teeth, and X rays to develop patient treatment plans. Diagnose teeth and jaw or other dental-facial abnormalities. Examine patients to assess abnormalities of jaw development, tooth position, and other dental-facial structures. Prepare diagnostic and treatment records. Adjust dental appliances

periodically to produce and maintain normal function. Provide patients with proposed treatment plans and cost estimates. Instruct dental officers and technical assistants in orthodontic procedures and techniques. Coordinate orthodontic services with other dental and medical services. Design and fabricate appliances, such as space maintainers, retainers, and labial and lingual arch wires.

Personality Type: Investigative. Investigative occupations frequently involve working with ideas and require an extensive amount of thinking. These occupations can involve searching for facts and figuring out problems mentally.

GOE—Interest Area: 08. Health Science. **Work Group:** 08.03. Dentistry. **Other Jobs in This Work Group:** Dental Assistants; Dental Hygienists; Dentists, General; Oral and Maxillofacial Surgeons; Prosthodontists.

Skills—Management of Financial Resources: Determining how money will be spent to get the work done and accounting for these expenditures. **Management of Personnel Resources:** Motivating, developing, and directing people as they work; identifying the best people for the job. **Equipment Selection:** Determining the kind of tools and equipment needed to do a job. **Management of Material Resources:** Obtaining and seeing to the appropriate use of equipment, facilities, and materials needed to do certain work. **Technology Design:** Generating or adapting equipment and technology to serve user needs. **Judgment and Decision Making:** Considering the relative costs and benefits of potential actions to choose the most appropriate one. **Instructing:** Teaching others how to do something. **Service Orientation:** Actively looking for ways to help people.

Education and Training Programs: Orthodontics/ Orthodontology (Cert, MS, PhD); Orthodontics Specialty. **Related Knowledge/Courses: Medicine and Dentistry:** The information and techniques needed to diagnose and treat human injuries, diseases, and deformities. This includes symptoms, treatment alternatives, drug properties and interactions, and preventive health-care measures. **Biology:** Plant and animal organisms and their tissues, cells, functions, interdependencies, and interactions with each other and the environment. **Sales and Marketing:** Principles and methods for showing, promoting, and selling products or services. This includes marketing strategy and tactics, product demonstration, sales techniques, and sales control systems. **Economics and Accounting:** Economic and accounting principles and practices, the financial markets, banking, and the analysis and reporting of financial data. **Personnel and Human Resources:** Principles and procedures for personnel recruitment, selection, training, compensation and benefits, labor relations and negotiation, and personnel information systems. **Customer and Personal Service:** Principles and processes for providing customer and personal services. This includes customer needs assessment, meeting quality standards for services, and evaluation of customer satisfaction.

Work Environment: Indoors; disease or infections; sitting; using hands on objects, tools, or controls; bending or twisting the body; repetitive motions.

Orthotists and Prosthetists

- Annual Earnings: $53,760
- Growth: 18.0%
- Annual Job Openings: Fewer than 500
- Education/Training Required: Bachelor's degree
- Self-Employed: 14.4%
- Part-Time: 18.2%

How the Job Improves the World: Contributes to health and well-being.

Assist patients with disabling conditions of limbs and spine or with partial or total absence of limb by fitting and preparing orthopedic braces or prostheses. Examine, interview, and measure patients in order to determine their appliance needs and to identify factors that could affect appliance fit. Fit, test, and evaluate devices on patients and make adjustments for proper fit, function, and comfort. Instruct patients in the use and care of orthoses and prostheses. Design orthopedic and prosthetic devices based on physicians' prescriptions and examination and measurement of patients. Maintain patients' records. Make and modify plaster casts of areas that will be fitted with prostheses or orthoses for use in the device construction process. Select materials and components to be used, based on device design. Confer with physicians to formulate specifications and prescriptions for orthopedic or prosthetic devices. Repair, rebuild, and modify prosthetic and orthopedic appliances. Construct and fabricate appliances or supervise others who are constructing the appliances. Train and supervise orthopedic and prosthetic assistants and technicians and other support staff. Update skills and knowledge by attending conferences and seminars. Show and explain orthopedic and prosthetic appliances to healthcare workers. Research new ways to construct and use orthopedic and prosthetic devices. Publish research findings and present them at conferences and seminars.

Personality Type: Social. Social occupations frequently involve working with, communicating with, and teaching people. These occupations often involve helping or providing service to others.

GOE—Interest Area: 08. Health Science. **Work Group:** 08.06. Medical Technology. **Other Jobs in This Work Group:** Biological Technicians; Cardiovascular Technologists and Technicians; Diagnostic Medical Sonographers; Medical and Clinical Laboratory Technicians; Medical and Clinical Laboratory Technologists; Medical Equipment Preparers; Medical Records and Health Information Technicians; Nuclear Medicine Technologists; Opticians, Dispensing; Radiologic Technicians;

Radiologic Technologists; Radiologic Technologists and Technicians.

Skills—Technology Design: Generating or adapting equipment and technology to serve user needs. **Management of Financial Resources:** Determining how money will be spent to get the work done and accounting for these expenditures. **Management of Material Resources:** Obtaining and seeing to the appropriate use of equipment, facilities, and materials needed to do certain work. **Service Orientation:** Actively looking for ways to help people. **Management of Personnel Resources:** Motivating, developing, and directing people as they work; identifying the best people for the job. **Operations Analysis:** Analyzing needs and product requirements to create a design. **Quality Control Analysis:** Conducting tests and inspections of products, services, or processes to evaluate quality or performance. **Social Perceptiveness:** Being aware of others' reactions and understanding why they react as they do.

Education and Training Programs: Orthotist/ Prosthetist; Assistive/Augmentative Technology and Rehabilitation Engineering. **Related Knowledge/ Courses: Engineering and Technology:** The practical application of engineering science and technology. This includes applying principles, techniques, procedures, and equipment to the design and production of various goods and services. **Medicine and Dentistry:** The information and techniques needed to diagnose and treat human injuries, diseases, and deformities. This includes symptoms, treatment alternatives, drug properties and interactions, and preventive health-care measures. **Design:** Design techniques, tools, and principles involved in production of precision technical plans, blueprints, drawings, and models. **Therapy and Counseling:** Principles, methods, and procedures for diagnosis, treatment, and rehabilitation of physical and mental dysfunctions and for career counseling and guidance. **Psychology:** Human behavior and performance; individual differences in ability, personality, and interests; learning and motivation; psychological

research methods; and the assessment and treatment of behavioral and affective disorders. **Production and Processing:** Raw materials, production processes, quality control, costs, and other techniques for maximizing the effective manufacture and distribution of goods.

Work Environment: Indoors; noisy; contaminants; disease or infections; hazardous equipment; using hands on objects, tools, or controls.

Park Naturalists

- Annual Earnings: $53,350
- Growth: 6.3%
- Annual Job Openings: 2,000
- Education/Training Required: Bachelor's degree
- Self-Employed: 9.0%
- Part-Time: 6.7%

The job openings listed here are shared with Range Managers and with Soil and Water Conservationists.

How the Job Improves the World: Contributes to education and natural environment.

Plan, develop, and conduct programs to inform public of historical, natural, and scientific features of national, state, or local park. Provide visitor services by explaining regulations; answering visitor requests, needs, and complaints; and providing information about the park and surrounding areas. Conduct field trips to point out scientific, historic, and natural features of parks, forests, historic sites, or other attractions. Prepare and present illustrated lectures and interpretive talks about park features. Perform emergency duties to protect human life, government property, and natural features of park. Confer with park staff to determine subjects and schedules for park programs. Assist with operations of general facilities, such as visitor centers. Plan, organize, and direct activities of

P

seasonal staff members. Perform routine maintenance on park structures. Prepare brochures and write newspaper articles. Construct historical, scientific, and nature visitor-center displays. Research stories regarding the area's natural history or environment. Interview specialists in desired fields to obtain and develop data for park information programs. Compile and maintain official park photographic and information files. Take photographs and motion pictures for use in lectures and publications and to develop displays. Survey park to determine forest conditions and distribution and abundance of fauna and flora. Plan and develop audiovisual devices for public programs.

Personality Type: Social. Social occupations frequently involve working with, communicating with, and teaching people. These occupations often involve helping or providing service to others.

GOE—Interest Area: 01. Agriculture and Natural Resources. **Work Group:** 01.01. Managerial Work in Agriculture and Natural Resources. **Other Jobs in This Work Group:** Aquacultural Managers; Crop and Livestock Managers; Farm Labor Contractors; Farm, Ranch, and Other Agricultural Managers; Farmers and Ranchers; First-Line Supervisors/Managers of Agricultural Crop and Horticultural Workers; First-Line Supervisors/Managers of Animal Husbandry and Animal Care Workers; First-Line Supervisors/ Managers of Aquacultural Workers; First-Line Supervisors/Managers of Construction Trades and Extraction Workers; First-Line Supervisors/Managers of Farming, Fishing, and Forestry Workers; First-Line Supervisors/Managers of Landscaping, Lawn Service, and Groundskeeping Workers; First-Line Supervisors/ Managers of Logging Workers; Nursery and Greenhouse Managers; Purchasing Agents and Buyers, Farm Products.

Skills—Management of Personnel Resources: Motivating, developing, and directing people as they work; identifying the best people for the job.

Management of Financial Resources: Determining how money will be spent to get the work done and accounting for these expenditures. **Service Orientation:** Actively looking for ways to help people. **Writing:** Communicating effectively in writing as appropriate for the needs of the audience. **Science:** Using scientific rules and methods to solve problems. **Management of Material Resources:** Obtaining and seeing to the appropriate use of equipment, facilities, and materials needed to do certain work. **Persuasion:** Persuading others to change their minds or behavior. **Instructing:** Teaching others how to do something.

Education and Training Programs: Natural Resources/Conservation, General; Water, Wetlands, and Marine Resources Management; Land Use Planning and Management/Development; Natural Resources Management and Policy, Other; Forestry, General; Forest Sciences and Biology; Forest Management/Forest Resources Management; Forestry, Other; Wildlife and Wildlands Science and Management; Natural Resources and Conservation, Other. **Related Knowledge/Courses: Biology:** Plant and animal organisms and their tissues, cells, functions, interdependencies, and interactions with each other and the environment. **History and Archeology:** Historical events and their causes, indicators, and effects on civilizations and cultures. **Geography:** Principles and methods for describing the features of land, sea, and air masses, including their physical characteristics; locations; interrelationships; and distribution of plant, animal, and human life. **Customer and Personal Service:** Principles and processes for providing customer and personal services. This includes customer needs assessment, meeting quality standards for services, and evaluation of customer satisfaction. **Sociology and Anthropology:** Group behavior and dynamics, societal trends and influences, human migrations, ethnicity, and cultures and their history and origins. **Communications and Media:** Media production, communication, and dissemination techniques and methods. This includes alternative ways to inform and entertain via written, oral, and visual media.

Work Environment: More often indoors than outdoors; very hot or cold; minor burns, cuts, bites, or stings; sitting; using hands on objects, tools, or controls.

Pediatricians, General

- Annual Earnings: $136,600
- Growth: 24.0%
- Annual Job Openings: 41,000
- Education/Training Required: First professional degree
- Self-Employed: 11.5%
- Part-Time: 9.6%

The job openings listed here are shared with Anesthesiologists; Family and General Practitioners; Internists, General; Obstetricians and Gynecologists; Psychiatrists; and Surgeons.

How the Job Improves the World: Contributes to health.

Diagnose, treat, and help prevent children's diseases and injuries. Examine patients or order, perform, and interpret diagnostic tests to obtain information on medical condition and determine diagnosis. Examine children regularly to assess their growth and development. Prescribe or administer treatment, therapy, medication, vaccination, and other specialized medical care to treat or prevent illness, disease, or injury in infants and children. Collect, record, and maintain patient information, such as medical history, reports, and examination results. Advise patients, parents or guardians, and community members concerning diet, activity, hygiene, and disease prevention. Treat children who have minor illnesses, acute and chronic health problems, and growth and development concerns. Explain procedures and discuss test results or prescribed treatments with patients and parents or guardians. Monitor patients' condition and progress and re-evaluate treatments as necessary. Plan and execute medical care programs to aid in the mental and physical growth and development of children and adolescents. Refer patient to medical specialist or other practitioner when necessary. Direct and coordinate activities of nurses, students, assistants, specialists, therapists, and other medical staff. Provide consulting services to other physicians. Plan, implement, or administer health programs or standards in hospital, business, or community for information, prevention, or treatment of injury or illness. Operate on patients to remove, repair, or improve functioning of diseased or injured body parts and systems. Conduct research to study anatomy and develop or test medications, treatments, or procedures to prevent or control disease or injury. Prepare reports for government or management of birth, death, and disease statistics; workforce evaluations; or medical status of individuals.

Personality Type: Investigative. Investigative occupations frequently involve working with ideas and require an extensive amount of thinking. These occupations can involve searching for facts and figuring out problems mentally.

GOE—Interest Area: 08. Health Science. **Work Group:** 08.02. Medicine and Surgery. **Other Jobs in This Work Group:** Anesthesiologists; Family and General Practitioners; Internists, General; Medical Assistants; Medical Transcriptionists; Obstetricians and Gynecologists; Pharmacists; Pharmacy Aides; Pharmacy Technicians; Physician Assistants; Psychiatrists; Registered Nurses; Surgeons; Surgical Technologists.

Skills—Science: Using scientific rules and methods to solve problems. **Social Perceptiveness:** Being aware of others' reactions and understanding why they react as they do. **Active Learning:** Understanding the implications of new information for both current and future problem-solving and decision-making. **Persuasion:** Persuading others to change their minds or behavior. **Critical Thinking:** Using logic and reasoning to identify the strengths and weaknesses of alternative solutions, conclusions, or approaches to problems. **Management of Financial Resources:** Determining how money will be spent to get the work done and accounting for these expenditures. **Reading Comprehension:** Understanding written sentences and paragraphs in work-related documents. **Negotiation:** Bringing others together and trying to reconcile differences.

Education and Training Programs: Child/Pediatric Neurology; Family Medicine; Neonatal-Perinatal Medicine; Pediatric Cardiology; Pediatric Endocrinology; Pediatric Hemato-Oncology; Pediatric Nephrology; Pediatric Orthopedics; Pediatric Surgery; Pediatrics. **Related Knowledge/Courses: Medicine and Dentistry:** The information and techniques needed to diagnose and treat human injuries, diseases, and deformities. This includes symptoms, treatment alternatives, drug properties and interactions, and preventive health-care measures. **Therapy and Counseling:** Principles, methods, and procedures for diagnosis, treatment, and rehabilitation of physical and mental dysfunctions and for career counseling and guidance. **Biology:** Plant and animal organisms and their tissues, cells, functions, interdependencies, and interactions with each other and the environment. **Psychology:** Human behavior and performance; individual differences in ability, personality, and interests; learning and motivation; psychological research methods; and the assessment and treatment of behavioral and affective disorders. **Chemistry:** The chemical composition, structure, and properties of substances and of the chemical processes and transformations that they undergo. This includes uses of chemicals and their danger signs, production techniques, and disposal methods. **Sociology and Anthropology:** Group behavior and dynamics, societal trends and influences, human migrations, ethnicity, and cultures and their history and origins.

Work Environment: Indoors; disease or infections; standing; using hands on objects, tools, or controls.

Personal and Home Care Aides

- Annual Earnings: $17,340
- Growth: 41.0%
- Annual Job Openings: 230,000
- Education/Training Required: Short-term on-the-job training
- Self-Employed: 4.5%
- Part-Time: 36.6%

How the Job Improves the World: Contributes to health and safety.

Assist elderly or disabled adults with daily living activities at the person's home or in a daytime non-residential facility. Duties performed at a place of residence may include keeping house (making beds, doing laundry, washing dishes) and preparing meals. May provide meals and supervised activities at non-residential care facilities. May advise families, the elderly, and disabled on such things as nutrition, cleanliness, and household utilities. Perform health care–related tasks, such as monitoring vital signs and medication, under the direction of registered nurses and physiotherapists. Administer bedside and personal care, such as ambulation and personal hygiene assistance. Prepare and maintain records of client progress and services performed, reporting changes in client condition to manager or supervisor. Perform housekeeping duties, such as cooking, cleaning, washing clothes and dishes, and running errands. Care for individuals and families during periods of incapacitation, family disruption, or convalescence, providing

PHCA

companionship, personal care, and help in adjusting to new lifestyles. Instruct and advise clients on issues such as household cleanliness, utilities, hygiene, nutrition, and infant care. Plan, shop for, and prepare nutritious meals or assist families in planning, shopping for, and preparing nutritious meals. Participate in case reviews, consulting with the team caring for the client, to evaluate the client's needs and plan for continuing services. Transport clients to locations outside the home, such as to physicians' offices or on outings, using a motor vehicle. Train family members to provide bedside care. Provide clients with communication assistance, typing their correspondence and obtaining information for them.

Personality Type: Social. Social occupations frequently involve working with, communicating with, and teaching people. These occupations often involve helping or providing service to others.

GOE—Interest Area: 10. Human Service. **Work Group:** 10.03. Child/Personal Care and Services. **Other Jobs in This Work Group:** Child Care Workers; Funeral Attendants; Nannies.

Skills—Social Perceptiveness: Being aware of others' reactions and understanding why they react as they do. **Persuasion:** Persuading others to change their minds or behavior. **Service Orientation:** Actively looking for ways to help people. **Learning Strategies:** Selecting and using training/instructional methods and procedures appropriate for the situation when learning or teaching new things. **Monitoring:** Monitoring/assessing your performance or that of other individuals or organizations to make improvements or take corrective action. **Coordination:** Adjusting actions in relation to others' actions. **Critical Thinking:** Using logic and reasoning to identify the strengths and weaknesses of alternative solutions, conclusions, or approaches to problems. **Active Listening:** Giving full attention to what other people are saying, taking time to understand the points being made, asking questions as appropriate, and not interrupting at inappropriate times.

Education and Training Program: Home Health Aide/Home Attendant. **Related Knowledge/Courses: Customer and Personal Service:** Principles and processes for providing customer and personal services. This includes customer needs assessment, meeting quality standards for services, and evaluation of customer satisfaction.

Work Environment: Disease or infections; standing.

Personal Financial Advisors

- Annual Earnings: $63,500
- Growth: 25.9%
- Annual Job Openings: 17,000
- Education/Training Required: Bachelor's degree
- Self-Employed: 38.9%
- Part-Time: 8.5%

How the Job Improves the World: Contributes to education.

Advise clients on financial plans, utilizing knowledge of tax and investment strategies, securities, insurance, pension plans, and real estate. Duties include assessing clients' assets, liabilities, cash flow, insurance coverage, tax status, and financial objectives to establish investment strategies. Open accounts for clients and disburse funds from account to creditors as agents for clients. Research and investigate available investment opportunities to determine whether they fit into financial plans. Recommend strategies clients can use to achieve their financial goals and objectives, including specific recommendations in such areas as cash management, insurance coverage, and investment planning. Sell financial products such as stocks, bonds, mutual funds, and insurance if licensed to do so. Collect information from students to determine their eligibility for specific financial aid programs.

P

Conduct seminars and workshops on financial planning topics such as retirement planning, estate planning, and the evaluation of severance packages. Contact clients' creditors to arrange for payment adjustments so that payments are feasible for clients and agreeable to creditors. Meet with clients' other advisors, including attorneys, accountants, trust officers, and investment bankers, to fully understand clients' financial goals and circumstances. Authorize release of financial aid funds to students. Participate in the selection of candidates for specific financial aid awards. Determine amounts of aid to be granted to students, considering such factors as funds available, extent of demand, and financial needs. Build and maintain client bases, keeping current client plans up to date and recruiting new clients on an ongoing basis. Review clients' accounts and plans regularly to determine whether life changes, economic changes, or financial performance indicate a need for plan reassessment. Prepare and interpret information for clients such as investment performance reports, financial document summaries, and income projections. Answer clients' questions about the purposes and details of financial plans and strategies. Contact clients periodically to determine if there have been changes in their financial status. Devise debt liquidation plans that include payoff priorities and timelines. Explain and document for clients the types of services that are to be provided and the responsibilities to be taken by the personal financial advisor.

Personality Type: Social. Social occupations frequently involve working with, communicating with, and teaching people. These occupations often involve helping or providing service to others.

GOE—Interest Area: 06. Finance and Insurance. **Work Group:** 06.05. Finance/Insurance Sales and Support. **Other Jobs in This Work Group:** Advertising Sales Agents; Insurance Sales Agents; Sales Agents, Financial Services; Sales Agents, Securities and Commodities; Securities, Commodities, and Financial Services Sales Agents.

Skills—No data available.

Education and Training Programs: Finance, General; Financial Planning and Services. **Related Knowledge/Courses: Economics and Accounting:** Economic and accounting principles and practices, the financial markets, banking, and the analysis and reporting of financial data. **Mathematics:** Arithmetic, algebra, geometry, calculus, and statistics and their applications.

Work Environment: Indoors; sitting.

Pharmacists

- Annual Earnings: $89,820
- Growth: 24.6%
- Annual Job Openings: 16,000
- Education/Training Required: First professional degree
- Self-Employed: 1.7%
- Part-Time: 21.1%

How the Job Improves the World: Contributes to health.

Compound and dispense medications, following prescriptions issued by physicians, dentists, or other authorized medical practitioners. Review prescriptions to assure accuracy, to ascertain the needed ingredients, and to evaluate their suitability. Provide information and advice regarding drug interactions, side effects, dosage and proper medication storage. Analyze prescribing trends to monitor patient compliance and to prevent excessive usage or harmful interactions. Order and purchase pharmaceutical supplies, medical supplies, and drugs, maintaining stock and storing and handling it properly. Maintain records, such as pharmacy files; patient profiles; charge system files; inventories; control records for radioactive nuclei; and registries of poisons, narcotics, and controlled drugs. Provide specialized services to help patients manage conditions such as diabetes, asthma, smoking cessation, or high blood pressure. Advise customers on the selection of medication brands, medical equipment, and health-care supplies. Collaborate with other health care professionals to plan, monitor, review, and evaluate the quality and effectiveness of drugs and drug regimens, providing advice on drug applications and characteristics. Compound and dispense medications as prescribed by doctors and dentists by calculating, weighing, measuring, and mixing ingredients or oversee these activities. Offer health promotion and prevention activities, for example, training people to use devices such as blood pressure or diabetes monitors. Refer patients to other health professionals and agencies when appropriate. Prepare sterile solutions and infusions for use in surgical procedures, emergency rooms, or patients' homes. Plan, implement, and maintain procedures for mixing, packaging, and labeling pharmaceuticals according to policy and legal requirements to ensure quality, security, and proper disposal. Assay radiopharmaceuticals, verify rates of disintegration, and calculate the volume required to produce the desired results to ensure proper dosages. Manage pharmacy operations, hiring and supervising staff, performing administrative duties, and buying and selling non-pharmaceutical merchandise. Work in hospitals, clinics, or for Health Management Organizations (HMOs), dispensing prescriptions, serving as a medical team consultant, or specializing in specific drug therapy areas such as oncology or nuclear pharmacotherapy.

Personality Type: Investigative. Investigative occupations frequently involve working with ideas and require an extensive amount of thinking. These occupations can involve searching for facts and figuring out problems mentally.

GOE—Interest Area: 08. Health Science. **Work Group:** 08.02. Medicine and Surgery. **Other Jobs in This Work Group:** Anesthesiologists; Family and General Practitioners; Internists, General; Medical Assistants; Medical Transcriptionists; Obstetricians and Gynecologists; Pediatricians, General; Pharmacy Aides; Pharmacy Technicians; Physician Assistants; Psychiatrists; Registered Nurses; Surgeons; Surgical Technologists.

Skills—Science: Using scientific rules and methods to solve problems. **Reading Comprehension:** Understanding written sentences and paragraphs in work-related documents. **Social Perceptiveness:** Being aware of others' reactions and understanding why they react as they do. **Active Listening:** Giving full attention to what other people are saying, taking time to understand the points being made, asking questions as appropriate, and not interrupting at inappropriate times. **Instructing:** Teaching others how to do something. **Mathematics:** Using mathematics to solve problems. **Speaking:** Talking to others to convey information effectively. **Critical Thinking:** Using logic and reasoning to identify the strengths and weaknesses of alternative solutions, conclusions, or approaches to problems.

Education and Training Programs: Pharmacy (PharmD [USA]; PharmD, BS/BPharm [Canada]); Pharmacy Administration and Pharmacy Policy and Regulatory Affairs (MS, PhD); Pharmaceutics and Drug Design (MS, PhD); Medicinal and Pharmaceutical Chemistry (MS, PhD); Natural Products Chemistry and Pharmacognosy (MS, PhD); Clinical and Industrial Drug Development (MS, PhD); Pharmacoeconomics/Pharmaceutical Economics (MS, PhD); Clinical, Hospital, and Managed Care Pharmacy (MS, PhD); others. **Related Knowledge/Courses: Medicine and Dentistry:** The information and techniques needed to diagnose and treat human injuries, diseases, and deformities. This includes symptoms, treatment alternatives, drug properties and interactions, and preventive health-care measures. **Chemistry:** The chemical composition, structure, and properties of substances and of the chemical processes and transformations that they undergo. This includes uses of chemicals and their danger signs, production techniques, and disposal

P

methods. **Therapy and Counseling:** Principles, methods, and procedures for diagnosis, treatment, and rehabilitation of physical and mental dysfunctions and for career counseling and guidance. **Biology:** Plant and animal organisms and their tissues, cells, functions, interdependencies, and interactions with each other and the environment. **Psychology:** Human behavior and performance; individual differences in ability, personality, and interests; learning and motivation; psychological research methods; and the assessment and treatment of behavioral and affective disorders. **Customer and Personal Service:** Principles and processes for providing customer and personal services. This includes customer needs assessment, meeting quality standards for services, and evaluation of customer satisfaction.

Work Environment: Indoors; disease or infections; standing; repetitive motions.

Pharmacy Technicians

- Annual Earnings: $24,390
- Growth: 28.6%
- Annual Job Openings: 35,000
- Education/Training Required: Moderate-term on-the-job training
- Self-Employed: 0.3%
- Part-Time: 23.2%

How the Job Improves the World: Contributes to health.

Prepare medications under the direction of a pharmacist. May measure, mix, count out, label, and record amounts and dosages of medications. Receive written prescription or refill requests and verify that information is complete and accurate. Maintain proper storage and security conditions for drugs. Answer telephones, responding to questions or requests. Fill bottles with prescribed medications and type and affix labels. Assist customers by answering simple questions, locating items, or referring them to the pharmacist for medication information. Price and file prescriptions that have been filled. Clean and help maintain equipment and work areas and sterilize glassware according to prescribed methods. Establish and maintain patient profiles, including lists of medications taken by individual patients. Order, label, and count stock of medications, chemicals, and supplies and enter inventory data into computer. Receive and store incoming supplies, verify quantities against invoices, and inform supervisors of stock needs and shortages. Transfer medication from vials to the appropriate number of sterile disposable syringes, using aseptic techniques. Under pharmacist supervision, add measured drugs or nutrients to intravenous solutions under sterile conditions to prepare intravenous (IV) packs. Supply and monitor robotic machines that dispense medicine into containers and label the containers. Prepare and process medical insurance claim forms and records. Mix pharmaceutical preparations according to written prescriptions. Operate cash registers to accept payment from customers. Compute charges for medication and equipment dispensed to hospital patients and enter data in computer. Deliver medications and pharmaceutical supplies to patients, nursing stations, or surgery. Price stock and mark items for sale. Maintain and merchandise home health-care products and services.

Personality Type: Conventional. Conventional occupations frequently involve following set procedures and routines. These occupations can include working with data and details more than with ideas. Usually there is a clear line of authority to follow.

GOE—Interest Area: 08. Health Science. **Work Group:** 08.02. Medicine and Surgery. **Other Jobs in This Work Group:** Anesthesiologists; Family and

General Practitioners; Internists, General; Medical Assistants; Medical Transcriptionists; Obstetricians and Gynecologists; Pediatricians, General; Pharmacists; Pharmacy Aides; Physician Assistants; Psychiatrists; Registered Nurses; Surgeons; Surgical Technologists.

Skills—No data available.

Education and Training Program: Pharmacy Technician/Assistant. **Related Knowledge/Courses: Medicine and Dentistry:** The information and techniques needed to diagnose and treat human injuries, diseases, and deformities. This includes symptoms, treatment alternatives, drug properties and interactions, and preventive health-care measures. **Chemistry:** The chemical composition, structure, and properties of substances and of the chemical processes and transformations that they undergo. This includes uses of chemicals and their danger signs, production techniques, and disposal methods. **Customer and Personal Service:** Principles and processes for providing customer and personal services. This includes customer needs assessment, meeting quality standards for services, and evaluation of customer satisfaction. **Mathematics:** Arithmetic, algebra, geometry, calculus, and statistics and their applications. **Clerical Practices:** Administrative and clerical procedures and systems such as word processing, managing files and records, stenography and transcription, designing forms, and other office procedures and terminology. **Computers and Electronics:** Circuit boards; processors; chips; electronic equipment; and computer hardware and software, including applications and programming.

Work Environment: Indoors; standing; using hands on objects, tools, or controls; repetitive motions.

Philosophy and Religion Teachers, Postsecondary

- Annual Earnings: $53,210
- Growth: 32.2%
- Annual Job Openings: 329,000
- Education/Training Required: Master's degree
- Self-Employed: 0.4%
- Part-Time: 27.3%

The job openings listed here are shared with 35 other postsecondary teaching occupations. For a complete list, see the beginning of this section.

How the Job Improves the World: Contributes to education and spiritual development.

Teach courses in philosophy, religion, and theology. Evaluate and grade students' classwork, assignments, and papers. Initiate, facilitate, and moderate classroom discussions. Prepare and deliver lectures to undergraduate and graduate students on topics such as ethics, logic, and contemporary religious thought. Prepare course materials such as syllabi, homework assignments, and handouts. Compile, administer, and grade examinations or assign this work to others. Keep abreast of developments in their field by reading current literature, talking with colleagues, and participating in professional conferences. Maintain student attendance records, grades, and other required records. Plan, evaluate, and revise curricula, course content, and course materials and methods of instruction. Maintain regularly scheduled office hours to advise and assist students. Select and obtain materials and supplies such as textbooks. Advise students on academic and vocational curricula and on career issues. Conduct research in a particular field of knowledge

P

and publish findings in professional journals, books, or electronic media. Perform administrative duties such as serving as department head. Serve on academic or administrative committees that deal with institutional policies, departmental matters, and academic issues. Collaborate with colleagues to address teaching and research issues. Participate in campus and community events. Participate in student recruitment, registration, and placement activities. Compile bibliographies of specialized materials for outside reading assignments. Supervise undergraduate and graduate teaching, internship, and research work. Act as advisers to student organizations. Write grant proposals to procure external research funding. Provide professional consulting services to government or industry.

Personality Type: No data available.

GOE—Interest Area: 05. Education and Training. **Work Group:** 05.03. Postsecondary and Adult Teaching and Instructing. **Other Jobs in This Work Group:** Adult Literacy, Remedial Education, and GED Teachers and Instructors; Agricultural Sciences Teachers, Postsecondary; Anthropology and Archeology Teachers, Postsecondary; Architecture Teachers, Postsecondary; Area, Ethnic, and Cultural Studies Teachers, Postsecondary; Art, Drama, and Music Teachers, Postsecondary; Atmospheric, Earth, Marine, and Space Sciences Teachers, Postsecondary; Biological Science Teachers, Postsecondary; Business Teachers, Postsecondary; Chemistry Teachers, Postsecondary; Communications Teachers, Postsecondary; Computer Science Teachers, Postsecondary; Criminal Justice and Law Enforcement Teachers, Postsecondary; Economics Teachers, Postsecondary; Education Teachers, Postsecondary; Engineering Teachers, Postsecondary; English Language and Literature Teachers, Postsecondary; Environmental Science Teachers, Postsecondary; Farm and Home Management Advisors; Foreign Language and Literature Teachers, Postsecondary; Forestry and Conservation Science Teachers, Postsecondary; Geography Teachers, Postsecondary; Graduate Teaching Assistants; Health Specialties Teachers, Postsecondary; History Teachers, Postsecondary; Home Economics Teachers, Postsecondary; Law Teachers, Postsecondary; Library Science Teachers, Postsecondary; Mathematical Science Teachers, Postsecondary; Nursing Instructors and Teachers, Postsecondary; Physics Teachers, Postsecondary; Political Science Teachers, Postsecondary; Psychology Teachers, Postsecondary; Recreation and Fitness Studies Teachers, Postsecondary; Self-Enrichment Education Teachers; Social Work Teachers, Postsecondary; Sociology Teachers, Postsecondary; Vocational Education Teachers, Postsecondary.

Skills—Instructing: Teaching others how to do something. **Writing:** Communicating effectively in writing as appropriate for the needs of the audience. **Critical Thinking:** Using logic and reasoning to identify the strengths and weaknesses of alternative solutions, conclusions, or approaches to problems. **Reading Comprehension:** Understanding written sentences and paragraphs in work-related documents. **Learning Strategies:** Selecting and using training/instructional methods and procedures appropriate for the situation when learning or teaching new things. **Speaking:** Talking to others to convey information effectively. **Social Perceptiveness:** Being aware of others' reactions and understanding why they react as they do. **Persuasion:** Persuading others to change their minds or behavior.

Education and Training Programs: Philosophy; Ethics; Philosophy, Other; Religion/Religious Studies; Buddhist Studies; Christian Studies; Hindu Studies; Philosophy and Religious Studies, Other; Bible/Biblical Studies; Missions/Missionary Studies and Missiology; Religious Education; Religious/Sacred Music; Theology/Theological Studies; Divinity/Ministry (BD, MDiv.); Pre-Theology/Pre-Ministerial Studies; others. **Related Knowledge/Courses: Philosophy and Theology:** Different philosophical systems and religions. This includes their basic principles, values, ethics, ways of thinking, customs, and practices and their impact on human culture. **History and Archeology:** Historical events and their causes, indicators, and effects on civilizations and cultures. **Sociology and Anthropology:** Group behavior and dynamics, societal trends and influences, human migrations, ethnicity, and cultures and their history and origins. **Education and Training:** Principles and methods for curriculum and training design, teaching and instruction for individuals and groups, and the measurement of training effects. **Foreign Language:** The structure and content of a foreign (non-English) language, including the meaning and spelling of words, rules of composition and grammar, and pronunciation. **English Language:** The structure and content of the English language, including the meaning and spelling of words, rules of composition, and grammar.

Work Environment: Indoors; sitting.

Physical Therapist Aides

- ◎ Annual Earnings: $21,510
- ◎ Growth: 34.4%
- ◎ Annual Job Openings: 5,000
- ◎ Education/Training Required: Short-term on-the-job training
- ◎ Self-Employed: 0.2%
- ◎ Part-Time: 28.6%

How the Job Improves the World: Contributes to health and well-being.

Under close supervision of a physical therapist or physical therapy assistant, perform only delegated, selected, or routine tasks in specific situations. These duties include preparing the patient and the treatment area. Clean and organize work area and disinfect equipment after treatment. Observe patients during treatment to compile and evaluate data on patients' responses and progress and report to physical therapist. Instruct, motivate, safeguard, and assist patients in practicing exercises and functional activities under direction of medical staff. Secure patients into or onto therapy equipment. Transport patients to and from treatment areas, using wheelchairs or providing standing support. Confer with physical therapy staff or others to discuss and evaluate patient information for planning, modifying, and coordinating treatment. Record treatment given and equipment used. Perform clerical duties, such as taking inventory, ordering supplies, answering telephone, taking messages, and filling out forms. Maintain equipment and furniture to keep it in good working condition, including performing the assembly and disassembly of equipment and accessories. Administer active and passive manual therapeutic exercises; therapeutic massage; and heat, light, sound, water, or electrical modality treatments such as ultrasound. Change linens, such as bed sheets and pillowcases. Arrange treatment supplies to keep them in order. Assist patients to dress; undress; and put on and remove supportive devices, such as braces, splints, and slings. Measure patient's range of joint motion, body parts, and vital signs to determine effects of treatments or for patient evaluations. Train patients to use orthopedic braces, prostheses, or supportive devices. Fit patients for orthopedic braces, prostheses, or supportive devices, adjusting fit as needed. Participate in patient care tasks, such as assisting with passing food trays, feeding residents, or bathing residents on bed rest. Administer traction to relieve neck and back pain, using intermittent and static traction equipment.

Personality Type: Social. Social occupations frequently involve working with, communicating with, and teaching people. These occupations often involve helping or providing service to others.

GOE—Interest Area: 08. Health Science. **Work Group:** 08.07. Medical Therapy. **Other Jobs in This Work Group:** Audiologists; Massage Therapists;

Occupational Therapist Aides; Occupational Therapist Assistants; Occupational Therapists; Physical Therapist Assistants; Physical Therapists; Radiation Therapists; Recreational Therapists; Respiratory Therapists; Respiratory Therapy Technicians; Speech-Language Pathologists.

Skills—Social Perceptiveness: Being aware of others' reactions and understanding why they react as they do. **Service Orientation:** Actively looking for ways to help people. **Operation Monitoring:** Watching gauges, dials, or other indicators to make sure a machine is working properly. **Equipment Maintenance:** Performing routine maintenance on equipment and determining when and what kind of maintenance is needed. **Time Management:** Managing one's own time and the time of others. **Learning Strategies:** Selecting and using training/instructional methods and procedures appropriate for the situation when learning or teaching new things. **Negotiation:** Bringing others together and trying to reconcile differences. **Persuasion:** Persuading others to change their minds or behavior.

Education and Training Program: Physical Therapist Assistant. **Related Knowledge/Courses: Psychology:** Human behavior and performance; individual differences in ability, personality, and interests; learning and motivation; psychological research methods; and the assessment and treatment of behavioral and affective disorders. **Medicine and Dentistry:** The information and techniques needed to diagnose and treat human injuries, diseases, and deformities. This includes symptoms, treatment alternatives, drug properties and interactions, and preventive health-care measures. **Therapy and Counseling:** Principles, methods, and procedures for diagnosis, treatment, and rehabilitation of physical and mental dysfunctions and for career counseling and guidance. **Customer and Personal Service:** Principles and processes for providing customer and personal services. This includes customer needs assessment, meeting quality standards for serv-

ices, and evaluation of customer satisfaction. **Clerical Practices:** Administrative and clerical procedures and systems such as word processing, managing files and records, stenography and transcription, designing forms, and other office procedures and terminology. **Education and Training:** Principles and methods for curriculum and training design, teaching and instruction for individuals and groups, and the measurement of training effects.

Work Environment: Indoors; disease or infections; standing; walking and running; using hands on objects, tools, or controls; repetitive motions.

Physical Therapist Assistants

- Annual Earnings: $39,490
- Growth: 44.2%
- Annual Job Openings: 7,000
- Education/Training Required: Associate degree
- Self-Employed: 0.2%
- Part-Time: 28.6%

How the Job Improves the World: Contributes to health and well-being.

Assist physical therapists in providing physical therapy treatments and procedures. May, in accordance with state laws, assist in the development of treatment plans, carry out routine functions, document the progress of treatment, and modify specific treatments in accordance with patient status and within the scope of treatment plans established by a physical therapist. Generally requires formal training. Instruct, motivate, safeguard, and assist patients as they practice exercises and functional activities. Confer with physical therapy staff or others to discuss and evaluate patient information for planning, modifying, and coordinating treatment. Administer active and passive manual therapeutic exercises; therapeutic massage; and heat, light, sound, water, and electrical modality treatments such as ultrasound. Observe patients during treatments to compile and evaluate data on patients' responses and progress and report to physical therapist. Measure patients' range of joint motion, body parts, and vital signs to determine effects of treatments or for patient evaluations. Secure patients into or onto therapy equipment. Fit patients for orthopedic braces, prostheses, and supportive devices such as crutches. Train patients in the use of orthopedic braces, prostheses, or supportive devices. Transport patients to and from treatment areas, lifting and transferring them according to positioning requirements. Monitor operation of equipment and record use of equipment and administration of treatment. Clean work area and check and store equipment after treatment. Assist patients to dress; undress; or put on and remove supportive devices such as braces, splints, and slings. Administer traction to relieve neck and back pain, using intermittent and static traction equipment. Perform clerical duties, such as taking inventory, ordering supplies, answering telephone, taking messages, and filling out forms. Prepare treatment areas and electrotherapy equipment for use by physiotherapists. Perform postural drainage, percussions, and vibrations and teach deep breathing exercises to treat respiratory conditions.

Personality Type: Social. Social occupations frequently involve working with, communicating with, and teaching people. These occupations often involve helping or providing service to others.

GOE—Interest Area: 08. Health Science. **Work Group:** 08.07. Medical Therapy. **Other Jobs in This Work Group:** Audiologists; Massage Therapists; Occupational Therapist Aides; Occupational Therapist Assistants; Occupational Therapists; Physical Therapist Aides; Physical Therapists; Radiation Therapists; Recreational Therapists; Respiratory Therapists; Respiratory Therapy Technicians; Speech-Language Pathologists.

Skills—Science: Using scientific rules and methods to solve problems. **Social Perceptiveness:** Being aware of others' reactions and understanding why they react as they do. **Service Orientation:** Actively looking for ways to help people. **Writing:** Communicating effectively in writing as appropriate for the needs of the audience. **Time Management:** Managing one's own time and the time of others. **Instructing:** Teaching others how to do something. **Speaking:** Talking to others to convey information effectively. **Reading Comprehension:** Understanding written sentences and paragraphs in work-related documents.

Education and Training Program: Physical Therapist Assistant. **Related Knowledge/Courses: Therapy and Counseling:** Principles, methods, and procedures for diagnosis, treatment, and rehabilitation of physical and mental dysfunctions and for career counseling and guidance. **Psychology:** Human behavior and performance; individual differences in ability, personality, and interests; learning and motivation; psychological research methods; and the assessment and treatment of behavioral and affective disorders. **Medicine and Dentistry:** The information and techniques needed to diagnose and treat human injuries, diseases, and deformities. This includes symptoms, treatment alternatives, drug properties and interactions, and preventive health-care measures. **Education and Training:** Principles and methods for curriculum and training design, teaching and instruction for individuals and groups, and the measurement of training effects. **Sociology and Anthropology:** Group behavior and dynamics, societal trends and influences, human migrations, ethnicity, and cultures and their history and origins. **Biology:** Plant and animal organisms and their tissues, cells, functions, interdependencies, and interactions with each other and the environment.

Work Environment: Indoors; disease or infections; standing; walking and running; using hands on objects, tools, or controls; bending or twisting the body.

Physical Therapists

- Annual Earnings: $63,080
- Growth: 36.7%
- Annual Job Openings: 13,000
- Education/Training Required: Master's degree
- Self-Employed: 4.5%
- Part-Time: 24.7%

How the Job Improves the World: Contributes to health and well-being.

Assess, plan, organize, and participate in rehabilitative programs that improve mobility, relieve pain, increase strength, and decrease or prevent deformity of patients suffering from disease or injury. Plan, prepare, and carry out individually designed programs of physical treatment to maintain, improve, or restore physical functioning; alleviate pain; and prevent physical dysfunction in patients. Perform and document an initial exam, evaluating data to identify problems and determine a diagnosis prior to intervention. Evaluate effects of treatment at various stages and adjust treatments to achieve maximum benefit. Administer manual exercises, massage, or traction to help relieve pain, increase patient strength, or decrease or prevent deformity or crippling. Instruct patient and family in treatment procedures to be continued at home. Confer with the patient, medical practitioners, and appropriate others to plan, implement, and assess the intervention program. Review physician's referral and patient's medical records to help determine diagnosis and physical therapy treatment required. Obtain patients' informed consent to proposed interventions. Record prognosis, treatment, response, and progress in patient's chart or enter information into computer.

Discharge patient from physical therapy when goals or projected outcomes have been attained and provide for appropriate follow-up care or referrals. Test and measure patient's strength, motor development and function, sensory perception, functional capacity, and respiratory and circulatory efficiency and record data. Identify and document goals, anticipated progress, and plans for reevaluation. Provide information to the patient about the proposed intervention, its material risks and expected benefits, and any reasonable alternatives. Inform patients when diagnosis reveals findings outside physical therapy and refer to appropriate practitioners. Direct, supervise, assess, and communicate with supportive personnel. Administer treatment involving application of physical agents, using equipment, moist packs, ultraviolet and infrared lamps, and ultrasound machines. Teach physical therapy students as well as those in other health professions. Evaluate, fit, and adjust prosthetic and orthotic devices and recommend modification to orthotist. Provide educational information about physical therapy and physical therapists, injury prevention, ergonomics, and ways to promote health.

Personality Type: Social. Social occupations frequently involve working with, communicating with, and teaching people. These occupations often involve helping or providing service to others.

GOE—Interest Area: 08. Health Science. **Work Group:** 08.07. Medical Therapy. **Other Jobs in This Work Group:** Audiologists; Massage Therapists; Occupational Therapist Aides; Occupational Therapist Assistants; Occupational Therapists; Physical Therapist Aides; Physical Therapist Assistants; Radiation Therapists; Recreational Therapists; Respiratory Therapists; Respiratory Therapy Technicians; Speech-Language Pathologists.

Skills—Science: Using scientific rules and methods to solve problems. **Reading Comprehension:** Understanding written sentences and paragraphs in work-related documents. **Social Perceptiveness:** Being aware of others' reactions and understanding why they react as they do. **Instructing:** Teaching others how to do something. **Learning Strategies:** Selecting and using training/instructional methods and procedures appropriate for the situation when learning or teaching new things. **Service Orientation:** Actively looking for ways to help people. **Monitoring:** Monitoring/assessing your performance or that of other individuals or organizations to make improvements or take corrective action. **Time Management:** Managing one's own time and the time of others.

Education and Training Programs: Physical Therapy/Therapist; Kinesiotherapy/Kinesiotherapist. **Related Knowledge/Courses: Therapy and Counseling:** Principles, methods, and procedures for diagnosis, treatment, and rehabilitation of physical and mental dysfunctions and for career counseling and guidance. **Medicine and Dentistry:** The information and techniques needed to diagnose and treat human injuries, diseases, and deformities. This includes symptoms, treatment alternatives, drug properties and interactions, and preventive health-care measures. **Psychology:** Human behavior and performance; individual differences in ability, personality, and interests; learning and motivation; psychological research methods; and the assessment and treatment of behavioral and affective disorders. **Biology:** Plant and animal organisms and their tissues, cells, functions, interdependencies, and interactions with each other and the environment. **Sociology and Anthropology:** Group behavior and dynamics, societal trends and influences, human migrations, ethnicity, and cultures and their history and origins. **Customer and Personal Service:** Principles and processes for providing customer and personal services. This includes customer needs assessment, meeting quality standards for services, and evaluation of customer satisfaction.

Work Environment: Indoors; contaminants; disease or infections; standing; walking and running; bending or twisting the body.

Physician Assistants

- Annual Earnings: $72,030
- Growth: 49.6%
- Annual Job Openings: 10,000
- Education/Training Required: Bachelor's degree
- Self-Employed: 1.3%
- Part-Time: 16.7%

How the Job Improves the World: Contributes to health.

Under the supervision of a physician, provide healthcare services typically performed by a physician. Conduct complete physicals, provide treatment, and counsel patients. May, in some cases, prescribe medication. Must graduate from an accredited educational program for physician assistants. Examine patients to obtain information about their physical condition. Make tentative diagnoses and decisions about management and treatment of patients. Interpret diagnostic test results for deviations from normal. Obtain, compile, and record patient medical data, including health history, progress notes, and results of physical examination. Administer or order diagnostic tests, such as X-ray, electrocardiogram, and laboratory tests. Prescribe therapy or medication with physician approval. Perform therapeutic procedures, such as injections, immunizations, suturing and wound care, and infection management. Instruct and counsel patients about prescribed therapeutic regimens, normal growth and development, family planning, emotional problems of daily living, and health maintenance. Provide physicians with assistance during surgery or complicated medical procedures. Supervise and coordinate activities of technicians and technical assistants. Visit and observe patients on hospital rounds or house calls, updating charts, ordering therapy, and reporting back to physician. Order medical and laboratory supplies and equipment.

Personality Type: Investigative. Investigative occupations frequently involve working with ideas and require an extensive amount of thinking. These occupations can involve searching for facts and figuring out problems mentally.

GOE—Interest Area: 08. Health Science. **Work Group:** 08.02. Medicine and Surgery. **Other Jobs in This Work Group:** Anesthesiologists; Family and General Practitioners; Internists, General; Medical Assistants; Medical Transcriptionists; Obstetricians and Gynecologists; Pediatricians, General; Pharmacists; Pharmacy Aides; Pharmacy Technicians; Psychiatrists; Registered Nurses; Surgeons; Surgical Technologists.

Skills—Science: Using scientific rules and methods to solve problems. **Social Perceptiveness:** Being aware of others' reactions and understanding why they react as they do. **Reading Comprehension:** Understanding written sentences and paragraphs in work-related documents. **Critical Thinking:** Using logic and reasoning to identify the strengths and weaknesses of alternative solutions, conclusions, or approaches to problems. **Active Listening:** Giving full attention to what other people are saying, taking time to understand the points being made, asking questions as appropriate, and not interrupting at inappropriate times. **Instructing:** Teaching others how to do something. **Time Management:** Managing one's own time and the time of others. **Writing:** Communicating effectively in writing as appropriate for the needs of the audience.

Education and Training Program: Physician Assistant. **Related Knowledge/Courses: Medicine and Dentistry:** The information and techniques needed to diagnose and treat human injuries, diseases, and deformities. This includes symptoms, treatment alternatives, drug properties and interactions, and preventive health-care measures. **Biology:** Plant and animal organisms and their tissues, cells, functions, interde-

pendencies, and interactions with each other and the environment. **Therapy and Counseling:** Principles, methods, and procedures for diagnosis, treatment, and rehabilitation of physical and mental dysfunctions and for career counseling and guidance. **Psychology:** Human behavior and performance; individual differences in ability, personality, and interests; learning and motivation; psychological research methods; and the assessment and treatment of behavioral and affective disorders. **Chemistry:** The chemical composition, structure, and properties of substances and of the chemical processes and transformations that they undergo. This includes uses of chemicals and their danger signs, production techniques, and disposal methods. **Customer and Personal Service:** Principles and processes for providing customer and personal services. This includes customer needs assessment, meeting quality standards for services, and evaluation of customer satisfaction.

Work Environment: Indoors; disease or infections; standing.

Physics Teachers, Postsecondary

- Annual Earnings: $65,880
- Growth: 32.2%
- Annual Job Openings: 329,000
- Education/Training Required: Master's degree
- Self-Employed: 0.4%
- Part-Time: 27.3%

The job openings listed here are shared with 35 other postsecondary teaching occupations. For a complete list, see the beginning of this section.

How the Job Improves the World: Contributes to education.

Teach courses pertaining to the laws of matter and energy. Includes both teachers primarily engaged in teaching and those who do a combination of both teaching and research. Evaluate and grade students' classwork, laboratory work, assignments, and papers. Prepare and deliver lectures to undergraduate and/or graduate students on topics such as quantum mechanics, particle physics, and optics. Compile, administer, and grade examinations or assign this work to others. Maintain student attendance records, grades, and other required records. Supervise students' laboratory work. Prepare course materials such as syllabi, homework assignments, and handouts. Maintain regularly scheduled office hours to advise and assist students. Supervise undergraduate and/or graduate teaching, internship, and research work. Keep abreast of developments in their field by reading current literature, talking with colleagues, and participating in professional conferences. Plan, evaluate, and revise curricula, course content, and course materials and methods of instruction. Initiate, facilitate, and moderate classroom discussions. Conduct research in a particular field of knowledge and publish findings in professional journals, books, and/or electronic media. Advise students on academic and vocational curricula and on career issues. Select and obtain materials and supplies such as textbooks and laboratory equipment. Collaborate with colleagues to address teaching and research issues. Participate in student recruitment, registration, and placement activities. Serve on academic or administrative committees that deal with institutional policies, departmental matters, and academic issues. Write grant proposals to procure external research funding. Perform administrative duties such as serving as department head. Act as advisers to student organizations. Provide professional consulting services to government and/or industry. Compile bibliographies of specialized materials for outside reading assignments. Participate in campus and community events.

Personality Type: Investigative. Investigative occupations frequently involve working with ideas and require an extensive amount of thinking. These occupations can involve searching for facts and figuring out problems mentally.

GOE—Interest Area: 05. Education and Training. **Work Group:** 05.03. Postsecondary and Adult Teaching and Instructing. **Other Jobs in This Work Group:** Adult Literacy, Remedial Education, and GED Teachers and Instructors; Agricultural Sciences Teachers, Postsecondary; Anthropology and Archeology Teachers, Postsecondary; Architecture Teachers, Postsecondary; Area, Ethnic, and Cultural Studies Teachers, Postsecondary; Art, Drama, and Music Teachers, Postsecondary; Atmospheric, Earth, Marine, and Space Sciences Teachers, Postsecondary; Biological Science Teachers, Postsecondary; Business Teachers, Postsecondary; Chemistry Teachers, Postsecondary; Communications Teachers, Postsecondary; Computer Science Teachers, Postsecondary; Criminal Justice and Law Enforcement Teachers, Postsecondary; Economics Teachers, Postsecondary; Education Teachers, Postsecondary; Engineering Teachers, Postsecondary; English Language and Literature Teachers, Postsecondary; Environmental Science Teachers, Postsecondary; Farm and Home Management Advisors; Foreign Language and Literature Teachers, Postsecondary; Forestry and Conservation Science Teachers, Postsecondary; Geography Teachers, Postsecondary; Graduate Teaching Assistants; Health Specialties Teachers, Postsecondary; History Teachers, Postsecondary; Home Economics Teachers, Postsecondary; Law Teachers, Postsecondary; Library Science Teachers, Postsecondary; Mathematical Science Teachers, Postsecondary; Nursing Instructors and Teachers, Postsecondary; Philosophy and Religion Teachers, Postsecondary; Political Science Teachers, Postsecondary; Psychology Teachers, Postsecondary; Recreation and Fitness Studies Teachers,

Postsecondary; Self-Enrichment Education Teachers; Social Work Teachers, Postsecondary; Sociology Teachers, Postsecondary; Vocational Education Teachers, Postsecondary.

Skills—Science: Using scientific rules and methods to solve problems. **Programming:** Writing computer programs for various purposes. **Instructing:** Teaching others how to do something. **Mathematics:** Using mathematics to solve problems. **Learning Strategies:** Selecting and using training/instructional methods and procedures appropriate for the situation when learning or teaching new things. **Critical Thinking:** Using logic and reasoning to identify the strengths and weaknesses of alternative solutions, conclusions, or approaches to problems. **Writing:** Communicating effectively in writing as appropriate for the needs of the audience. **Reading Comprehension:** Understanding written sentences and paragraphs in work-related documents.

Education and Training Programs: Physics, General; Atomic/Molecular Physics; Elementary Particle Physics; Plasma and High-Temperature Physics; Nuclear Physics; Optics/Optical Sciences; Solid State and Low-Temperature Physics; Acoustics; Theoretical and Mathematical Physics; Physics, Other. **Related Knowledge/Courses: Physics:** Physical principles and laws and their interrelationships and applications to understanding fluid, material, and atmospheric dynamics and mechanical, electrical, atomic, and subatomic structures and processes. **Mathematics:** Arithmetic, algebra, geometry, calculus, and statistics and their applications. **Education and Training:** Principles and methods for curriculum and training design, teaching and instruction for individuals and groups, and the measurement of training effects. **Chemistry:** The chemical composition, structure, and properties of substances and of the chemical processes and transformations that they undergo. This includes uses of chemicals and their danger signs, production techniques, and disposal methods. **Engineering and**

Technology: The practical application of engineering science and technology. This includes applying principles, techniques, procedures, and equipment to the design and production of various goods and services. **Computers and Electronics:** Circuit boards; processors; chips; electronic equipment; and computer hardware and software, including applications and programming.

Work Environment: Indoors; sitting.

Podiatrists

- Annual Earnings: $100,550
- Growth: 16.2%
- Annual Job Openings: 1,000
- Education/Training Required: First professional degree
- Self-Employed: 19.8%
- Part-Time: 22.4%

How the Job Improves the World: Contributes to health.

Diagnose and treat diseases and deformities of the human foot. Treat bone, muscle, and joint disorders affecting the feet. Diagnose diseases and deformities of the foot, using medical histories, physical examinations, X rays, and laboratory test results. Prescribe medications, corrective devices, physical therapy, or surgery. Treat conditions such as corns, calluses, ingrown nails, tumors, shortened tendons, bunions, cysts, and abscesses by surgical methods. Advise patients about treatments and foot care techniques necessary for prevention of future problems. Refer patients to physicians when symptoms indicative of systemic disorders, such as arthritis or diabetes, are observed in feet and legs. Correct deformities by means of plaster casts and strapping. Make and fit prosthetic appliances. Perform administrative duties such as hiring employees, ordering supplies, and keeping records.

Educate the public about the benefits of foot care through techniques such as speaking engagements, advertising, and other forums. Treat deformities, using mechanical methods, such as whirlpool or paraffin baths, and electrical methods, such as shortwave and low-voltage currents.

Personality Type: Social. Social occupations frequently involve working with, communicating with, and teaching people. These occupations often involve helping or providing service to others.

GOE—Interest Area: 08. Health Science. **Work Group:** 08.04. Health Specialties. **Other Jobs in This Work Group:** Chiropractors; Optometrists.

Skills—Science: Using scientific rules and methods to solve problems. **Active Listening:** Giving full attention to what other people are saying, taking time to understand the points being made, asking questions as appropriate, and not interrupting at inappropriate times. **Complex Problem Solving:** Identifying complex problems and reviewing related information to develop and evaluate options and implement solutions. **Management of Financial Resources:** Determining how money will be spent to get the work done and accounting for these expenditures. **Reading Comprehension:** Understanding written sentences and paragraphs in work-related documents. **Active Learning:** Understanding the implications of new information for both current and future problem-solving and decision-making. **Equipment Selection:** Determining the kind of tools and equipment needed to do a job. **Judgment and Decision Making:** Considering the relative costs and benefits of potential actions to choose the most appropriate one.

Education and Training Program: Podiatric Medicine/Podiatry (DPM). **Related Knowledge/Courses: Medicine and Dentistry:** The information and techniques needed to diagnose and treat human injuries, diseases, and deformities. This includes symptoms, treatment alternatives, drug properties and in-

teractions, and preventive health-care measures. **Biology:** Plant and animal organisms and their tissues, cells, functions, interdependencies, and interactions with each other and the environment. **Therapy and Counseling:** Principles, methods, and procedures for diagnosis, treatment, and rehabilitation of physical and mental dysfunctions and for career counseling and guidance. **Sales and Marketing:** Principles and methods for showing, promoting, and selling products or services. This includes marketing strategy and tactics, product demonstration, sales techniques, and sales control systems. **Chemistry:** The chemical composition, structure, and properties of substances and of the chemical processes and transformations that they undergo. This includes uses of chemicals and their danger signs, production techniques, and disposal methods. **Customer and Personal Service:** Principles and processes for providing customer and personal services. This includes customer needs assessment, meeting quality standards for services, and evaluation of customer satisfaction.

Work Environment: Indoors; contaminants; disease or infections; sitting; using hands on objects, tools, or controls; repetitive motions.

Poets, Lyricists, and Creative Writers

- Annual Earnings: $46,420
- Growth: 17.7%
- Annual Job Openings: 14,000
- Education/Training Required: Bachelor's degree
- Self-Employed: 67.7%
- Part-Time: 30.7%

The job openings listed here are shared with Copy Writers.

How the Job Improves the World: Contributes to the arts.

Create original written works, such as scripts, essays, prose, poetry, or song lyrics, for publication or performance. Revise written material to meet personal standards and to satisfy needs of clients, publishers, directors, or producers. Choose subject matter and suitable form to express personal feelings and experiences or ideas or to narrate stories or events. Plan project arrangements or outlines and organize material accordingly. Prepare works in appropriate format for publication and send them to publishers or producers. Follow appropriate procedures to get copyrights for completed work. Write fiction or nonfiction prose such as short stories, novels, biographies, articles, descriptive or critical analyses, and essays. Develop factors such as themes, plots, characterizations, psychological analyses, historical environments, action, and dialogue to create material. Confer with clients, editors, publishers, or producers to discuss changes or revisions to written material. Conduct research to obtain factual information and authentic detail, using sources such as newspaper accounts, diaries, and interviews. Write narrative, dramatic, lyric, or other types of poetry for publication. Attend book launches and publicity events or conduct public readings. Write words to fit musical compositions, including lyrics for operas, musical plays, and choral works. Adapt text to accommodate musical requirements of composers and singers. Teach writing classes. Write humorous material for publication or for performances such as comedy routines, gags, and comedy shows. Collaborate with other writers on specific projects.

Personality Type: Artistic. Artistic occupations frequently involve working with forms, designs, and patterns. They often require self-expression, and the work can be done without following a clear set of rules.

GOE—Interest Area: 03. Arts and Communication. **Work Group:** 03.02. Writing and Editing. **Other Jobs in This Work Group:** Copy Writers; Editors; Technical Writers; Writers and Authors.

Skills—Writing: Communicating effectively in writing as appropriate for the needs of the audience. **Social Perceptiveness:** Being aware of others' reactions and understanding why they react as they do. **Persuasion:** Persuading others to change their minds or behavior. **Management of Financial Resources:** Determining how money will be spent to get the work done and accounting for these expenditures. **Active Listening:** Giving full attention to what other people are saying, taking time to understand the points being made, asking questions as appropriate, and not interrupting at inappropriate times. **Reading Comprehension:** Understanding written sentences and paragraphs in work-related documents. **Speaking:** Talking to others to convey information effectively. **Critical Thinking:** Using logic and reasoning to identify the strengths and weaknesses of alternative solutions, conclusions, or approaches to problems.

Education and Training Programs: Communication Studies/Speech Communication and Rhetoric; Mass Communication/Media Studies; Family and Consumer Sciences/Human Sciences Communication; English Composition; Creative Writing; Playwriting and Screenwriting. **Related Knowledge/Courses: Fine Arts:** The theory and techniques required to compose, produce, and perform works of music, dance, visual art, drama, and sculpture. **Communications and Media:** Media production, communication, and dissemination techniques and methods. This includes alternative ways to inform and entertain via written, oral, and visual media. **Philosophy and Theology:** Different philosophical systems and religions. This includes their basic principles, values, ethics, ways of thinking, customs, and practices and their impact on human culture. **Sociology and Anthropology:** Group behavior and dynamics, societal trends and influences, human migrations, ethnicity, and cultures and their history and origins. **Sales and Marketing:** Principles and methods for showing, promoting, and selling products or services. This includes marketing strategy and tactics, product demonstration, sales techniques, and sales control systems. **English Language:** The structure and content of the English language, including the meaning and spelling of words, rules of composition, and grammar.

Work Environment: Indoors; sitting; using hands on objects, tools, or controls; repetitive motions.

Police Detectives

- Annual Earnings: $55,790
- Growth: 16.3%
- Annual Job Openings: 9,000
- Education/Training Required: Work experience in a related occupation
- Self-Employed: 0.0%
- Part-Time: 2.5%

The job openings listed here are shared with Criminal Investigators and Special Agents; Immigration and Customs Inspectors; and Police Identification and Records Officers.

How the Job Improves the World: Contributes to justice and law enforcement.

Conduct investigations to prevent crimes or solve criminal cases. Examine crime scenes to obtain clues and evidence, such as loose hairs, fibers, clothing, or weapons. Secure deceased body and obtain evidence from it, preventing bystanders from tampering with it prior to medical examiner's arrival. Obtain evidence from suspects. Provide testimony as a witness in court. Analyze completed police reports to determine what additional information and investigative work is needed. Prepare charges, responses to charges, or information for court cases according to formalized procedures. Note, mark, and photograph location of objects found, such as footprints, tire tracks, bullets, and bloodstains, and take measurements of the scene. Obtain facts or statements from complainants, witnesses, and accused persons and record interviews, us-

ing recording device. Obtain summary of incident from officer in charge at crime scene, taking care to avoid disturbing evidence. Examine records and governmental agency files to find identifying data about suspects. Prepare and serve search and arrest warrants. Block or rope off scene and check perimeter to ensure that entire scene is secured. Summon medical help for injured individuals and alert medical personnel to take statements from them. Provide information to lab personnel concerning the source of an item of evidence and tests to be performed. Monitor conditions of victims who are unconscious so that arrangements can be made to take statements if consciousness is regained. Secure persons at scene, keeping witnesses from conversing or leaving the scene before investigators arrive. Preserve, process, and analyze items of evidence obtained from crime scenes and suspects, placing them in proper containers and destroying evidence no longer needed. Record progress of investigation, maintain informational files on suspects, and submit reports to commanding officer or magistrate to authorize warrants. Organize scene search, assigning specific tasks and areas of search to individual officers and obtaining adequate lighting as necessary. Take photographs from all angles of relevant parts of a crime scene, including entrance and exit routes and streets and intersections.

Personality Type: Enterprising. Enterprising occupations frequently involve starting up and carrying out projects. These occupations can involve leading people and making many decisions. They sometimes require risk taking and often deal with business.

GOE—Interest Area: 12. Law and Public Safety. **Work Group:** 12.04. Law Enforcement and Public Safety. **Other Jobs in This Work Group:** Bailiffs; Correctional Officers and Jailers; Criminal Investigators and Special Agents; Detectives and Criminal Investigators; Fire Investigators; Forensic Science Technicians; Parking Enforcement Workers; Police and Sheriff's Patrol Officers; Police Identification and Records Officers; Police Patrol

Officers; Sheriffs and Deputy Sheriffs; Transit and Railroad Police.

Skills—Persuasion: Persuading others to change their minds or behavior. **Negotiation:** Bringing others together and trying to reconcile differences. **Social Perceptiveness:** Being aware of others' reactions and understanding why they react as they do. **Coordination:** Adjusting actions in relation to others' actions. **Speaking:** Talking to others to convey information effectively. **Active Listening:** Giving full attention to what other people are saying, taking time to understand the points being made, asking questions as appropriate, and not interrupting at inappropriate times. **Service Orientation:** Actively looking for ways to help people. **Writing:** Communicating effectively in writing as appropriate for the needs of the audience.

Education and Training Programs: Criminal Justice/Police Science; Criminalistics and Criminal Science. **Related Knowledge/Courses: Public Safety and Security:** Relevant equipment, policies, procedures, and strategies to promote effective local, state, or national security operations for the protection of people, data, property, and institutions. **Law and Government:** Laws, legal codes, court procedures, precedents, government regulations, executive orders, agency rules, and the democratic political process. **Psychology:** Human behavior and performance; individual differences in ability, personality, and interests; learning and motivation; psychological research methods; and the assessment and treatment of behavioral and affective disorders. **Therapy and Counseling:** Principles, methods, and procedures for diagnosis, treatment, and rehabilitation of physical and mental dysfunctions and for career counseling and guidance. **Philosophy and Theology:** Different philosophical systems and religions. This includes their basic principles, values, ethics, ways of thinking, customs, and practices and their impact on human culture. **Education and Training:** Principles and methods for curriculum and training design, teaching and instruc-

tion for individuals and groups, and the measurement of training effects.

Work Environment: More often indoors than outdoors; very hot or cold; sitting.

Police Patrol Officers

- ◎ Annual Earnings: $46,290
- ◎ Growth: 15.5%
- ◎ Annual Job Openings: 47,000
- ◎ Education/Training Required: Long-term on-the-job training
- ◎ Self-Employed: 0.0%
- ◎ Part-Time: 1.4%

The job openings listed here are shared with Sheriffs and Deputy Sheriffs.

How the Job Improves the World: Contributes to justice and law enforcement.

Patrol assigned area to enforce laws and ordinances, regulate traffic, control crowds, prevent crime, and arrest violators. Provide for public safety by maintaining order, responding to emergencies, protecting people and property, enforcing motor vehicle and criminal laws, and promoting good community relations. Identify, pursue, and arrest suspects and perpetrators of criminal acts. Record facts to prepare reports that document incidents and activities. Review facts of incidents to determine if criminal act or statute violations were involved. Render aid to accident victims and other persons requiring first aid for physical injuries. Testify in court to present evidence or act as witness in traffic and criminal cases. Evaluate complaint and emergency-request information to determine response requirements. Patrol specific area on foot, horseback, or motorized conveyance, responding promptly to calls for assistance. Monitor, note, report, and investigate suspicious persons and situations, safety hazards, and unusual or illegal activity in patrol area. Investigate traffic accidents and other accidents to determine causes and to determine whether a crime has been committed. Photograph or draw diagrams of crime or accident scenes and interview principals and eyewitnesses. Monitor traffic to ensure that motorists observe traffic regulations and exhibit safe driving procedures. Relay complaint and emergency-request information to appropriate agency dispatchers. Issue citations or warnings to violators of motor vehicle ordinances. Direct traffic flow and reroute traffic in case of emergencies. Inform citizens of community services and recommend options to facilitate longer-term problem resolution. Provide road information to assist motorists. Process prisoners and prepare and maintain records of prisoner bookings and prisoner status during booking and pre-trial process. Inspect public establishments to ensure compliance with rules and regulations. Act as official escorts, such as when leading funeral processions or firefighters.

Personality Type: Social. Social occupations frequently involve working with, communicating with, and teaching people. These occupations often involve helping or providing service to others.

GOE—Interest Area: 12. Law and Public Safety. **Work Group:** 12.04. Law Enforcement and Public Safety. **Other Jobs in This Work Group:** Bailiffs; Correctional Officers and Jailers; Criminal Investigators and Special Agents; Detectives and Criminal Investigators; Fire Investigators; Forensic Science Technicians; Parking Enforcement Workers; Police and Sheriff's Patrol Officers; Police Detectives; Police Identification and Records Officers; Sheriffs and Deputy Sheriffs; Transit and Railroad Police.

Skills—Persuasion: Persuading others to change their minds or behavior. **Negotiation:** Bringing others together and trying to reconcile differences. **Judgment and Decision Making:** Considering the relative costs and benefits of potential actions to choose the most appropriate one. **Social Perceptiveness:** Being aware of

others' reactions and understanding why they react as they do. **Service Orientation:** Actively looking for ways to help people. **Active Listening:** Giving full attention to what other people are saying, taking time to understand the points being made, asking questions as appropriate, and not interrupting at inappropriate times. **Complex Problem Solving:** Identifying complex problems and reviewing related information to develop and evaluate options and implement solutions. **Speaking:** Talking to others to convey information effectively.

Education and Training Programs: Criminal Justice/Police Science; Criminalistics and Criminal Science. **Related Knowledge/Courses: Public Safety and Security:** Relevant equipment, policies, procedures, and strategies to promote effective local, state, or national security operations for the protection of people, data, property, and institutions. **Law and Government:** Laws, legal codes, court procedures, precedents, government regulations, executive orders, agency rules, and the democratic political process. **Psychology:** Human behavior and performance; individual differences in ability, personality, and interests; learning and motivation; psychological research methods; and the assessment and treatment of behavioral and affective disorders. **Therapy and Counseling:** Principles, methods, and procedures for diagnosis, treatment, and rehabilitation of physical and mental dysfunctions and for career counseling and guidance. **Customer and Personal Service:** Principles and processes for providing customer and personal services. This includes customer needs assessment, meeting quality standards for services, and evaluation of customer satisfaction. **Telecommunications:** Transmission, broadcasting, switching, control, and operation of telecommunications systems.

Work Environment: Outdoors; noisy; very hot or cold; contaminants; hazardous equipment; using hands on objects, tools, or controls.

Police, Fire, and Ambulance Dispatchers

◉ Annual Earnings: $30,060
◉ Growth: 15.9%
◉ Annual Job Openings: 12,000
◉ Education/Training Required: Moderate-term on-the-job training
◉ Self-Employed: 1.3%
◉ Part-Time: 6.9%

How the Job Improves the World: Contributes to health and safety.

Receive complaints from public concerning crimes and police emergencies. Broadcast orders to police patrol units in vicinity of complaint to investigate. Operate radio, telephone, or computer equipment to receive reports of fires and medical emergencies and relay information or orders to proper officials. Determine response requirements and relative priorities of situations and dispatch units in accordance with established procedures. Record details of calls, dispatches, and messages. Question callers to determine their locations and the nature of their problems to determine type of response needed. Enter, update, and retrieve information from teletype networks and computerized data systems regarding such things as wanted persons, stolen property, vehicle registration, and stolen vehicles. Scan status charts and computer screens and contact emergency response field units to determine emergency units available for dispatch. Relay information and messages to and from emergency sites, to law enforcement agencies, and to all other individuals or groups requiring notification. Receive incoming telephone or alarm system calls regarding emergency and non-emergency police and fire service, emergency ambulance service, information, and after-hours calls for departments within a city.

Maintain access to, and security of, highly sensitive materials. Observe alarm registers and scan maps to determine whether a specific emergency is in the dispatch service area. Maintain files of information relating to emergency calls such as personnel rosters and emergency call-out and pager files. Monitor various radio frequencies such as those used by public works departments, school security, and civil defense to keep apprised of developing situations. Learn material and pass required tests for certification. Read and effectively interpret small-scale maps and information from a computer screen to determine locations and provide directions. Answer routine inquiries and refer calls not requiring dispatches to appropriate departments and agencies. Provide emergency medical instructions to callers. Monitor alarm systems to detect emergencies such as fires and illegal entry into establishments. Test and adjust communication and alarm systems and report malfunctions to maintenance units. Operate and maintain mobile dispatch vehicles and equipment.

Personality Type: Social. Social occupations frequently involve working with, communicating with, and teaching people. These occupations often involve helping or providing service to others.

GOE—Interest Area: 03. Arts and Communica-tion. **Work Group:** 03.10. Communications Technology. **Other Jobs in This Work Group:** Air Traffic Controllers; Airfield Operations Specialists; Dispatchers, Except Police, Fire, and Ambulance; Telephone Operators.

Skills—Active Listening: Giving full attention to what other people are saying, taking time to understand the points being made, asking questions as appropriate, and not interrupting at inappropriate times. **Speaking:** Talking to others to convey information effectively. **Social Perceptiveness:** Being aware of others' reactions and understanding why they react as they do. **Judgment and Decision Making:** Considering the relative costs and benefits of potential actions to choose the most appropriate one. **Critical Thinking:** Using logic and reasoning to identify the strengths and weaknesses of alternative solutions, conclusions, or approaches to problems. **Service Orientation:** Actively looking for ways to help people. **Active Learning:** Understanding the implications of new information for both current and future problem-solving and decision-making. **Coordination:** Adjusting actions in relation to others' actions.

Education and Training Program: No related programs. **Related Knowledge/Courses: Telecommunications:** Transmission, broadcasting, switching, control, and operation of telecommunications systems. **Customer and Personal Service:** Principles and processes for providing customer and personal services. This includes customer needs assessment, meeting quality standards for services, and evaluation of customer satisfaction. **Clerical Practices:** Administrative and clerical procedures and systems such as word processing, managing files and records, stenography and transcription, designing forms, and other office procedures and terminology. **Public Safety and Security:** Relevant equipment, policies, procedures, and strategies to promote effective local, state, or national security operations for the protection of people, data, property, and institutions. **Law and Government:** Laws, legal codes, court procedures, precedents, government regulations, executive orders, agency rules, and the democratic political process. **Computers and Electronics:** Circuit boards; processors; chips; electronic equipment; and computer hardware and software, including applications and programming.

Work Environment: Indoors; noisy; sitting; using hands on objects, tools, or controls; repetitive motions.

Political Science Teachers, Postsecondary

- Annual Earnings: $59,850
- Growth: 32.2%
- Annual Job Openings: 329,000
- Education/Training Required: Master's degree
- Self-Employed: 0.4%
- Part-Time: 27.3%

The job openings listed here are shared with 35 other postsecondary teaching occupations. For a complete list, see the beginning of this section.

How the Job Improves the World: Contributes to education.

Teach courses in political science, international affairs, and international relations. Initiate, facilitate, and moderate classroom discussions. Prepare and deliver lectures to undergraduate or graduate students on topics such as classical political thought, international relations, and democracy and citizenship. Evaluate and grade students' classwork, assignments, and papers. Compile, administer, and grade examinations or assign this work to others. Prepare course materials such as syllabi, homework assignments, and handouts. Keep abreast of developments in their field by reading current literature, talking with colleagues, and participating in professional conferences. Plan, evaluate, and revise curricula, course content, and course materials and methods of instruction. Maintain student attendance records, grades, and other required records. Maintain regularly scheduled office hours in order to advise and assist students. Advise students on academic and vocational curricula and on career issues. Select and obtain materials and supplies such as textbooks.

Conduct research in a particular field of knowledge and publish findings in professional journals, books, and electronic media. Supervise undergraduate and graduate teaching, internship, and research work. Collaborate with colleagues to address teaching and research issues. Serve on academic or administrative committees that deal with institutional policies, departmental matters, and academic issues. Participate in student recruitment, registration, and placement activities. Participate in campus and community events. Compile bibliographies of specialized materials for outside reading assignments. Act as advisers to student organizations. Perform administrative duties such as serving as department head. Write grant proposals to procure external research funding. Provide professional consulting services to government and industry.

Personality Type: Social. Social occupations frequently involve working with, communicating with, and teaching people. These occupations often involve helping or providing service to others.

GOE—Interest Area: 05. Education and Training. **Work Group:** 05.03. Postsecondary and Adult Teaching and Instructing. **Other Jobs in This Work Group:** Adult Literacy, Remedial Education, and GED Teachers and Instructors; Agricultural Sciences Teachers, Postsecondary; Anthropology and Archeology Teachers, Postsecondary; Architecture Teachers, Postsecondary; Area, Ethnic, and Cultural Studies Teachers, Postsecondary; Art, Drama, and Music Teachers, Postsecondary; Atmospheric, Earth, Marine, and Space Sciences Teachers, Postsecondary; Biological Science Teachers, Postsecondary; Business Teachers, Postsecondary; Chemistry Teachers, Postsecondary; Communications Teachers, Postsecondary; Computer Science Teachers, Postsecondary; Criminal Justice and Law Enforcement Teachers, Postsecondary; Economics Teachers, Postsecondary; Education Teachers, Postsecondary; Engineering Teachers, Postsecondary; English Language and Literature Teachers, Postsecondary; Environmental Science Teachers, Postsecondary; Farm and Home Management Advisors; Foreign Language and Literature Teachers, Postsecondary; Forestry and Conservation Science Teachers, Postsecondary; Geography Teachers, Postsecondary; Graduate Teaching Assistants; Health Specialties Teachers, Postsecondary; History Teachers, Postsecondary; Home Economics Teachers, Postsecondary; Law Teachers, Postsecondary; Library Science Teachers, Postsecondary; Mathematical Science Teachers, Postsecondary; Nursing Instructors and Teachers, Postsecondary; Philosophy and Religion Teachers, Postsecondary; Physics Teachers, Postsecondary; Psychology Teachers, Postsecondary; Recreation and Fitness Studies Teachers, Postsecondary; Self-Enrichment Education Teachers; Social Work Teachers, Postsecondary; Sociology Teachers, Postsecondary; Vocational Education Teachers, Postsecondary.

Skills—Instructing: Teaching others how to do something. **Writing:** Communicating effectively in writing as appropriate for the needs of the audience. **Persuasion:** Persuading others to change their minds or behavior. **Learning Strategies:** Selecting and using training/instructional methods and procedures appropriate for the situation when learning or teaching new things. **Reading Comprehension:** Understanding written sentences and paragraphs in work-related documents. **Critical Thinking:** Using logic and reasoning to identify the strengths and weaknesses of alternative solutions, conclusions, or approaches to problems. **Speaking:** Talking to others to convey information effectively. **Active Learning:** Understanding the implications of new information for both current and future problem-solving and decision-making.

Education and Training Programs: Social Science Teacher Education; Political Science and Government, General; American Government and Politics (United States); Political Science and Government, Other. **Related Knowledge/Courses: History and Archeology:** Historical events and their causes, indicators, and effects on civilizations and cultures. **Philosophy and Theology:** Different philosophical systems and religions. This includes their basic principles, values, ethics, ways of thinking, customs, and practices and their impact on human culture. **Sociology and Anthropology:** Group behavior and dynamics, societal trends and influences, human migrations, ethnicity, and cultures and their history and origins. **Geography:** Principles and methods for describing the features of land, sea, and air masses, including their physical characteristics; locations; interrelationships; and distribution of plant, animal, and human life. **Law and Government:** Laws, legal codes, court procedures, precedents, government regulations, executive orders, agency rules, and the democratic political process. **Education and Training:** Principles and methods for curriculum and training design, teaching and instruction for individuals and groups, and the measurement of training effects.

Work Environment: Indoors; sitting.

Preschool Teachers, Except Special Education

- ⊚ Annual Earnings: $21,990
- ⊚ Growth: 33.1%
- ⊚ Annual Job Openings: 77,000
- ⊚ Education/Training Required: Postsecondary vocational training
- ⊚ Self-Employed: 1.4%
- ⊚ Part-Time: 25.1%

How the Job Improves the World: Contributes to education.

Instruct children (normally up to 5 years of age) in activities designed to promote social, physical, and intellectual growth needed for primary school in preschool, day care center, or other child development facility. **May be required to hold state certification.** Provide a variety of materials and resources for children to explore, manipulate, and use, both in learning activities and in imaginative play. Attend to children's basic needs by feeding them, dressing them, and changing their diapers. Establish and enforce rules for behavior and procedures for maintaining order. Read books to entire classes or to small groups. Teach basic skills such as color, shape, number, and letter recognition; personal hygiene; and social skills. Organize and lead activities designed to promote physical, mental, and social development, such as games, arts and crafts, music, storytelling, and field trips. Observe and evaluate children's performance, behavior, social development, and physical health. Meet with parents and guardians to discuss their children's progress and needs, determine their priorities for their children, and suggest ways that they can promote learning and development. Identify children showing signs of emotional, developmental, or health-related problems and discuss them with supervisors, parents or guardians, and child development specialists. Enforce all administration policies and rules governing students. Prepare materials and classrooms for class activities. Serve meals and snacks in accordance with nutritional guidelines. Teach proper eating habits and personal hygiene. Assimilate arriving children to the school environment by greeting them, helping them remove outerwear, and selecting activities of interest to them. Adapt teaching methods and instructional materials to meet students' varying needs and interests. Establish clear objectives for all lessons, units, and projects and communicate those objectives to children. Demonstrate activities to children. Arrange indoor and outdoor space to facilitate creative play, motor-skill activities, and safety. Plan and conduct activities for a balanced program of instruction, demonstration, and work time that provides students with opportunities to observe, question, and investigate. Maintain accurate and complete student records as required by laws, district policies, and administrative regulations.

P

Personality Type: Social. Social occupations frequently involve working with, communicating with, and teaching people. These occupations often involve helping or providing service to others.

GOE—Interest Area: 05. Education and Training. **Work Group:** 05.02. Preschool, Elementary, and Secondary Teaching and Instructing. **Other Jobs in This Work Group:** Elementary School Teachers, Except Special Education; Kindergarten Teachers, Except Special Education; Middle School Teachers, Except Special and Vocational Education; Secondary School Teachers, Except Special and Vocational Education; Special Education Teachers, Middle School; Special Education Teachers, Preschool, Kindergarten, and Elementary School; Special Education Teachers, Secondary School; Teacher Assistants; Vocational Education Teachers, Middle School; Vocational Education Teachers, Secondary School.

Skills—No data available.

Education and Training Programs: Montessori Teacher Education; Early Childhood Education and Teaching; Child Care and Support Services Management. **Related Knowledge/Courses: Philosophy and Theology:** Different philosophical systems and religions. This includes their basic principles, values, ethics, ways of thinking, customs, and practices and their impact on human culture. **Sociology and Anthropology:** Group behavior and dynamics, societal trends and influences, human migrations, ethnicity, and cultures and their history and origins. **Customer and Personal Service:** Principles and processes for providing customer and personal services. This includes customer needs assessment, meeting quality standards for services, and evaluation of customer satisfaction. **Psychology:** Human behavior and performance; individual differences in ability, personality, and interests; learning and motivation; psychological research methods; and the assessment and treatment of behavioral and affective disorders.

Education and Training: Principles and methods for curriculum and training design, teaching and instruction for individuals and groups, and the measurement of training effects.

Work Environment: Indoors; standing; walking and running; bending or twisting the body.

Private Detectives and Investigators

- Annual Earnings: $32,650
- Growth: 17.7%
- Annual Job Openings: 7,000
- Education/Training Required: Work experience in a related occupation
- Self-Employed: 23.7%
- Part-Time: 16.1%

How the Job Improves the World: Contributes to justice and law enforcement.

Detect occurrences of unlawful acts or infractions of rules in private establishment or seek, examine, and compile information for client. Question persons to obtain evidence for cases of divorce, child custody, or missing persons or information about individuals' character or financial status. Conduct private investigations on a paid basis. Confer with establishment officials, security departments, police, or postal officials to identify problems, provide information, and receive instructions. Observe and document activities of individuals to detect unlawful acts or to obtain evidence for cases, using binoculars and still or video cameras. Investigate companies' financial standings or locate funds stolen by embezzlers, using accounting skills. Monitor industrial or commercial properties to enforce conformance to establishment rules and to protect people or property. Search computer databases, credit reports, public records, tax and legal filings, and other resources to locate persons or to compile information for investigations. Write reports and case summaries to document investigations. Count cash and review transactions, sales checks, and register tapes to verify amounts and to identify shortages. Perform undercover operations such as evaluating the performance and honesty of employees by posing as customers or employees. Expose fraudulent insurance claims or stolen funds. Alert appropriate personnel to suspects' locations. Conduct background investigations of individuals, such as pre-employment checks, to obtain information about an individual's character, financial status, or personal history. Testify at hearings and court trials to present evidence. Warn troublemakers causing problems on establishment premises and eject them from premises when necessary. Obtain and analyze information on suspects, crimes, and disturbances to solve cases, to identify criminal activity, and to gather information for court cases. Apprehend suspects and release them to law enforcement authorities or security personnel.

Personality Type: Enterprising. Enterprising occupations frequently involve starting up and carrying out projects. These occupations can involve leading people and making many decisions. They sometimes require risk taking and often deal with business.

GOE—Interest Area: 12. Law and Public Safety. **Work Group:** 12.05. Safety and Security. **Other Jobs in This Work Group:** Animal Control Workers; Crossing Guards; Gaming Surveillance Officers and Gaming Investigators; Lifeguards, Ski Patrol, and Other Recreational Protective Service Workers; Security Guards; Transportation Security Screeners.

Skills—No data available.

Education and Training Program: Criminal Justice/Police Science. **Related Knowledge/Courses: Public Safety and Security:** Relevant equipment, policies, procedures, and strategies to promote effective local, state, or national security operations for the protection of people, data, property, and institutions. **Law and Government:** Laws, legal codes, court pro-

cedures, precedents, government regulations, executive orders, agency rules, and the democratic political process.

Work Environment: More often indoors than outdoors; standing; walking and running.

Probation Officers and Correctional Treatment Specialists

- Annual Earnings: $40,210
- Growth: 12.8%
- Annual Job Openings: 14,000
- Education/Training Required: Bachelor's degree
- Self-Employed: 0.1%
- Part-Time: 16.0%

How the Job Improves the World: Contributes to justice and law enforcement.

Provide social services to assist in rehabilitation of law offenders in custody or on probation or parole. Make recommendations for actions involving formulation of rehabilitation plan and treatment of offender, including conditional release and education and employment stipulations. Prepare and maintain case folder for each assigned inmate or offender. Write reports describing offenders' progress. Inform offenders or inmates of requirements of conditional release, such as office visits, restitution payments, or educational and employment stipulations. Discuss with offenders how such issues as drug and alcohol abuse and anger management problems might have played roles in their criminal behavior. Gather information about offenders' backgrounds by talking to offenders, their families and friends, and other people who have relevant information. Develop rehabilitation programs for assigned offenders or inmates, establishing rules of conduct, goals, and objectives. Develop liaisons and networks with other parole officers, community agencies, staff in correctional institutions, psychiatric facilities, and after-care agencies to make plans for helping offenders with life adjustments. Arrange for medical, mental health, or substance abuse treatment services according to individual needs and court orders. Provide offenders or inmates with assistance in matters concerning detainers, sentences in other jurisdictions, writs, and applications for social assistance. Arrange for post-release services such as employment, housing, counseling, education, and social activities. Recommend remedial action or initiate court action when terms of probation or parole are not complied with. Interview probationers and parolees regularly to evaluate their progress in accomplishing goals and maintaining the terms specified in their probation contracts and rehabilitation plans. Supervise people on community-based sentences, including people on electronically monitored home detention. Assess the suitability of penitentiary inmates for release under parole and statutory release programs and submit recommendations to parole boards. Investigate alleged parole violations, using interviews, surveillance, and search and seizure. Conduct prehearing and presentencing investigations and testify in court regarding offenders' backgrounds and recommended sentences and sentencing conditions.

Personality Type: Social. Social occupations frequently involve working with, communicating with, and teaching people. These occupations often involve helping or providing service to others.

GOE—Interest Area: 10. Human Service. **Work Group:** 10.01. Counseling and Social Work. **Other Jobs in This Work Group:** Child, Family, and School Social Workers; Clinical Psychologists; Clinical, Counseling, and School Psychologists; Counseling Psychologists; Marriage and Family Therapists; Medical and Public Health Social Workers; Mental Health and Substance Abuse Social Workers; Mental Health Counselors; Rehabilitation Counselors;

Residential Advisors; Social and Human Service Assistants; Substance Abuse and Behavioral Disorder Counselors.

Skills—Social Perceptiveness: Being aware of others' reactions and understanding why they react as they do. **Persuasion:** Persuading others to change their minds or behavior. **Negotiation:** Bringing others together and trying to reconcile differences. **Management of Personnel Resources:** Motivating, developing, and directing people as they work; identifying the best people for the job. **Time Management:** Managing one's own time and the time of others. **Monitoring:** Monitoring/assessing your performance or that of other individuals or organizations to make improvements or take corrective action. **Learning Strategies:** Selecting and using training/instructional methods and procedures appropriate for the situation when learning or teaching new things. **Writing:** Communicating effectively in writing as appropriate for the needs of the audience.

Education and Training Program: Social Work. **Related Knowledge/Courses: Therapy and Counseling:** Principles, methods, and procedures for diagnosis, treatment, and rehabilitation of physical and mental dysfunctions and for career counseling and guidance. **Psychology:** Human behavior and performance; individual differences in ability, personality, and interests; learning and motivation; psychological research methods; and the assessment and treatment of behavioral and affective disorders. **Sociology and Anthropology:** Group behavior and dynamics, societal trends and influences, human migrations, ethnicity, and cultures and their history and origins. **Philosophy and Theology:** Different philosophical systems and religions. This includes their basic principles, values, ethics, ways of thinking, customs, and practices and their impact on human culture. **Law and Government:** Laws, legal codes, court procedures, precedents, government regulations, executive orders, agency rules, and the democratic political process. **Public Safety and Security:** Relevant equipment, policies, procedures, and strategies to promote effective local, state, or national security operations for the protection of people, data, property, and institutions.

Work Environment: More often indoors than outdoors; very hot or cold; disease or infections; sitting.

Prosthodontists

- Annual Earnings: More than $145,600
- Growth: 13.6%
- Annual Job Openings: Fewer than 500
- Education/Training Required: First professional degree
- Self-Employed: 38.2%
- Part-Time: 22.4%

How the Job Improves the World: Contributes to health.

Construct oral prostheses to replace missing teeth and other oral structures to correct natural and acquired deformation of mouth and jaws; to restore and maintain oral function, such as chewing and speaking; and to improve appearance. Replace missing teeth and associated oral structures with permanent fixtures, such as crowns and bridges, or removable fixtures, such as dentures. Fit prostheses to patients, making any necessary adjustments and modifications. Design and fabricate dental prostheses or supervise dental technicians and laboratory bench workers who construct the devices. Measure and take impressions of patients' jaws and teeth to determine the shape and size of dental prostheses, using face bows, dental articulators, recording devices, and other materials. Collaborate with general dentists, specialists, and other health professionals to develop solutions to dental and oral health concerns. Repair, reline, and/or rebase dentures. Restore function and aesthetics to traumatic injury victims or to individuals with

diseases or birth defects. Use bonding technology on the surface of the teeth to change tooth shape or to close gaps. Treat facial pain and jaw joint problems. Place veneers onto teeth to conceal defects. Bleach discolored teeth to brighten and whiten them.

Personality Type: Investigative. Investigative occupations frequently involve working with ideas and require an extensive amount of thinking. These occupations can involve searching for facts and figuring out problems mentally.

GOE—Interest Area: 08. Health Science. **Work Group:** 08.03. Dentistry. **Other Jobs in This Work Group:** Dental Assistants; Dental Hygienists; Dentists, General; Oral and Maxillofacial Surgeons; Orthodontists.

Skills—Management of Financial Resources: Determining how money will be spent to get the work done and accounting for these expenditures. **Science:** Using scientific rules and methods to solve problems. **Social Perceptiveness:** Being aware of others' reactions and understanding why they react as they do. **Reading Comprehension:** Understanding written sentences and paragraphs in work-related documents. **Active Learning:** Understanding the implications of new information for both current and future problem-solving and decision-making. **Equipment Selection:** Determining the kind of tools and equipment needed to do a job. **Complex Problem Solving:** Identifying complex problems and reviewing related information to develop and evaluate options and implement solutions. **Judgment and Decision Making:** Considering the relative costs and benefits of potential actions to choose the most appropriate one.

Education and Training Programs: Prosthodontics/Prosthodontology (Cert, MS, PhD); Prosthodontics Specialty. **Related Knowledge/ Courses: Medicine and Dentistry:** The information and techniques needed to diagnose and treat human injuries, diseases, and deformities. This includes symptoms, treatment alternatives, drug properties and interactions, and preventive health-care measures. **Biology:** Plant and animal organisms and their tissues, cells, functions, interdependencies, and interactions with each other and the environment. **Chemistry:** The chemical composition, structure, and properties of substances and of the chemical processes and transformations that they undergo. This includes uses of chemicals and their danger signs, production techniques, and disposal methods. **Psychology:** Human behavior and performance; individual differences in ability, personality, and interests; learning and motivation; psychological research methods; and the assessment and treatment of behavioral and affective disorders. **Sales and Marketing:** Principles and methods for showing, promoting, and selling products or services. This includes marketing strategy and tactics, product demonstration, sales techniques, and sales control systems. **Engineering and Technology:** The practical application of engineering science and technology. This includes applying principles, techniques, procedures, and equipment to the design and production of various goods and services.

Work Environment: Indoors; noisy; contaminants; disease or infections; hazardous equipment; using hands on objects, tools, or controls.

Psychiatrists

- ⊚ Annual Earnings: More than $145,600
- ⊚ Growth: 24.0%
- ⊚ Annual Job Openings: 41,000
- ⊚ Education/Training Required: First professional degree
- ⊚ Self-Employed: 11.5%
- ⊚ Part-Time: 9.6%

The job openings listed here are shared with Anesthesiologists; Family and General Practitioners; Internists, General; Obstetricians and Gynecologists; Pediatricians, General; and Surgeons.

How the Job Improves the World: Contributes to health.

Diagnose, treat, and help prevent disorders of the mind. Analyze and evaluate patient data and test findings to diagnose nature and extent of mental disorder. Prescribe, direct, and administer psychotherapeutic treatments or medications to treat mental, emotional, or behavioral disorders. Collaborate with physicians, psychologists, social workers, psychiatric nurses, or other professionals to discuss treatment plans and progress. Gather and maintain patient information and records, including social and medical history obtained from patients, relatives, and other professionals. Counsel outpatients and other patients during office visits. Design individualized care plans, using a variety of treatments. Examine or conduct laboratory or diagnostic tests on patient to provide information on general physical condition and mental disorder. Advise and inform guardians, relatives, and significant others of patients' conditions and treatment. Review and evaluate treatment procedures and outcomes of other psychiatrists and medical professionals. Teach, conduct research, and publish findings to increase understanding of mental, emotional, and behavioral states and disorders. Prepare and submit case reports and summaries to government and mental health agencies. Serve on committees to promote and maintain community mental health services and delivery systems.

Personality Type: Investigative. Investigative occupations frequently involve working with ideas and require an extensive amount of thinking. These occupations can involve searching for facts and figuring out problems mentally.

GOE—Interest Area: 08. Health Science. **Work Group:** 08.02. Medicine and Surgery. **Other Jobs in This Work Group:** Anesthesiologists; Family and General Practitioners; Internists, General; Medical Assistants; Medical Transcriptionists; Obstetricians and Gynecologists; Pediatricians, General; Pharmacists; Pharmacy Aides; Pharmacy Technicians;

Physician Assistants; Registered Nurses; Surgeons; Surgical Technologists.

Skills—Social Perceptiveness: Being aware of others' reactions and understanding why they react as they do. **Science:** Using scientific rules and methods to solve problems. **Persuasion:** Persuading others to change their minds or behavior. **Systems Analysis:** Determining how a system should work and how changes in conditions, operations, and the environment will affect outcomes. **Active Learning:** Understanding the implications of new information for both current and future problem-solving and decision-making. **Active Listening:** Giving full attention to what other people are saying, taking time to understand the points being made, asking questions as appropriate, and not interrupting at inappropriate times. **Complex Problem Solving:** Identifying complex problems and reviewing related information to develop and evaluate options and implement solutions. **Negotiation:** Bringing others together and trying to reconcile differences.

Education and Training Programs: Child Psychiatry; Psychiatry; Physical Medical and Rehabilitation/Psychiatry. **Related Knowledge/Courses: Therapy and Counseling:** Principles, methods, and procedures for diagnosis, treatment, and rehabilitation of physical and mental dysfunctions and for career counseling and guidance. **Medicine and Dentistry:** The information and techniques needed to diagnose and treat human injuries, diseases, and deformities. This includes symptoms, treatment alternatives, drug properties and interactions, and preventive health-care measures. **Psychology:** Human behavior and performance; individual differences in ability, personality, and interests; learning and motivation; psychological research methods; and the assessment and treatment of behavioral and affective disorders. **Biology:** Plant and animal organisms and their tissues, cells, functions, interdependencies, and interactions with each other and the environment. **Philosophy and Theology:** Different

philosophical systems and religions. This includes their basic principles, values, ethics, ways of thinking, customs, and practices and their impact on human culture. **Sociology and Anthropology:** Group behavior and dynamics, societal trends and influences, human migrations, ethnicity, and cultures and their history and origins.

Work Environment: Indoors; disease or infections; sitting.

Psychology Teachers, Postsecondary

- Annual Earnings: $56,370
- Growth: 32.2%
- Annual Job Openings: 329,000
- Education/Training Required: Master's degree
- Self-Employed: 0.4%
- Part-Time: 27.3%

The job openings listed here are shared with 35 other postsecondary teaching occupations. For a complete list, see the beginning of this section.

How the Job Improves the World: Contributes to education and mental health.

Teach courses in psychology, such as child, clinical, and developmental psychology, and psychological counseling. Prepare and deliver lectures to undergraduate and/or graduate students on topics such as abnormal psychology, cognitive processes, and work motivation. Evaluate and grade students' classwork, laboratory work, assignments, and papers. Initiate, facilitate, and moderate classroom discussions. Compile, administer, and grade examinations or assign this work to others. Keep abreast of developments in their field by reading current literature, talking with colleagues, and participating in professional conferences. Prepare course materials such as syllabi, homework assignments, and handouts. Plan, evaluate, and revise curricula, course content, and course materials and methods of instruction. Maintain student attendance records, grades, and other required records. Supervise undergraduate and/or graduate teaching, internship, and research work. Maintain regularly scheduled office hours to advise and assist students. Conduct research in a particular field of knowledge and publish findings in professional journals, books, and electronic media. Advise students on academic and vocational curricula and on career issues. Select and obtain materials and supplies such as textbooks. Collaborate with colleagues to address teaching and research issues. Serve on academic or administrative committees that deal with institutional policies, departmental matters, and academic issues. Compile bibliographies of specialized materials for outside reading assignments. Participate in student recruitment, registration, and placement activities. Supervise students' laboratory work. Perform administrative duties such as serving as department head. Act as advisers to student organizations. Write grant proposals to procure external research funding. Participate in campus and community events. Provide professional consulting services to government and industry.

Personality Type: Social. Social occupations frequently involve working with, communicating with, and teaching people. These occupations often involve helping or providing service to others.

GOE—Interest Area: 05. Education and Training. **Work Group:** 05.03. Postsecondary and Adult Teaching and Instructing. **Other Jobs in This Work Group:** Adult Literacy, Remedial Education, and GED Teachers and Instructors; Agricultural Sciences Teachers, Postsecondary; Anthropology and Archeology Teachers, Postsecondary; Architecture Teachers, Postsecondary; Area, Ethnic, and Cultural Studies Teachers, Postsecondary; Art, Drama, and Music Teachers, Postsecondary; Atmospheric, Earth, Marine, and Space Sciences Teachers, Postsecondary;

Biological Science Teachers, Postsecondary; Business Teachers, Postsecondary; Chemistry Teachers, Postsecondary; Communications Teachers, Postsecondary; Computer Science Teachers, Postsecondary; Criminal Justice and Law Enforcement Teachers, Postsecondary; Economics Teachers, Postsecondary; Education Teachers, Postsecondary; Engineering Teachers, Postsecondary; English Language and Literature Teachers, Postsecondary; Environmental Science Teachers, Postsecondary; Farm and Home Management Advisors; Foreign Language and Literature Teachers, Postsecondary; Forestry and Conservation Science Teachers, Postsecondary; Geography Teachers, Postsecondary; Graduate Teaching Assistants; Health Specialties Teachers, Postsecondary; History Teachers, Postsecondary; Home Economics Teachers, Postsecondary; Law Teachers, Postsecondary; Library Science Teachers, Postsecondary; Mathematical Science Teachers, Postsecondary; Nursing Instructors and Teachers, Postsecondary; Philosophy and Religion Teachers, Postsecondary; Physics Teachers, Postsecondary; Political Science Teachers, Postsecondary; Recreation and Fitness Studies Teachers, Postsecondary; Self-Enrichment Education Teachers; Social Work Teachers, Postsecondary; Sociology Teachers, Postsecondary; Vocational Education Teachers, Postsecondary.

Skills—Science: Using scientific rules and methods to solve problems. **Learning Strategies:** Selecting and using training/instructional methods and procedures appropriate for the situation when learning or teaching new things. **Instructing:** Teaching others how to do something. **Social Perceptiveness:** Being aware of others' reactions and understanding why they react as they do. **Writing:** Communicating effectively in writing as appropriate for the needs of the audience. **Reading Comprehension:** Understanding written sentences and paragraphs in work-related documents. **Active Learning:** Understanding the implications of new information for both current and future problem-solving and decision-making. **Critical Thinking:** Using logic and reasoning to identify the strengths and weaknesses of alternative solutions, conclusions, or approaches to problems.

Education and Training Programs: Social Science Teacher Education; Psychology Teacher Education; Psychology, General; Clinical Psychology; Cognitive Psychology and Psycholinguistics; Community Psychology; Comparative Psychology; Counseling Psychology; Developmental and Child Psychology; Experimental Psychology; Industrial and Organizational Psychology; Personality Psychology; Physiological Psychology/Psychobiology; others. **Related Knowledge/Courses: Therapy and Counseling:** Principles, methods, and procedures for diagnosis, treatment, and rehabilitation of physical and mental dysfunctions and for career counseling and guidance. **Psychology:** Human behavior and performance; individual differences in ability, personality, and interests; learning and motivation; psychological research methods; and the assessment and treatment of behavioral and affective disorders. **Sociology and Anthropology:** Group behavior and dynamics, societal trends and influences, human migrations, ethnicity, and cultures and their history and origins. **Philosophy and Theology:** Different philosophical systems and religions. This includes their basic principles, values, ethics, ways of thinking, customs, and practices and their impact on human culture. **Education and Training:** Principles and methods for curriculum and training design, teaching and instruction for individuals and groups, and the measurement of training effects. **English Language:** The structure and content of the English language, including the meaning and spelling of words, rules of composition, and grammar.

Work Environment: Indoors; sitting.

Radiation Therapists

- Annual Earnings: $62,340
- Growth: 26.3%
- Annual Job Openings: 1,000
- Education/Training Required: Associate degree
- Self-Employed: 0.0%
- Part-Time: 6.0%

How the Job Improves the World: Contributes to health.

Provide radiation therapy to patients as prescribed by a radiologist according to established practices and standards. Duties may include reviewing prescription and diagnosis; acting as liaison with physician and supportive care personnel; preparing equipment, such as immobilization, treatment, and protection devices; and maintaining records, reports, and files. May assist in dosimetry procedures and tumor localization. Administer prescribed doses of radiation to specific body parts, using radiation therapy equipment according to established practices and standards. Position patients for treatment with accuracy according to prescription. Enter data into computer and set controls to operate and adjust equipment and regulate dosage. Follow principles of radiation protection for patient, self, and others. Maintain records, reports and files as required, including such information as radiation dosages, equipment settings, and patients' reactions. Review prescription, diagnosis, patient chart, and identification. Conduct most treatment sessions independently in accordance with the long-term treatment plan and under the general direction of the patient's physician. Check radiation therapy equipment to ensure proper operation. Observe and reassure patients during treatment and report unusual reactions to physician or turn equipment off if unexpected adverse reactions occur. Check for side effects such as skin irritation, nausea, and hair loss to assess patients' reaction to treatment. Educate, prepare, and reassure patients and their families by answering questions, providing physical assistance, and reinforcing physicians' advice regarding treatment reactions and post-treatment care. Calculate actual treatment dosages delivered during each session. Prepare and construct equipment, such as immobilization, treatment, and protection devices. Photograph treated area of patient and process film. Help physicians, radiation oncologists, and clinical physicists to prepare physical and technical aspects of radiation treatment plans, using information about patient condition and anatomy. Train and supervise student or subordinate radiotherapy technologists. Provide assistance to other health care personnel during dosimetry procedures and tumor localization. Implement appropriate follow-up care plans. Act as liaison with physicist and supportive care personnel. Store, sterilize, or prepare the special applicators containing the radioactive substance implanted by the physician. Assist in the preparation of sealed radioactive materials, such as cobalt, radium, cesium, and isotopes, for use in radiation treatments.

Personality Type: Social. Social occupations frequently involve working with, communicating with, and teaching people. These occupations often involve helping or providing service to others.

GOE—Interest Area: 08. Health Science. **Work Group:** 08.07. Medical Therapy. **Other Jobs in This Work Group:** Audiologists; Massage Therapists; Occupational Therapist Aides; Occupational Therapist Assistants; Occupational Therapists; Physical Therapist Aides; Physical Therapist Assistants; Physical Therapists; Recreational Therapists; Respiratory Therapists; Respiratory Therapy Technicians; Speech-Language Pathologists.

Skills—Operation Monitoring: Watching gauges, dials, or other indicators to make sure a machine is working properly. **Operation and Control:** Controlling operations of equipment or systems. **Technology Design:** Generating or adapting equip-

ment and technology to serve user needs. **Time Management:** Managing one's own time and the time of others. **Science:** Using scientific rules and methods to solve problems. **Management of Personnel Resources:** Motivating, developing, and directing people as they work; identifying the best people for the job. **Service Orientation:** Actively looking for ways to help people. **Social Perceptiveness:** Being aware of others' reactions and understanding why they react as they do.

Education and Training Program: Medical Radiologic Technology/Science—Radiation Therapist. **Related Knowledge/Courses: Medicine and Dentistry:** The information and techniques needed to diagnose and treat human injuries, diseases, and deformities. This includes symptoms, treatment alternatives, drug properties and interactions, and preventive health-care measures. **Biology:** Plant and animal organisms and their tissues, cells, functions, interdependencies, and interactions with each other and the environment. **Physics:** Physical principles and laws and their interrelationships and applications to understanding fluid, material, and atmospheric dynamics and mechanical, electrical, atomic, and subatomic structures and processes. **Psychology:** Human behavior and performance; individual differences in ability, personality, and interests; learning and motivation; psychological research methods; and the assessment and treatment of behavioral and affective disorders. **Therapy and Counseling:** Principles, methods, and procedures for diagnosis, treatment, and rehabilitation of physical and mental dysfunctions and for career counseling and guidance. **Customer and Personal Service:** Principles and processes for providing customer and personal services. This includes customer needs assessment, meeting quality standards for services, and evaluation of customer satisfaction.

Work Environment: Indoors; disease or infections; standing; walking and running; using hands on objects, tools, or controls; repetitive motions.

Radiologic Technicians

- Annual Earnings: $45,950
- Growth: 23.2%
- Annual Job Openings: 17,000
- Education/Training Required: Associate degree
- Self-Employed: 0.4%
- Part-Time: 17.2%

The job openings listed here are shared with Radiologic Technologists.

How the Job Improves the World: Contributes to health.

Maintain and use equipment and supplies necessary to demonstrate portions the human body on X-ray film or fluoroscopic screen for diagnostic purposes. Use beam-restrictive devices and patient-shielding techniques to minimize radiation exposure to patient and staff. Position X-ray equipment and adjust controls to set exposure factors, such as time and distance. Position patient on examining table and set up and adjust equipment to obtain optimum view of specific body area as requested by physician. Determine patients' X-ray needs by reading requests or instructions from physicians. Make exposures necessary for the requested procedures, rejecting and repeating work that does not meet established standards. Process exposed radiographs, using film processors or computer-generated methods. Explain procedures to patients to reduce anxieties and obtain cooperation. Perform procedures such as linear tomography; mammography; sonograms; joint and cyst aspirations; routine contrast studies; routine fluoroscopy; and examinations of the head, trunk, and extremities under supervision of physician. Prepare and set up X-ray room for patient. Assure that sterile supplies, contrast materials, catheters, and other required equipment are present and in working order, requisitioning materials as necessary. Maintain records of patients examined, examinations performed, views taken, and technical factors used. Provide assistance to physicians or other technologists in the performance of more complex procedures. Monitor equipment operation and report malfunctioning equipment to supervisor. Provide students and other technologists with suggestions of additional views, alternate positioning, or improved techniques to ensure the images produced are of the highest quality. Coordinate work of other technicians or technologists when procedures require more than one person. Assist with on-the-job training of new employees and students and provide input to supervisors regarding training performance. Maintain a current file of examination protocols. Operate mobile X-ray equipment in operating room, in emergency room, or at patient's bedside. Provide assistance in radiopharmaceutical administration, monitoring patients' vital signs and notifying the radiologist of any relevant changes.

Personality Type: Realistic. Realistic occupations frequently involve work activities that include practical, hands-on problems and solutions. They often deal with plants; animals; and real-world materials such as wood, tools, and machinery. Many of the occupations require working outside and do not involve a lot of paperwork or working closely with others.

GOE—Interest Area: 08. Health Science. **Work Group:** 08.06. Medical Technology. **Other Jobs in This Work Group:** Biological Technicians; Cardiovascular Technologists and Technicians; Diagnostic Medical Sonographers; Medical and Clinical Laboratory Technicians; Medical and Clinical Laboratory Technologists; Medical Equipment Preparers; Medical Records and Health Information Technicians; Nuclear Medicine Technologists; Opticians, Dispensing; Orthotists and Prosthetists; Radiologic Technologists; Radiologic Technologists and Technicians.

Skills—Science: Using scientific rules and methods to solve problems. **Operation Monitoring:** Watching gauges, dials, or other indicators to make sure a machine is working properly. **Operation and Control:** Controlling operations of equipment or systems. **Service Orientation:** Actively looking for ways to help people. **Equipment Selection:** Determining the kind of tools and equipment needed to do a job. **Negotiation:** Bringing others together and trying to reconcile differences. **Active Listening:** Giving full attention to what other people are saying, taking time to understand the points being made, asking questions as appropriate, and not interrupting at inappropriate times. **Speaking:** Talking to others to convey information effectively.

Education and Training Programs: Medical Radiologic Technology/Science—Radiation Therapist; Radiologic Technology/Science—Radiographer; Allied Health Diagnostic, Intervention, and Treatment Professions, Other. **Related Knowledge/Courses: Medicine and Dentistry:** The information and techniques needed to diagnose and treat human injuries, diseases, and deformities. This includes symptoms, treatment alternatives, drug properties and interactions, and preventive health-care measures. **Clerical Practices:** Administrative and clerical procedures and systems such as word processing, managing files and records, stenography and transcription, designing forms, and other office procedures and terminology. **Psychology:** Human behavior and performance; individual differences in ability, personality, and interests; learning and motivation; psychological research methods; and the assessment and treatment of behavioral and affective disorders. **Physics:** Physical principles and laws and their interrelationships and applications to understanding fluid, material, and atmospheric dynamics and mechanical, electrical, atomic, and subatomic structures and processes. **Biology:** Plant and animal organisms and their tissues, cells, functions, interdependencies, and interactions with each other and the environment. **Chemistry:** The chemical composition, structure, and properties of substances and of the chemical processes

and transformations that they undergo. This includes uses of chemicals and their danger signs, production techniques, and disposal methods.

Work Environment: Indoors; radiation; disease or infections; standing; walking and running; using hands on objects, tools, or controls.

Radiologic Technologists

- Annual Earnings: $45,950
- Growth: 23.2%
- Annual Job Openings: 17,000
- Education/Training Required: Associate degree
- Self-Employed: 0.4%
- Part-Time: 17.2%

The job openings listed here are shared with Radiologic Technicians.

How the Job Improves the World: Contributes to health.

Take X rays and Computerized Axial Tomography (CAT or CT) scans or administer nonradioactive materials into patient's bloodstream for diagnostic purposes. Includes technologists who specialize in other modalities, such as computed tomography, ultrasound, and magnetic resonance. Review and evaluate developed X rays, videotape, or computer-generated information to determine if images are satisfactory for diagnostic purposes. Use radiation safety measures and protection devices to comply with government regulations and to ensure safety of patients and staff. Explain procedures and observe patients to ensure safety and comfort during scan. Operate or oversee operation of radiologic and magnetic imaging equipment to produce images of the body for diagnostic purposes. Position and immobilize patient on examining table. Position imaging equipment and adjust controls to set exposure time and distance according to specification of examination. Key commands and data into computer to document and specify scan sequences, adjust transmitters and receivers, or photograph certain images. Monitor video display of area being scanned and adjust density or contrast to improve picture quality. Monitor patients' conditions and reactions, reporting abnormal signs to physician. Prepare and administer oral or injected contrast media to patients. Set up examination rooms, ensuring that all necessary equipment is ready. Take thorough and accurate patient medical histories. Remove and process film. Record, process, and maintain patient data and treatment records and prepare reports. Coordinate work with clerical personnel or other technologists. Demonstrate new equipment, procedures, and techniques to staff and provide technical assistance. Provide assistance in dressing or changing seriously ill, injured, or disabled patients. Move ultrasound scanner over patient's body and watch pattern produced on video screen. Measure thickness of section to be radiographed, using instruments similar to measuring tapes. Operate fluoroscope to aid physician to view and guide wire or catheter through blood vessels to area of interest. Assign duties to radiologic staff to maintain patient flows and achieve production goals. Collaborate with other medical team members, such as physicians and nurses, to conduct angiography or special vascular procedures. Perform administrative duties such as developing departmental operating budget, coordinating purchases of supplies and equipment, and preparing work schedules.

Personality Type: Realistic. Realistic occupations frequently involve work activities that include practical, hands-on problems and solutions. They often deal with plants; animals; and real-world materials such as wood, tools, and machinery. Many of the occupations require working outside and do not involve a lot of paperwork or working closely with others.

GOE—Interest Area: 08. Health Science. **Work Group:** 08.06. Medical Technology. **Other Jobs in**

This Work Group: Biological Technicians; Cardiovascular Technologists and Technicians; Diagnostic Medical Sonographers; Medical and Clinical Laboratory Technicians; Medical and Clinical Laboratory Technologists; Medical Equipment Preparers; Medical Records and Health Information Technicians; Nuclear Medicine Technologists; Opticians, Dispensing; Orthotists and Prosthetists; Radiologic Technicians; Radiologic Technologists and Technicians.

Skills—Operation Monitoring: Watching gauges, dials, or other indicators to make sure a machine is working properly. **Social Perceptiveness:** Being aware of others' reactions and understanding why they react as they do. **Instructing:** Teaching others how to do something. **Reading Comprehension:** Understanding written sentences and paragraphs in work-related documents. **Service Orientation:** Actively looking for ways to help people. **Active Listening:** Giving full attention to what other people are saying, taking time to understand the points being made, asking questions as appropriate, and not interrupting at inappropriate times. **Speaking:** Talking to others to convey information effectively. **Science:** Using scientific rules and methods to solve problems.

Education and Training Programs: Medical Radiologic Technology/Science—Radiation Therapist; Radiologic Technology/Science—Radiographer; Allied Health Diagnostic, Intervention, and Treatment Professions, Other. **Related Knowledge/Courses: Medicine and Dentistry:** The information and techniques needed to diagnose and treat human injuries, diseases, and deformities. This includes symptoms, treatment alternatives, drug properties and interactions, and preventive health-care measures. **Biology:** Plant and animal organisms and their tissues, cells, functions, interdependencies, and interactions with each other and the environment. **Physics:** Physical principles and laws and their interrelationships and applications to understanding fluid, material, and atmospheric dynamics and mechanical, electrical, atomic, and subatomic structures and processes. **Psychology:** Human behavior and performance; individual differences in ability, personality, and interests; learning and motivation; psychological research methods; and the assessment and treatment of behavioral and affective disorders. **Chemistry:** The chemical composition, structure, and properties of substances and of the chemical processes and transformations that they undergo. This includes uses of chemicals and their danger signs, production techniques, and disposal methods. **Customer and Personal Service:** Principles and processes for providing customer and personal services. This includes customer needs assessment, meeting quality standards for services, and evaluation of customer satisfaction.

Work Environment: Indoors; disease or infections; standing; walking and running; using hands on objects, tools, or controls; repetitive motions.

Range Managers

- Annual Earnings: $53,350
- Growth: 6.3%
- Annual Job Openings: 2,000
- Education/Training Required: Bachelor's degree
- Self-Employed: 9.0%
- Part-Time: 6.7%

The job openings listed here are shared with Park Naturalists and with Soil and Water Conservationists.

How the Job Improves the World: Contributes to natural environment.

Research or study range land management practices to provide sustained production of forage, livestock, and wildlife. Regulate grazing and help ranchers plan and organize grazing systems to manage, improve, and protect rangelands and maximize their use. Measure and assess vegetation resources for biological assess-

ment companies, environmental impact statements, and rangeland monitoring programs. Maintain soil stability and vegetation for non-grazing uses, such as wildlife habitats and outdoor recreation. Mediate agreements among rangeland users and preservationists as to appropriate land use and management. Study rangeland management practices and research range problems to provide sustained production of forage, livestock, and wildlife. Manage forage resources through fire, herbicide use, or revegetation to maintain a sustainable yield from the land. Offer advice to rangeland users on water management, forage production methods, and control of brush. Plan and direct construction and maintenance of range improvements such as fencing, corrals, stock-watering reservoirs, and soil-erosion control structures. Tailor conservation plans to landowners' goals, such as livestock support, wildlife, or recreation. Develop technical standards and specifications used to manage, protect, and improve the natural resources of rangelands and related grazing lands. Study grazing patterns to determine number and kind of livestock that can be most profitably grazed and to determine the best grazing seasons. Plan and implement revegetation of disturbed sites. Study forage plants and their growth requirements to determine varieties best suited to particular range. Develop methods for protecting range from fire and rodent damage and for controlling poisonous plants. Manage private livestock operations. Develop new and improved instruments and techniques for activities such as range reseeding.

Personality Type: Investigative. Investigative occupations frequently involve working with ideas and require an extensive amount of thinking. These occupations can involve searching for facts and figuring out problems mentally.

GOE—Interest Area: 01. Agriculture and Natural Resources. **Work Group:** 01.02. Resource Science/Engineering for Plants, Animals, and the Environment. **Other Jobs in This Work Group:** Agricultural Engineers; Animal Scientists;

Conservation Scientists; Environmental Engineers; Foresters; Mining and Geological Engineers, Including Mining Safety Engineers; Petroleum Engineers; Soil and Plant Scientists; Soil and Water Conservationists; Zoologists and Wildlife Biologists.

Skills—Negotiation: Bringing others together and trying to reconcile differences. **Science:** Using scientific rules and methods to solve problems. **Management of Financial Resources:** Determining how money will be spent to get the work done and accounting for these expenditures. **Persuasion:** Persuading others to change their minds or behavior. **Coordination:** Adjusting actions in relation to others' actions. **Systems Evaluation:** Identifying measures or indicators of system performance and the actions needed to improve or correct performance relative to the goals of the system. **Complex Problem Solving:** Identifying complex problems and reviewing related information to develop and evaluate options and implement solutions. **Writing:** Communicating effectively in writing as appropriate for the needs of the audience.

Education and Training Programs: Natural Resources/Conservation, General; Natural Resources Management and Policy; Water, Wetlands, and Marine Resources Management; Land Use Planning and Management/Development; Natural Resources Management and Policy, Other; Forestry, General; Forest Sciences and Biology; Forest Management/Forest Resources Management; Forestry, Other; Wildlife and Wildlands Science and Management; others. **Related Knowledge/Courses: Biology:** Plant and animal organisms and their tissues, cells, functions, interdependencies, and interactions with each other and the environment. **Geography:** Principles and methods for describing the features of land, sea, and air masses, including their physical characteristics; locations; interrelationships; and distribution of plant, animal, and human life. **Food Production:** Techniques and equipment for planting, growing, and harvesting food products (both plant and animal) for consumption, including storage/handling techniques. **History and Archeology:** Historical events and their causes, indicators, and effects on civilizations and cultures. **Law and Government:** Laws, legal codes, court procedures, precedents, government regulations, executive orders, agency rules, and the democratic political process. **Engineering and Technology:** The practical application of engineering science and technology. This includes applying principles, techniques, procedures, and equipment to the design and production of various goods and services.

Work Environment: More often outdoors than indoors; noisy; very hot or cold; minor burns, cuts, bites, or stings; sitting.

Recreation and Fitness Studies Teachers, Postsecondary

- Annual Earnings: $45,890
- Growth: 32.2%
- Annual Job Openings: 329,000
- Education/Training Required: Master's degree
- Self-Employed: 0.4%
- Part-Time: 27.3%

The job openings listed here are shared with 35 other postsecondary teaching occupations. For a complete list, see the beginning of this section.

How the Job Improves the World: Contributes to education and physical fitness.

Teach courses pertaining to recreation, leisure, and fitness studies, including exercise physiology and facilities management. Evaluate and grade students' classwork, assignments, and papers. Maintain student attendance records, grades, and other required records. Prepare and deliver lectures to undergraduate and graduate students on topics such as anatomy, therapeutic recreation, and conditioning theory. Prepare course materials such as syllabi, homework assignments, and handouts. Maintain regularly scheduled office hours to advise and assist students. Compile, administer, and grade examinations or assign this work to others. Plan, evaluate, and revise curricula, course content, and course materials and methods of instruction. Initiate, facilitate, and moderate classroom discussions. Keep abreast of developments in their field by reading current literature, talking with colleagues, and participating in professional conferences. Advise students on academic and vocational curricula and on career issues. Participate in student recruitment, registration, and placement activities. Collaborate with colleagues to address teaching and research issues. Select and obtain materials and supplies such as textbooks. Participate in campus and community events. Serve on academic or administrative committees that deal with institutional policies, departmental matters, and academic issues. Compile bibliographies of specialized materials for outside reading assignments. Supervise undergraduate or graduate teaching, internship, and research work. Perform administrative duties such as serving as department heads. Prepare students to act as sports coaches. Conduct research in a particular field of knowledge and publish findings in professional journals, books, or electronic media. Act as advisers to student organizations. Write grant proposals to procure external research funding. Provide professional consulting services to government or industry.

Personality Type: No data available.

GOE—Interest Area: 05. Education and Training. **Work Group:** 05.03. Postsecondary and Adult Teaching and Instructing. **Other Jobs in This Work Group:** Adult Literacy, Remedial Education, and GED Teachers and Instructors; Agricultural Sciences Teachers, Postsecondary; Anthropology and Archeology Teachers, Postsecondary; Architecture Teachers, Postsecondary; Area, Ethnic, and Cultural Studies Teachers, Postsecondary; Art, Drama, and Music Teachers, Postsecondary; Atmospheric, Earth, Marine, and Space Sciences Teachers, Postsecondary; Biological Science Teachers, Postsecondary; Business Teachers, Postsecondary; Chemistry Teachers, Postsecondary; Communications Teachers, Postsecondary; Computer Science Teachers, Postsecondary; Criminal Justice and Law Enforcement Teachers, Postsecondary; Economics Teachers, Postsecondary; Education Teachers, Postsecondary; Engineering Teachers, Postsecondary; English Language and Literature Teachers, Postsecondary; Environmental Science Teachers, Postsecondary; Farm and Home Management Advisors; Foreign Language and Literature Teachers, Postsecondary; Forestry and Conservation Science Teachers, Postsecondary; Geography Teachers, Postsecondary; Graduate Teaching Assistants; Health Specialties Teachers, Postsecondary; History Teachers, Postsecondary; Home Economics Teachers, Postsecondary; Law Teachers, Postsecondary; Library Science Teachers, Postsecondary; Mathematical Science Teachers, Postsecondary; Nursing Instructors and Teachers, Postsecondary; Philosophy and Religion Teachers, Postsecondary; Physics Teachers, Postsecondary; Political Science Teachers, Postsecondary; Psychology Teachers, Postsecondary; Self-Enrichment Education Teachers; Social Work Teachers, Postsecondary; Sociology Teachers, Postsecondary; Vocational Education Teachers, Postsecondary.

Skills—Instructing: Teaching others how to do something. **Learning Strategies:** Selecting and using training/instructional methods and procedures appropriate for the situation when learning or teaching new things. **Science:** Using scientific rules and methods to solve problems. **Social Perceptiveness:** Being aware of others' reactions and understanding why they react as they do. **Persuasion:** Persuading others to change their minds or behavior. **Time Management:** Managing one's own time and the time of others. **Management of Financial Resources:** Determining how money will be spent to get the work done and accounting for these expenditures. **Writing:** Communicating effectively in writing as appropriate for the needs of the audience.

Education and Training Programs: Parks, Recreation, and Leisure Studies; Health and Physical Education, General; Sport and Fitness Administration/Management. **Related Knowledge/Courses: Education and Training:** Principles and methods for curriculum and training design, teaching and instruction for individuals and groups, and the measurement of training effects. **Psychology:** Human behavior and performance; individual differences in ability, personality, and interests; learning and motivation; psychological research methods; and the assessment and treatment of behavioral and affective disorders. **Philosophy and Theology:** Different philosophical systems and religions. This includes their basic principles, values, ethics, ways of thinking, customs, and practices and their impact on human culture. **Therapy and Counseling:** Principles, methods, and procedures for diagnosis, treatment, and rehabilitation of physical and mental dysfunctions and for career counseling and guidance. **Medicine and Dentistry:** The information and techniques needed to diagnose and treat human injuries, diseases, and deformities. This includes symptoms, treatment alternatives, drug properties and interactions, and preventive health-care measures. **Personnel and Human Resources:** Principles and procedures for personnel recruitment, selection, training, compensation and benefits, labor relations and negotiation, and personnel information systems.

Work Environment: More often indoors than outdoors; standing.

Recreation Workers

- Annual Earnings: $20,110
- Growth: 17.3%
- Annual Job Openings: 69,000
- Education/Training Required: Short-term on-the-job training
- Self-Employed: 6.7%
- Part-Time: 41.3%

How the Job Improves the World: Contributes to health and fitness.

Conduct recreation activities with groups in public, private, or volunteer agencies or recreation facilities. Organize and promote activities such as arts and crafts, sports, games, music, dramatics, social recreation, camping, and hobbies, taking into account the needs and interests of individual members. Enforce rules and regulations of recreational facilities to maintain discipline and ensure safety. Organize, lead, and promote interest in recreational activities such as arts, crafts, sports, games, camping, and hobbies. Manage the daily operations of recreational facilities. Administer first aid according to prescribed procedures and notify emergency medical personnel when necessary. Ascertain and interpret group interests, evaluate equipment and facilities, and adapt activities to meet participant needs. Greet new arrivals to activities, introducing them to other participants, explaining facility rules, and encouraging participation. Complete and maintain time and attendance forms and inventory lists. Explain principles, techniques, and safety procedures to participants in recreational activities and demonstrate use of materials and equipment. Evaluate recreation areas, facilities, and services to determine if they are producing desired results. Confer with management to discuss and resolve participant complaints. Supervise and coordinate the work activities of personnel, such as training staff members and assigning work duties. Meet and collaborate with agency personnel, community organizations, and other professional personnel to plan balanced recreational programs for participants. Schedule maintenance and use of facilities. Direct special activities or events such as aquatics, gymnastics, or performing arts. Meet with staff to discuss rules, regulations, and work-related problems. Provide for entertainment and set up related decorations and equipment. Encourage participants to develop their own activities and leadership skills through group discussions. Serve as liaison between park or recreation administrators and activity instructors. Evaluate staff performance, recording evaluations on appropriate forms. Oversee the purchase, planning, design, construction, and upkeep of recreation facilities and areas.

Personality Type: Social. Social occupations frequently involve working with, communicating with, and teaching people. These occupations often involve helping or providing service to others.

GOE—Interest Area: 09. Hospitality, Tourism, and Recreation. **Work Group:** 09.02. Recreational Services. **Other Jobs in This Work Group:** Amusement and Recreation Attendants; Gaming and Sports Book Writers and Runners; Gaming Dealers; Locker Room, Coatroom, and Dressing Room Attendants; Motion Picture Projectionists; Slot Key Persons; Ushers, Lobby Attendants, and Ticket Takers.

Skills—Management of Financial Resources: Determining how money will be spent to get the work done and accounting for these expenditures. **Management of Personnel Resources:** Motivating, developing, and directing people as they work; identifying the best people for the job. **Service Orientation:** Actively looking for ways to help people. **Management of Material Resources:** Obtaining and seeing to the appropriate use of equipment, facilities, and materials needed to do certain work. **Social Perceptiveness:** Being aware of others' reactions and understanding why they react as they do. **Time Management:** Managing one's own time and the time

of others. **Writing:** Communicating effectively in writing as appropriate for the needs of the audience. **Systems Evaluation:** Identifying measures or indicators of system performance and the actions needed to improve or correct performance relative to the goals of the system.

Education and Training Programs: Parks, Recreation, and Leisure Studies; Parks, Recreation, and Leisure Facilities Management; Sport and Fitness Administration/Management; Health and Physical Education/Fitness, Other; Parks, Recreation, Leisure, and Fitness Studies, Other. **Related Knowledge/ Courses: Psychology:** Human behavior and performance; individual differences in ability, personality, and interests; learning and motivation; psychological research methods; and the assessment and treatment of behavioral and affective disorders. **Customer and Personal Service:** Principles and processes for providing customer and personal services. This includes customer needs assessment, meeting quality standards for services, and evaluation of customer satisfaction. **Therapy and Counseling:** Principles, methods, and procedures for diagnosis, treatment, and rehabilitation of physical and mental dysfunctions and for career counseling and guidance. **Sociology and Anthropology:** Group behavior and dynamics, societal trends and influences, human migrations, ethnicity, and cultures and their history and origins. **Sales and Marketing:** Principles and methods for showing, promoting, and selling products or services. This includes marketing strategy and tactics, product demonstration, sales techniques, and sales control systems. **Clerical Practices:** Administrative and clerical procedures and systems such as word processing, managing files and records, stenography and transcription, designing forms, and other office procedures and terminology.

Work Environment: Indoors; noisy; more often standing than sitting; using hands on objects, tools, or controls.

Registered Nurses

- Annual Earnings: $54,670
- Growth: 29.4%
- Annual Job Openings: 229,000
- Education/Training Required: Associate degree
- Self-Employed: 0.7%
- Part-Time: 24.1%

How the Job Improves the World: Contributes to health.

Assess patient health problems and needs, develop and implement nursing care plans, and maintain medical records. Administer nursing care to ill, injured, convalescent, or disabled patients. May advise patients on health maintenance and disease prevention or provide case management. Licensing or registration required. Includes advance practice nurses, such as nurse practitioners, clinical nurse specialists, certified nurse midwives, and certified registered nurse anesthetists. Advanced practice nursing is practiced by RNs who have specialized formal, post-basic education and who function in highly autonomous and specialized roles. Maintain accurate, detailed reports and records. Monitor, record, and report symptoms and changes in patients' conditions. Record patients' medical information and vital signs. Modify patient treatment plans as indicated by patients' responses and conditions. Consult and coordinate with health care team members to assess, plan, implement, and evaluate patient care plans. Order, interpret, and evaluate diagnostic tests to identify and assess patient's condition. Monitor all aspects of patient care, including diet and physical activity. Direct and supervise less-skilled nursing or health care personnel or supervise a particular unit. Prepare patients for, and assist with, examinations and treatments. Observe nurses and visit patients to ensure proper nursing care. Assess the needs of individuals, families, or communities, including assessment of individuals' home or work environments, to identify potential health or safety problems. Instruct individuals, families, and other groups on topics such as health education, disease prevention, and childbirth; develop health improvement programs. Prepare rooms, sterile instruments, equipment, and supplies and ensure that stock of supplies is maintained. Inform physician of patient's condition during anesthesia. Deliver infants and provide prenatal and postpartum care and treatment under obstetrician's supervision. Administer local, inhalation, intravenous, and other anesthetics. Provide health care, first aid, immunizations, and assistance in convalescence and rehabilitation in locations such as schools, hospitals, and industry. Conduct specified laboratory tests. Perform physical examinations, make tentative diagnoses, and treat patients en route to hospitals or at disaster site triage centers. Hand items to surgeons during operations. Prescribe or recommend drugs; medical devices; or other forms of treatment, such as physical therapy, inhalation therapy, or related therapeutic procedures. Direct and coordinate infection control programs, advising and consulting with specified personnel about necessary precautions. Perform administrative and managerial functions, such as taking responsibility for a unit's staff, budget, planning, and long-range goals.

Personality Type: Social. Social occupations frequently involve working with, communicating with, and teaching people. These occupations often involve helping or providing service to others.

GOE—Interest Area: 08. Health Science. **Work Group:** 08.02. Medicine and Surgery. **Other Jobs in This Work Group:** Anesthesiologists; Family and General Practitioners; Internists, General; Medical Assistants; Medical Transcriptionists; Obstetricians and Gynecologists; Pediatricians, General; Pharmacists; Pharmacy Aides; Pharmacy Technicians; Physician Assistants; Psychiatrists; Surgeons; Surgical Technologists.

Skills—Social Perceptiveness: Being aware of others' reactions and understanding why they react as they do. **Service Orientation:** Actively looking for ways to help people. **Science:** Using scientific rules and methods to solve problems. **Time Management:** Managing one's own time and the time of others. **Monitoring:** Monitoring/assessing your performance or that of other individuals or organizations to make improvements or take corrective action. **Instructing:** Teaching others how to do something. **Critical Thinking:** Using logic and reasoning to identify the strengths and weaknesses of alternative solutions, conclusions, or approaches to problems. **Reading Comprehension:** Understanding written sentences and paragraphs in work-related documents.

Education and Training Programs: Nursing—Registered Nurse Training (RN, ASN, BSN, MSN); Adult Health Nurse/Nursing; Nurse Anesthetist; Family Practice Nurse/Nurse Practitioner; Maternal/Child Health and Neonatal Nurse/Nursing; Nurse Midwife/Nursing Midwifery; Nursing Science (MS, PhD); Pediatric Nurse/Nursing; Psychiatric/Mental Health Nurse/Nursing; Public Health/Community Nurse/Nursing; others. **Related Knowledge/Courses: Medicine and Dentistry:** The information and techniques needed to diagnose and treat human injuries, diseases, and deformities. This includes symptoms, treatment alternatives, drug properties and interactions, and preventive health-care measures. **Psychology:** Human behavior and performance; individual differences in ability, personality, and interests; learning and motivation; psychological research methods; and the assessment and treatment of behavioral and affective disorders. **Therapy and Counseling:** Principles, methods, and procedures for diagnosis, treatment, and rehabilitation of physical and mental dysfunctions and for career counseling and guidance. **Biology:** Plant and animal organisms and their tissues, cells, functions, interdependencies, and interactions with each other and the environment. **Sociology and**

Anthropology: Group behavior and dynamics, societal trends and influences, human migrations, ethnicity, and cultures and their history and origins. **Philosophy and Theology:** Different philosophical systems and religions. This includes their basic principles, values, ethics, ways of thinking, customs, and practices and their impact on human culture.

Work Environment: Indoors; noisy; contaminants; disease or infections; standing; using hands on objects, tools, or controls.

Residential Advisors

- Annual Earnings: $21,850
- Growth: 28.9%
- Annual Job Openings: 22,000
- Education/Training Required: Moderate-term on-the-job training
- Self-Employed: 0.0%
- Part-Time: 19.0%

How the Job Improves the World: Contributes to education.

Coordinate activities for residents of boarding schools, college fraternities or sororities, college dormitories, or similar establishments. Order supplies and determine need for maintenance, repairs, and furnishings. May maintain household records and assign rooms. May refer residents to counseling resources if needed. Enforce rules and regulations to ensure the smooth and orderly operation of dormitory programs. Provide emergency first aid and summon medical assistance when necessary. Mediate interpersonal problems between residents. Administer, coordinate, or recommend disciplinary and corrective actions. Communicate with other staff to resolve problems with individual students. Counsel students in the handling of issues such as family, financial, and educational problems. Make regular rounds to ensure that residents and areas are safe and secure. Observe students to detect and report unusual behavior. Determine the need for facility maintenance and repair and notify appropriate personnel. Collaborate with counselors to develop counseling programs that address the needs of individual students. Develop program plans for individuals or assist in plan development. Hold regular meetings with each assigned unit. Direct and participate in on- and off-campus recreational activities for residents of institutions, boarding schools, fraternities or sororities, children's homes, or similar establishments. Assign rooms to students. Provide requested information on students' progress and the development of case plans. Confer with medical personnel to better understand the backgrounds and needs of individual residents. Answer telephones and route calls or deliver messages. Supervise participants in work-study programs. Process contract cancellations for students who are unable to follow residence hall policies and procedures. Sort and distribute mail. Supervise the activities of housekeeping personnel. Order supplies for facilities. Supervise students' housekeeping work to ensure that it is done properly. Chaperone group-sponsored trips and social functions. Compile information such as residents' daily activities and the quantities of supplies used to prepare required reports. Accompany and supervise students during meals. Provide transportation or escort for expeditions such as shopping trips or visits to doctors or dentists. Inventory, pack, and remove items left behind by former residents.

Personality Type: Social. Social occupations frequently involve working with, communicating with, and teaching people. These occupations often involve helping or providing service to others.

GOE—Interest Area: 10. Human Service. **Work Group:** 10.01. Counseling and Social Work. **Other Jobs in This Work Group:** Child, Family, and School Social Workers; Clinical Psychologists; Clinical, Counseling, and School Psychologists; Counseling Psychologists; Marriage and Family Therapists; Medical and Public Health Social Workers; Mental Health and Substance Abuse Social Workers; Mental Health Counselors; Probation Officers and Correctional Treatment Specialists; Rehabilitation Counselors; Social and Human Service Assistants; Substance Abuse and Behavioral Disorder Counselors.

Skills—Social Perceptiveness: Being aware of others' reactions and understanding why they react as they do. **Monitoring:** Monitoring/assessing your performance or that of other individuals or organizations to make improvements or take corrective action. **Management of Personnel Resources:** Motivating, developing, and directing people as they work; identifying the best people for the job. **Persuasion:** Persuading others to change their minds or behavior. **Time Management:** Managing one's own time and the time of others. **Service Orientation:** Actively looking for ways to help people. **Management of Financial Resources:** Determining how money will be spent to get the work done and accounting for these expenditures. **Negotiation:** Bringing others together and trying to reconcile differences.

Education and Training Program: Hotel/Motel Administration/Management. **Related Knowledge/Courses: Therapy and Counseling:** Principles, methods, and procedures for diagnosis, treatment, and rehabilitation of physical and mental dysfunctions and for career counseling and guidance. **Philosophy and Theology:** Different philosophical systems and religions. This includes their basic principles, values, ethics, ways of thinking, customs, and practices and their impact on human culture. **Sociology and Anthropology:** Group behavior and dynamics, societal trends and influences, human migrations, ethnicity, and cultures and their history and origins. **Psychology:** Human behavior and performance; individual differences in ability, personality, and interests; learning and motivation; psychological research methods; and the assessment and treatment of behavioral and affective disorders. **Personnel and Human Resources:** Principles and procedures for personnel recruitment, selection, training, compensation and benefits, labor relations and negotiation, and personnel information systems. **Customer and Personal Service:** Principles and processes for providing customer and personal services. This includes customer needs assessment, meeting quality standards for services, and evaluation of customer satisfaction.

Work Environment: Indoors; noisy; sitting.

Respiratory Therapists

- Annual Earnings: $45,140
- Growth: 28.4%
- Annual Job Openings: 7,000
- Education/Training Required: Associate degree
- Self-Employed: 0.4%
- Part-Time: 15.9%

How the Job Improves the World: Contributes to health.

Assess, treat, and care for patients with breathing disorders. Assume primary responsibility for all respiratory care modalities, including the supervision of respiratory therapy technicians. Initiate and conduct therapeutic procedures; maintain patient records; and select, assemble, check, and operate equipment. Set up and operate devices such as mechanical ventilators, therapeutic gas administration apparatus, environmental control systems, and aerosol generators, following specified parameters of treatment. Provide emergency care, including artificial respiration, external cardiac massage, and assistance with cardiopulmonary resuscitation. Determine requirements for treatment, such as type, method, and duration of therapy; precautions to be taken; and medication and dosages, compatible with physicians' orders. Monitor patient's physiological responses to therapy, such as vital signs, arterial blood gases, and blood chemistry

changes, and consult with physician if adverse reactions occur. Read prescription, measure arterial blood gases, and review patient information to assess patient condition. Work as part of a team of physicians, nurses, and other health care professionals to manage patient care. Enforce safety rules and ensure careful adherence to physicians' orders. Maintain charts that contain patients' pertinent identification and therapy information. Inspect, clean, test, and maintain respiratory therapy equipment to ensure equipment is functioning safely and efficiently, ordering repairs when necessary. Educate patients and their families about their conditions and teach appropriate disease management techniques, such as breathing exercises and the use of medications and respiratory equipment. Explain treatment procedures to patients to gain cooperation and allay fears. Relay blood analysis results to a physician. Perform pulmonary function and adjust equipment to obtain optimum results in therapy. Perform bronchopulmonary drainage and assist or instruct patients in performance of breathing exercises. Demonstrate respiratory care procedures to trainees and other health care personnel. Teach, train, supervise, and utilize the assistance of students, respiratory therapy technicians, and assistants. Make emergency visits to resolve equipment problems. Use a variety of testing techniques to assist doctors in cardiac and pulmonary research and to diagnose disorders. Conduct tests, such as electrocardiograms (EKGs), stress testing, and lung capacity tests, to evaluate patients' cardiopulmonary functions.

Personality Type: Investigative. Investigative occupations frequently involve working with ideas and require an extensive amount of thinking. These occupations can involve searching for facts and figuring out problems mentally.

GOE—Interest Area: 08. Health Science. **Work Group:** 08.07. Medical Therapy. **Other Jobs in This Work Group:** Audiologists; Massage Therapists; Occupational Therapist Aides; Occupational Therapist Assistants; Occupational Therapists;

Physical Therapist Aides; Physical Therapist Assistants; Physical Therapists; Radiation Therapists; Recreational Therapists; Respiratory Therapy Technicians; Speech-Language Pathologists.

Skills—Science: Using scientific rules and methods to solve problems. **Operation Monitoring:** Watching gauges, dials, or other indicators to make sure a machine is working properly. **Mathematics:** Using mathematics to solve problems. **Instructing:** Teaching others how to do something. **Active Learning:** Understanding the implications of new information for both current and future problem-solving and decision-making. **Reading Comprehension:** Understanding written sentences and paragraphs in work-related documents. **Troubleshooting:** Determining causes of operating errors and deciding what to do about them. **Service Orientation:** Actively looking for ways to help people.

Education and Training Program: Respiratory Care Therapy/Therapist. **Related Knowledge/Courses: Medicine and Dentistry:** The information and techniques needed to diagnose and treat human injuries, diseases, and deformities. This includes symptoms, treatment alternatives, drug properties and interactions, and preventive health-care measures. **Biology:** Plant and animal organisms and their tissues, cells, functions, interdependencies, and interactions with each other and the environment. **Psychology:** Human behavior and performance; individual differences in ability, personality, and interests; learning and motivation; psychological research methods; and the assessment and treatment of behavioral and affective disorders. **Customer and Personal Service:** Principles and processes for providing customer and personal services. This includes customer needs assessment, meeting quality standards for services, and evaluation of customer satisfaction. **Therapy and Counseling:** Principles, methods, and procedures for diagnosis, treatment, and rehabilitation of physical and mental dysfunctions and for career counseling and guidance. **Chemistry:** The chemical composition, structure, and

properties of substances and of the chemical processes and transformations that they undergo. This includes uses of chemicals and their danger signs, production techniques, and disposal methods.

Work Environment: Indoors; disease or infections; standing.

School Psychologists

- Annual Earnings: $57,170
- Growth: 19.1%
- Annual Job Openings: 10,000
- Education/Training Required: Doctoral degree
- Self-Employed: 38.2%
- Part-Time: 22.8%

The job openings listed here are shared with Clinical Psychologists and with Counseling Psychologists.

How the Job Improves the World: Contributes to mental health.

Investigate processes of learning and teaching and develop psychological principles and techniques applicable to educational problems. Compile and interpret students' test results, along with information from teachers and parents, to diagnose conditions and to help assess eligibility for special services. Report any pertinent information to the proper authorities in cases of child endangerment, neglect, or abuse. Assess an individual child's needs, limitations, and potential, using observation, review of school records, and consultation with parents and school personnel. Select, administer, and score psychological tests. Provide consultation to parents, teachers, administrators, and others on topics such as learning styles and behavior modification techniques. Promote an understanding of child development and its relationship to learning and behavior. Collaborate with other educational professionals to develop teaching strategies and school programs. Counsel children and families to help solve conflicts and problems in learning and adjustment. Develop individualized educational plans in collaboration with teachers and other staff members. Maintain student records, including special education reports, confidential records, records of services provided, and behavioral data. Serve as a resource to help families and schools deal with crises, such as separation and loss. Attend workshops, seminars, or professional meetings to remain informed of new developments in school psychology. Design classes and programs to meet the needs of special students. Refer students and their families to appropriate community agencies for medical, vocational, or social services. Initiate and direct efforts to foster tolerance, understanding, and appreciation of diversity in school communities. Collect and analyze data to evaluate the effectiveness of academic programs and other services, such as behavioral management systems. Provide educational programs on topics such as classroom management, teaching strategies, or parenting skills. Conduct research to generate new knowledge that can be used to address learning and behavior issues.

Personality Type: Investigative. Investigative occupations frequently involve working with ideas and require an extensive amount of thinking. These occupations can involve searching for facts and figuring out problems mentally.

GOE—Interest Area: 15. Scientific Research, Engineering, and Mathematics. **Work Group:** 15.04. Social Sciences. **Other Jobs in This Work Group:** Anthropologists; Anthropologists and Archeologists; Archeologists; Economists; Historians; Industrial-Organizational Psychologists; Political Scientists; Sociologists.

Skills—Social Perceptiveness: Being aware of others' reactions and understanding why they react as they do. **Negotiation:** Bringing others together and trying to reconcile differences. **Learning Strategies:** Selecting

and using training/instructional methods and procedures appropriate for the situation when learning or teaching new things. **Persuasion:** Persuading others to change their minds or behavior. **Writing:** Communicating effectively in writing as appropriate for the needs of the audience. **Active Listening:** Giving full attention to what other people are saying, taking time to understand the points being made, asking questions as appropriate, and not interrupting at inappropriate times. **Service Orientation:** Actively looking for ways to help people. **Active Learning:** Understanding the implications of new information for both current and future problem-solving and decision-making.

Education and Training Programs: Educational Assessment, Testing, and Measurement; Psychology, General; Clinical Psychology; Counseling Psychology; Developmental and Child Psychology; School Psychology; Psychoanalysis and Psychotherapy. **Related Knowledge/Courses: Therapy and Counseling:** Principles, methods, and procedures for diagnosis, treatment, and rehabilitation of physical and mental dysfunctions and for career counseling and guidance. **Psychology:** Human behavior and performance; individual differences in ability, personality, and interests; learning and motivation; psychological research methods; and the assessment and treatment of behavioral and affective disorders. **Sociology and Anthropology:** Group behavior and dynamics, societal trends and influences, human migrations, ethnicity, and cultures and their history and origins. **Philosophy and Theology:** Different philosophical systems and religions. This includes their basic principles, values, ethics, ways of thinking, customs, and practices and their impact on human culture. **Education and Training:** Principles and methods for curriculum and training design, teaching and instruction for individuals and groups, and the measurement of training effects. **Customer and Personal Service:** Principles and processes for providing customer and personal services. This includes customer needs assessment, meeting quality standards for services, and evaluation of customer satisfaction.

Work Environment: Indoors; sitting.

Secondary School Teachers, Except Special and Vocational Education

- Annual Earnings: $46,060
- Growth: 14.4%
- Annual Job Openings: 107,000
- Education/Training Required: Bachelor's degree
- Self-Employed: 0.0%
- Part-Time: 9.2%

How the Job Improves the World: Contributes to education.

Instruct students in secondary public or private schools in one or more subjects at the secondary level, such as English, mathematics, or social studies. May be designated according to subject matter specialty, such as typing instructors, commercial teachers, or English teachers. Establish and enforce rules for behavior and procedures for maintaining order among the students for whom they are responsible. Instruct through lectures, discussions, and demonstrations in one or more subjects such as English, mathematics, or social studies. Establish clear objectives for all lessons, units, and projects and communicate those objectives to students. Prepare, administer, and grade tests and assignments to evaluate students' progress. Prepare materials and classrooms for class activities. Adapt teaching methods and instructional materials to meet students' varying needs and interests. Assign and grade classwork and homework. Maintain accurate and complete student records as required by laws, dis-

trict policies, and administrative regulations. Enforce all administration policies and rules governing students. Observe and evaluate students' performance, behavior, social development, and physical health. Plan and conduct activities for a balanced program of instruction, demonstration, and work time that provides students with opportunities to observe, question, and investigate. Prepare students for later grades by encouraging them to explore learning opportunities and to persevere with challenging tasks. Guide and counsel students with adjustment and/or academic problems or special academic interests. Instruct and monitor students in the use and care of equipment and materials to prevent injuries and damage. Prepare for assigned classes and show written evidence of preparation upon request of immediate supervisors. Meet with parents and guardians to discuss their children's progress and to determine their priorities for their children and their resource needs. Confer with parents or guardians, other teachers, counselors, and administrators in order to resolve students' behavioral and academic problems. Use computers, audiovisual aids, and other equipment and materials to supplement presentations. Prepare objectives and outlines for courses of study, following curriculum guidelines or requirements of states and schools. Meet with other professionals to discuss individual students' needs and progress.

Personality Type: Social. Social occupations frequently involve working with, communicating with, and teaching people. These occupations often involve helping or providing service to others.

GOE—Interest Area: 05. Education and Training. **Work Group:** 05.02. Preschool, Elementary, and Secondary Teaching and Instructing. **Other Jobs in This Work Group:** Elementary School Teachers, Except Special Education; Kindergarten Teachers, Except Special Education; Middle School Teachers, Except Special and Vocational Education; Preschool Teachers, Except Special Education; Special Education Teachers, Middle School; Special

S

Education Teachers, Preschool, Kindergarten, and Elementary School; Special Education Teachers, Secondary School; Teacher Assistants; Vocational Education Teachers, Middle School; Vocational Education Teachers, Secondary School.

Skills—Learning Strategies: Selecting and using training/instructional methods and procedures appropriate for the situation when learning or teaching new things. **Persuasion:** Persuading others to change their minds or behavior. **Social Perceptiveness:** Being aware of others' reactions and understanding why they react as they do. **Instructing:** Teaching others how to do something. **Monitoring:** Monitoring/assessing your performance or that of other individuals or organizations to make improvements or take corrective action. **Time Management:** Managing one's own time and the time of others. **Negotiation:** Bringing others together and trying to reconcile differences. **Service Orientation:** Actively looking for ways to help people.

Education and Training Programs: Junior High/Intermediate/Middle School Education and Teaching; Secondary Education and Teaching; Teacher Education, Multiple Levels; Waldorf/Steiner Teacher Education; Agricultural Teacher Education; Art Teacher Education; Business Teacher Education; Driver and Safety Teacher Education; English/Language Arts Teacher Education; Foreign Language Teacher Education; Health Teacher Education; others. **Related Knowledge/Courses: Education and Training:** Principles and methods for curriculum and training design, teaching and instruction for individuals and groups, and the measurement of training effects. **History and Archeology:** Historical events and their causes, indicators, and effects on civilizations and cultures. **Philosophy and Theology:** Different philosophical systems and religions. This includes their basic principles, values, ethics, ways of thinking, customs, and practices and their impact on human culture. **Sociology and Anthropology:** Group behavior and dynamics, societal trends and influences,

human migrations, ethnicity, and cultures and their history and origins. **Geography:** Principles and methods for describing the features of land, sea, and air masses, including their physical characteristics; locations; interrelationships; and distribution of plant, animal, and human life. **Therapy and Counseling:** Principles, methods, and procedures for diagnosis, treatment, and rehabilitation of physical and mental dysfunctions and for career counseling and guidance.

Work Environment: Indoors; noisy; standing.

Security Guards

- Annual Earnings: $20,760
- Growth: 12.6%
- Annual Job Openings: 230,000
- Education/Training Required: Short-term on-the-job training
- Self-Employed: 0.7%
- Part-Time: 17.1%

How the Job Improves the World: Contributes to safety and security.

Guard, patrol, or monitor premises to prevent theft, violence, or infractions of rules. Patrol industrial or commercial premises to prevent and detect signs of intrusion and ensure security of doors, windows, and gates. Answer alarms and investigate disturbances. Monitor and authorize entrance and departure of employees, visitors, and other persons to guard against theft and maintain security of premises. Write reports of daily activities and irregularities such as equipment or property damage, theft, presence of unauthorized persons, or unusual occurrences. Call police or fire departments in cases of emergency, such as fire or presence of unauthorized persons. Circulate among visitors, patrons, or employees to preserve order and protect property. Answer telephone calls to take messages, answer questions, and provide information during non-business hours or when switchboard is closed. Warn persons of rule infractions or violations and apprehend or evict violators from premises, using force when necessary. Operate detecting devices to screen individuals and prevent passage of prohibited articles into restricted areas. Escort or drive motor vehicle to transport individuals to specified locations or to provide personal protection. Inspect and adjust security systems, equipment, or machinery to ensure operational use and to detect evidence of tampering. Drive or guard armored vehicle to transport money and valuables to prevent theft and ensure safe delivery. Monitor and adjust controls that regulate building systems, such as air conditioning, furnace, or boiler.

Personality Type: Social. Social occupations frequently involve working with, communicating with, and teaching people. These occupations often involve helping or providing service to others.

GOE—Interest Area: 12. Law and Public Safety. **Work Group:** 12.05. Safety and Security. **Other Jobs in This Work Group:** Animal Control Workers; Crossing Guards; Gaming Surveillance Officers and Gaming Investigators; Lifeguards, Ski Patrol, and Other Recreational Protective Service Workers; Private Detectives and Investigators; Transportation Security Screeners.

Skills—No data available.

Education and Training Programs: Security and Loss Prevention Services; Securities Services Administration/Management. **Related Knowledge/Courses: Public Safety and Security:** Relevant equipment, policies, procedures, and strategies to promote effective local, state, or national security operations for the protection of people, data, property, and institutions. **Customer and Personal Service:** Principles and processes for providing customer and personal services. This includes customer needs assessment, meeting quality standards for services, and evaluation of customer satisfaction. **Telecommunications:** Transmission, broadcasting, switching, control, and operation of telecommunications systems. **Law and Government:** Laws, legal codes, court procedures, precedents, government regulations, executive orders, agency rules, and the democratic political process. **Clerical Practices:** Administrative and clerical procedures and systems such as word processing, managing files and records, stenography and transcription, designing forms, and other office procedures and terminology. **Transportation:** Principles and methods for moving people or goods by air, rail, sea, or road, including the relative costs and benefits.

Work Environment: More often outdoors than indoors; noisy; very hot or cold; more often sitting than standing.

Self-Enrichment Education Teachers

- Annual Earnings: $32,360
- Growth: 25.3%
- Annual Job Openings: 74,000
- Education/Training Required: Work experience in a related occupation
- Self-Employed: 31.1%
- Part-Time: 45.6%

How the Job Improves the World: Contributes to education.

Teach or instruct courses other than those that normally lead to an occupational objective or degree. Courses may include self-improvement, nonvocational, and nonacademic subjects. Teaching may or may not take place in a traditional educational institution. Adapt teaching methods and instructional materials to meet students' varying needs and interests. Conduct classes, workshops, and demonstrations and provide individual instruction to teach topics and skills such as cooking, dancing, writing, physical fitness, photography, personal finance, and flying.

Monitor students' performance to make suggestions for improvement and to ensure that they satisfy course standards, training requirements, and objectives. Observe students to determine qualifications, limitations, abilities, interests, and other individual characteristics. Instruct students individually and in groups, using various teaching methods such as lectures, discussions, and demonstrations. Establish clear objectives for all lessons, units, and projects and communicate those objectives to students. Instruct and monitor students in use and care of equipment and materials to prevent injury and damage. Prepare students for further development by encouraging them to explore learning opportunities and to persevere with challenging tasks. Prepare materials and classrooms for class activities. Enforce policies and rules governing students. Plan and conduct activities for a balanced program of instruction, demonstration, and work time that provides students with opportunities to observe, question, and investigate. Prepare instructional program objectives, outlines, and lesson plans. Maintain accurate and complete student records as required by administrative policy. Participate in publicity planning and student recruitment. Plan and supervise class projects, field trips, visits by guest speakers, contests, or other experiential activities and guide students in learning from those activities. Attend professional meetings, conferences, and workshops in order to maintain and improve professional competence. Meet with other instructors to discuss individual students and their progress. Confer with other teachers and professionals to plan and schedule lessons promoting learning and development. Attend staff meetings and serve on committees as required. Prepare and administer written, oral, and performance tests and issue grades in accordance with performance.

Personality Type: Social. Social occupations frequently involve working with, communicating with, and teaching people. These occupations often involve helping or providing service to others.

GOE—Interest Area: 05. Education and Training. **Work Group:** 05.03. Postsecondary and Adult Teaching and Instructing. **Other Jobs in This Work Group:** Adult Literacy, Remedial Education, and GED Teachers and Instructors; Agricultural Sciences Teachers, Postsecondary; Anthropology and Archeology Teachers, Postsecondary; Architecture Teachers, Postsecondary; Area, Ethnic, and Cultural Studies Teachers, Postsecondary; Art, Drama, and Music Teachers, Postsecondary; Atmospheric, Earth, Marine, and Space Sciences Teachers, Postsecondary; Biological Science Teachers, Postsecondary; Business Teachers, Postsecondary; Chemistry Teachers, Postsecondary; Communications Teachers, Postsecondary; Computer Science Teachers, Postsecondary; Criminal Justice and Law Enforcement Teachers, Postsecondary; Economics Teachers, Postsecondary; Education Teachers, Postsecondary; Engineering Teachers, Postsecondary; English Language and Literature Teachers, Postsecondary; Environmental Science Teachers, Postsecondary; Farm and Home Management Advisors; Foreign Language and Literature Teachers, Postsecondary; Forestry and Conservation Science Teachers, Postsecondary; Geography Teachers, Postsecondary; Graduate Teaching Assistants; Health Specialties Teachers, Postsecondary; History Teachers, Postsecondary; Home Economics Teachers, Postsecondary; Law Teachers, Postsecondary; Library Science Teachers, Postsecondary; Mathematical Science Teachers, Postsecondary; Nursing Instructors and Teachers, Postsecondary; Philosophy and Religion Teachers, Postsecondary; Physics Teachers, Postsecondary; Political Science Teachers, Postsecondary; Psychology Teachers, Postsecondary; Recreation and Fitness Studies Teachers, Postsecondary; Social Work Teachers, Postsecondary; Sociology Teachers, Postsecondary; Vocational Education Teachers, Postsecondary.

Skills—Instructing: Teaching others how to do something. **Learning Strategies:** Selecting and using training/instructional methods and procedures appropriate for the situation when learning or teaching new things. **Social Perceptiveness:** Being aware of others' reactions and understanding why they react as they do. **Service Orientation:** Actively looking for ways to help people. **Monitoring:** Monitoring/assessing your performance or that of other individuals or organizations to make improvements or take corrective action. **Speaking:** Talking to others to convey information effectively. **Persuasion:** Persuading others to change their minds or behavior. **Time Management:** Managing one's own time and the time of others.

Education and Training Program: Adult and Continuing Education and Teaching. **Related Knowledge/Courses: Fine Arts:** The theory and techniques required to compose, produce, and perform works of music, dance, visual art, drama, and sculpture. **Education and Training:** Principles and methods for curriculum and training design, teaching and instruction for individuals and groups, and the measurement of training effects. **Psychology:** Human behavior and performance; individual differences in ability, personality, and interests; learning and motivation; psychological research methods; and the assessment and treatment of behavioral and affective disorders. **Customer and Personal Service:** Principles and processes for providing customer and personal services. This includes customer needs assessment, meeting quality standards for services, and evaluation of customer satisfaction. **Sales and Marketing:** Principles and methods for showing, promoting, and selling products or services. This includes marketing strategy and tactics, product demonstration, sales techniques, and sales control systems. **Administration and Management:** Business and management principles involved in strategic planning, resource allocation, human resources modeling, leadership techniques, production methods, and coordination of people and resources.

Work Environment: Indoors; standing.

Set and Exhibit Designers

- Annual Earnings: $37,390
- Growth: 9.3%
- Annual Job Openings: 2,000
- Education/Training Required: Bachelor's degree
- Self-Employed: 27.6%
- Part-Time: 21.3%

How the Job Improves the World: Contributes to the arts and education.

Design special exhibits and movie, television, and theater sets. May study scripts, confer with directors, and conduct research to determine appropriate architectural styles. Examine objects to be included in exhibits to plan where and how to display them. Acquire, or arrange for acquisition of, specimens or graphics required to complete exhibits. Prepare rough drafts and scale working drawings of sets, including floor plans, scenery, and properties to be constructed. Confer with clients and staff to gather information about exhibit space, proposed themes and content, timelines, budgets, materials, and promotion requirements. Estimate set- or exhibit-related costs, including materials, construction, and rental of props or locations. Develop set designs based on evaluation of scripts, budgets, research information, and available locations. Direct and coordinate construction, erection, or decoration activities to ensure that sets or exhibits meet design, budget, and schedule requirements. Inspect installed exhibits for conformance to specifications and satisfactory operation of special effects components. Plan for location-specific issues such as space limitations, traffic flow patterns, and safety concerns. Submit plans for approval and adapt plans to serve intended purposes or to conform to budget or fabrication restrictions. Prepare preliminary renderings of proposed exhibits, including detailed construction, layout, and material specifications and diagrams relating to aspects such as special effects and lighting. Select and purchase lumber and hardware necessary for set construction. Collaborate with those in charge of lighting and sound so that those production aspects can be coordinated with set designs or exhibit layouts. Research architectural and stylistic elements appropriate to the time period to be depicted, consulting experts for information as necessary. Design and produce displays and materials that can be used to decorate windows, interior displays, or event locations such as streets and fairgrounds. Coordinate the removal of sets, props, and exhibits after productions or events are complete. Select set props such as furniture, pictures, lamps, and rugs. Confer with conservators to determine how to handle an exhibit's environmental aspects, such as lighting, temperature, and humidity, so that objects will be protected and exhibits will be enhanced.

Personality Type: Artistic. Artistic occupations frequently involve working with forms, designs, and patterns. They often require self-expression, and the work can be done without following a clear set of rules.

GOE—Interest Area: 03. Arts and Communication. **Work Group:** 03.05. Design. **Other Jobs in This Work Group:** Commercial and Industrial Designers; Fashion Designers; Floral Designers; Graphic Designers; Interior Designers; Merchandise Displayers and Window Trimmers.

Skills—Persuasion: Persuading others to change their minds or behavior. **Installation:** Installing equipment, machines, wiring, or programs to meet specifications. **Management of Material Resources:** Obtaining and seeing to the appropriate use of equipment, facilities,

and materials needed to do certain work. **Management of Personnel Resources:** Motivating, developing, and directing people as they work; identifying the best people for the job. **Operations Analysis:** Analyzing needs and product requirements to create a design. **Negotiation:** Bringing others together and trying to reconcile differences. **Management of Financial Resources:** Determining how money will be spent to get the work done and accounting for these expenditures. **Coordination:** Adjusting actions in relation to others' actions.

Education and Training Programs: Design and Visual Communications, General; Illustration; Design and Applied Arts, Other; Technical Theatre/Theatre Design and Technology. **Related Knowledge/Courses: Fine Arts:** The theory and techniques required to compose, produce, and perform works of music, dance, visual art, drama, and sculpture. **Design:** Design techniques, tools, and principles involved in production of precision technical plans, blueprints, drawings, and models. **History and Archeology:** Historical events and their causes, indicators, and effects on civilizations and cultures. **Communications and Media:** Media production, communication, and dissemination techniques and methods. This includes alternative ways to inform and entertain via written, oral, and visual media. **Sociology and Anthropology:** Group behavior and dynamics, societal trends and influences, human migrations, ethnicity, and cultures and their history and origins. **Computers and Electronics:** Circuit boards; processors; chips; electronic equipment; and computer hardware and software, including applications and programming.

Work Environment: Indoors; sitting; using hands on objects, tools, or controls.

Sheriffs and Deputy Sheriffs

- Annual Earnings: $46,290
- Growth: 15.5%
- Annual Job Openings: 47,000
- Education/Training Required: Long-term on-the-job training
- Self-Employed: 0.0%
- Part-Time: 1.4%

The job openings listed here are shared with Police Patrol Officers.

How the Job Improves the World: Contributes to justice and law enforcement.

Enforce law and order in rural or unincorporated districts or serve legal processes of courts. May patrol courthouse, guard court or grand jury, or escort defendants. Drive vehicles or patrol specific areas to detect law violators, issue citations, and make arrests. Investigate illegal or suspicious activities. Verify that the proper legal charges have been made against law offenders. Execute arrest warrants, locating and taking persons into custody. Record daily activities and submit logs and other related reports and paperwork to appropriate authorities. Patrol and guard courthouses, grand jury rooms, or assigned areas to provide security, enforce laws, maintain order, and arrest violators. Notify patrol units to take violators into custody or to provide needed assistance or medical aid. Place people in protective custody. Serve statements of claims, subpoenas, summonses, jury summonses, orders to pay alimony, and other court orders. Take control of accident scenes to maintain traffic flow, to assist accident victims, and to investigate causes. Question individuals entering secured areas to determine their business, directing and rerouting individuals as necessary. Transport or escort prisoners and defendants en route to courtrooms, prisons or jails, attorneys' offices, or medical facilities. Locate and confiscate real or personal property, as directed by court order. Manage jail operations and tend to jail inmates.

Personality Type: Social. Social occupations frequently involve working with, communicating with, and teaching people. These occupations often involve helping or providing service to others.

GOE—Interest Area: 12. Law and Public Safety. **Work Group:** 12.04. Law Enforcement and Public Safety. **Other Jobs in This Work Group:** Bailiffs; Correctional Officers and Jailers; Criminal Investigators and Special Agents; Detectives and Criminal Investigators; Fire Investigators; Forensic Science Technicians; Parking Enforcement Workers; Police and Sheriff's Patrol Officers; Police Detectives; Police Identification and Records Officers; Police Patrol Officers; Transit and Railroad Police.

Skills—Negotiation: Bringing others together and trying to reconcile differences. **Persuasion:** Persuading others to change their minds or behavior. **Social Perceptiveness:** Being aware of others' reactions and understanding why they react as they do. **Service Orientation:** Actively looking for ways to help people. **Complex Problem Solving:** Identifying complex problems and reviewing related information to develop and evaluate options and implement solutions. **Judgment and Decision Making:** Considering the relative costs and benefits of potential actions to choose the most appropriate one. **Coordination:** Adjusting actions in relation to others' actions. **Equipment Selection:** Determining the kind of tools and equipment needed to do a job.

Education and Training Programs: Criminal Justice/Police Science; Criminalistics and Criminal Science. **Related Knowledge/Courses: Public Safety and Security:** Relevant equipment, policies, procedures, and strategies to promote effective local, state, or national security operations for the protection of people, data, property, and institutions. **Law and Government:** Laws, legal codes, court procedures, precedents, government regulations, executive orders, agency rules, and the democratic political process. **Telecommunications:** Transmission, broadcasting, switching, control, and operation of telecommunications systems. **Psychology:** Human behavior and performance; individual differences in ability, personality, and interests; learning and motivation; psychological research methods; and the assessment and treatment of behavioral and affective disorders. **Therapy and Counseling:** Principles, methods, and procedures for diagnosis, treatment, and rehabilitation of physical and mental dysfunctions and for career counseling and guidance. **Customer and Personal Service:** Principles and processes for providing customer and personal services. This includes customer needs assessment, meeting quality standards for services, and evaluation of customer satisfaction.

Work Environment: More often outdoors than indoors; very hot or cold; contaminants; disease or infections; sitting.

Social and Community Service Managers

- ◎ Annual Earnings: $49,500
- ◎ Growth: 25.5%
- ◎ Annual Job Openings: 17,000
- ◎ Education/Training Required: Bachelor's degree
- ◎ Self-Employed: 2.2%
- ◎ Part-Time: 12.5%

How the Job Improves the World: Contributes to social well-being.

Plan, organize, or coordinate the activities of a social service program or community outreach organization. Oversee the program or organization's budget and policies regarding participant involvement, program requirements, and benefits. Work may involve directing social workers, counselors, or probation officers. Establish and maintain relationships with other agencies and organizations in community to meet community needs and to ensure that services are not duplicated. Prepare and maintain records and reports, such as budgets, personnel records, or training manuals. Direct activities of professional and technical staff members and volunteers. Evaluate the work of staff and volunteers to ensure that programs are of appropriate quality and that resources are used effectively. Establish and oversee administrative procedures to meet objectives set by boards of directors or senior management. Participate in the determination of organizational policies regarding such issues as participant eligibility, program requirements, and program benefits. Research and analyze member or community needs to determine program directions and goals. Speak to community groups to explain and interpret agency purposes, programs, and policies. Recruit, interview, and hire or sign up volunteers and staff. Represent organizations in relations with governmental and media institutions. Plan and administer budgets for programs, equipment, and support services. Analyze proposed legislation, regulations, or rule changes to determine how agency services could be impacted. Act as consultants to agency staff and other community programs regarding the interpretation of program-related federal, state, and county regulations and policies. Implement and evaluate staff training programs. Direct fundraising activities and the preparation of public relations materials.

Personality Type: Social. Social occupations frequently involve working with, communicating with, and teaching people. These occupations often involve helping or providing service to others.

GOE—Interest Area: 07. Government and Public Administration. **Work Group:** 07.01. Managerial Work in Government and Public Administration. **Other Jobs in This Work Group:** No other jobs in this group.

Skills—**Management of Personnel Resources:** Motivating, developing, and directing people as they work; identifying the best people for the job. **Social Perceptiveness:** Being aware of others' reactions and understanding why they react as they do. **Negotiation:** Bringing others together and trying to reconcile differences. **Service Orientation:** Actively looking for ways to help people. **Systems Evaluation:** Identifying measures or indicators of system performance and the actions needed to improve or correct performance relative to the goals of the system. **Persuasion:** Persuading others to change their minds or behavior. **Monitoring:** Monitoring/assessing your performance or that of other individuals or organizations to make improvements or take corrective action. **Management of Financial Resources:** Determining how money will be spent to get the work done and accounting for these expenditures.

Education and Training Programs: Human Services, General; Community Organization and Advocacy; Public Administration; Business/Commerce, General; Business Administration and Management, General; Non-Profit/Public/Organizational Management; Entrepreneurship/Entrepreneurial Studies; Business, Management, Marketing, and Related Support Services, Other. **Related Knowledge/Courses: Sociology and Anthropology:** Group behavior and dynamics, societal trends and influences, human migrations, ethnicity, and cultures and their history and origins. **Therapy and Counseling:** Principles, methods, and procedures for diagnosis, treatment, and rehabilitation of physical and mental dysfunctions and for career counseling and guidance. **Psychology:** Human behavior and performance; individual differences in ability, personality, and interests; learning and motivation; psychological research methods; and the assessment and treatment of behavioral and affective disorders. **Education and Training:** Principles and methods for curriculum and training design, teaching and instruction for individuals and groups, and the measurement of training effects. **Philosophy and**

Theology: Different philosophical systems and religions. This includes their basic principles, values, ethics, ways of thinking, customs, and practices and their impact on human culture. **Clerical Practices:** Administrative and clerical procedures and systems such as word processing, managing files and records, stenography and transcription, designing forms, and other office procedures and terminology.

Work Environment: Indoors; noisy; sitting.

Social and Human Service Assistants

- ◉ Annual Earnings: $25,030
- ◉ Growth: 29.7%
- ◉ Annual Job Openings: 61,000
- ◉ Education/Training Required: Moderate-term on-the-job training
- ◉ Self-Employed: 0.1%
- ◉ Part-Time: 16.0%

How the Job Improves the World: Contributes to social well-being.

Assist professionals from a wide variety of fields, such as psychology, rehabilitation, or social work, to provide client services, as well as support for families. May assist clients in identifying available benefits and social and community services and help clients obtain them. May assist social workers with developing, organizing, and conducting programs to prevent and resolve problems relevant to substance abuse, human relationships, rehabilitation, or adult daycare. Provide information and refer individuals to public or private agencies or community services for assistance. Keep records and prepare reports for owner or management concerning visits with clients. Visit individuals in homes or attend group meetings to provide information on agency services, requirements, and procedures. Advise clients regarding food stamps, child care, food, money management, sanitation, or housekeeping. Submit reports and review reports or problems with superior. Oversee day-to-day group activities of residents in institution. Interview individuals and family members to compile information on social, educational, criminal, institutional, or drug history. Meet with youth groups to acquaint them with consequences of delinquent acts. Transport and accompany clients to shopping areas or to appointments, using automobile. Explain rules established by owner or management, such as sanitation and maintenance requirements and parking regulations. Observe and discuss meal preparation and suggest alternate methods of food preparation. Demonstrate use and care of equipment for tenant use. Consult with supervisor concerning programs for individual families. Monitor free, supplementary meal program to ensure cleanliness of facility and that eligibility guidelines are met for persons receiving meals. Observe clients' food selections and recommend alternate economical and nutritional food choices. Inform tenants of facilities such as laundries and playgrounds. Care for children in client's home during client's appointments. Assist in locating housing for displaced individuals. Assist clients with preparation of forms, such as tax or rent forms. Assist in planning of food budget, using charts and sample budgets.

Personality Type: Social. Social occupations frequently involve working with, communicating with, and teaching people. These occupations often involve helping or providing service to others.

GOE—Interest Area: 10. Human Service. **Work Group:** 10.01. Counseling and Social Work. **Other Jobs in This Work Group:** Child, Family, and School Social Workers; Clinical Psychologists; Clinical, Counseling, and School Psychologists; Counseling Psychologists; Marriage and Family Therapists; Medical and Public Health Social Workers; Mental Health and Substance Abuse Social Workers; Mental Health Counselors; Probation Officers and Correctional Treatment Specialists; Rehabilitation Counselors; Residential Advisors; Substance Abuse and Behavioral Disorder Counselors.

Skills—Social Perceptiveness: Being aware of others' reactions and understanding why they react as they do. **Management of Financial Resources:** Determining how money will be spent to get the work done and accounting for these expenditures. **Service Orientation:** Actively looking for ways to help people. **Speaking:** Talking to others to convey information effectively. **Judgment and Decision Making:** Considering the relative costs and benefits of potential actions to choose the most appropriate one. **Active Listening:** Giving full attention to what other people are saying, taking time to understand the points being made, asking questions as appropriate, and not interrupting at inappropriate times. **Time Management:** Managing one's own time and the time of others. **Learning Strategies:** Selecting and using training/instructional methods and procedures appropriate for the situation when learning or teaching new things.

Education and Training Program: Mental and Social Health Services and Allied Professions, Other. **Related Knowledge/Courses: Therapy and Counseling:** Principles, methods, and procedures for diagnosis, treatment, and rehabilitation of physical and mental dysfunctions and for career counseling and guidance. **Psychology:** Human behavior and performance; individual differences in ability, personality, and interests; learning and motivation; psychological research methods; and the assessment and treatment of behavioral and affective disorders. **Philosophy and Theology:** Different philosophical systems and religions. This includes their basic principles, values, ethics, ways of thinking, customs, and practices and their impact on human culture. **Sociology and Anthropology:** Group behavior and dynamics, societal trends and influences, human migrations, ethnicity, and cultures and their history and origins. **Clerical Practices:** Administrative and clerical procedures and systems such as word processing, managing files and records, stenography and transcription, designing forms, and other office procedures and terminology. **Customer and Personal Service:** Principles and processes for providing customer and personal services. This includes customer needs assessment, meeting quality standards for services, and evaluation of customer satisfaction.

Work Environment: Indoors; noisy; sitting.

Social Work Teachers, Postsecondary

- Annual Earnings: $52,660
- Growth: 32.2%
- Annual Job Openings: 329,000
- Education/Training Required: Master's degree
- Self-Employed: 0.4%
- Part-Time: 27.3%

The job openings listed here are shared with 35 other postsecondary teaching occupations. For a complete list, see the beginning of this section.

How the Job Improves the World: Contributes to education, health, and social welfare.

Teach courses in social work. Initiate, facilitate, and moderate classroom discussions. Evaluate and grade students' classwork, assignments, and papers. Prepare and deliver lectures to undergraduate or graduate students on topics such as family behavior, child and adolescent mental health, and social intervention evaluation. Keep abreast of developments in their field by reading current literature, talking with colleagues, and participating in professional conferences. Supervise students' laboratory work and fieldwork. Conduct research in a particular field of knowledge and publish findings in professional journals, books, or electronic media. Prepare course materials such as syllabi, homework assignments, and handouts. Maintain regularly scheduled office hours to advise

and assist students. Supervise undergraduate or graduate teaching, internship, and research work. Plan, evaluate, and revise curricula, course content, and course materials and methods of instruction. Collaborate with colleagues and with community agencies to address teaching and research issues. Compile, administer, and grade examinations or assign this work to others. Advise students on academic and vocational curricula and on career issues. Maintain student attendance records, grades, and other required records. Write grant proposals to procure external research funding. Serve on academic or administrative committees that deal with institutional policies, departmental matters, and academic issues. Perform administrative duties such as serving as department head. Compile bibliographies of specialized materials for outside reading assignments. Select and obtain materials and supplies such as textbooks and laboratory equipment. Participate in student recruitment, registration, and placement activities. Participate in campus and community events. Provide professional consulting services to government and industry. Act as advisers to student organizations.

Personality Type: No data available.

GOE—Interest Area: 05. Education and Training. **Work Group:** 05.03. Postsecondary and Adult Teaching and Instructing. **Other Jobs in This Work Group:** Adult Literacy, Remedial Education, and GED Teachers and Instructors; Agricultural Sciences Teachers, Postsecondary; Anthropology and Archeology Teachers, Postsecondary; Architecture Teachers, Postsecondary; Area, Ethnic, and Cultural Studies Teachers, Postsecondary; Art, Drama, and Music Teachers, Postsecondary; Atmospheric, Earth, Marine, and Space Sciences Teachers, Postsecondary; Biological Science Teachers, Postsecondary; Business Teachers, Postsecondary; Chemistry Teachers, Postsecondary; Communications Teachers, Postsecondary; Computer Science Teachers, Postsecondary; Criminal Justice and Law Enforcement Teachers, Postsecondary; Economics Teachers, Postsecondary;

Education Teachers, Postsecondary; Engineering Teachers, Postsecondary; English Language and Literature Teachers, Postsecondary; Environmental Science Teachers, Postsecondary; Farm and Home Management Advisors; Foreign Language and Literature Teachers, Postsecondary; Forestry and Conservation Science Teachers, Postsecondary; Geography Teachers, Postsecondary; Graduate Teaching Assistants; Health Specialties Teachers, Postsecondary; History Teachers, Postsecondary; Home Economics Teachers, Postsecondary; Law Teachers, Postsecondary; Library Science Teachers, Postsecondary; Mathematical Science Teachers, Postsecondary; Nursing Instructors and Teachers, Postsecondary; Philosophy and Religion Teachers, Postsecondary; Physics Teachers, Postsecondary; Political Science Teachers, Postsecondary; Psychology Teachers, Postsecondary; Recreation and Fitness Studies Teachers, Postsecondary; Self-Enrichment Education Teachers; Sociology Teachers, Postsecondary; Vocational Education Teachers, Postsecondary.

Skills—Social Perceptiveness: Being aware of others' reactions and understanding why they react as they do. **Service Orientation:** Actively looking for ways to help people. **Instructing:** Teaching others how to do something. **Learning Strategies:** Selecting and using training/instructional methods and procedures appropriate for the situation when learning or teaching new things. **Complex Problem Solving:** Identifying complex problems and reviewing related information to develop and evaluate options and implement solutions. **Writing:** Communicating effectively in writing as appropriate for the needs of the audience. **Critical Thinking:** Using logic and reasoning to identify the strengths and weaknesses of alternative solutions, conclusions, or approaches to problems. **Negotiation:** Bringing others together and trying to reconcile differences.

Education and Training Programs: Teacher Education and Professional Development, Specific Subject Areas, Other; Social Work; Clinical/Medical Social Work. **Related Knowledge/Courses: Therapy and Counseling:** Principles, methods, and procedures for diagnosis, treatment, and rehabilitation of physical and mental dysfunctions and for career counseling and guidance. **Sociology and Anthropology:** Group behavior and dynamics, societal trends and influences, human migrations, ethnicity, and cultures and their history and origins. **Psychology:** Human behavior and performance; individual differences in ability, personality, and interests; learning and motivation; psychological research methods; and the assessment and treatment of behavioral and affective disorders. **Education and Training:** Principles and methods for curriculum and training design, teaching and instruction for individuals and groups, and the measurement of training effects. **Philosophy and Theology:** Different philosophical systems and religions. This includes their basic principles, values, ethics, ways of thinking, customs, and practices and their impact on human culture. **English Language:** The structure and content of the English language, including the meaning and spelling of words, rules of composition, and grammar.

Work Environment: Indoors; sitting.

Sociology Teachers, Postsecondary

- Annual Earnings: $54,320
- Growth: 32.2%
- Annual Job Openings: 329,000
- Education/Training Required: Master's degree
- Self-Employed: 0.4%
- Part-Time: 27.3%

The job openings listed here are shared with 35 other postsecondary teaching occupations. For a complete list, see the beginning of this section.

How the Job Improves the World: Contributes to education and social harmony.

Teach courses in sociology. Evaluate and grade students' classwork, assignments, and papers. Prepare and deliver lectures to undergraduate and graduate students on topics such as race and ethnic relations, measurement and data collection, and workplace social relations. Initiate, facilitate, and moderate classroom discussions. Prepare course materials such as syllabi, homework assignments, and handouts. Compile, administer, and grade examinations or assign this work to others. Keep abreast of developments in their field by reading current literature, talking with colleagues, and participating in professional conferences. Maintain student attendance records, grades, and other required records. Maintain regularly scheduled office hours in order to advise and assist students. Plan, evaluate, and revise curricula, course content, and course materials and methods of instruction. Advise students on academic and vocational curricula and on career issues. Collaborate with colleagues to address teaching and research issues. Conduct research in a particular field of knowledge and publish findings in professional journals, books, or electronic media. Select and obtain materials and supplies such as textbooks and laboratory equipment. Supervise undergraduate and graduate teaching, internship, and research work. Serve on academic or administrative committees that deal with institutional policies, departmental matters, and academic issues. Participate in student recruitment, registration, and placement activities. Perform administrative duties such as serving as department head. Supervise students' laboratory work and fieldwork. Write grant proposals to procure external research funding. Act as advisers to student organizations. Compile bibliographies of specialized materials for outside reading assignments. Participate in campus and community events. Provide professional consulting services to government and industry.

Personality Type: Social. Social occupations frequently involve working with, communicating with, and teaching people. These occupations often involve helping or providing service to others.

GOE—Interest Area: 05. Education and Training. **Work Group:** 05.03. Postsecondary and Adult Teaching and Instructing. **Other Jobs in This Work Group:** Adult Literacy, Remedial Education, and GED Teachers and Instructors; Agricultural Sciences Teachers, Postsecondary; Anthropology and Archeology Teachers, Postsecondary; Architecture Teachers, Postsecondary; Area, Ethnic, and Cultural Studies Teachers, Postsecondary; Art, Drama, and Music Teachers, Postsecondary; Atmospheric, Earth, Marine, and Space Sciences Teachers, Postsecondary; Biological Science Teachers, Postsecondary; Business Teachers, Postsecondary; Chemistry Teachers, Postsecondary; Communications Teachers, Postsecondary; Computer Science Teachers, Postsecondary; Criminal Justice and Law Enforcement Teachers, Postsecondary; Economics Teachers, Postsecondary; Education Teachers, Postsecondary; Engineering Teachers, Postsecondary; English Language and Literature Teachers, Postsecondary; Environmental Science Teachers, Postsecondary; Farm and Home Management Advisors; Foreign Language and Literature Teachers, Postsecondary; Forestry and Conservation Science Teachers, Postsecondary; Geography Teachers, Postsecondary; Graduate Teaching Assistants; Health Specialties Teachers, Postsecondary; History Teachers, Postsecondary; Home Economics Teachers, Postsecondary; Law Teachers, Postsecondary; Library Science Teachers, Postsecondary; Mathematical Science Teachers, Postsecondary; Nursing Instructors and Teachers, Postsecondary; Philosophy and Religion Teachers, Postsecondary; Physics Teachers, Postsecondary; Political Science Teachers, Postsecondary; Psychology Teachers, Postsecondary; Recreation and Fitness Studies Teachers, Postsecondary; Self-Enrichment Education Teachers; Social Work Teachers,

Postsecondary; Vocational Education Teachers, Postsecondary.

Skills—Instructing: Teaching others how to do something. **Learning Strategies:** Selecting and using training/instructional methods and procedures appropriate for the situation when learning or teaching new things. **Writing:** Communicating effectively in writing as appropriate for the needs of the audience. **Science:** Using scientific rules and methods to solve problems. **Social Perceptiveness:** Being aware of others' reactions and understanding why they react as they do. **Critical Thinking:** Using logic and reasoning to identify the strengths and weaknesses of alternative solutions, conclusions, or approaches to problems. **Active Learning:** Understanding the implications of new information for both current and future problem-solving and decision-making. **Speaking:** Talking to others to convey information effectively.

Education and Training Programs: Social Science Teacher Education; Sociology. **Related Knowledge/Courses: Sociology and Anthropology:** Group behavior and dynamics, societal trends and influences, human migrations, ethnicity, and cultures and their history and origins. **Philosophy and Theology:** Different philosophical systems and religions. This includes their basic principles, values, ethics, ways of thinking, customs, and practices and their impact on human culture. **History and Archeology:** Historical events and their causes, indicators, and effects on civilizations and cultures. **Education and Training:** Principles and methods for curriculum and training design, teaching and instruction for individuals and groups, and the measurement of training effects. **English Language:** The structure and content of the English language, including the meaning and spelling of words, rules of composition, and grammar. **Psychology:** Human behavior and performance; individual differences in ability, personality, and interests; learning and motivation; psychological research methods; and the assessment and treatment of behavioral and affective disorders.

Work Environment: Indoors; sitting.

Soil and Water Conservationists

- Annual Earnings: $53,350
- Growth: 6.3%
- Annual Job Openings: 2,000
- Education/Training Required: Bachelor's degree
- Self-Employed: 9.0%
- Part-Time: 6.7%

The job openings listed here are shared with Park Naturalists and with Range Managers.

How the Job Improves the World: Contributes to natural environment.

Plan and develop coordinated practices for soil erosion control, soil and water conservation, and sound land use. Develop and maintain working relationships with local government staff and board members. Advise land users such as farmers and ranchers on conservation plans, problems, and alternative solutions and provide technical and planning assistance. Apply principles of specialized fields of science, such as agronomy, soil science, forestry, or agriculture, to achieve conservation objectives. Plan soil management and conservation practices, such as crop rotation, reforestation, permanent vegetation, contour plowing, or terracing, to maintain soil and conserve water. Visit areas affected by erosion problems to seek sources and solutions. Monitor projects during and after construction to ensure projects conform to design specifications. Compute design specifications for implementation of conservation practices, using survey and field information technical guides, engineering manuals, and calculator. Revisit land users to view implemented land use practices and plans. Coordinate and implement technical, financial, and administrative assistance programs for local government units to ensure efficient program implementation and timely responses to requests for assistance. Analyze results of investigations to determine measures needed to maintain or restore proper soil management. Participate on work teams to plan, develop, and implement water and land management programs and policies. Develop, conduct, and/or participate in surveys, studies, and investigations of various land uses, gathering information for use in developing corrective action plans. Survey property to mark locations and measurements, using surveying instruments. Compute cost estimates of different conservation practices based on needs of land users, maintenance requirements, and life expectancy of practices. Provide information, knowledge, expertise, and training to government agencies at all levels to solve water and soil management problems and to assure coordination of resource protection activities. Respond to complaints and questions on wetland jurisdiction, providing information and clarification. Initiate, schedule, and conduct annual audits and compliance checks of program implementation by local government.

Personality Type: Investigative. Investigative occupations frequently involve working with ideas and require an extensive amount of thinking. These occupations can involve searching for facts and figuring out problems mentally.

GOE—Interest Area: 01. Agriculture and Natural Resources. **Work Group:** 01.02. Resource Science/Engineering for Plants, Animals, and the Environment. **Other Jobs in This Work Group:** Agricultural Engineers; Animal Scientists; Conservation Scientists; Environmental Engineers; Foresters; Mining and Geological Engineers, Including Mining Safety Engineers; Petroleum Engineers; Range Managers; Soil and Plant Scientists; Zoologists and Wildlife Biologists.

Skills—Persuasion: Persuading others to change their minds or behavior. **Operations Analysis:** Analyzing

needs and product requirements to create a design. **Science:** Using scientific rules and methods to solve problems. **Quality Control Analysis:** Conducting tests and inspections of products, services, or processes to evaluate quality or performance. **Judgment and Decision Making:** Considering the relative costs and benefits of potential actions to choose the most appropriate one. **Installation:** Installing equipment, machines, wiring, or programs to meet specifications. **Mathematics:** Using mathematics to solve problems. **Active Learning:** Understanding the implications of new information for both current and future problem-solving and decision-making.

Education and Training Programs: Natural Resources/Conservation, General; Natural Resources Management and Policy; Water, Wetlands, and Marine Resources Management; Land Use Planning and Management/Development; Natural Resources Management and Policy, Other; Forestry, General; Forest Sciences and Biology; Forest Management/Forest Resources Management; Forestry, Other; Wildlife and Wildlands Science and Management; others. **Related Knowledge/Courses: Geography:** Principles and methods for describing the features of land, sea, and air masses, including their physical characteristics; locations; interrelationships; and distribution of plant, animal, and human life. **Biology:** Plant and animal organisms and their tissues, cells, functions, interdependencies, and interactions with each other and the environment. **Engineering and Technology:** The practical application of engineering science and technology. This includes applying principles, techniques, procedures, and equipment to the design and production of various goods and services. **Design:** Design techniques, tools, and principles involved in production of precision technical plans, blueprints, drawings, and models. **History and Archeology:** Historical events and their causes, indicators, and effects on civilizations and cultures. **Physics:** Physical principles and laws and their interrelationships and applications to understanding fluid, material, and atmospheric dynamics and mechanical, electrical, atomic, and subatomic structures and processes.

Work Environment: More often outdoors than indoors; contaminants; sitting.

Sound Engineering Technicians

- Annual Earnings: $38,390
- Growth: 18.4%
- Annual Job Openings: 2,000
- Education/Training Required: Postsecondary vocational training
- Self-Employed: 6.5%
- Part-Time: 18.3%

How the Job Improves the World: Contributes to the arts.

Operate machines and equipment to record, synchronize, mix, or reproduce music, voices, or sound effects in sporting arenas, theater productions, recording studios, or movie and video productions. Confer with producers, performers, and others in order to determine and achieve the desired sound for a production such as a musical recording or a film. Set up, test, and adjust recording equipment for recording sessions and live performances; tear down equipment after event completion. Regulate volume level and sound quality during recording sessions, using control consoles. Prepare for recording sessions by performing activities such as selecting and setting up microphones. Report equipment problems and ensure that required repairs are made. Mix and edit voices, music, and taped sound effects for live performances and for prerecorded events, using sound mixing boards. Synchronize and equalize prerecorded dialogue, music, and sound effects with visual action of motion pictures or television productions, using control consoles.

Record speech, music, and other sounds on recording media, using recording equipment. Reproduce and duplicate sound recordings from original recording media, using sound editing and duplication equipment. Separate instruments, vocals, and other sounds; then combine sounds later during the mixing or post-production stage. Keep logs of recordings. Create musical instrument digital interface programs for music projects, commercials, or film post-production.

Personality Type: Realistic. Realistic occupations frequently involve work activities that include practical, hands-on problems and solutions. They often deal with plants; animals; and real-world materials such as wood, tools, and machinery. Many of the occupations require working outside and do not involve a lot of paperwork or working closely with others.

GOE—Interest Area: 03. Arts and Communication. **Work Group:** 03.09. Media Technology. **Other Jobs in This Work Group:** Audio and Video Equipment Technicians; Broadcast Technicians; Camera Operators, Television, Video, and Motion Picture; Film and Video Editors; Multi-Media Artists and Animators; Photographers; Radio Operators.

Skills—Technology Design: Generating or adapting equipment and technology to serve user needs. **Operation Monitoring:** Watching gauges, dials, or other indicators to make sure a machine is working properly. **Operation and Control:** Controlling operations of equipment or systems. **Installation:** Installing equipment, machines, wiring, or programs to meet specifications. **Equipment Maintenance:** Performing routine maintenance on equipment and determining when and what kind of maintenance is needed. **Troubleshooting:** Determining causes of operating errors and deciding what to do about them. **Management of Material Resources:** Obtaining and seeing to the appropriate use of equipment, facilities, and materials needed to do certain work. **Social Perceptiveness:** Being aware of others' reactions and understanding why they react as they do.

Education and Training Programs: Communications Technology/Technician; Recording Arts Technology/Technician. **Related Knowledge/Courses: Fine Arts:** The theory and techniques required to compose, produce, and perform works of music, dance, visual art, drama, and sculpture. **Communications and Media:** Media production, communication, and dissemination techniques and methods. This includes alternative ways to inform and entertain via written, oral, and visual media. **Telecommunications:** Transmission, broadcasting, switching, control, and operation of telecommunications systems. **Computers and Electronics:** Circuit boards; processors; chips; electronic equipment; and computer hardware and software, including applications and programming. **Customer and Personal Service:** Principles and processes for providing customer and personal services. This includes customer needs assessment, meeting quality standards for services, and evaluation of customer satisfaction. **Production and Processing:** Raw materials, production processes, quality control, costs, and other techniques for maximizing the effective manufacture and distribution of goods.

Work Environment: Indoors; noisy; sitting; using hands on objects, tools, or controls; repetitive motions.

Special Education Teachers, Middle School

- Annual Earnings: $45,490
- Growth: 19.9%
- Annual Job Openings: 8,000
- Education/Training Required: Bachelor's degree
- Self-Employed: 0.5%
- Part-Time: 10.5%

How the Job Improves the World: Contributes to education.

Teach middle school subjects to educationally and physically handicapped students. Includes teachers who specialize and work with audibly and visually handicapped students and those who teach basic academic and life processes skills to the mentally impaired. Establish and enforce rules for behavior and policies and procedures to maintain order among students. Maintain accurate and complete student records and prepare reports on children and activities as required by laws, district policies, and administrative regulations. Prepare materials and classrooms for class activities. Confer with parents, administrators, testing specialists, social workers, and professionals to develop individual educational plans designed to promote students' educational, physical, and social development. Develop and implement strategies to meet the needs of students with a variety of handicapping conditions. Teach socially acceptable behavior, employing techniques such as behavior modification and positive reinforcement. Modify the general education curriculum for special-needs students based upon a variety of instructional techniques and instructional technology. Employ special educational strategies and techniques during instruction to improve the development of sensory- and perceptual-motor skills, language, cognition, and memory. Confer with parents or guardians, other teachers, counselors, and administrators to resolve students' behavioral and academic problems. Instruct through lectures, discussions, and demonstrations in one or more subjects such as English, mathematics, or social studies. Coordinate placement of students with special needs into mainstream classes. Meet with parents and guardians to discuss their children's progress and to determine their priorities for their children and their resource needs. Guide and counsel students with adjustment or academic problems or special academic interests. Prepare, administer, and grade tests and assignments to evaluate students' progress. Observe and evaluate students' performance, behavior, social development, and physical health. Establish clear objectives for all lessons, units, and projects and communicate those objectives to students. Teach students personal development skills such as goal setting, independence, and self-advocacy. Plan and conduct activities for a balanced program of instruction, demonstration, and work time that provides students with opportunities to observe, question, and investigate.

Personality Type: Social. Social occupations frequently involve working with, communicating with, and teaching people. These occupations often involve helping or providing service to others.

GOE—Interest Area: 05. Education and Training. **Work Group:** 05.02. Preschool, Elementary, and Secondary Teaching and Instructing. **Other Jobs in This Work Group:** Elementary School Teachers, Except Special Education; Kindergarten Teachers, Except Special Education; Middle School Teachers, Except Special and Vocational Education; Preschool Teachers, Except Special Education; Secondary School Teachers, Except Special and Vocational Education; Special Education Teachers, Preschool, Kindergarten, and Elementary School; Special Education Teachers, Secondary School; Teacher Assistants; Vocational Education Teachers, Middle School; Vocational Education Teachers, Secondary School.

Skills—Learning Strategies: Selecting and using training/instructional methods and procedures appropriate for the situation when learning or teaching new things. **Social Perceptiveness:** Being aware of others' reactions and understanding why they react as they do. **Instructing:** Teaching others how to do something. **Monitoring:** Monitoring/assessing your performance or that of other individuals or organizations to make improvements or take corrective action. **Persuasion:** Persuading others to change their minds or behavior. **Negotiation:** Bringing others together and trying to reconcile differences. **Writing:** Communicating effectively in writing as appropriate for the needs of the audience. **Time Management:** Managing one's own time and the time of others.

Education and Training Programs: Special Education and Teaching, General; Education/Teaching of the Gifted and Talented; Education/Teaching of Individuals Who Are Developmentally Delayed; Education/Teaching of Individuals in Early Childhood Special Education Programs. **Related Knowledge/Courses: Geography:** Principles and methods for describing the features of land, sea, and air masses, including their physical characteristics; locations; interrelationships; and distribution of plant, animal, and human life. **History and Archeology:** Historical events and their causes, indicators, and effects on civilizations and cultures. **Psychology:** Human behavior and performance; individual differences in ability, personality, and interests; learning and motivation; psychological research methods; and the assessment and treatment of behavioral and affective disorders. **Therapy and Counseling:** Principles, methods, and procedures for diagnosis, treatment, and rehabilitation of physical and mental dysfunctions and for career counseling and guidance. **Sociology and Anthropology:** Group behavior and dynamics, societal trends and influences, human migrations, ethnicity, and cultures and their history and origins. **Education and Training:** Principles and methods for curriculum and training design, teaching and instruction for individuals and groups, and the measurement of training effects.

Work Environment: Indoors; noisy; standing.

Special Education Teachers, Preschool, Kindergarten, and Elementary School

- Annual Earnings: $44,630
- Growth: 23.3%
- Annual Job Openings: 18,000
- Education/Training Required: Bachelor's degree
- Self-Employed: 0.5%
- Part-Time: 10.5%

How the Job Improves the World: Contributes to education.

Teach elementary and preschool school subjects to educationally and physically handicapped students. Includes teachers who specialize and work with audibly and visually handicapped students and those who teach basic academic and life processes skills to the mentally impaired. Instruct students in academic subjects, using a variety of techniques such as phonetics, multisensory learning, and repetition to reinforce learning and to meet students' varying needs and interests. Employ special educational strategies and techniques during instruction to improve the development of sensory- and perceptual-motor skills, language, cognition, and memory. Teach socially acceptable behavior, employing techniques such as behavior modification and positive reinforcement. Modify the general education curriculum for special-needs students based upon a variety of instructional techniques and technologies. Meet with parents and guardians to discuss their children's progress and to determine their priorities for their children and their resource needs. Plan and conduct activities for a balanced program of instruction, demonstration, and work time that provides students with opportunities to observe, question, and investigate. Establish and enforce rules for behavior and policies and procedures to maintain order among the students for whom they are responsible. Confer with parents, administrators, testing specialists, social workers, and professionals to develop individual educational plans designed to promote students' educational, physical, and social development. Maintain accurate and complete student records and prepare reports on children and activities as required by laws, district policies, and administrative regulations. Establish clear objectives for all lessons, units, and projects and communicate those objectives to students. Develop and implement strategies to meet the needs of students with a variety of handicapping conditions. Prepare classrooms for class activities and provide a variety of materials and resources for children to explore, manipulate, and use, both in learning activities and imaginative play. Confer with parents or guardians, teachers, counselors, and administrators to resolve students' behavioral and academic problems. Observe and evaluate students' performance, behavior, social development, and physical health. Teach students personal development skills such as goal setting, independence, and self-advocacy.

Personality Type: Social. Social occupations frequently involve working with, communicating with, and teaching people. These occupations often involve helping or providing service to others.

GOE—Interest Area: 05. Education and Training. **Work Group:** 05.02. Preschool, Elementary, and Secondary Teaching and Instructing. **Other Jobs in This Work Group:** Elementary School Teachers, Except Special Education; Kindergarten Teachers, Except Special Education; Middle School Teachers, Except Special and Vocational Education; Preschool Teachers, Except Special Education; Secondary School Teachers, Except Special and Vocational Education; Special Education Teachers, Middle School; Special Education Teachers, Secondary School; Teacher

Assistants; Vocational Education Teachers, Middle School; Vocational Education Teachers, Secondary School.

Skills—Learning Strategies: Selecting and using training/instructional methods and procedures appropriate for the situation when learning or teaching new things. **Instructing:** Teaching others how to do something. **Social Perceptiveness:** Being aware of others' reactions and understanding why they react as they do. **Monitoring:** Monitoring/assessing your performance or that of other individuals or organizations to make improvements or take corrective action. **Negotiation:** Bringing others together and trying to reconcile differences. **Time Management:** Managing one's own time and the time of others. **Coordination:** Adjusting actions in relation to others' actions. **Speaking:** Talking to others to convey information effectively.

Education and Training Programs: Special Education and Teaching, General; Education/Teaching of Individuals with Hearing Impairments, Including Deafness; Education/Teaching of the Gifted and Talented; Education/Teaching of Individuals with Emotional Disturbances; Education/Teaching of Individuals with Mental Retardation; Education/Teaching of Individuals with Multiple Disabilities; Education/Teaching of Individuals with Orthopedic and Other Physical Health Impairments; others. **Related Knowledge/Courses: Psychology:** Human behavior and performance; individual differences in ability, personality, and interests; learning and motivation; psychological research methods; and the assessment and treatment of behavioral and affective disorders. **History and Archeology:** Historical events and their causes, indicators, and effects on civilizations and cultures. **Therapy and Counseling:** Principles, methods, and procedures for diagnosis, treatment, and rehabilitation of physical and mental dysfunctions and for career counseling and guidance. **Geography:** Principles and methods for describing the features of land, sea, and air masses, including their physical characteristics; locations; interrelationships; and distribu-

tion of plant, animal, and human life. **Philosophy and Theology:** Different philosophical systems and religions. This includes their basic principles, values, ethics, ways of thinking, customs, and practices and their impact on human culture. **Sociology and Anthropology:** Group behavior and dynamics, societal trends and influences, human migrations, ethnicity, and cultures and their history and origins.

Work Environment: Indoors; noisy; standing.

Special Education Teachers, Secondary School

- Annual Earnings: $46,820
- Growth: 17.9%
- Annual Job Openings: 11,000
- Education/Training Required: Bachelor's degree
- Self-Employed: 0.5%
- Part-Time: 10.5%

How the Job Improves the World: Contributes to education.

Teach secondary school subjects to educationally and physically handicapped students. Includes teachers who specialize and work with audibly and visually handicapped students and those who teach basic academic and life processes skills to the mentally impaired. Maintain accurate and complete student records and prepare reports on children and activities as required by laws, district policies, and administrative regulations. Prepare materials and classrooms for class activities. Teach socially acceptable behavior, employing techniques such as behavior modification and positive reinforcement. Establish and enforce rules for behavior and policies and procedures to maintain order among students. Confer with parents, administrators, testing specialists, social workers, and professionals to develop individual educational plans designed to promote students' educational, physical, and social development. Instruct through lectures, discussions, and demonstrations in one or more subjects such as English, mathematics, or social studies. Employ special educational strategies and techniques during instruction to improve the development of sensory- and perceptual-motor skills, language, cognition, and memory. Plan and conduct activities for a balanced program of instruction, demonstration, and work time that provides students with opportunities to observe, question, and investigate. Prepare students for later grades by encouraging them to explore learning opportunities and to persevere with challenging tasks. Teach personal development skills such as goal setting, independence, and self-advocacy. Establish clear objectives for all lessons, units, and projects and communicate those objectives to students. Develop and implement strategies to meet the needs of students with a variety of handicapping conditions. Modify the general education curriculum for special-needs students based upon a variety of instructional techniques and technologies. Meet with other professionals to discuss individual students' needs and progress. Confer with parents or guardians, other teachers, counselors, and administrators to resolve students' behavioral and academic problems. Meet with parents and guardians to discuss their children's progress and to determine their priorities for their children and their resource needs. Guide and counsel students with adjustment or academic problems or special academic interests.

Personality Type: Social. Social occupations frequently involve working with, communicating with, and teaching people. These occupations often involve helping or providing service to others.

GOE—Interest Area: 05. Education and Training. **Work Group:** 05.02. Preschool, Elementary, and Secondary Teaching and Instructing. **Other Jobs in This Work Group:** Elementary School Teachers, Except Special Education; Kindergarten Teachers, Except Special Education; Middle School Teachers, Except Special and Vocational Education; Preschool Teachers, Except Special Education; Secondary School Teachers, Except Special and Vocational Education; Special Education Teachers, Middle School; Special Education Teachers, Preschool, Kindergarten, and Elementary School; Teacher Assistants; Vocational Education Teachers, Middle School; Vocational Education Teachers, Secondary School.

Skills—Learning Strategies: Selecting and using training/instructional methods and procedures appropriate for the situation when learning or teaching new things. **Social Perceptiveness:** Being aware of others' reactions and understanding why they react as they do. **Negotiation:** Bringing others together and trying to reconcile differences. **Instructing:** Teaching others how to do something. **Persuasion:** Persuading others to change their minds or behavior. **Service Orientation:** Actively looking for ways to help people. **Time Management:** Managing one's own time and the time of others. **Monitoring:** Monitoring/assessing your performance or that of other individuals or organizations to make improvements or take corrective action.

Education and Training Programs: Special Education and Teaching, General; Education/Teaching of the Gifted and Talented; Education/Teaching of Individuals Who Are Developmentally Delayed; Education/Teaching of Individuals in Early Childhood Special Education Programs. **Related Knowledge/Courses: Therapy and Counseling:** Principles, methods, and procedures for diagnosis, treatment, and rehabilitation of physical and mental dysfunctions and for career counseling and guidance. **History and Archeology:** Historical events and their causes, indicators, and effects on civilizations and cultures. **Geography:** Principles and methods for describing the features of land, sea, and air masses, including their physical characteristics; locations; interrelationships; and distribution of plant, animal, and human life. **Psychology:** Human behavior and performance;

individual differences in ability, personality, and interests; learning and motivation; psychological research methods; and the assessment and treatment of behavioral and affective disorders. **Philosophy and Theology:** Different philosophical systems and religions. This includes their basic principles, values, ethics, ways of thinking, customs, and practices and their impact on human culture. **Sociology and Anthropology:** Group behavior and dynamics, societal trends and influences, human migrations, ethnicity, and cultures and their history and origins.

Work Environment: Indoors; noisy; standing.

Speech-Language Pathologists

◎ Annual Earnings: $54,880

◎ Growth: 14.6%

◎ Annual Job Openings: 5,000

◎ Education/Training Required: Master's degree

◎ Self-Employed: 6.0%

◎ Part-Time: 30.2%

How the Job Improves the World: Contributes to health and education.

Assess and treat persons with speech, language, voice, and fluency disorders. May select alternative communication systems and teach their use. May perform research related to speech and language problems. Monitor patients' progress and adjust treatments accordingly. Evaluate hearing and speech/language test results and medical or background information to diagnose and plan treatment for speech, language, fluency, voice, and swallowing disorders. Administer hearing or speech and language evaluations, tests, or examinations to patients to collect information on type and degree of impairments, using written and oral tests and special instruments.

Record information on the initial evaluation, treatment, progress, and discharge of clients. Develop and implement treatment plans for problems such as stuttering, delayed language, swallowing disorders, and inappropriate pitch or harsh voice problems, based on own assessments and recommendations of physicians, psychologists, or social workers. Develop individual or group programs in schools to deal with speech or language problems. Instruct clients in techniques for more effective communication, including sign language, lip reading, and voice improvement. Teach clients to control or strengthen tongue, jaw, face muscles, and breathing mechanisms. Develop speech exercise programs to reduce disabilities. Consult with and advise educators or medical staff on speech or hearing topics, such as communication strategies or speech and language stimulation. Instruct patients and family members in strategies to cope with or avoid communication-related misunderstandings. Design, develop, and employ alternative diagnostic or communication devices and strategies. Conduct lessons and direct educational or therapeutic games to assist teachers dealing with speech problems. Refer clients to additional medical or educational services if needed. Participate in conferences or training, or publish research results, to share knowledge of new hearing or speech disorder treatment methods or technologies. Communicate with non-speaking students, using sign language or computer technology. Provide communication instruction to dialect speakers or students with limited English proficiency. Use computer applications to identify and assist with communication disabilities.

Personality Type: Social. Social occupations frequently involve working with, communicating with, and teaching people. These occupations often involve helping or providing service to others.

GOE—Interest Area: 08. Health Science. **Work Group:** 08.07. Medical Therapy. **Other Jobs in This Work Group:** Audiologists; Massage Therapists; Occupational Therapist Aides; Occupational

Therapist Assistants; Occupational Therapists; Physical Therapist Aides; Physical Therapist Assistants; Physical Therapists; Radiation Therapists; Recreational Therapists; Respiratory Therapists; Respiratory Therapy Technicians.

Skills—Instructing: Teaching others how to do something. **Learning Strategies:** Selecting and using training/instructional methods and procedures appropriate for the situation when learning or teaching new things. **Social Perceptiveness:** Being aware of others' reactions and understanding why they react as they do. **Speaking:** Talking to others to convey information effectively. **Monitoring:** Monitoring/assessing your performance or that of other individuals or organizations to make improvements or take corrective action. **Service Orientation:** Actively looking for ways to help people. **Time Management:** Managing one's own time and the time of others. **Active Learning:** Understanding the implications of new information for both current and future problem-solving and decision-making.

Education and Training Programs: Communication Disorders, General; Speech-Language Pathology/Pathologist; Audiology/Audiologist and Speech-Language Pathology/Pathologist; Communication Disorders Sciences and Services, Other. **Related Knowledge/Courses: Therapy and Counseling:** Principles, methods, and procedures for diagnosis, treatment, and rehabilitation of physical and mental dysfunctions and for career counseling and guidance. **Psychology:** Human behavior and performance; individual differences in ability, personality, and interests; learning and motivation; psychological research methods; and the assessment and treatment of behavioral and affective disorders. **Education and Training:** Principles and methods for curriculum and training design, teaching and instruction for individuals and groups, and the measurement of training effects. **Sociology and Anthropology:** Group behavior and dynamics, societal trends and influences, human migrations, ethnicity, and cultures and their history and

origins. **Medicine and Dentistry:** The information and techniques needed to diagnose and treat human injuries, diseases, and deformities. This includes symptoms, treatment alternatives, drug properties and interactions, and preventive health-care measures. **English Language:** The structure and content of the English language, including the meaning and spelling of words, rules of composition, and grammar.

Work Environment: Indoors; disease or infections; sitting.

Substance Abuse and Behavioral Disorder Counselors

- Annual Earnings: $32,580
- Growth: 28.7%
- Annual Job Openings: 11,000
- Education/Training Required: Master's degree
- Self-Employed: 5.0%
- Part-Time: 16.7%

How the Job Improves the World: Contributes to mental health.

Counsel and advise individuals with alcohol; tobacco; drug; or other problems, such as gambling and eating disorders. May counsel individuals, families, or groups or engage in prevention programs. Counsel clients and patients individually and in group sessions to assist in overcoming dependencies, adjusting to life, and making changes. Complete and maintain accurate records and reports regarding the patients' histories and progress, services provided, and other required information. Develop client treatment plans based on research, clinical experience, and client histories. Review and evaluate clients' progress in relation to measurable goals described in treatment and care plans. Interview clients, review records, and confer with other professionals to evaluate individuals' mental and physical condition and to determine their suitability for participation in a specific program. Intervene as advocate for clients or patients to resolve emergency problems in crisis situations. Provide clients or family members with information about addiction issues and about available services and programs, making appropriate referrals when necessary. Modify treatment plans to comply with changes in client status. Coordinate counseling efforts with mental health professionals and other health professionals such as doctors, nurses, and social workers. Attend training sessions to increase knowledge and skills. Plan and implement follow-up and aftercare programs for clients to be discharged from treatment programs. Conduct chemical dependency program orientation sessions. Counsel family members to assist them in understanding, dealing with, and supporting clients or patients. Participate in case conferences and staff meetings. Act as liaisons between clients and medical staff. Coordinate activities with courts, probation officers, community services, and other post-treatment agencies. Confer with family members or others close to clients to keep them informed of treatment planning and progress. Instruct others in program methods, procedures, and functions. Follow progress of discharged patients to determine effectiveness of treatments. Develop, implement, and evaluate public education, prevention, and health promotion programs, working in collaboration with organizations, institutions, and communities.

Personality Type: Social. Social occupations frequently involve working with, communicating with, and teaching people. These occupations often involve helping or providing service to others.

GOE—Interest Area: 10. Human Service. **Work Group:** 10.01. Counseling and Social Work. **Other Jobs in This Work Group:** Child, Family, and School Social Workers; Clinical Psychologists; Clinical, Counseling, and School Psychologists; Counseling Psychologists; Marriage and Family Therapists;

Medical and Public Health Social Workers; Mental Health and Substance Abuse Social Workers; Mental Health Counselors; Probation Officers and Correctional Treatment Specialists; Rehabilitation Counselors; Residential Advisors; Social and Human Service Assistants.

Skills—Social Perceptiveness: Being aware of others' reactions and understanding why they react as they do. **Persuasion:** Persuading others to change their minds or behavior. **Service Orientation:** Actively looking for ways to help people. **Negotiation:** Bringing others together and trying to reconcile differences. **Learning Strategies:** Selecting and using training/instructional methods and procedures appropriate for the situation when learning or teaching new things. **Active Listening:** Giving full attention to what other people are saying, taking time to understand the points being made, asking questions as appropriate, and not interrupting at inappropriate times. **Instructing:** Teaching others how to do something. **Complex Problem Solving:** Identifying complex problems and reviewing related information to develop and evaluate options and implement solutions.

Education and Training Programs: Substance Abuse/Addiction Counseling; Clinical/Medical Social Work; Mental and Social Health Services and Allied Professions, Other. **Related Knowledge/Courses: Therapy and Counseling:** Principles, methods, and procedures for diagnosis, treatment, and rehabilitation of physical and mental dysfunctions and for career counseling and guidance. **Psychology:** Human behavior and performance; individual differences in ability, personality, and interests; learning and motivation; psychological research methods; and the assessment and treatment of behavioral and affective disorders. **Sociology and Anthropology:** Group behavior and dynamics, societal trends and influences, human migrations, ethnicity, and cultures and their history and origins. **Philosophy and Theology:** Different philosophical systems and religions. This includes their basic principles, values, ethics, ways of thinking, customs, and practices and their impact on human culture. **Customer and Personal Service:** Principles and processes for providing customer and personal services. This includes customer needs assessment, meeting quality standards for services, and evaluation of customer satisfaction. **Education and Training:** Principles and methods for curriculum and training design, teaching and instruction for individuals and groups, and the measurement of training effects.

Work Environment: Indoors; disease or infections; sitting.

Surgeons

- Annual Earnings: More than $145,600
- Growth: 24.0%
- Annual Job Openings: 41,000
- Education/Training Required: First professional degree
- Self-Employed: 11.5%
- Part-Time: 9.6%

The job openings listed here are shared with Anesthesiologists; Family and General Practitioners; Internists, General; Obstetricians and Gynecologists; Pediatricians, General; and Psychiatrists.

How the Job Improves the World: Contributes to health.

Treat diseases, injuries, and deformities by invasive methods, such as manual manipulation, or by using instruments and appliances. Analyze patient's medical history, medication allergies, physical condition, and examination results to verify operation's necessity and to determine best procedure. Operate on patients to correct deformities, repair injuries, prevent and treat diseases, or improve or restore patients' functions. Follow established surgical techniques during the operation. Prescribe preoperative and postoperative treat-

ments and procedures, such as sedatives, diets, antibiotics, and preparation and treatment of the patient's operative area. Examine patient to provide information on medical condition and surgical risk. Diagnose bodily disorders and orthopedic conditions and provide treatments, such as medicines and surgeries, in clinics, hospital wards, and operating rooms. Direct and coordinate activities of nurses, assistants, specialists, residents, and other medical staff. Provide consultation and surgical assistance to other physicians and surgeons. Refer patient to medical specialist or other practitioners when necessary. Examine instruments, equipment, and operating room to ensure sterility. Prepare case histories. Manage surgery services, including planning, scheduling and coordination, determination of procedures, and procurement of supplies and equipment. Conduct research to develop and test surgical techniques that can improve operating procedures and outcomes.

Personality Type: Investigative. Investigative occupations frequently involve working with ideas and require an extensive amount of thinking. These occupations can involve searching for facts and figuring out problems mentally.

GOE—Interest Area: 08. Health Science. **Work Group:** 08.02. Medicine and Surgery. **Other Jobs in This Work Group:** Anesthesiologists; Family and General Practitioners; Internists, General; Medical Assistants; Medical Transcriptionists; Obstetricians and Gynecologists; Pediatricians, General; Pharmacists; Pharmacy Aides; Pharmacy Technicians; Physician Assistants; Psychiatrists; Registered Nurses; Surgical Technologists.

Skills—Science: Using scientific rules and methods to solve problems. **Reading Comprehension:** Understanding written sentences and paragraphs in work-related documents. **Judgment and Decision Making:** Considering the relative costs and benefits of potential actions to choose the most appropriate one. **Management of Financial Resources:** Determining how money will be spent to get the work done and accounting for these expenditures. **Complex Problem Solving:** Identifying complex problems and reviewing related information to develop and evaluate options and implement solutions. **Critical Thinking:** Using logic and reasoning to identify the strengths and weaknesses of alternative solutions, conclusions, or approaches to problems. **Active Learning:** Understanding the implications of new information for both current and future problem-solving and decision-making. **Active Listening:** Giving full attention to what other people are saying, taking time to understand the points being made, asking questions as appropriate, and not interrupting at inappropriate times.

Education and Training Programs: Colon and Rectal Surgery; Critical Care Surgery; General Surgery; Hand Surgery; Neurological Surgery/Neurosurgery; Orthopedics/Orthopedic Surgery; Otolaryngology; Pediatric Orthopedics; Pediatric Surgery; Plastic Surgery; Sports Medicine; Thoracic Surgery; Urology; Vascular Surgery; Adult Reconstructive Orthopedics (Orthopedic Surgery); Orthopedic Surgery of the Spine. **Related Knowledge/Courses: Medicine and Dentistry:** The information and techniques needed to diagnose and treat human injuries, diseases, and deformities. This includes symptoms, treatment alternatives, drug properties and interactions, and preventive health-care measures. **Biology:** Plant and animal organisms and their tissues, cells, functions, interdependencies, and interactions with each other and the environment. **Therapy and Counseling:** Principles, methods, and procedures for diagnosis, treatment, and rehabilitation of physical and mental dysfunctions and for career counseling and guidance. **Psychology:** Human behavior and performance; individual differences in ability, personality, and interests; learning and motivation; psychological research methods; and the assessment and treatment of behavioral and affective disorders. **Chemistry:** The chemical composition, structure, and properties of substances and of the chemical processes and transformations that they un-

dergo. This includes uses of chemicals and their danger signs, production techniques, and disposal methods. **Customer and Personal Service:** Principles and processes for providing customer and personal services. This includes customer needs assessment, meeting quality standards for services, and evaluation of customer satisfaction.

Work Environment: Indoors; contaminants; radiation; disease or infections; standing; using hands on objects, tools, or controls.

Surgical Technologists

- Annual Earnings: $34,830
- Growth: 29.5%
- Annual Job Openings: 12,000
- Education/Training Required: Postsecondary vocational training
- Self-Employed: 0.3%
- Part-Time: 23.2%

How the Job Improves the World: Contributes to health.

Assist in operations under the supervision of surgeons, registered nurses, or other surgical personnel. May help set up operating room; prepare and transport patients for surgery; adjust lights and equipment; pass instruments and other supplies to surgeons and surgeon's assistants; hold retractors; cut sutures; and help count sponges, needles, supplies, and instruments. Count sponges, needles, and instruments before and after operation. Hand instruments and supplies to surgeons and surgeons' assistants, hold retractors and cut sutures, and perform other tasks as directed by surgeon during operation. Scrub arms and hands and assist the surgical team in scrubbing and putting on gloves, masks, and surgical clothing. Position patients on the operating table and cover them with sterile surgical drapes to prevent exposure.

Provide technical assistance to surgeons, surgical nurses, and anesthesiologists. Wash and sterilize equipment, using germicides and sterilizers. Prepare, care for, and dispose of tissue specimens taken for laboratory analysis. Clean and restock the operating room, placing equipment and supplies and arranging instruments according to instruction. Prepare dressings or bandages and apply or assist with their application following surgery. Operate, assemble, adjust, or monitor sterilizers, lights, suction machines, and diagnostic equipment to ensure proper operation. Monitor and continually assess operating room conditions, including patient and surgical team needs. Observe patients' vital signs to assess physical condition. Maintain supply of fluids, such as plasma, saline, blood, and glucose, for use during operations. Maintain files and records of surgical procedures.

Personality Type: Realistic. Realistic occupations frequently involve work activities that include practical, hands-on problems and solutions. They often deal with plants; animals; and real-world materials such as wood, tools, and machinery. Many of the occupations require working outside and do not involve a lot of paperwork or working closely with others.

GOE—Interest Area: 08. Health Science. **Work Group:** 08.02. Medicine and Surgery. **Other Jobs in This Work Group:** Anesthesiologists; Family and General Practitioners; Internists, General; Medical Assistants; Medical Transcriptionists; Obstetricians and Gynecologists; Pediatricians, General; Pharmacists; Pharmacy Aides; Pharmacy Technicians; Physician Assistants; Psychiatrists; Registered Nurses; Surgeons.

Skills—Troubleshooting: Determining causes of operating errors and deciding what to do about them. **Equipment Selection:** Determining the kind of tools and equipment needed to do a job. **Instructing:** Teaching others how to do something. **Operation Monitoring:** Watching gauges, dials, or other indicators to make sure a machine is working properly. **Science:** Using scientific rules and methods to solve problems. **Reading Comprehension:** Understanding written sentences and paragraphs in work-related documents. **Learning Strategies:** Selecting and using training/instructional methods and procedures appropriate for the situation when learning or teaching new things. **Active Learning:** Understanding the implications of new information for both current and future problem-solving and decision-making.

Education and Training Programs: Pathology/Pathologist Assistant; Surgical Technology/Technologist. **Related Knowledge/Courses: Medicine and Dentistry:** The information and techniques needed to diagnose and treat human injuries, diseases, and deformities. This includes symptoms, treatment alternatives, drug properties and interactions, and preventive health-care measures. **Chemistry:** The chemical composition, structure, and properties of substances and of the chemical processes and transformations that they undergo. This includes uses of chemicals and their danger signs, production techniques, and disposal methods. **Philosophy and Theology:** Different philosophical systems and religions. This includes their basic principles, values, ethics, ways of thinking, customs, and practices and their impact on human culture. **Psychology:** Human behavior and performance; individual differences in ability, personality, and interests; learning and motivation; psychological research methods; and the assessment and treatment of behavioral and affective disorders. **Customer and Personal Service:** Principles and processes for providing customer and personal services. This includes customer needs assessment, meeting quality standards for services, and evaluation of customer satisfaction. **Therapy and Counseling:** Principles, methods, and procedures for diagnosis, treatment, and rehabilitation of physical and mental dysfunctions and for career counseling and guidance.

Work Environment: Indoors; contaminants; disease or infections; hazardous conditions; standing; using hands on objects, tools, or controls.

Talent Directors

- Annual Earnings: $53,860
- Growth: 16.6%
- Annual Job Openings: 11,000
- Education/Training Required: Long-term on-the-job training
- Self-Employed: 30.4%
- Part-Time: 8.1%

The job openings listed here are shared with Directors—Stage, Motion Pictures, Television, and Radio; Producers; Program Directors; and Technical Directors/Managers.

How the Job Improves the World: Contributes to the arts.

Audition and interview performers to select most appropriate talent for parts in stage, television, radio, or motion picture productions. Review performer information such as photos, resumes, voice tapes, videos, and union membership to decide whom to audition for parts. Read scripts and confer with producers to determine the types and numbers of performers required for a given production. Select performers for roles or submit lists of suitable performers to producers or directors for final selection. Serve as liaisons between directors, actors, and agents. Audition and interview performers to match their attributes to specific roles or to increase the pool of available acting talent. Maintain talent files that include information such as performers' specialties, past performances, and availability. Prepare actors for auditions by providing scripts and information about roles and casting requirements. Attend or view productions to maintain knowledge of available actors. Negotiate contract agreements with performers, with agents, or between performers and agents or production companies. Contact agents and actors to provide notification of audition and performance opportunities and to set up audition times. Hire and supervise workers who help locate people with specified attributes and talents. Arrange for or design screen tests or auditions for prospective performers. Locate performers or extras for crowd and background scenes and stand-ins or photo doubles for actors by direct contact or through agents.

Personality Type: Artistic. Artistic occupations frequently involve working with forms, designs, and patterns. They often require self-expression, and the work can be done without following a clear set of rules.

GOE—Interest Area: 03. Arts and Communication. **Work Group:** 03.07. Music. **Other Jobs in This Work Group:** Music Composers and Arrangers; Music Directors; Music Directors and Composers; Musicians and Singers; Musicians, Instrumental; Singers.

Skills—Management of Financial Resources: Determining how money will be spent to get the work done and accounting for these expenditures. **Management of Personnel Resources:** Motivating, developing, and directing people as they work; identifying the best people for the job. **Persuasion:** Persuading others to change their minds or behavior. **Social Perceptiveness:** Being aware of others' reactions and understanding why they react as they do. **Negotiation:** Bringing others together and trying to reconcile differences. **Judgment and Decision Making:** Considering the relative costs and benefits of potential actions to choose the most appropriate one. **Time Management:** Managing one's own time and the time of others. **Management of Material Resources:** Obtaining and seeing to the appropriate use of equipment, facilities, and materials needed to do certain work.

Education and Training Programs: Radio and Television; Drama and Dramatics/Theatre Arts, General; Directing and Theatrical Production; Theatre/Theatre Arts Management; Dramatic/ Theatre Arts and Stagecraft, Other; Film/Cinema Studies; Cinematography and Film/Video

Production. **Related Knowledge/Courses: Fine Arts:** The theory and techniques required to compose, produce, and perform works of music, dance, visual art, drama, and sculpture. **Communications and Media:** Media production, communication, and dissemination techniques and methods. This includes alternative ways to inform and entertain via written, oral, and visual media. **Clerical Practices:** Administrative and clerical procedures and systems such as word processing, managing files and records, stenography and transcription, designing forms, and other office procedures and terminology. **Computers and Electronics:** Circuit boards; processors; chips; electronic equipment; and computer hardware and software, including applications and programming. **Sales and Marketing:** Principles and methods for showing, promoting, and selling products or services. This includes marketing strategy and tactics, product demonstration, sales techniques, and sales control systems. **Telecommunications:** Transmission, broadcasting, switching, control, and operation of telecommunications systems.

Work Environment: Indoors; noisy; sitting.

Teacher Assistants

- Annual Earnings: $20,090
- Growth: 14.1%
- Annual Job Openings: 252,000
- Education/Training Required: Short-term on-the-job training
- Self-Employed: 0.2%
- Part-Time: 38.5%

How the Job Improves the World: Contributes to education.

Perform duties that are instructional in nature or deliver direct services to students or parents. Serve in a position for which a teacher or another professional has ultimate responsibility for the design and implementation of educational programs and services. Provide extra assistance to students with special needs, such as non-English-speaking students or those with physical and mental disabilities. Tutor and assist children individually or in small groups to help them master assignments and to reinforce learning concepts presented by teachers. Supervise students in classrooms, halls, cafeterias, school yards, and gymnasiums or on field trips. Enforce administration policies and rules governing students. Observe students' performance and record relevant data to assess progress. Discuss assigned duties with classroom teachers to coordinate instructional efforts. Instruct and monitor students in the use and care of equipment and materials to prevent injuries and damage. Present subject matter to students under the direction and guidance of teachers, using lectures, discussions, or supervised role-playing methods. Organize and label materials and display students' work in a manner appropriate for their eye levels and perceptual skills. Distribute tests and homework assignments and collect them when they are completed. Type, file, and duplicate materials. Distribute teaching materials such as textbooks, workbooks, papers, and pencils to students. Use computers, audiovisual aids, and other equipment and materials to supplement presentations. Attend staff meetings and serve on committees as required. Prepare lesson materials, bulletin board displays, exhibits, equipment, and demonstrations. Carry out therapeutic regimens such as behavior modification and personal development programs under the supervision of special education instructors, psychologists, or speech-language pathologists. Provide disabled students with assistive devices, supportive technology, and assistance accessing facilities such as restrooms. Assist in bus loading and unloading. Take class attendance and maintain attendance records. Grade homework and tests, and compute and record results, using answer sheets or electronic marking devices. Organize and supervise games and other recreational activities to promote physical, mental, and social development.

Personality Type: Social. Social occupations frequently involve working with, communicating with, and teaching people. These occupations often involve helping or providing service to others.

GOE—Interest Area: 05. Education and Training. **Work Group:** 05.02. Preschool, Elementary, and Secondary Teaching and Instructing. **Other Jobs in This Work Group:** Elementary School Teachers, Except Special Education; Kindergarten Teachers, Except Special Education; Middle School Teachers, Except Special and Vocational Education; Preschool Teachers, Except Special Education; Secondary School Teachers, Except Special and Vocational Education; Special Education Teachers, Middle School; Special Education Teachers, Preschool, Kindergarten, and Elementary School; Special Education Teachers, Secondary School; Vocational Education Teachers, Middle School; Vocational Education Teachers, Secondary School.

Skills—Social Perceptiveness: Being aware of others' reactions and understanding why they react as they do. **Learning Strategies:** Selecting and using training/instructional methods and procedures appropriate for the situation when learning or teaching new things. **Instructing:** Teaching others how to do something. **Persuasion:** Persuading others to change their minds or behavior. **Active Listening:** Giving full attention to what other people are saying, taking time to understand the points being made, asking questions as appropriate, and not interrupting at inappropriate times. **Negotiation:** Bringing others together and trying to reconcile differences. **Service Orientation:** Actively looking for ways to help people. **Writing:** Communicating effectively in writing as appropriate for the needs of the audience.

Education and Training Programs: Teacher Assistant/Aide; Teaching Assistants/Aides, Other. **Related Knowledge/Courses: Geography:** Principles and methods for describing the features of land, sea, and air masses, including their physical characteristics; locations; interrelationships; and distribution of plant, animal, and human life. **History and Archeology:** Historical events and their causes, indicators, and effects on civilizations and cultures. **Psychology:** Human behavior and performance; individual differences in ability, personality, and interests; learning and motivation; psychological research methods; and the assessment and treatment of behavioral and affective disorders. **Therapy and Counseling:** Principles, methods, and procedures for diagnosis, treatment, and rehabilitation of physical and mental dysfunctions and for career counseling and guidance. **Sociology and Anthropology:** Group behavior and dynamics, societal trends and influences, human migrations, ethnicity, and cultures and their history and origins. **English Language:** The structure and content of the English language, including the meaning and spelling of words, rules of composition, and grammar.

Work Environment: Indoors; noisy; standing.

Tour Guides and Escorts

- Annual Earnings: $19,990
- Growth: 16.6%
- Annual Job Openings: 5,000
- Education/Training Required: Moderate-term on-the-job training
- Self-Employed: 14.4%
- Part-Time: 29.8%

How the Job Improves the World: Contributes to safety, education, and intercultural understanding.

Escort individuals or groups on sightseeing tours or through places of interest such as industrial establishments, public buildings, and art galleries. Conduct educational activities for schoolchildren. Escort individuals or groups on cruises; on sightseeing tours; or through places of interest such as industrial establishments, public buildings, and art galleries.

Describe tour points of interest to group members and respond to questions. Monitor visitors' activities to ensure compliance with establishment or tour regulations and safety practices. Greet and register visitors and issue any required identification badges or safety devices. Distribute brochures, show audiovisual presentations, and explain establishment processes and operations at tour sites. Provide directions and other pertinent information to visitors. Provide for physical safety of groups, performing such activities as providing first aid and directing emergency evacuations. Research environmental conditions and clients' skill and ability levels to plan expeditions, instruction, and commentary that are appropriate. Provide information about wildlife varieties and habitats, as well as any relevant regulations, such as those pertaining to hunting and fishing. Collect fees and tickets from group members. Teach skills, such as proper climbing methods, and demonstrate and advise on the use of equipment. Select travel routes and sites to be visited based on knowledge of specific areas. Solicit tour patronage and sell souvenirs. Speak foreign languages to communicate with foreign visitors. Assemble and check the required supplies and equipment prior to departure. Perform clerical duties such as filing, typing, operating switchboards, and routing mail and messages. Drive motor vehicles to transport visitors to establishments and tour site locations.

Personality Type: Social. Social occupations frequently involve working with, communicating with, and teaching people. These occupations often involve helping or providing service to others.

GOE—Interest Area: 09. Hospitality, Tourism, and Recreation. **Work Group:** 09.03. Hospitality and Travel Services. **Other Jobs in This Work Group:** Baggage Porters and Bellhops; Concierges; Flight Attendants; Hotel, Motel, and Resort Desk Clerks; Janitors and Cleaners, Except Maids and Housekeeping Cleaners; Maids and Housekeeping Cleaners; Reservation and Transportation Ticket Agents and Travel Clerks; Transportation Attendants, Except Flight Attendants and Baggage Porters; Travel Agents; Travel Guides.

Skills—No data available.

Education and Training Program: Tourism and Travel Services Management. **Related Knowledge/Courses: History and Archeology:** Historical events and their causes, indicators, and effects on civilizations and cultures. **Fine Arts:** The theory and techniques required to compose, produce, and perform works of music, dance, visual art, drama, and sculpture. **Philosophy and Theology:** Different philosophical systems and religions. This includes their basic principles, values, ethics, ways of thinking, customs, and practices and their impact on human culture. **Sociology and Anthropology:** Group behavior and dynamics, societal trends and influences, human migrations, ethnicity, and cultures and their history and origins. **Customer and Personal Service:** Principles and processes for providing customer and personal services. This includes customer needs assessment, meeting quality standards for services, and evaluation of customer satisfaction. **Communications and Media:** Media production, communication, and dissemination techniques and methods. This includes alternative ways to inform and entertain via written, oral, and visual media.

Work Environment: Standing.

Traffic Technicians

- Annual Earnings: $37,070
- Growth: 14.1%
- Annual Job Openings: 1,000
- Education/Training Required: Short-term on-the-job training
- Self-Employed: 0.0%
- Part-Time: No data available

How the Job Improves the World: Contributes to safety.

Conduct field studies to determine traffic volume, speed, effectiveness of signals, adequacy of lighting, and other factors influencing traffic conditions under direction of traffic engineer. Interact with the public to answer traffic-related questions; respond to complaints and requests; or discuss traffic control ordinances, plans, policies, and procedures. Prepare drawings of proposed signal installations or other control devices, using drafting instruments or computer automated drafting equipment. Plan, design, and improve components of traffic control systems to accommodate current and projected traffic and to increase usability and efficiency. Analyze data related to traffic flow, accident rate data, and proposed development to determine the most efficient methods to expedite traffic flow. Prepare work orders for repair, maintenance, and changes in traffic systems. Study factors affecting traffic conditions, such as lighting and sign and marking visibility, to assess their effectiveness. Visit development and worksites to determine projects' effect on traffic and the adequacy of plans to control traffic and maintain safety and to suggest traffic control measures. Lay out pavement markings for striping crews. Operate counters and record data to assess the volume, type, and movement of vehicular and pedestrian traffic at specified times. Provide technical supervision regarding traffic control devices to other traffic technicians and laborers. Gather and compile data from hand-count sheets, machine-count tapes, and radar speed checks and code data for computer input. Place and secure automatic counters, using power tools, and retrieve counters after counting periods end. Measure and record the speed of vehicular traffic, using electrical timing devices or radar equipment. Study traffic delays by noting times of delays, the numbers of vehicles affected, and vehicle speed through the delay area. Review traffic control/barricade plans to issue permits for parades and other special events and for construction work that affects rights-of-way, providing assistance with plan preparation or revision as necessary. Prepare graphs, charts, diagrams, and other aids to illustrate observations and conclusions.

Personality Type: Realistic. Realistic occupations frequently involve work activities that include practical, hands-on problems and solutions. They often deal with plants; animals; and real-world materials such as wood, tools, and machinery. Many of the occupations require working outside and do not involve a lot of paperwork or working closely with others.

GOE—Interest Area: 16. Transportation, Distribution, and Logistics. **Work Group:** 16.07. Transportation Support Work. **Other Jobs in This Work Group:** Bridge and Lock Tenders; Cargo and Freight Agents; Cleaners of Vehicles and Equipment; Laborers and Freight, Stock, and Material Movers, Hand; Railroad Brake, Signal, and Switch Operators.

Skills—Operation Monitoring: Watching gauges, dials, or other indicators to make sure a machine is working properly. **Coordination:** Adjusting actions in relation to others' actions. **Technology Design:** Generating or adapting equipment and technology to serve user needs. **Systems Evaluation:** Identifying measures or indicators of system performance and the actions needed to improve or correct performance relative to the goals of the system. **Systems Analysis:** Determining how a system should work and how changes in conditions, operations, and the environment will affect outcomes. **Writing:** Communicating effectively in writing as appropriate for the needs of the audience. **Judgment and Decision Making:** Considering the relative costs and benefits of potential actions to choose the most appropriate one. **Active Learning:** Understanding the implications of new information for both current and future problem-solving and decision-making.

Education and Training Program: Traffic, Customs, and Transportation Clerk/Technician. **Related Knowledge/Courses: Design:** Design techniques, tools, and principles involved in production of precision technical plans, blueprints, drawings, and models. **Building and Construction:** The materials, methods, and tools involved in the construction or repair of houses, buildings, or other structures such as highways and roads. **Engineering and Technology:** The practical application of engineering science and technology. This includes applying principles, techniques, procedures, and equipment to the design and production of various goods and services. **Customer and Personal Service:** Principles and processes for providing customer and personal services. This includes customer needs assessment, meeting quality standards for services, and evaluation of customer satisfaction. **Law and Government:** Laws, legal codes, court procedures, precedents, government regulations, executive orders, agency rules, and the democratic political process. **Public Safety and Security:** Relevant equipment, policies, procedures, and strategies to promote effective local, state, or national security operations for the protection of people, data, property, and institutions.

Work Environment: More often indoors than outdoors; noisy; very hot or cold; hazardous equipment; sitting.

Transit and Railroad Police

- Annual Earnings: $48,850
- Growth: 9.2%
- Annual Job Openings: Fewer than 500
- Education/Training Required: Long-term on-the-job training
- Self-Employed: 0.0%
- Part-Time: 1.4%

How the Job Improves the World: Contributes to justice, law enforcement, and safety.

Protect and police railroad and transit property, employees, or passengers. Patrol railroad yards, cars, stations, and other facilities to protect company property and shipments and to maintain order. Examine credentials of unauthorized persons attempting to enter secured areas. Apprehend or remove trespassers or thieves from railroad property or coordinate with law enforcement agencies in apprehensions and removals. Prepare reports documenting investigation activities and results. Investigate or direct investigations of freight theft, suspicious damage or loss of passengers' valuables, and other crimes on railroad property. Direct security activities at derailments, fires, floods, and strikes involving railroad property. Direct and coordinate the daily activities and training of security staff. Interview neighbors, associates, and former employers of job applicants to verify personal references and to obtain work history data. Record and verify seal numbers from boxcars containing frequently pilfered items, such as cigarettes and liquor, to detect tampering. Plan and implement special safety and preventive programs, such as fire and accident prevention. Seal empty boxcars by twisting nails in door hasps, using nail twisters.

Personality Type: Enterprising. Enterprising occupations frequently involve starting up and carrying out projects. These occupations can involve leading people and making many decisions. They sometimes require risk taking and often deal with business.

GOE—Interest Area: 12. Law and Public Safety. **Work Group:** 12.04. Law Enforcement and Public Safety. **Other Jobs in This Work Group:** Bailiffs; Correctional Officers and Jailers; Criminal Investigators and Special Agents; Detectives and Criminal Investigators; Fire Investigators; Forensic Science Technicians; Parking Enforcement Workers; Police and Sheriff's Patrol Officers; Police Detectives; Police Identification and Records Officers; Police Patrol Officers; Sheriffs and Deputy Sheriffs.

Skills—Persuasion: Persuading others to change their minds or behavior. **Service Orientation:** Actively

T

looking for ways to help people. **Social Perceptiveness:** Being aware of others' reactions and understanding why they react as they do. **Negotiation:** Bringing others together and trying to reconcile differences. **Active Listening:** Giving full attention to what other people are saying, taking time to understand the points being made, asking questions as appropriate, and not interrupting at inappropriate times. **Writing:** Communicating effectively in writing as appropriate for the needs of the audience. **Complex Problem Solving:** Identifying complex problems and reviewing related information to develop and evaluate options and implement solutions. **Speaking:** Talking to others to convey information effectively.

Education and Training Programs: Security and Loss Prevention Services; Security and Protective Services, Other. **Related Knowledge/Courses: Public Safety and Security:** Relevant equipment, policies, procedures, and strategies to promote effective local, state, or national security operations for the protection of people, data, property, and institutions. **Transportation:** Principles and methods for moving people or goods by air, rail, sea, or road, including the relative costs and benefits. **Telecommunications:** Transmission, broadcasting, switching, control, and operation of telecommunications systems. **English Language:** The structure and content of the English language, including the meaning and spelling of words, rules of composition, and grammar. **Law and Government:** Laws, legal codes, court procedures, precedents, government regulations, executive orders, agency rules, and the democratic political process. **Geography:** Principles and methods for describing the features of land, sea, and air masses, including their physical characteristics; locations; interrelationships; and distribution of plant, animal, and human life.

Work Environment: More often indoors than outdoors; noisy; very hot or cold; very bright or dim lighting; hazardous conditions.

Urban and Regional Planners

- Annual Earnings: $55,170
- Growth: 15.2%
- Annual Job Openings: 3,000
- Education/Training Required: Master's degree
- Self-Employed: 0.0%
- Part-Time: 9.9%

How the Job Improves the World: Contributes to physical and natural environment.

Develop comprehensive plans and programs for use of land and physical facilities of local jurisdictions such as towns, cities, counties, and metropolitan areas. Design, promote, and administer government plans and policies affecting land use, zoning, public utilities, community facilities, housing, and transportation. Hold public meetings and confer with government, social scientists, lawyers, developers, the public, and special interest groups to formulate and develop land use or community plans. Recommend approval, denial, or conditional approval of proposals. Determine the effects of regulatory limitations on projects. Assess the feasibility of proposals and identify necessary changes. Create, prepare, or requisition graphic and narrative reports on land use data, including land area maps overlaid with geographic variables such as population density. Conduct field investigations, surveys, impact studies, or other research to compile and analyze data on economic, social, regulatory, and physical factors affecting land use. Advise planning officials on project feasibility, cost-effectiveness, regulatory conformance, and possible alternatives. Discuss with planning officials the purpose of land use projects such as transportation, conservation, residential, commercial, industrial, and community use. Keep informed about economic and legal issues involved in zoning codes, building codes, and environmental regulations. Mediate community disputes and assist in developing alternative plans and recommendations for programs or projects. Coordinate work with economic consultants and architects during the formulation of plans and the design of large pieces of infrastructure. Review and evaluate environmental impact reports pertaining to private and public planning projects and programs. Supervise and coordinate the work of urban planning technicians and technologists. Investigate property availability.

Personality Type: Investigative. Investigative occupations frequently involve working with ideas and require an extensive amount of thinking. These occupations can involve searching for facts and figuring out problems mentally.

GOE—Interest Area: 07. Government and Public Administration. **Work Group:** 07.02. Public Planning. **Other Jobs in This Work Group:** City and Regional Planning Aides.

Skills—Complex Problem Solving: Identifying complex problems and reviewing related information to develop and evaluate options and implement solutions. **Persuasion:** Persuading others to change their minds or behavior. **Coordination:** Adjusting actions in relation to others' actions. **Writing:** Communicating effectively in writing as appropriate for the needs of the audience. **Service Orientation:** Actively looking for ways to help people. **Speaking:** Talking to others to convey information effectively. **Judgment and Decision Making:** Considering the relative costs and benefits of potential actions to choose the most appropriate one. **Time Management:** Managing one's own time and the time of others.

Education and Training Program: City/Urban, Community, and Regional Planning. **Related Knowledge/Courses: Design:** Design techniques, tools, and principles involved in production of precision technical plans, blueprints, drawings, and models. **Building and Construction:** The materials, methods, and tools involved in the construction or repair of houses, buildings, or other structures such as highways and roads. **Geography:** Principles and methods for describing the features of land, sea, and air masses, including their physical characteristics; locations; interrelationships; and distribution of plant, animal, and human life. **Customer and Personal Service:** Principles and processes for providing customer and personal services. This includes customer needs assessment, meeting quality standards for services, and evaluation of customer satisfaction. **History and Archeology:** Historical events and their causes, indicators, and effects on civilizations and cultures. **Law and Government:** Laws, legal codes, court procedures, precedents, government regulations, executive orders, agency rules, and the democratic political process.

Work Environment: Indoors; noisy; very bright or dim lighting; sitting; using hands on objects, tools, or controls; repetitive motions.

Veterinarians

- Annual Earnings: $68,910
- Growth: 17.4%
- Annual Job Openings: 8,000
- Education/Training Required: First professional degree
- Self-Employed: 20.7%
- Part-Time: 10.8%

How the Job Improves the World: Contributes to animal and human health.

Diagnose and treat diseases and dysfunctions of animals. May engage in a particular function, such as research and development, consultation, administration, technical writing, sale or production of commercial products, or rendering of technical services to commercial firms or other organizations. Includes veterinarians who inspect livestock. Examine animals to detect and determine the nature of diseases or injuries. Treat sick or injured animals by prescribing medication, setting bones, dressing wounds, or performing surgery. Inoculate animals against various diseases such as rabies and distemper. Collect body tissue, feces, blood, urine, or other body fluids for examination and analysis. Operate diagnostic equipment such as radiographic and ultrasound equipment and interpret the resulting images. Advise animal owners regarding sanitary measures, feeding, and general care necessary to promote health of animals. Educate the public about diseases that can be spread from animals to humans. Train and supervise workers who handle and care for animals. Provide care to a wide range of animals or specialize in a particular species, such as horses or exotic birds. Euthanize animals. Establish and conduct quarantine and testing procedures that prevent the spread of diseases to other animals or to humans and that comply with applicable government regulations. Conduct postmortem studies and analyses to determine the causes of animals' deaths. Perform administrative duties such as scheduling appointments, accepting payments from clients, and maintaining business records. Drive mobile clinic vans to farms so that health problems can be treated or prevented. Direct the overall operations of animal hospitals, clinics, or mobile services to farms. Specialize in a particular type of treatment such as dentistry, pathology, nutrition, surgery, microbiology, or internal medicine. Inspect and test horses, sheep, poultry, and other animals to detect the presence of communicable diseases. Research diseases to which animals could be susceptible. Plan and execute animal nutrition and reproduction programs. Inspect animal housing facilities to determine their cleanliness and adequacy. Determine the effects of drug therapies, antibiotics, or new surgical techniques by testing them on animals.

Personality Type: Investigative. Investigative occupations frequently involve working with ideas and require an extensive amount of thinking. These occupations can involve searching for facts and figuring out problems mentally.

GOE—Interest Area: 08. Health Science. **Work Group:** 08.05. Animal Care. **Other Jobs in This Work Group:** Animal Breeders; Animal Trainers; Nonfarm Animal Caretakers; Veterinary Assistants and Laboratory Animal Caretakers; Veterinary Technologists and Technicians.

Skills—Science: Using scientific rules and methods to solve problems. **Management of Financial Resources:** Determining how money will be spent to get the work done and accounting for these expenditures. **Reading Comprehension:** Understanding written sentences and paragraphs in work-related documents. **Judgment and Decision Making:** Considering the relative costs and benefits of potential actions to choose the most appropriate one. **Complex Problem Solving:** Identifying complex problems and reviewing related information to develop and evaluate options and implement solutions. **Management of Personnel Resources:** Motivating, developing, and directing people as they work; identifying the best people for the job. **Instructing:** Teaching others how to do something. **Active Learning:** Understanding the implications of new information for both current and future problem-solving and decision-making.

Education and Training Programs: Veterinary Medicine (DVM); Veterinary Sciences/Veterinary Clinical Sciences, General (Cert, MS, PhD); Veterinary Anatomy (Cert, MS, PhD); Veterinary Physiology (Cert, MS, PhD); Veterinary Microbiology and Immunobiology (Cert, MS, PhD); Veterinary Pathology and Pathobiology (Cert, MS, PhD); Veterinary Toxicology and Pharmacology (Cert, MS, PhD); Large Animal/Food Animal and Equine Surgery and Medicine (Cert, MS, PhD); others. **Related Knowledge/Courses: Biology:** Plant and animal organisms and their tissues, cells, functions, interdependencies, and interactions with each other and the environment. **Medicine and Dentistry:** The information and techniques needed to diagnose and treat human injuries, diseases, and deformities. This includes symptoms, treatment alternatives, drug properties and interactions, and preventive health-care measures. **Chemistry:** The chemical composition, structure, and properties of substances and of the chemical processes and transformations that they undergo. This includes uses of chemicals and their danger signs, production techniques, and disposal methods. **Therapy and Counseling:** Principles, methods, and procedures for diagnosis, treatment, and rehabilitation of physical and mental dysfunctions and for career counseling and guidance. **Sales and Marketing:** Principles and methods for showing, promoting, and selling products or services. This includes marketing strategy and tactics, product demonstration, sales techniques, and sales control systems. **Customer and Personal Service:** Principles and processes for providing customer and personal services. This includes customer needs assessment, meeting quality standards for services, and evaluation of customer satisfaction.

Work Environment: Indoors; noisy; contaminants; disease or infections; standing; using hands on objects, tools, or controls.

Veterinary Assistants and Laboratory Animal Caretakers

- ◎ Annual Earnings: $19,610
- ◎ Growth: 21.0%
- ◎ Annual Job Openings: 14,000
- ◎ Education/Training Required: Short-term on-the-job training
- ◎ Self-Employed: 2.7%
- ◎ Part-Time: 27.5%

How the Job Improves the World: Contributes to animal and human health.

Feed, water, and examine pets and other nonfarm animals for signs of illness, disease, or injury in laboratories and animal hospitals and clinics. Clean and disinfect cages and work areas and sterilize laboratory and surgical equipment. May provide routine post-operative care, administer medication orally or topically, or prepare samples for laboratory examination under the supervision of veterinary or laboratory animal technologists or technicians, veterinarians, or scientists. Monitor animals recovering from surgery and notify veterinarians of any unusual changes or symptoms. Administer anesthetics during surgery and monitor the effects on animals. Clean, maintain, and sterilize instruments and equipment. Administer medication, immunizations, and blood plasma to animals as prescribed by veterinarians. Provide emergency first aid to sick or injured animals. Clean and maintain kennels, animal holding areas, examination and operating rooms, and animal loading/unloading facilities to control the spread of disease. Hold or restrain animals during veterinary procedures. Perform routine laboratory tests or diagnostic tests such as taking and developing X rays. Fill medication prescriptions. Collect laboratory specimens such as blood, urine, and feces for testing. Examine animals to detect behavioral changes or clinical symptoms that could indicate illness or injury. Assist veterinarians in examining animals to determine the nature of illnesses or injuries. Prepare surgical equipment and pass instruments and materials to veterinarians during surgical procedures. Perform enemas, catheterization, ear flushes, intravenous feedings, and gavages. Prepare feed for animals according to specific instructions such as diet lists and schedules. Exercise animals and provide them with companionship. Record information relating to animal genealogy, feeding schedules, appearance, behavior, and breeding. Educate and advise clients on animal health care, nutrition, and behavior problems. Perform hygiene-related duties such as clipping animals' claws and cleaning and polishing teeth. Prepare examination or treatment rooms by stocking them with appropriate supplies. Provide assistance with euthanasia of animals and disposal of corpses. Perform office reception duties such as scheduling appointments and helping customers. Dust, spray, or bathe animals to control insect pests. Write reports, maintain research information, and perform clerical duties. Perform accounting duties, including bookkeeping, billing customers for services, and maintaining inventories. Assist professional personnel with research projects in commercial, public health, or research laboratories.

Personality Type: Realistic. Realistic occupations frequently involve work activities that include practical, hands-on problems and solutions. They often deal with plants; animals; and real-world materials such as wood, tools, and machinery. Many of the occupations require working outside and do not involve a lot of paperwork or working closely with others.

GOE—Interest Area: 08. Health Science. **Work Group:** 08.05. Animal Care. **Other Jobs in This Work Group:** Animal Breeders; Animal Trainers; Nonfarm Animal Caretakers; Veterinarians; Veterinary Technologists and Technicians.

Skills—Science: Using scientific rules and methods to solve problems. **Operation Monitoring:** Watching gauges, dials, or other indicators to make sure a machine is working properly. **Active Listening:** Giving full attention to what other people are saying, taking time to understand the points being made, asking questions as appropriate, and not interrupting at inappropriate times. **Reading Comprehension:** Understanding written sentences and paragraphs in work-related documents. **Instructing:** Teaching others how to do something. **Equipment Maintenance:** Performing routine maintenance on equipment and determining when and what kind of maintenance is needed. **Troubleshooting:** Determining causes of operating errors and deciding what to do about them.

Service Orientation: Actively looking for ways to help people.

Education and Training Program: Veterinary/Animal Health Technology/Technician and Veterinary Assistant. **Related Knowledge/Courses: Medicine and Dentistry:** The information and techniques needed to diagnose and treat human injuries, diseases, and deformities. This includes symptoms, treatment alternatives, drug properties and interactions, and preventive health-care measures. **Biology:** Plant and animal organisms and their tissues, cells, functions, interdependencies, and interactions with each other and the environment. **Chemistry:** The chemical composition, structure, and properties of substances and of the chemical processes and transformations that they undergo. This includes uses of chemicals and their danger signs, production techniques, and disposal methods. **Clerical Practices:** Administrative and clerical procedures and systems such as word processing, managing files and records, stenography and transcription, designing forms, and other office procedures and terminology.

Work Environment: Indoors; disease or infections; minor burns, cuts, bites, or stings; standing; walking and running; using hands on objects, tools, or controls.

Vocational Education Teachers, Postsecondary

- Annual Earnings: $41,750
- Growth: 32.2%
- Annual Job Openings: 329,000
- Education/Training Required: Work experience in a related occupation
- Self-Employed: 0.4%
- Part-Time: 27.3%

The job openings listed here are shared with 35 other postsecondary teaching occupations. For a complete list, see the beginning of this section.

How the Job Improves the World: Contributes to education.

Teach or instruct vocational or occupational subjects at the postsecondary level (but at less than the baccalaureate) to students who have graduated or left high school. Includes correspondence school instructors; industrial, commercial, and government training instructors; and adult education teachers and instructors who prepare persons to operate industrial machinery and equipment and transportation and communications equipment. Teaching may take place in public or private schools whose primary business is education or in a school associated with an organization whose primary business is other than education. Supervise and monitor students' use of tools and equipment. Observe and evaluate students' work to determine progress, provide feedback, and make suggestions for improvement. Present lectures and conduct discussions to increase students' knowledge and competence, using visual aids such as graphs, charts, videotapes, and slides. Administer oral, written, or performance tests to measure progress and to evaluate training effectiveness. Prepare reports and maintain records such as student grades, attendance rolls, and training activity details. Supervise independent or group projects, field placements, laboratory work, or other training. Determine training needs of students or workers. Provide individualized instruction and tutorial or remedial instruction. Conduct on-the-job training, classes, or training sessions to teach and demonstrate principles, techniques, procedures, and methods of designated subjects. Develop curricula and plan course content and methods of instruction. Prepare outlines of instructional programs and training schedules and establish course goals. Integrate academic and vocational curricula so that students can obtain a variety of skills. Develop teaching aids such as instructional software, multimedia visual aids, or study materials. Select and assemble books, materials, supplies, and equipment for training, courses, or projects. Advise students on course selection, career decisions, and other academic and vocational concerns. Participate in conferences, seminars, and training sessions to keep abreast of developments in the field and integrate relevant information into training programs. Serve on faculty and school committees concerned with budgeting, curriculum revision, and course and diploma requirements. Review enrollment applications and correspond with applicants to obtain additional information. Arrange for lectures by experts in designated fields.

Personality Type: Social. Social occupations frequently involve working with, communicating with, and teaching people. These occupations often involve helping or providing service to others.

GOE—Interest Area: 05. Education and Training. **Work Group:** 05.03. Postsecondary and Adult Teaching and Instructing. **Other Jobs in This Work Group:** Adult Literacy, Remedial Education, and GED Teachers and Instructors; Agricultural Sciences Teachers, Postsecondary; Anthropology and Archeology Teachers, Postsecondary; Architecture Teachers, Postsecondary; Area, Ethnic, and Cultural Studies Teachers, Postsecondary; Art, Drama, and Music Teachers, Postsecondary; Atmospheric, Earth, Marine, and Space Sciences Teachers, Postsecondary; Biological Science Teachers, Postsecondary; Business Teachers, Postsecondary; Chemistry Teachers, Postsecondary; Communications Teachers, Postsecondary; Computer Science Teachers, Postsecondary; Criminal Justice and Law Enforcement Teachers, Postsecondary; Economics Teachers, Postsecondary; Education Teachers, Postsecondary; Engineering Teachers, Postsecondary; English Language and Literature Teachers, Postsecondary; Environmental Science Teachers, Postsecondary; Farm and Home Management Advisors; Foreign Language and Literature Teachers, Postsecondary; Forestry and

Conservation Science Teachers, Postsecondary; Geography Teachers, Postsecondary; Graduate Teaching Assistants; Health Specialties Teachers, Postsecondary; History Teachers, Postsecondary; Home Economics Teachers, Postsecondary; Law Teachers, Postsecondary; Library Science Teachers, Postsecondary; Mathematical Science Teachers, Postsecondary; Nursing Instructors and Teachers, Postsecondary; Philosophy and Religion Teachers, Postsecondary; Physics Teachers, Postsecondary; Political Science Teachers, Postsecondary; Psychology Teachers, Postsecondary; Recreation and Fitness Studies Teachers, Postsecondary; Self-Enrichment Education Teachers; Social Work Teachers, Postsecondary; Sociology Teachers, Postsecondary.

Skills—Instructing: Teaching others how to do something. **Learning Strategies:** Selecting and using training/instructional methods and procedures appropriate for the situation when learning or teaching new things. **Social Perceptiveness:** Being aware of others' reactions and understanding why they react as they do. **Service Orientation:** Actively looking for ways to help people. **Speaking:** Talking to others to convey information effectively. **Time Management:** Managing one's own time and the time of others. **Persuasion:** Persuading others to change their minds or behavior. **Writing:** Communicating effectively in writing as appropriate for the needs of the audience.

Education and Training Programs: Agricultural Teacher Education; Business Teacher Education; Technology Teacher Education/Industrial Arts Teacher Education; Sales and Marketing Operations/Marketing and Distribution Teacher Education; Technical Teacher Education; Trade and Industrial Teacher Education; Health Occupations Teacher Education; Teacher Education and Professional Development, Specific Subject Areas, Other. **Related Knowledge/Courses: Education and Training:** Principles and methods for curriculum and training design, teaching and instruction for individuals and groups, and the measurement of training effects.

Psychology: Human behavior and performance; individual differences in ability, personality, and interests; learning and motivation; psychological research methods; and the assessment and treatment of behavioral and affective disorders. **Therapy and Counseling:** Principles, methods, and procedures for diagnosis, treatment, and rehabilitation of physical and mental dysfunctions and for career counseling and guidance. **Computers and Electronics:** Circuit boards; processors; chips; electronic equipment; and computer hardware and software, including applications and programming. **Sales and Marketing:** Principles and methods for showing, promoting, and selling products or services. This includes marketing strategy and tactics, product demonstration, sales techniques, and sales control systems. **Design:** Design techniques, tools, and principles involved in production of precision technical plans, blueprints, drawings, and models.

Work Environment: Indoors; standing; using hands on objects, tools, or controls.

Vocational Education Teachers, Secondary School

- Annual Earnings: $47,090
- Growth: 9.1%
- Annual Job Openings: 10,000
- Education/Training Required: Work experience plus degree
- Self-Employed: 0.0%
- Part-Time: 9.2%

How the Job Improves the World: Contributes to education.

Teach or instruct vocational or occupational subjects at the secondary school level. Prepare materials and classroom for class activities. Maintain accurate and complete student records as required by law, district policy, and administrative regulations. Instruct students individually and in groups, using various teaching methods such as lectures, discussions, and demonstrations. Observe and evaluate students' performance, behavior, social development, and physical health. Establish and enforce rules for behavior and procedures for maintaining order among the students for whom they are responsible. Instruct and monitor students the in use and care of equipment and materials to prevent injury and damage. Plan and conduct activities for a balanced program of instruction, demonstration, and work time that provides students with opportunities to observe, question, and investigate. Prepare, administer, and grade tests and assignments to evaluate students' progress. Enforce all administration policies and rules governing students. Assign and grade classwork and homework. Instruct students in the knowledge and skills required in a specific occupation or occupational field, using a systematic plan of lectures; discussions; audiovisual presentations; and laboratory, shop, and field studies. Establish clear objectives for all lessons, units, and projects and communicate those objectives to students. Use computers, audiovisual aids, and other equipment and materials to supplement presentations. Plan and supervise work-experience programs in businesses, industrial shops, and school laboratories. Prepare students for later grades by encouraging them to explore learning opportunities and to persevere with challenging tasks. Confer with parents or guardians, other teachers, counselors, and administrators in order to resolve students' behavioral and academic problems. Guide and counsel students with adjustment or academic problems or special academic interests. Prepare objectives and outlines for courses of study, following curriculum guidelines or requirements of states and schools. Keep informed about trends in education and subject matter specialties.

Personality Type: Social. Social occupations frequently involve working with, communicating with, and teaching people. These occupations often involve helping or providing service to others.

GOE—Interest Area: 05. Education and Training. **Work Group:** 05.02. Preschool, Elementary, and Secondary Teaching and Instructing. **Other Jobs in This Work Group:** Elementary School Teachers, Except Special Education; Kindergarten Teachers, Except Special Education; Middle School Teachers, Except Special and Vocational Education; Preschool Teachers, Except Special Education; Secondary School Teachers, Except Special and Vocational Education; Special Education Teachers, Middle School; Special Education Teachers, Preschool, Kindergarten, and Elementary School; Special Education Teachers, Secondary School; Teacher Assistants; Vocational Education Teachers, Middle School.

Skills—Management of Financial Resources: Determining how money will be spent to get the work done and accounting for these expenditures. **Learning Strategies:** Selecting and using training/instructional methods and procedures appropriate for the situation when learning or teaching new things. **Social Perceptiveness:** Being aware of others' reactions and understanding why they react as they do. **Instructing:** Teaching others how to do something. **Management of Material Resources:** Obtaining and seeing to the appropriate use of equipment, facilities, and materials needed to do certain work. **Persuasion:** Persuading others to change their minds or behavior. **Management of Personnel Resources:** Motivating, developing, and directing people as they work; identifying the best people for the job. **Service Orientation:** Actively looking for ways to help people.

Education and Training Program: Technology Teacher Education/Industrial Arts Teacher Education. **Related Knowledge/Courses: Education and Training:** Principles and methods for curriculum and training design, teaching and instruction for individuals and groups, and the measurement of training effects. **Therapy and Counseling:** Principles, methods, and procedures for diagnosis, treatment, and rehabilitation of physical and mental dysfunctions and for career counseling and guidance. **Sociology and Anthropology:** Group behavior and dynamics, societal trends and influences, human migrations, ethnicity, and cultures and their history and origins. **Psychology:** Human behavior and performance; individual differences in ability, personality, and interests; learning and motivation; psychological research methods; and the assessment and treatment of behavioral and affective disorders. **Design:** Design techniques, tools, and principles involved in production of precision technical plans, blueprints, drawings, and models. **Clerical Practices:** Administrative and clerical procedures and systems such as word processing, managing files and records, stenography and transcription, designing forms, and other office procedures and terminology.

Work Environment: Indoors; noisy; standing; using hands on objects, tools, or controls.

APPENDIX A

Resources for Further Exploration

The facts and pointers in this book provide a good beginning to the subject of jobs that make a better world. If you want additional details, we suggest you consult some of the resources listed here.

Facts About Careers

The *Occupational Outlook Handbook* (or the *OOH*) (JIST): Updated every two years by the U.S. Department of Labor, this book provides descriptions for almost 270 major jobs covering more than 85 percent of the workforce.

The *Enhanced Occupational Outlook Handbook* (JIST): Includes all descriptions in the *OOH* plus descriptions of more than 6,300 more-specialized jobs related to them.

The *O*NET Dictionary of Occupational Titles* (JIST): The only printed source of the more than 900 jobs described in the U.S. Department of Labor's Occupational Information Network database. It covers all the jobs in the book you're now reading, but it offers more topics than we were able to fit here.

The *New Guide for Occupational Exploration* (JIST): An important career reference that allows you to explore all major O*NET jobs based on your interests.

Career Decision Making and Planning

Overnight Career Choice, by Michael Farr (JIST): This book can help you choose a career goal based on a variety of criteria, including skills, interests, and values. It is part of the *Help in a Hurry* series, so it is designed to produce quick results.

50 Best Jobs for Your Personality by Michael Farr and Laurence Shatkin, Ph.D. (JIST): Built around the six Holland personality types, this book includes an assessment to help you identify your dominant and secondary personality types, plus lists and descriptions of high-paying and high-growth civilian jobs linked to those personality types.

Job Hunting

Same-Day Resume, by Michael Farr (JIST): Learn in an hour how to write an effective resume. This book includes dozens of sample resumes from professional writers and even offers advice on cover letters, online resumes, and more.

Seven-Step Job Search, by Michael Farr (JIST): In seven easy steps, learn what it takes to land the right job fast. Quick worksheets will help you identify your skills, define your ideal job, use the most effective job search methods, write a superior resume, organize your time to get two interviews a day, dramatically improve your interviewing skills, and follow up on all job leads effectively.

Idealist.org: This Web site lets you search for openings in world-improving jobs and volunteer opportunities with nonprofit organizations, including overseas positions.

Job Banks by Occupation: This is a set of links offered by America's Career InfoNet. At www.acinet.org, find the Career Tools box, click Career Resource Library, and then click Job & Resume Banks. The Job Banks by Occupation link leads you to groups of jobs such as "Healthcare Practitioners and Technical Occupations" and "Legal Occupations," which in turn lead you to more specific job titles and occupation-specific job-listing sites maintained by various organizations.

APPENDIX B

The GOE Interest Areas and Work Groups

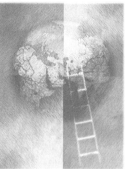

As Part I explains, the GOE is a way of organizing the world of work into large interest areas and more-specific work groups containing jobs that have a lot in common. Part I defines the 16 GOE interest areas, and Part II also lists the work groups for each job described. We thought you would want to see the complete GOE taxonomy so you would understand how any job that interests you fits into this structure.

Interest areas have two-digit code numbers; work groups have four-digit code numbers beginning with the code number for the interest area in which they are classified. These are the 16 GOE interest areas and work groups:

01 Agriculture and Natural Resources

    01.01 Managerial Work in Agriculture and Natural Resources

    01.02 Resource Science/Engineering for Plants, Animals, and the Environment

    01.03 Resource Technologies for Plants, Animals, and the Environment

    01.04 General Farming

    01.05 Nursery, Groundskeeping, and Pest Control

    01.06 Forestry and Logging

    01.07 Hunting and Fishing

    01.08 Mining and Drilling

02 Architecture and Construction

      02.01 Managerial Work in Architecture and Construction

      02.02 Architectural Design

      02.03 Architecture/Construction Engineering Technologies

      02.04 Construction Crafts

      02.05 Systems and Equipment Installation, Maintenance, and Repair

      02.06 Construction Support/Labor

03 Arts and Communication

      03.01 Managerial Work in Arts and Communication

      03.02 Writing and Editing

      03.03 News, Broadcasting, and Public Relations

      03.04 Studio Art

      03.05 Design

      03.06 Drama

      03.07 Music

      03.08 Dance

      03.09 Media Technology

      03.10 Communications Technology

      03.11 Musical Instrument Repair

04 Business and Administration

      04.01 Managerial Work in General Business

      04.02 Managerial Work in Business Detail

      04.03 Human Resources Support

      04.04 Secretarial Support

      04.05 Accounting, Auditing, and Analytical Support

      04.06 Mathematical Clerical Support

      04.07 Records and Materials Processing

      04.08 Clerical Machine Operation

05 Education and Training

      05.01 Managerial Work in Education

      05.02 Preschool, Elementary, and Secondary Teaching and Instructing

      05.03 Postsecondary and Adult Teaching and Instructing

      05.04 Library Services

      05.05 Archival and Museum Services

      05.06 Counseling, Health, and Fitness Education

06 Finance and Insurance

        06.01 Managerial Work in Finance and Insurance

        06.02 Finance/Insurance Investigation and Analysis

        06.03 Finance/Insurance Records Processing

        06.04 Finance/Insurance Customer Service

        06.05 Finance/Insurance Sales and Support

07 Government and Public Administration

        07.01 Managerial Work in Government and Public Administration

        07.02 Public Planning

        07.03 Regulations Enforcement

        07.04 Public Administration Clerical Support

08 Health Science

        08.01 Managerial Work in Medical and Health Services

        08.02 Medicine and Surgery

        08.03 Dentistry

        08.04 Health Specialties

        08.05 Animal Care

        08.06 Medical Technology

        08.07 Medical Therapy

        08.08 Patient Care and Assistance

        08.09 Health Protection and Promotion

09 Hospitality, Tourism, and Recreation

        09.01 Managerial Work in Hospitality and Tourism

        09.02 Recreational Services

        09.03 Hospitality and Travel Services

        09.04 Food and Beverage Preparation

        09.05 Food and Beverage Service

        09.06 Sports

        09.07 Barber and Beauty Services

10 Human Service

        10.01 Counseling and Social Work

        10.02 Religious Work

        10.03 Child/Personal Care and Services

        10.04 Client Interviewing

11 Information Technology

        11.01 Managerial Work in Information Technology

        11.02 Information Technology Specialties

        11.03 Digital Equipment Repair

12 Law and Public Safety

        12.01 Managerial Work in Law and Public Safety

        12.02 Legal Practice and Justice Administration

        12.03 Legal Support

        12.04 Law Enforcement and Public Safety

        12.05 Safety and Security

        12.06 Emergency Responding

        12.07 Military

13 Manufacturing

        13.01 Managerial Work in Manufacturing

        13.02 Machine Setup and Operation

        13.03 Production Work, Assorted Materials Processing

        13.04 Welding, Brazing, and Soldering

        13.05 Production Machining Technology

        13.06 Production Precision Work

        13.07 Production Quality Control

        13.08 Graphic Arts Production

        13.09 Hands-On Work, Assorted Materials

        13.10 Woodworking Technology

        13.11 Apparel, Shoes, Leather, and Fabric Care

        13.12 Electrical and Electronic Repair

        13.13 Machinery Repair

        13.14 Vehicle and Facility Mechanical Work

        13.15 Medical and Technical Equipment Repair

        13.16 Utility Operation and Energy Distribution

        13.17 Loading, Moving, Hoisting, and Conveying

14 Retail and Wholesale Sales and Service

        14.01 Managerial Work in Retail/Wholesale Sales and Service

        14.02 Technical Sales

        14.03 General Sales

        14.04 Personal Soliciting

        14.05 Purchasing

        14.06 Customer Service

15 Scientific Research, Engineering, and Mathematics

        15.01 Managerial Work in Scientific Research, Engineering, and Mathematics

        15.02 Physical Sciences

        15.03 Life Sciences

        15.04 Social Sciences

        15.05 Physical Science Laboratory Technology

        15.06 Mathematics and Data Analysis

        15.07 Research and Design Engineering

        15.08 Industrial and Safety Engineering

        15.09 Engineering Technology

16 Transportation, Distribution, and Logistics

        16.01 Managerial Work in Transportation

        16.02 Air Vehicle Operation

        16.03 Truck Driving

        16.04 Rail Vehicle Operation

        16.05 Water Vehicle Operation

        16.06 Other Services Requiring Driving

        16.07 Transportation Support Work

Index

G

H

I

J